Eugene O'Neill

Eugene O'Neill

An Annotated International Bibliography, 1973 through 1999

by
Madeline C. Smith
and Richard Eaton

McFarland & Company, Inc., Publishers
Jefferson, North Carolina, and London

Acknowledgments: Many have helped us to acquire and present our materials. West Virginia University, its English department, the University library and its staff (notably the Interlibrary Loan, Reference, and Periodicals departments) have all been especially generous with their time, support, advice, and patience — this last so necessary in the face of our often so cranky frustrations. California University of Pennsylvania also made its contribution in several ways, especially through the labors of two of its former graduate students, Tina Szalay and Alfreida Smith, who helped to gather material during the semester they were enrolled in an O'Neill seminar. To all of them, our thanks.

ISBN 0-7864-1036-1 (library binding : 50# alkaline paper)

Library of Congress cataloguing data are available

British Library cataloguing data are available

Manufactured in the United States of America

McFarland & Company, Inc., Publishers
Box 611, Jefferson, North Carolina 28640
America.www.mcfarlandpub.com

Contents

Abbreviations

We avoid abbreviations except for the standard ones used in conventional bibliographical entries (U for University, P for Press) and therefore known to everyone — or, at least, everyone likely to use this work. So most of our entries give the full names for the journals (though without the preliminary definite articles). The exceptions are publications, especially eastern European ones, whose unabbreviated forms we have been unable to discover or unravel. With these latter we have probably made some serious (and, maybe, to the initiated even humorous) gaffes, confusing fugitive news items with more enduring matters. Because very frequent reference is made to O'Neill's plays we do abridge most play titles of more than one word.

Ah, Wilderness!	*Wilderness*	*Lazarus Laughed*	*Lazarus*
All God's Chillun Got Wings	*Chillun*	*Long Day's Journey*	
The Ancient Mariner	*Mariner*	*into Night*	*Journey*
"Anna Christie"	*Anna*	*The Long Voyage Home*	*Voyage*
Before Breakfast	*Breakfast*	*Marco Millions*	*Marco*
Beyond the Horizon	*Horizon*	*A Moon for the Misbegotten*	*Misbegotten*
Bound East for Cardiff	*Cardiff*	*The Moon of the Caribbees*	*Caribbees*
Chris Christopherson	*Chris*	*More Stately Mansions*	*Mansions*
Days Without End	*Days*	*Mourning Becomes Electra*	*Electra*
Desire Under the Elms	*Desire*	*Strange Interlude*	*Interlude*
The Dreamy Kid	*Dreamy*	*A Touch of the Poet*	*Touch*
The Emperor Jones	*Jones*	*Where the Cross Is Made*	*Cross*
The Great God Brown	*Brown*	*A Wife for a Life*	*Wife*
The Hairy Ape	*Ape*		
The Iceman Cometh	*Iceman*		
In the Zone	*Zone*		

Introduction

This work was originally designed to update the 1973 edition of Jordan Y. Miller's *Eugene O'Neill and the American Critic.* But as our digging deepened, our circumference widened. Professor Miller had directed his attention to the matter of *American* O'Neilliana and O'Neillians. That was appropriate since his work was an outgrowth of activities begun in the early 1950s when O'Neill was almost exclusively the province of the American theater, and American theater historians, critics and scholars. In the last half century, however, the American theater has become much more a part of the global theatrical community. And the many productions of O'Neill's work outside of the United States both in English-speaking countries and elsewhere, as well as the large number of published translations of even his minor plays, give ample testimony to O'Neill's growing *internationality.*

As a result, in taking up where Professor Miller stopped, 1973, and carrying on through the end of 1999, we have tried also to range beyond the English-speaking world in our survey of the O'Neill experience. We should note that we have included a few items that pre-date 1973, items that escaped the Miller bibliography (in 1973, remember, WorldCat, MLAIB, and DAI were not online and instantly updated).

Miller's bibliography also included productions and reviews. But productions for him meant usually first productions only. And of course *first* means also normally (though not absolutely in O'Neill's case) American. Here we take a new direction. We have, first, widened American to mean English-language productions and, second, included as many as we could find. Then in a separate section we have tried to do the same for productions in foreign languages. Of course many, possibly most, have escaped our notice — those by community theaters, summer stock companies, college and university theaters. And few newspapers that might review or, at the least, notice their productions publish indexes or preserve their fugitive lives in microfilm. But the conclusions capable (we hope) of being drawn from the production information we have garnered should be *indicative,* or, at the least, *suggestive,* of the O'Neill condition in America and, we hope, the world in the last quarter of the twentieth century.

A word about reviews. A bibliography about a writer usually only contains primary and secondary material. Reviews are tertiary. They can, however, be illuminating, especially when they point towards interpretations. Here they enter the area of criticism — not just of performance, but of text. So we have listed some reviews, even at times with annotations.

The Bibliography

A. Periodical Publications (English)

A1 Abbott, Michael. "The Curse of the Misbegotten: The Wanton Son in the Plays of Eugene O'Neill and Sam Shepard." *Eugene O'Neill Review* 18.1-2 (1994): 193-98.

Though articulating several points of similarity between O'Neill and Shepard, Abbott focuses on "their depiction of the wanton son, their most complex and directly autobiographical character," which renders Shepard "O'Neill's most direct descendant."

A2 Acharya, Shanta. "Beyond the 'New Woman' in O'Neill's *Strange Interlude*." *Triveni: A Journal of the Indian Renaissance* 49.4 (1980): 57-65.

Nina is the "new woman" who revolts against restrictions, forging her own destiny.

A3 _____. "Beyond the 'New Woman' in O'Neill's *Strange Interlude*." *Abstracts of English Studies* (June 1986); and *Eugene O'Neill Newsletter* 10.2 (1986): 47.

Abstracts the article published in *Triveni: A Journal of the Indian Renaissance* 49.4 (1980): 57-65.

A4 Ackerly, Chris. "Lowry and O'Neill: Cows and Pigs and Chickens." *Malcolm Lowry Review* 19-20 (1986-87): 129-30.

Yank's dream of a farm in *Cardiff* is echoed by Yvonne in *Under the Volcano*.

A5 Adler, Thomas P. "'Through a Glass Darkly': O'Neill's Aesthetic Theory as Seen through His Writer Characters." *Arizona Quarterly* 32 (1976): 171-83.

Referencing nine O'Neill writer-characters, Adler shows that from the poet in *Fog* to Edmund in *Journey*, O'Neill demonstrated that writers can lift man from confusion to truth.

A6 _____. "Two Plays for Puritans." *Tennessee Williams Newsletter* 1.1 (1978): 5-7.

Finds that "the numerous correspondences in plot, stage setting, characters, language, imagery, use of biblical allusions and the Oedipal motif, and even similar quasi-religious, religious or philosophical attitudes all suggest that Tennessee Williams had O'Neill's *Desire* at least unconsciously in mind when he wrote *Kingdom of Earth* (*The Seven Descents of Myrtle*)." Concludes, though, that *Kingdom* fails as a play while *Desire* succeeds.

A7 _____. "The Mirror as Stage Prop in Modern Drama." *Comparative Drama* 14 (1980): 355-73.

Discusses four dramas — Pirandello's *It Is So! (If You Think So)*, Camus' *Caligula*, Genet's *The Balcony*, and *Touch* — and three musicals — *Man of La Mancha*, *Cabaret*, and *A Chorus Line* — in terms of the mirror as prop. When Con Melody first stands in front of the mirror, he tries to erase the "son of a thievin' shebeen keeper" but in his last appearance, he parodies his earlier performance as major.

A8 _____. "A Cabin in the Woods, A Summerhouse in a Garden: Closure and Enclosure in O'Neill's *More Stately Mansions*." *Eugene O'Neill Newsletter* 9.2 (1985): 23-27.

In *Mansions* "O'Neill achieves closure through multiple images of enclosure." Act II, for example, ends as Simon is encircled by his mother and his wife. The play ends as Sara locks herself in the cabin and Deborah entombs herself in the summerhouse. Suggests that *Electra* and *Journey* also achieve closure through enclosure.

A9 _____. "'Daddy Spoke to Me!': Gods Lost and Found in *Long Day's Journey* *into Night* and *Through a Glass Darkly.*" *Comparative Drama* 20 (1986): 341-48.

Finds similarities between O'Neill's play and the Bergman film: both are plays of four figures; in both plays the crisis in faith is bound up with a failure in vocation; both plays move from darkness into light (however momentarily); women characters in these plays see the image of a male God as threatening, etc.

A10 _____. "Beyond Synge: O'Neill's *Anna Christie.*" *Eugene O'Neill Newsletter* 12.1 (1988): 34-39.

In his opening paragraph Adler outlines what he will do in this article: 1) look at *Riders to the Sea* for "visual and verbal texture" that appealed to O'Neill; 2) examine *Anna* to see how Synge's work was "personalized" by O'Neill; 3) consider the theme of personal freedom in this play as one that appealed to O'Neill throughout his canon.

A11 _____. "The Legacy of Eugene O'Neill According to Stark Young." *Eugene O'Neill Review* 20.1-2 (1996): 64-70.

Critiques the critic, searching for the basis of Young's admiration for O'Neill. Adler determines that the myth-making and soul-baring qualities of the drama are what endear it to Young. Ultimately, Young's assessment of O'Neill can be found in the "Critic's Diary": "whatever [O'Neill's] faults and limitations, he breaks your heart."

A12 Alvarez, Carmen Gago. "O'Neill and Tragedy — A Longing to Die." *Estudos Anglo-Americanos* [Sao Paulo, Brazil] 12-13 (1988-89): 24-29.

In *Iceman, Journey* and *Electra* the characters are in love with death and that death gives meaning to their lives — their only solution for dissatisfaction with themselves and their plights.

A13 _____. "'Hybris and the Mannons': A Study of Eugene O'Neill's Trilogy *Mourning Becomes Electra.*" *Estudos Anglo-Americanos* [Sao Paulo, Brazil] 17-18 (1993-94): 23-41.

Alvarez's intent is "to prove that O'Neill's trilogy, *Mourning Becomes Electra*, deals with the tragedy of self, or we might say referring back to Greek tragedy, that it is a tragedy of hybris — not the wanton insolence in the Greek sense of the word — but a tragedy of pride, the Mannons' tragic flaw." The work is about the search for self, one which leads to "frustration and self destruction."

A14 Alvis, John. "On the American

Line: O'Neill's *Mourning Becomes Electra* and the Principles of the Founding." *Southern Review* 22.1 (1986): 69-85.

Argues that "twentieth-century American drama reflects the reduction of equality and liberty accomplished by the determinist historians and by the followers of Freud"—plays tend to be either economic parables or Freudian analyses. But a few plays move beyond these limits to achieve "artistic honesty." Looks at *Electra* as a play in which "O'Neill goes some distance toward reestablishing a moral meaning for equality and liberty."

A15 Antush, John V. "Eugene O'Neill: Modern and Postmodern." *Eugene O'Neill Review* 13.1 (1989): 14-26.

In the playwright's attack on the superficial realism of the stage we find O'Neill's contribution to modernism and his anticipation of postmodernism as well since "the more radical postmodernism questions the codes, myths, techniques of modernism." *Anna* furnishes the evidence.

A16 Applebome, Peter. "The *Iceman* of Kevin Spacey." *New York Times* 4 Apr. 1999, sec. 2: 1+

Spacey says of *Iceman*, "You know, it's crazy. The play has everything going against it. It's too long, it's clunky, it's got all its difficulties. But one reason I've fallen in love with it is because O'Neill not only knew these people, he loved them, and he wrote about them with clarity and with an outrageous sense of humor that allows them to rib each other and be in on the joke." (The interview also reveals that Spacey supports an egalitarian approach to acting: he receives the same minimal-scale wage as the other actors.)

A17 Apseloff, Stanford S. "Eugene O'Neill: An Early Letter." *Resources for American Literary Study* 1 (1981): 109-11.

See Primary Works section, G10.

A18 Ardolino, Frank. "Irish Myth and Legend in *Long Day's Journey into Night* and *A Moon for the Misbegotten.*" *Eugene O'Neill Review* 22.1-2 (1998): 63-69.

Edmund's anecdote about the Shaughnessy-Harker conflict in *Journey,* that becomes the centerpiece of *Misbegotten,* is presented as a microcosm of struggles and triumphs of Irish history and myth. Sean O'Faolain's *The Great O'Neill* (no, not about Eugene) enters the plot.

A19 Astington, John H. "Shakespe-herian Rags." *Modern Drama* 31 (1988): 73-80.

In an intriguing if sometimes strained discussion of *Journey*, Astington details what he sees as Shakespearean influences on the play. Contends that the particularly biographical themes of *Journey* prompted O'Neill "unconsciously or not" to hint at the imagery of *Antony and Cleopatra* as well as *Romeo and Juliet*.

A20 Badino, Margareth M. Scarton. "The Self Destructiveness of an Idealist: A Study of Mary Tyrone in Eugene O'Neill's *Long Day's Journey into Night.*" *Estudos Anglo-Americanos* [Sao Paulo, Brazil] 5-6 (1981): 118-36.

Explains Mary Tyrone's symbolic regression at the end of the play as a search "for lost innocence." Memories and illusions provide no comfort, however, and "she finishes as a loser when attempting to regain ... [her innocence] by retreating to her past."

A21 Bagchee, Shyamal. "On Blake and O'Neill." *Eugene O'Neill Review* 14.1-2 (1990): 25-38.

"The aim of this essay is quite limited: to describe as clearly as possible the probable grounds of imaginative contact and similarity between O'Neill and Blake"; Blake's legendary Irish/O'Neil heritage, the poet's romanticism (his idealism, his social conscience) and other "confluences" are discussed herein.

A22 Bak, John S. "Eugene O'Neill and John Reed: Recording the Body Politic, 1913-1922." *Eugene O'Neill Review* 20.1-2 (1996): 17-35.

Investigates the literary exchange between Reed and O'Neill, one which has been overlooked except for the influence of Reed on O'Neill's *Movie Man*. "This essay, then, examines how both men recorded their societies' responses to the rapidly evolving world around them — technologically, artistically, and politically." Both address women's issues, the workers' struggle, and the atrocities of World War I, though O'Neill was content with exposing them and Reed committed to reform.

A23 Barbera, Jack Vincent. "Pipe Dreams, Games and Delusions." *Southern Review* 13.2 (1980): 120-28.

Concerns the opposition between Transactional Analysis and Alcoholics Anonymous as they relate to the compelling alcoholism of John Barrymore. O'Neill's *Iceman* is used to illustrate the determinism of AA.

A24 Barlow, Judith E. "*Long Day's Journey into Night*: From Early Notes to Finished Play." *Modern Drama* 22 (1979): 19-28.

In early versions of *Journey*, the characters are bitter and selfish. Final version tones down some of the bitterness.

A25 _____. "No He-Men Need Apply: A Look at O'Neill's Heroes." *Eugene O'Neill Review* 19.1-2 (1995): 110-21.

While granting that O'Neill offers only a narrow view of woman in his plays, Barlow looks at his male characters for what is not there. O'Neill's male characters do not subscribe to traditional notions of masculinity — "virility, competition, ruthlessness, materialism, stoicism."

A26 Basile, Michael. "Semiotic Transformability in *All God's Chillun Got Wings*." *Eugene O'Neill Review* 16.1 (1992): 25-37.

Imposing title aside, this article is a lucid discussion of the reasons for the play's neglect. Attributes lack of critical attention and production to "racial and artistic" prejudice. Defining artistic prejudice as the predilection for "stylistic homogeneity," Basile explains why the play does not live up to expectations in that regard and proposes a reassessment sans the bias.

A27 Basney, Lionel. "Eugene O'Neill: Earthbound Aspiration." *Christianity Today* 23 Nov. 1973: 17-22.

A 2,000-word introductory essay on O'Neill's themes, career, reception, and techniques with short summaries of *Marco, Brown, Lazarus, Electra* that focus on O'Neill's religious orientation. Finds O'Neill's religious statements insubstantial. O'Neill sees tragedy as resting in the failure of man's aspirations to find the truth he so mistakenly seeks.

A28 Bauersfeld, Erik. "*The Hairy Ape*: Introduction to the José Quintero Rehearsal Notes." [Also indexed under Travis Bogard, ed. "Directing a Radio Production of Eugene O'Neill's *The Hairy Ape*," and under Quintero.] *Theatre Journal* 43 (1991): 337-40; inclusive of the program notes, 337-59.

A short assessment of the concerns/problems Quintero faced as he adapted *Ape* for radio. Acoustic considerations, naturally, are the focus, adjustments being made as Quintero began rehearsals.

A29 Ben-Zvi, Linda. "*Exiles, The Great God Brown* and the Specter of Nietzsche." *Modern Drama* 24 (1981): 251-69.

Full form of a paper presented at the Eugene O'Neill-James Joyce Session of the James Joyce Symposium, in Provincetown, Massachusetts, June 1980. Points to the numerous similarities between the writers and suggests that Joyce's play *Exiles* may have influenced O'Neill's *Brown*.

A30 _____. "Susan Glaspell and Eugene O'Neill." *Eugene O'Neill Newsletter* 6.2 (1982): 21-29.

Suggests that Glaspell is not just a footnote in O'Neill studies: that O'Neill respected her opinions — she was, after all, an established writer when they met — and that her play *The Verge* may have influenced O'Neill's *Ape*.

A31 _____. "Eugene O'Neill and Film." *Eugene O'Neill Newsletter* 7.1 (1983): 3-10.

Discusses the changes made when O'Neill's plays were adapted for film. Plays treated include: *Anna, Wilderness, Ape, Breakfast, Jones, Interlude, Journey, Iceman, Electra.*

A32 _____. "Susan Glaspell and Eugene O'Neill: The Imagery of Gender." *Eugene O'Neill Newsletter* 10.1 (1986): 22-27.

Discusses Susan Glaspell's genesis and "possible influence" on O'Neill — her play *The Verge* and O'Neill's *Ape*.

A33 _____. "Freedom and Fixity in the Plays of Eugene O'Neill." *Modern Drama* 31 (1988): 16-27.

Examines the tension between the search for freedom and the search for stability in a number of O'Neill's better known works. Argues that despite protestations to the contrary, characters prefer home to the sea. In the later plays, freedom comes only through stability. Ben-Zvi's most compelling observation concerns gender; she claims that O'Neill's female characters handle the tensions better than male characters do.

A34 _____. "O'Neill's Cape(d) Compatriot." *Eugene O'Neill Review* 19.1-2 (1995): 129-38.

Takes a look at Susan Glaspell's contribution to American theater and influence on O'Neill.

A35 Berkvist, Robert. "Hello, Columbus: A Playwright Explores Wonder and Terror." *New Catholic World* 218 (1975): 23-27.

A general essay with two references to O'Neill. Of little importance to O'Neill scholarship.

A36 _____. "Liv Ullmann's Love Affair

with Eugene O'Neill." *New York Times* 10 Apr. 1977, sec. 2: 1+.

Interviews Liv Ullmann in Washington, DC, while *Anna* is on tour before going to Broadway. Ullmann sees Anna as a stronger woman than is Ibsen's Nora — as rather like Josie Hogan — and says O'Neill's success in Scandinavian countries is the result of their people's capacity to accept symbols. Ullmann thinks the play reflects a modern attitude about women — Anna is seeking freedom "in the face of terrible male chauvinism."

A37 _____. "Theater." *New York Times* 25 Dec. 1977, sec. 2: 2.

Brief description of the relationship between *Touch* and the cycle that was to be called *The Calms of Capricorn.*

A38 Berlin, Normand. "Ghosts of the Past: O'Neill and Hamlet." *Massachusetts Review* 20 (1979): 312-23.

Enumerates the many similarities between the mad scene in *Hamlet* and scenes in *Journey*. Also cites Jamie's association of his mother with a whore as similar to Hamlet's, and compares Jamie's and Hamlet's death wish. Makes a case for the psychic pressures on O'Neill exerted by an extensive knowledge of *Hamlet* and for Jamie as self portrait.

A39 _____. "The Beckettian O'Neill." *Modern Drama* 31 (1988): 28-34.

Argues that Beckett was such an influence on *Iceman* that the play could be called *Waiting for Hickey*. Sees philosophical similarities in the work of the playwrights and credits the concurrent Broadway openings of *Iceman* and *Godot* with the former play's success. Also maintains that Beckett influenced *Journey*, but his argument here is not as fully developed.

A40 _____. "O'Neill and Comedy: *The Iceman Cometh.*" *Eugene O'Neill Newsletter* 12.3 (1988): 3-8.

Having witnessed audience appreciation of the comic in two O'Neill productions (Keith Hack's *Interlude* and José Quintero's *Iceman*), Berlin rethinks his assessment of O'Neill's work, and of the latter play specifically, as he plumbs the play's ties to the comic tradition.

A41 _____. "O'Neill's Shakespeare." *Eugene O'Neill Review* 13.1 (1989): 5-13.

Hamlet, King Lear, Macbeth, Othello— they're all in *Journey*, though Shakespeare's influence O'Neill never acknowledged.

A42 _____. "O'Neill the 'Novelist.'" *Modern Drama* 34 (1991): 49-58.

Argues that "O'Neill's novelistic impulse carried him too far away from his instinctive theatrical strengths, and that only by tempering this novelistic impulse was he able to create his finest work." Focuses on *Interlude* to show that O'Neill's novelistic impulse was working against his theatrical instincts.

A43 _____. "Olivier's Tyrone." *Eugene O'Neill Review* 18.1-2 (1994): 135-42.

Explains Olivier's personal connection with the role which the actor called "autobiographical" [his] and critiques Olivier in the National Theatre production of *Journey*. Olivier's portrayal of the miserly Tyrone earns Berlin's "unqualified admiration."

A44 Bermel, Albert. "The Liberation of Eugene O'Neill." *American Theatre* (July-Aug. 1984): 4-9+

Comments on O'Neill's plays that were associated with José Quintero, Geraldine Fitzgerald, Colleen Dewhurst, James Earl Jones, Katherine Hepburn, George Ferencz, and Arvin Brown.

A45 _____. "A Crutch of the Poet." *Eugene O'Neill Newsletter* 11.1 (1987): 10-14.

In his discussion of *Touch* Bermel distinguishes between pipe dreams and dreams and suggests that, in the character of Con Melody, O'Neill was embodying not just personal pride but nationalism.

A46 _____. "O'Neill's Funny Valentine." *Eugene O'Neill Newsletter* 12.2 (1988): 18-22.

Explores the dark side of *Wilderness*, which he calls a "toxic nectar."

A47 Bernstein, Matthew. "Hollywood's 'Arty Cinema': John Ford's *The Long Voyage Home*." *Wide Angle* 10.1 (1988): 30-45.

The essay bridges the gap between literature and film as it investigates the history and technique behind director John Ford's film version of *The Long Voyage Home*, based on O'Neill's sea plays. Ford's vision contends that men are helpless in the face of what the sea, that "cruel mistress," ordains. Although the film alters certain scenes and formats from the sea play canon, it nevertheless complements O'Neill's vision by retaining the plays' starkness in the movie's black-and-white format.

A48 Bernstein, Samuel J. "*Hughie*: Inner Dynamics and Canonical Relevance." *Eugene O'Neill Review* 22.1-2 (1998): 77-103.

Though O'Neill's plays are very dark, we can yet find in them "images of transcendence" for "the pain and suffering of earthly life." And in the late plays, especially in *Hughie*, "camaraderie, particularly among men, and love suggest a mystical connection among suffering humanity and a source of goodness and salvation in the universe."

A49 Berry, David W. "Albee and the Iceman: O'Neill's Influence on *Who's Afraid of Virginia Woolf*?" *Eugene O'Neill Newsletter* 11.3 (1987): 18-21.

While most critics look to European Theatre of the Absurd as Albee's foundation, Berry "would argue that Albee's deepest roots are really much nearer home." To that end, he looks to *Iceman* as a source for *Who's Afraid of Virginia Woolf*?

A50 Billington, Michael. "Why Are American Plays Suddenly Popular in Britain?" *New York Times* 23 Mar. 1980, sec. 2: 5.

Maintains that the "collapse of the gentleman-code of English drama" has opened the way for more "uninhibited" self expression. Among American plays in Britain are *Hughie, Voyage*, and *Iceman*.

A51 Billman, Carol. "Language as Theme in Eugene O'Neill's *Hughie*." *Notes on Modern American Literature* 3 (1979): Item 25.

O'Neill's sense of dialogue and use of dialect in *Hughie* dramatize his theme that human beings can get through to one another by means of language, the failure of which is the cause of violence in other one-acts: Albee's *Zoo Story* and Amiri Baraka's *Dutchman*.

A52 Black, Cheryl. "Ida Rauh: Power Player at Provincetown." *Journal of American Drama and Theatre* 6.2-3 (1994): 63-80.

A background piece on Rauh and her affiliation with the Provincetown Players, this essay, for the O'Neillian, is of interest in its comments on the relationship between the budding playwright and the actress. Black mentions that Rauh directed *Dreamy* and *Cross*, before bowing out of the company.

A53 Black, Stephen A. "Ella O'Neill's Addiction." *Eugene O'Neill Newsletter* 9.1 (1985): 24-26.

Theorizes that Ella O'Neill's addiction was due to fear of pregnancy and attributes her cure at the age of 56 to the release from that fear.

A54 _____. "Letting the Dead Be Dead:

A Reinterpretation of *A Moon for the Misbe-gotten.*" *Modern Drama* 29 (1986): 544-55.

Sees the central character as Josie Hogan, not Jim Tyrone, and says the play is about Josie's mourning Jim rather than Jim's mourning his mother.

A55 _____. "America's First Tragedy." *English Studies in Canada* 13.2 (1987): 195-203.

Tries to resurrect *Horizon*'s reputation, calling it "the first play by an American that can be justly called a tragedy."

A56 _____. "O'Neill's Dramatic Process." *American Literature* 59 (1987): 58–70.

Analyzes the "symphonic" quality of *Journey*: the first movement begins adagio and slows to andante; the second and third movements, lento; the fourth movement, rubato.

A57 _____. "The War Among the Ty-rones." *Eugene O'Neill Newsletter* 11.2 (1987): 29-31.

To explain the "poetic," "musical," or "rhythmic" effect of *Journey*, Black looks at the family dynamic as moving from alliances (harmony) to contrapuntal rejections (discord), which give the play a "symphonic-like structure."

A58 _____. "Eugene O'Neill in Mourning." *Biography: An Interdisciplinary Quarterly* 11.1 (1988): 16-34.

Focusing on *Iceman* and *Journey*, Black discusses how personal losses and grieving affected O'Neill's plays so that the writing process became for the playwright inseparable from the grieving process.

A59 _____. "Reality and Its Vicissi-tudes: The Problem of Understanding in *Long Day's Journey into Night.*" *Eugene O'Neill Review* 16.2 (1992): 57-72.

"Argues that O'Neill makes the Tyrones embody the values, achievements and failures of Western culture in ways that link the play to its tragic tradition; and that, in so doing, O'Neill delineates the specific qualities of tragedy in our time."

A60 _____. "On Jason Robards as O'Neill's Nietzschean Iceman." *Eugene O'Neill Review* 17.1-2 (1993): 149-56.

A long tribute to Jason Robards' 1960 interpretation of the role of Hickey. Concludes that "O'Neill and Robards conspire to make Hickey's madness less psychiatric than Dionysian. Jason Robards helps us to know how great a play *The Iceman Cometh* is."

A61 _____. "O'Neill and the Old Ham." *Eugene O'Neill Review* 17.1-2 (1993): 77-81.

Taking a psychoanalytic approach, Black finds that despite prevailing opinion that the playwright was "'an emotional hemophiliac whose family-inflicted wounds never healed' O'Neill did in fact reach a state of psychic emancipation in the two years before his father's death."

A62 _____. "Eugene O'Neill in Mourning." *Eugene O'Neill Review* 18.1-2 (1994): 171-88.

A reprint with additional notes. See A58.

A63 _____. "O'Neill's Early Reckless-ness." *Eugene O'Neill Review* 20.1-2 (1996): 11-16.

Takes a look at an O'Neill play that gets no respect — *Recklessness* — for signs of the genius who would appear just five years later in *Horizon*. Concludes that there are hints of "personal coherence" in the playwright's self-psychoanalysis contained therein.

A64 _____. "Episodes from a Life of O'Neill." *Eugene O'Neill Review* 22.1-2 (1998): 6-22.

Three papers delivered at the 1997, 1998, 1999 O'Neill sessions of the ALA as foreshad-owings of Black's *Eugene O'Neill: Beyond Mourning and Tragedy* (1999), for which see B50.

A65 Blank, Martin. "Eugene O'Neill in South Africa: Margaret Webster's Produc-tion of *A Touch of the Poet.*" *Theatre Survey* 29. 1 (1988): 113-15.

Sheds light on the 1961 South African production of O'Neill's play, directed by British-American Margaret Webster. While the play was generally well received by both critics and audience in Johannesburg, when it went on tour, the fact that it played to segre-gated audiences precipitated protest.

A66 Blau, Eleanor. "News of the The-ater." *New York Times* 11 Mar. 1981, sec. C: 19.

Announces the removal of Geraldine Fitzgerald's *Journey* from the Theater at St. Peter's Church to Joseph Papp's Anspacher — to open there 18 Mar. 1981.

A67 Blesch, Edwin J., Jr. "O'Neill's *Hughie*: A Misconceived Experiment?" *The Nassau Review: The Journal of Nassau Com-munity College Devoted to Arts, Letters, and Sci-ences* 2 (1974): 1-8.

The problem with the play is that it is more like a monologue than a drama.

A68 _____. "Lots of Desire, No Elms: A Consideration of Eugene O'Neill's *Desire Under the Elms* on Film." *The Nassau Review: The Journal of Nassau Community College Devoted to Arts, Letters, and Sciences* 4 (1981): 14-22.

Examines the 1958 Paramount film of *Desire*. Based both on the original play and on a screenscript begun by M. L. Davis and completed by Irwin Shaw (which was based on a 13-page scenario done by O'Neill in 1928), the film is widely divergent from the original play. It is a drama of lust and greed but one lacking the mythic dimension of *Desire*. Finds the film inept in technical execution, interpretation of roles, casting, and artistic conception.

A69 Bliss, Matt. "'So happy for a time': A Cultural Poetics of Eugene O'Neill's *Long Day's Journey into Night*." *American Drama* 7.1 (1997): 1-17.

Sees the tragedy of the play in the Americanization of Tyrone — in his need for property, his work ethic, his denigration of his Irish tenant — and the impact it has on his wife's and sons' dreams.

A70 Bloom, Steven F. "The Role of Drinking and Alcoholism in O'Neill's Late Plays." *Eugene O'Neill Newsletter* 8.1 (1984): 22-27.

Studies O'Neill's use of alcohol in *Iceman, Touch, Journey*, and *Misbegotten* and concludes that though the characters who drink are seeking transcendence, they find disappointment and emptiness.

A71 _____. "Drinking and Drunkenness in *The Iceman Cometh*: A Response to Mary McCarthy." *Eugene O'Neill Newsletter* 9.1 (1985): 3-11.

Bloom refutes Mary McCarthy's criticism of *Iceman* (the Martin Beck Theatre's 1947 production) that the characters show "virtually no evidence in the performance of the effects that such an amount of drinking as occurs in the play would actually have on human beings." O'Neill was very aware of what hardened drunks were like and depicted them accurately in *Iceman*.

A72 _____. "Waiting for the Dough: O'Neill's *Hughie*." *Eugene O'Neill Newsletter* 12.3 (1988): 28-35.

Although at first glance *Hughie* may seem Godotesque, upon "closer examination it is unmistakably O'Neillian."

A73 _____. "Alcoholism and Intoxication in *A Touch of the Poet*." *Dionysos* 2.3 (1991): 31-39.

Points out that in O'Neill's later plays "intoxication is both romantic metaphor and naturalistic detail." At the end of *Touch* "we are confronted with O'Neill's vision of the lonely emptiness and purposelessness of human life surrounded by drunken voices of desperation trying to escape from it."

A74 _____. "The Lingering (Comic?) Legacy of Eugene O'Neill." *Eugene O'Neill Review* 20.1-2 (1996): 139-46.

Admits that it may seem a bit of a stretch to find the influence of O'Neill on two Jewish-American comic writers, but Bloom does. Recent plays by Neil Simon and Woody Allen "have suggested a strong 'O'Neill connection.'"

A75 Bogard, Travis. "C.W.D.'s at Tao House." *Eugene O'Neill Newsletter* 1.1 (1977): 3-5.

Tao House, where O'Neill worked from 1937 to 1944, was the setting of O'Neill's most intense work. At the end of each month O'Neill would note in his journal "C.W.D. 30," which meant 30 creative working days. The only breaks in creativity were caused by illness. It was here he wrote *Touch, Mansions, Journey, Misbegotten, Hughie, Iceman*, as well as worked on the 11-play cycle. Traces the subsequent history of the house, to its presently becoming a historic site.

A76 _____. "'My Yosephine': The Music from *Anna Christie*." *Eugene O'Neill Newsletter* 8.3 (1984): 12-13.

No song of this title was copyrighted, but apparently O'Neill borrowed it from a bartender at the Hell Hole, who made it up. A letter from O'Neill to Agnes Boulton indicates as much.

A77 _____. "Eugene O'Neill in the West." *Eugene O'Neill Newsletter* 9.2 (1985): 11-16.

Discusses O'Neill's conception of California in plays O'Neill envisioned and those he realized. Concludes that "so far as the west itself was concerned, O'Neill made little use of it, other than as a poetic, thematic image. California writer though he was [for a time], he remained an easterner in thought and deed."

A78 _____. "First Love: Eugene O'Neill and 'Boutade.'" *Eugene O'Neill Newsletter* 12.1 (1988): 3-9.

See Primary Works section, G18.

A79 _____. "Little Orphan Annie Christie." New Haven: Long Wharf Theatre Program Note, Mar. 1990.

Looks at the history of the play, from the real life inspirations for the characters, to the earlier version, to the finished product, to critical reaction.

A80 _____, ed. "Directing a Radio Production of Eugene O'Neill's *The Hairy Ape*." *Theatre Journal* 43 (1991): 337-59.

See Bauersfeld A28.

A81 _____. "Alice and Alla." *Eugene O'Neill Review* 18.1-2 (1994): 65-77.

Provides some background/anecdotal material on the women who starred in the premiere of *Electra*— Alla Nazimova (Christine) and Alice Brady (Lavinia)— not to mention on the youthful Bogard. Both actresses Bogard saw on stage in his adolescence, though not in the O'Neill play.

A82 _____. "Edna Kenton." *Eugene O'Neill Review* 21.1-2 (1997): 6-13.

Serves as preface to the *Review*'s publication of Edna Kenton's *The Provincetown Players and the Playwrights' Theatre*, an insider's look at the historic theater movement. Bogard explains the inexplicable, Edna Kenton's connections with and functions within the group, her devotion to the Cooks and their vision, and her break with the group, that came with its inevitable move toward a commercially viable theater.

A83 _____, and Jackson R. Bryer. "A Comradeship-in-Arms: A Letter from Eugene O'Neill to Arthur Miller, introduced by Travis Bogard and Jackson L. Bryer." *Eugene O'Neill Review* 17.1-2 (1993): 121-23.

See Primary Works section, G8.

A84 Booth, Willard. "Haunting Fragments from Eugene O'Neill." *Adam* 39 (1973): 37-40.

The article occurs in a section entitled "Views and Reviews" and suggests that O'Neill may have reserved *Touch* and *Mansions* for a later trilogy. Stresses that O'Neill's thesis was that we are what we are because our parents were what they were.

A85 Bordewyk, Gordon, and Michael McGowan. "Another Source of Eugene O'Neill's *The Emperor Jones*." *Notes on Modern American Literature* 6 (1982): Item 2.

O'Neill found his model for Brutus Jones in Marcus Garvey, whose Universal Negro Improvement Association had its spectacular convention in Harlem during August 1920, while O'Neill was in New York, when Garvey spoke before 20,000-25,000 people in Madison Square Garden and, dressed in a dazzling uniform, took part in a parade several miles long. Finds that Jones and Garvey had similar personalities.

A86 Bower, Martha. "The Cycle Women and Carlotta Monterey O'Neill." *Eugene O'Neill Newsletter* 10.2 (1986): 29-33.

While admitting that the women in most O'Neill plays are "angels of destruction," Bower says that the women in the Cycle plays, "although maintaining the same destructive tendencies and deference to the male ego, achieve a self-determination, an independence of spirit and an uncharacteristic ability to succeed in the materialistic male world of business and profit taking." Sees in Sara Melody (*Touch*), Leda Cade (*The Calms of Capricorn*), and Bessie Bowen (*Hair of the Dog*) a penchant for masculine roles, which may have been inspired by Carlotta O'Neill's character.

A87 _____. "Carlotta Monterey and Eugene O'Neill: A Specular Collaboration." *Eugene O'Neill Review* 19.1-2 (1995): 139-49.

Looks at O'Neill's personal/psychological dependency on Carlotta and concludes that she, unlike Agnes Boulton, was essential for his creativity.

A88 _____. "Upstairs/Downstairs: Dueling Triangles in *A Touch of the Poet*." *Eugene O'Neill Review* 20.1-2 (1996): 97-101.

Asserting that the play is a "superbly crafted theatrical piece, Bower analyzes alterations O'Neill made in his original conception to render it so. Removing Simon as a visible presence so that the action can focus on family relationships was a brilliant stroke.

A89 Bowles, Patrick. "Another Biblical Parallel in *Desire Under the Elms*." *Eugene O'Neill Newsletter* 2.3 (1979): 10-12

Likens Eben to Adonijah, who infuriated Solomon by asking for Abishag's hand. Both stories tell of a young man in competition with his master. Eben, like Adonijah, will presumably be executed. Abbie is like Abishag, who was brought to warm King David in his old age.

A90 _____. "*The Hairy Ape* as Existential Allegory." *Eugene O'Neill Newsletter* 3.1 (1979): 2-3.

Yank represents "the human self which is

prior to either primitive or civilized consciousness." He is like the Heideggerian man, who "can never belong since he is ever a human becoming and never a human being." Yank is "spreadeagled between ape and essence."

A91 Brooks, Marshall. "New London: A Mental Traveller's Note." *Eugene O'Neill Newsletter* 3.2 (1979): 7-8.

Description and pictures of Monte Cristo Cottage.

A92 _____. "Harry Kemp: Lest We Forget." *Eugene O'Neill Newsletter* 4.1-2 (1980): 15-17.

Remembers the eccentric Kemp, a footnote to O'Neill biography, who played the part of the poet in the 1916 Wharf Theatre production of *Cardiff*. Kemp "knew, abused, or bored the right people."

A93 _____. "Eugene O'Neill's Boston." *Eugene O'Neill Newsletter* 8.2 (1984): 19-21.

A walking tour of O'Neill's Boston, which points out places where O'Neill lived and places which he frequented when he lived in Boston as a student at Harvard and toward the end of his life.

A94 Brown, Carolyn T. "Creative Imitation: Hung Shen's Cultural Translation of Eugene O'Neill's *The Emperor Jones.*" *Comparative Literature Studies* 22 (1985): 147-55.

Recognizing David Chen's and Marián Gálik's earlier studies of the influence of O'Neill on Hung Shen, this essay examines the cultural implications suggested by the similarities between and differences in *Jones* and *Yama Chao*. Sees Jones as the "master" of his destiny, reflecting the classical ideal of hero struggling with fate, while Yama Chao is the "victim" of his destiny—a view which reflects in a radical form, a traditional eastern attitude.

A95 Brucher, Richard. "O'Neill, *Othello* and Robeson." *Eugene O'Neill Review* 18.1-2 (1994): 45-58.

While *Chillun* may not have influenced the Theatre Guild's *Othello*, O'Neill's play may have paved the way for it. Moreover, "*All God's Chillun* ... travesties Shakespeare's *Othello* in an appropriately twentieth-century way, and Robeson's Othello rebuts the disturbing ending of O'Neill's Jim Crow tragedy." Finally, sees in *Journey* parody of the roles of Jim Harris and Othello in James Tyrone.

A96 Bryer, Jackson R., and Ruth M. Alvarez. "American Drama, 1918-1940: A Survey of Research and Criticism." *American Quarterly* 30 (1978): 298-330.

Includes thirty or so items on or related to O'Neill.

A97 Burke, Tom. *New York Times* 15 May 1977, sec. 2: 5+.

About Mary McCarty, who played Marthy Owen in Quintero's *Anna*.

A98 Burlingame, Michael. "O'Neill Recalled Warmly." *Day* [New London, CT] 21 July 1988, sec. E: 1+.

Earle Johnson, who helped the O'Neills decorate their Marblehead home and became one of their last friends, shares "for the first time" his recollections of the playwright's final years. There is nothing surprising to our understanding of O'Neill or his relationship with Carlotta, though some of the anecdotes are new.

A99 Butler, Robert. "Artifice and Art: Words in *The Iceman Cometh* and *Hughie.*" *Eugene O'Neill Newsletter* 5.1 (1981): 3-6.

The verbal and moral disintegration in *Iceman* is reversed in *Hughie*. In *Hughie* O'Neill allows characters to overcome the silence and alienation by creating with words a fictive world, which could be the source of useful illusions. Whereas Hickey's illusions about Evelyn are debilitating, Erie's are creative.

A100 Butler, Ron. "O'Neill's New London Turns Back." *Boston Herald America* 22 Feb. 1981, sec. B: 10.

Reports on various restoration projects taking place in New England, including work on Monte Cristo Cottage.

A101 Cahill, Gloria. "Mothers and Whores: The Process of Integration in the Plays of Eugene O'Neill." *Eugene O'Neill Review* 16.1 (1992): 5-23.

Beginning with the premise that "the playwright's quest for a return to the womb was closely connected to his desire to bridge the gap between two mother figures who dominated his life" (Ella O'Neill and Sarah Sandy), Cahill discusses O'Neill's attempt to integrate the polarities of mother and whore in his characters. In charting the process of integration, she looks at *Anna, Chillun, Brown, Desire,* and *Misbegotten.*

A102 Cardullo, Bert. "The Function of Simon Harford in *A Touch of the Poet.*" *Eugene O'Neill Newsletter* 8.1 (1984): 27-28.

Simon Harford is a foil to Con Melody.

Simon is a symbol of truth, while Con is a symbol of deception. In *Mansions* Simon ceases to be a symbol of truth.

A103 _____. "Parallelism and Divergence: The Case of *She Stoops to Conquer* and *Long Day's Journey into Night*." *Eugene O'Neill Newsletter* 9.2 (1985): 31-34.

Both plays have a maid Bridget, who is absent, lazy, and cantankerous; both Hardcastle and Tyrone are nostalgic and thrifty; and both plays use disguise.

A104 _____. "Dreams of Journey." *Eugene O'Neill Review* 18.1-2 (1994): 132-34.

Gives us a brief look at *Journey* as a dream play.

A105 _____. "Two Short Articles: Dreams of Journey." *Moderna Sprak* 89.1 (1995): 30-32.

A short article/note that looks at *Journey* as a dream play. See previous entry.

A106 _____. "Dreams of Journey: *Long Day's Journey into Night*." *Notes on Contemporary Literature* 26 (1996): 3-5.

A short article/note that looks at *Journey* as a dream play. See previous entries.

A107 Carpenter, Charles A. "Elusive Articles, Books, and Parts of Books about O'Neill, 1966-78: Addenda to Miller." *Eugene O'Neill Newsletter* 2.3 (1979): 29-31.

A supplement to Miller's *Eugene O'Neill and the American Critic*. Over 50 additions.

A108 _____. "American Drama: A Bibliographic Essay." *American Studies International* 21.5 (1983): 3-52.

A general bibliographical essay on American dramatic literature. Concentrates on dramatic literature rather than performances, books rather than articles, and, especially, books published after 1950. Pages 24-28 concern O'Neill. The importance of O'Neill to the larger work is indicated by the way the essay is divided: playwrights before O'Neill and playwrights after O'Neill.

A109 Carpenter, Frederic I. "The Enduring O'Neill: The Early Plays." *Eugene O'Neill Newsletter* 1.1 (1977): 1-3.

Defends O'Neill's early plays: Carpenter saw in the original performances many things which moved and continue to move him strongly. *Desire, Beyond, Anna, Interlude, Jones, Wilderness* are, he is certain, enduring works.

A110 _____. "*Hughie*: By Way of Obit." *Eugene O'Neill Newsletter* 2.2 (1978): 1-3.

Hughie is a "parable of the creative imagination," and is also highly autobiographical in that Smith's struggle to reach his audience parallels O'Neill's.

A111 _____. "*Strange Interlude—* Strange Criticism." *Eugene O'Neill Newsletter* 8.3 (1984): 22-24.

The receptions of recent London productions of *Interlude* and *Journey*, the first panned by critics and loved by audiences, the second applauded by critics but unsuccessful, lead Carpenter to reflect on the standards critics use to judge the works. Decides that *Journey*, which abides by the unities, is appreciated for that reason, unlike *Interlude*, which is more experimental. Inveighs against a narrowness of perception that finds only the *Poetics'* standards acceptable. See A346.

A112 _____. "Eugene O'Neill and the Orient: A Forward Glance." *Eugene O'Neill Review* 13.1 (1989): 27-28.

A preface to articles by Frank R. Cunningham ("'Authentic Tidings of Invisible Things': Beyond James Robinson's *Eugene O'Neill and Oriental Thought*") and James Robinson ("O'Neill's Indian *Elms*"), which are, says the politic Carpenter, complementary.

A113 Cawthon, Daniel. "Eugene O'Neill: Progenitor of a New Religious Drama." *Theatre and Religion* 1 (1992): 21-30.

"O'Neill's theatre, from beginning to end, documents his attempt to create a new symbol-system, a new mythology, for expressing 'the Force behind—Fate, God, our biological past … Mystery certainly.'" Ultimately, it is the poet, the priest, "who stands amid the rubble of fallen humanity and sees 'Behind Life.'" O'Neill "forged a religious theatre for modern times, creating a unique way of perceiving the relationship of man to God."

A114 "Celebrating the O'Neill Centennial." *Sunset* 181 (Sept. 1988): 16.

A brief description of Tao House and its accessibility during this the centennial year of O'Neill's birth. It also notes some California stage productions of *Marco, Electra, Anna, Brown*, and "selections" from the sea plays.

A115 Chabrowe, Leonard. "An Open Letter to John Henry Raleigh." *Eugene O'Neill Newsletter* 1.2 (1977): 8-10.

A defense of his book *Ritual and Pathos: The Theater of O'Neill* against Raleigh's review in *American Literature*. See B91.

A116 Chandran, S. Subhash. "Life and Death at War: A Study of Eugene O'Neill's *Hughie*." *Indian Journal of American Studies* [Hyderabad] 27.1 (1997): 47-53.

If *Iceman* "equates pipe dreams with life … *Hughie* depicts the horrors of human existence without pipe dreams." Thereafter *Hughie* shows "that life and death are equally potential winners in a struggle for domination."

A117 Chioles, John. "Aeschylus and O'Neill: A Phenomenological View." *Comparative Drama* 14 (1980): 159-87.

Discusses *Electra* as phenomenological in the sense that it places man at the center of the world. Also considers O'Neill's concept of trilogy, use of masks, and use of chorus vis-à-vis Aeschylus' use of the same.

A118 Chothia, Jean. "'Native Eloquence': Multiple Voices in *Long Day's Journey into Night*." *Eugene O'Neill Newsletter* 12.3 (1988): 24-28.

Focuses on *Journey* to justify O'Neill's use of language and concludes that "Using an unusually extensive range of registers and speech forms, O'Neill has found scenic and linguistic means to explore the themes of alienation, inarticulacy, and dispossession, experienced by people striving for something more."

A119 _____. "O'Neill in London —*A Touch of the Poet*." *Recorder* 3.1 (1989): 67-72.

Discovers, in "the first ever London staging" of *Touch*, that the play, when responded to sensitively by director and actors, "shares a surprising amount of ground" with O'Neill's most finished last plays, *Iceman* and *Journey*. Though "it lacks the depth and scale" of those two, it has a "remarkable tonal range," that moves from "broad farce" to "bleak despair."

The casting of Vanessa Redgrave as Nora is a "bold" move that gives us a different balance and tension than is usually sensed in the play.

A120 _____. "Questions of Significance: Some Recent Work in O'Neill Studies." *Journal of American Studies* 23 (1989): 311-14.

Review-essay assesses five then-recently-published books, including *The Unknown O'Neill* (ed. Travis Bogard), *Eugene O'Neill at Work* (ed. Virginia Floyd), *Eugene O'Neill: Comments on the Drama and the Theater* (ed. Ulrich Halfmann), *Eugene O'Neill: The Unfin-* ished Plays (ed. Virginia Floyd), and *O'Neill's The Iceman Cometh: Reconstructing the Premiere* (by Gary Vena). After explaining why 1988 was the annus mirabilis of O'Neill's revival, Chothia turns to the publications which marked the centennial of O'Neill's birth. Halfmann's and Bogard's books are "largely complementary": the former "a meticulously annotated volume, which will become an essential handbook," the latter containing "Bogard's unfailingly intelligent and good-humoured annotations." Vena's reconstruction of the 1946 *Iceman* is "a notable contribution to this kind of criticism." Of Floyd's work, Chothia says that while *Eugene O'Neill at Work* provides "invaluable earlier versions of the finished plays," *The Unfinished Plays* reminds us that "scholars can lose sight of the realities of theatre." Disputes some of Floyd's assessments of O'Neill's fragmentary notes.

A121 Ciancio, Ralph A. "Richard Wright, Eugene O'Neill and the Beast in the Skull." *Modern Language Studies* 23.3 (1993): 45-59.

Looks at O'Neill's *Ape* as a possible influence on Richard Wright's *Native Son*. Ciancio allows for the possibility that Wright may have drawn on the work subconsciously.

A122 Clarity, James F. Rev. of the *Great Soviet Encyclopedia*. *New York Times* 9 Jan. 1975: 4.

In the most recent volume of the *Great Soviet Encyclopedia*, O'Neill is treated without moral or social comment, whereas in the 1954 edition he was described as a "decadent American playwright." *Iceman* is no longer viewed as "a complete degradation."

A123 Cline, Francis X. "O'Neill's Words Echo and Play at Sea View Hospital." *New York Times* 12 June 1979, sec. B: 3.

Describes a dress rehearsal of *Misbegotten* that took place at the Sea View Hospital, the municipal nursing home on Staten Island, on 6 June 1979.

A124 Clurman, Harold. "What Was Broadway's All-Time Best Season?" *New York Times* 9 Mar. 1980, sec. 2: 1+.

Considers what might have been Broadway's greatest season, even though Clurman concedes this is highly speculative. Suggests that 1919-20 season, when *Horizon* played at the Morosco Theater, might be a contender, but says his favorite season was 1924-25, when *Desire* appeared: the number of plays that season coupled with the stature of the actors determines his choice.

A125 Codde, Philippe. " 'Dat ole davil, sea': Cowardice and Redemption in Eugene O'Neill's *Anna Christie.*" *Eugene O'Neill Review* 22.1-2 (1998): 23-32.

Using the Sartrean assumption that in a godless, existential world all who do not accept responsibility for themselves are cowards, Codde shows how the one character in *Anna* who is not a coward, Mat, leads Anna into behaving courageously — that is, into accepting responsibility for herself.

A126 Colakis, Marianthe. "Eugene O'Neill's *The Emperor Jones* as Senecan Tragedy." *Classical and Modern Literature* 10.2 (1990): 153-59.

Offers another possible influence on O'Neill's play — Seneca. "It is therefore quite appropriate to compare him with the ancient dramatist most directly concerned with philosophical questions. Both Seneca and O'Neill dramatized power and its abuses by enacting a character's hopes, fears, and delusions before our eyes." Looks to *Jones* to prove the point.

A127 Combs, Robert. "O'Neill's (and Others') Characters as Others." *Eugene O'Neill Review* 20.1-2 (1996): 119-25.

Addresses the admittedly slippery subject of "otherness" in O'Neill's canon to find that in the later plays "the futile struggle against becoming an Other is explored with great compassion and a sort of artistic ruthlessness. As the boundaries between self and other disappear, there comes epiphany."

A128 Como, Robert M. "O'Neill, Beckett, and Dürrenmatt: The Shared Genre." *Eugene O'Neill Review* 13.2 (1989): 63-72.

Finding common ground in O'Neill's later work (*Iceman*) and the work of Absurdists Beckett (*Godot*) and Dürrenmatt (*The Visit*), Como looks at the plays as "impure" genres, mixing elements of tragedy and comedy.

A129 Conklin, Robert. "The Expression of Character in O'Neill's *The Emperor Jones* and *The Hairy Ape.*" *Philological Papers* 39 (1993): 101-07.

Points out the contradiction behind these plays — that characterization conflicts with the Expressionistic form of the plays. This results in the playwright's attempt to model the literary movements occurring in Europe (hence his Expressionism) and to escape the melodramatic theater of his predecessors (hence character development marks his plays). The clash of these literary impulses in O'Neill's work makes for a watershed moment in theater history.

A130 Connolly, Thomas F. "Was Good Old Nathan Reliable?" *Eugene O'Neill Review* 20.1-2 (1996): 72-79.

While most of George Jean Nathan's critical judgments of O'Neill's plays are sound, we must scrutinize carefully the image of the man that Nathan labored to create. O'Neill's friend was working hard to counter the playwright's public "sourball" image. To understand Nathan, Connolly delves into the critic's biography.

A131 Cooley, John R. "*The Emperor Jones* and the Harlem Renaissance." *Studies in the Literary Imagination* 7 (1974): 73-83.

While O'Neill showed considerable interest in the problem of blacks between 1914 and 1924, it should be remembered that the roles of blacks on the stage were usually played by whites in blackface. Cooley reevaluates *Jones* in terms of the Harlem Renaissance New Negro Movement (which celebrated black achievement and declared freedom from white myths and stereotypes of blacks). In this context he sees O'Neill's picture of Jones as a combination of a number of white stereotypes.

A132 Cooper, Gary. "Sharks." *Theatre Crafts* 14.3 (1980): 40+.

About the special effects used in a University of Wisconsin experimental production of *Thirst.* The most challenging problem was creating the illusion of sharks moving on the stage floor. One photograph.

A133 Cooperman, Robert. "*Marco Millions*: O'Neill's Other Comedy." *Eugene O'Neill Review* 13.2 (1989): 39-44.

Examines the comic elements and ending of O'Neill's often overlooked comedy. "The play may fail as poetry, and it may even have defied most attempts at staging it. But it is surely time for *Marco Millions* to take its rightful place beside *Ah, Wilderness!* as O'Neill's other (and more sophisticated) comedy."

A134 _____. "Unacknowledged Familiarity: Jean Toomer and Eugene O'Neill." *Eugene O'Neill Review* 16.1 (1992): 39-41.

Admitting that he is on tenuous ground, Cooperman nonetheless makes a case for the mutual influence of contemporaries Jean Toomer and Eugene O'Neill, focusing on the similarities between Ella Downey in *Chillun* and Toomer creations.

A135 Coppenger, Royston. "The Incomplete Plays of Eugene O'Neill: Floyd's *Eugene O'Neill at Work*." *Theater* 13.3 (1982): 65-69.

A review-essay which finds that the "book's major shortcomings" stem from the editor's enthusiasm for O'Neill: she sees his art in the details of his life; she engages in "facile psychologizing"; she finds "self references lurking" everywhere. And she misses seeing O'Neill in history, in his contemporary world, as an evolving artist, as a man of great energy and imagination, and as a man with deep concern for the oppressed and a profound spirituality. For the book being reviewed see Primary Works section, G11.

A136 Cordaro, Joseph. "Long Day's Journey into Frankenstein." *Eugene O'Neill Review* 18.1-2 (1994): 116-28.

Explains the implications of Jamie Tyrone's confusion of creator and creation in his allusion to Mary Shelley's *Frankenstein*— or is it O'Neill's confusion?

A137 Corey, James. "O'Neill's *The Emperor Jones*." *American Notes and Queries* 12 (1974): 156-57.

A line-by-line comparison of how O'Neill patterned his witch doctor scene in *Jones* after a scene in Conrad's *Heart of Darkness*.

A138 Costello, Donald P. "Forgiveness in O'Neill." *Modern Drama* 34(1991): 499-512.

Argues that in life and art O'Neill searched first for pity, then understanding, and finally forgiveness. Discusses *Horizon, Iceman, Journey* and *Misbegotten* as plays which mark the playwright's progress toward forgiveness.

A139 _____. "Sidney Lumet's *Long Day's Journey into Night*." *Literature Film Quarterly* 22.2 (1994): 78-92.

Justifies his belief that Lumet's adaptation of O'Neill's masterpiece is "the best movie ever made of an American play."

A140 Costley, Bill. "Spithead Revisited, 1979." *Eugene O'Neill Newsletter* 3.3 (1979): 5-6.

Brief recounting of author's 1979 visit to Spithead [Bermuda], a former O'Neill residence.

A141 _____. "Black Bread vs. *Strange Interlude*: O'Neill Parodied." *Eugene O'Neill Newsletter* 4.3 (1980): 14.

Calls attention to a parody/synopsis of *Interlude* by Eric Linklater, Scottish novelist and dramatist, in his book *Juan in America* (1931). Some slight attention to the Marx Brothers' one-reeler *Strange Innertube*.

A142 Coy, Stephen C., and Barbara Gelb. Letters. *New York Times* 8 Apr. 1973, sec. 2: 21.

Exchange of letters between Coy and Gelb about her 4 Mar. 1973 article in the *Times*. Gelb said she thought James Tyrone custodial yet resentful of Mary; Coy disagrees.

A143 Cranston, Alan. "A Living Monument to Eugene O'Neill." *New York Times* 24 Oct. 1976, sec. 2: 7-8.

Cranston (U.S. Senator from California) describes O'Neill's association with Tao House and the six-year struggle to get government support for the landmark.

A144 Cunningham, Frank R. "*The Great God Brown* and O'Neill's Romantic Vision." *Ball State University Forum* 14.3 (1973): 69-78.

The goal of society (Billy Brown) to destroy Dion Anthony's creativity, and the psychic conflict in Dion create the tension of the play. The source of O'Neill's thought — Nietzsche's doctrine of eternal recurrence — is reflected in the play's structure and technique, and in the similarities between the prologue and the epilogue.

A145 _____. "*Lazarus Laughed*: A Study in O'Neill's Romanticism." *Studies in the Twentieth Century* 15 (1975): 51-75.

Argues the difficulty of imagining in dramatic literature, "save Goethe's *Faust II*, an attempt to create the ideal and of bringing to fruition" the fusion of Nietzsche and Buddha.

A146 _____. "*The Ancient Mariner* and the Genesis of O'Neill's Romanticism." *Eugene O'Neill Newsletter* 3.1 (1979): 6-9.

O'Neill's early adaptation of Coleridge's poem, dramatizing the reconciliation of man with nature, revealed an interest which the playwright never lost.

A147 _____. "'Authentic Tidings of Invisible Things': Beyond James Robinson's *Eugene O'Neill and Oriental Thought*." *Eugene O'Neill Review* 13.1 (1989): 29-39.

Taking issue that for O'Neill's characters transcendence lies in an "orientally or occidentally conceived static beatitude beyond the horizon," Cunningham argues it is found in "a strengthened, more enlightened self that can better join with the oneness of the universe." He sees less promise in the pursuit of Orientalism as a means of understanding the playwright's canon than in an examination of Western Romanticism and pre-Existential thought.

A148 _____. "Eugene O'Neill in Our Time: Overcoming Student Resistance." *Eugene O'Neill Review* 16.2 (1992): 45-55.

Looks at possible reasons for student indifference to O'Neill's work, considers what is available in anthologies to be taught, lists possible approaches to the canon, and ultimately justifies the playwright's modernism.

A149 _____. "O'Neill's Beginnings and the Birth of Modernism in American Drama." *Eugene O'Neill Review* 17.1-2 (1993): 11-20.

Contends O'Neill's power derives from "his unique capacity to drive us deep into the unknown within ourselves ... in his ability to synthesize apparently contradictory aspects of experience into imaginatively subtle and arresting art, like other great writers more widely acknowledged than O'Neill as in the Modernist tradition." The author of this article examines some of O'Neill's early efforts to demonstrate these modernist leanings.

A150 _____. "A Newly Discovered Fourth Production of O'Neill's *Lazarus Laughed*." *Eugene O'Neill Review* 22.1-2 (1998): 114-22.

Reports on a fourth production of O'Neill's unwieldy play, a 1963 production mounted at Mercy College, in Detroit, wherein Lazarus' laughter was "in part sung, somewhat on the model of Gregorian chant." An appendix provides a typescript of the program.

A151 Curran, Ronald T. "Insular Typees: Puritanism and Primitivism in *Mourning Becomes Electra*." *Revue des Langues Vivantes* [Belgium] 41 (1975): 371-77.

The allusions to *Typee* and to the Blessed Isles in *Electra* are O'Neill's attempts to re-employ "in various forms the conventional image of exotic islands in order to gain a universally-conditioned response from his audience — escape from unpleasant reality." But whatever the islands mean to the audience, there is no escape for O'Neill's characters. For them, escape (the islands) is not only freedom but sexual license as well, and any suggestion

of the latter revivifies the curse of their ancestral New England puritanism.

A152 Curtis, Anthony. "London." *Drama: The Quarterly Theatre Review* 133 (1979): 46-47.

Argues *The Long Voyage Home* (includes *Voyage, Zone,* and *Caribbees*) is good early O'Neill, enriched by incidents from his own life and worked up with "a certainty of touch."

A153 Dai, Gang. "Eugene O'Neill in China." *Beijing Review* 1 Aug. 1988: 24-26.

Describes the "artistic tributes" and other cultural activities celebrating the 100th anniversary of the birth of O'Neill, the "father of modern American drama," especially performances of a dozen O'Neill plays and the meeting of the international O'Neill Society at the Eugene O'Neill Festival in Nanjing and Shanghai, 6-14 June. There is also a brief survey, going back to 1935, of the history of the China-O'Neill connection.

A154 Dallett, Athenaide. "Old Beauty and Gutter Tramps: O'Neill on Stage." *Eugene O'Neill Review* 18.1-2 (1994): 13-20.

Summarizes the 12 May 1995 panel "O'Neill on Stage," a session of the conference "O'Neill's People" (at Suffolk University), which featured O'Neill actor Jason Robards and director José Quintero.

A155 Dawes, James R. "Drama and Ethics, Grief and Privacy: The Case of Eugene O'Neill." *Eugene O'Neill Review* 17.1-2 (1993): 83-92.

Prefacing his discussion by noting O'Neill's dread of personal revelation, Dawes looks at the playwright's giving birth to so highly personal a play as *Journey* and concludes that "representation is therapy" since "it removes the psychic wound, transforming pain into language and then disentangling the language from the self."

A156 Dee, James H. "Orestes and Electra in the Twentieth Century." *Classical Bulletin* 55.6 (1979): 81-87.

Examines five 20th-century plays that use the Orestes-Electra myth: Hofmannsthal's *Elektra*, O'Neill's *Electra*, Giradoux's *Electre*, Sartre's *Les Mouches*, and Richardson's *The Prodigal*. All five plays exhibit the playwrights' "own programmatic concerns" at the expense of the issues raised in their sources. Though the characters in O'Neill's trilogy are "impressive as projections of the intense forces struggling inside O'Neill himself," "the love-hate relations among the characters ... have an exaggerately precise symmetry that borders on the comical."

A157 Ditsky, John M. "All Irish Here: The 'Irishman' in Modern Drama." *Dalhousie Review* 54 (1974): 94-102.

Discusses characteristics of the Irish in plays by Miller, Pinter, and O'Neill (*Ape, Touch* and *Iceman*). The Irishman is displaced, a wanderer, a dreamer-poet, an interpreter of life, a fighter, a drinker, and a loser.

He is incompatible with the American success ethic. But he is part of our heritage, so we all identify with him.

A158 Doloff, Steven. "'O'Neill's 'Ice-Man.'" *Eugene O'Neill Review* 17.1-2 (1993): 231-32.

An onomastic note on the significance of the name *Hickey*, deriving from the Irish root for *cure* or *physician*.

A159 _____. "Hickey's Name in Eugene O'Neill's *The Iceman Cometh*." *Onomastica Canadiana* 78.1 (1996): 26.

See the annotation for A158.

A160 Dougherty, Dru, and María Francisca Vilches de Frutos. "Eugene O'Neill in Madrid, 1918-1936." *Eugene O'Neill Review* 17.1-2 (1993): 157-64.

Discusses Spanish translations of O'Neill's work and performances between the wars and concludes that while not many translations appeared nor productions were staged, "O'Neill's presence there takes on a significance that surpasses first impressions."

A161 Drucker, Trudy. "Sexuality as Destiny: The Shadow Lives of O'Neill's Women." *Eugene O'Neill Newsletter* 6.2 (1982): 7-10.

Comments on O'Neill's limited view of women, despite the fact that he was exposed to some of the most avant-garde women of his day.

A162 _____. "The Return of O'Neill's 'Play of Old Sorrow.'" *Eugene O'Neill Newsletter* 10.3 (1986): 21-23.

A review-essay, responding to the televised version of the Jonathan Miller/Jack Lemmon/Bethel Leslie/Kevin Spacey/Peter Gallagher *Journey*. Lemmon was the "best of all the fine actors" she had seen in the role of James; faulted several directorial decisions — Mary's wearing instead of carrying the wedding dress in the last act, the pace of delivery of her speech to Cathleen in the third act —

but found the overlapping dialogue "true to the spirit of the play." See also E325.

A163 Dubost, Thierry. "The Last of Ireland: Becoming American Irish in O'Neill's Plays." *Études Irlandaises* 23.2 (1998): 9-29.

Focuses on *Touch, Ape, Misbegotten,* and *Journey* to demonstrate the thesis: that Irish-Americans had to contend with the loss of their identity (and their religion) in their transformation to American-Irish.

A164 Duclos, Donald P. "A Plank in Faulkner's 'Lumber Room': *The Emperor Jones* and *Light in August*." *Eugene O'Neill Newsletter* 11.2 (1987): 8-13.

Thinks O'Neill's influence on Faulkner is uncharted territory, despite Faulkner's acknowledging the influence. Attempts to rectify the oversight by looking to *Jones* and *Light in August*.

A165 Dunning, Jennifer. "Quintero Takes on an Early O'Neill." *New York Times* 7 June 1981, sec. 2: 5+.

Surveys the autobiographical character of *Welded* and the original critical reception. Interviews Quintero who cut no words and sought "to capture the sense of ritual in movement that is a little stylized, in almost the way of dance." Also talks about Quintero's relationship with his cast.

A166 Dutta, Ujjal. "*The Iceman Cometh*: O'Neill's Theatre of Alien Vision." *Journal of the Department of English* [Calcutta] 17.2 (1982): 72-78.

Argues that *Iceman*, rather than being a tragedy, belongs to the Theatre of Alien Vision, a genre anticipating the work of Ionesco, Pinter, Beckett, and Albee in which the artist views "life as essentially fragmentary," speaks from a "background of nullity," denies "all possibilities of positive structure," and "attributes to death an autonomous significance."

A167 Dymkowski, Christine. "On the Edge: The Plays of Susan Glaspell." *Modern Drama* 31 (1988): 91-105.

Examines some plays of O'Neill's associate and fellow playwright Susan Glaspell. Claims that Glaspell's female characters are often seen in marginal places on stage and occupy marginal roles in dramatic action. Yet this treatment makes the women more vital to the action since Glaspell believed that the most important actions in drama happen beyond the confines of the stage. Although it has little to do with O'Neill, the book is a rewarding read in adding to the O'Neill-Provincetown Players ambience.

A168 Eder, Richard. "Missing Power." *New York Times* 26 Jan. 1977, sec. C: 15.

About Liv Ullmann and the upcoming production of *Anna*. When Quintero is directing, he suffers and imposes that suffering on his actors.

A169 Egri, Péter. "Eugene O'Neill: *The Iceman Cometh*." *Hungarian Studies in English* 11 (1977): 95-105.

Drawing comparisons among *Iceman*, Ibsen's *The Wild Duck*, and Gorky's *The Lower Depths*, Egri concludes that *Iceman* is a tragicomedy of illusion and despair. Also discusses *Iceman* in terms of Goethe's progressive/retrogressive motifs, the former furthering the action and the latter retarding it.

A170 _____. "O'Neill in Hungary: A Letter." *Eugene O'Neill Newsletter* 1.1 (1977): 15-16.

Notes there is a great deal of interest in O'Neill in Hungary. The works by O'Neill which have been translated into Hungarian include *Jones, Desire, Electra, Iceman, Journey, Misbegotten, Touch, Mansions, Movie Man, Hughie.* Comments on some scholarly treatments of O'Neill.

A171 _____. "O'Neill Productions in Hungary: A Chronological Record." *Eugene O'Neill Newsletter* 2.2 (1978): 14.

Lists O'Neill productions and years.

A172 _____. "The Short Story in the Drama: Chekhov and O'Neill." *Acta Litteraria Academiæ Scientiarum Hungaricæ* 20 (1978): 3-28.

Discusses the connection between the short story and drama in Chekhov's and O'Neill's plays. Mentions that several O'Neill one-act plays developed out of short stories he had written or others he had read. O'Neill used "short story-like dramatic units" early in his career to help him structure multiple-act plays—for instance, *Servitude*. Discusses *Misbegotten* as a play with an "unmistakable Chekhovian atmosphere"—the Janus-like quality of the characters, the lyricism of the play, the use of symbols, and the open-endedness of the acts.

A173 _____. "The Genetic and Generic Aspect of Stephen Crane's *The Red Badge of Courage*." *Acta Litteraria Academiæ Scientiarum Hungaricæ* 22 (1980): 333-48.

Explains why Crane's novel is neither historical nor naturalistic fiction, nor epic. Only the last two pages mention O'Neill, where Egri compares the charge led by Orin Mannon mentioned in *Electra* to that of Henry Fleming: both react as if they were in a trance, both suffer head wounds, and both react with a certain barbarism.

A174 _____. "The Reinterpretation of the Chekhovian Mosaic Design in O'Neill's *Long Day's Journey into Night*." *Acta Litteraria Academiæ Scientiarum Hungaricæ* 22 (1980): 29-71.

A discussion of *Journey* in terms of the short story patterns he sees in the play—the "collision between material gain and spiritual loss; the conflict of illusion and reality; the constant oscillation of emotions between the poles of attraction and repulsion, love and hate; and the confrontation of human aspirations and the workings of fate"—as they apply to the characters in the play.

A175 _____. "A Touch of the Story-Teller: The Dramatic Function of the Short Story Model in Chekhov's *Uncle Vanya* and O'Neill's *A Touch of the Poet*." *Hungarian Studies in English* 13 (1980): 93-113.

Applies the theory expressed in his *The Short Story in the Drama* to *Uncle Vanya* and *Touch*. Finds that the dramatic function of the short story as it relates to the two plays is in turning them into tragi-comedies by bringing about a concurrence of the high point of emotional tension, the turning point of the plot and the "culminating point of the dramatic action": at the "penultimate structural unit (rather than at the end) of the play."

A176 _____. "European Origins and American Originality: The Case of Drama." *Zeitschrift für Anglistik und Amerikanistik* 29 (1981): 197-206.

See the following item.

A177 _____. "*The Iceman Cometh*: European Origins and American Originality." *Eugene O'Neill Newsletter* 5.3 (1981): 5-10; 6.1 (1982): 16-24; 6.2 (1982): 30-36.

Three-part article that shows parallels between Ibsen's *The Wild Duck* and *Iceman*, and *Iceman* and Gorky's *The Lower Depth*. Also notes an affinity between O'Neill's play and Synge's "The Well of the Saints" and Conrad's short story "Tomorrow," which later became a one-act play, "One Day More." Concludes that *Iceman* draws from works by Ibsen, Gorky, Synge, Chekhov, and Conrad.

A178 _____. "The Merger of the Dramatic and the Lyric in Chekhov's *The Sea-Gull* and O'Neill's *Long Day's Journey into Night*." *Annales, Universitatis Scientiarum Budapestinensis: Sectio Philologica Moderna* 12 (1981): 65-86.

By "lyric" is meant what belongs to the tradition of poetry. The "merging" in the title is achieved by the two playwrights' use of symbolic leitmotifs (poetic or lyric devices) in their plays (the dramatic). The leitmotif for the two "is not simply a means of characterization but much rather a structural device."

A179 _____. "The Plight of War and the Predicament of Revolution: Eugene O'Neill's *The Personal Equation*." *Acta Litteraria Academiæ Scientiarum Hungaricæ* 23 (1981): 249-60.

Plot synopsis of *Equation* to which are appended some observations about the play — that it anticipates later plays (*Voyage, Horizon, Chris, The Ole Davil, Anna, Dynamo, Straw, Iceman, Electra*) and that it is a play built on antitheses.

A180 _____. "'Belonging' Lost: Alienation and Dramatic Form in Eugene O'Neill's *The Hairy Ape*." *Acta Litteraria Academiæ Scientiarum Hungaricæ* 24.1 (1982): 157-90.

Discusses *Ape* scene by scene as a play in which the protagonist moves from a state in which he believes he belongs, to one in which he realizes that he does not, to a state of mind that leads him to search for whatever it will take for him to belong. Also deals with the effect that stage directions have on the play and O'Neill's repetition of vowel and consonant sounds.

A181 _____. "The Dramatic Role of the Fog/Foghorn Leitmotif in Eugene O'Neill's *Long Day's Journey into Night*." *Amerikastudien* 27 (1982): 445-55.

Discusses "the central conflict and leitmotif-technique" of *Journey*, which is seen as alienation versus the desire for communion with others. Related are the tensions between materialism and spiritual loss, love and hate, illusion and reality, and human aspiration and fate. The characters' attitudes toward the fog and foghorn are "intimately connected with these forms of conflict."

A182 _____. "Beneath *The Calms of Capricorn*: O'Neill's Adoption and Naturalization of European Modes." *Eugene O'Neill Newsletter* 7.2 (1983): 6-17.

Studies the embryonic text of *Calms* for influences. Concludes that O'Neill's work was influenced by Shakespeare, Ibsen, the well-made melodrama, the well-made farce, Wildean comedy, Shavian comedy, Symbolist tragedy, the morality play, Chekhov, Strindberg, and Expressionistic and Absurdist drama.

A183 _____. "O'Neill's Genres: Early Performance and Late Achievement." *Eugene O'Neill Newsletter* 8.2 (1984): 9-11.

Speculates on how O'Neill integrated non-dramatic forms into his drama — the novel, the lyric, and the short story.

A184 _____. "Epic Retardation and Diversion: Hemingway, Strindberg, and O'Neill." *Zeitschrift für Anglistik und Amerikanistik* 33.4 (1985): 324-30.

A recasting of Egri's "The Origins and Originality of American Culture: The Case of Drama" and "The Epic Tradition of the European Drama and the Birth of American Tragedy." Discusses retarding motifs in drama — factors which "hold up the pace" of the action. Egri distinguishes between retarding motifs and retrogressive ones, which "divert the action from its goal." Finds examples of retrogressive motifs in Hemingway's *A Farewell to Arms* and *For Whom the Bell Tolls*. Epic retardation is found in Sillitoe's "The Loneliness of the Long Distance Runner" and Strindberg's *The Dance of Death*. But he concentrates on O'Neill's *Interlude*, discussing a number of instances of "epic retardation." The "novelistic building up and relinquishing of motive" help us to understand character. O'Neill's own youth provided ample opportunity to witness how ambitions are thwarted. Finds that in *Interlude* the epic and dramatic fuse.

A185 _____. "The Fusion of the Epic and Dramatic: Hemingway, Strindberg and O'Neill." *Eugene O'Neill Newsletter* 10.1 (1986): 16-21.

A reprint; see A184 and A187.

A186 _____. "The Social and Spiritual History of the American Dream: Eugene O'Neill, *A Tale of Possessors Self-Dispossessed*." *Acta Litteraria Academiæ Scientiarum Hungaricæ* 28.1-2 (1986): 65-89.

Discusses the conditions surrounding O'Neill's writing of the unfinished 11-play cycle and concludes that the "novelistic aspect of the dramatic project shattered the framework of the drama sequence. O'Neill's failure to complete the cycle is not a personal but an epic fiasco." Nonetheless, the failure resulted in O'Neill's turning to the dramatic pattern that furnished his masterpieces.

A187 _____. "Epic Retardation and Diversion: Hemingway, Strindberg and O'Neill." *Neohelicon* 14.1 (1987): 9-20.

Originally published in *Zeitschrift für Anglistik* 33.4 (1985): 324-30, it was reprinted as "The Fusion of the Epic and Dramatic: Hemingway, Strindberg and O'Neill," *Eugene O'Neill Newsletter* 10.1 (1986): 16-21.

See A184 and A186.

A188 _____. "The Aftermath of World War I and the Fictionalization of Drama." *Acta Litteraria Academiæ Scientiarum Hungaricæ* 29.1-2 (1987): 75-96.

Maintains that in *Interlude* O'Neill moved toward psychological realism and epic drama, attributable to the playwright's "increased awareness of alienation, which became a mass experience during and after World War I."

A189 _____. "Critical Approaches to the Birth of Modern American Tragedy: The Significance of Eugene O'Neill." *Acta Litteraria Academiæ Scientiarum Hungaricæ* 30.3-4 (1988): 243-71.

An essay in literary history that places O'Neill in context by discussing what preceded him. Concludes that, although O'Neill was profoundly influenced by European literature, he was in turn to alter its course.

A190 _____. "The Psychology of Alienation, or What Parodies are Good for: A Note on O'Neill's Modernity." *Recorder* 3.1 (1989): 37-44.

Briefly surveys the question of whether modern psychology influenced O'Neill's writing, O'Neill's denial that it did, some amusing responses of critics, and concludes that O'Neill's position as "America's foremost modern dramatist with universal appeal" is the result of his "presenting the psychological as an aspect of the social."

A191 _____. "Dramatic Exposition and Resolution in O'Neill, Williams, Miller, and Albee." *Neohelicon* 19.1 (1992): 175-84.

Mainly about Albee (he receives more lines than the other three together). Points out that O'Neill, Williams, Miller take much time to establish the expository conditions of their plays (Shakespeare and Sophocles, by contrast, "get things moving" quite speedily). The rea-

son: they are writing about "characters ... dominated by their situations." Albee's expository passages are much shorter: his characters "step over their limitations ... momentarily suspending and delaying determinism." Briefly surveys the question of whether modern psychology influenced O'Neill's writing, O'Neill's denial that it did, some of the amusing responses of critics. Concludes that O'Neill's position as "America's foremost modern dramatist with universal appeal" is the result of his "presenting the psychological as an aspect of the social."

A192 Eincnkel, Robert. "Long Day's Journey toward Separation: The Mary-Edmund Struggle." *Eugene O'Neill Newsletter* 9.1: (1985): 14-23.

Edmund, at the start of the play, is the only family member who can believe in Mary's redemption from addiction. He may be dying — his redemption looks to her redemption. Therefore, he must separate himself from the immortal son that she sees him as. The article discusses four scenes between mother and son. Edmund's dropping of Mary's hand in their last scene together symbolizes his releasing her forever.

A193 Eisen, Kurt. "Eugene O'Neill's Joseph: A Touch of the Dreamer." *Comparative Drama* 23 (1989): 344-58.

Looks to a role that James O'Neill enacted, Joseph, in *Joseph and His Brethren*, to find a prototype for the dreamer who permeates the playwright's canon.

A194 _____. "Novelization and the Drama of Consciousness in *Strange Interlude*." *Eugene O'Neill Review* 14.1-2 (1990): 39-46.

Argues that "through Bakhtin's critique of Freud, along with his closely related theory of discourse in the novel, we can understand how O'Neill makes *Strange Interlude* a specifically novelistic response to Freudian psychology — in a play which, as always with O'Neill, deeply implicates the playwright himself."

A195 _____. "'The Writing on the Wall': Novelization and the Critique of History in *The Iceman Cometh*." *Modern Drama* 34 (1991): 59-73.

Beginning with Bonamy Dobrée's objection to the novelistic elements of the play, Eisen launches into a justification of their use and of the play's purpose. Concludes that "this dissolution of the barrier between the audience and tragic action serves as the most compelling justification of O'Neill's attempts to novelize the drama."

A196 Elliott, Thomas S. "Altar Ego: O'Neill's Sacrifice of Self and Character in *The Great God Brown.*" *Eugene O'Neill Review* 18.1-2 (1994): 59-64.

Punning on alter/altar, Elliott is nonetheless serious about seeing in the characters of Dion Anthony/Billy Brown autobiographical characters (alter egos), who are "sacrificed to appease the God O'Neill can't find" (altar egos).

A197 Ellis, Ted R., III. "The Materialization of Ghosts in *Strange Interlude.*" *American Notes and Queries* 19 (1981): 110-14.

Contends that the third act of the nine-act *Interlude* was influenced by Ibsen's *Ghosts.*

A198 Erben, Rudolf. "Mourning Becomes Regina: Lillian Hellman's Unfinished Trilogy." *Maske und Kothurn: Internationale Beiträge zur Theaterwissenschaft* [Vienna] 33.3-4 (1987): 125-52.

Essentially a comparison/contrast between two modern American dramas: O'Neill's *Electra* and Hellman's *The Little Foxes,* an unfinished trilogy. In the 1930s American audiences, scarred by the depression and frightened by reports from an unstable Europe, were strangely attracted to the Greek drama's theme of retributive justice. O'Neill and Hellman were, for many theater-goers, messengers whose stories of family turmoil and revenge helped to explain the trauma that America was experiencing. Asserts that O'Neill and Hellman modernized the ancient Greek drama by substituting the plight of personal responsibility and psychological motivation for the supernatural elements of classical tragedy.

A199 Erens, Pamela. "Portrait of the Playwright as a Young Man." *Connecticut Magazine* Feb. 1988: 82+.

A background piece, aimed at the general audience, of received opinion on the family, ethnicity, and early life of the playwright. Relies heavily on Louis Sheaffer's biography, but adds to it from local sources — New London Public Library, Gaylord Hospital. Pictures accompany the text.

A200 Fairservis, Walter. "Managing the Magic of *Marco Millions.*" *Eugene O'Neill Newsletter* 2.3 (1979): 18-21.

How he staged his August 1978 produc-tion of *Marco* at the Sharon Playhouse, in Connecticut (see E376): he used the stage manager, minimized scenery, and pared down speeches.

A201 Fambrough, Preston. "The Tragic Cosmology of O'Neill's *Desire Under the Elms.*" *Eugene O'Neill Newsletter* 10.2 (1986): 25-29.

Looks at *Desire* to show that O'Neill's vision was tragic — since the playwright admits to "an irreducible core of mystery at the center of the human experience."

A202 Feldman, Robert. "The Longing for Death in O'Neill's *Strange Interlude* and *Mourning Becomes Electra.*" *Literature and Psychology* 31.1 (1981): 39-48.

Supported by Arthur Nethercot's articles (see A466, A467, A468) which have shown that the extent of Freud's influence on O'Neill is debatable, Feldman takes issue with those critics who stress the Freudian Oedipal element in O'Neill's work. Sees the Freudian death instinct, however, as apparent in *Caribbees, Horizon, Interlude,* and *Electra.*

A203 Fichera, Anthony. "*Ah, Wilderness!:* O'Neill's True Family?" *Yale Reports* 12.5 (1988): 2+.

A playbill-like account, by the production dramaturg, for the Yale Rep production of *Wilderness,* Spring 1988.

A204 Field, Brad. "Corrections in O'Neill." *Eugene O'Neill Review* 17.1-2 (1993): 93-105.

Meanders through O'Neill's texts finding example after example of one character's verbally dismissing another, correcting another or correcting self. Calling these retractive devices "fingerprints" of O'Neill's style, Field concludes that "the corrections are his tools with which players may replicate the pain of communicating feelings even as speakers doubt their authenticity."

A205 _____. "Characterization in O'Neill: Self-doubt as an Aid to Art." *Eugene O'Neill Review* 20.1-2 (1996): 126-31.

Looks at characterization, the process of creating character, in the canon and suggests that readers should question the sincerity of the characters — especially in the later plays. Clues to their honesty can be found in the reactions of other characters, even in the subtleties of the blocking.

A206 Fiet, Lowell A. "O'Neill's Modification of Traditional American Themes in *A*

Touch of the Poet." *Educational Theatre Journal* 27 (1975): 508-15.

Goes back to James Steele MacKaye's *Hazel Kirke* and James A. Herne's *Shore Acres* to point out that O'Neill was still linked to nineteenth-century attitudes, particularly in regard to the nuclear family.

A207 Filipowicz, Halina. "Dream and Death in Gerhart Hauptmann's *Vor Sonnenaufgang* and Eugene O'Neill's *Beyond the Horizon.*" *Acta Universitatis Wratislaviensis* 233 (1974): 69-83.

Compares Hauptmann's and O'Neill's use of nonverbal devices — gesture, movement, music, lighting, coloring, and stage design — in two plays that are similar in their interchange of indoor with outdoor scenes throughout. Finds that O'Neill is more visually than verbally oriented and that his dialogue supports or interprets what his settings, stage design, and lighting have already suggested.

A208 Filipowicz-Findlay, Halina. "O'Neill's Plays in Poland." *Eugene O'Neill Newsletter* 3.1 (1979): 9-11.

Traces the history of O'Neill's plays on the Polish stage and notes that while theater historians in Poland have considered O'Neill one of the foremost playwrights, theaters have been very slow in introducing him to audiences. Investigates possible reasons for this and concludes that O'Neill's work is still terra incognita to Polish theater-goers.

A209 Fisher, James. "Eugene O'Neill and Edward Gordon Craig." *Eugene O'Neill Newsletter* 10.1 (1986): 27-30.

The son of Ellen Terry, Craig worked toward a "unified, symbolic and anti-naturalistic theatre." While he never met O'Neill, he did comment on the playwright's stage directions and contributions to the theater.

A210 _____. "Tender Men: The Acquaintanceship of Eugene O'Neill and Sherwood Anderson." *Eugene O'Neill Review* 17.1-2 (1993): 135-47.

Chronicles the relationship between Anderson and O'Neill — providing correspondence and circumstances of their meetings — and makes clear their mutual high regard.

A211 Fitzgerald, Brian. "Ghost, Writer." *Eugene O'Neill Review* 22.1-2 (1998): 170-73.

Has the ghost of O'Neill taken residence at Shelton Hall's Suite 401, where the play-

wright died almost 50 years ago? Unexplained events at that location may suggest O'Neill is still with us.

A212 Fjelde, Rolf. "Eugene O'Neill and Henrik Ibsen: Struggle, Fate, Freedom." *Theater Three* 5 (1988): 67-74.

Originally a talk given as part of the Nanjing-Shanghai Eugene O'Neill Centennial Festival (June 1988). Sees Ibsen's "tetralogy" (Fjelde's term) — *Master Builder, Little Eyolf, Borkman, When We Dead Awaken* — as joining in influence with "A Tale of Possessors Self-Dispossessed" to form and shape O'Neill's own tetralogic *Comédie Humaine* — *Iceman, Journey, Misbegotten, Hughie.*

A213 Fleming, Robert E. "O'Neill's *The Hairy Ape* as a source for *Native Son.*" *College Language Association Journal* 28.4 (1985): 434-43.

Ape influenced Richard Wright "in his creation of Bigger Thomas and Mary Dalton, in his attacks on religion and leftist political movements, and perhaps even in certain surrealistic elements in the setting of *Native Son.*"

A214 Floyd, Virginia. "Behind Life Forces in Eugene O'Neill." *Eugene O'Neill Newsletter* 1.1 (1977): 5-13.

Summarizes the papers presented at the 1976 MLA session on Irish Catholicism, New England Puritan and Humanistic concerns in the plays of O'Neill: John Henry Raleigh's "Irish Catholicism in O'Neill's Later Plays"; Frederick Wilkins' "'Stones Atop O' Stones,' the Pressure of Puritanism in O'Neill's New England Plays" (see B459); Esther M. Jackson's "O'Neill the Humorist," later published (see A331); and Albert Bermel's "Theatre Poetry and Mysticism in O'Neill," later published (see B41).

A215 _____. "Eugene O'Neill: Citizen of the World, Man Without a Country." *Eugene O'Neill Newsletter* 2.1 (1978): 6-9.

Gives highlights of three papers delivered at the 1977 MLA Convention: Tom Olsson's "O'Neill and the Royal Dramatic" (see A485); Timo Tiusanen's "O'Neill's Significance: A Scandinavian and European View" (see B424); and Péter Egri's "An East-European View of O'Neill: The Uses of the Short Story in O'Neill's and Chekhov's Plays (see A172)."

A216 _____. "The Search for Self in *The Hairy Ape*: An Exercise in Futility?" *Eugene O'Neill Newsletter* 1.3 (1978): 4-7.

Yank's quest is for the reality and fullness of himself. It is this quest that the modern world refuses to let him (modern man) engage in.

A217 _____. "O'Neill at Work: A Pen in Trust to Art." *Eugene O'Neill Newsletter* 12.2 (1988): 33-38.

Looks at the role of art in the life of the playwright. "Art influenced every major decision of the author's life," Floyd contends.

A218 _____. "Eugene O'Neill: Gift of a Celtic Legacy." *Recorder* 3.1 (1989): 5-14.

O'Neill is painted as the reactor to two forces, his New England and his Irish heritage, the spiritual and social consequences of both being reflected in his early life and his art, and in his later years coming full circle to appear most artistically in his last plays: *Touch, Mansions, Journey,* and *Iceman.*

A219 Fluckiger, Stephen L. "The Idea of Puritanism in the Plays of Eugene O'Neill." *Renascence* 30 (1978): 152-62.

O'Neill's plays suggest the puritan mentality and attitudes partly through setting and partly through rhetoric. In the latter case puritanism is sometimes treated half humorously — though usually it is seen as repressive. Comments on *Diff'rent, Iceman, Electra, Dynamo,* and *Brown,* but especially on *Horizon* and *Desire.*

A220 Fludernik, Monika. "Byron, Napoleon, and the Thorough-bred Mares: Symbolism and Semiosis in Eugene O'Neill's *A Touch of the Poet.*" *Sprachkunst* 21.2 (1990): 335-52.

Provides a linguistic/semiotic study of *Touch,* looking at the "image clusters and symbols" in the play. To some extent the article is a refutation of the charge that the play's symbolism is heavy-handed.

A221 _____. "The Illusion of Truth in Eugene O'Neill's *A Touch of the Poet.*" *Amerikastudien* 36.3 (1991): 317-35.

Looks at the binary oppositions of truth and illusion in *Touch* to conclude that despite the emphasis on this theme no resolution is achieved.

A222 Flynn, Joyce. "Melting Plots: Patterns of Racial and Ethnic Amalgamation in American Drama Before O'Neill." *American Quarterly* 38.3 (1986): 417-38.

The title of this article may be a red herring in that O'Neill and *Iceman* are mentioned only in passing. A bibliographic essay that looks to pre-O'Neill plays in light of their depiction of racial and ethnic mix.

A223 Forseth, Roger. "Denial as Tragedy: The Dynamics of Addiction in O'Neill's *The Iceman Cometh* and *Long Day's Journey into Night.*" *Dionysos* 1.1 (1989): 10-18.

The thesis: "I propose to examine *The Iceman* and *Long Day's Journey* as dramatic tragedies — the former of tragic farce and the latter of classical tragedy — by demonstrating how, variously, the addictive patterns and behaviors are central to O'Neill's artistic accomplishment."

A224 Frank, Glenda. "The Tiger as Daddy's Girl: A Feminist Reading of Lavinia Mannon." *Eugene O'Neill Review* 19.1-2 (1995): 55-65.

After showing Lavinia's affinities with her literary predecessors, Frank explains her uniqueness, her power. She is "the captain of her soul and master of the mansion."

A225 Frazer, Winifred L. "O'Neill's Iceman — Not Ice Man." *American Literature* 44 (1973): 677-78.

O'Neill would have known the slang of the underworld of 1912 — the period in which *Iceman* is set. *Iceman* meant an inmate whose promises were not to be relied upon or someone who bore worthless or trivial gifts, according to the *Dictionary of American Underworld Lingo.* Shows how these definitions are applicable to Hickey.

A226 _____. "A Lost Poem by Eugene O'Neill." *Eugene O'Neill Newsletter* 3.1 (1979): 4-6.

See Primary Works section, G32.

A227 _____. "Revolution in *The Iceman Cometh.*" *Modern Drama* 22 (1979): 1-8.

Shows that a poem called "Revolution" by the 19th-century German revolutionary and lyric poet Ferdinand Freiligrath is the source for two important lines from *Iceman*: "The days grow hot, O Babylon!/ 'Tis cool beneath thy willow trees!" Besides supporting the love-death bridegroom-iceman connotations of the play, the lines illustrate that revolution is one of the foolish ways by which men try to improve society.

A228 _____. "O'Neill's Stately Mansions: A Visitor's Reminiscences." *Eugene O'Neill Newsletter* 8.3 (1984): 15-21.

First an account of her aborted attempt to link O'Neill's residences with the work he produced. Later she makes a connection between *Iceman* and the farmhouse that Emma Goldman lived at in Ossining, NY. Goldman allowed Terry Carlin and Donald Vose to live there. Vose subsequently obtained the address of liberal Matthew Schmidt and betrayed it to the police. Like Rosa Parritt, Goldman felt betrayed.

A229 Freedman, Samuel G. "Lemmon revives the Past in O'Neill's *Journey*." *New York Times* 27 Apr. 1986, sec. 2:1.

An interview with Jack Lemmon on the eve of his opening in *Journey* provides insight into the actor's view of his character. "Lemmon regards his Tyrone as a decent man with some indecent traits, a faded dandy aware of his self-delusions, as much victim as victimizer." To find the character of Tyrone, Lemmon looked in part to his own father — his parsimony, his love for the stage. Lemmon took the role because he knew that Jonathan Miller's production would not be "just another revival."

A230 Frenz, Horst. "Eugene O'Neill: A Contemporary American Playwright." *Eigo Seinen* [Tokyo] 122 (1976): 34-39.

Originally a paper delivered before the American Literary Society of Japan (Kagoshima, 26 Oct. 1975). Stresses O'Neill's universality. O'Neill, open to experimentation, strives to express his deepest fears in order "to cope with the basic questions of existence, problems and questions ... which are still relevant today."

A231 _____. "Three European Productions of *The Hairy Ape*." *Eugene O'Neill Newsletter* 1.3 (1978): 10-12.

Looking back on the early European response to O'Neill's plays, Frenz finds that the playwright scored his first real success with *Ape* in London, Paris, and Berlin.

A232 _____. "Eugene O'Neill and China." *Tamkang Review* 10 (1979): 5-16.

A look at reciprocal influences: China's on O'Neill and O'Neill's on Chinese playwrights. In addition to comments on *Marco Million*'s orientalism (O'Neill admired Chinese philosophy, but felt it incompatible with the aspirations of Western man), Frenz points out the influence of *Jones* on Hung Sheng's *Chao — the King of Hell*, of *Dynamo* on Ts'ao Yü's *Sunrise*, and of *Desire* on the latter's *Thunderstorm*. But "it is in the primitive jungles of Ts'ao Yü's *The Wilderness* that O'Neill will be remembered as the first dramatist who

inspired the transplantation of Western expressionism into Chinese drama."

A233 _____. "*Marco Millions*: O'Neill's Chinese Experience and Chinese Drama." *Comparative Literature Studies* 18 (1981): 362-67.

Lightly touches on O'Neill's Chinese associations and then summarizes O'Neill's influence on important Chinese dramatists Hung Sheng and Ts'ao Yü.

A234 Fuchs, E. "O'Neill's Poet: Touched by Ibsen." *Educational Theatre Journal* 30 (1978): 513-16.

A re-thinking of Ibsen may have been responsible for the change in O'Neill's dramaturgy between *Days* and *Iceman*. Sees *Touch* as a pivotal play.

A235 Fukushima, Osamu. "The Tragic Tone of *Mourning Becomes Electra*." *Kyushu American Literature* 15 (1974): 1-9.

A general discussion of alienation in *Electra* and of the symbolic tension created by the references to the South Sea Islands and the Mannon residence.

A236 Fulford, Robert. "A Theatrical Journey into Long-Lost Lingo." *Eugene O'Neill Review* 18.1-2 (1994): 129-31.

Though included with the essays in the *Review*, Fulford's article is more a response to the Stratford Festival's 1994 production of *Journey*. The author observes that, ironically, the play's archaic language takes on even more power with the passage of time.

A237 Gabbard, Lucina P. "At the Zoo: From O'Neill to Albee." *Modern Drama* 19 (1976): 365-74.

Ape and *Zoo Story* are both plays about men imprisoned within themselves — men who recall for us animals caged in a zoo. Stresses the differences between the plays as well.

A238 Gálik, Marián. "*Chao-the King of Hell* and *The Emperor Jones*: Two Plays by Hung Shen and O'Neill." *Asian and African Studies* 12 (1976): 123-31.

Hung Shen studied under George Pierce Baker in 1919-20. He probably saw *Jones* in the U.S.; certainly he had read it. Its influence shows in *Chao — the King of Hell* (1923) in scenic structure, character roles, forest setting, visions, sound effects, and in the finale. The difference is that Hung's expressionism was purely technical, not like O'Neill's. And so, his attempt to bring O'Neill to China — through imitation — failed.

A239 Gallup, Donald. "The Eugene O'Neill Collection at Yale." *Eugene O'Neill Newsletter* 9.2 (1985): 3-11.

Indicates the extent of the holdings at Yale and explains the circumstances of their acquisition. Carlotta O'Neill's interest in gifts to Yale and her relationship with Gallup are explained in detail, as is her decision to give publication rights of *Journey* to Yale.

A24 _____. "O'Neill's Original 'Epilogue' for *A Touch of the Poet*." *Eugene O'Neill Review* 15.2 (1991): 93-107.

See Primary Works section, G39.

A241 _____. "'Greed of the Meek': O'Neill's Scenario for Act One of the First Play of His Eight-Play Cycle." *Eugene O'Neill Review* 16.2 (1992): 5-11.

See Primary Works section, G25.

A242 Gannon, Barbara C. "Little Theater in America: 1890-1920." *Bulletin of Bibliography* 40 (1983): 189-92.

A bibliography on the subject. Includes three categories: (1) Books published about or touching on, and published between 1911 and 1978; (2) periodicals and newspapers published between 1891 and 1958; (3) dissertations published between 1937 and 1974. A total of 90 items, most of them contemporary with the Little Theater Movement.

A243 Gannon, Frank. "Long Day's Journey into Abs." *New Yorker* 17 Mar. 1997: 124.

The heading, an observation by the Associated Press that "Infomercials disguised as actual programming are becoming more and more subtle," is illustrated by a one one-page parody of *Journey* which aims at selling a Personal Fitness Plan ("three easy payments"). Presumably any *New Yorker* reader would spot the allusion.

A244 Garvey, Sheila Hickey. "Recreating a Myth: *The Iceman Cometh* in Washington, 1985." *Eugene O'Neill Newsletter* 9.3 (1985): 17-23.

Considers Quintero's 1985 production of *Iceman*. Provides background and makes observations about this production vis-à-vis the 1956 production.

A245 _____. "Rethinking O'Neill." *Eugene O'Neill Newsletter* 10.3 (1986): 13-20.

An interview with Peter Gallagher, who played Edmund in the Jonathan Miller/Jack Lemmon 1986 production of *Journey*. The actor shows himself a spirited defender of the production.

A246 _____. "The Origins of the O'Neill Renaissance: A History of the 1956 Productions of *The Iceman Cometh* and *Long Day's Journey into Night*." *Theatre Survey* 29.1 (1988): 51-67.

Gives the chronology of events leading up to the landmark 1956 productions of *Iceman* and *Journey*. Garvey bases her article, in part, on interviews with some of the principals.

A247 _____. "Desecrating an Idol: *Long Day's Journey into Night* as Directed by José Quintero and Jonathan Miller." *Recorder* 3.1 (1989): 73-85.

Quintero's *Journey* (1956) plays to an audience for whom the story of O'Neill's family history is a revelation, and one exploited by the director. Miller's version (1986) tries to give us almost any dysfunctional family. The two approaches are realized by the choice of actors: in Quintero's, "Tyrone becomes the play's centerpiece because of the towering performance of Frederic March"; but by casting Jack Lemmon, Miller "deflated Tyrone, who was left to scramble along with his offspring for the crumbs of Mary Tyrone's affection."

A248 _____. "*Anna Christie* in New Haven: A Theatrical Odyssey." *Eugene O'Neill Review* 14.1-2 (1990): 52-70.

A bird's eye view of the history of the 1990 New Haven Long Wharf Theatre's production of *Anna*. Included are comments on earlier productions.

A249 _____. "*Anna Christie* and the 'Fallen Woman Genre.'" *Eugene O'Neill Review* 19.1-2 (1995): 66-80.

Considers the gender stereotypes of the "fallen woman genre" and then approaches *Anna* from three feminist perspectives: Radical Feminism, Material or Marxist Feminism, and Cultural Feminism.

A250 Garzilli, Enrico F. "*Long Day's Journey into Night* (Mary) and *Streetcar Named Desire* (Blanche): An Inquiry into Compassion." *Theatre Annual* 33 (1977): 7-23.

Journey and *Streetcar* reflect a particular decade's sensibilities. Still, though, they are able to "elicit in us … compassion and pity." Compares the two plays for the influence of the past on the characters Mary and Blanche, their lost innocence, the elusiveness of affection and protection, and their homelessness.

A251 Gatta, John, Jr. "The American Subject: Moral History as Tragedy in the Plays of Eugene O'Neill." *Essays in Literature* 6 (1979): 227-39.

Discusses the American origins of O'Neill's vision and his rootedness in a native literary tradition, by examining *Desire, Electra, Touch*, and *Mansions*. Describes the conflict in many of O'Neill's characters between self-reliance and greed.

A252 Gauss, Rebecca B. "O'Neill, Gruenberg and *The Emperor Jones.*" *Eugene O'Neill Review* 18.1-2 (1994): 38-44.

Plumbs the problematic circumstances surrounding the adaptation of *Jones* to opera by composer Louis Gruenberg.

A253 Gelb, Arthur, and Barbara Gelb. "The Twisted Path to *More Stately Mansions.*" *Eugene O'Neill Review* 22.1-2 (1998): 105-09.

A look at how the play came to be published, since it was the express wish of its author that his unfinished cycle should be destroyed, and a lament over the "cannibalizing" of O'Neill's uncompleted work.

A254 Gelb, Barbara. "Written in Tears and Blood...." *New York Times* 4 Mar. 1973, sec. 2: 19-20.

Points out that when *Journey* was first performed, the recognition that it was about O'Neill's own family led to reconsideration of his other plays — especially *Chillun, Desire, Brown, Electra*, and *Touch*— and recognition of the autobiographical elements in them.

A255 _____. "Jason Jamie Robards Tyrone." *New York Times* 20 Jan. 1974, sec. 6: 14+.

Covers Robards' career and points out similarities between him and James O'Neill, Jr., and between Robards and Eugene O'Neill. Includes his response to Lee Marvin's being chosen for the film *Iceman*.

A256 _____. "Touch of the Tragic." *New York Times Magazine* 11 Dec. 1977: 43+.

As Quintero and Robards prepare for *Touch*'s opening (25 Dec. 1977), Barbara Gelb interviews them. Stresses Quintero's identification with O'Neill.

A257 _____. "O'Neill's *Iceman* Sprang from the Ashes of His Youth." *New York Times* 29 Sept. 1985, sec. 2: 1+.

Looks at the play in light of the Quintero-Robards revival. Notes that the play is highly autobiographical — that O'Neill is reminiscing about his days at Jimmy-the-Priest's — and suggests that Willie Oban is partly O'Neill. Recaps others' observations about the play.

A258 _____. "O'Neill's Father Shaped His Son's Vision." *New York Times* 27 Apr. 1986, sec. 2: 1.

Provides background on James O'Neill, the roles he assumed, his successes, comparing him to Richard Burton. The point? That ultimately James O'Neill was eclipsed, but not forgotten, by his son, who immortalized his father in an immortal role.

A259 _____. "In Search of O'Neill." *Eugene O'Neill Newsletter* 12.2 (1988): 3-8.

Anecdotal material drawn from Barbara and Arthur Gelb's research for their biography of O'Neill. Some of the material contained is reprised in *Eugene O'Neill Review* 18.1-2 (1994): 9-12.

A260 _____. "Interviewing Ghosts." *Eugene O'Neill Review* 18.1-2 (1994): 9-12.

Recounts some amusing anecdotes regarding the roadblocks she and husband/ writer Arthur Gelb encountered in researching O'Neill's background and suggests that it may be time to revisit her subject.

A261 _____. "Historic Houses: Eugene O'Neill." *Architectural Digest* 52.11 (1995): 96+.

The history of O'Neill's connection with Monte Cristo Cottage and an update on the restoration work in progress. *Journey* served as the "blueprint" for the museum's curators in their efforts to return the home to the way it looked when the O'Neills moved in. Perhaps more impressive than the text are the visuals, the pictures of Monte Cristo Cottage, newly and ninety-percent renovated, showing O'Neill's early home inside and out to best advantage. The text provides a history of the house, explains about the playwright's life there, and credits Sally Thomas Pavetti and Lois Erickson McDonald with the undertaking.

A262 _____. "Concealing While Revealing: O'Neill's Way with Truth." *New York Times* 4 Apr. 1999, sec. 2: 5+.

Pulls together the realities (factualities?) of O'Neill's life and the characters and themes of *Iceman*. Inspired by the Davies-Spacey production.

A263 _____. "In Search of Memory." *Eugene O'Neill Review* 22.1-2 (1998): 110-13.

Describes an interview with Lillian Brennan, Ella's second cousin and possible inspiration for Lily Miller and Emma Crosby. Though suffering from senile dementia at the time of the interview, Brennan was still able to provide some insight into her cousin's character.

A264 _____. "Tribute to José Quintero." *Eugene O'Neill Review* 22.1-2 (1998): 4-5.

A touching recollection of the last few days of the director whose sympathies seemed most in tune with O'Neill's sensibility.

A265 _____, **and Tony Randall.** Letters. *New York Times* 24 Feb. 1974, sec. 6: 70.

Exchange of letters between Gelb and Randall concerning her "Jason Jamie Robards Tyrone" article in 20 Jan. 1974 issue of the *New York Times.*

A266 Gillespie, Michael. "Eugene O'Neill: The Theatrical Quest." *Claudel Studies* 9 (1982): 43-51.

Discusses O'Neill's use of the mask in *Brown,* to reveal the divided self, then turns to *Journey,* where O'Neill used dialogue, not stage techniques, to achieve the same result.

A267 Gilmore, Thomas B. "*The Iceman Cometh* and the Anatomy of Alcoholism." *Comparative Drama* 18 (1984): 335-47.

Looks at *Iceman* in terms of the theories of Alcoholics Anonymous and Vernon Johnson. Sees Hickey's new-found sobriety and his reasoning about it as a travesty of AA. Harry Hope's patrons are sociopaths — "drunks without guilt"; Hickey and Slade are alcoholics — drunks who see their obsession as a violation of some right. Hickey, though controlling his drink, does so without self knowledge and so unbalances himself. Slade's problem is the conflict between his desire to be a thoughtless drunkard and his inability to reject the demands put on him by his conscience.

A268 Going, William T. "Eugene O'Neill, American." *Papers on Language and Literature* 12 (1976): 384-401.

Makes a well-documented case for O'Neill as a playwright in the mainstream of American authors, which include Frost, Melville, and Hawthorne. Describes O'Neill's plays as romantic in themes, techniques, and setting and finds some of the romantic in O'Neill's life. Ultimately, though, O'Neill's orientation was American and 20th-century — American in his rootlessness, in his need to dissolve family ties, in his search for a moral

center to replace lost religion, and in his themes: miscegenation, concern with prostitutes, with the sea, with New England, with the decline of urban life.

A269 Goldhurst, William. "Misled by a Box: Variations on a Theme from Poe." *Clues: A Journal of Detection* 3.1 (1982): 31-37.

Studies the use of the box — "a starting point for speculation about the Unknown" — in Poe's "The Oblong Box," Arthur Conan Doyle's "The Little Square Box," and O'Neill's *In the Zone.* (Notes that John Colt's murder of Samuel Adams, covered in the newspapers in 1841, may have been Poe's source.)

A270 Goldman, Arnold. "The Culture of the Provincetown Players." *Journal of American Studies* 12 (1978): 291-310.

Gives a history of the early days of the Provincetown Players, who "preserved something of a progressive social vision, focused it, prompted it and passed it on as a legacy to later artists, and to the intellectual community, and to the public."

A271 Gomez, Andrea A. "Modern Tragedies." *Research Journal* [St. Louis U] 19.1 (1988): 35-84.

Discusses Arthur Miller's *Death of a Salesman* and O'Neill's *Ape* and concludes that they are modern tragedies of "the inability of man to cope with the demands of a fast-paced technological system."

A272 Gonzales, José B. "Homecoming: O'Neill's New London in *Long Day's Journey into Night.*" *New England Quarterly* 66.3 (1993): 450-57.

Attributes the "see-sawing of emotions" in O'Neill's masterpiece in part to the characters' New England environment, to their ambivalence toward their New London home.

A273 Gordenstein, Arnold. "A Few Thousand Battered Books: Eugene O'Neill's Use of Myth in *Desire Under the Elms* and *Mourning Becomes Electra.*" *Ilha Do Desterro* 15-16.1-2 (1986): 134-46.

Looks at the interplay of Greek and biblical myth in these plays to conclude that O'Neill used the Greek model in both works, "with the story of Adam and Eve ... acting as either an alternative or as reconfirmation."

A274 Gramm, Julie M. "'Tomorrow': From Whence the Iceman Cometh." *Eugene O'Neill Review* 15.1 (1991): 78-92.

Concludes that "'Tomorrow' began as a relatively uncomplicated story of one man's tomorrow-fantasies and his subsequent suicide. It grew into a much more complex story of men, women, pipe-dreams and self delusion which was not told in its entirety until the completion of *The Iceman Cometh* over twenty years later."

A275 Grecco, Stephen R. "High Hopes: Eugene O'Neill and Alcohol." *Yale French Studies* 50 (1974): 142-49.

O'Neill's early drinking kept him from understanding himself. After he conquered his alcoholism, he wrote more understandingly and more strongly. Some observations about *Caribbees* and *Iceman*.

A276 Green, Charmian S. "Wolfe, O'Neill, and the Mask of Illusion." *Papers on Language and Literature* 14 (1978): 87-90.

In Thomas Wolfe's play *Mannerhouse*, as in O'Neill's expressionistic plays of the 1920s, characters are alienated: in *Brown* by masked faces and in *Mannerhouse* by a cynical expression. Also, in *Look Homeward Angel*, Eugene Gant's encounter with the ghosts of his emerging identity may pay homage to O'Neill, whom Wolfe admired. Wolfe may have seen O'Neill's *Mariner* in which masks were used. *Mannerhouse* (1925) and *Brown* (1926) bear striking similarities in their themes (paradox of illusion and reality) and in their use of the divided character. *Look Homeward Angel*, which again deals with the paradox of illusion and reality, may also reflect a debt to O'Neill.

A277 Griffin, Ernest G. "O'Neill and the Tragedy of Culture." *Modern Drama* 37 (1988): 1-15.

Focuses on the O'Neill plays dealing with a modern rendering of fate — *Electra, Journey, Iceman*, and *Misbegotten* — to show how O'Neill tranferred the ancient Greek sense of fate from the external (all-powerful, supernatural gods meddling in the lives of humans) to the internal (the inescapable psychological realism that determines our lives).

A278 Grimm, Reinhold. "The Hidden Heritage: Repercussions of Nietzsche in Modern Theater and its Theory." *Nietzsche Studien: Internationales Jahrbuch für die Nietzsche-Forschung* 12 (1983): 355-71.

Deals mainly with Nietzsche — only incidental references to his influence on O'Neill.

A279 _____. "A Note on O'Neill, Nietzsche and Naturalism: *Long Day's Journey*

into Night in European Perspective." *Modern Drama* 26 (1983): 331-34.

Sees *Journey* as reflecting the tightly knit structure of any classic Ibsen play ("say, *Ghosts*") — family drama, "naturalistic" setting and language, the three unities, even a similar symbolism. But the endings are different. The "naturalistic" touch of optimism is missing from *Journey* (using optimism to mean, rather, realism). Here O'Neill dramatizes the tragic world-view of Nietzsche, as expressed by Edmund — in an imagery recognizable as coming from *The Birth of Tragedy*.

A280 Gross, Robert F. "O'Neill's Queer Interlude: Epicene Excess and Camp Pleasures." *Journal of Dramatic Theory and Criticism* 12.1 (1997): 3-22.

Wonders why *Interlude* generated such hostility from critics when the play was "enormously" successful on stage. "Perhaps the anxiety of male critics is not surprising since *Strange Interlude* is a play structured around the loss of heroic masculinity." What follows is a discussion of *Interlude* as "camp" — the kind of art that proposes itself seriously, but cannot be taken altogether seriously because it is "too much."

A281 Gurewitsch, Matthew. "A Country of Lesser Giants." *New York Times* 4 Apr. 1999, sec. 2: 1+.

A consideration of Spacey's *Iceman* and Brian Dennehy's *Death of a Salesman* leads Gurewitsch to reflections on the twentieth-century American obsession with loser heroes.

A282 Guruprasad, Thakur. "Experimentation with Dramatic Technique in O'Neill's *The Hairy Ape*." *Indian Journal of English Studies* 14 (1973): 44-54.

A view of the multifarious [and long-noted] types of experimentation involved in *Ape*.

A283 Gussow, Mel. "José Quintero's Long Journey Back." *New York Times* 28 Jan. 1974: 134.

Recounts the peaks and valleys of Quintero's career — now at a peak with the success of *Misbegotten*.

A284 _____. "José Quintero: Saving O'Neill and Himself." *New York Times* 26 Aug. 1998, sec. E: 1+.

Discusses with the famous O'Neill director the vicissitudes of his professional and personal lives: his bouts with alcoholism and cancer, and his many theatrical successes.

Quotes Quintero as saying that "one reason for his success is that he never thought of [O'Neill] as a realistic playwright." Of *Misbegotten* [with Robards, Dewhurst and Flanders] Quintero said, the production "will live in my imagination as long as I live."

A285 Hall, Ann C. "High Anxiety: Women in Eugene O'Neill's *The Iceman Cometh*." *Recorder* 3.1 (1989): 45-51.

O'Neill, explaining why he so often looks at himself in a mirror, says, "I just want to make sure that I'm here." The women of *Iceman* are seen as mirrors whose function is to give the men of the play an opportunity to validate themselves.

A286 Hamilton, J. W. "Early Trauma, Dreaming and Creativity: the Works of Eugene O'Neill." *International Review of Psychoanalysis* 3 [London] (1976): 341-64.

Tries to correlate biographical data and writing "to demonstrate how certain intrapsychic conflicts of predominantly pre-oedipal origin specifically affected O'Neill's career as a dramatist." Important terms are *pregenital themes, oral-sadistic rage,* and *narcissistic repair.* Though many early plays are touched on, most attention is given to *Mansions, Iceman,* and *Journey.*

A287 _____. "Transitional Phenomena and the Early Writings of Eugene O'Neill." *International Review of Psychoanalysis* [London] 6 (1979): 49-60.

A look at O'Neill's relationship with Bee Ashe during [the year he was studying at Harvard under George Pierce Baker]. His loneliness and the intensity of his feelings, as expressed in his letters to her, are seen as the psychological underpinning of his later creativity.

A288 Hammerman, Harley J. "On Collecting O'Neill." *Eugene O'Neill Review* 13.1 (1989): 47-54.

Explains how he became a collector of O'Neilliana — specifically how he acquired the Robert Sisk and León Mirlas materials.

A289 _____. "On Collecting O'Neill." *Eugene O'Neill Review* 15.1 (1991): 93-96.

Describes the author's acquisition of O'Neilliana, primarily how he came into possession of letters from the playwright to Richard Madden, O'Neill's literary agent.

A290 Hamner, Robert. "Dramatizing the New World's African King: O'Neill, Walcott and Césaire on Christophe." *Journal of West Indian Literature* 5.1-2 (1992): 30-47.

Looks at the depiction of Henri Christophe in plays by O'Neill *(Jones),* Derek Walcott *(Henri Christophe),* and Aimé Césaire *(La Tragédie du Roi Christophe)* only to conclude that neither the Caribbean authors nor the American depicts the protagonist with much sympathy.

A291 Han, Kim. "*Lazarus Laughed*: Dionysus and *The Birth of Tragedy*." *English Language and Literature* 37.4 (1991): 993-1005.

Looks at the Nietzschean influence on (despite the title of the essay) both *Lazarus* and *Brown.* "Like Nietzsche O'Neill regarded Greek tragedy as the unsurpassed example of art" and tried to recreate the Greek spirit in modern life.

A292 Hanson, Philip J. "*The Emperor Jones*: Naturalistic Tragedy in Hemispheric Perspective." *American Drama* 5.2 (1996): 23-43.

Provides historical and cultural background to show that "Jones' tragedy emerges as a collision of centuries of accumulated tragic African-American experience with the local experience of the black descendants of slaves from the era of Dessalines and Toussaint L'Ouverture." The play is less about a character's bad choice than about "larger external forces beyond the character's control." It is a play of hemispheric tragedy that continues to our time.

A293 Hardin, Michael. "Fair Maiden and Dark Lady in *The Great God Brown*: Inverting the Standard Representations." *Eugene O'Neill Review* 22.1-2 (1998): 42-47.

Maintains that in the process of donning and shedding masks the two heroines of *Brown,* Margaret and Cybel, become the opposites of the qualities and values we traditionally associate with the light and dark ladies of story and lore.

A294 Harris, Andrew B., Jr. "A Tangible Confrontation: *Welded*." *Theatre News* 13.7 (1981): 9-10.

The producer of Columbia University's production of *Welded* addresses the reasons Quintero chose this play. Although critical reception of the play was unfavorable, the choice proved valuable as a learning experience for the students. Discusses too Quintero's vision of the play — that the relationship depicted was like that of Carlotta and O'Neill but that Eleanor is modeled on Agnes Boulton.

A295 Hart, Doris. "Whose Play is this, Anyway?— Interpreting Mary and James Tyrone." *Recorder* 3.1 (1989): 115-22.

Compares the roles of Mary and Tyrone as interpreted in the first three New York productions of *Journey*— Frederic March/Florence Eldridge (1956), Robert Ryan/Geraldine Fitzgerald (1971), and Jason Robards, Jr./Zoe Caldwell (1976)— and finds herself agreeing with Prideaux "that the drama is a 'stretch-fit' masterpiece, able to accommodate different interpretations."

A296 Harvey, Sally. "O'Neill's *Hughie* and Albee's *The Zoo Story*: Two Tributes to the Teller and his Tale." *Journal of American Drama and Theatre* 3.2 (1991): 14-26.

Looks at the similarities and differences in the above works from their common interest in the storyteller. Despite the differences in the playwrights' opinions as to the possibility of meaningful communication reflected in *Hughie* and *The Zoo Story* (the latter suggesting the impossibility of such) both O'Neill and Albee pay tribute to the storyteller.

A297 Hawley, William. "*The Iceman Cometh* and the Critics —1946, 1956, 1973." *Eugene O'Neill Newsletter* 9.3 (1985): 5-9.

Compares three American productions, focusing on the role of Hickey. The 1946 production had a strong ensemble, but a weak Hickey; 1973 production had a strong Hickey, but a weak ensemble; and the 1956 production was strong in both.

A298 Hayes, Richard. "Eugene O'Neill: The Tragic in Exile." *Theater-Week* 26 Mar. 1990: 34-38.

A reprint of an essay which appeared in *Theatre Arts* in 1963.

A299 Hays, Peter L. "Child Murder and Incest in American Drama." *Twentieth-Century Literature* 36 (1990): 434-48.

Comments on the frequency of the above theme in three plays by O'Neill *(Abortion, Desire,* and *Interlude)*, in two plays by Edward Albee, and in one by Sam Shepard. Hays notes that infanticide in these plays may serve merely to complicate the plot or to criticize society, but in combination with incest it is "an attempt to show the perversion of our values, the immediate gratification at the cost of long-range, social development."

A300 _____. "O'Neill and Hellman." *Eugene O'Neill Review* 18.1-2 (1994): 189-92.

Draws comparisons between *Electra* and Lillian Hellman's *The Little Foxes*.

A301 _____. "Hemingway's 'A Clean Well-Lighted Place' and O'Neill's *Iceman*." *Eugene O'Neill Review* 22.1-2 (1998): 70-76.

We know O'Neill's settings and characters have a "long history" in his life, but the similarities in detail between *Iceman* and Hemingway's story make us want to find some kind of connection. Or are we left with nothing more than a "confluence"?

A302 Hedderel, Vance Philip. "Sibling Rivalry in *Mourning Becomes Electra* and *The Little Foxes*." *Eugene O'Neill Review* 17.1-2 (1993): 60-65.

Argues that there are several reasons why these two plays should be considered together but most significant is the fact that "both feature a psychological overlay in the construction of the mother-daughter relationships which are the crux of the two dramas."

A303 Highsmith, James Milton. "*The Personal Equation*: Eugene O'Neill's Abandoned Play." *Southern Humanities Review* 8 (1974): 195-212.

Summarizes the play and shows how echoes of this early O'Neill reverberate in later plays. Draws parallels between the characters of *Equation*, its themes and concerns, and numerous other O'Neill plays.

A304 Hill, Philip G. "A New Look at Mary Cavan Tyrone." *Southern Theatre* 21.1 (1977): 11-17.

Argues that a close reading of *Journey* and careful study of O'Neill's relations with his own mother suggest that Mary Tyrone was not the "sweet but victimized, saintly and long suffering, lovable old lady" as usually portrayed but was "in fact ... a twisted, bitter, vicious woman who is herself the cause of most of her family's troubles." Evidence of O'Neill's feelings toward his mother is derived from Sheaffer's biography.

A305 Hinden, Michael. "*The Birth of Tragedy* and *The Great God Brown*." *Modern Drama* 16 (1973): 129-40.

Nietzsche's interest in a fundamental unity principle underlying all phenomena fascinated O'Neill continually — even in his darker years when the vision had slipped through his grasp. Thinks O'Neill responded to the influence of *Birth* even in his sea plays, although some critics think O'Neill had not mastered the book by the time he wrote *Brown,* which elaborates most on *Birth.*

A306 _____. "Liking O'Neill." *Forum* 2.3 (1973): 59-66.

Evaluates O'Neill's strengths and weaknesses. O'Neill was a self-acknowledged "stammerer." His handling of language was often inept — "language fails to meet our expectations." Notes that the language often improves as play progresses and that language of the middle-class is often plodding, but that the vernacular can be effective. Recognizing his limitations, O'Neill concentrated on characterization and construction. Acknowledges that O'Neill's plays are not plays of ideas but of ritual, "a place for illumination of inner life." They are not mere social diatribes.

A307 _____. "Ritual and Tragic Action: A Synthesis of Current Theory." *Journal of Aesthetics and Art Criticism* 32 (1974): 357-73.

O'Neill and *Jones, Electra,* and *Desire* receive a couple of mentions but only in the company of other playwrights and a dozen other plays, as illustrations.

A308 _____. "Ironic Use of Myth in *The Hairy Ape.*" *Eugene O'Neill Newsletter* 1.3 (1978): 2-4.

Sees the myth of Dionysus as presented by Nietzsche treated ironically in *Ape*: the modern world, which is without a mythic center, prevents the ancient triumph of Dionysus.

A309 _____. "*Desire Under the Elms*: O'Neill and the American Romance." *Forum* 15 (1979): 44-51.

Desire is probably one of O'Neill's most significant works in relation to the American tradition. Ties it to works by Emerson, Hawthorne, Melville, and Whitman.

A310 _____. "'Splendid Twaddle': O'Neill and Richard Middleton." *Eugene O'Neill Newsletter* 2.3 (1979): 13-16.

The poetry of Richard Middleton, which O'Neill knew and quoted, according to Agnes Boulton, may have affected the young O'Neill, possibly providing the name for Richard in *Wilderness*. Middleton, a suicide at 29, wrote moody, love-sick verse, which, for very good reasons, is quite forgotten today.

A311 _____. "Desire and Forgiveness: O'Neill's Diptych." *Comparative Drama* 14 (1980): 240-50.

Shows a change in O'Neill's attitude and technique between his early and late plays. Citing many similarities between *Desire* and *Misbegotten*, Hinden illustrates the autobiographical nature of both and the different attitude O'Neill had toward his mother, father and Jamie when he wrote the later play.

A312 _____. "*The Emperor Jones*: O'Neill, Nietzsche, and the American Past."

Eugene O'Neill Newsletter 3.3 (1980): 2-4.

Brutus Jones represents not specifically the black man but all Americans who have forgotten in their acquisitiveness the liberating principles upon which this country was founded. Thus, the protagonist, of any race, enslaves his spirit and tragically brings about his own destruction.

A313 _____. "The Transitional Nature of *All God's Chillun Got Wings.*" *Eugene O'Neill Newsletter* 4.1-2 (1980): 3-5.

Jim Harris may be thought the son of Brutus Jones, struggling at the center of society rather than on an island, torn between his desire for success in the white world and his allegiance to his ethnic past.

A314 _____. "When Playwrights Talk to God: Peter Shaffer and the Legacy of O'Neill." *Comparative Drama* 16 (1982): 49-63.

Discusses Peter Shaffer as O'Neill's successor. Like O'Neill, Shaffer experiments with thought-asides, masks, mime, the split protagonist, spectacle, and theme.

A315 _____. "Paradise Lost: O'Neill and American History." *Eugene O'Neill Newsletter* 12.1 (1988): 39-48.

Taking issue with critics who denigrate O'Neill's early work to praise his later, Hinden revisits the plays of the 1920s to find their common thread — "They comprise a series on an epic theme that has occupied American writers since the nineteenth century: the myth of America as a new Eden, its discovery and loss."

A316 _____. "Missing Lines in *Long Day's Journey into Night.*" *Modern Drama* 32.1 (1989): 178-82.

The history of the text of the play: 1) O'Neill wrote his pencil version, which he edited; 2) then Carlotta produced a typescript, which O'Neill also edited; 3) from this Carlotta produced a second typescript, which O'Neill did not edit; 4) professional copies of this last were made, without any revisions; 5) from these came the Yale edition. Between the second and third stages four lines of text were lost — one discovered by Judith Barlow (see her *Final Acts*), the others by Hinden. The nut of this essay shows how these lines alter our interpretation of *Journey*.

A317 _____. "The Pharmacology of *Long Day's Journey into Night.*" *Eugene O'Neill Review* 14.1-2 (1990): 47-51.

Recent medical research indicating that patients who are given morphine to control pain rarely become addicted sheds new light on *Journey*.

A318 Holmberg, Arthur. "Fallen Angels at Sea: Garbo, Ullmann, Richardson, and the Contradictory Prostitute in *Anna Christie*." *Eugene O'Neill Review* 20.1-2 (1996): 43-63.

Looks at the conflicting images of the prostitute in art and literature — the spiritualized Romantic view and the very material Naturalistic image. Then he examines the performances of three of the great Anna Christies — Greta Garbo, Liv Ullmann, and Natasha Richardson — to find that all three actresses were able to project "the contradictory traditions embodied in Anna."

A319 Holton, Deborah Wood. "Revealing Blindness, Revealing Vision: Interpreting O'Neill's Black Female Characters in *Moon of the Caribbees, The Dreamy Kid* and *All God's Chillun Got Wings*." *Eugene O'Neill Review* 19.1-2 (1995): 29-44.

Finding that sometimes O'Neill hits and sometimes misses in his depiction of black characters in the three plays, Holton nevertheless concedes that O'Neill "cast light, however dim, on aspects of black life."

A320 Hoover, Marjorie L. "Three O'Neill Plays in 1920's Productions by Tairov's Kamerny Theater." *Theatre History Studies* 11 (1991): 123-27.

Alexander Tairov and the Kamerny Theater's productions of *Desire, Chillun,* and *Ape* are the focus of this article. Concludes that "while the O'Neill plays still belong to Kamerny's true artistic achievement, they also mark a turning point towards increasing capitulation to realism and to ideological preachment against the very Westernism which brought Kamerny to the height of its earlier best years."

A321 Hori, Mariko. "Aspects of Noh Theatre in Three Late O'Neill Plays." *Eugene O'Neill Review* 18.1-2 (1994): 143-48.

Noh drama "begins when all action has ended; in other words, action has occurred in the past and the events of the past are told and revealed in the present, during the course of the play." In light of this description of Noh drama, Hori looks at *Journey, Iceman,* and *Hughie*.

A322 Hornby, Richard. "O'Neill's Death of a Salesman." *Journal of Dramatic Theory and Criticism* 2.2 (1988): 53-59.

Providing the folklore surrounding the Yankee peddler/salesman, Hornby then compares/contrasts three salesman characters — Willy Loman, Stanley Kowalski, and Hickey — to find that *Iceman* is a better play than *Salesman* "because O'Neill realized … that the tragedy of America is not a tragedy of failure but rather one of success."

A323 _____. "O'Neill's Metadrama." *Eugene O'Neill Newsletter* 12.2 (1988): 13-18.

Looks at O'Neill's ambivalence toward the theater as reflected in the kind of drama he wrote, metadrama, a combination of realism and theatricalism. Assuming that O'Neill's plays were "not just employing theatre as a medium" but were "about theatre" explains some of what critics have termed O'Neill's weaknesses — melodramatic plot devices, "stagey dialects," etc.

A324 Horovitz, Israel. "The Legacy of O'Neill." *Eugene O'Neill Newsletter* 11.1 (1987): 3-10.

In an amusing address to attendees of the 1986 "Eugene O'Neill: The Later Years" Conference, Boston, playwright Horovitz tells what it was like maturing artistically in O'Neill's shadow.

A325 Houchin, John H. "Eugene O'Neill's 'Woman Play' in Boston." *Eugene O'Neill Review* 22.1-2 (1998): 48-62.

Prudery and Politics: or, why *Strange Interlude* opened in Quincy rather than Boston during its 1929 run. Detailed, informative and amusing.

A326 Hsia, An Min. [O'Neill and the Tao]. *Chung Wai Literary Monthly* [Taiwan] Dec. 1978: 104-09.

Based on a dissertation and an earlier study, this essay grants that Doris Alexander is correct in pointing to the East to find the source of O'Neill's mysticism. Says, though, that it is Tao, *Light on the Path,* which influenced O'Neill (the underlying principle of Taoism is the return of all existence). Argues that we see Tao influence in O'Neill's Kukachin, Marco, Nina, Miriam, Lavinia, Mary, *Iceman* characters, etc. Reprinted in Frenz and Tuck's *Eugene O'Neill's Critics,* see B174.

A327 Hughes, Ann D. "Biblical Allusions in *The Hairy Ape*." *Eugene O'Neill Newsletter* 1.3 (1978): 7-9.

Identifies the ship's great furnaces with those of Moloch, which were fed by human lives. O'Neill is implying that the workers are sacrificed to industrialism. Mildred's references to a leopard's spots, her father as president of Nazareth Steel, and Dr. Caiaphas point to Yank's alienation from heaven.

A328 Ikcuchi, Yasuko. "*Ah, Wilderness!* and *Desire Under the Elms* in Japan." *Recorder* 3.1 (1989): 105-14.

Describes Murayama's 1937 redaction of *Wilderness* (called *First Love*), which aimed at, and was criticized for, "subverting traditional [Japanese] values and the patriarchal hierarchy within the family," and for which its author, Tomoyoshi Murayama, was imprisoned. Then segues to *Desire* and to the reasons it is O'Neill's most popular play in post-war Japan. The treatments are framed by a brief history of O'Neill's reception in Japan.

A329 Innes, Christopher. "The Salesman of the Stage: A Study in the Social Influence on Drama." *English Studies in Canada* 3 (1977): 336-50.

Discusses *Death of a Salesman, Iceman,* and Jack Gelber's *The Connection* as plays dealing with salesmen and materialism.

A330 Isaac, Dan. "Founding Father: O'Neill's Correspondence with Arthur Miller and Tennessee Williams." *Eugene O'Neill Review* 17.1-2 (1993): 124-33.

See Primary Works section, G19.

A331 Jackson, Esther M. "O'Neill the Humanist." *Eugene O'Neill Newsletter* 1.2 (1977): 1-4.

Sees O'Neill as following in the tradition of New Humanists (Irving Babbitt, Paul Elmer More), treating the same themes of democracy, freedom, and crisis of faith and eventually exhibiting the same "tragic humanism." Surveys plays from *Thirst* to *Journey.*

A332 _____. "Eugene O'Neill's *More Stately Mansions*: Studies in Dramatic Form at the University of Wisconsin-Madison." *Eugene O'Neill Newsletter* 5.2 (1981): 21-26.

Sums up findings of a research seminar on dramatic form in *More Stately Mansions.* The seminar was conducted by Jackson and John D. Ezell.

A333 _____. "Dramatic Form in Eugene O'Neill's *The Calms of Capricorn.*" *Eugene O'Neill Newsletter* 12.3 (1988): 35-42.

Argues that in *Touch* and *Mansions* O'Neill used forms that derived from European literary traditions: romantic in the former and experimental in the latter. But in *The Calms of Capricorn* "he appears to have attempted the creation of a more original form, a heroic saga, with characteristics drawn from the emerging traditions of American literature, music, dance, and painting, as well as others drawn from the popular art of the film."

A334 Jaidev. "Realities from the Margins: A Deconstruction of *Mourning Becomes Electra.*" *Panjab University Research Bulletin (Arts)* [Chandigarh, India] 20.1 (1989): 25-32.

Views O'Neill's choral characters as if they formed a *classical* Greek chorus — that is, as representing proper or normal values. These are values which Jaidev thinks we will, at least temporarily — during our suspension of disbelief— also share as we watch the central characters and their story from the choral stance — from the margins of the action.

A335 "Jason Robards: Of Dreams and Lies." *New York Times* 4 Apr. 1999, sec. 2: 25.

Revisits the subject of *Iceman* productions now that, of the "O'Neill trinity" (Dewhurst, Robards, Quintero), only Robards survives. Inspired by the Davies-Spacey revival.

A336 Jenckes, Norma. "O'Neill's Use of Irish-Yankee Stereotypes in *A Touch of the Poet.*" *Eugene O'Neill Newsletter* 9.2 (1985): 34-38.

Discusses Irish stereotypes in early American theater and song. In *Touch* O'Neill "redrew the stereotypes to suggest not merely their inadequacy but also their culpability, as part of a propaganda of assimilation, in generating a false consciousness and raising false hopes of ultimate equality and acceptance."

A337 Jiji, Vera. "Reviewers' Responses to the Early Plays of Eugene O'Neill: A Study in Influence." *Theatre Survey* 29.1 (1988): 69-86.

Plumbs the reasons behind the lack of critical enthusiasm for O'Neill's early plays, which she attributes in part to the playwright's violating "prevalent taboos." Looks at the reception of *Jones, Ape, Desire,* et al., to conclude that reviewers were "sometimes inconsistent, persistently naive, almost always provincial."

A338 _____. "Another Look at *The Hairy Ape.*" *Recorder* 3.1 (1989): 141-43.

Students in Professor Jiji's seminar decide that the jail scene is the "crucial turning point for Yank: culmination of his loss of his old identity and the start of his search for a new one, as well as the hint of the ultimate futility of that desperate search."

A339 Jinglan, Zhu. "Feelings in O'Neill's plays: An Actress Analyzes Abbie in *Desire Under the Elms.*" *Recorder* 3.1 (1989): 123-26.

Four passages from *Desire* are chosen to illustrate how an actress must use her own sensibility — her "feelings" — as the basis for her interpretation of the roles she plays. In these "feelings" the "complex psychological conflicts of the character are revealed."

A340 Jones, Edward T. "The Tyrones as TV Family: O'Neill's *Long Day's Journey into Night*, Primetime." *Literature and Film Quarterly* 22.2 (1994): 93-97.

Looks at the television versions of *Journey*, those directed by Jonathan Miller and Peter Woods, and finds advantages the medium offers over the theater experience.

A341 Josephs, Lois S. "The Women of Eugene O'Neill: Sex Role Stereotypes." *Ball State University Forum* 14.3 (1973): 3-8.

O'Neill never reached beyond traditional sex roles after *Horizon*. Women in O'Neill plays belong to men and serve their needs.

A342 Jurich, Joseph. "Jack London, and *The Hairy Ape.*" *Eugene O'Neill Newsletter* 3.3 (1980): 6-8.

Compares the disillusionment of Yank with that of the hero of *Martin Eden* both of whom die without hope of finding love or success. Both protagonists are rejected by society and both are lower-class seamen. Both O'Neill and London were torn between concern for the masses and rugged individualism.

A343 Jurich, Marilyn. "Men of Iron, Beasts of Clay: The Confluence of Folk-Tale and Drama in "Joe Magarac" and *The Hairy Ape.*" *Eugene O'Neill Newsletter* 12.2 (1988): 38-45.

Considers *Ape* in light of the folk-tale "Joe Magarac," finding in the two similar attitudes toward industry and labor.

A344 Kakutani, Michiko. [No Title]. *New York Times* 15 Oct. 1979, sec. C: 15.

Describes an evening at the Public Theater (14 Oct. 1979), in which O'Neill's birthday was celebrated by a reading of Barbara Gelb's "O'Neill and Carlotta," written for the occasion. The work was a dramatic collage of O'Neill's and Carlotta's own words from letters, papers, *Journey, Iceman,* and *Misbegotten.* Recordings of Carlotta's voice were included.

The readers were Jason Robards, Colleen Dewhurst, José Quintero, Geraldine Fitzgerald, Philip Anglim, and Madeline Kahn. The director was Robert Allan Ackerman, and the producer was Joseph Papp. (Most of those on stage were members of the Theater Committee for Eugene O'Neill.)

A345 _____. "Hospital Remembers Rebirth of O'Neill." *New York Times* 18 Oct. 1982, sec. C: 14.

The occasion of the Gaylord Sanitarium's 80th anniversary gives us the opportunity to hear O'Neill's response to his stay there. The article also considers how Gaylord influenced O'Neill's writing (*Straw*) and furthered his career (he read Synge, Ibsen, Yeats, Lady Gregory, Brieux, and Hauptmann while there).

A346 Kalson, Albert E. "When Strangers Meet: A Response to Frederick I. Carpenter." *Eugene O'Neill Newsletter* 8.3 (1984): 24-26.

Defends his reviews of the London productions of *Interlude* and *Journey* against Carpenter's charge of elitism and of sticking too closely to the unities (see A111).

A347 _____. "Up-staged and off-staged by the Director and Designer: *The Hairy Ape* and *Desire Under the Elms* in London." *Eugene O'Neill Newsletter* 11.2 (1987): 36-40.

Kalson's advice to West Germany's Schaubühne Company (which produced *Ape* in May 1987) and to England's Greenwich Theatre (which produced *Desire* at the same time) is "Place your trust in the dramatist you are supposedly honoring, not in the ingenuity of a 'creative' concept." He finds the sets and the addition of men and women in gorilla suits at the end of *Ape* derisive and the set of *Desire* at odds with the playwright's lines.

A348 _____, and Lisa M. Schwerdt. "Eternal Recurrence and the Shaping of O'Neill's Dramatic Structures." *Comparative Drama* 24 (1990): 133-50.

Contends that O'Neill's aesthetic can be understood only by a look at the element of Nietzschean philosophy (eternal recurrence) that attracted him to Strindberg's cyclical form.

A349 Kauffmann, Stanley. "Notes on Some New York Theaters." *Performance* 1.6 (1973): 82-87.

Some comments on the inadequacies of the new location of the Circle in the Square company for staging *Electra*, a play "that was dead before the playwright finished writing it."

A350 Kaul, R. K. "Tragedy and O'Neill." *Jadavpur Journal of Comparative Literature* 11 (1973): 93-106.

Sets O'Neill against the whole tradition of tragedy — Greek, Renaissance, and modern — and then briefly comments on how *Electra, Lazarus, Brown, Interlude, Desire,* and *Journey* fit within the genre. Finds that O'Neill gives too much attention to explanation, leaves too little room for inference. Still "in fairness it must be added that he falls short because he aims too high."

A351 Kehl, D. G. "The 'Big Subject' in *The Hairy Ape*: A New Look at Scene Five." *Eugene O'Neill Review* 17.1-2 (1993): 39-43.

"If nostalgic romantics like Paddy falsify the past, and if Long's socialist, Wobbly radicals, self-serving capitalists, and instinctive animals displace him in the present, the high society religionists rob Yank not only of spiritual reality in the present but also of transcendent hope for the future."

A352 Kellar, Deborah. "Staging *A Touch of the Poet*." *Eugene O'Neill Newsletter* 4.1-2 (1980): 10-12.

Describes her experience directing *Touch* at Centralia College, in Washington, and discusses the improvisations that budgetary constraints necessitated.

A353 Keller, James R. "Rage Against Order: O'Neill's Yank and Milton's Satan." *Eugene O'Neill Review* 17.1-2 (1993): 45-52.

O'Neill's play and Milton's epic are alike in structure and theme. "Like Milton's Satan, Yank ... is portrayed as an outsider who is entrapped and tormented by forces beyond his control and who yearns for an unattainable bliss — a yearning that plunges him into a vengeful quest that ultimately proves degrading rather than fulfilling." In *Paradise Lost*, O'Neill "found a paradigm for the alienation and dehumanization of the modern industrial worker."

A354 _____. "Eugene O'Neill's Stokehole and Edmund Spenser's Cave of Mammon." *English Language Notes* 31.3 (1994): 66-73.

"The purpose of this discussion is to add one more potential influence to the list [of works that may have influenced O'Neill's *The Hairy Ape*] — Edmund Spenser's *The Fairie Queene*."

A355 Kellman, Alice J. "*The Emperor Jones* and *The Hairy Ape:* A Beginning and an End." *Eugene O'Neill Newsletter* 2.1 (1978): 9-10.

Notes that whereas *Jones* brought the Provincetown Players into the limelight, *Ape* marked an end to their experimentation.

A356 Kennedy, Andrew K. "Natural, Mannered, and Parodic Dialogue." *Yearbook of English Studies* 9 (1979): 28-54.

Although it is often listed in O'Neill bibliographies, this lengthy article only briefly mentions O'Neill.

A357 Kennedy, Joyce D. "O'Neill's Lavinia Mannon and the Dickinson Legend." *American Literature* 49 (1977): 108-13.

Suggests that Emily Dickinson and her sister Lavinia served as models for Lavinia Mannon. Draws numerous parallels between the sisters and O'Neill's Lavinia.

A358 _____. "Pierre's Progeny: O'Neill and the Melville Revival." *English Studies in Canada* 3 (1977): 103-17.

Compares Melville's *Pierre* to O'Neill's *Electra* and concludes that O'Neill was influenced by Melville's work, but admits there is no direct evidence that O'Neill owned or had read the book.

A359 Kenton, Edna. *The Provincetown Players and the Playwrights' Theatre 1915-1922.* Eds. Travis Bogard and Jackson R. Bryer. *Eugene O'Neill Review* 21.1-2 (1997): 16-160.

This seven-chapter history of the Provincetown Players, by someone who lived the history, went unpublished when Helen Deutsch and Stella Hanau's *The Provincetown* beat it to the publisher in 1931. In it we learn of the group's vision, formation, and membership, its successful, though short-lived seasons, and its demise. Reconstructs events from "the old constitutions and minutes; old programs and projected bills; old manifestos of great aims and purposes; old budgets of what we would like to do blue-pencilled down to the bone of what we could do; old plans for the glass-walled Dome Theatre we were sometime to build overnight on land we had already chosen for ours in Washington Square South; above all, as sign of our general looseness, old annual financial reports" to recount the group's seven-year history.

A360 King, W. D. "'It Brought the World to this Coast': The World Premiere of Eugene O'Neill's *Lazarus Laughed* at the

Pasadena Community Playhouse." *Theatre Survey* 29.1 (1988): 1-34.

Referring to O'Neill's correspondence with Kenneth Macgowan, King revisits the premiere of play which failed to result in a New York production and explains why.

A361 Knight, Michael. "Design for New Theater Picked in Provincetown." *New York Times* 20 Nov. 1978, sec. C: 16.

Discusses the choosing of architectural plans for a new (the fourth) Wharf Playhouse in Provincetown, MA.

A362 Kolin, Philip C. "*All God's Chillun Got Wings* and *Macbeth*." *Eugene O'Neill Newsletter* 12.1 (1988): 55-61.

Argues that the relationship between husband and wife in *Macbeth* may have influenced O'Neill's depiction of Ella and Jim Harris.

A363 _____. "Parallels Between *Desire Under the Elms* and *Sweet Bird of Youth*." *Eugene O'Neill Review* 13.2 (1989): 23-35.

The title of this article says it all. Looking at similarities in the characters of Ephraim Cabot and Boss Finley, in the relevance of the setting (elms and palm trees), and the inclusion in both plays of a woman called Min of suspect reputation, Kolin concludes that Williams was influenced by O'Neill when he wrote *Sweet Bird*.

A364 Krafchick, Marcelline. "Film and Fiction in O'Neill's *Hughie*." *Arizona Quarterly* 39 (1983): 47-61.

Argues that *Hughie* can be a successful play through the use of film and technological audio devices to handle those points of the stage directions that cannot be presented through normal staging. Disagrees with Raleigh, Scheibler, and Tiusanen who say, in effect, that *Hughie* is unperformable.

A365 _____. "*Hughie*: Some Light on O'Neill's *Moon*." *Eugene O'Neill Newsletter* 8.3 (1984): 8-11.

Sees *Hughie*'s affinities to *Misbegotten*. Although *Misbegotten, Hughie, Iceman,* and *Journey* all try to salvage from despair, in *Iceman* and *Journey* the efforts end in calamity and self-revelations are thwarted. However, both Josie and Erie are able to convert their pain into a life-creating force.

A366 _____. "*Hughie* and *The Zoo Story*." *Eugene O'Neill Newsletter* 10.1 (1986): 15-16.

Acknowledging that there is no evidence that Albee read *Hughie*, Krafchick, nonetheless, finds similarities in these plays of "rhetorical seduction"—which lure recalcitrant listeners into participants.

A367 Krasner, David. "Whose Role Is It Anyway? Charles Gilpin and the Harlem Renaissance." *African American Review* 29.3 (1995): 483-96.

A justification of why Gilpin changed O'Neill's lines when he played Brutus Jones, offering aesthetic, as well as cultural, reasons for the alterations.

A368 Krimsky, John. "*The Emperor Jones*: Robeson and O'Neill on Film." *Connecticut Review* 7 (1974): 94-99.

Provides insights into the troubles O'Neill faced with censorship and racial prejudice during the 1933 film production of *Jones*.

A369 Labelle, Maurice M. "Dionysus and Despair: The Influence of Nietzsche upon O'Neill's Drama." *Educational Theatre Journal* 25 (1973): 436-42.

Discusses the Apollonian-Dionysian conflict, which is seen to deepen in *Desire*.

A370 Lai, Sheng-chuan. "Mysticism and Noh in O'Neill." *Theatre Journal* 35 (1983): 74-87.

Discusses the influence on O'Neill of Mabel Collins' *Light on the Path*, which O'Neill read around 1915. Says the book misunderstands the Eastern philosophy it tries to present. This misunderstanding appears in O'Neill's experimental plays, which failed, partly as a result. Thinks the last plays reflect the influence of Noh drama, which O'Neill had known from the 1920s. Finds *Journey, Iceman, Hughie, Touch* similar to Noh drama in theme and form, though, of course, not in style.

A371 Lang, William A. "Power in the Theatre: O'Neill's *Long Day's Journey into Night*." *Lubelskie Materialy Neofilologiczne* [Lublin, Poland] 18 (1994): 91-95.

No matter how you look at the play, as cultural statement, as classical tragedy, its power derives from its subject — the universal yet personal experience that all Americans have in common, the family.

A372 Lapisardi, Frederick S. "Not-So-Random Notes on Masks in Yeats and O'Neill." *Eugene O'Neill Review* 20.1-2 (1996): 132-38.

Conceding that there is no direct evidence of Yeats's influence on O'Neill in terms of their mutual interest in dramatic masks, Lapisardi posits a possible link, common influence, in the person of Gordon Craig, whose *The Theatre Advancing* O'Neill had read. Craig was indisputably an influence on Yeats.

A373 Larson, Kelli A. "O'Neill's Tragic Quest for Belonging: Psychological Determinism in the *S.S. Glencairn* Quartet." *Eugene O'Neill Review* 13.2 (1989): 12-22.

Looks at *Caribbees, Zone, Cardiff,* and *Voyage,* concluding that "in his quest for belonging, each of the Glencairn protagonists reaches beyond the end of his tether, only to be jerked back sharply by the playwright's deterministic reality."

A374 Lask, Thomas. "Publishing: Robards on the Touch of O'Neill." *New York Times* 1 June 1979, sec. C: 22.

From a column on publishing news we hear that Robards, at the urging of Nan Talese, a vice president of Simon and Schuster, may do a book about the "place and influence of O'Neill on his life."

A375 Lauder, Robert E. "The Renegade Haunted by God: Eugene O'Neill's Dream of Forgiveness." *Commonweal* 14 Dec. 1984: 690-92.

A priest responds to the 1984 Broadway production of *Misbegotten.* Notes O'Neill's inability to "get the church out of" himself. Sees *Misbegotten* as an expression in Catholic symbols of O'Neill's belief in "the Force behind" and man's struggle "to make the Force express him … instead of being … an infinitesimal incident in its expression." Calls attention to the scene in which Leveau's lighting suggests the Pietà. See E416.

A376 Lawson, Carol. "Broadway." *New York Times* 27 Mar. 1981, sec. C: 2.

An interview with Earle Hyman, the James Tyrone of Geraldine Fitzgerald's *Journey.* Hyman comments on the universality of the play. See E305.

A377 _____. "Broadway." *New York Times* 10 Apr. 1981, sec. C: 2.

Announces that José Quintero will lend himself to the Eugene O'Neill Festival at Columbia University by giving three lectures and directing a summer production of *Welded* to open 10 June for a four-week run.

A378 _____. "Broadway Celebrates Eugene O'Neill's Birthday." *New York Times* 20 Oct. 1981, sec. C: 9.

Discusses the doings at the third annual celebration of Eugene O'Neill's birthday at the Circle in the Square Theatre (Fri., 16 Oct.). Quintero received the gold O'Neill birthday medal.

A379 Lawson, Steve. "José, Jason, and Gene." *Horizon* 21 (1978): 36-42.

Attributes to O'Neill the position of "foremost American dramatist" in response to the collaboration of Jason Robards and José Quintero in *Iceman* (May '56), *Journey* (Fall, '56), and later in *Hughie,* and *Misbegotten,* and on the occasion for this article, the production of *Touch.*

A380 Leadbeater, Lewis W. "Aristophanes and O'Neill: Hickey as Comic Hero." *Classical and Modern Literature* 12.4 (1992): 361-74.

Hickey becomes the hero in "a comedy of despair," according to Leadbeater, who applies Aristotle's definition of comedy to *Iceman.* His citations from Aristophanes' *The Birds* and *The Frogs,* in Greek, are sure to send a few scurrying for translations. Still, his case is convincing.

A381 LeClaire, Anne. "Provincetown Awaits Rebirth of Playhouse." *Boston Sunday Globe* 12 Nov. 1978, sec. A: 20.

Discusses the early stages in the rebuilding of the Provincetown Playhouse, destroyed by arson in 1977. The first steps include the assembling of various architectural firms in Provincetown and the briefing of these representatives on the history of the area.

A382 Leech, Michael. "Miller's Journey." *Plays and Players* 396 (1986): 11-13.

As he prepares for the opening of *Journey* in London, Jonathan Miller gives his opinion of the play and answers questions about its previous reception in New York. Miller finds *Journey* a great play, but not, as often thought, "quintessentially Irish" or of epic "magnitude." See E325.

A383 Lemanis, Mara. "*Desire Under the Elms* and Tragic Form: A Study of Misalliance." *South Dakota Review* 16.3 (1978): 46-55.

While the characteristics of tragedy are found in *Desire,* the play is closer to disaster, as defined by Robert B. Heilman, than to tragedy. Conclusion is reached by study of the dialogue and actions surrounding Abbie's murder of her child. Ephraim has tragic stature, but experiences no rebirth. Abbie, on the other hand, experiences the rebirth but lacks awareness. Such a "hybrid" results in a "miscegenated tragedy."

A384 Leonard, Hugh. "Can a Playwright Truly Depict Himself?" *New York Times* 23 Nov. 1980, sec. 2: 5.

Discusses the factualness of autobiography, and more especially of autobiographical fictions. *Journey* is criticized, not as a play, but as dishonest. All the characters in the play, save Edmund, are seen as betrayers, who finally are absolved by Edmund. Claims that O'Neill could not accept responsibility for betrayals.

A385 Levitt, H. N. "Comedy in the Plays of Eugene O'Neill." *Players Magazine* 51 (1976): 92-95.

Analyzes O'Neill's plays according to Alan Reynolds Thompson's classification in *The Anatomy of Drama* (1942) of the six sources of laughter: comic taboo, physical movement and slapstick, plot, verbal characters, and ideas. Charts 45 plays.

A386 Lewis, Ward B. "O'Neill and Hauptmann: A Study in Mutual Admiration." *Comparative Literary Studies* 22 (1985): 231-43.

Plumbs the affinities between these playwrights, before O'Neill's creativity found a new path and prior to Hauptmann's death in 1946: their political interest, their desire to create innovative theater, their naturalism. The article also describes their meeting — after the American premiere of *Electra* — and their mutual regard, as well as the German reception of O'Neill's early plays.

A387 Linney, Romulus. "About O'Neill." *Eugene O'Neill Newsletter* 6.3 (1982): 3-5.

Reflects upon his exposure to O'Neill when an undergraduate and O'Neill's reputation was at an ebb. Recalls also his response to the Frederic March-Florence Eldridge-Jason Robards *Journey.*

A388 Liu, Haiping. "Eugene O'Neill in China." *Theatre Survey* 29.1 (1988): 87-101.

Charts O'Neill's popularity in China (translations of his work, influence on other writers) from its inception in the late 1920s and rise, to its 30-year nadir from 1949-1979 when O'Neill was neither read nor performed, to recent renewed interest.

A389 _____. "Taoism in O'Neill's Tao House Plays." *Eugene O'Neill Newsletter* 12.2 (1988): 28-33.

Contends that from a general interest in Orientalism, O'Neill moved to Taoism specifically. The transcendence achieved in his later plays derives from O'Neill's rejecting of dualism and subscribing to the tenets of Taoism.

A390 _____. "The Invisible: A Study of Eugene O'Neill's Offstage Characters." *Eugene O'Neill Review* 18.1-2 (1994): 149-61.

Studies those O'Neill creations who don't appear on stage but who affect the play's action nonetheless. In Yvette (*A Wife for a Life*), in Ephraim Cabot's second wife (*Desire*), in Rosa Parritt and Evelyn Hickman (*Iceman*) Liu finds "facets of the playwright's perception or understanding of his own mother."

A391 Lloyd, D. W. "Mystical Experience in *Long Day's Journey into Night.*" *Unisa English Studies* 24.2 (1986): 17-21.

O'Neill's mysticism breathes hot and cold. We find it hinted at in *Cardiff*, rejected in *Jones* (that is Jones's tragedy), at the center and Christianized in *Lazarus*, but rejected again in *Electra*. Hot again in *Journey* with Edmund's famous "Like a saint's vision of beatitude" speech. Evidence outside the plays are among others his A. H. Quinn letter—"I am always acutely conscious,"—the Nietzschean Apollonian/Dionysian tensions known to O'Neill, and the similarities between Edmund's experiences and others' mystical encounters.

A392 Lock, Charles. "Maurice Browne and the Chicago Little Theatre." *Modern Drama* 31 (1988): 106-16.

O'Neill, whose plays were produced in the Chicago Little Theatre, by Browne, features only marginally in this study.

A393 Lucow, Ben. "O'Neill's Use of Realism in *Ah, Wilderness!*" *Notes on Modern American Literature* 1 (1977): Item 10.

Sees an implied criticism of the small town in the play. Richard must give up the wilderness for civilization, the individual for society.

A394 MacQueen, Scott. "Rise and Fall of *The Emperor Jones*, 1933." *American Cinematographer* 71 (Feb. 1990): 34-40.

Addresses the making of the film version of *Jones*, critical responses, script deletions, its place in the beginnings of race-oriented films, and the Paul Robeson connection. Considerable plot summary. No bibliography. The "Credits" section identifies the production staff and cast.

A395 Mandal, Somdatta. "Eugene O'Neill and Film." *Indian Journal of American Studies* 25.2 (1995): 135-41.

Argues that O'Neill's attitude towards the filming of his plays was not simply a matter of money — despite what O'Neill himself said. Movies and plays of the early decades of the century stressed the visual, stressed technical experimentation (nearly everything film makers did was for the first time), and, as far as early O'Neill plays are concerned, slavishly followed plot formulas.

A396 Mandl, Bette. "Absence as Presence: The Second Sex in *The Iceman Cometh.*" *Eugene O'Neill Newsletter* 6.2 (1982): 10-15.

Revelations about women in *Iceman* reveal hatred. Women are expected to betray men, and even Larry Slade must admit that the reason he left the movement was disgust at Rosa's infidelity.

A397 _____. "Family Ties: Landscape and Gender in *Desire Under the Elms.*" *Eugene O'Neill Newsletter* 11.2 (1987): 19-23.

In a feminist interpretation of *Desire,* Mandl looks to Sherry Ortner's essay "Is Female to Male as Nature to Culture?" with its contention that women in literature tend to be associated with nature and men with culture to find the conflict over land and woman at the play's center.

A398 _____. "Wrestling with the Angel in the House: Mary Tyrone's Long Journey." *Eugene O'Neill Newsletter* 12.3 (1988): 19-24.

Argues that in the character of Mary Tyrone we see "an authentic representation of a woman at odds … with home and family as they were structured in her day." Mary is "in uneasy relation to those virtues associated with … womanhood: 'piety, purity, submissiveness and domesticity.'"

A399 _____. "Gender as Design in Eugene O'Neill's *Strange Interlude.*" *Eugene O'Neill Review* 19.1-2 (1995): 123-38.

Looks at what O'Neill called his "woman play" as a "theatrical allegory of gender." Mandl argues that "the presence of Marsden, though it highlights the homosocial preoccupations of the men, also disrupts, the binarism that structures the rigidities of the gender arrangements the play otherwise reflects."

A400 Manheim, Michael. "Dialogue Between Son and Mother in Chekhov's *The Sea Gull* and O'Neill's *Long Day's Journey into Night.*" *Eugene O'Neill Newsletter* 6.1 (1982): 24-29.

Studies the similarities between the mother-son relationships in the two plays. Rejection, addiction, and suicide are central to both plays.

A401 _____. "O'Neill's Transcendence of Melodrama in *A Touch of the Poet* and *A Moon for the Misbegotten.*" *Comparative Drama* 16 (1982): 238-50.

Early O'Neill plays were not melodramatic, but after the deaths of his parents in 1920s, they became so. Later, in the 1930s, O'Neill came to terms with his memories of his family. Melodrama is treated humorously thereafter, as in *Touch* and *Misbegotten.*

A402 _____. "Eugene O'Neill: America's National Playwright." *Eugene O'Neill Newsletter* 9.2 (1985): 17-23.

Tries to define a national playwright by showing what he is not — an apologist or a regionalist. His voice should be a broad cross-section of the population, and he must be well known. O'Neill's reputation as a national playwright rests on the plays at the end of his career. The characters' dialect in these plays is recognizably American, as is their temperament.

A403 _____. "O'Neill's Early Debt to David Belasco." *Theatre History Studies* 6 (1986): 124-31.

Argues O'Neill came under Belasco's influence as we see in O'Neill's use of stage directions, in his dramatic action, dialogue and acting style, and in particular in his use of the supernatural and the fallen woman motif.

A404 _____. "Confession as Artifice in the Plays of Eugene O'Neill." *Renascence* 39.3 (1987): 430-41.

Taking a look at *Iceman, Journey, Misbegotten,* Manheim asserts that O'Neill used the theater as "his own artistic confessional," revealing through his characters his friends', his family's, or his own sins and offering through the drama absolution.

A405 _____. "O'Neill's Transcendence of Melodrama in the Late Plays." *Eugene O'Neill Newsletter* 12.2 (1988): 22-28.

Building on Robert Heilman's definition of melodrama found in *Tragedy and Melodrama* — that it "involves intrigue, a mystery wherein key information is withheld until the final moments of work" and that it contains "polar opposition of clear conceptions of good and evil"— Manheim shows that *Misbegotten, Iceman* and *Journey* are not of the genre.

A406 _____. "*The Great God Brown* in the Light of O'Neill's Last Plays." *Eugene O'Neill Review* 14.1-2 (1990): 5-15.

Argues convincingly for *Brown* as precursor to *Misbegotten* and *Journey*, especially in light of the relationship between Jamie and Edmund as reflected in the dichotomous Dion Anthony-Billy Brown relationship.

A407 _____. "At Home with the Harfords." *Eugene O'Neill Review* 20.1-2 (1996): 102-09.

A reviewer's comment on his then still-to-be-published *Eugene O'Neill's New Language of Kinship* sparks this meditation in which Manheim considers *Mansions* as a play wherein "opposed sides of individual personalities might establish 'alliances' with their counterparts in other divided personalities." Concludes that it is in O'Neill's last plays that characters separated by feelings of distrust or hostility appeal for understanding from others and find it, however temporarily. The late plays are "the true language of kinship plays," which complete what O'Neill began in *Mansions*.

A408 Mann, Bruce J. "O'Neill's 'Presence' in *Long Day's Journey into Night*." *Theatre Annual* 43 (1988): 15-30.

Argues the mature playwright is present in *Journey*, which is suggested by point of view. Using Robert Brustein's observation that there is a fifth character in the play (the aging O'Neill), Mann contends that O'Neill the elder is the subtle narrator of the play.

A409 _____. "An FBI Memorandum on O'Neill." *Eugene O'Neill Review* 15.1 (1991): 58-63.

Mann's sleuthing pays off when he discovers and publishes herein the FBI file on O'Neill.

A410 Mann, Theodore. "José Quintero: A Life that was Art." *New York Times* 7 Mar. 1999, sec. 2: 10.

An obituary written for Quintero by his friend and collaborator. Recalls first meeting Quintero in 1947 — Mann's initial impressions of the director's intensity. And he reminisces too about their early success, Tennessee Williams' *Summer and Smoke*.

A411 Mason, Jeffrey D. "The Metatheatre of O'Neill: Actor as Metaphor in *A Touch of the Poet*." *Theatre Annual* 43 (1988): 53-66.

In *Touch* O'Neill, in using the figure of the actor, went beyond recreating his father in the role of Con Melody and beyond symbolizing mankind: "the play transcends biography as father, actor and theatre all become conceptually linked to produce O'Neill's metatheatrical response to his personal memories and to the melodramatic tradition against which he rebelled."

A412 Massa, Ann. "Intention and Effect in *The Hairy Ape*." *Modern Drama* 31 (1988): 41-51.

Can any but an American audience appreciate the nuances of *Ape* is the question that Massa poses in this review of the Schaubühne Company's Berlin production. Apparently not, she concludes. This play's language and theme do not translate easily. Moreover, director Peter Stein's vision violates O'Neill's intention.

A413 Maufort, Marc. "The Legacy of Melville's *Pierre*: Family Relationships in *Mourning Becomes Electra*." *Eugene O'Neill Newsletter* 11.2 (1987): 23-28.

Bypassing the more obvious classical influences on O'Neill's play, Maufort goes to the overlooked Melville novel *Pierre* to find its impact on *Electra*.

A414 _____. "Eugene O'Neill and Poetic Realism: Tragic form in the Belgian Premiere of *Long Day's Journey into Night*." *Theatre Survey* 29.1 (1988): 117-25.

To write this review/essay Maufort looks at the Belgian production's promptbook and conducts interviews with the director and the actress who played Mary to conclude that "the 1970 Charleroi production of *Long Day's Journey into Night* was a masterpiece of poetic realism, notwithstanding the fact that the director concentrated excessively on the figure of the mother and effected a few unjustified cuts."

A415 _____. "Eugene O'Neill's Innovative Craftsmanship in the 'Glencairn' Cycle (1914-1917)." *Eugene O'Neill Newsletter* 12.1 (1988): 27-33.

Looks at soliloquy in the sea plays, which, Maufort concludes, is O'Neill's dramatic answer to the novelistic interior monologue and proffers Henry James's influence on the playwright.

A416 _____. "Mariners and Mystics: Echoes of *Moby Dick* in O'Neill." *Theatre Annual* 43 (1988): 31-52.

Statements the playwright made and O'Neill's library holdings provide evidence of the playwright's appreciation of Melville. Then Maufort looks at *Electra, Ile, Cross,* and *Journey* for echoes of the novelist.

A417 _____. "O'Neill's Variations on an Obituary Motif in *Bound East for Cardiff* and *Hughie.*" *Revue Belge de Philologie et d'Histoire/Belgisch Tijdschrift voor Filologie en Geschiedenis*[Wezembeek, Belgium] 46.3 (1988): 602-12.

"A comparison between the settings, modes of characterization, and thematic substance of *Bound East for Cardiff* and *Hughie*" "evinces their kinship." In both plays O'Neill treats of death, paying tribute to departed friends.

A418 _____. "Tragedy and Solipsism: The Kinship of *Moby Dick* and *The Iceman Cometh.*" *Recorder* 3.1 (1989): 27-36.

Argues that when O'Neill characters fail to reach out to others, they fail to achieve their tragic potential, and when they do, they attain tragic nobility. Maufort then looks at *Iceman* and finds Melville's influence. "Both Melville and O'Neill regarded man's inner division between solipsism and human love as an important factor of tragedy and expressed this theme in strikingly convergent artistic terms."

A419 _____. "The Playwright as Lord of Touraine: O'Neill and French Civilization." *English Studies* [Lisse, Netherlands] 71.6 (1990): 501-08.

A "pilgrimage" to the chateau Le Plessis near Saint Antoine du Rocher in the Loire Valley — O'Neill and Carlotta's first home together — inspires musings on the influence of French culture on O'Neill's plays. "The echoes of French history resonate throughout O'Neill's canon" but mainly in *Iceman, Journey,* where we see the shades of Balzac and Proust, and in *Electra* and *Mansions,* where we find echoes of the physical Le Plessis itself.

A420 _____. "O'Neill's 'Passage to India': Spiritual Discovery of America in *The Fountain.*" *Belgian Essays on Language and Literature* [Liège] (1993): 61-67.

Another confluence? Yes, indeed. This time Whitman's and O'Neill's affinities (and dissimilarities) are unmasked. *Fountain* is found to be "comparable to Whitman's 'Passage to India' and 'The Prayer of Columbus' in its vision of the discovery of America as a spiritual enterprise."

A421 _____. "'Sometimes — There's God — So Quickly!': Imprints of Eugene O'Neill in A *Streetcar Named Desire.*" *Tennessee Williams Literary Journal* 3.1 (1993-94): 23-30.

Taking a well trodden path, Maufort finds "confluences" — "affinities in aesthetic and philosophical vision" — between O'Neill's *Iceman* and Williams' play.

A422 _____. "The Legacy of the American Romance in O'Neill's Expressionist Drama." *English Studies* 5 (1994): 32-45.

O'Neill's expressionism, though indebted to the German, is distinctively American in its blend of realism and the poetic-mystical. This blending is "readily observable" in *Cardiff, Journey, Iceman,* but also "obliquely" in *Ape, Chillun, Dynamo.* Parallels between the latter three plays and *Moby-Dick,* where we find the same blending, are then described.

A423 _____. "Exorcisms of the Past: Avatars of the O'Neillian Monologue in Modern Drama." *Eugene O'Neill Review* 22.1-2 (1998): 123-36.

"In these pages, I propose to concentrate on the avatars of a more specific aspect of O'Neill's novelistic imagination, namely his attempts to offer us visions of his characters' consciousness in dramatic equivalent of novelistic 'interior monologues.' I shall argue that his use of novelistic monologues ... has had a significant impact on subsequnt American playwrights." Tennessee Williams' *A Streetcar Named Desire* and *Suddenly Last Summer,* Albee's *The Zoo Story* and *The American Dream,* and Sam Shepard's *Buried Child* and *Curse of the Starving Class* provide the evidence.

A424 Mayberry, Robert. "Sterile Wedding: The Comic Structure of O'Neill's *Hughie.*" *Massachusetts Studies in English* 7 (1980): 10-19.

Shows *Hughie* in a comic tradition, having its roots in ancient ritual: comic in structure, because death is at the end denied when Erie finds a successor to the dead Hughie; comic in order, because rebirth and continuance are finally celebrated; and comic in tone, in that there is final relief from tension. The *wedding* of the title of the article refers to the final handshake between Hughie and Erie; thereafter, they have a friendship which suggests a kind of wedding. The pattern of Erie's behavior is one of courtship.

A425 McCown, Cynthia. "*The Great God Brown*: A Diagnostic of Commercialism's Ills." *Eugene O'Neill Review* 17.1-2 (1993): 53-59.

Assails the paradox of why a play which attacks American materialism was commercially viable when it debuted.

A426 McDermott, Dana S. "Robert Edmond Jones and Eugene O'Neill: Two American Visionaries." *Eugene O'Neill Newsletter* 8.1 (1984): 3-10.

Reviews the artistic relationship between Robert Edmond Jones and Eugene O'Neill in productions of *Desire, Iceman, Electra.*

A427 McDonald, David. "The Phenomenology of the Glance in *Long Day's Journey into Night.*" *Theatre Journal* 31 (1979): 343-56.

The essence of *Journey* is "watchers being watched." The three men watch Mary, and she watches them until she escapes their glances through drugs. Discusses the effect of seeing and being seen on the identity and outcome of each character.

A428 McDonough, Carole, and Brian McDonough. "*Mourning Becomes Electra*: A Study of the Conflict between Puritanism and Paganism." *English Review* [Salem State College] 3 (1975): 6-19.

Discusses pagan and Puritan elements in the play — the house, the Mannon ancestors, and the Mannons themselves. Argues that the trilogy pits the "devastating effects of Puritanism" against the "free-seeking, life-loving forces of paganism." The play's ending — Lavinia's reversion to Puritanism — "demonstrates O'Neill's admiration for the Puritan character" ... "though he may not have agreed with its principles."

A429 McIlvaine, Robert. "Crane's *Maggie*: A Source for *The Hairy Ape.*" *Eugene O'Neill Newsletter* 2.3 (1979): 8-10.

Compares Crane's work and O'Neill's. The dialect Maggie and Jimmie use parallels Yank's as do Yank's and Jimmie's childhoods. Also, there is a hint of the hairy ape imagery in *Maggie.*

A430 McKelly, James C. "Ain't it the Truth: *Hughie* and the Power of Fiction." *Eugene O'Neill Newsletter* 11.1 (1987): 15-19.

A refutation of Ruby Cohn's criticism of O'Neill as a writer of dialogue and creator of character. McKelly looks to *Hughie* to prove O'Neill's adeptness at both.

A431 McLaughlin, Bruce W. "*Strange Interlude* and *The Divine Comedy.*" *The Theatre Journal* [Albany] 12.2 (1973): 20-30.

The author finds support for this thesis, that *The Divine Comedy* influenced O'Neill's *Interlude*, in Robert J. Andreach's work, which found a correspondence between O'Neill's plays *Ape* and *Fountain* and Dante's work. Finds parallels in the structuring of the two works, in the use of the symbolic number three, in their concern with broken commandments, in their ethical concern, in their dependence upon characters who do not appear (Gordon Shaw and Beatrice).

A432 McQueen, Joan. "O'Neill as Seth in *Mourning Becomes Electra.*" *Eugene O'Neill Newsletter* 9.3 (1985): 32-34.

Seth is modeled after the playwright himself. Both speak of the sea, are privy to family secrets.

A433 McVeigh, Terrance A. "A Tragic Senex Amans: O'Neill's Ephraim Cabot." *Classical and Modern Literature* 11.1 (1990): 67-75.

Sees in Ephraim Cabot a "stereotypical comic figure in classical literature and drama, the version of the senex amans most familiar to readers of English literature as January in Chaucer's *Merchant's Tale*" — "which mocks the emotional and physical weaknesses of old men."

A434 Meade, Robert. "Incest Fantasy and the Hero in *A Touch of the Poet.*" *Eugene O'Neill Review* 18.1-2 (1994): 79-94.

Traces Con Melody's posturing to Byron's poetry — Lucifer in *Cain*, the protagonist in *Don Juan* and the speaker in *Childe Harold's Pilgrimage* — and then looks to Jungian theory to explain Con's fantasies. Ultimately "the manifestation of Con's repressed shadow in the form of the inferior persona of the peasant saloon keeper, though inferior to the Major, can now go on living a life among the common men sitting at the bar."

A435 Meaney, Geraldine. "*Long Day's Journey into Night*: Modernism, Post-Modernism and Maternal Loss." *Irish University Review* 21.2 (1991): 204-18.

Most interpretations of *Journey* see the play as one dealing with loss of the mother figure, but "that loss is rarely seen in the context of a more general 'loss,' a cultural loss of legitimacy and authenticity, endemic in and enabling modernism, articulated as 'disinheritance' by an other 'coded as feminine.'" Concludes that until the last act *Journey* is "resolutely post-modern; it 'puts forward the unpresentable in presentation itself.'" Only in

Mary's last speech does it yield to the nostalgia which characterizes modernism.

A436 Meyer, Evelyn S. "Honoring Eugene O'Neill (1888-1953): A Centennial Review of Literature." *Reference Services Review* (Spring 1989): 33-41.

An occasional piece, a general assessment of O'Neill's place in American drama, of the vicissitudes of his reputation, of his background. Most helpful is the selected bibliography.

A437 Mikoś Michael, and David Mulroy. "Reymont's *The Peasants*: A Probable Influence on *Desire Under the Elms*." *Eugene O'Neill Newsletter* 10.1 (1986): 4-15.

Wladyslaw Reymont's *The Peasants*, a 1902 Polish novel, is the only work "that could have provided O'Neill in one text with the setting, characters and plot combining the themes of ancient myths with descriptions of village life, and of incestuous love with the struggle for land in a remote rural community."

A438 Miliora, Maria. "Narcissistic Fantasies in *A Touch of the Poet*: A Self-Psychological Study." *Eugene O'Neill Review* 18.1-2 (1994): 95-107.

A professor of chemistry and lecturer in psychology takes a look at Con Melody's psyche and concludes that he is "a picture-perfect presentation of the narcissistically disordered personality" made manifest by his arrogance, fantasies, need for an audience, etc.

A439 _____. "A Self Psychological Study of Dehumanization in Eugene O'Neill's *The Hairy Ape*." *Clinical Social Work Journal* 24.4 (1996): 415-27.

Applies "the constructs of self psychology, particularly those relating to selfobjects and the selfobject milieu" to *Ape* in order to study the fragmentation of the character. Literature, Miliora contends, can provide insights for the clinician. Her diagnosis? "A radical shift in one's sense of 'home' can alter one's sense of self. Displacement from the familiar, where one felt sustained and a sense of belonging, is disquieting and perhaps disorienting." The application for the therapist is clear: he/she needs to create a "selfobject milieu to support the displaced client."

A440 _____. "A Self-Psychological Study of a Shared Gambling Fantasy in Eugene O'Neill's *Hughie*." *Journal of Gambling Studies* 13.2 (1997): 105-23.

By "applying the constructs of self psychology, [Miliora shows that] the play illustrates … the narcissistic features and the emotional and behavioral characteristics of compulsive gamblers," which affect the "mood" of the play's characters, helping them "to experience a sense of camaraderie, humanness, and the illusion of kinship."

A441 Miller, Eileen. "The Turks on O'Neill: Putting the Iceman on Ice." *Eugene O'Neill Review* 20.1-2 (1996): 88-96.

An attempt to understand the reviews of Eric Bentley and Mary McCarthy of the original production of *Iceman*. While both reviewers were scathing in their criticism, at least Bentley attempted to understand the work in his informative review — something McCarthy did not do.

A442 Miller, Gabriel. "The Visionary Moment in the Plays of Eugene O'Neill." *Annals of Scholarship* 9.3 (1992): 293-306.

Argues that O'Neill's approach to theater is "painterly" in that in his canon "setting design and the arrangement of stage space, like the frame of a painting or a film, may provide significant visual metaphors for the protagonist's thoughts and emotional state." Looking at the work of O'Neill's contemporaries Winslow Homer and Edward Hopper, Miller shows how tension between interior and exterior states seen in select paintings is mirrored in *Cardiff, Caribbees, Horizon, Brown, Wilderness,* and *Misbegotten*.

A443 Miller, Jordan Y. "From Nobody to the Nobel: Two Decades of First Night O'Neill Criticism." *Eugene O'Neill Newsletter* 12.2 (1988): 8-13.

Considers first-night reaction to O'Neill's plays of the 1920s and 30s and concludes that critical response was consistent only in its inconsistency: "ecstatic praise to utter condemnation, irrespective of the play under consideration."

A444 Miller, Ronald R. "History as Image: Approaches to the Staging of Eugene O'Neill's *More Stately Mansions*." *Eugene O'Neill Newsletter* 5.2 (1981): 26-32.

Discusses the stage reading production of the play at the University of Wisconsin, conducted by Esther M. Jackson and John D. Ezell.

A445 Moin-UI-Islam. "O'Neill and the Expressionistic Techniques of Drama." *Journal of Research: Humanities* [U of the Punjab] 14 (1979): 59-69.

An introductory-level treatment of O'Neill as experimental dramatist. Finds him Americanizing European notions and theatrical techniques, and thereby freeing the American theater from its earlier commercial and unimaginative chains. Exemplifies his point by reference to *Jones, Ape,* and *Brown*.

A446 Moleski, Joseph J. "Eugene O'Neill and the Cruelty of Theater." *Comparative Drama* 15 (1981): 327-42.

Argues that in view of the philosophy of Jacques Derrida and the dramatic theory of Antonin Artaud, O'Neill's work can be "resituated" within the tradition of Western metaphysics as an example of the logocentric quest for presence: the self-sufficient presence of song as pure sound undiluted by meaning, the desire to forget past and future in fulfillment of a living present, and the self-presence of the "self-possessed" individual. O'Neill's defense of the possibility of presence and the present is both structural and thematic. It dictates the construction of the plays as well as an alternation of dualities in which the "musical" rhythm of alternation is itself the "subject" of the work (hope and despair in *Iceman),* and it is the basis for the notion that the present can be restored even if only through the articulation of its loss *(Interlude).* O'Neill's later work reflects "the obverse of the doctrine of presence," the recognition of "fate," the immutable, inviolable past as a time of origins *(Journey).*

A447 _____, **and John H. Stroupe.** "Jean Anouilh and Eugene O'Neill: Repetition as Negativity." *Comparative Drama* 20 (1986): 315-26.

A look at Anouilh's *Antigone, Becket,* and *Eurydice* and O'Neill's *Interlude, Ape,* and *Iceman* to find that both playwrights "create meaning in a world not possessing it as an inherent attribute and where the very forms from which meaning derives destroy it," but while O'Neill's characters find meaning, Anouilh's are forced to reject it. Quoting Derrida, Moleski and Stroupe find repetition in Anouilh's "death rehearsal," which in O'Neill is "repetition of life."

A448 Mongia, Sunanda. "'Marital Hell' in the Plays of O'Neill." *Panjab University Research Bulletin (Arts)* [Chandigarh, India] 20.1 (1989): 57-63.

Examines the marital relationships cursorily in several O'Neill plays *(The First Man, Elec-tra, Days, Diff'rent, Chillun, Wilderness, Desire, Welded)* to conclude that 1) O'Neill's writing was influenced by his personal relationships with women, and 2) that his couples "may be loving but they are never well-adjusted."

A449 Monteiro, George. "Jorge de Sena, Eugene O'Neill's Critic and Translator." *Eugene O'Neill Review* 17.1-2 (1993): 165-66.

Provides background on the writer who translated *Journey* into Portuguese in one month's time.

A450 Moorton, Richard F. "What's in a Name? The Significance of 'Mannon' in *Mourning Becomes Electra.*" *Eugene O'Neill Newsletter* 12.3 (1988): 42-44.

A note on the significance of the name Mannon — to suggest steadfast.

A451 _____. "The Author as Oedipus in *Mourning Becomes Electra* and *Long Day's Journey into Night.*" *Papers on Language and Literature* 25.3 (1989): 304-25.

Looks at the affinities among *Electra, Journey,* and the *Oresteia.* "In both *Mourning Becomes Electra* and *Long Day's Journey into Night* Eugene O'Neill thus inserted oedipal portraits of himself, his father, and his mother."

A452 _____. "Eugene O'Neill's American *Eumenides.*" *Classical and Modern Literature* 10.4 (1990): 359-72.

"In spite of his statement to the contrary O'Neill consciously or unconsciously followed Aeschylus to the end by patterning the third play of his American trilogy on the third play of the Greek trilogy which he had made his model."

A453 Morrison, Kristin. "Conrad and O'Neill as Playwrights of the Sea." *Eugene O'Neill Newsletter* 2.1 (1978): 3-5.

Possibly O'Neill read Conrad's play *One Day More.* Points out similarities between it and *Ile, Caribbees,* and *Voyage.* Observes that Conrad was not a good playwright, whereas O'Neill was.

A454 Mullaly, Edward. "O'Neill and the Perfect Pattern." *Dalhousie Review* 52 (1973): 603-10.

Analyzes *Mansions* in terms of what O'Neill called the perfect pattern — an upright man gains power, abuses it, and this abuse leads to his downfall. Such is Simon Harford's lot.

A455 Murphy, Brenda. "O'Neill's Realism: A Structural Approach." *Eugene O'Neill Newsletter* 7.2 (1983): 3-6.

From the realistic viewpoint O'Neill's career was a development of two earlier needs — the need for theatrical ways to depict the deepest reality of his characters within dramatic forms and the need for a dramatic form that would give true shape to his realistic dramatic action. These were fulfilled only in *Iceman, Journey, Misbegotten, Touch*. Discusses *Iceman* in terms of structural realism.

A456 _____. "*Beyond the Horizon*'s Narrative Sentence: An American Intertext for O'Neill." *Theatre Annual* 41 (1986): 49-62.

Sees *Horizon* as a play coming out of an American context. Traces the motif of two brothers in love with the same woman to plays by James A. Herne and David Belasco (who, in turn, "borrowed" it). Attributes O'Neill's long term success to his iconoclasm. Rather than support the notion that virtue, self-sacrifice, the family unit provide joy abounding, O'Neill's work debunks the middle-class values.

A457 _____. "Interpreting *Marco Millions*: Two New York Productions." *Recorder* 3.1 (1989): 127-33.

Sets the 1928 Theater Guild *Marco* (directed by Rouben Mamoulian, with Alfred Lunt) against the 1964 ANTA Lincoln Center Repertory's (director José Quintero, with Hal Holbrook). The Guild's production "probably" reflected "a fuller understanding of O'Neill's intentions." Suggests reasons.

A458 _____. "Fetishizing the Dynamo: Henry Adams and Eugene O'Neill." *Eugene O'Neill Review* 16.1 (1992): 85-90.

Takes a closer look at the affinities and discrepancies between Adams' *Education* and O'Neill's *Dynamo*; finds that while Adams "embraced what he conceived of as the new 'multiverse' of the twentieth century," O'Neill rejected the power of science, as he had religion, as destructive.

A459 _____. "*McTeague*'s Dream and *The Emperor Jones*: O'Neill's Move from Naturalism to Modernism." *Eugene O'Neill Review* 17.1-2 (1993): 21-29.

Argues that though *Jones* shares much with the naturalistic writings of the time (*McTeague* in particular), it differs in that O'Neill is not so concerned with the explanation of Jones's regression as he is with the process. Viewed subjectively, rather than objectively, Jones's experience constitutes a shift from Naturalism to Modernism.

A460 Murray, David Aaron. "O'Neill's Transvaluation of Pessimism in *The Iceman Cometh*." *Eugene O'Neill Review* 16.2 (1992): 73-79.

Contends that *Iceman* reflects O'Neill's first-hand knowledge of Nietzsche, what many critics of O'Neill lack. And that "far from embodying a despairing creed, [*Iceman*] recapitulates O'Neill's return to realism — a realism that no longer claims any ideological justification beyond the artist's will to create."

A461 Murray, Joel K., and Michael S. Bowman. "The Desire for Structure: A Deconstructive Analysis of *Desire Under the Elms*." *Theater Three* 5 (1988): 75-80.

The authors have a handle on Derrida and Husserl, but not on O'Neill. In their penultimate sentence, they refer, rightly, to "our inability to say what we mean, mean what we say." Their managing of O'Neill bibliography in their "References" section adds further disheartenment. Did Törnqvist only "edit" his *Drama Of Souls?*

A462 Murray, Keat. "O'Neill's *The Hairy Ape* and Rodin's *The Thinker*." *Journal of Evolutionary Psychology* 19.1-2 (1998): 108-15.

Traces, through the play's allusions to *The Thinker*, Yank's "progression toward an existence demanding expression." As the play's end approaches "Yank briefly becomes an art form and accepts uncertainty as the requisite for the struggle with the one unalterable reality: the fact that he is human."

A463 Myers, Andrew B. "Hysteria Night in the Sophomore Dormitory: Eugene O'Neill's *Days Without End*." *Columbia Library Columns* 28.2 (1979): 3-13.

Touches on the reception of *Days* by theater critics, the public and O'Neill's publisher. The failure of the production and the book resulted "obviously because O'Neill had no clear line of thought." Quotes from correspondence between O'Neill and Bennett Cerf and says that "it seems likely" there is unpublished material [more correspondence] in the Random House archives.

A464 Narey, Wayne. "Eugene O'Neill's Attic Spirit: *Desire Under the Elms*." *Eugene O'Neill Review* 16.1 (1992): 49-54.

Fathoms the sources of O'Neill's play and finds them in Euripides' *Hippolytus* and *Medea*.

A465 Nelson, Doris. "O'Neill's Women." *Eugene O'Neill Newsletter* 6.2 (1982): 3-7.

Women in O'Neill's plays are defined by their biological roles and by their relationship to men. O'Neill's women characters search for the perfect husband and marriage, where men seek beyond the domestic realm. In women, men look for lovers or parents, not intellectual companions.

A466 Nethercot, Arthur H. "The Psychoanalyzing of Eugene O'Neill: P.P.S." *Modern Drama* 16 (1973): 35-48.

A second P.S.— he had published an article in two parts in *Modern Drama* in 1960 and 1961 and a postscript to them, after the Gelb biography, in 1965. Charming search for a book mentioned by Malcolm Cowley that O'Neill may have read by 1923 — which contains case histories in psychoanalysis. Surveys briefly the building of the Yale collections of O'Neill's library. Also surveys the scholarly treatment of the influence on O'Neill of modern psychology.

A467 _____. "Madness in the Plays of Eugene O'Neill." *Modern Drama* 18 (1975): 259-79.

In 42 of 45 published plays there is some form of mental instability. Categorizes sources of the disorders in O'Neill's plays.

A468 _____. "O'Neill's *More Stately Mansions*." *Educational Theatre Journal* 27 (1975): 161-69.

O'Neill's themes of madness, loneliness, and mysticism are well developed in this last rough play.

A469 Neu, Jerome. "Life Lies and Pipe Dreams: Self-Deception in Ibsen's *The Wild Duck* and O'Neill's *The Iceman Cometh*." *Philosophical Forum* 19.4 (1988): 241-69.

Argues that despite prevailing preference for honesty and openness, Ibsen's work and O'Neill's are suggesting that we cannot live without illusions. Neu looks to *The Wild Duck* and *Iceman* to prove his point.

A470 *New York Times* 14 Oct. 1973, sec. 7: 1.

Article on house in Marblehead, MA, that once belonged to Eugene O'Neill (1948-51).

A471 *New York Times* 29 Apr. 1974: 48.

Note on the purchase of Monte Cristo Cottage by the Eugene O'Neill Memorial Theater Center.

A472 *New York Times* 5 May 1974, sec. 2: 1.

Comments on the controversy over the disposition of the O'Neill estate.

A473 Nickel, John. "Racial Degeneration and *The Hairy Ape*." *Eugene O'Neill Review* 22.1-2 (1998): 33-40.

Describes an O'Neill who, despite himself, lacked the political correctness of the 21st century. *Ape, Jones,* and *Chillun* reveal an "inability to break free completely from dominant racial prejudices," exhibiting "the deeply-conflicted view of race prevalent" in his times. The documentation is wide and deep.

A474 Nolan, Patrick J. "*The Emperor Jones*: A Jungian View of the Origin of Fear in the Black Race." *Eugene O'Neill Newsletter* 4.1-2 (1980): 6-9.

Sees *Jones* as a play about a black man undermined by the materialistic goals of the whites. The fear arising from the loss of his old God and the psychological destruction of the new brings about Jones's personal and racial downfall.

A475 _____. "*Desire Under the Elms*: Characters by Jung." *Eugene O'Neill Newsletter* 5.2 (1981): 5-10.

Points to the Jungian influence on O'Neill's play and to examples of the influence — the polarities, the god of materialism versus the god of love. Unlike Jung, O'Neill offers no resolution.

A476 Norton, Elliot. "30 Years Later, a Look at Eugene O'Neill's *Long Day's Journey into Night*." *Boston Sunday Globe* 27 Nov. 1983: 85, 89.

Five to six hundred words on O'Neill's years with Carlotta: their spats, his/her warts, and the impact on his writing. Good journalism, for an uninformed audience.

A477 Novick, Julius. An essay on Arvin Brown. *New York Times* 12 Oct. 1975, sec. 2: 1+.

Brown has so invigorated the Long Wharf Theater company (New Haven, CT) that two of their productions have been viewed nationwide on public television and six have been transferred to New York, including *Wilderness.*

A478 Nugent, Georgia S. "Masking Becomes Electra: O'Neill, Freud, and the Feminine." *Comparative Drama* 22 (1988): 37-55.

Argues "that O'Neill, in the process of writing and rewriting the play [*Electra*], consistently cut passages revealing feminine desire or sexual activity and replaced them with passages that displace and conceal that activity, and, moreover, that suppressed sexuality ... is displaced onto the author's own writing"; that the playwright uses Freud, not to reveal, but to mask female sexuality. She concludes that "mastery of authorship becomes a means of confronting feminine desire." For reprints see B224 and B299.

A479 O'Connor, John J. "Lemmon in O'Neill Drama." *New York Times* 13 Apr. 1987, sec. C: 18.

Written in anticipation of the "Broadway on Showtime" cable production of Jonathan Miller's *Journey*. Crediting Lemmon with "one of the most ambitious and admirable performances of his career," O'Connor notes with irritation the overlapping dialogue.

A480 OhAodha, Micheal. "O'Neill and the Anatomy of the Stage Irishman." *Eugene O'Neill Newsletter* 1.2 (1977): 13-14.

Suggests that the early O'Neill Irishmen were stage Irishmen but that later Irish characters, such as the Tyrones, were more real.

A481 Ohkawa, Tetsuo. "Gothicism in Some Plays of Eugene O'Neill." *Chu Shikoko/Studies in American Literature* [Hiroshima] 26 (1990): 76-83.

Unavailable.

A482 Oku, Yasuko. "An Analysis of the Fourth Act of O'Neill's *Long Day's Journey into Night*: Mainly His Application of the Comic Perspective." *Studies in English Literature* 58 (1982): 43-61.

Mary is the "symbol of tragic suffering." O'Neill, in order to make Mary's suffering appear universal, drew four parallel images of suffering and reduced her comicality. The fourth act takes us beyond despair to an affirmation of life.

A483 Oliver, R. W. "From the Exotic to the Real: The Evolution of Black Characterization in Three Plays by Eugene O'Neill." *Forum* 13 (1976): 56-61.

Illustrates the playwright's progress toward realism from Brutus Jones through Jim Harris to Joe Mott.

A484 Oliver, Roger W. "Bergman's Trilogy: Tradition and Innovation." *Performing Arts Journal* 40 (1992): 75-86.

Considering the Bergman-directed, Brooklyn Academy of Music productions of *Miss Julie*, *Journey*, and *A Doll House*, Oliver

notes the Naturalistic directorial approach. Comments on the impact of Bergman's providing only one intermission, dividing *Journey* between the third and fourth act, the effect being to divide the part of the play dominated by Mary from that of the three Tyrone men. Quotes Peter Stormare, who played Edmund, as saying that Bergman's purpose was to emphasize the "'dream that becomes a revelation in the night.'"

A485 Olsson, Tom J. A. "The O'Neill Tradition at Stockholm's Royal Dramatic Theatre." *Recorder* 3.1 (1989): 86-99.

A lean, mean history of the O'Neill-Sweden love affair.

A486 O'Neill, Michael. "Confession as Artifice in the Plays of Eugene O'Neill." *Renascence* 39.3 (1987): 430-41.

Maintains that O'Neill "made it his business as a playwright to reveal the secrets of the confessional to those assembled in his one, true church, which became, in time, the theater." O'Neill found the stage perfectly suited to confessing his life through artifice. Looking at *Days*, *Desire*, *Journey*, and *Misbegotten*, Michael O'Neill finds that the power of the last play comes from forgiveness extended not by a god outside or inside of us, but by one another.

A487 Onunwa, Father Paschal. "Eugene O'Neill: A Voice for Racial Justice." *Recorder* 3.1 (1989): 15-24.

O'Neill is presented as an early "voice for racial justice and brotherhood." This "voice" expresses a concern that grows out of his own background — parents, home, heredity. The treatment of the Irish on both sides of the Atlantic "led O'Neill to identify throughout his life with the outcasts and victims of injustice." Hence his sympathy with black people, as seen in *Thirst*, *The Dreamy Kid*, *Jones*, *Chillun*, *Iceman*.

A488 Ouyang, Ji. "Daoist Ideas in O'Neill's Play about Marco Polo." *China Reconstructs* (North American Edition) 36 (June 1987): 26-28.

Tenets of Daoism — the mystical unity of man and spirit in a universe of flux; the passive resignation to destiny; the suspicion that the self and the objective are illusions — these are found in *Marco*.

A489 Pace, Eric. "Preserving the Homes Where O'Neill Lived and Worked." *New York Times* 8 Feb. 1981, sec. D: 5, 18.

Discusses the restorations of the family cottage in Connecticut and the taking over of Tao House by the National Park Service, as well as the plans for a new Provincetown Playhouse: speculation as to why the renewed interest in O'Neill.

A490 Packard, Frederick C., Jr. "Eugene O'Neill Dramatic Innovator." *Eugene O'Neill Newsletter* 3.2 (1979): 9-12.

Reprint of an article first published in *Chrysalis,* now a defunct publication. Discusses Eugene O'Neill's major contributions to theater technique by showing the innovations of his most acclaimed plays — masks in *Brown,* asides in *Interlude,* and range and scope in *Electra.*

A491 Pavlov, Grigor. "Structure and Meaning in Eugene O'Neill's *Mourning Becomes Electra.*" *Annuaire de l'Université de Sofia: Faculté des Lettres* 68.1 (1974): 213-85.

Begins with a survey of criticism since 1931, reflecting two approaches: O'Neill's concern with the relationship between man and God and O'Neill's social-economic criticism. Concludes that O'Neill's trilogy is too complex for "pat and ready formulae." Then, devoting a section to each, Pavlov analyzes the three parts of O'Neill's *Electra.* Finds in the three plays a pattern of repetition of situation, dialogue, and speech that in *Homecoming* grows naturally out of character and situation and focuses on socio-economic factors, but that in *The Haunted* "leads him to a mechanistic treatment of his characters" that "runs counter to the complex dialectic conception of human nature he achieves dramatically in *Homecoming.*" In effect, a failure in the attempt to fuse the social, moral, and psychological.

A492 Pecile, Jordan. "Where the Long Day's Journey Began: The O'Neill House Restoration." *Hartford Current Magazine* 28 Dec. 1980: 4-7.

Brief account for the general reader of the connection between the O'Neills and New London. The focus is on Monte Cristo. Illustrated.

A493 Peel, Sylvia Terrill. "Mildred Shivers." *Eugene O'Neill Review* 16.1 (1992): 142.

In this note on *Ape* Peel says Mildred "falters" and "shivers," words which, within the context of the play, hint at the failure of the strength of character her ancestors presumably bequeathed her.

A494 Perrin, Robert. "O'Neill's Use of Language in *Where the Cross is Made.*" *Eugene O'Neill Newsletter* 6.3 (1982): 12-13.

Analyzes the syntax of Nat's language and discovers that his syntax is normal when he is talking to those he doesn't fear. However, when threatened by his father and when he begins to lose control, his syntax is less mature and less consistent.

A495 _____. "Bringing O'Neill's Works to Life in the Drama Classroom." *Eugene O'Neill Newsletter* 8.3 (1984): 13-14.

A plea for producing O'Neill's plays. They are filled with strong characters, who have strong emotions; filled with extended monologues and scenes between pairs of characters; filled with smaller self-contained units within the longer works; filled with experiments with language that provide range for actors.

A496 Perry, Thomas Amherst. "The Contribution of Petru Comarnescu to Romanian-American Relationships." *Southeastern Europe/l'Europe du Sud-Est* 7.1 (1980): 91-98.

Describes the efforts of Comarnescu, the Romanian scholar-critic to acquaint his country with American literature and drama. Touches on Comarnescu's special interest in O'Neill and on translations of O'Neill's plays into Romanian.

A497 Peters, John G. "Ghosts and Guilt: *Mourning Becomes Electra* and its Mythic Tradition." *Midwest Quarterly* 32 (1991): 474-83.

Instead of considering the similarities between O'Neill's play and Greek myth, Peters looks at the differences: in setting, characterization, plot, relationships.

A498 Peterson, William M. "A Portrait of O'Neill's Electra." *Eugene O'Neill Review* 17.1-2 (1993): 66-75.

O'Neill may have had in mind a portrait of Carlotta, by Abram Poole, in her role of Mlle. Clairon (Voltaire), when he conceived of Christine/Lavinia Mannon in *Electra.*

A499 _____. "O'Neill's Divided Agonists." *Eugene O'Neill Review* 20. 1-2 (1996): 110-18.

Argues that while in his early plays O'Neill attempted to create psychological complexity by using polarized characters, with the advent of *Desire,* the playwright "utilized mythological plots and the devices of Greek tragedies, combined with psychological models derived from or related to them, to create resonance, the echoing reverberations of shifting reality."

A500 Petite, Joseph. "The Paradox of Power in *More Stately Mansions.*" *Eugene O'Neill Newsletter* 5.3 (1981): 2-5.

Studies the play by itself rather than trying to fit it into some preconceived notions about O'Neill's work.

A501 Pettegrove, J. P. "'Snuff'd Out by an Article': *Anna Christie* in Berlin." *Maske und Kothurn: Internationale Beiträge zur Theaterwissenschaft* 27 (1981): 335-45.

Examines the impact on O'Neill scholars (especially Frenz, the Gelbs, and Sheaffer) of Rudolf Kommer's 1924 *New York Times* article on the reception of *Anna* in Germany. Shows that Kommer's slick writing concealed his ignorance of matters theatrical and his incompetence as a judge of English-German translations. Finds that the first German *Anna* was based on *The Ole Davil.*

A502 Phillips, David. "Eugene O'Neill's Fateful Maine Interlude." *Down East* 28 (Aug. 1981): 84+.

A detailed look at the summer (June-Oct. 1926) O'Neill spent at Belgrade Lakes, in Maine. Reveals the imminent family breakup, discusses O'Neill's work on *Interlude*, and calls the summer a turning point in O'Neill's personal and professional lives.

A503 Pond, Gloria Dribble. "A Family Disease." *Eugene O'Neill Newsletter* 9.1 (1985): 12-14.

Discusses alcoholism as a family disease in *Journey.* The Tyrones reinforce one another's addictions and "use morphine, whoring, and greed as opiates analogous to alcohol."

A504 Poole, Gabriele. "'Blarsted Nigers!': *The Emperor Jones* and Modernism's Encounter with Africa." *Eugene O'Neill Review* 18.1-2 (1994): 21-37.

Maintains that neither "black discourse" nor "white discourse" is "clearly privileged" in *Jones* and that the complexity of the play derives, in part, from the shifting between the two. In the end, the play is unable to "break out of a reductive binary opposition between a petty and violent white world, and a mysterious, perhaps fascinating, but equally destructive black one."

A505 Porter, Laurin R. "*The Iceman*

Cometh as Crossroad in O'Neill's Long Journey." *Modern Drama* 31 (1988): 52-62.

Addresses the role of familial responsibility in this article in which she argues that *Iceman* is structured around the family unit, much as is *Journey.* There are two families depicted in *Iceman*: the larger one of the boarders under Harry's paternal eye and the smaller unit consisting of Larry and Parritt, who, tied to one another by their ties to Rosa, find a kindred soul in Hickey, who recognizes something familiar about Parritt.

A506 _____. "Bakhtin's Chronotope: Time and Space in *A Touch of the Poet* and *More Stately Mansions.*" *Modern Drama* 34 (1991): 369-82.

Looks at the O'Neill plays named in her title to find, as chronotopes, "the intrinsic connectedness of temporal and spatial relationships in literature." Finds in *Touch* the bar, the dining room and the mirror "focus the issues and function as signifiers" as do Simon's office, the Harford mansion and Deborah's garden in *Mansions.*

A507 _____. "Modern and Postmodern Wastelands: *Long Day's Journey into Night* and Shepard's *Buried Child.*" *Eugene O'Neill Review* 17.1-2 (1993): 106-19.

Fathoming numerous comparisons in the unlikely pairing of Shepard's *Buried Child* and O'Neill's masterpiece, Porter concludes that ultimately they differ in "their philosophical underpinnings." "The midnight of *Long Day's Journey*'s final scene, though devastating, at least casts a shadow; the dawn of *Buried Child*'s conclusion, with its ironic references to the sun, is total eclipse."

A508 _____. "Self and Other: The Problem of Possession in O'Neill's Historical Cycle." *Eugene O'Neill Review* 18.1-2 (1994): 109-15.

Though many writers have addressed American materialism in their work, O'Neill brings to the subject "an understanding of the ways in which the desire to possess leads to self-dispossession." Looks at *Touch*, *Mansions*, and *The Calms of Capricorn* to illustrate the point and concludes that for O'Neill the desire for possession is a "spiritual malady."

A509 _____. "The Banished Prince Revisited: A Feminist Rereading of *More Stately Mansions.*" *Eugene O'Neill Review* 19.1-2 (1995): 7-27.

The task of a feminist critic is to "unmask the encoding of male dominance, female inferiority, biases and limitations in gender roles, prejudicial attitudes toward sexuality, and other cultural distortions and reveal them for what they are: social constructs rather than biological mandates or metaphysical truths." Approaching *Mansions* from this vantage point, Porter finds several "cultural distortions," which she addresses. Finally, she takes issue with feminists who see the play as about two strong women; it is about the angst in Simon's soul.

A510 Powers, Dennis. "The Russians Said Hello to Dolly Levi." *New York Times* 5 Sept. 1976, sec. 2: 5, 24.

About the reception given to the American Conservatory Theater in Russia. Its two productions — including *Desire* (*Lyubov pod Viasami*) — were excerpted in film for Soviet TV. Played the Lensoviet Palace of Culture in Leningrad. Mentions that two O'Neill plays are in rehearsal in Russian theaters.

A511 Prasad, Hari Mohan. "The Symbolism of the Sea in Eugene O'Neill's Plays." *Journal of the Karnatak University: Humanities* 22 (1978): 108-13.

The sea is an ambivalent symbol in O'Neill's canon. In the sea plays, it is a personification of the life force and a "device for emotional pressure." The rhythm and beauty of the sea is mentioned in *Electra*. In *Horizon* it is a motivating force. The sea is a presence in *Journey* and *Wilderness*, and in *Anna* it is life.

A512 _____. "Symbols of Fog and Home in the Plays of Eugene O'Neill." *Rajasthan Journal of English Studies* 10 (1979): 1-9.

Explores several possibilities of the symbolism of fog in O'Neill's plays: as indicator of the characters' inner natures (*Fog, Journey*), of death (*Cardiff, Interlude, Electra, Fountain*), or as cleansing agent (*Anna*). The fog symbol achieves "greater complexity and a more universal sense" in *Journey*. Also touches on the symbolism of home in *Cardiff, Chillun, Interlude, Desire, Electra, Beyond, Touch, Misbegotten,* and *Journey*. In O'Neill's work "the whole history of man's disinheritance, which is the central message" of the plays is "wrought in this symbol."

A513 _____. "The Tragic Mode: A Study in Eugene O'Neill's *Beyond the Horizon, The Emperor Jones,* and *The Hairy Ape.*"

Osmania Journal of English Studies [Hyderabad] 15 (1979): 21-30.

Tragedy for O'Neill lives in the failure of his central character to preserve his illusions in the face of the onslaught of reality. "The tragic character awakens to the truth that he is human and learns through suffering that to be human is to be fully tragic." *Horizon, Jones,* and *Ape* are examined.

A514 _____. "Nuances of Soliloquy in the Theatre of Eugene O'Neill." *Commonwealth Quarterly* 5.7 (1980): 48-59.

Discusses O'Neill's use of soliloquies, monologues and thought asides in both his early and late plays. Maintains that these devices reveal character, and give significance to the plot. Emphasis is given to *Interlude, Iceman, Journey*.

A515 Proehl, Geoffrey S. "Foucault on Discourse: O'Neill as Discourse: LDJN (4: 125-154), Tyrone and Edmund." *Journal of Dramatic Theory and Criticism* 4.1 (1990): 51-62.

Foucault meets O'Neill: Proehl looks at the discourse of quotation, accusation, and autobiography in Edmund's and Tyrone's speeches in Act IV of *Journey* to find that autobiography is a process (with quotation and accusation) by which the subject creates a self.

A516 Qazi, Munir A. "O'Neill: Aristotelian Tragedy in America." *Journal of Research (Humanities)* [Lahore U of the Punjab] 21 (1986): 17-36.

An introductory-level essay on Greek tragedy and its elements in O'Neill's plays from *Cardiff* and *Voyage* on. Sees O'Neill's tragedy as developing in three stages: from the political-economic, through the psychological, to the "conflict with God." In the bibliography the most recent item of secondary criticism is Gassner's 1964 *O'Neill: A Collection of Critical Essays*.

A517 Qian, Jiaoru. "A Long Day's Journey That Tries But Fails to Get Beyond the Horizon." *Waiguoyu* [Beijing] 2.60 (1989): 34-39.

Thesis: "in this trouble-ridden and sinful world which we inhabit" O'Neill sought the meaning of life, a quest which "tries but fails to get beyond the horizon." The author cites several plays — *Cardiff, Desire, Ape, Horizon, Iceman, Journey* — and refers to pervasive imagery — cage, night/darkness — to prove the point.

A518 Quinby, George H. "O'Neill in Iran." *Eugene O'Neill Newsletter* 1.2 (1977): 10-12.

Comments on the performances of O'Neill plays in Farsi and English in Iran when Quinby was there in 1956-57 and 1962-63. Explains what Iranians could and couldn't understand of O'Neill. Lists the O'Neill plays translated into Farsi: the *Sea Plays, Wilderness, Journey, Straw.*

A519 _____. "A Humanitarian Playwright." *Eugene O'Neill Newsletter* 2.2 (1978): 8-11.

The speech Quinby delivered in Feb. 1923 at Bowdoin College. In *Jones, Anna, Ape* we are taken to "such heights of tragic emotion that we are made to sympathize with the lowest strata of society." Applauds O'Neill's choice of characters and emotionalism.

A520 Quintero, José. "Directing a Radio Production of Eugene O'Neill's *The Hairy Ape*." Ed. Travis Bogard. *Theatre Journal* 43.3 (1991): 341-59.

Provides scene-by-scene commentary on the play and how Quintero envisions the scenes should be delivered. The text was "distilled from Quintero's general observations on the play and his instructions to the actors as a group and as individuals during rehearsals." See Bogard and Bauersfeld.

A521 Radel, Nicholas F. "Provincetown Plays: Women Writers and O'Neill's American Intertext." *Essays in Theatre* 9.1 (1990): 31-43.

Argues for the preferability of looking to the cultural and literary ambience which surrounded the writer, rather than to a particular influence. Refers to the works of Provincetown playwrights Susan Glaspell, Neith Boyce, and Louise Bryant to show that their early works dealt with some of the same issues as O'Neill's. These early Provincetown efforts are part of O'Neill's "intertexts."

A522 Ràfols, Wifredo de. "Non-worded Words and Unmentionable Pharmaka in O'Neill and Valle-Inclan." *Comparative Drama* 31 (1997): 193-212.

Theorizing from Derrida's *La Pharmacie de Platon*, Rafols examines the role of gesture and nonverbal communication in O'Neill's *Journey* and Valle-Inclan's *Las galas del difunto.*

A523 Raleigh, John Henry. "Strindberg in Andrew Jackson's America: O'Neill's *More Stately Mansions*." *CLIO: A Journal of Literature, History, and the Philosophy of History* 13.1 (1983): 1-15.

Studies O'Neill's evolution as an historical dramatist from *Electra* to *Touch* to *Mansions*. Sees the relationships of the characters in *Mansions* as reflecting what was happening to America in the 1830s — the period of economic speculation. It was a time of monetary instability, predatoriness, a scrambling for control, and a shifting of power. The relationships in the play mirror the larger world.

A524 _____. "Communal, Familial, and Personal Memories in O'Neill's *Long Day's Journey Into Night*." *Modern Drama* 31 (1988): 63-72.

Looks at O'Neill's play from the perspective of human memory, which Raleigh considers tri-fold: communal, familial and individual. Formed against a backdrop of the Irish Catholic identity, the play focuses on family history and individual memory. Recalling the same historical/communal truths differently, the Tyrone family bond as a family yet emerge as individuals.

A525 Ramamoorthy, Parasuram. "Perform/Interpret: The Director in the Post-Modernist Theatre." *Indian Journal of American Studies* [Hyderabad] 26.2 (1996): 22-26.

The author has presented a performance of *Breakfast* as part of a seminar he is is directing. Now we hear his comments on what he was trying to do, or would like to have tried to do, with the play. For instance, what about adding music? How might that be used to give "shape" to the play. Some observations about *Servitude* also.

A526 Ranald, Margaret Loftus. "When They Weren't Playing O'Neill: The Antithetical Career of Carlotta Monterey." *Theatre History Studies* 11 (1991): 81-106.

What was life like for Carlotta before she met O'Neill? Ranald looks at the actress's stage career and concludes that it wasn't brilliant.

A527 Rao, C. R. Visweswara. "*Mourning Becomes Electra*: The Play's Design." *Indian Journal of American Studies* [Hyderabad] 26.2 (1996): 59-63.

Sees *Electra* as an "elaborately constructed theatrical piece, showing that the material of drama consists in the interrelatedness of ethical systems [ancient and modern] amplifying and accentuating the rhythm of the modern."

A528 Raphael, Jay E. "On Directing *Long Day's Journey into Night*." *Eugene O'Neill Newsletter* 5.1 (1981): 7-10.

Journey is a fusion of techniques O'Neill used in earlier plays; Raphael plans to use mystical lighting and sparse sets when he directs the play at University of Virginia.

A529 Ratliff, Gerald L. "*Fog:* An O'Neill Theological Miscellany." *Eugene O'Neill Newsletter* 6.3 (1982): 5-20.

Considers *Fog* in terms of the biblical parable: "when the inevitability of suffering is grasped, and misery and despair are understood as part of the divine pattern of transfiguration, the darker side of life must appear to us permeated by a renewed belief in the immortality of the human soul."

A530 Ready, Robert. "The Play of the Misbegotten." *Modern Drama* 31 (1988): 81-90.

Examines references, explicit and implicit, to acting in *Misbegotten.* "The three main characters act out the parts they create in order to know themselves and each other." In reflecting on their need to theatricalize, the characters impart poignancy to the moment.

A531 Redlon, Rebecca. "'Significant Beauty': Eugene O'Neill's Portrayal of Women." *Essays and Studies by Students of Simmons College* 1.2 (1993): 9-12.

Looks at four O'Neill women characters — Mrs. Keeney, Abbie Putnam, Anna Christopherson, and Mary Tyrone — to conclude that O'Neill was sensitive to the plight of women and that they are often the most sympathetic characters in his plays.

A532 Reed, Terry. "O'Neill's Nausikka Episode." *Eugene O'Neill Newsletter* 11.3 (1987): 8-9.

Finds that O'Neill "source stalkers" have overlooked the influence of the *Odyssey* on *Anna.*

A533 Regenbaum, Shelly. "Wrestling with God: Old Testament Themes in *Beyond the Horizon.*" *Eugene O'Neill Newsletter* 8.3 (1984): 2-8.

An analysis of O'Neill's play in terms of the Jacob and Esau story. The Mayos are like the biblical brothers, but whereas the existence of God is never in doubt in the biblical story, it is in question in this O'Neill play.

A534 Reilly, Kevin P. "Pitching the Mansion and Pumping the Morphine: Eugene O'Neill's *Long Day's Journey into Night.*" *Gypsy Scholar* 5 (1978): 22-33.

A psychoanalysis of Mary Tyrone aimed at revealing the reason behind her addiction. Mary's drug-taking seems to be "an attempt to escape the excrementalized bodily self of the present into the vision of the spiritualized self of the past." She is one of O'Neill's divided characters. She feels sullied by marriage, and her suicide attempt could be seen as an attempt to cleanse the body. Embarrassed by self, she sees James's coaxing her into marriage as a betrayal. Mary Tyrone's inability to come to terms with excremental self is the cause of her addiction.

A535 Reinhardt, Nancy. "Formal Patterns in *The Iceman Cometh.*" *Modern Drama* 16 (1973): 119-28.

Aural and visual patterns and "purposeful patterning" facilitate an understanding of O'Neill's play. Visual patterns include the symbolic positioning of tables and chairs and characters, and aural patterns include the repeated choral refrains, barroom songs, and antiphonal dialogue. These patterns reflect the play's paradoxical theme.

A536 Remshardt, Ralf Erik. "Masks and Permutations: The Construction of Character in O'Neill's Earlier Plays." *Essays in Theatre* 8.2 (1990): 127-36.

Remshardt limits himself to O'Neill plays pre-*Interlude* for a look at patterns in the creation of character. In O'Neill plays we see characters suffering from guilt and loneliness reverting to innocence, paired characters, use of masks, etc.

A537 Rice, Joseph. "The Blinding of Mannon House: O'Neill, Electra, and Oedipus." *Text and Presentation: The Journal of the Comparative Drama Conference* [Gainesville, FL] 13 (1992): 45- 51.

Argues that "though *Mourning Becomes Electra* owes a great debt to Aeschylus' *Oresteia,* the fact remains that O'Neill has also incorporated into his work a Sophoclean thread — a thread that finds its beginnings in the concept of house as mask."

A538 Rich, Frank. "A Short Day's Journey to Eugene O'Neill's Childhood Home." *New York Times* 6 Aug. 1981, sec. C: 15.

Rich spent a July 1981 weekend visiting Monte Cristo Cottage, in New London, and the O'Neill Theatre Center, in Waterford. Thinks that there American theaters past and present intersect because the home is the setting of *Wilderness* and *Journey,* and the O'Neill Theatre Center gives opportunities to rising playwrights to see and hear their work done.

A539 Richardson, Brian. "*The Great God Brown* and the Theory of Character." *Eugene O'Neill Review* 14.1-2 (1990): 17-24.

Counters the prevailing modernist trend to ignore or marginalize O'Neill's theatrical innovation by looking at *Brown* and creation of character. Concludes that this critically unacclaimed play derives from the "cunning, audacious and playful" O'Neill at work.

A540 Richardson, Jack. "O'Neill Reconsidered." *Commentary* Jan. 1974: 52-54.

Uses the occasion of the publication of Sheaffer's second volume to elaborate on O'Neill's career. Finds O'Neill's work prior to *Journey, Iceman,* and *Misbegotten* lacking because of O'Neill's desire to be a poet, his hope to restore antique forms of tragedy for modern use, and his desire to make "dramatically compelling" the prevailing philosophical and scientific notions. Success in later plays was due to distance between O'Neill and his subject.

A541 Roberts, Nancy L. "The Cottage with a Glimpse of Eugene O'Neill." *Boston Sunday Globe* 5 May 1985: 25-26.

Eighteen hundred words on Monte Cristo Cottage ("Hours: Monday through Thursday, 1-4 p.m. and by appointment") and the O'Neill connection. For the general reader.

A542 Robinson, James A. "O'Neill's Grotesque Dancers." *Modern Drama* 19 (1976): 34-49.

Covers *Jones, Ape, Desire, Brown, Lazarus.* All dances and choreographed movements within the plays enforce or define the themes of the plays.

A543 _____. "Christianity and *All God's Chillun Got Wings.*" *Eugene O'Neill Newsletter* 2.1 (1978): 1-3.

Contrary to received opinion, Robinson asserts that the play's ending is not inconsistent with what has come before. Racism, madness, and Christianity are closely connected in Act I. Jim is ultimately duped by his own racism and religion into becoming a slave to a white woman.

A544 _____. "O'Neill and Albee." *Philological Papers* [West Virginia U] 25 (1979): 38-45.

Finds many parallels between the theaters of O'Neill and Albee — concern with the American family, the dead child motif, urban alienation, Strindbergian sexual conflicts, symbolic or allegorical characters, thin treatment of the loss of the Christian God. Some may result from having similar family and personal histories; some from the similarity of the 1920s to the 1960s; but some, "the confessional monologue and a similar treatment of the illusion-reality theme, demonstrate an undeniable O'Neill influence on Albee's work."

A545 _____. "O'Neill's Symbolic Sounds." *Modern Language Studies* 9 (1979): 36-45.

Analyzes sound effects in *Jones, Ape, Lazarus,* and *Dynamo* in terms of function and symbolic meaning.

A546 _____. "Taoism and O'Neill's *Marco Millions.*" *Comparative Drama* 14 (1980): 251-62.

Reviews the extent to which Taoist thought is exemplified in *Marco's* Kukachin, Kublai, and, especially, in the advisor, Chu Yin.

A547 _____. "Convergences and Divergences: Father and Son in *A Touch of the Poet* and *The Iceman Cometh.*" *American Literature* 59.3 (1987): 323-40.

Argues that both *Touch* and *Iceman* "contain indirect portraits of James O'Neill as a performer, thereby serving as preparations for the more direct, domestic portrait that was soon to emerge in *Long Day's Journey into Night.*"

A548 _____. "Ghost Stories: *Iceman's* Absent Women and Mary Tyrone." *Eugene O'Neill Newsletter* 12.3 (1988): 14-19.

Expanding on Michael Manheim's argument that the absent women in *Iceman* represent O'Neill's varying attitudes toward his mother, Robinson further suggests that these absent women anticipate the character of Mary Tyrone.

A549 _____. "O'Neill's Indian *Elms.*" *Eugene O'Neill Review* 13.1 (1989): 40-46.

Having left *Desire* out of his book *Eugene O'Neill and Oriental Thought,* Robinson rethinks his omission, finding in the play "general Indian doctrines of detachment and liberation, and the Vedantic Hindu belief in the unity of all existence."

A550 _____. "The Masculine Primitive and *The Hairy Ape.*" *Eugene O'Neill Review* 19.1-2 (1995): 95-109.

Argues that O'Neill's rebellion against authority — specifically paternal and middle class — which was hinted at in the sea plays is developed in *Ape.*

A551 Robinson, Leroy. "John Harold Lawson on Eugene O'Neill, Man and Playwright." *Eugene O'Neill Newsletter* 3.2 (1979): 12-14.

Summarizes previously unpublished comments by Lawson on O'Neill and on *Dynamo,* a play which bears a close resemblance to Lawson's earlier play *Nirvana.*

A552 _____. "John Howard Lawson's 'Souls': A Harbinger of *Strange Interlude*." *Eugene O'Neill Newsletter* 4.3 (1980): 12-13.

Finds in Lawson's "Souls" (unpublished and unproduced) a curious anticipation of O'Neill's *Interlude*. In the development of Act II and the use of asides O'Neill may have been influenced by Lawson.

A553 Roediger, David. "White Looks: Hairy Apes, True Stories and Limbaugh's Laughs." *Minnesota Review: A Journal of Committed Writing* [Greenville, NC] 47 (1997): 37-47.

In an essay that pits Mark Twain's "genius" against Rush Limbaugh's "banality" in terms of their depiction of race, Roediger makes room for a discussion of O'Neill's *Ape*. The fact that Mildred Douglas "looks" Yank into nonwhiteness is plausible, Roediger says, in light of the highly publicized Bronx Zoo exhibition of the African Ota Benga who was housed with the monkeys and apes, in the early 1900s.

A554 Rogalus, Paul W. "Shepard's *Tooth of Crime*, O'Neill's *Emperor Jones*, and the Contemporary American Tragic Hero." *Notes on Contemporary Literature* 22.2 (1992): 2-3.

Asserts that in *Tooth of Crime* Shepard follows in the footsteps of O'Neill in imparting to his protagonist Hoss the stature of Brutus Jones. In these characters, we have modern tragic heroes.

A555 Rollyson, Carl, Jr. "O'Neill's Mysticism: From His Historical Trilogy to *Long Day's Journey into Night*." *Studies in Mystic Literature* [Taiwan] 1 (1981): 218-36.

Examines *Fountain, Marco, Lazarus,* in discussing O'Neill's mysticism. These plays are not successful because they rely too heavily on spectacle and because they do not invite us to identify with the characters. Their language is also abstract. But in *Journey* O'Neill relies on language rather than staging and effects to communicate the mystical experience and so it is "his best attempt to render the mystical experience in dramatic form."

A556 Rose, Lloyd. "Turning Points of a Century / Theater." *Washington Post* 26 Dec. 1999, sec. G: 13.

In a century's-end assessment of American drama, O'Neill is seen as the one who inspired playwrights to grow up.

A557 Rothenberg, Albert, and Eugene D. Shapiro. "The Defense of Psychoanalysis in Literature: *Long Day's Journey into Night* and *A View from the Bridge*." *Comparative Drama* 7 (1973): 51-67.

Contrasts the simple tension of Miller's play with the complex defensive sequence of O'Neill's.

A558 Rothstein, Mervyn. "O'Neill Lauded in His Own Words." *New York Times* 18 Oct. 1988, sec. C: 20.

Describes a centennial birthday party for O'Neill in New York City. Among the celebrants are B. Gelb, T. Mann, J. Papp, C. Dewhurst, J. Robards, others. The celebration includes performances of scenes, favorite monologues, and songs from O'Neill plays.

A559 _____, and Richard Severo. "José Quintero, Director Who Exalted O'Neill, Dies at 74." *New York Times* 27 Feb. 1999: 1+.

Quintero's revival of *Iceman* in 1956 "shattered" the view that O'Neill had "become outdated." Surveys Quintero's life, but especially the connection between Quintero and O'Neill.

A560 Rutenberg, Michael E. "Bob Smith Ain't So Dumb." *Eugene O'Neill Newsletter* 3.3 (1980): 11-15.

Explains the problems of making Yank a sympathetic character.

A561 _____. "Eugene O'Neill, Fidei Defensor: An Eschatological Study of *The Great God Brown*." *Eugene O'Neill Newsletter* 8.2 (1984): 12-16.

Studies *Brown* as one of O'Neill's Catholic plays. The play's "subject matter is God, Christ, and the subsequent evolution of man's Catholic religiosity."

A562 Ryan, Pat M. "Stockholm Revives O'Neill." *Scandinavian Review* 65.1 (1977): 8-23.

About the circumstances leading to Karl Ragnar Gierow's production of *Journey* in Stockholm, 1956, and, subsequently, to other dramatic productions of *Touch, Hughie, Mansions*. The information rests, in part, on an interview between the author and Gierow and on letters from Carlotta O'Neill in the archives of the Royal Dramatic Theater.

A563 _____. "*Long Day's Journey* was the 'Wrong' Play." *Theatre Survey* 29.1 (1988): 103-12.

Translates Karl Ragnar Gierow's version of how he was able to obtain from O'Neill's literary estate, and from Carlotta specifically, *Journey*, *Hughie*, and *Touch* for the Swedish Royal Dramatic Theatre. As Gierow observed, "I had cast for a pike, there was a bite, and I had caught a salmon."

A564 Ryan, Paul. "Eugene O'Neill: A Hundred Years On." *Drama* 170 (1988): 27-30.

One of the many tributes to O'Neill in this the centennial year of his birth, Ryan's piece asserts the importance of O'Neill to modern drama and includes comments from Jason Robards, Marcella Markham, and Amanda Byer, all of whom have acted in O'Neill plays. Markham (Cora in the original *Iceman*), recalls meeting the playwright, Robards debunks the stereotype of O'Neill as a morose playwright, and Byer speaks to the O'Neill play she currently stars in, *Touch*.

A565 Sabinson, Harvey. "A Coronet for O'Neill." *Theatregoers' Guide* (advertising supplement to the *New York Times*) 7 Sept. 1980: 12+.

Recounts a meeting he had with Carlotta in August 1959 in order to get her permission for his client Lester Osterman to rename his theater, the Coronet, after O'Neill. Taken from Sabinson's book *Darling You Were Wonderful*.

A566 Saiz, Peter R. "The Colonial Story in *The Emperor Jones*." *Eugene O'Neill Review* 17.1-2 (1993): 31-38.

Looks at the sociological implications of a play which depicts a master-slave relationship under colonialism. "In Brutus Jones, O'Neill has personified the dual nature of the colonial subject. He is both the colonizer and the colonized."

A567 Sánchez, Marta. "*Desire Under The Elms* as a Celebration of Life: A View in the Light of Nietzsche's *Birth of Tragedy*." *Filología y Lingüística* 15.2 (1989): 31-35.

Applying Nietzsche's theory of eternal recurrence to *Desire*, Sánchez sees in Cabot a Dionysian figure who "defies time and becomes, like time, eternal." The "son of the farm" becomes symbolic of the triumph of life over death, and even the death of Abbie's son

"carries the deepest ritualistic meaning.... It represents the return of Dionysus, the triumph of life. The child's return to the earth, the depths of life, provokes Abbie's and Eben's capability to emerge from conflict and the depths of death."

A568 Saqqaf, Abdulaziz Yassin. "The Nature of Conflict in *The Hairy Ape*." *Journal of English* [Sana'a U] [no vol.] (1975): 77-84.

Unavailable.

A569 Sarlós, Robert K. "Response to the Preview Issue: A Letter." *Eugene O'Neill Newsletter* 1.1 (1977): 14-15.

Unhappy about the panel evaluation of O'Neill's plays (see Wilkins, et al.) Sarlós asserts that the plays should be seen and evaluated in terms of their potential for production. Finds merit in *Interlude, Electra, Cardiff, Caribbees, Rope*.

A570 _____. "Nina Moise Directs Eugene O'Neill's *The Rope*." *Eugene O'Neill Newsletter* 6.3 (1982): 9-12.

A reconstruction of the Apr. 26, 1918, production of *The Rope*. Though there are no photographs of it, Sarlós turns to Heywood Broun's review of that production and 1963 conversations with Nina Moise and Charles Ellis.

A571 _____. "'Writing a Dance': *Lazarus Laughed* as O'Neill's Dithyramb of the Western Hemisphere." *Theatre Survey* 29.1 (1988): 37-49.

Reexamines O'Neill's play "'for an imaginative theatre' based on the conviction ... that a dramatic text is not a work of art, 'but only written directions for manufacturing one.'" Providing a summary of the distinctive theatrical means O'Neill used in the play, Sarlós then argues that "certain autobiographical, philosophical-theological, and aesthetic factors implicit in the script demand corresponding production values also rooted in O'Neill's artistic collaboration with [George Cram] Cook."

A572 Saur, Pamela S. "Classifying Rural Dramas: O'Neill's *Desire Under the Elms* and Schönherr's *Erde*." *Modern Austrian Literature* 26.3-4 (1993): 101-11.

Uses these plays to show "how literary works that are similar in content may be judged differently depending upon differing cultural, literary and historical contexts."

A573 Sayre, Nora. "*Iceman* Film does Justice to the Play." *New York Times* 30 Oct. 1973: 36.

Lee Marvin "has the salesman's slick authority, the talent for hustling ... for invading privacy, but lacks the necessary touch of the maniac spellcaster." The film close-ups destroy the ensemble impact of the group.

A574 Scanlan, Tom. "The Domestication of Rip Van Winkle: Joe Jefferson's play as Prologue to Modern American Drama." *Virginia Quarterly Review* 50 (1974): 51-62.

Argues that Jefferson's adaptation of Irving's story so softens and sentimentalizes as to give greater emphasis on the importance of the family structure thus prefiguring the family of O'Neill, Arthur Miller, and Tennessee Williams.

A575 Scheibler, Rolf. "*Hughie*: A One-Act Play for the Imaginary Theatre." *English Studies* [Amsterdam] 54 (1973): 231-48.

Comments on the difficulties of staging the play which can reach its full development only in the imaginary stage of the reader's mind.

A576 Scheick, William J. "The Ending of O'Neill's *Beyond the Horizon*." *Modern Drama* 20 (1977): 293-98.

Robert Mayo, articulate about his dreams at the beginning of the play, dies inarticulate. The loss of his verbal gift is a result of disillusionment rather than illumination.

A577 _____. "Two Letters by Eugene O'Neill." *Resources for American Literary Study* 8 (1978): 73-80.

See Primary Works section, G54.

A578 Schmitt, Patrick. "*Marco Millions* and O'Neill's Vision of America." *Canadian Review of American Studies* 20.1 (1989): 31-39.

Finds in *Marco* a critique of American life and significance in the fact that in this "powerful and comic representation of O'Neill's scathing vision" the playwright "first established the connections between history and the unredeemably tragic condition of contemporary American society."

A579 Schvey, Henry I. "'The Past is the Present, Isn't it?' Eugene O'Neill's *Long Day's Journey into Night*." *Dutch Quarterly Review of Anglo-American Letters* 10 (1980): 80-99.

A general discussion of the play with reference to O'Neill biography. Sees the Tyrones as simultaneously jailers and prisoners.

A580 _____. "The Master and the Double: Eugene O'Neill and Sam Shepard."

Journal of Dramatic Theory and Criticism 5.2 (1991): 49-60.

Finds affinities between two ostensibly different playwrights in their classical sensibilities, their obsession with family and in particular the father figure, and their treatment of father-son relations. *Desire* and *Buried Child* are Schvey's foci.

A581 Scrimgeour, James R. "From Loving to the Misbegotten: Despair in the Drama of Eugene O'Neill." *Modern Drama* 20 (1977): 37-53.

Discusses O'Neill's treatment of the despairing human consciousness throughout his career, showing the characteristics of the human being in despair that changed and those that didn't. In O'Neill plays despair arises from pride, anger and self-contempt, which may lead to suicide. John Loving, Dion Anthony, Caligula, characters in *Iceman*, and Jamie are characters who despair.

A582 _____. "Photo of Eugene and Carlotta O'Neill: 1929 (poem)." *Eugene O'Neill Review* 15.2 (1991): 108.

See H50.

A583 Selmon, Malcolm. "Past, Present, and Future Converged: The Place of *More Stately Mansions* in Eugene O'Neill's Canon." *Modern Drama* 28 (1985): 553-62.

Mansions is a "watershed" play in O'Neill's canon in that even in its imcomplete form, its themes, character types, techniques repeat those seen in earlier plays or anticipate those of later plays, thus helping to clarify the continuity of that career — and especially in its "growing concern for the immediate past ... in O'Neill's drama."

A584 _____. "'Like ... So Many Small Theatres': The Panoptic and the Theatric in *Long Day's Journey into Night*." *Modern Drama* 40(1997): 526-39.

Deals with "the interaction of gazes": "the tension generated when the domestic surveillance ... itself becomes an object of audience scrutiny"; and explores the way the "panoptic" gaze which, as Foucault claims, "pervades the modern world" — involving "an interaction between cultural history and the specific strategies O'Neill employs." Each member of the Tyrone family, under the gaze of all the others, is trapped into performing roles the others demand, and struggles to escape the power of the gaze (the reason, for example, Mary takes dope). The panopticon is

Jeremy Bentham's idea — no longer should punishment be in a dark dungeon, but rather in a glass cell, the prisoner always visible to the gaze.

A585 Sen, Krishna. "Eugene O'Neill and the Concept of 'Psychic Fate.'" *Journal of the Department of English* [U of Calcutta] 21.1-2 (1986-87): 55-66.

Yes, O'Neill is trying to bring his audience as close as he can to the classical sense of tragedy, but, still, the impact of Freud cannot be ignored. Not only was Freudianism "in the air," but O'Neill knew about it — had read more deeply in it than he was willing to admit. A good summary but a dated bibliography.

A586 Sewall, Richard B. "*Long Day's Journey into Night*." *Cross Currents* 29 (1979): 446-56.

A new chapter in the new edition of Sewall's *The Vision of Tragedy. Journey* as O'Neill's *Lear, Job,* and *Karamozov.* The tragedy is, however, neither heroic nor "great" (no curse or ancestral sin).

A587 Shafer, Yvonne. "In Ibsen's Back Room: Related Patterns in *The Iceman Cometh* and *The Wild Duck*." *Eugene O'Neill Newsletter* 12.3 (1988): 8-14.

Looks at the influence of Ibsen's *The Wild Duck* on *Iceman* in terms of setting, conflict, and "architectonic similarities."

A588 _____. "A Berlin Diary: *The Iceman Cometh*." *Eugene O'Neill Review* 16.2 (1992): 80-103.

Chronicles Shafer's involvement with the Berlin Deutsches Theater's 1993 production of *Iceman* from conception to execution. Several pictures of the production are included.

A589 _____. "Interview with Edward Petherbridge." *Eugene O'Neill Review* 21.1-2 (1997): 163-71.

Petherbridge played Marsden on the London and New York stages as well as on TV. The interview reveals the actor's initial indifference to the role, his apprehension regarding what he believed were stagy devices, and his subsequent appreciation of the character of Charlie, of *Interlude,* and of the playwright who created them.

A590 _____. "The Chain Lightning Theatre." *Eugene O'Neill Review* 22.1-2 (1998): 174-84.

An interview with Claire Higgins, who with her husband, Kricker James, founded the Chain Lightning Theatre that has launched several O'Neill productions, and with David Travis, who directed *Horizon* for the company.

A591 Sharma, Ghanshiam. "The Theme of Self-Transcendence in Marlowe, Shakespeare and Eugene O'Neill." *Meerut Journal of Comparative Literature and Language* [Meerut, India] 2.1 (1989): 1-21.

Unavailable.

A592 Shaughnessy, Edward L. "Question and Answer in *Hughie*." *Eugene O'Neill Newsletter* 2.2 (1978): 3-7.

Hughie is a play of the spiritually and psychologically broken, who never quite bridge the gap between them. Nonetheless, they are not completely adrift. The handshake and roll of dice are symbols of rapport.

A593 _____. "The Iceman Melteth." *Eugene O'Neill Newsletter* 3.2 (1979): 3-6.

In *Iceman* and *Journey* O'Neill tapped his creative powers by searching familial and cultural roots for inspiration. Doesn't suggest that O'Neill became Catholic again, but that he used Catholicism to his plays' advantage.

A594 _____. "Eugene O'Neill: The Development of the Negro Portraiture." *MELUS* 11.2 (1984): 87-91.

Considers O'Neill's plays which portray blacks (*Dreamy, Caribbees, Jones, Chillun, Iceman*). In O'Neill's short plays, blacks are often one-dimensional, while in the longer plays, they "are more complex, showing a great depth of emotional capability which is only suggested in the early plays." Thinks that O'Neill's sensitivity to blacks grew, even though he still relied on stereotypes in *Iceman.*

A595 _____. "Masks in the Dramaturgy of Yeats and O'Neill." *Irish University Review* 14 (1984): 205-20.

Considers how Yeats's plays and O'Neill's make use of the mask. Looking at *Brown* and the Cuchulain plays, Shaughnessy concludes that while both playwrights used masks "to reveal tensions between the inner and outer selves, their dramaturgical intentions differed radically. For Yeats, only a kind of disembodied voice is required behind the mask since it is an image assigned to men by the poet." "For O'Neill, the personality of the actor is needed to give plausibility to the dramatization."

A596 _____. "A Connecticut Yankee in the Wilderness: The Sterner Stuff of O'Neill's Comedy." *Recorder* 3.2 (1989): 89-99.

Looks for the "sterner stuff," the "muscle," the "tragic hidden undertones" that make *Wilderness* a real O'Neill play and give it "endurance quotient" (what will make it live on) and finds them. The "tragic possibilities" are "present" but "muted"—spectres that are, however, "viewed with kindly tolerance."

A597 _____. "Ella, James and Jamie O'Neill." *Eugene O'Neill Review* 15.2 (1991): 5-92.

In a worthy follow-up to Louis Sheaffer's O'Neill biography, Shaughnessy provides supplemental biographical detail on the O'Neills, including photographs, letters, Jamie's poetry, etc.

A598 _____. "O'Neill's Catholic Dilemma in *Days Without End*." *Eugene O'Neill Review* 15.1 (1991): 5-26.

Revisits the play, which garnered criticism even from O'Neill's strongest supporters, to stress the importance of "what the play means in term of its own logic and what it seems to have revealed about O'Neill's own state of mind."

A599 _____. "Ella O'Neill and the Imprint of Faith." *Eugene O'Neill Review* 16.2 (1992): 29-43.

Expanding on what is known about Ella Quinlan's youth and education, Shaughnessy sheds light on her faith by placing it in its cultural context.

A600 _____. "Brutus Jones in the Heartland: *The Emperor Jones* in Indianapolis, 1921." *Eugene O'Neill Review* 20.1-2 (1996): 36-42.

Delves into production history, unearthing what is known about the 1921 Little Theatre performances. Notes that the production was extraordinary in three respects: in the play's experimental nature, in its controversial subject matter, and in the presence of the talented black actor Arthur T. Long.

A601 _____. "O'Neill in Ireland: An Update." *Eugene O'Neill Review* 22.1-2 (1998): 137-56.

In an update on his 1988 *Eugene O'Neill in Ireland*, Shaughnessy lists and describes six more professional Irish productions of O'Neill plays—*Hughie*, *Iceman* (twice), *Misbegotten*, *Journey*, and *Anna*. The appendix lists the actors in these productions.

A602 Shea, Laura. "A Note on *Long Day's Journey Into Night*." *Notes on Contemporary Literature* 23.3 (1993): 4-5.

Argues that Jamie becomes the Frankenstein he intended Edmund to be. "More than brothers," "they are one and the same."

A603 Sheaffer, Louis. "Saxe Commins and the O'Neills." *Eugene O'Neill Newsletter* 2.2 (1978): 7-8.

A note that is also a review of *What is an Editor? Saxe Commins at Work* (see B107). "Mrs. Commins [the book's editor], who writes well, has smoothly woven into her narrative ... excerpts from her husband's writings" to flesh out the picture of a friendship between O'Neill and Saxe Commins—for if anyone knew O'Neill, "it surely was Saxe Commins."

A604 _____. "O'Neill's Way." *Confrontation* 17 (1979): 169-70.

In reconstructing conversations between O'Neill and others in his biography on O'Neill, Sheaffer "invented nothing" and "borrowed everything" and took an attitude of skepticism toward the playwright's own claims about himself.

A605 _____. "Correcting Some Errors in the Annals of O'Neill." *Eugene O'Neill Newsletter* 7.3 (1983): 13-25.

Corrects many misconceptions about O'Neill's life, some of them promulgated by O'Neill himself, other mistakes by biographers. For the continuation see next entry.

A606 _____. "Correcting Some Errors in the Annals of O'Neill (Part II)." *Eugene O'Neill Newsletter* 8.1 (1984): 16-21.

As the title suggests, the article clarifies some misconceptions about O'Neill biography. Includes information on the sources of O'Neill's plays, on Jamie's romance with Pauline Frederick, on O'Neill's drinking, and on his plans for *Journey*. See previous entry.

A607 _____. "Correcting some Errors in Annals of O'Neill." *Comparative Drama* 17 (1984): 201-32.

In two parts in *Eugene O'Neill Newsletter* 7.3 (1983): 13-24 and 8.1 (1984): 16-21. See A605 and A606.

A608 _____. "O'Neill's First Wife Defamed." *Eugene O'Neill Newsletter* 9.1 (1985): 26-29.

Corrects some of Bennett Cerf's stories about O'Neill's drinking (including the story of O'Neill's marrying his first wife following a night of carousing). Takes Donald Hall to task as editor of *The Oxford Book of American Literary Anecdotes* for reprinting the myth.

A609 ____. "Eugene O'Neill, Closet Poet." *American Voice* 3 (Summer 1986): 118-28.

Despite the kudos O'Neill received for his dramaturgy the playwright always considered himself a poet. This article demonstrates O'Neill's lingering interest in poetry.

A610 ____. "Taasinge or Tharsing?" *Eugene O'Neill Newsletter* 11.1 (1987): 26.

A note in which Sheaffer ends the "confusion among O'Neill's chroniclers and critics as to the original name of his third and final wife, Carlotta Monterey."

A611 Simon, Bennett. "Poetry, Tragic Dialogue and the Killing of Children in Eugene O'Neill's *Long Day's Journey into Night.*" *Hebrew University Studies in Literature and the Arts* 14 (1986): 66-105.

Taking an "endopoetic" critical stance ("studying the characters and actions as if they were living, autonomous people"), Simon, in this protracted article, focuses on how the Tyrones verbally assail (kill) one another and then attempt to rebuild a family "in the world of poetry, a family which both replicates and improves upon the family within the play." Identifies this essay as part of a longer work on the subject which he will put forth.

A612 Simon, John. "Brothers Under the Skin: O'Neill and Williams." *Hudson Review* 39.4 (1987): 553-65.

Looks at America's most celebrated playwrights and the "Williams-O'Neill nexus" to conclude that they are writers who should be seen as complementing rather than competing with each other. Whether O'Neill actually wrote to Williams or Williams just imagined he did matters less than the fact that Williams felt the strong presence of his predecessor.

A613 Simon, Marc. "Eugene O'Neill's Introduction to Hart Crane's *White Buildings*: Why he 'would have done it in a minute but....'" *Eugene O'Neill Review* 15.1 (1991): 41-58.

See Primary Works section, G17.

A614 Singh, Avadhesh Kumar. "Mythical Elements in Eugene O'Neill's *The Hairy Ape.*" *Indian Scholar* 12.2 (1990): 25-33.

Discusses what he terms a kind of heroic mythic form in *Ape*, which is characterized by 1) the appearance of evil (capitalism); 2) society's inability to cope with the evil; 3) the arrival of a hero to combat the evil; 4) the disappearance of the hero.

A615 Singh, Veena. "O'Neill's Yank and Jones — the Dislocated Characters." *Panjab University Research Bulletin: Arts* 18.1 (1987): 45-54.

Operating from the standpoint that man is a social animal, that he needs to belong to a reality larger than himself, Singh focuses on two O'Neill characters: Yank in *Ape* and Brutus Jones in *Jones*, describing the pair as "rootless and alienated," searching for identities in an absurd world which only heightens their feelings of alienation.

A616 Sinha, C. P. "Eugene O'Neill and the Tragic Vision." *Journal of the Bhagalpur University* 6.2 (1975): 89-95.

Argues O'Neill's vision was tragic and ties the playwright's vision to his biography; contends further that only in *Lazarus* and *Wilderness* did O'Neill strike a hopeful note. *Misbegotten* and *Journey* express his "eternal anguish." Nonetheless, to O'Neill, as to Nietzsche, tragedy is an affirmation, a celebration of life. O'Neill both wrote and lived tragedies.

A617 Sipple, William L. "From Stage to Screen: *The Long Voyage Home* and *Long Day's Journey into Night.*" *Eugene O'Neill Newsletter* 7.1 (1983): 10-14.

John Ford's *The Long Voyage Home*, adapted from four O'Neill one-acts, and *Long Day's Journey into Night*, directed by Sidney Lumet, successfully transfer O'Neill's stage dramas to screen. Discusses why those films are successful by considering aural and visual images.

A618 Smith, Madeline Catherine. "*The Emperor Jones* and Confession." *Bulletin of the West Virginia Association of College English Teachers* 8 (1983): 17-22.

"In *The Emperor Jones* O'Neill, consciously or not, drew on Catholic ritual to resolve dramatic conflict and reconcile man to himself and man to God." As a penitent, Brutus Jones admits his faults, regrets his sins, and accepts Penance.

A619 ____. "Anna Christie's Baptism." *Recorder* 3.1 (1989): 57-63.

Gathers together, after a brief exposition of the sacramental nature of baptism, the hints, the echoes, the allusions in the play to show how they and the sacrament itself help to shape *Anna*. Matter from *Iceman* and *Wilderness* is included to demonstrate that this is not a one-off exercise of O'Neill's.

A620 _____, **and Richard Eaton.**
"Four Letters by Eugene O'Neill." *Eugene O'Neill Newsletter* 11.3 (1987): 12-18.

See Primary Works section, G20.

A621 _____. "Lewys v. O'Neill Again — or, Who Was That Lady?" *Eugene O'Neill Review* 13.2 (1989): 44-54.

Expands on the little that is known of writer Georges Lewys (Gladys Adelina Lewis) whose plagiarism suit against O'Neill came to naught. The authors conclude that if Lewys' life "was obscure, it certainly wasn't unproductive."

A622 _____. "Land and Sea: *Long Day's Journey into Night* and the Humorous Tyrones." *Philological Papers* [West Virginia U] 37 (1991): 123-30.

Looks at O'Neill's masterpiece as a play which draws on correspondences and the humours theory, the main characters associated with earth, air, fire, and water.

A623 _____. "More Roads to Xanadu." *Eugene O'Neill Review* 15.1 (1991): 27-39.

Explores several possible sources for O'Neill's play. Beyond the accepted Henry Yule edition of *The Book of Ser Marco Polo, the Venetian, Concerning Kingdoms and the Marvels of the East*, O'Neill's work may also have drawn on William Marsden's *The Travels of Marco Polo the Venetian* and on Donn Byrne's novel *Messer Marco Polo*.

A624 _____. "Everything's Up to Date in Kansas City." *Eugene O'Neill Review* 16.1 (1992): 71-84.

Discusses the bruhaha that might have occurred (but didn't) over the staging of the controversial *Interlude* in conservative Kansas City (the real life version of Middletown, USA). Telegraph messages between attorneys representing the Theatre Guild's interest (published here for the first time) suggest their fear that the play would draw widespread protest.

A625 _____. "The O'Neill-Komroff Connection: Thirteen Letters from Eugene O'Neill." *Eugene O'Neill Review* 16.2 (1992): 13-28.

See Primary Works section, G37.

A626 _____. "O'Neill's 'Suitable' Comments on *Strange Interlude*." *Philological Papers* [West Virginia U] 38 (1992): 125-33.

In heretofore unpublished letters and court documents pertaining to the plagiarism suit brought by Georges Lewys, O'Neill responds to Lewys' charges and provides insight into his play *Interlude*.

A627 _____. "The Truth About Hogan." *Eugene O'Neill Review* 18.1-2 (1994): 163-70.

How O'Neill revised biographical matter in *Misbegotten*: the life and times of Dirty John Dolan, Phil Hogan's prototype.

A628 _____. "Harold DePolo: Pulp Fiction's Dark Horse." *Eugene O'Neill Review* 20.1-2 (1996): 80-87.

Based on interviews with relatives, some of the 3000-plus stories written by DePolo, and Louis Sheaffer's exchanges with the pulp fiction writer, the authors shed light on DePolo's talent and relationship with O'Neill.

A629 _____. "Classico-Buffo: Classical Parody in the Plays of Eugene O'Neill." *Memory and History: European Identity at the Millenium*. Proc. of the International Society for the Study of European Ideas. 19-24 Aug. 1996 [Utrecht]. C-D Rom, 1996.

Phil Hogan, a pig farmer, and Brutus Jones, an ex-con, are viewed as parodies of the classical hero.

A630 _____. "Con-Fusion: Con Melody's Identity Crisis." *South Carolina Review* 32.1 (1999): 228-32.

Philip Guedalla's *Wellington*, a 1931 Literary Guild selection, is seen as the "principal" source of *Touch*. "Not only did the work provide [O'Neill] with the facts of [the battle of Talavera] but also provided an inspiration for the fiction." Ultimately the character, values, and appearance of Con Melody were spun off those of the Iron Duke himself.

A631 Smith, Robert S. "O'Neill, Wilder, and American Drama." *Canadian Review of American Studies* 17.4 (1986): 469-74.

Uses the occasion of the publication of five works on Wilder and O'Neill to spawn this essay. C.W.E. Bigsby's *A Critical Introduction to Twentieth Century American Drama, Volume One*; Jackson R. Bryer's edition of the letters of Eugene O'Neill to Kenneth Macgowan ("*The Theatre We Worked For*"); Horst Frenz and Susan Tuck's *Eugene O'Neill: Voices From Abroad*; Gilbert A. Harrison's *The Enthusiast: A Life of Thornton Wilder*; and Linda Simon's *Thornton Wilder: His World* spark this essay/reflection on the importance of the dramatists to American theater. Concludes that the playwrights' works were complementary.

A632 Smith, Susan Harris. "Twentieth-Century Plays Using Classical Mythic Themes: A Checklist." *Modern Drama* 29 (1986): 110-34.

An ambitious listing of plays (1898 and after) which are based on classical myth. Grouped according to myth subject, the plays are identified by the nationality of the authors. O'Neill, alas, does not feature prominently here.

A633 _____. "Inscribing the Body: Lavinia Mannon as the Site of Struggle." *Eugene O'Neill Review* 19.1-2 (1995): 45-54.

A feminist reading of *Electra*, which focuses on Lavinia's physical self as the site of dramatic conflict and finds that the character is "uniquely gendered, degendered and regendered by O'Neill's dialogue and stage directions describing her physical body." Concludes that "Lavinia fails in her attempt to become self-authenticating because she cannot authorize her own voice and her woman's body as subject."

A634 _____. "Trying to Like Sam Shepard: Or, The Emperor's New Dungarees." *Contemporary Theatre Review* 8.3 (1998): 31-40.

From Shepard to experimentation to American literary tradition to O'Neill.

A635 Snyder, Phillip A. "A Wanderer's Tether: The Meaning of Home in O'Neill's *Ah Wilderness!* and *Long Day's Journey into Night*." *Encyclia: The Journal of the Utah Academy of Sciences Arts and Letters* 57 (1980): 103-09.

Discusses the two autobiographical plays in terms of the depiction of home in each. Finds that, although the atmospheres of the plays differ, in both home is where you can expect to find sympathy and understanding.

A636 Sohn, Dong-Ho. "*The Emperor Jones*: Cinematic Imagination and Modern Spatiality." *English Language and Literature* 41.4 (1995): 1083-1098.

Sohn's objective is "to examine the way O'Neill explores the schizophrenia of modern man in the disintegration of Jones's personality, which evolves to be one of the most extensively employed theatrical methods in the twentieth century."

A637 Spånberg, Sven-Johan. "*A Moon For the Misbegotten* as Elegy: An Intertextual Reading." *Studia Neophilologica* 61 (1989): 23-36.

Takes a close look at Jim Tyrone's use of literary quotations — the "web of allusions and echoes that helps to define the character of Jim Tyrone, his grief and despair."

A638 Sprinchorn, Evert. "O'Neill's Myth Plays for the God-Forsaken." *Theater Three* 5 (1988): 55-66.

Looks at O'Neill, not as a playwright who had a religious affiliation that could be gleaned from his canon, but as one who wrote about man's religious impulse. Under discussion are *Days, Interlude, Brown, Dynamo*, and *Iceman*. In these plays, says Sprinchorn, O'Neill recapitulated the religious history of man (*Brown*), considered the reasons behind man's religious impulse, contemplates human love as a suitable alternative to spiritual fervor (*Days*), and finally abandoned the myth for reality (*Iceman*).

A639 Sproxton, Birk. "Eugene O'Neill, Masks and Demons." *Sphinx* [U of Regina] 3 (1975): 57-62.

A review of Sheaffer's newly released biographies. Sproxton finds the volumes' "chief merit" in the "handling of O'Neill and psychology." Also credits Sheaffer with adding "many documents to the record" and creating a picture of O'Neill's life through family interrelationships and "in a larger context."

A640 Stanich, Linda K. "*The Iceman Cometh* as Ethnographic Text." *Eugene O'Neill Review* 13.2 (1989): 55-61.

Looks at this play as a multi-cultural work evidencing the four phases of social drama defined by Victor Turner: "breech, crisis, regressive action, and reintegration."

A641 Stephens, Judith L. "Subverting the Demon-Angel Dichotomy: Innovation and Feminist Intervention in Twentieth-Century Drama." *Text and Performance Quarterly* 9.1 (1989): 53-64.

Discusses a number of plays in which the demon-angel dichotomy appears, including O'Neill's *Brown*, which furnishes support for Stephens' contention that the American audience accepts this persistent stereotype of women.

A642 St. Pierre, Ronald. "'So Happy for a Time': O'Neill and the Idea of Belonging." *Shoin Literary Review* [Shoin U, Japan] 16 (1982): 53-79.

Unavailable.

A643 Strickland, Edward. "Baudelaire's 'Portraits de maîtresses' and O'Neill's *The Iceman Cometh*." *Romance Notes* 22 (1982): 291-94.

Suggests the influence of Baudelaire's collection of prose poems *Le Spleen de Paris* (Paris, 1869) on O'Neill's *Iceman*. Draws parallels between the settings, climactic suicides, and both writers' questioning of the excruciating perfection of women. Although no complete translation of the work was available in O'Neill's time, the Modern Library had published an abridged version, translated by Arthur Symons. O'Neill knew some of the poems; in fact he quotes from "Envirez-vous" in *Journey*.

A644 Stroupe, John H. "The Abandonment of Ritual: Jean Anouilh and Eugene O'Neill." *Renascence* 28 (1976): 147-54.

Claims that the renunciation of rituals is the renunciation of life itself. Whereas Anouilh's characters, Antigone, Becket, Orpheus, perish when they refuse to yield to rituals which violate their ethics, O'Neill's characters accept social programming and survive. For O'Neill the stress is not on the quality of life but living.

A645 Stuart, Otis. "Backstage with the Tyrone Brothers." *Theater Week* 25-31 July 1988: 30-35.

An interview with two of the actors in the 1988 revival of *Journey*, Campbell Scott (Edmund) and Jamey Sheridan (Jamie), who interpret their "characters" for us. Edmund is seen as sharing in the family's guilt, Jamie as less of the Cain figure than some interpretations hold him to be.

A646 Sullivan, Kevin. "O'Neill: The Irish Dimension." *Recorder* 1.1 (1985): 4-21.

A detailed look at O'Neill's ethnicity — his affinities to Irish and Irish-American authors, his Irish themes, his temperament, his family. Ultimately it is the playwright's inability to be easily classified as Irish or otherwise and his interest in "the big subject" that render him an artist.

A647 Sun, Baimei. "In Commemoration of the Centenary of Eugene O'Neill." *Waiguoyu* 6.58 (1988): 33-36.

A short, introductory and general background piece.

A648 Swortzell, Lowell. "O'Neill and the Marionette: Über and Otherwise." *Eugene O'Neill Newsletter* 11.3 (1987): 3-7.

Discusses O'Neill's interest in the use of marionettes in theater, inspired by the Federal Theatre Project's successful production of *Jones*, employing marionettes, and by a book he received on puppetry in 1939. Marionette productions of O'Neill's plays were not the "novelties we might expect."

A649 _____. "O'Neill in China: A Report on the Centenary Celebration." *Recorder* 3.1 (1989): 100-04.

O'Neillians, some 200 and more, from 10 countries gather in Nanjing, PRC, June, 1988, for a four-day conference: 30 presentations, panel discussions, performances of plays, involving scholars, directors, designers, actors. *Jones, Horizon, Journey* in Chinese, with interesting "spins," and *Hughie* in English, all well received. Notes of enthusiasm.

A650 Szabó, Klára. "O'Neill Double-Bills of Multiple Interest in Classroom Teaching." *Recorder* 3.1 (1989): 136-40.

How to teach O'Neill one-act plays in a college-level teacher training program in Hungary. The seven plays of the sea are paired in four groups (*In the Zone* does double service) thereby allowing for fuller development of character and theme when subjected to classroom analysis. The students can begin to anticipate in the later, more subtle, more developed O'Neill.

A651 Szilassy, Zoltán. "The Stanislavsky Heritage in the American Theatre." *Studies in English and American* [Budapest] 4 (1978): 201-12.

Touches very lightly on the perseverence of Stanislavsky's influence in America, first felt with the American visit of the Moscow Art Theatre. Its impact on the American Laboratory Theatre, then the Group Theatre, and the Actors' Studio was manifest in the growing concern with the creative participation, in plays, of both actor and audience, in the concern with existential problems, and in the use of tragicomic characters. References very general and slight to *Iceman, Journey, Days,* and *Lazarus*.

A652 Theriot, Ibry G-F. "The Bitch Archetype." *Journal of Dramatic Theory and Criticism* 9.1 (1994): 119-33.

Using Jung's anima/animus as his point of departure, Theriot describes the "bitch" character as one whose animus overtakes her — causing her to be dominated by the masculine element of her personality. In addition to Hedda Gabler and Maggie (*Cat on a Hot Tin Roof*), Abbie (*Desire*) is analyzed as one of the great "bitches."

A653 Thompson, Leslie M. "The Multiple Uses of the Lazarus Motif in Modern Literature." *Christian Scholar's Review* 7 (1977): 306-29.

Ranges widely over the literature of the 19th and 20th centuries. Pages 311-19 are on plays; pages 312-14 on O'Neill's *Lazarus*. Sees

Lazarus as illustrating "the complexity of modern life and the existential leap of faith necessary for belief in the miraculous" and reflecting "the increasing secularization and demythologization of Christianity" as well as "man's perennial concern with death and the variety of his responses to it."

A654 Timár, Esther. "Possible Sources for Two O'Neill One-Acts." *Eugene O'Neill Newsletter* 6.3 (1982): 20-23.

Suggests that *Recklessness* may be based on a novella in Boccaccio's *Decameron* and that *In the Zone* may be based on Conan Doyle's "That Little Square Box" or Poe's "The Oblong Box."

A655 Titcomb, Caldwell. "O'Neill's People." *Eugene O'Neill Review* 18.1-2 (1994): 5-8.

Naming the article after the conference described, Titcomb provides some of the highlights of the 11-14 May 1995 Eugene O'Neill conference, held at Suffolk University, Boston.

A656 Törnqvist, Egil. "Miss Julie and O'Neill." *Modern Drama* 19 (1976): 351-64.

Points out similarities between the *Electra* trilogy and *Miss Julie*. Also considers in much detail the influence of Strindberg on O'Neill's early works.

A657 _____. "O'Neill's Work Method." *Studia Neophilologica: A Journal of Germanic and Romance Languages and Literature* 49 (1977): 43-58.

"A slightly different version" of an essay he wrote in Swedish ("O'Neill's arbetssat." In *Drama och Teater.* Ed. Egil Törnqvist. Stockholm: Almqvist and Wiksell, 1968). Describes what writing meant to O'Neill; where he did it best; when and for how long at a time; the evolution of a play from draft to draft; overlapping creativity; the differences between the production and the published version, etc.

A658 _____. "Ingmar Bergman Directs *Long Day's Journey into Night.*" *New Theatre Quarterly* 5.20 (1989): 374-83.

Looks at Bergman's 1988 production, explaining the directorial cuts and adaptations and giving reasons for the production's success. Reprinted with minor changes in Liu and Swortzell's *Eugene O'Neill in China* (1992), see B263.

A659 _____. "O'Neill's Firstborn." *Eugene O'Neill Review* 13.2 (1989): 5-11.

Takes issue with Arthur and Barbara

Gelb's assertion that *A Wife for a Life* does not presage O'Neill's promise as premier American playwright. Looking to autobiographical, classical and contemporary influences on the writer, Törnqvist spots the themes and influences found rudimentarily in this play and developed in his later work. Concludes that "O'Neill's firstborn is not stillborn."

A66 _____. "Strindberg, O'Neill, Norén: A Swedish-American Triangle." *Eugene O'Neill Review* 15.1 (1991): 64-77.

Looks at Strindberg's influence on O'Neill and O'Neill's influence on Lars Norén, finding in the latter (and the intertextual echoes) the completion of a circle.

A661 _____. "To Speak the Unspoken: Audible Thinking in O'Neill's Plays." *Eugene O'Neill Review* 16.1 (1992): 55-70.

Revisiting *Interlude* for a look at the thought asides/soliloquies, Törnqvist finds O'Neill's inspiration for this device in Joyce's *Ulysses.* Concludes that the soliloquy in *Interlude* marked an important development in O'Neill's use of language. "Having tried it out, O'Neill could discard it in favor of more dramatic types of audible thinking."

A662 Tuck, Susan. "Electricity is God Now: D. H. Lawrence and O'Neill." *Eugene O'Neill Newsletter* 5.2 (1981): 10-15.

Suggests that Lawrence's *Women in Love,* and particularly the chapter on "The Industrial Magnate," may have been an influence on Eugene O'Neill's *Dynamo.* Although there was no copy of Lawrence's book in O'Neill's library, Carlotta had one. Both Reuben Light and Gerald Crich try to understand this godless world through a display of the power found in electricity. Both feared their fathers, and both scorned Christianity. Finally, both substituted science for religion and were brought to the brink of insanity.

A663 _____. "House of Compson, House of Tyrone: Faulkner's Influence on O'Neill." *Eugene O'Neill Newsletter* 5.3 (1981): 10-16.

Finds the Compsons of *The Sound and the Fury* and the Tyrones similar. The two families are both held together by a common past of betrayal. Both works have quadripartite structures, and both focus on a family destroying itself.

A664 _____. "O'Neill and Frank Wedekind." *Eugene O'Neill Newsletter* 6.1 (1982): 29-35 and 6.2 (1982): 17-21.

Part One notes the similarities in the backgrounds of the two playwrights. O'Neill may have seen Wedekind's work in New York City and points out the similarities between *Frühlings Erwachen* and *Wilderness*. Part Two compares *Erdgeist* to *Interlude* in terms of character and common elements in scenes.

A665 _____. "White Dreams, Black Nightmares: *All God's Chillun Got Wings* and *Light in August.*" *Eugene O'Neill Newsletter* 12.1 (1988): 48-55.

In terms of the depiction of the black man, O'Neill's play and Faulkner's novel have much in common. Unlike most works that predate these, *All God's Chillun* and *Light in August* recognize the humanity of their characters.

A666 Updike, John. "A Case of Melancholia." *New Yorker* 20 Feb. 1989: 112-20.

A look at the life, art, and suicide of Ralph Barton, Carlotta's third husband.

A667 Usui, Masami. "Mary Tyrone's Drug Addiction and Quest for Truth in Eugene O'Neill's *Long Day's Journey into Night.*" *Gengo bunka kenkyu* [*Studies in Languages and Cultures*]16 (1990): 109-22.

Sees the "facts" of Mary's life and addiction as leading to revelations of an "inner truth"—the revelations played out by husband and sons in their confessional scenes. Badly edited.

A668 Van Laan, Thomas F. "Singing in the Wilderness: A Dark vision of O'Neill's Only Mature Comedy." *Modern Drama* 22 (1979): 9-18.

Wilderness has undertones of criticism of the family life it seems to extol: satirizes the sentimental characters and their responses to the Fourth of July. To recognize that O'Neill's attitude differs from those of his characters is to recognize the richness of his play.

A669 Van Leer, David. "The Showman Cometh." *New Republic* 13 Nov. 1989: 29-30.

Surveys some of the activities at the centennial of the birth of O'Neill—"our greatest playwright," whom "nobody much likes," whose plays "do not hold up in print," and who depends on "strong performances by powerful actors and imaginative directors to make his characters live."

A670 Vena, Gary. "Chipping at the *Iceman*: The Text and the 1946 Theatre Guild Production." *Eugene O'Neill Newsletter* 9.3 (1985): 11-17.

Considers the changes in dialogue made in the 1946 Theatre Guild production. The length of the play necessitated some cutting; some changes were made to suit the physical attributes of the actors. Most of the alterations in dialogue were made in Hickey's lines.

A671 _____. "Congruency and Coincidence in O'Casey's *Juno* and O'Neill's *Journey.*" *English Studies* 68 (June 1987): 249-63.

Prefaces observations on the similarities between O'Casey's play and O'Neill's by relating the circumstances under which the playwrights met. Concludes that "As fated victims of alcohol, betrayal, economics, breaches of religious faith, and disintegrating sociometric environments, these stage characters [*Journey's* and *Juno's*] are ultimately the creations of playwrights who were influenced by a shared Irish heritage."

A672 Vera, Yvonne. "Observation as System in Eugene O'Neill's *The Iceman Cometh.*" *Modern Drama* 39 (1996): 448-56.

Arguing that O'Neill's play "lends itself to an analysis of power relations, spatial presence, and punishment," Vera looks at the characters as they look at other characters and concludes that *Iceman* "yields an elaboration of the impact of observation among characters, and the motivation of personal freedom rising from reciprocal relations of control and domestication among them."

A673 Viswanathan, R. "The Ship Scene in *The Emperor Jones.*" *Eugene O'Neill Newsletter* 4.3 (1980): 3-5.

Points out that the imaginary ship in Scene VI isn't a slave ship, but appears to be a Jungian symbol of Jones's regression to his roots. The sea setting is reflective of Jung's conception of the water as the archetypal symbol of the soul and the return to it as representative of the desire to be united with one's spiritual self, to "disinherit" one's "native tradition," one's lost cultural legacy."

A674 _____. "*The Jungle Books* and O'Neill." *Eugene O'Neill Newsletter* 11.2 (1987): 3-7.

Though O'Neill acknowledged the influence of Kipling on his poetry, he said nothing of the British writer's influence on his plays. *Ape* and *Jones* are analyzed for their Kiplingesque motifs.

A675 Vobozil, Róza. "Fatalism in Eugene O'Neill's *Long Day's Journey into Night.*" *Folia Litteraria* 18 (1987): 149-60.

Looks at *Journey* in light of its dramatic tension and irony to conclude that the tragedy of the play "consists in their [the characters'] coming to awareness about the hopeless predicament in which they are trapped."

A676 Voelker, Paul D. "Eugene O'Neill and George Pierce Baker: A Reconsideration." *American Literature* 49 (1977): 206-20.

Counters the prevailing notions about Baker's influence on O'Neill (especially Travis Bogard's) by suggesting that Baker's influence on O'Neill was a positive one.

A677 _____. "O'Neill and George Pierce Baker." *Eugene O'Neill Newsletter* 1.2 (1977): 4-6.

Abstract of Voelker's dissertation "The Early Plays of Eugene O'Neill, 1913-1915." But see C126.

A678 _____. "Eugene O'Neill's Aesthetic of the Drama." *Modern Drama* 21 (1978): 87-99.

While O'Neill's theories are expounded informally in interviews and letters, they exist. Essay concerns itself with four areas of his aesthetic — realism and expressionism, tragedy, production techniques, and the affective aspect of plays. Notes O'Neill stressed the play as written work.

A679 _____. "The Uncertain Origins of Eugene O'Neill's *Bound East for Cardiff*." *Studies in Bibliography: Papers of the Bibliographical Society of the University of Virginia* 32 (1979): 273-81.

First discusses the changes O'Neill made when he rewrote *Children of the Sea* into *Cardiff*. O'Neill softened coarse elements and heightened softer ones. Attempts to pinpoint the date of revision and theorizes that the date of composition O'Neill gave (1914) might be an autobiographical fiction. Theorizes 1915-16 is the more probable date and speculates that O'Neill may have invented the earlier date so as to deny the influence of George Pierce Baker on his writing.

A680 _____. "An Agenda for O'Neill Studies." *Eugene O'Neill Newsletter* 8.1 (1984): 11-15.

Surveys recent achievements in O'Neill scholarship — the publication of documents and letters hitherto unavailable, work by Törnqvist, Halfmann, and Tiusanen on O'Neill's staging — and considers directions for the future — publication of an authoritative complete works of O'Neill, more productions of O'Neill plays, and the restoration of Monte Cristo and Tao House.

A681 _____. "Politics, but Literature: The Example of Eugene O'Neill's Apprenticeship." *Eugene O'Neill Newsletter* 8.2 (1984): 3-8.

Considers the political/social elements in O'Neill's early plays (*The Web, A Wife for a Life, Thirst, Recklessness, Cardiff, Bread and Butter, Abortion, The Personal Equation*) and concludes that *The Personal Equation* reflects O'Neill's criticism of political activists — that they are self-seeking. O'Neill opted for changes within the individual as a way of bettering society.

A682 _____. "Conspicuous by his Absence: O'Neill and a 1987 Provincetown Conference." *Eugene O'Neill Newsletter* 11.3 (1987): 10-12.

In what is essentially a conference review, Voelker applauds the opportunity to see four infrequently produced plays which were performed for the first time at the Provincetown Playhouse in 1915 — *Suppressed Desires* (George Cram Cook and Susan Glaspell), *Constancy* (Neith Boyce), *Change Your Style* (George Cram Cook), and *Contemporaries* (Wilbur Daniel Steele) — but bemoans the lack of O'Neill.

A683 _____. "O'Neill's First Families: *Warnings* through *The Personal Equation*." *Eugene O'Neill Newsletter* 11.2 (1987): 13-18.

Looks to O'Neill's early plays to find the roots of the interest in the family unit. *Warnings* is his first play to dramatize at length relationships between parents, children and siblings, but even in the earlier works — *Wife, The Web, Thirst,* and *Recklessness* — we witness the influence of the family. Sees two themes in the early family plays — the family under attack from outside forces and the male who is destroyed by the demands of family.

A684 _____. "Biography, Autobiography and Artistry in *A Wife for a Life*." *Eugene O'Neill Newsletter* 12.1 (1988): 10-17.

Finds this "anomalous" play a foreshadowing of the strengths and weaknesses of his canon.

A685 Voglino, Barbara. "'Games' the Tyrones Play." *Eugene O'Neill Review* 16.1 (1992): 91-103.

Using Eric Berne's definition of "game" as "a recurring set of transactions, not necessarily imply[ing] fun or even enjoyment, but characterized by a concealed motivation that progresses to a well-defined, predictable outcome," Voglino looks at the "games" the Tyrones play in *Journey*. In an effort to avoid the cruel facts of Edmund's illness, Mary's addiction, etc., the characters resort to role playing.

A686 Vorlicky, Robert. "'No Use Gabbin' Here All Night': Male Talk and Silence in *Hughie*." *Eugene O'Neill Review* 19.1-2 (1995): 81-94.

Hughie is the "first critically acclaimed American male-cast play that utilizes the dynamic of unsuccessful communication as its source of dramatic form and content"—which is achieved through "pervasive reliance on silence." While applauding the playwright's mastery in depicting the lack of intimacy between the characters, Vorlicky regrets that O'Neill opts not for meaningful communication at the end, but for "clichéd behavior."

A687 _____. "O'Neill's First Play: *A Wife For A Life*." *Eugene O'Neill Review* 20.1-2 (1996): 5-10.

Dismissing prevailing opinion, Vorlicky argues that "*A Wife for a Life* is, in fact, a very revealing first work in its handling of American male characters who interact with one another amidst the absence of women—an interaction that is the sole dynamic of the play." In the play appear the forerunners of the taciturn and inarticulate American male characters who populate the century's drama.

A688 Vyzga, Bernard. "Designing O'Neill's *The Hairy Ape*." *Eugene O'Neill Newsletter* 1.3 (1980): 15-16.

Explains how he conveyed the central idea of *Ape*—man's movement toward suicide—through set design, in the summer 1979 production at Dartmouth. Comments on his reliance upon monochromatic colors and steel.

A689 Wainscott, Ronald H. "Harnessing O'Neill's Furies: Philip Moeller Directs *Dynamo*." *Eugene O'Neill Newsletter* 10.3 (1986): 3-13.

Even if the play *Dynamo* was not a success, Philip Moeller's 1929 production was. Moeller's enthusiasm for the play was infectious, and the cast mounted "an impressive, trenchant spectacle."

A690 _____. "Exploring the Religion of the Dead: Philip Moeller Directs *Mourning Becomes Electra*." *Theatre History Studies* 7 (1987): 28-39.

A performance review written 36 years after the performance. It describes the original production of *Electra,* crediting that production with establishing the play as a success. Focuses on the collaborative vision of O'Neill and Moeller and proves useful for those interested in production history.

A691 Wasserstrom, William. "Notes on Electricity: Henry Adams and Eugene O'Neill." *Psychocultural Review* 1 (1977): 161-78.

Reflecting on *Dynamo* after a production at Syracuse University, Wasserstrom says that the play reveals the playwright's attraction to the optimism of Walter Lippman and Charles Beard in contrast to the pessimism of Henry Adams and D.H. Lawrence concerning the effect of modern mechanization on the human psyche. Ultimately, O'Neill renounced an easy faith in progress.

A692 Waterstradt, Jean Anne. "Another View of Ephraim Cabot: A Footnote to *Desire Under the Elms*." *Eugene O'Neill Newsletter* 9.2 (1985): 27-31.

Ephraim not hard and unyielding but rather "the most creative, the most fulfilled member of the Cabot family." The stones with which Ephraim is identified are suggestive of his unity and strength. He has experienced "something eternal."

A693 Watson, James G. "The Theater in *The Iceman Cometh*: Some Modernist Implications." *Arizona Quarterly* 34 (1978): 230-38.

Finds that *Iceman* is not about illusions but about theater. Hickey almost kills theater, but when he assumes the role of a madman, he restores it.

A694 Watt, Stephen M. "The 'Formless Fear' of O'Neill's *Emperor* and Tennyson's *King*." *Eugene O'Neill Newsletter* 6.3 (1982): 14-15.

Did O'Neill borrow the phrase "formless fear" from Tennyson's "The Passing of Arthur" in *Idylls of the King*.

A695 _____. "O'Neill and Otto Rank: Doubles, 'Death Instinct,' and the Trauma of Birth." *Comparative Drama* 20 (1986): 211-30.

Asserts that it is not his intention "to establish Otto Rank as a direct source of O'Neill's drama, but merely to urge that the former's best-known works—*The Double, The Trauma of Birth* ... and *Will Therapy*—constitute a means by which we might explore

O'Neill's split or identical characters." Though Watt focuses on *Electra*, he draws on other O'Neill plays as well.

A696 Weales, Gerald. "The Postman Cometh." *Gettysburg Review* 2.4 (1989): 647-57.

Assesses O'Neill as letter writer in an essay/review of Travis Bogard and Jackson R. Bryer's *Selected Letters*. Weales grants that while the playwright's letters give insight into his mission, message and means, this volume disappoints in its index and documentation which "too much of the time" takes the editors "between no information and pointless identifications."

A697 Wedge, George F. "Mixing Memory with Desire: The Family of the Alcoholic in Three Mid-Century Plays." *Dionysos* 1.1 (1989): 10-18.

Provides a clinician's view of the alcoholism at center in *A Streetcar Named Desire*, *Come Back, Little Sheba*, and *Journey*. Concludes that in these plays alcoholism, rather than being depicted as a moral failing, is shown to have sprung "from an illness characterized not by depravity but by an obsessive desire to recapture a time of innocence, to relive the first blush of pure love."

A698 Weinstein, Katherine. "Towards a Theatre of Creative Imagination: Alexander Tairov's O'Neill Productions." *Eugene O'Neill Review* 22.1-2 (1998): 157-70.

Provides the background to the 1920s Russian productions, directed by Alexander Tairov, of *Chillun*, *Ape*, and *Desire*. Weinstein disputes Maya Koreneva's contention that it was O'Neill's political/social views that attracted Tairov to him. Instead, she argues, "It was their kindred belief in a 'theatre of creative imagination'" that gave birth to these productions.

A699 Weiss, Samuel A. "O'Neill, Nietzsche, and Cows." *Modern Drama* 34 (1991): 494-98.

To find the inspiration for Ephraim Cabot's bovine enthusiasm, Weiss looks to Nietzsche's *Thus Spake Zarathustra* and *Ecco Homo* for passages in which the philosopher speaks of the warmth and comfort the animals provide.

A700 Weixlmann, Joe. "Staged Segregation: Baldwin's *Blues for Mister Charlie* and O'Neill's *All God's Chillun Got Wings*." *Black American Literature Forum* 11 (1977): 35-36.

Baldwin's play, blending symbolism and setting in an effort to point out the separation of white and black people, finds its inspiration in O'Neill's *Chillun*. But, where Baldwin generally makes his points "with words instead of actions," O'Neill "allows physical effects to substitute for verbal ones." *Chillun* is seen as a failure because 1) "racial attitudes … cause the play to crumble at the end," 2) O'Neill did not know enough of Negro life, and 3) the characters' behavior (especially Jim's) was implausible.

A701 Welch, Dennis M. "Hickey as a Satanic Force in *The Iceman Cometh*." *Arizona Quarterly* 34 (1978): 219-29.

Perhaps a case can be made for Hickey as an image of Milton's Lucifer. Hickey, after all, is a rebel against man's God — illusion.

A702 Werner, Bette Charlene. "Eugene O'Neill's *Paradise Lost*: The Theme of the Islands in *Mourning Becomes Electra*." *Forum* 26.1 (1985): 46-52.

Focuses on *Electra*, which is seen as a play about the breaking of the mother-child bond. "Maternal abandonment is the original sin" precipitating the fall from innocence.

A703 Wertheim, Albert. "Gaspard the Miser in O'Neill's *Long Day's Journey into Night*." *American Notes and Queries* 18 (1979): 39-42.

Points out the many connotations of the reference to old Gaspard the miser in *Journey*. The allusion mocks Tyrone, not only for his penuriousness, but also for playing melodrama.

A704 _____. "Eugene O'Neill's *Days Without End* and the Tradition of the Split Character in Modern American and British Drama." *Eugene O'Neill Newsletter* 6.3 (1982): 5-9.

Notes the problem of drama's demonstrating a divided inner and outer self. Later O'Neill learned that character could be more effective than special effects. In *Touch*, *Misbegotten*, and *Iceman* he is more successful at demonstrating the split character than in his earlier plays. May have gotten the idea for *Days* from Alice Gerstenberg's play *Overtones*. *Days* is important because in it O'Neill uses a technique which is now being refined successfully by others.

A705 Wharton, Don. "Eugene O'Neill: The Man Behind the Genius." *Reader's Digest* May 1975: 112+.

Strings together predictable glimpses of O'Neill — from O'Neill's own words and those of family, wives, and acquaintances.

A706 White, George C. "Directing O'Neill in China." *Eugene O'Neill Newsletter* 9.1 (1985): 29-36.

White explains the problems he encountered directing *Anna* in Beijing and comments on the adaptations made in that 1984 production. See B457.

A707 White, Leslie. "Eugene O'Neill and the Federal Theatre Project." *Resources for American Literary Study* 17.1 (1990): 63-85.

Looks at the reception of several O'Neill plays produced by the Federal Theatre Project — *Wilderness, Anna, Horizon, Jones*, the sea plays, *The First Man, The Straw, Days, Welded, Diff'rent, Cross, Breakfast*, and *Dreamy* — and credits the group with bringing O'Neill to the uninitiated.

A708 Whitlatch, Michael. "Eugene O'Neill and Class Consciousness in *The Hairy Ape*." *Zeitschrift für Anglistik und Amerikanistik* 35.3 (1987): 223-27.

Sees in the characters of Mildred and Yank symbols of "opposing factions of society."

A709 Wiles, Timothy J. "Tammanyite, Progressive, and Anarchist: Political Communities in *The Iceman Cometh*." *CLIO: A Journal of Literature, History, and the Philosophy of History* 9 (1979): 179-96.

Rejects the notion that *Iceman* is only a private tragedy or to be seen only in universal terms and examines it to find a middle ground of social and political concerns: leftist radicalism, establishmentarianism and reform.

A710 Wilkins, Frederick C., et al. "The Enduring O'Neill: Which Plays Will Survive?" *Eugene O'Neill Newsletter*. Preview issue (1977): 2-15.

Based on an MLA panel discussion of 27 Dec. 1975. Considers the criteria to be used to judge the best of O'Neill's plays. Panelists include John Henry Raleigh, Doris Falk, Virginia Floyd, Esther M. Jackson, and Frederick C. Wilkins. Some of the criteria for judging O'Neill decided on by the panelists were O'Neill's use of dramatic technique, his ability to translate his own life into drama, and his adherence to the more conventional of European stage forms.

A711 Wilkins, Frederick C. "Lawson and Cole Revisited." *Eugene O'Neill Newsletter* 7.2 (1983): 23-27.

Recaps the responses of Marxist critics to O'Neill's work shortly after his death. Lester Cole attacked O'Neill and was vituperative in his response to John Howard Lawson's analysis of O'Neill's work.

A712 _____. "*Hughie* — By Way of Intro." *Eugene O'Neill Newsletter* 8.3 (1984): 27.

Finds that *Hughie* is like *Cardiff* in that at "each play's central core is a nighttime duet for two men whose spiritual and emotional communion provides comfort and solace against the surrounding menaces of life and death."

A713 _____. "Publications by and about Eugene O'Neill, 1980-1983." *Eugene O'Neill Newsletter* 8.2 (1984): 22-28.

Bibliography of O'Neill publications, 1980-1983.

A714 _____. "O'Neill at 100." *Americana* July-Aug. 1988: 47-52.

An entertainingly written background piece on O'Neill, meant to remind the general reader of O'Neill's contributions to American drama and to herald the upcoming celebrations marking the centennial of his birth. Pictures of Monte Cristo Cottage and Tao House accompany the text — both locations the sites of O'Neill festivities.

A715 _____. "O'Neill's Secular Saints." *Eugene O'Neill Review* 14.1-2 (1990): 71-78.

Examines those more placid O'Neill characters, whom Wilkins refers to, admittedly hyperbolically, as secular saints, and whose balance offers an alternative to the angst-torn protagonists of the canon.

A716 Williams, Gary Jay. "Turned Down in Provincetown: O'Neill's Debut Reexamined." *Theatre Journal* 37.2 (1985): 155-66.

Citing letters by Hutchins Hapgood and Harry Kemp, Williams raises questions about Susan Glaspell's account of O'Neill's arrival at Provincetown. The evidence suggests that O'Neill arrived in June, not July, 1916. Wonders why, if O'Neill's talents were immediately recognized by George Cram Cook and Glaspell, no play of his appeared on the first billing (July 13). Did Glaspell exaggerate their reception of O'Neill to gain for her husband a sound place in the history of O'Neill's career? Also discusses O'Neill's changes in his turning *Children of the Sea* into *Cardiff* — changes that may have resulted from his seeing the former in production.

A717 _____. "*The Dreamy Kid*: O'Neill's Darker Brother." *Theatre Annual* 43 (1988): 3-14.

Posits that Abe of *Dreamy* may have been inspired by Jamie O'Neill and even the playwright himself. Looks to biographical sources to prove his case.

A718 _____. "Turned Down in Provincetown: O'Neill's Debut Re-Examined." *Eugene O'Neill Newsletter* 12.1 (1988): 17-27.

Takes another look at O'Neill's legendary and theatrical discovery by the Provincetown Players. Finds fiction amid the fact.

A719 Wilmer, Steve. "Censoring Eugene O'Neill." *Gramma: Journal of Theory and Criticism* 2 (1993): 199-211.

Looks at O'Neill's battle with the censors—*Chillun, Ape*—to conclude that it was "because O'Neill undermined American hegemonic social values that the authorities sought to censor him."

A720 Wishnia, Kenneth. "Myth, Non-Linear time and Self-Negation: Demetrio Aguilera Malta's *El Tigre* and Eugene O'Neill's *The Emperor Jones*." *Hispanic Journal* 15.2 (1994): 257-69.

Refers to the similarities between O'Neill's play and Ecuadorian author Aguilera Malta's one-act in his discussion of the latter. His focus is on *El Tigre*'s "two irreconcilable realities, one mythic and atemporal, one banal, materialistic and chronological, inhabiting the same 3-D space." Calling *El Tigre* "magical realism," Wishnia concludes that while the reasons for the Emperor's downfall are fathomable, the result of the conflict between pagan and Christian, the two forces in Aguilera Malta's play do not confront each other but merely coexist in the same space. "The loser, unfortunately, is the poor soul whose homeland must play unwilling host to the two of them." *Jones* gets only brief treatment here.

A721 Wittenberg, Judith B. "Faulkner and Eugene O'Neill." *Mississippi Quarterly* 33 (1980): 327-41.

Faulkner's personal and professional lives gave him "access" to the work of Eugene O'Neill. Faulkner had a strong interest in drama and was acquainted with at least five O'Neill plays: *Anna, Straw, Gold, Jones*, and *Diff'rent*. Compares some of these plays to works by Faulkner. Thinks that perhaps *Interlude* influenced *The Sound and the Fury*, and *Electra* influenced *As I Lay Dying* and *Absalom, Absalom!*

A722 Woertendyke, Ruis. "Directing *A Moon for the Misbegotten* at Pace University." *Recorder* 3.1 (1989): 144-50.

Some college students, most not even theater majors, are led unwillingly into playing O'Neill, and eventually develop an "interest in, understanding of, and, finally, love" for the playwright as they work on a production of *Misbegotten*.

A723 Wolter, Jürgen. "O'Neill's Open Boat." *Litteratur in Wissenschaft und Unterricht* 11 (1978): 222-29.

Points out parallels between Crane's "Open Boat" and O'Neill's early work, especially *Thirst* and *Fog*.

A724 Ximen, Lusha. "Eugene O'Neill Revival." *China Reconstructs* (North American Edition) 36 (June 1987): 24-25.

A short history of how O'Neill's plays were first introduced to China, including mention of director George White's 1984 visit to Beijing to assist in the production of *Anna*, an assessment of O'Neill's popularity in China, and a reflection on the 1987 O'Neill symposium held in Beijing.

A725 Young, William. "Mother and Daughter in *Mourning Becomes Electra*." *Eugene O'Neill Newsletter* 6.2 (1982): 15-17.

Since Vinnie is blind to her desire to be like her mother, she is more pathetic than tragic. Christine, on the other hand, has a mind of her own and realizes she has wasted much of her life. She is more tragic.

A726 Yu, Zhao. "O'Neill's Tragedies: A Chinese View." *Recorder* 3.1 (1989): 52-56.

In the 1980s a number of professional productions of O'Neill plays hint at a resurgence of interest in the playwright's work. *Desire* and *Homecoming*, from *Electra*, were especially important because they were eventually shown on Chinese national television. The critical and scholarly interest in the two that resulted is the concern of this essay.

A727 Zapf, Hubert. "O'Neill's *Hairy Ape* and the Reversal of Hegelian Dialectics." *Modern Drama* 31 (1988): 35-40.

Assuming that O'Neill was familiar with Hegel's philosophy as a result of either the playwright's interest in Nietzsche or his flirtation with Marx, Zapf looks at *Ape* "as a

critical exploration of this progressive-dialec-
tic model of the mind (Hegel) and of society
(Marx)." Concludes that "O'Neill reverses in
The Hairy Ape the Hegelian-Marxist model of
dialectics, of man's intellectual-historical self-
realization, and thus deconstructs, in the
medium of the drama, the ideology of progress
which this model, in its uncritical application
to modern reality, implies."

B. Books and Parts
of Books (English)

B1 Aarseth, Inger. "A Drama of Life and Death Impulses: A Thematical Analysis of *Mourning Becomes Electra*." In *Americana-Norvegica*. Vol. 4. *Norwegian Contributions to American Studies Dedicated to Sigmund Skard*. Ed. Brita Seyerstad. Oslo: Universitetsforlaget, 1973. 291-304.

Concerned with the "metaphysical aspect" of *Electra*: "the mythical-religious and symbolic implications of the major conflict"; "the grey puritanism" of the Mannons versus "the green 'paganism' of the South Sea Islanders"— conflicts between and within characters, especially Ezra and Lavinia. Implications of the conflicts include life-death/ spiritual immortality vs. life here and now (with immortality found only in the life cycle). Sees the house as a prison, and the moon as romance, love and sexual freedom. Finds validity in O'Neill's assertion that *Electra* is "the drama of the life and death impulses." *Ape* and *Brown* help to explicate themes.

B2 Abbott, Anthony S. *The Vital Lie: Reality and Illusion in Modern Drama.* Tuscaloosa: U of Alabama P, 1989.

In his discussion of modern drama's theme of the conflict between reality and illusion, Abbott includes an introductory-level chapter on O'Neill. The chapter concludes that O'Neill was a "frustrated idealist."

Connolly, Thomas F. Rev. *Eugene O'Neill Review* 13.2 (1989): 105-09.

B3 _____. "Themes in O'Neill's Plays." In *Readings on Eugene O'Neill.* Ed. Thomas Siebold. The Greenhaven Press Literary Companion Series. San Diego: Greenhaven, 1998. 51-59.

Reprinted from *The Vital Lie: Reality and Illusion in Modern Drama*, 1989; see B2.

B4 Adam, Julie. *Versions of Heroism in Modern American Drama: Redefinitions by Miller, Williams, O'Neill, and Anderson.* New York: St. Martin's, 1991.

Her 1988 University of Toronto dissertation; see C1.

Bloom, Steven F. Rev. *Eugene O'Neill Review* 17.1-2 (1993): 198-205.

B5 Adler, Thomas P. *Mirror on the Stage: The Pulitzer Plays as an Approach to American Drama.* West Lafayette, IN: Purdue UP, 1987.

Surveying the 57 Pulitzer-prize plays between 1917 and 1986 in 171 pages, Adler is restricted in the coverage he can to give any one of them. There are 10 essays, in which O'Neill's four prize winners are given two or three pages each. *Horizon* is treated (pp. 26-28) in an essay entitled "Supportive Illusions/Romantic Delusions"; *Interlude* (pp. 48-51) in "The Ethic of Happiness"; *Anna* (pp. 117-18) in "The Varieties of Religious Experience"; and *Journey* (pp. 146-49) in "From Modernism to Metatheatre—Art and Artists in Modern American Drama."

Connolly, Thomas F. Rev. *Eugene O'Neill Newsletter* 12.2 (1988): 65-67.

B6 _____. *American Drama, 1940-1960: A Critical History.* Twayne Critical History of American Drama Series. New York: Twayne, 1994. 21-42.

Adler's second chapter is entitled "Eugene O'Neill: 'Faithful Realism' with a Poet's Touch." Because of the limits imposed by the series itself, O'Neill is restricted to a period that allows coverage for only his last plays (*Touch*,

Mansions, Iceman, Journey, Misbegotten and *Hughie*). Adler links them as attempts to use the world of objective reality in ways that hint at characters' inner beings and worlds.

Bloom, Steven F. Rev. *Eugene O'Neill Review* 17.1-2 (1993): 198-205.

B7 Ahuja, Chaman. *Tragedy, Modern Temper and O'Neill.* Atlantic Highlands, NJ: Humanities, 1984.

Carefully analyzes all of O'Neill's published plays, usually working chronologically, to demonstrate the thesis that though O'Neill had "a noble conception of the theatre, and a noble aim of reviving the spirit of Greek tragedy … in terms of achievement his success was of such a modest level that it did not satisfy even himself." Finds that though he was "a colossus in the modern theater — vital and strong — O'Neill lacked the finesse that brings greatness," the reason lying in his inability to reconcile his inclinations — towards modernism, towards irony — with the demands of tragedy. True there are masterpieces — *Ape, Jones, Brown, Interlude, Electra, Iceman, Journey,* and *Misbegotten* — but not as tragedies. It is only when they are approached as "plays" that O'Neill's "range, variety, theatrical experiment and dramatic power" can be appreciated.

B8 Alexander, Doris. *Eugene O'Neill's Creative Struggle: The Decisive Decade, 1924-1933.* University Park: Pennsylvania State UP, 1992.

Desire, Marco, Brown, Lazarus, Interlude, Dynamo, Electra, Wilderness, and *Days* are the plays under consideration in this volume which tries to "discover the whys and wherefores" of the creative process. Arguing that for O'Neill writing plays was a way "to confront and solve a pressing life problem," Alexander shows how even in what are accounted his less autobiographical works, the playwright and his problem are at the fore.

Bloom, Steven F. Rev. *Eugene O'Neill Review* 17.1-2 (1993): 93-96.

B9 *American Playwrights, 1880-1945: A Research and Production Sourcebook.* Ed. William W. Demastes. Westport, CT: Greenwood P, 1995. 323-47.

See Ranald, B351.

B10 Anniah Gowda, Hennur H. *Dramatic Poetry from Mediaeval to Modern Times: A Philosophic Inquiry into the Nature of Poetic Drama in England, Ireland and the United States of America.* Rev. ed. Madras: Macmillan, 1979.

In a chapter entitled "Twentieth Century America: The Progressives" (331-62) five pages are devoted to *Lazarus,* which, we are told, succeeds like O'Neill's other plays despite, rather than because of, its language. In brief O'Neill lacks mastery "of any form of verbal expression." Still *Lazarus* is "remarkable for its moving and poetic spectacle and for its reasoned and scholarly statement." It "demonstrates" that "even the widely agnostic twentieth century" can "create admirable religious and metaphysical drama." But still O'Neill fails to give his actors words with "poetic connotation" or grandeur equal to the poetic stature of his play's goals.

B11 Apte, Madhvi. "Three O'Neill translations in Marathi." In *T. S. Eliot & Eugene O'Neill: The Dream and the Nightmare.* Eds. V. R. N. Prasad, et al. New Delhi: Ajanta, 1991. 133-40.

Discusses the difficulties in translating and looks at *Wilderness, Electra,* and *Interlude* — all of which have been translated into Marathi. Of the three translations, Apte concludes that S. G. Malshe's treatment of *Interlude* most successfully captures the original.

B12 Asselineau, Roger. "*Desire Under the Elms: A Phase of O'Neill's Philosophy.*" In *Eugene O'Neill: A Collection of Criticism.* Ed. Ernest G. Griffin. New York: McGraw, 1976. 59-66.

The central interest is *Desire,* where we find an animalistic interpretation of human behavior in conflict with a spiritual interpretation: the feeling between Abbie and Eben changes from lust to spiritual love, something that transcends the body. [Reprinted from *Festschrift Rudolf Stamm.* Eds. Eduart Kolb and Jorg Hasler. Bern: Franke Verlag, 1969. 277-83.]

B13 _____. "Eugene O'Neill's Transcendental Phase." In *The Transcendental Constant in American Literature.* New York: New York UP, 1980. 115-23.

A reprint; see B12.

B14 Atkinson, Brooks, and Albert Hirschfeld. *The Lively Years — 1920-1973.* New York: Associated, 1973.

Eighty-two essays (between 800 and 1000 words each) introducing 82 plays produced in New York during the period 1920-73. Includes essays on *Anna, Ape, Interlude, Desire,* and *Iceman.* Illustrations by Hirschfeld.

B15 Atkinson, Jennifer M. *Eugene O'Neill: A Descriptive Bibliography.* Pittsburgh: U of Pittsburgh P, 1974.

Takes up where the Sanborn and Clark bibliography left off in 1931. Appendices include all published acting scripts, O'Neill's contributions to newspapers and periodicals, promo blurbs, auction material and book dealer catalogues, and a listing of plays in anthologies and of film, radio and musical adaptations.

B16 Austin, Gayle. *Feminist Theories for Dramatic Criticism.* Ann Arbor: U of Michigan P, 1990.

Basing her work on Judith Fetterley's *The Resisting Reader,* Austin provides a feminist interpretation of *Iceman* (as well as of plays by Arthur Miller, Lillian Hellman and others) and concludes that O'Neill's play is in a sense "a justification of murder" since the reader/viewer is invited to sympathize with the perpetrator (Hickey) at the expense of the victim (Evelyn). Since women readers/viewers can neither identify with the male perspective presented nor sympathize with the thinly drawn female characters, they might assign blame to womankind for men's problems. Austin provides some production suggestions to circumvent that possibility.

Bloom, Steven F. Rev. *Eugene O'Neill Review* 17.1-2 (1993): 198-205.

B17 Avram, Rachmael ben. "Eugene O'Neill in the Divided Stream." In *Naturalisme Americain.* Eds. Jean Cazemajou and Jean-Claude Barat. Bordeaux-Talence: Maisons des Sciences de l'Homme d'Aquitaine, 1976. 38-47.

A general assessment of O'Neill's place in American theater, which concludes that his work "seemed to fail to arrive at the promised end" (*Journey* being the exception). Referring to Charles Walcutt's *American Literary Naturalism, a Divided Stream,* Avram says that "O'Neill was reacting to the forces which formed the naturalistic movement in the novel, by creating a drama which embodied the very forms Prof. Walcutt describes."

B18 Avrich, Paul. *Anarchist Portraits.* Princeton, NJ: Princeton UP, 1988.

A history of anarchism organized around a series of essays on leading anarchists. Emma Goldman is treated in Chapter 13 ("Jewish Anarchism in the United States," pp.176-99).

Alexander Berkman's career receives its own chapter (Chapter 14, pp. 200-07). V. M. Eikhenbaum, alias Volin, who with Berkman translated *Lazarus* into Russian, receives a chapter (Chapter 8, pp. 125-34). Though there is no reference to *Iceman,* O'Neill appears in the index twice.

B19 Bagchee, Shyamal, ed. *Perspectives on Eugene O'Neill: New Essays.* English Language Studies Monograph Series. Victoria, BC: U of Victoria P, 1988.

A collection of seven essays celebrating the O'Neill centennial. The editor stresses that the mainly biographical and textual approaches are missing from the volume. The essays are:

Shyamal Bagchee's "Reading O'Neill's Poetry" (See B20)

Judith E. Barlow's "O'Neill's Many Mothers: Mary Tyrone, Josie Hogan, and their Antecedents" (See B23)

Stephen A. Black's "Tragic Anagnorisis in *The Iceman Cometh*" (See B47)

Marcia Blumberg's "Eloquent Stammering in the Fog: O'Neill's Heritage in Mamet" (See B57)

Péter Egri's "The Electra Complex of Puritan Morality and the Epic Ambition of O'Neillian Tragedy" (See B142)

Michael Manheim's "The Transcendence of Melodrama in *Long Day's Journey into Night*" (See B269)

James A. Robinson's "The Metatheatrics of *A Moon for the Misbegotten* " (See B361)

Wilkins, Frederick C. Rev. *Eugene O'Neill Review* 13.1 (1989): 81-83.

B20 _____. "Reading O'Neill's Poetry." In *Perspectives on Eugene O'Neill: New Essays.* Ed. Shyamal Bagchee. Victoria, BC: U of Victoria P, 1988. 76-96.

Revisits the playwright's poetry, speculates on why it has been summarily dismissed, reassessing its value, and seeing in it a key to O'Neill's creative temperament.

B21 Baker, George Pierce. *Dramatic Technique.* 1919. New York: Capo, 1976.

A reprint.

B22 Barlow, Judith E. *Final Acts: The Creation of Three Late O'Neill Plays.* Athens: U of Georgia P, 1985.

The product of 12 years of research, *Final Acts* analyzes *Iceman, Journey,* and *Misbegotten,* utilizing O'Neill's notes, drafts, and scenarios. The introduction says the book is "not intended simply as a technical account of O'Neill's composition method in his later years," but also shows the extent of the changes and when the changes were made. Suggests that knowing the playwright's original ideas can explain why a play succeeds or fails and can help us focus on what we might have overlooked in the finished product. See C7.

B23 _____. "O'Neill's Many Mothers: Mary Tyrone, Josie Hogan, and their Antecedents." In *Perspectives On Eugene O'Neill: New Essays*. Ed. Shyamal Bagchee. Victoria, BC: U of Victoria P, 1988. 7-16.

A romp through the canon and a look at the playwright's female characters reveal that "in at least one way O'Neill remained traditional and conservative. His depiction of women only rarely strays from the narrow limits of the conventional male view prevalent in Western culture and literature, or in fact from much of the Catholic ethos with which he grew up." O'Neill's view of women is the outsider's; he imbues them with maternal feeling or condemns them for its lack. Josie is O'Neill's ideal: measured against her all other women are found wanting.

B24 _____. "Mother, Wife, Friend, and Collaborator: Carlotta Monterey and *Long Day's Journey into Night*." In *Eugene O'Neill and the Emergence of American Drama*. Ed. Marc Maufort. Costerus New Series, 75. Amsterdam: Rodopi, 1989. 123-31.

Thinks there is a kinship between Mary Tyrone and Carlotta Monterey and wonders whether *Journey* would have been written had it not been for Carlotta, who may well have influenced the character of Mary.

B25 _____. "Building Characters: Eugene O'Neill's Composition Process." In *Eugene O'Neill in China: An International Centenary Celebration*. Eds. Haiping Liu and Lowell Swortzell. Westport, CT: Greenwood, 1992. 149-55.

Looking at *Iceman's* Hickey and Larry Slade, Barlow addresses O'Neill's creation of character. Out of fact (his life) O'Neill created fiction.

B26 _____. "O'Neill's Female Characters." In *The Companion to Eugene O'Neill*. Ed. Michael Manheim. Cambridge Companions to Literature series. Cambridge: Cambridge UP, 1998. 164-77.

Tracks O'Neill's women characters from his earliest to his last plays. Attention is given to the scholarly-critical debate about whether he really understood women, and whether his treatment of them changed after he met Carlotta.

B27 Behrendt, Patricia Flanagan. "Images of Women and the Burden of Myth: Plagues on the Houses of Gorky and O'Neill." In *Drama and Philosophy*. Themes in Drama, no. 12. Ed. James Redmond. Cambridge: Cambridge UP, 1990. 161-69.

Looks at *The Lower Depths* and *Iceman* in terms of the female image and discovers a similarity in their representation of women; that is, women in these works are seen as destructive, "life-crushing tyrants."

B28 Benchley, Robert. *Benchley at the Theatre: Dramatic Criticism, 1920-1940, by Robert Benchley*. Ed. Charles Getchell. Ipswich, MA: Ipswich P, 1985.

Includes reprints of Benchley's reviews of first productions of *Chillun, Desire, Interlude, Brown, Dynamo*, and *Electra*.

B29 Ben-Zvi, Linda. "'Home Sweet Home': Deconstructing the Masculine Myth of the Frontier in Modern American Drama." In *The Frontier Experience and the American Dream: Essays on American Literature*. College Station: Texas A & M UP, 1989. 217-25.

Looks at O'Neill's work and Arthur Miller's *Death of a Salesman* to find reinforcement for the frontier myth, a myth which, of course, suggests the marginalizing of women and the exalting of men.

B30 _____. "O'Neill and Absurdity." In *Around the Absurd: Essays on Modern and Postmodern Drama*. Eds. Enoch Brater and Ruby Cohn. Ann Arbor: U of Michigan P, 1990. 33-55.

Concerns O'Neill's ties to the Theatre of the Absurd. In staging and visual imagery, in character delineation, in dramatic language and in theatrical artifice we see the connectedness.

B31 _____, ed. *Susan Glaspell: Essays on Her Theatre and Fiction*. Ann Arbor: U of Michigan P, 1995.

A collection of essays the focus of which is not, nor was meant to be, O'Neill. Nonetheless, while he is peripheral, the friendship between the playwrights in O'Neill's formative years makes this volume on Susan Glaspell of interest to O'Neill devotees.

Mandl, Bette. Rev. *Eugene O'Neill Review* 20.1-2 (1996): 153-55.

B32 Bergman, Ingrid. "A Meeting with O'Neill." In *Eugene O'Neill: A World View.* Ed. Virginia Floyd. New York: Ungar, 1979. 293-95.

Ingrid Bergman recalls her meeting with O'Neill in 1941: he talked about his nine-play American-history cycle and his hope of founding a company that would be willing to do all the plays. Such a company, he envisioned, would need to stay together for four years.

B33 Berkowitz, Gerald M. *New Broadways: Theatre Across America 1950-80.* Totowa, NJ: Rowman and Littlefield, 1982.

Useful in putting the O'Neill revival into a context of Off-Broadway activities of the late 1950s and 60s.

B34 _____. *American Drama of the Twentieth Century.* Longman Literature in English Series. London: Longman, 1992.

Surveys twentieth-century American theater history in 200-plus pages. O'Neill has sections in three of the six chapters (pp. 16-21, 30-42, 66-69, 105-14) and some 30 other references. In all, 39 of his plays are touched on. A good introduction for readers who know the plays but not the whole picture. Much back matter (index, bibliography, biography, chronology) makes this handy for students.

B35 Berlin, Normand. *The Secret Cause: A Discussion of Tragedy.* Amherst: U of Massachusetts P, 1981.

A series of chapters ("essays") concerned with seeing the "essence" of tragedy — the operations of fate (the "force behind") which express to us the incomprehensible mystery at the core of things. Chapter 3, "Passion: *Hippolytus, Phaedra, Desire,"* (pp. 33-63) analyzes first Euripides' play, then Racine's, comparing the two, then O'Neill's, comparing it with the other two. *Desire* "has captured the tragic spirit," because "necessity hangs over the play ... in the 'sinister maternity' of two large elms." Eben is seen as Hamlet-like in his role of avenger of the past.

B36 _____. *Eugene O'Neill.* New York: Grove, 1982.

An introductory treatment touching lightly on biography in analyzing O'Neill's major plays. First discusses *Journey* as O'Neill's greatest achievement. Then considers his chief works in chronological order in terms of art and tragic vision: especially *Anna, Ape, Days, Desire, Horizon, Iceman, Jones, Misbegotten,* and *Electra.*

B37 _____, **ed.** *Eugene O'Neill: Three Plays:* Mourning Becomes Electra, The Iceman Cometh, Long Day's Journey into Night: *A Casebook.* London: Macmillan, 1989.

The book is divided into three parts, one part for each play. Within each the procedure is fixed: first O'Neill's own comments (from letters, interviews, work diary); then excerpts from reviews of productions (American and English) by the better-known reviewers; and finally excerpts from critical studies, most by academics. The more recent items are from 1985 (two). Berlin's introduction (pp. 10-18) briefly puts the plays in the context of O'Neill's career, summarizes received opinion about the three and concludes, quoting from O'Neill's famous letter to A. H. Quinn, that each play 1) is "a realistic presentation of life," 2) shows life as ultimately deterministic, and 3) is fundamentally a tragedy.

Mandl, Bette. Rev. *Eugene O'Neill Review* 14.1-2 (1990): 108-10.

B38 _____. *O'Neill's Shakespeare.* Ann Arbor: U of Michigan P, 1993.

Taking the important half of O'Neill's canon for reference and analysis, Berlin finds that a life forged by the fire of Shakespeare's presence cannot escape reproducing, rethinking and reshaping Shakespearean thoughts, values, and dramatic forms. Though the book is highly subjective, Berlin's credentials and experience with both Shakespeare and O'Neill are too solid for his opinions to be taken casually. Good bibliography and index.

Frank, Glenda. Rev. *Theatre Survey* 36.2 (1995): 109-11.

Wilkins, Frederick C. Rev. *Eugene O'Neill Review* 17.1-2 (1993): 196-97.

B39 _____. "The Late Plays." In *The Companion to Eugene O'Neill.* Ed. Michael Manheim. Cambridge Companions to Literature series. Cambridge: Cambridge UP, 1998. 82-95.

Treats of the last six plays — *Touch, Mansions, Iceman, Journey, Misbegotten, Hughie*— in terms of O'Neill's despair at America's loss of spirituality: the world's greatest tragedy, since America had had more than any other nation to start with.

B40 Bermel, Albert. *Contrary Characters: An Interpretation of Modern Theatre.* New York: Dutton, 1973. 105-21.

In the chapter "The Family as Villain" Bermel tries to establish who is ultimately responsible for the problems with the Tyrone family. After finding excuses for or redeeming features in Edmund, Jamie, and Tyrone, he opts for Mary: the play is Mary's tragedy; and she has inflicted the deepest wounds.

B41 _____. "Poetry and Mysticism in O'Neill." In *Eugene O'Neill: A World View*. Ed. Virginia Floyd. New York: Ungar, 1979. 245-51.

Poetry in this case means the yearning of the characters in *Journey*. Mysticism refers to the union they yearn for. The stage imagery in the characters' speeches is used to support the author's thesis that O'Neill was a mystic.

B42 Bernstein, Samuel J. *The Strands Entwined: A New Direction in American Drama*. Boston: Northeastern UP, 1980.

Only passing references to O'Neill.

B43 Bigsby, C. W. E. *A Critical Introduction to Twentieth-Century American Drama*. Vol. 1 (1900-1940). Cambridge: Cambridge UP, 1982.

Chapter 1 ("Provincetown: The Birth of Twentieth-Century American Drama," pp. 1-35) is especially useful in describing the ground in which O'Neill had his roots. Chapter 2 ("Eugene O'Neill," pp. 36-119) is a sensitive, thoughtful survey of O'Neill's career with analyses (and some censuring) of important works. Though not tendentious, it contributes to the understanding of the main themes of O'Neill's achievement. In Appendices 1, 2, and 3 are lists of "Harvard 47 plays, 1913-17;" "Washington Square Players' Productions, 1915-18"; and "Provincetown Plays: 1915-27."

B44 _____. "O'Neill's Endgame." In *Eugene O'Neill and the Emergence of American Drama*. Ed. Marc Maufort. Costerus New Series, 75. Amsterdam: Rodopi, 1989. 159-68.

Iceman and *Hughie* are viewed as plays in which the aging playwright is able creatively to revisit his past. A dry run for the next entry.

B45 _____. *Modern American Drama, 1945-1990*. Cambridge UP, 1992.

In his "reflections on American drama in the second half of the twentieth century" Bigsby offers essays on six playwrights. Chapter Two (pp. 14-31) is entitled "Eugene O'Neill's Endgame." Just after World War II, O'Neill appears as "a ghost haunting an American theatre that had discovered new enthusiasms and new authors." But then O'Neill's last plays —*Journey*, *Iceman* and *Misbegotten*—

are discovered. The final third of the essay attends mostly to *Hughie*, seeing the play as bringing O'Neill close to the Absurdists and to Beckett—in a humor that depends on the nonsequitur, and a language that is purposefully "clotted, clogged and inarticulate" (Bigsby quoting O'Neill). Mention is made of Foucault, Bakhtin and Balthus, but just in passing.

B46 Birko, Alexander S., comp. *Soviet Cinema: Directors and Films*. Hamden, CT: Archon, 1976. 330.

Mentions that the Soviet film *Woman from the Fair* (1928), directed by G. Makarov, and later banned in Russia, was based on O'Neill's *Desire*. It concerned an Italian revolutionary movement.

B47 Black, Stephen A. "Tragic Anagnorisis in *The Iceman Cometh*." In *Perspectives on Eugene O'Neill: New Essays*. Ed. Shyamal Bagchee. Victoria, BC: U of Victoria P, 1988. 17-32.

Looks at *Iceman* as a play which "shows the development of Parritt's insight into his crime, a tragic anagnorisis that leads and permits the youth to seek and accept a fit punishment and exorcism."

B48 _____, comp. *File on O'Neill*. Writer-Files series. London: Methuen, 1993.

A handy pocketbook on O'Neill, part of a series documenting the work of major dramatists of the last 100 years. Each volume of the series contains "a detailed performance history, excerpted reviews and a selection of the writer's own comments on his work."

B49 _____. " 'Celebrant of Loss': Eugene O'Neill 1888-1953." In *The Companion to Eugene O'Neill*. Ed. Michael Manheim. Cambridge Companions to Literature series. Cambridge: Cambridge UP, 1998. 4-17.

The kickoff to the volume and so about O'Neill's life, especially as it is reflected in his plays. A bibliographical note assesses the various biographical works.

B50 _____. *Eugene O'Neill: Beyond Mourning and Tragedy*. New Haven: Yale UP, 1999.

"What is new in this biography is the interpretations made both of numerous small matters and of the large patterns of O'Neill's life, interpretations that grow partly out of their author's professional training and experience as a literary scholar, a psychoanalytic researcher, and, for a time, a clinician." Black argues that O'Neill used his creativity as "a form of self-psychoanalysis," allowing the playwright to mourn his dead. With "object relations theory" as the basis for his approach, Black examines O'Neill's whole life and career. Though there are eight-plus pages of bibliography, it is assumed that the reader will know the major studies of O'Neill's life. Indexed.

B51 Bloom, Harold, ed. *Eugene O'Neill.* Modern Critical Views series. New York: Chelsea House, 1987.

An introduction focusing on *Iceman* and *Journey* that finds O'Neill, even at his best, lacking: he is not really American, Irish Catholic, an artist, a good writer, though more so, or better than, etc., etc. Contains reprints of "a representative collection of the best criticism available upon the plays." Only Van Laan's falls within the scope of this work. The essays are:

C. W. E. Bigsby's "Four Early Plays"

Travis Bogard's "The Historian: *Mourning Becomes Electra* and *Ah, Wilderness!*"

Jean Chothia's "Long Day's Journey into Night: The Dramatic Effectiveness of Supposedly Neutral Dialogue"

Doris Falk's "Fatal Balance: O'Neill's Last Plays"

Arnold Goldman's "The Vanity of Personality: The Development of Eugene O'Neill"

Robert C. Lee's "Evangelism and Anarchy in *The Iceman Cometh* "

Michael Manheim's "Remnants of a Cycle: *A Touch of the Poet* and *More Stately Mansions*"

Lionel Trilling's "Eugene O'Neill"

Thomas F. Van Laan's "Singing in the Wilderness: The Dark Vision of O'Neill's Only Mature Comedy" (See A668)

Wilkins, Frederick C. Rev. *Eugene O'Neill Newsletter* 12.2 (1988): 64-65.

B52 _____, **ed.** *Eugene O'Neill's* Long Day's Journey into Night. Modern Critical Interpretations series. New York: Chelsea House, 1987.

In his eight-page introduction Bloom justifies the playwright's reputation with quotations from O'Neill's most famous play. The book contains a selected bibliography, a chronology of the playwright's life, and ten essays. The essays are all reprints and only two — Orr's and Sewall's — fall within the scope of this work.

C.W.E. Bigsby's "The Retreat Behind Language"

Travis Bogard's "The Door and the Mirror"

Robert Brustein's "The Theatre of Revolt"

Jean Chothia's "Significant Form: *Long Day's Journey into Night* "

Doris V. Falk's "*Long Day's Journey* "

John Orr's "Eugene O'Neill: The Life Remembered" (See B317)

Robert B. Sewall's "*Long Day's Journey into Night* " (See A586)

Timo Tiusanen's "Through the Fog into the Monologue"

Egil Törnqvist's "Life in Terms of Lives"

Raymond Williams' "*Long Day's Journey into Night*: Eugene O'Neill"

Wilkins, Frederick C. Rev. *Eugene O'Neill Newsletter* 12.2 (1988): 64-65.

B53 _____, **ed.** *Eugene O'Neill's* The Iceman Cometh. Modern Critical Interpretations series. New York: Chelsea House, 1987.

Essays on *Iceman* by some eminent O'Neill scholars, all published, originally, too early for this work.

Normand Berlin's "Endings"

Travis Bogard's "The Door and the Mirror: *The Iceman Cometh* "

Jean Chothia's "The Late Plays and the Development of Significant Form: *The Iceman Cometh* "

Cyrus Day's "The Iceman and the Bridegroom"

Robert B. Heilman's "The Drama of Disaster"

Robert C. Lee's "Evangelism and Anarchy in *The Iceman Cometh* "

John Orr's "*The Iceman Cometh* and Modern Society"

Timo Tiusanen's "Composition for Solos and a Chorus: *The Iceman Cometh* "

Bloom in his introductory essay (pp. 1-7) ranges far afield. But when he focuses on *Iceman* (though finding O'Neill unrivaled — except for Dreiser — for "sheer bad writing," to be ignored when he talks about tragedy, and lacking "strength" in "stance" and "style"), he discovers O'Neill to be strong in the dramatic representation of illusions and despair and in the persuasive imitation of human personality, particularly in its self-destructive weaknesses.

Wilkins, Frederick C. Rev. *Eugene O'Neill Newsletter* 12.2 (1988): 64-65.

B54 Bloom, Steven F. "Empty Bottles, Empty Dreams: O'Neill's Use of Drinking and Alcoholism in *Long Day's Journey into Night.*" In *Critical Essays on Eugene O'Neill.* Ed. James J. Martine. Boston: G. K. Hall, 1984. 159-77.

Applies some of the characteristics of alcoholism (self-hatred, denial, cyclical patterns of behavior) to the four Tyrones to show that there is "a vital connection between the [play's] repetitiousness, the vision, and alcoholism."

B55 _____. "Alcoholism and Addiction in *Long Day's Journey into Night.*" In *Readings on Eugene O'Neill.* Ed. Thomas Siebold. The Greenhaven Press Literary Companion Series. San Diego: Greenhaven, 1988.

A reprint; see B54.

B56 Blum, Daniel. *A Pictorial History of the American Theatre: 1860-1976.* 4th ed. enlarged and revised by John Willis. New York: Crown, 1977.

A coffee-table book which includes many pictures of O'Neill and his father and scenes from O'Neill's plays.

B57 Blumberg, Marcia. "Eloquent Stammering in the Fog: O'Neill's Heritage in Mamet." In *Perspectives on Eugene O'Neill: New Essays.* Ed. Shyamal Bagchee. Victoria, BC: U of Victoria P, 1988. 97-111.

Looks at *American Buffalo, Glengarry Glen Ross* and *Edmond* vis-à-vis O'Neill's *Iceman* and concludes that while both playwrights concern themselves with the failure of the American Dream and society's spiritual bankruptcy, their works reveal "variations in leitmotif, tone and emphasis, while their use of language exposes the differing zeitgeist."

B58 Bogard, Travis. "Dreams of Joy, Dreams of Pain." *Eugene O'Neill.* N.p.: n.p., 1978.

Program distributed by Milwaukee Repertory Theater Co. to the audience for the Midwestern and Western tour of *Wilderness* and *Journey.* Literary content supervised by Paul Voelker.

B59 _____. *Contour in Time: The Plays of Eugene O'Neill.* Rev. ed. New York: Oxford UP, 1988.

The significant revisions in this edition of Bogard's 1972 seminal work have to do with the analysis of "A Tale of Possessors Self-Dispossessed," the full text of *Mansions* and *The Calms of Capricorn* having been previously unavailable to the author, and the correction of what Bogard terms "a serious error," the confusion of O'Neill's Bessie Bowen with Mme. Stephen Jumel, also Bessie Bowen.

B60 _____, **ed.** *Eugene O'Neill: The Complete Plays.* New York: Library of America, 1988.

See Primary Works section, G7.

B61 _____. *The Unknown O'Neill.* New Haven: Yale UP, 1988.

See Primary Works section, G55.

B62 _____. *Eugene O'Neill at Tao House.* Tucson, AZ: Southwest Parks and Monuments Association, 1989. Paperback.

Brochure (for the tourists) describing Tao House and the O'Neills' association with it. Pictures.

B63 _____, **ed.** *The Eugene O'Neill Songbook.* Theater and Dramatic Studies 56. Berkeley, CA: East Bay Books, 1993.

The words and music scores to all the songs sung or referred to in O'Neill's plays.

Frank, Glenda. Rev. *Theatre Survey* 36.2 (1995): 111-12.

B64 _____. "*From the Silence of Tao House*": Essays about Eugene and Carlotta O'Neill and the Tao House Plays.* Danville, CA: The Eugene O'Neill Foundation, Tao House, 1993. Hardback and paperback editions.

This book, a gift to the Eugene O'Neill Foundation, Tao House, collects a number of Bogard's writings on O'Neill and his plays that would otherwise be hard to come by: papers read before nonprofessional as well as professional groups (the MLA, the ALITA), program notes, commentaries for NPR as introductions to radio versions of some O'Neill plays. Bogard writes of the Sea Plays, *Jones, Anna, Ape, Touch,* and includes some pages from his *Contour in Time* on *Iceman* and *Hughie.* His longest essay — "O'Neill in Love" (pp. 35-63) — in surveying O'Neill's love life gives a unity to its development not often seen — as if Carlotta were the logical, inevitable and rightful culmination of it. Though not aimed at the scholar, there are six pages of notes and a two-page bibliography.

B65 Bogard, Travis, Richard Moody and Walter J. Meserve. *American Drama.* The "Revels" History of Drama in English, 8. London: Methuen, 1977.

Part 1, Chapters 2 (pp. 24-42) and 4 (pp. 66-76), covers O'Neill and experimental theater under the heading of "Art and Politics."

Part III, Chapter 10 (pp. 219-26), surveys O'Neill's career, giving most attention to the years from *Horizon* on. Solid throughout, but the scope of the book precludes the possibility of its being more than a survey based on received opinion.

B66 Bogard, Travis, and Jackson R. Bryer, eds. *Selected Letters of Eugene O'Neill.* New Haven: Yale UP, 1988.

See Primary Works section, G44.

B67 Bonin, Jane F. *Major Themes in Prize-Winning American Drama.* Metuchen, NJ: Scarecrow, 1975.

Scattered references to O'Neill's plays — *Anna, Interlude, Horizon,* and *Journey.* The themes include: "Women and Marriage" (*Anna* "presupposes the inability of women to survive outside marriage"; *Interlude* "suggests that the role of women is to give themselves to men, to live through men, and to bear children"; *Horizon* presents marriage as "the spoiler of hopes"); "Work and Material Rewards" (*Interlude* denigrates "the get-ahead gospel and upholds the need for vocation"; Tyrone in *Journey* sacrifices his talent for money); "Religion" (*Journey* "seems to underscore the impossibility of finding strength or solace through religion").

B68 Bower, Martha Gilman, ed. *Eugene O'Neill,* More Stately Mansions: *The Unexpurgated Edition.* New York: Oxford UP, 1988.

See Primary Works section, G35.

B69 _____. *Eugene O'Neill's Unfinished* Threnody *and Process of Invention in Four Cycle Plays.* Lewiston, NY: Edwin Mellen, 1992.

Includes transcriptions and summaries of O'Neill's notes and drafts for *Touch, Mansions, The Calms of Capricorn,* and "Hair of the Dog" to show the process by which the plays evolved. The thrust of the work is Bower's comments on and assessment of the playwright's decision-making. In the "Foreword" her former adviser (this book is based on her 1986 doctoral dissertation, for which see C12) describes the work as a companion piece to Judith Barlow's *Final Acts.*

Black, Stephen A. Rev. *Eugene O'Neill Review* 19.1-2 (1995): 150-152.

B70 _____. "The Pathology of Resistance to Cultural Assimilation in Eugene O'Neill's Late Plays." In *Staging Difference*: *Cultural Pluralism in American Theatre and Drama.* Ed. Marc Maufort. American Uni-

versity Studies Series 25. New York: Peter Lang, 1995. 111-19.

Looks to social and cultural analyses of the Irish community to shed light on the behavior of characters in *Journey* and *Touch.* Concludes that "the O'Neill family, the Tyrones, and the Melodys were unable to move beyond their oppositional desires — of wanting to belong and wanting not to belong."

B71 Bradby, David. "Blacking Up — Three Productions by Peter Stein." In *A Radical Stage: Theatre in Germany in the 1970's and 1980's.* Ed. W. G. Sebald. Oxford: Berg, 1988. 18-30.

A look at Schaubühne director Peter Stein's work. Includes a discussion of his 1986 *Ape*, a production which revealed Stein's "crushing pessimism." "Stein's stage images repeatedly stressed the individual's inability to make sense of his life." The use of "a whole arsenal of Expressionist production methods" marked the effort.

B72 Brevda, William. *Harry Kemp: The Last Bohemian.* Lewisburg, PA: Bucknell UP, 1986.

An important fixture in the village and Provincetown community during the O'Neill years, Kemp was an intimate of O'Neill's circle and a familiar of the scenes and artistic life that helped to form O'Neill's life and career between 1915 and 1930. Mostly for background but O'Neill figures amusingly in Kemp's roman à clef *Love Among the Cape Enders* (1931). Solid academic biography, good literary history, and an admirable bibliography. Indexed.

Brooks, Marshall. Rev. *Eugene O'Neill Newsletter* 11.1 (1987): 51.

B73 Brockett, Oscar G., and Robert R. Findley. *Century of Innovation: A History of European and American Theatre and Drama Since 1870.* Englewood Cliffs, NJ: Prentice-Hall, 1973.

A richly detailed and illustrated book of over 800 pages offering what its subtitle says. The sections on America during the period of O'Neill's career, though not directed at O'Neill, do much to establish the context of his work.

B74 Brown, Arvin. "Staging O'Neill's 'Simple Play.'" In *Eugene O'Neill: A World View.* Ed. Virginia Floyd. New York: Ungar, 1979. 288-89.

Concerns the two productions of *Journey* Brown directed (1965 and 1971) and the growth of his understanding of the play.

B75 Brown, John Russell, ed. *The Oxford Illustrated History of Theatre.* Oxford: Oxford UP, 1997.

In a book that "tells the history of theatre from its various beginnings to the present day," the references to O'Neill are predictably sporadic. Two pages (413-14) — and some of that is taken up with a picture from Peter Stein's 1986 production of *Ape* — constitute the only sustained discussion of his achievement.

B76 Brown, Roger. "Causality in O'Neill's Late Masterpieces." In *Eugene O'Neill's Century: Centennial Views on America's Foremost Tragic Dramatist.* Ed. Richard F. Moorton, Jr. Westport, CT: Greenwood, 1991. 41-54.

Notes that in *Misbegotten*, *Journey* and *Iceman*, characters revisit the past — albeit unwillingly — in what Freud called "repetition compulsion" and that references to the past substitute for the action of earlier plays.

B77 Bruccoli, Matthew J., and C. E. Frazer Clark, Jr., comps. *First Printings of Americans Authors: Contributions Towards a Descriptive Checklist.* Vol. 1. Detroit: Gale, 1977.

Lists first editions of plays and collections of plays and non-dramatic works in England and America. Covers O'Neill, pp. 291-96.

B78 Brucher, Richard. "Pernicious Nostalgia in *Glengarry Glen Ross.*" In *David Mamet's* Glengarry Glen Ross: *Text and Performance.* Ed. Leslie Kane. Garland Reference Library of the Humanities/Studies in Modern Drama. New York: Garland, 1996. 211-25.

Since the theme is nostalgia, *Iceman* and *Death of a Salesman* must enter for comparison's sake.

B79 Brüning, Eberhard. "Relations Between Progressive American and German Drama in the Twenties and Thirties." In *Actes du VIIIe Congrès de l'Association internationale de Littérature Comparée/Proceedings of the 8th Congress of the International Comparative Literature Association.* Eds. Bela Köpeczi and György M. Vajda. Vol. 1. Stuttgart: Bieber, 1980. 789-95.

Sees the German and American theaters of the 1920s and 1930s as belonging to an international theatrical scene. The "relations" of the title are the result of socio-economic experiences common to the Western World that propel the various nations' theaters to express similar values, using similar experimental techniques. "The same kind of environment, the same kind of social conditions, the same aims and ideological positions led to similar themes and techniques, made an inspiring exchange of material and experience possible and produced similar effects in different places." Among many references are some to *Jones, Ape, Brown,* and *Chillun.*

B80 Bryan, George B., and Wolfgang Mieder, comps. *The Proverbial Eugene O'Neill: An Index to Proverbs in the Works of Eugene Gladstone O'Neill.* Westport, CT: Greenwood, 1995.

In a 77-page introductory essay Bryan and Mieder, theater historian and folklorist, address O'Neill's use of proverbs — their sources and context. But the book's meat is the encyclopedic key-word index, identifying what the authors term O'Neill's "astonishing" use of proverbs, their precise location in the canon and the date of utterance. Also included in this 359-page study are appendices indicating distribution and frequency.

Bloom, Steven F. Rev. *Eugene O'Neill Review* 17.1-2 (1993): 198-205.

B81 Bryer, Jackson R., ed. *"The Theatre We Worked For": The Letters of Eugene O'Neill to Kenneth Macgowan.* New Haven: Yale UP, 1982.

See Primary Works section, G49.

B82 _____. "'Peace is an Exhausted Reaction to Normal': O'Neill's Letters to Dudley Nichols." In *Critical Essays on Eugene O'Neill.* Ed. James J. Martine. Boston: G. K. Hall, 1984. 33-55.

See Primary Works section, G40.

B83 _____. "O'Neill's Letters to Donald Pace: A Newly DiscoveredCorrespondence." In *Eugene O'Neill and the Emergence of American Drama.* Ed. Marc Maufort. Costerus New Series, 75. Amsterdam: Rodopi, 1989. 133-48.

See Primary Works section, G38.

B84 Bryfonski, Dedria, and Phyllis Carmel Mendelson, eds. *Twentieth-Century Literary Criticism.* Vol. 1. Detroit: Gale, 1978. 381-407.

Reprints excerpts from a selection of criticism — both contemporarily with O'Neill's career and posthumously — from Alexander Woollcott's 1920 review of *Horizon* to Carl Tucker's 1976 review of *Journey.*

B85 Burkman, Katherine H. *The Arrival of Godot: Ritual Patterns in Modern Drama.* Rutherford, NJ: Fairleigh Dickinson UP [Associated U Presses], 1986.

The introduction (Chapter One) shows us *The Wild Duck* and *Iceman* as aids to an understanding of Beckett: his ritualism (in Ibsen and O'Neill a birthday party) and theme (the arrival of someone who brings salvation — or damnation). Scattered remarks thereafter.

Connolly, Thomas F. Rev. *Eugene O'Neill Newsletter* 12.2 (1988): 65-67.

B86 Burns, Morris U. *The Dramatic Criticism of Alexander Woollcott.* Metuchen, NJ: Scarecrow, 1980. 85-92.

The 180-page text includes Woollcott's comments on some 18 O'Neill plays. The 95-page appendix — a list of over 1500 play reviews by Woollcott — includes citations for reviews of 14 original O'Neill productions up to 1928. The appendix, arranged alphabetically by play title, is not covered by the index.

B87 Burr, Suzanne. "O'Neill's Ghostly Women." In *Feminist Rereadings of Modern American Drama.* Ed. June Schlueter. Rutherford, NJ: Fairleigh Dickinson UP, 1989. 37-47.

Taking issue with conventional wisdom that O'Neill's absent women provide proof of his misogyny, and therefore of his affinity to Strindberg, Burr suggests that O'Neill empathizes with the women, acknowledging the power they have over men, an approach which aligns him with Ibsen. She looks at *Desire, Ile, Anna,* and *Journey* in arguing her thesis.

B88 Carpenter, Frederic I. *Eugene O'Neill.* 2nd ed. Boston: Twayne, 1979.

A revision of the 1964 edition. The advances in scholarship and criticism of the preceding 15 years are mainly handled in endnotes and in a new critique of *Hughie.*

B89 _____. *Eugene O'Neill.* Rev. ed. Twayne's United States Authors Series, 66. Twayne, 1991. Computer Optical Disc; 4 3/4 in. + 5 System requirements: IBM PC or PS/2 and compatibles; 640K RAM; 512.7K available memory; DOS 3.1 or higher; MS DOS extensions 2.0 or higher; hard disk drive (or card); compact disc drive.

Disk version of the 1979 edition.

B90 Cerf, Bennett. *At Random: The Reminiscences of Bennett Cerf.* New York: Random House, 1977.

A construction, apparently by Phyllis Cerf Wagner and Albert Erskine, based principally on a number of interviews as part of the Columbia Oral History program. Scattered recollections of contacts with the O'Neills by his publisher (see especially pp. 81-89).

B91 Chabrowe, Leonard. *Ritual and Pathos: The Theater of O'Neill.* Lewisburg, PA: Bucknell UP, 1976.

An expansion of his "Dionysus in *The Iceman Cometh*" (*Modern Drama* 4 [1962]: 377-88). Considers O'Neill's theory of tragedy as ritual, and finds that O'Neill's greatest works are cathartic in effect and move the audience to pathos.

Raleigh, John Henry. Rev. *American Literature* 49.1 (1977): 132-34.

B92 Chaplin, Patrice. *Hidden Star: Oona O'Neill Chaplin: A Memoir.* London: Richard Cohen Books, 1995.

Patrice Chaplin's memories of her former ex mother-in-law, Oona O'Neill, extend from 1965 until Oona's death in 1991. Though we receive no enlightenment about Eugene O'Neill (what is presented here is received wisdom or second, third-hand "scuttlebutt"), we are "entertained" with the continuing saga of the O'Neill family curse — drugs, booze and depression.

B93 Chatterji, Ruby. "Existentialist Approach to Modern American Drama." In *Existentialism in American Literature.* Ed. Ruby Chatterji. Atlantic Highlands, NJ: Humanities, 1983. 80-98. [Papers read at, or contributed to, a seminar held at Hindu College, Delhi U, in Oct. 1980.]

Deals some with Albee and Arthur Miller, but gives most attention to O'Neill and carefully analyzes *Iceman* and *Journey.* Sees both plays as reflecting in many ways the existential vision — an illusionless view of life. But O'Neill does not accept the final existential position, feeling that recognition of a need for hope justifies belief in illusions. However, both Larry, in *Iceman,* and Edmund, in *Journey,* achieve a sense of "authenticity of self and a mental state of revolt" — a state existentialists advocate.

B94 Chothia, Jean. *Forging a Language: A Study of the Plays of Eugene O'Neill.* Cambridge: Cambridge UP, 1979.

Shows O'Neill's handling of a range of language: colloquial American in his early plays, standard American in the middle plays, and Irish dialect and Broadway slang in the later plays. Appendices contain a list of

O'Neill's reading before 1914, notes on works that influenced his plays, and a good bibliography.

B95 _____. "Theatre Language: Word and Image in *The Hairy Ape*." In *Eugene O'Neill and the Emergence of American Drama*. Ed. Marc Maufort. Costerus New Series, 75. Amsterdam: Rodopi, 1989. 31-40.

The recent Schaubühne (Berlin) Company's successful production of *Ape* inspires Chothia's discussion of scenic effects in the play, which are "thematic not casual."

B96 _____. "Register and Idiolect in *The Iceman Cometh* and *Long Day's Journey into Night*." In *Eugene O'Neill in China: An International Centenary Celebration*. Eds. Haiping Liu and Lowell Swortzell. Westport, CT: Greenwood, 1992. 157-63.

Definitions: *register* refers to the range of languages one may speak (from the colloquial to the literary); *idiolect* to those features of language that distinguish one speaker from all others. The characters in *Iceman* reflect the latter; those in *Journey* the former. "O'Neill's sense of the way phatic elements of conversation suggest relationships between speakers, his responsiveness to the patterns of actual conversation, and his capacity to transform these elements into dramatic dialogue, to create words in action, is [sic] fundamental to his drama and helps [sic] establish his claim to being one of the major world dramatists."

B97 _____. "Trying to Write the Family Play: Autobiography and the Dramatic Imagination." In *The Companion to Eugene O'Neill*. Ed. Michael Manheim. Cambridge Companions to Literature series. Cambridge: Cambridge UP, 1998. 192-205.

Shows how O'Neill's means of skating around his true life story in his early plays become the foundation for the shaping of *Journey,* so that he can finally speak his tale directly. And as he had "absorbed [his] shaping devices from Ibsen, Tolstoi and Synge, so his dramatic tropes and motifs have been absorbed into subsequent American drama where secrets and concealments abound."

B98 Choudhuri, A. D. *The Face of Illusion in American Drama*. Atlantic Highlands, NJ: Humanities, 1979. 74-93.

Studies the manipulation of illusion in modern American drama (that is, the first half of the twentieth century)—the great dream in conflict with the pursuit of materialism. Be-sides *Iceman*, Choudhari treats of Rice's *The Adding Machine*, Miller's *Death of a Salesman*, Odets' *Golden Boy*, Williams' *The Glass Menagerie,* and Albee's *Who's Afraid of Virginia Woolf?* Sees *Iceman* as rejecting middle class values and aspirations, emphasizing the importance of illusions, minimizing the importance of truth.

B99 Clurman Harold. *The Divine Pastime*. 1946. New York: Macmillan, 1974.

A reprint with additions. One addition—on O'Neill—was a review, first printed 10 May 1971, of the film of *Journey*.

B100 Cobb, Mel. "O'Neill or Sunny Days and Starry Nights: An Original Play." In *Eugene O'Neill and the Emergence of American Drama*. Ed. Marc Maufort. Costerus New Series, 75. Amsterdam: Rodopi, 1989. 181-204.

See H9.

B101 Cohn, Ruby. "Oh, God, I Hate This Job." In *Approaches to Teaching Miller's Death of a Salesman*. Ed. Matthew C. Roudane. Approaches to Teaching World Literature. New York: MLA, 1995. 155-62.

Looks at the salesmen and selling in *Iceman, Death of a Salesman,* and Mamet's *Glengarry Glen Ross*.

B102 Colburn, Steven E. "*The Long Voyage Home*: Illusion and the Tragic Pattern of Fate in O'Neill's *S. S. Glencairn* Cycle." In *Critical Essays on Eugene O'Neill*. Ed. James J. Martine. Boston: G. K. Hall, 1984. 55-65.

Finds in *Caribbees, Cardiff, Zone,* and *Voyage* unity in that they have the same central conflict, one between the forces of illusion and actuality. In each play the protagonist tries to preserve his illusion. Also notes the Nietzschean influence in these plays.

B103 Cole, Susan Letzler. *The Absent One: Mourning Ritual, Tragedy, and the Performance of Ambivalence*. University Park: Pennsylvania State UP, 1985.

Looks at tragedy in the light of rituals of mourning. "The collective death of the characters is the unacknowledged situation of the play. The refusal to admit, and mourn, what is dead in the lives of each of the characters is the refusal to recover what is still living." *Iceman* appears only in the last chapter, as one of a short list of plays that "resist [Cole's] theory of tragedy" (pp. 160-65). Hickey's plea of insanity is what ultimately releases the characters from their mourning to restore their pipedreams.

Black, Stephen A. Rev. *Eugene O'Neill Newsletter* 12.2 (1988): 67-68.

B104 ____. *The Absent One: Mourning Ritual, Tragedy, and the Performance of Ambivalence.* 1985. University Park: Pennsylvania State UP, 1991.

Paperback reprint of the 1985 work.

B105 Columbia Literary History of the United States. Gen. ed. Emory Elliott. New York: Columbia UP, 1988.

In a work which gives Henry Adams a longer chapter than it does Hawthorne, Melville, Whitman, Dickinson, Twain or Henry James, there is little space left for O'Neill or, indeed, for American drama. Among twentieth-century writers, Hemingway, Fitzgerald, Gertrude Stein, Pound, Eliot, W. C. Williams, Wallace Stevens and Frost are prioritized by chapter headings. Frost even gets a chapter all to himself— 25 pages. O'Neill gets two-plus pages in the one chapter devoted to American drama. And those two-plus pages cover 16 O'Neill plays. O'Neill thrice chewed.

B106 Combs, Robert. "O'Neill and Horovitz: Toward Home." In *Israel Horovitz: A Collection of Critical Essays.* Ed. Leslie Kane. Westport, CT: Greenwood, 1994. 39-49.

Traces themes in Horovitz's work back to O'Neill: the unfulfilled promise, the prodigal son, materialism, etc.

B107 Commins, Dorothy. *What Is an Editor? Saxe Commins at Work.* Chicago: Chicago UP, 1978.

Two chapters deal exclusively with the relationship between O'Neill and Commins. Some letters are included as well as insights into O'Neill's life with Carlotta and his writing of *Journey*. See A603.

Sheaffer, Louis. Rev.-note. *Eugene O'Neill Newsletter* 2.2 (1978): 7-8.

B108 ____, ed. *"Love and Admiration and Respect": The O'Neill-Commins Correspondence.* Durham: Duke UP, 1986.

See Primary Works section, G33.

B109 Cooley, John R. *Savages and Naturals: Black Portraits by White Writers in Modern American Literature.* Newark: U of Delaware P, 1982. 59-72.

Despite the praise heaped upon O'Neill for moving the depiction of a black man "beyond the level of the minstrel show" in *Jones*, Cooley says the play still "exploits those stereotypes in the white imagination which associate blacks with the savage and a jungle landscape."

B110 ____. "In Pursuit of the Primitive: Black Portraits by Eugene O'Neill and other Village Bohemians." In *The Harlem Renaissance Re-Examined.* Ed. Victor A. Kramer. New York: AMS, 1987. 51-64.

Focuses on how white writers of the 1920s drew black characters and especially on how O'Neill created the characters in *Jones*. Concludes that "Despite the new consciousness that was growing in Harlem, we have seen that some of the old stereotypes of blacks persisted in white literature, and that certain new ones were created. No matter how complimentary the intention, the result is a quality of racial predisposition that impedes realistic depiction of black lives."

B111 ____. "White Writers and the Harlem Renaissance." In *The Harlem Renaissance: Revaluations.* Eds. Amritjit Singh, et al. New York: Garland, 1989. 13-22.

No matter how sophisticated black culture of the Harlem Renaissance was, for many white writers, including Eugene O'Neill, it furnished "portraits in the primitive." Cooley refers to O'Neill's *Jones* as proof.

B112 Cooper, Burton L. "Some Problems in Adapting O'Neill for Film." In *Eugene O'Neill's Century: Centennial Views on America's Foremost Tragic Dramatist.* Ed. Richard F. Moorton, Jr. Westport, CT: Greenwood, 1991. 73-86.

Tries "to account for the failure of films (both movies and television versions) and to indicate some things these adaptations reveal about the nature of O'Neill's art." Concludes that better versions would require "freer" adaptations, so that the director would not be constrained by the text but would capture the essence of the play.

B113 Counts, Michael L. *Coming Home: The Soldier's Return in Twentieth-Century American Drama.* America University Studies: Series 4, English Language and Literature, no. 63. New York: Peter Lang, 1988.

Examines 55 twentieth-century American plays including *Electra*. In Chapter Three "the plays are analyzed for common thematic concerns." The analysis is ordered into sections dealing with the homecomer's "Physical and Mental Handicaps" and "Altered Perceptions of Society," with "Society's Reception" of him, with his "Spouse, Fiancée, Loved One," and with him as "Ghost/Spirit." Only two of the plays antedate *Electra*. An appendix lists non-American plays with homecomer themes, of which 28 antedate *Electra*. In its original form this book was a dissertation ("The Twentieth-Century Homecomer Play," CUNY, 1983).

B114 Cronin, Harry C. *Eugene O'Neill: Irish and American: A Study in Cultural Context.* New York: Arno, 1977.

Stresses those features traditionally associated with the Irish (their Catholicism, their concern with family, their loquacity) and applies them to the canon. Finds that although Irish Catholicism is not the only, or necessary, consideration, it adds a meaningful dimension to the appreciation of O'Neill. Originally a doctoral dissertation ("The Plays of Eugene O'Neill in the Cultural Context of Irish American Catholicism," U of Minnesota, 1968).

B115 Cunningham, Frank R. "Romantic Elements in Early O'Neill." In *Critical Essays on Eugene O'Neill.* Ed. James J. Martine. Boston: G. K. Hall, 1984. 65-72.

Discusses *Horizon, Anna, Jones, Ape, Desire,* and *Mariner* in terms of "Romantic motifs and mythic patterns: dynamic organicism, the creative imagination as the basic process of Romantic affirmation of the organic universe, man's archetypal journey from stasis to recognition of the existence of such a universe, the concept of timelessness or Edenic time, and the cyclical nature of existence."

B116 _____. *Sidney Lumet: Film and Literary Vision.* Lexington: U of Kentucky P, 1991.

Looks at Lumet's work — *The Pawnbroker, Twelve Angry Men, Equus* — and, of particular interest to O'Neillians, at the film version of *Journey,* for which he has only "raves." Points out Lumet's alterations of/departures from the text, alterations/departures which give Mary a prominence that influences the viewer's interpretation of the play.

Johnson, Robert K. Rev. *Eugene O'Neill Review* 16.1 (1992): 124-26.

B117 Dahl, Liisa. "The Connective Links between the Dialogue and the Interior Monologue Passages in Eugene O'Neill's *Strange Interlude.*" In *Studies in Classical and Modern Philology Presented to Y. M. Biese on the Occasion of his Eightieth Birthday 4.1.1983.* Eds. Iiro Kajanto, et al. Helsinki: Suomalainen Tiedeakademia, 1982. 23-32.

Builds on Tiusanen and a 1963 study by Y. M. Biese as well as on semantic studies by Erik Andersson, M. A. K. Halliday, R. Hasan, Nils Erik Enkvist, and Jan-Ola Ostman to examine "the connective links between the dialogue and the interior monologue passages" and those between the stage directions and the interior monologues of *Interlude.* Finds "a number of text-linguistic and stylistic features" functioning as such links and contributing to the "coherence of the text of the play."

B118 D'Andrea, Paul. "Thou Starre of Poets: Shakespeare as DNA." In *Shakespeare: Aspects of Influence.* Harvard English Studies 7. Ed. G. B. Evans. Cambridge, MA: Harvard UP, 1976. 163-91.

Deals with Tom Stoppard, Slowomir Mrozek, and O'Neill. The O'Neill section (pp. 179-88) argues that the two icons of *Journey* are the Virgin and Shakespeare. Points out the frequency of the Shakespeare allusions. Edmund's control is the sea, Mary's the Virgin, and James's Shakespeare. Shakespeare appears to us as "living and life-giving power."

B119 Dardis, Thomas A. "Turn Back the Universe and Give Me Yesterday." In *The Thirsty Muse.* New York: Ticknor and Fields, 1989. 211-56.

One section in this book on alcoholic writers is devoted appropriately to O'Neill, wherein we look at the playwright's relationship to alcohol and the effect it had on his productivity. For most writers alcohol, we are told, diminishes artistic creativity. O'Neill overcame his addiction and wrote his greatest plays sober.

Bloom, Steven F. Rev. *Eugene O'Neill Review* 13.2 (1989): 97-105.

B120 _____. *Firebrand: The Life of Horace Liveright.* New York: Random House, 1995.

As head of Boni and Liveright, Liveright was O'Neill's first real publisher. His professional and social worlds overlapped with O'Neill's. Though Dardis has had access to sources (for example, Manuel Komroff's unpublished life of the publisher) which were not available when Walker Gilmer wrote his 1970 study, Dardis adds nothing to our knowledge of O'Neill. However seeing O'Neill *in the background* is a good reminder of the value of perspective.

B121 Davis, Walter A. *Get the Guests: Psychoanalysis, Modern American Drama, and* *the Audience*. Madison: U of Wisconsin P, 1994.

Chapters One and Four treat of *Iceman* ("Souls on Ice," pp. 13-59) and *Journey* ("Drug of Choice," pp. 147-208) respectively. The other chapters deal with *A Streetcar Named Desire*, *Death of a Salesman*, and *Who's Afraid of Virginia Woolf?* Davis assumes that the readers/viewers/critics study texts/performances in order to conquer them so that plays won't subvert their illusions about themselves: in effect literary theory is a defense mechanism. Davis' goal is to reverse the process of literary criticism and to "retrieve the hidden drama that is at the heart of all dramas." *Iceman* gives us "an in-depth analysis of group psychology by dramatizing the process whereby the repressed truths of group behavior come to light." Ultimately we are made "to confront death as the truth binding groups." *Journey* is "a drama where no one gets off the hook," not even the audience whose sympathies keep shifting with the focus on the characters. In *Journey* we see how familial ties are used for destructive ends.

B122 Dearborn, Mary V. *Queen of Bohemia: The Life of Louise Bryant.* Boston: Houghton Mifflin, 1996.

A solid, scholarly biography, strong on primary sources, but including all important secondary studies in the documentation. The O'Neill connection is given its proper weight and place in Bryant's history. Nothing new except the perspective, since with the Gelbs, Sheaffer, Boulton, Baskin and Rosenstone, the data, as well as the perspectives of O'Neill, Agnes, and John Reed, are already on record. The association between the artistic and journalistic worlds in the second decade of the twentieth century is well illuminated.

B123 Deshpande, Satish. "The Sense of Guilt in *The Emperor Jones*." In *T. S. Eliot & Eugene O'Neill: The Dream and the Nightmare*. Eds. V. R. N. Prasad, et al. New Delhi: Ajanta, 1991. 129-32.

Sees Jones's flight as "a product of his sense of guilt."

B124 Dewhurst, Colleen. *Colleen Dewhurst: Her Autobiography.* Tom Viola (Contributor). New York: Scribner, 1997.

By her death in 1991, Colleen Dewhurst had "roughed out" about two-thirds of this work. Viola, who had helped till then, took over and added from interviews. The book is enlightening about O'Neill, less so about her contributions to the roles she played in *Desire*, *Wilderness*, *Journey* and *Misbegotten*.

B125 Ditsky, John. "O'Neill's Evangel of Peace: *The Iceman Cometh*." In *The Onstage Christ: Studies in the Persistence of a Theme*. London: Vision, 1980. 93-110.

Essays on plays both modern and contemporary which contain Christ-figures. *Iceman*'s biblical overtones lead to the conclusion that the Christhood is "diffused" in the play. Both Parritt and Hickey are in ways Christ-like.

B126 Duberman, Martin Bauml. *Paul Robeson.* New York: Knopf, 1988.

Readable, sizeable (over 800 pages), scholarly (with 200 pages of very useful notes), thorough (Duberman not only used the "indispensable" Sheaffer volumes, but drew, also, from his correspondence with Sheaffer). For most of the O'Neill connection the reader may turn to Chapter Four—"The Provincetown Playhouse (1922-1924)." Robeson, we remember, played, with critical success, in *Jones* (O'Neill preferred Gilpin), *Chillun*, and *Ape*.

B127 Dubost, Thierry. *Struggle, Defeat or Rebirth: Eugene O'Neill's Vision of Humanity.* Jefferson, NC: McFarland, 1997.

Dubost's subject is "humanity confronted with the world in the theatre of Eugene O'Neill." Looking at 49 of O'Neill's plays, Dubost argues that what links the plays together is the theme of man's relationship to his world. The book, based on his dissertation (Université de Paris–Sorbonne, see D226), is divided into three parts: man's relationship to his family, the relationship between couples, and the conflict between the need to find one's self and the need to escape. He concludes that what gives unity to the plays is rebirth and that O'Neill is not the consummate pessimist critics would have him to be.

B128 Dunning, John. *Tune in Yesterday: The Ultimate Encyclopedia of Old-Time Radio, 1925-1976.* Englewood Cliffs, NJ: Prentice-Hall, 1976.

Several references to 1930s and 1940s radio dramatizations of O'Neill's plays.

B129 Durnell, Mazel B. "Eugene O'Neill and the Far East." *Japanese Cultural Influences on American Poetry and Drama*. Tokyo: Hokuseido, 1983. 147-64.

Introductory-level essay on O'Neill's interest in the Far East, a mention of plays which refer to the area, and a look at the relevant parts of his biography. Mention is made of O'Neill's interest in oriental philosophy as reflected in *Mansions*. References to *Touch, Journey, Electra,* and *Lazarus.*

B130 Eben, Michael C. "Georg Kaiser's *Von Morgens bis Mitternachts* and Eugene O'Neill's *Emperor Jones*: Affinities in Flight." In *Georg Kaiser: eine Aufsatzsammlung nach einem Symposium in Edmonton, Kanada.* Eds. Holger A. Pausch and Ernest Reinhold. Berlin: Agora, 1980. 263-76.

Compares Kaiser's play to O'Neill's in terms of characterization, use of expressionistic techniques, and structure.

B131 Eddleman, Floyd Eugene, comp. *American Theatre Criticism: Supplement II.* Hamden, CT: Shoe String, 1976.

Offers a highly selective list of readings and, where possible, reviews of major productions for each of O'Neill's plays. Organized alphabetically by play title. O'Neill material, pp. 119-29.

B132 Egan, Leona Rust. *Provincetown as a Stage: Provincetown, The Provincetown Players, and the Discovery of Eugene O'Neill.* Orleans, MA: Parnassus Imprints, 1994.

Here is a history of the town and its association with the bohemians who inhabited that remote section of the Cape at a critical period. Egan describes the town's ambience, depicts the quirks of character of the Provincetown lot, explains the complicated relationships among the players, and suggests their achievement. Though O'Neill's love life is given a rather more sensational treatment than strict accuracy would call for, the coverage of his association with Provincetown is useful. The bibliography is an intelligent one; much use of special collections and archives. Notes, index, and an appendix containing a listing of the Players' 1915 and 1916 seasons are included.

Wilkins, Frederick C. Rev. *Eugene O'Neill Review* 17.1-2 (1993): 207-08.

B133 Egri, Péter. "The Social and Psychological Aspects of the Conflict in Eugene O'Neill's *Mourning Becomes Electra*." In *Studies in English and American.* Eds. Erzsebet Perenyi and Tibor Frank. Vol. 2. Budapest: Dept. of English, L. Eotvos UP, 1975. 171-214.

A loosely-structured discussion of a variety of motifs in *Electra* (fate, puritanism,

Oedipal and Electra complexes) and of the structure of the epic. Concludes that the characters are "balanced"—eliciting neither approval nor condemnation.

B134 _____. "The Use of the Short Story in O'Neill's and Chekhov's One-Act Plays: A Hungarian View of O'Neill." In *Eugene O'Neill: A World View.* Ed. Virginia Floyd. New York: Ungar, 1979. 115-44.

Although as a young man O'Neill was fond of reading Chekhov, his similarities to Chekhov are in his later work. These similarities are based on an intellectual and emotional rapport and a tendency to think in terms of the short story before dramatizing. Includes a list of Hungarian productions from 1928-78.

B135 _____. "The Epic Tradition of the European Drama and the Birth of the American Tragedy." In *Actes du VIIIe Congrès de l'Association Internationale de Littérature comparée/Proceedings of the 8th Congress of the International Comparative Literature Association/ Trois grandes mutations Littéraires: Renaissance, Lumières, début de vingtième siècle/ Three Epoch-Making Literary Changes: Renaissance, Enlightenment, Early Twentieth Century.* Eds. Bela Köpeczi and György M. Vajda. Stuttgart: Bieber, 1980. 753-59.

Sees *Interlude* as "indicative of the crystallization of a formal pattern ... whose operation is ... laid down in Hegel's philosophy of history" wherein an "historical tendency is the sum total of individual behaviors," a sum, however, "different from the conflicting wishes of the individuals." In the foreground of *Interlude*, the concern is with alienation; in the background, we know that the "mass-character of alienation" has its source in "the inhumanity of World War I."

B136 _____. "'Belonging' Lost: Alienation and Dramatic Form in Eugene O'Neill's *The Hairy Ape*." In *Critical Essays on Eugene O'Neill.* Ed. James J. Martine. Boston: G. K. Hall, 1984. 77-111.

A reprint; see A180.

B137 _____. "European Origins and American Originality: The Case of Drama." In *American Culture.* Ed. Tibor Frank. Budapest: Akadémiai Kiadó, 1984. 405-22.

Although he does not define terms, Egri uses the word *epic* to mean *large-scale*. His article discusses O'Neill's *Iceman, Interlude,* and "A Tale of Possessors Self-Dispossessed" as epic works. Explains that, though the epic is a European creation, Americans have "received and reshaped" it so that they in turn have provided inspiration to European writers.

B138 _____. *Chekhov and O'Neill: The Uses of the Short Story in Chekhov's and O'Neill's Plays.* Budapest: Akadémiai Kiadó, 1986.

While focusing on the affinities between short stories and the two playwrights' dramas, Egri addresses the larger question of the connections between the genres. There are four ways to incorporate the elements of the short story into the drama, according to Egri: a short story can be transformed into a short play, the turn in the tale becoming the dramatic climax; "the cascade connection, metamorphosing short dramatic units into a cogent whole"; "shaping the peak of the dramatic structure by making use of a short-story-like culmination involving a sudden change in the direction of the action"; and the mosaic design, which entails restructuring short story motifs and elements into a new dramatic whole. By way of arguing his thesis — that both playwrights used these short story devices in their drama — Egri shows Chekhov's influence on O'Neill and provides detailed discussions of a number of O'Neill's [and Chekhov's] plays: *Touch, Misbegotten, Iceman, Journey, Hughie.*

B139 _____. "High Culture and Popular Culture in Eugene O'Neill (*Strange Interlude.*)" In *High and Low in American Culture.* Ed. Charlotte Kretzoi. Budapest: L. Eötvös UP, 1986. 55-76.

Interlude marks a departure for O'Neill in two respects: its depiction in realistic detail of the aftermath of World War I and its incorporation of the novel into the drama. Egri discusses "the interchange of the epic and dramatic motivations of *Interlude*'s action" and contends that the play is a good example of both high and low culture because "it melds the classicism of epic drama with the psychological realism of the modern novel. "

B140 _____. "Synge and O'Neill: Inspiration and Influence." In *Literary Interrelations: Ireland, England and the World.* Eds. Wolfgang Zach and Heinz Kosok. Tübingen: Gunter Narr, 1987. 261-68.

Finds that "the scope of similarities between Synge and O'Neill ranges from inspiration to influence; from typological convergence to parallels of theme, treatment, mood and motif."

B141 _____. *The Birth of American Tragedy.* Budapest: Tankönyvkiadó, 1988.

Though the title may suggest a broader scope, the book focuses on O'Neill. In a work that tries to address the question of why drama in America was a late-bloomer and that makes a case for the unfolding of American tragedy as a combination of European origins and Yankee originality, Egri analyzes several of O'Neill's plays. Chapter One discusses the influence of Shakespeare on American drama. Chapter Two is entitled "Critical Approaches to the Birth of Modern American Tragedy: The Significance of Eugene O'Neill." Chapter Three examines *The Personal Equation.* In Chapter Four *Ape* is discussed. Chapter Five, includes discussions of *Interlude, Electra,* "A Tale of Possessors Self-Dispossessed," *Touch, Mansions,* and *The Calms of Capricorn,* and Chapter Six, "Alienation and Tragedy," looks at *Journey.* Extensive notes, including a "thematic bibliography," are included.

Wilkins, Frederick C. Rev. *Eugene O'Neill Review* 13.1 (1989): 83-86.

B142 _____. "The Electra Complex of Puritan Morality and the Epic Ambition of O'Neillian Tragedy." In *Perspectives on Eugene O'Neill: New Essays.* Ed. Shyamal Bagchee. Victoria, BC: U of Victoria P, 1988. 43-60.

Argues that all 13 acts of the vast trilogy are patterned by an underlying central opposition: "the fatal and inevitable conflict between the deadly austerity of New England Puritanism and the explosion of emotions revolting against it." Though the revolt is doomed, the audience is in sympathy with those seeking emotional freedom.

B143 Eisen, Kurt. *The Inner Strength of Opposites: O'Neill's Novelistic Drama and the Melodramatic Imagination.* Athens: U of Georgia P, 1994.

O'Neill's goal was "to write novelistic drama" which would recapitulate "the nineteenth-century novel's simultaneous assimilation and disruption of a melodramatic code, presenting post-melodramatic images of self, marriage, and the family." So "the ideology of melodrama" would become "both the subject of history, and a critique that forms the powerful subtext" of his later plays. Eisen draws on the canon, but devotes their own chapters to *Journey, Iceman,* and *Hughie.* Notes and a bibliography. See C31.

Manheim, Michael. Rev. *Eugene O'Neill Review* 19.1-2 (1995): 53-56.

B144 ____. "O'Neill on Screen." In *The Companion to Eugene O'Neill*. Ed. Michael Manheim. Cambridge Companions to Literature series. Cambridge: Cambridge UP, 1998. 116-34.

After a consideration of which adapts itself more sympathetically to plays, television or film (television wins), there follows an account and survey of adaptations of O'Neill plays from the 1923 silent *Anna* on. Useful bibliography.

B145 Eldridge, Florence. "Reflections on *Long Day's Journey into Night:* First Curtain Call for Mary Tyrone." In *Eugene O'Neill: A World View*. Ed. Virginia Floyd. New York: Ungar, 1979. 286-87.

Florence Eldridge, who played Mary in the American premiere of *Journey*, recalls preparing for her role.

B146 Elsom, John, ed. *Post-War British Theatre Criticism*. London: Routledge, 1981. 209-16.

Includes excerpts of reviews of *Journey* that opened at the Old Vic (National Theatre) 21 Dec. 1971, starring Laurence Olivier.

B147 Elwood, William R. "Eugene O'Neill's *Dynamo* and the Expressionist Canon." In *Eugene O'Neill in China: An International Centenary Celebration*. Eds. Haiping Liu and Lowell Swortzell. Westport, CT: Greenwood, 1992. 129-36.

Addresses German expressionistic elements in *Dynamo*, the O'Neill play which most clearly shows their influence.

B148 Englund, Claes, and Gunnel Bergström, eds. *Strindberg, O'Neill and the Modern Theatre*. Addresses and Discussions at a Nobel Symposium at the Royal Dramatic Theatre, Stockholm. Jönköping [Sweden]: Tryckeri AB Småland, 1990.

Records the events of a symposium held in May of 1988, that celebrated the bicentenary of the Royal Dramatic Theatre. Includes the texts of six presentations on Strindberg, summarizes others, three of them on O'Neill (J.H. Raleigh's "Strindberg and O'Neill as Historical Playwrights," Virginia Floyd's "Eugene O'Neill: An Autobiographical Dramatist against a Catholic Background," and a third, untitled, in which Gary Vena "spoke of O'Neill's highly detailed specifications concerning actors, props, and fidelity to the text").

However the texts of two of the presentations — Egil Törnqvist's "Strindberg and O'Neill and their Impact on the Dramatists of Today" and Peter Sellars' "The Importance of Being Unproducible"— were included in full. For annotations see under their names, this section.

B149 Erlich, Alan. "A Streetcar Named Desire Under the Elms: A Study of Dramatic Space in *A Streetcar Named Desire* and *Desire Under the Elms*." In *Tennessee Williams: A Tribute*. Ed. Jac L. Tharpe. Jackson: UP of Mississippi, 1977. 126-36.

Sees the two plays as having identical subjects — the threat to a "family unit by the presence of desire." An outsider appears and tries to redefine the family unit — succeeds in *Desire*, fails in *Streetcar*. In both, the family is defined visually as a home.

B150 Estrin, Mark W. *Conversations with Eugene O'Neill*. Jackson: UP of Mississippi, 1990.

Over 30 interviews with the playwright. Deriving principally from newspapers (all were previously published), the interviews span the period 1920 to 1948. Also included are an introduction and a chronology.

Cunningham, Frank R. Rev. *Modern Drama* 36 (1993): 169-70.

Wilkins, Frederick C. Rev. *Eugene O'Neill Review* 15.1 (1991): 105-06.

B151 Evans, Gareth Lloyd. "American Connections — O'Neill, Miller, Williams, and Albee." In *The Language of Modern Drama*. Totowa, NJ: Rowman and Littlefield, 1977. 177-204.

Contends that the four playwrights in the title aspired to write in a "heightened" language. Now man is more aware of his own deficiencies than when O'Neill wrote, but the playwright tried to be "pathetically eloquent" in his "dramatic inarticulations," and like the others he succeeded with an American rhetoric that is almost reminiscent of old fashioned pulpit oratory — "bold in its calculated artistry and its assault on the emotions."

B152 Falb, Lewis W. *American Drama in Paris, 1945-1970: A Study of Its Critical Reception*. Chapel Hill: U of North Carolina P, 1973. 7-23.

Discusses the reception of *Jones, Chillun, Desire, Electra, Ape, Cardiff, Welded,* and *Journey*. Finds the French ambivalent about O'Neill. They recognize his stature, but have not taken to him: acclaim for *Journey,* but earlier works received mixed reviews. Acknowledges that French exposure to O'Neill is limited.

B153 Falk, Candace. *Love, Anarchy, & Emma Goldman.* New York: Holt, 1984.

O'Neill is not included in the index although *Wilderness,* the Gelbs' *O'Neill* and Sheaffer's *Son and Playwright* appear in the bibliography.

B154 Falk, Doris. *Eugene O'Neill and the Tragic Tension.* 1958. 2nd ed. New York: Gordian, 1982.

Only appreciable difference between the first and second editions is the inclusion in the latter of an "Afterword," reflecting on changes in society which alter our reading of O'Neill, and a brief list of indispensable books on O'Neill.

B155 Field, B. S., Jr. "Concrete Images of the Vague in the Plays of Eugene O'Neill." In *Critical Essays on Eugene O'Neill.* Ed. James J. Martine. Boston: G. K. Hall, 1984. 188-96.

"Vagueness in O'Neill's style is not merely a regrettable defect." Considers O'Neill's canon in terms of setting, language, characterization, and use of jokes. When O'Neill became overly concerned with what he wrote, he tended to shun words that communicated precisely what he meant, opting for more ambiguous words, which he saw as less melodramatic. These plays baffled the audiences. As he became less preoccupied with the precise word (in his later plays), he wrote less ambiguously.

B156 Fink, Ernest O. "Audience Aids for Non-Literary Allusions? Observations on the Transposition of Essential Technicalities in the Sea Plays of Eugene O'Neill." In *The Languages of the Theatre: Problems in the Translation and Transposition of Drama.* Ed. Ortrun Zuber. Oxford: Pergamon, 1980. 69-81.

Finds three voices in O'Neill's sea plays — of men, of things, of nature. Argues that the voice of things needs to be updated for the plays to be meaningful to a contemporary audience. That is, conditions, technicalities, situations must be given the assistance of stage machinery, something that wasn't necessary when the plays were first produced.

B157 Fischer, Heinz-Dietrich. Introduction to *Drama/Comedy Awards 1917-1996: From Eugene O'Neill and Tennessee Williams to Richard Rodgers and Edward Albee.* Vol. 12 of *The Pulitzer Prize Archive: A History and Anthology of Award-winning Materials in Journalism, Letters, and Arts.* Eds. Heinz-Dietrich Fischer and Erika J. Fischer. Munich: K. G. Saur, 1998. ix-xxxiv.

A brief history of the Pulitzer awards for play writing, with summaries of the judges' reasoning and who cast what votes for which plays. Speculates as to why O'Neill won for *Horizon, Anna, Interlude, Journey* and did not for *Iceman.*

B158 Fitzgerald, Geraldine. "Another Neurotic Electra: A New Look at Mary Tyrone." In *Eugene O'Neill: A World View.* Ed. Virginia Floyd. New York: Ungar, 1979. 290-92.

Fitzgerald, who under Arvin Brown's direction played Mary in the 1971 production of *Journey,* recalls her rather startling interpretation of the role.

B159 Fjelde, Rolf. "Structure of Forgiveness: The Endings of *A Moon for the Misbegotten* and Ibsen's *Peer Gynt.*" In *O'Neill in China: An International Centenary Celebration.* Eds. Haiping Liu and Lowell Swortzell. Westport, CT: Greenwood, 1992. 51-57.

Sees in *Peer Gynt* and *Misbegotten* plays which are their authors' final statements about redemption and forgiveness and notes that ironically there is none.

B160 Flèche, Anne. "'A Monster of Perfection': O'Neill's Stella." In *Feminist Rereadings of Modern American Drama.* Ed. June Schlueter. Rutherford, NJ: Fairleigh Dickinson. UP, 1989. 25-36.

Considers the character of Mary Tyrone and concludes that *Journey* is an Oedipal narrative: "its struggle for origins is revealed through the character of the woman who, motivating these things, is herself unmotivated, thrust into a role that is neither character nor narrator, but both." She exists "because Oedipal narrativity demands its mother, its monster, its prophet."

B161 _____. *Mimetic Disillusion: Eugene O'Neill, Tennessee Williams, and U.S. Dramatic Realism.* Tuscaloosa: U of Alabama P, 1997.

Mimesis involves "contradictory" goals: the attempt to reconcile the representation of superficial reality with the need to lead the viewer/reader to what lies beyond the "imperfect transparency" of realistic representation. O'Neill is seen as struggling to control these contradictions. The second and third chapters treat of "character, dialogue and time, and O'Neill's desire to represent non-being." *Journey* "challenges the realistic notion of representation as the mutual corroboration of text and mise en scène." *Iceman* "exposes the temporal promise of realism: that the present can be represented, and that historical lines of causality ultimately deliver discovery, climax, and meaning." The book is based on the author's dissertation; see C36.

Bak, John S. Rev. *Modern Drama* 41 (1998): 162-66.

B162 Floyd, Virginia, ed. *Eugene O'Neill: A World View.* New York: Ungar, 1979. See next entry.

Nineteen previously unpublished essays, listed below.

Ingrid Bergman's "A Meeting with O'Neill" (See B32)

Albert Bermel's "Poetry and Mysticism in O'Neill" (See B41)

Arvin Brown's "Staging O'Neill's 'Simple Play'" (See B74)

Péter Egri's "The Use of the Short Story in O'Neill's and Chekhov's One-Act Plays: A Hungarian View of O'Neill" (See B134)

Florence Eldridge's "First Curtain Call for Mary Tyrone" (See B145)

Geraldine Fitzgerald's "Another Neurotic Electra: A New Look at Mary Tyrone" (See B158)

Virginia Floyd's Three Introductions (See B163)

Horst Frenz's "Eugene O'Neill and Georg Kaiser" (See B172)

Esther M. Jackson's "O'Neill the Humanist" (See B229)

Josef Jařab's "The Lasting Challenge of Eugene O'Neill: A Czechoslovak View" (See B230)

Maya Koreneva's "One Hundred Percent American Tragedy: A Soviet View." (See B247)

Clifford Leech's "O'Neill in England — From *Anna Christie* to *Long Day's Journey into Night:* 1923-1958" (See B257)

Tom Olsson's "O'Neill and the Royal Dramatic" (See B314)

John Henry Raleigh's "The Irish Atavism of *A Moon for the Misbegotten* " and "The Last Confession: O'Neill and the Catholic Confessional" (See B346 and B347)

J. Dennis Rich's "Exile Without Remedy: The Late Plays of Eugene O'Neill" (See B357)

Marta Sienicka's "O'Neill in Poland" (See B396)

Timo Tiusanen's "O'Neill's Significance: A Scandinavian and European View" (See B424)

Egil Törnqvist's "Platonic Love in O'Neill's *Welded*" (See B426)

Frederick Wilkins' "The Pressure of Puritanism in O'Neill's New England Plays" (See B459)

B163 _____. "Introduction." In *Eugene O'Neill: A World View.* New York: Ungar, 1979. 3-33, 189-211, 279-85.

There are three sections to the book: "The European Perspective," "The American Perspective," and "Four People of the Theatre." The first section, nine essays, reflects the thinking about O'Neill and his work of scholar-critics from various European countries. The second section contains six essays by American scholars. In these two sections the significant feature is the ethnicity of the scholar, stressing the range of O'Neill's appeal, rather than holding to a single theme. The third section — four essays — reflects the interest of the practical stage to O'Neill: three actresses, one director speak. Introductions for each section serve as rehearsals for what was to be done more fully in *Eugene O'Neill at Work* (1981).

B164 _____, **ed.** *Eugene O'Neill at Work: Newly Released Ideas for Plays.* New York: Ungar, 1981.

See Primary Works section, G11.

B165 _____. *Eugene O'Neill: A New Assessment.* New York: Ungar, 1985.

An "introductory study designed to bring contemporary students and general readers to an understanding of Eugene O'Neill, the man and the playwright." Analyzes 50 plays, approached in four chronological sections: "Early Plays and Beginnings," "Experimental Plays and Maturation," "'Self' Plays and the Cycle," and "The Late Great Plays." Gives plot summary and some analysis, but is aimed, as the author says, at the basic level.

B166 _____, **ed.** *Eugene O'Neill: The Unfinished Plays.* New York: Continuum, 1988.

See Primary Works section, G15.

B167 _____. "Eugene O'Neill's Tao Te Ching: The Spiritual Evolution of a Mystic." In *Eugene O'Neill in China: An International*

Centenary Celebration. Eds. Haiping Liu and Lowell Swortzell. Westport, CT: Greenwood, 1992. 3-12.

An overview of O'Neill's personal and professional interest in Taoism.

B168 Frank, Glenda. "Fun House Mirrors: The Neil Simon-Eugene O'Neill Dialogue." In *Neil Simon: A Casebook.* Ed. Gary Konas. New York: Garland, 1997. 109-25.

As the title suggests this is O'Neill reflected in Simon — *Come Blow Your Horn* and the Brighton Beach trilogy as spins on *Wilderness* and *Journey*, with a soupçon of *Caribbees.* The parallels we are shown in the work of the two are numerous: "Simon's attraction to O'Neill is based on a sympathy of mind."

B169 Frazer, Winifred. *E.G. and E.G.O.: Emma Goldman and The Iceman Cometh.* Gainesville: Florida UP, 1974.

Studies how radical Emma Goldman influenced O'Neill and his plays. One chapter is devoted to *Iceman* (pp. 23-64) in which Emma and Alexander Berkman and the movement have left their spoor; the rest of the approximately 100 pages explains the milieu, the interlocking O'Neill-Goldman circles, their shared vision. A devotee of the theater (she had published a series of essays in *The Social Significance of the Drama*), she and O'Neill had much in common.

B170 _____. *Mabel Dodge Luhan.* Boston: G. K. Hall, 1984.

A thorough survey of Luhan's life and publications based on published materials. (Rudnick's book had not been published yet, but her dissertation had been used). One reference to O'Neill. Chapter 3 covers the New York City period when Luhan and O'Neill moved in the same world.

B171 Frenz, Horst. "Alexander Tairov and the 1930 World Tour of the Kamerny Theatre." In *Studies in Theatre and Drama: Essays in Honor of Hubert C. Heffner.* Ed. Oscar G. Brockett. New York: Humanities, 1973. 177-94.

Tairov's interest in experimental theater attracted him early to O'Neill's work. At the same time, he saw theatre as reflecting the ideologies of its society. The two O'Neill plays that were drawn into the Kamerny Theatre's 8-play repertory were *Desire* and *Chillun.* Discusses the treatment Tairov's production of *Chillun* received and the changes wrought in

the two plays (there was also a production of *Ape* which did not go on tour). Tairov's comments are also in Frenz and Tuck's *Eugene O'Neill's Critics: Voices from Abroad,* for which see below.

B172 _____. "Eugene O'Neill and Georg Kaiser." In *Eugene O'Neill: A World View.* Ed. Virginia Floyd. New York: Ungar, 1979. 172-85.

Despite O'Neill's denial, it is likely that the expressionism of his early days was influenced by Georg Kaiser.

B173 _____. "Eugene O'Neill and the European Connection." In *Literary Communication and Reception. Actes du IXe Congrès de l'Association Internationale de Littérature comparée.* Eds. Zoran Konstantinovic, Manfred Naumann and Hans Robert Jauss. Innsbruck: AMOE, 1980. 385-90.

Surveys O'Neill's reception in Europe in order to show his kinship with European drama. Indeed the many "affinities" between him and Shaw, Strindberg, and Ibsen, "made it easy for European audiences to accept the American playwright, for they discovered echoes" of their own writers in him.

B174 _____, and Susan Tuck, eds. *Eugene O'Neill's Critics: Voices from Abroad.* Carbondale: Southern Illinois UP, 1984.

Eclectic group of essays (written 1922 on) about O'Neill's international reputation. Only three of the 26 authors' essays fall within this book's scope: Catherine Mounier's, An Min Hsia's, and Timo Tiusanen's.

Alexander Anikst's "Preface to Russian Translations of O'Neill"

St. John Ervine's "Counsels of Despair"

Rudolf Haas' "A Literary-Historical Assessment of O'Neill"

Per Hallström's "Nobel Prize Presentation"

Hugo von Hofmannsthal's "Dramaturgical Reflections" and "The Beggar and *The Hairy Ape* "

An Min Hsia's "Cycle of Return: O'Neill and the Tao" (See A326)

Richard Jennings' "Drama of Monomania"

Toshio Kimura's "O'Neill's 'Whited Sepulchre'"

B. Nagy László's "The O'Neill Legend"

Maurice Le Breton's "Eugene O'Neill and the American Theatre"

Dorothy Macardle's "The Dual Nature of Man"

Gabriel Marcel's "Interpretations by a Philosopher"

León Mirlas' "The Scope of O'Neill's Drama"

Eugenio Montale's "O'Neill and the Future of the Theatre"

Catherine Mounier's "Notes on the 1967 French Production of *The Iceman Cometh*" (See B305 and D177))

Sean O'Casey's "Three Tributes to O'Neill"

Wojciech Natanson's "O'Neill's Comeback"

Erik Reger's "The Georg Kaiser of America"

Lennox Robinson's "*Beyond the Horizon* Versus *Gold*"

Alfonso Sastre's "On the Death of Eugene O'Neill"

Oscar Fritz Schuh's "O'Neill's Dramatic Work: His Image of Humanity"

Frederik Schyberg's "American Tragedy of Fate"

Alexander Tairov's "*Negr*: Director's Notes" and "The Creative Work of Eugene O'Neill"

Frank Tetauer's "Raw, Brutal Visions" and "The Tragic Wandering of a Great Dramatist"

Timo Tiusanen's "O'Neill and Wuolijoki: A Counter-Sketch to *Electra*" (See B425)

Kenneth Tynan's "The Heights and Depths" and "Massive Masterpiece"

B175 Fuhrmann, Manfred. "Notes on Eugene O'Neill in France." In *Texte und Kontexte: Studien zur deutschen und vergleichenden Litteraturwissenschaft*. Eds. Manfred Durzak, et al. Bern: Francke, 1973. 59-72.

Surveys the history of French productions of O'Neill's plays, from *Jones* (1923) to *Iceman* (1967). Also evaluates the translations of O'Neill's work (34 plays published between 1963 and 1965). Nonetheless, finds the French slow to appreciate O'Neill.

B176 _____. "Myth as a Recurrent Theme in Greek Tragedy and Twentieth-Century Drama." In *New Perspectives in German Literary Criticism: A Collection of Essays*. Eds. Richard E. Amacher and Victor Lange. Trans. David Henry Wilson, et al. Princeton: Princeton UP, 1979. 295-319.

Describes ancient Greeks' handling of myth in tragedy — "bound to the traditional skeleton of the story" but "free as regards mo-

tivation." Modern handling in one case assumes the audience is "familiar with the classical model and its standard interpretation ... [even to] a scene-for-scene comparison with the ... original." Asserts that O'Neill's *Electra*, Anouilh's *Antigone* and *Medée*, Giraudoux's *Amphitrion 38* and *Electra*, and Sartre's *Les Mouches*, following this concept, form almost a genre — first, by following the plot, and second, by developing a unique interpretation of motivation. These are "relative" dramas when "the events of the myth are merely an external, visual manifestation" while "each interpretation ... is the actual meaning of the myth." Originally published in German in Vol. 4 of *Poetik und Hermeneutik* (Munich: Wilhelm Fink, 1971).

B177 Furomoto, Toshi. "Problems of Irish Immigrants in Eugene O'Neill's *Long Day's Journey into Night*." In *The Classical World and the Mediterranean*. Eds. Giuseppe Serpillo and Donatella Abbate Badin. Cagliari [Italy]: Università di Sassari/Tema, 1996. 261-64.

Looks at Irish references/associations, explicit or implicit, in the play: blarney, brogue, confessions, guilt, etc., to conclude that "here the Irish-Americans are more like the Irish than the Irish themselves." Part of the proceedings of a conference (IASAIL, 1994) held in Sardinia.

B178 Gage, Nicholas. *A Place for Us.* Boston: Houghton Mifflin, 1989.

A note in Gage's memoir recalls his reading in the, then, new Gelb biography of the O'Neills' burning papers in their Shelton Hotel fireplace, a fact which Gage later disproved by visiting the room and discovering that no such fireplace existed or had existed. Instead, he learned that Carlotta, with staff assistance, had carried the papers to the basement, where they were incinerated.

B179 Gálik, Marián. "O'Neill, Baker, and Hung Shen." In *Actes du VIIIe Congrès de l'Association Internationale de Littérature comparée/Proceedings of the 8th Congress of the International Comparative Literature Association: Trois grandes mutations Littéraires: Renaissance, Lumières, début de vingtième siècle/Three Epoch-Making Literary Changes: Renaissance, Enlightenment, Early Twentieth Century*. Eds. Bela Köpeczi and György M. Vajda. Stuttgart: Bieber, 1980. 381-85.

Centers on the Chinese playwright Hung Shen's relationships with George Pierce Baker, his teacher, and O'Neill, whose work influenced Shen. Points out, but does not analyze, the influence of *Jones* on *Chao Ta*. In the foreword to his plays, Shen enjoys a fictional conversation with O'Neill, wherein he expresses admiration for the latter's work but reproaches him for borrowing heavily from Aeschylus when writing *Electra*.

B180 Gallup, Donald C. *Pigeons on the Granite: Memories of a Yale Librarian.* New Haven, CT: Yale UP, 1988.

A chapter devoted to Carlotta (pp. 282-310) covers the years 1954 to 1970 when Gallup, representing Yale, had most contact with her. These were the O'Neill renaissance years, the years of Gierow and Quintero, when *Journey, Misbegotten, Touch, Hughie,* and *Mansions* were first staged. Gallup is more sympathetic with Carlotta than many so that sometimes we are getting the "other side of the story": he was a trustee of her estate during the last years of her life — one of the seven people who attended her funeral. His account includes nearly eight pages of notes he took of conversations with her — her memories of her life before and with O'Neill.

B181 _____. *Eugene O'Neill and His Eleven-Play Cycle, A Tale of Possessors Self-Dispossessed.* The Henry McBride Series of Modernism and Modernity. New Haven, CT: Yale UP, 1998.

A study that covers the period (1931-1940) of O'Neill's life that was concerned with the evolution of the cycle of plays he never completed, the 200-year history of an American family. Gallup's narrative weaves together O'Neill's life, creative and otherwise, with summaries of the 11 plays. His familiarity with the resources of the Beinecke Library has given Gallup the opportunity to mine its gold much to the advantage of O'Neillians. Forty pages of back matter include a four-page chronology of the cycle's composition. The 14-page bibliography is mostly devoted to unpublished manuscripts in the Beinecke.

B182 _____. "A Tale of Possessors Self-Dispossessed." In *The Companion to Eugene O'Neill.* Ed. Michael Manheim. Cambridge Companions to Literature series. Cambridge: Cambridge UP, 1998. 178-91.

As a note (p. 190) informs us, this essay is adapted from Gallup's *Eugene O'Neill and His Eleven-Play Cycle*; for an annotation of see the preceding entry, B181.

B183 Gardner, Virginia. *"Friend and Lover": The Life of Louise Bryant.* New York: Horizon, 1982.

Chapters 2-5 (pp. 29-67) cover the Provincetown and Washington Square period when Louise Bryant's life crossed with O'Neill's. O'Neill falls in love with Louise. Louise helps O'Neill to control his drinking. Louise falls in love with O'Neill, but won't forsake Reed for him. Over a dozen of the relevant sources are unpublished materials: four interviews with Dorothy Day, one with Conrad Aiken, several with Andrew Dagsburg and Heaton Vorse; the Granville Hicks Collection at Syracuse University, and the John Reed Collection at Harvard.

B184 Gayford, Norman R. "The Artist as Antaeus: Lovecraft and Modernism." In *An Epicure in the Terrible: A Centennial Anthology of Essays in Honor of H. P. Lovecraft.* Eds. David E. Schultz and S. T. Joshi. Rutherford, NJ: Fairleigh Dickinson UP, 1991. 273-97.

Much on H. P. Lovecraft's modernism, little on O'Neill: *Jones* as a work which Lovecraft admired.

B185 Geddes, Virgil. *The Melodramadness of Eugene O'Neill.* 1934. Norwood, PA: Norwood, 1977.

Reprint of the 1934 edition published by the Brookfield Players, Brookfield, CT.

B186 Gelb, Arthur, and Barbara Gelb. *O'Neill.* 2nd ed. New York: Harper & Row, 1973.

One of the two most important biographies of O'Neill, this was originally published in 1962. New material is added in an epilogue, an account of Carlotta O'Neill's final years.

B187 _____. *O'Neill.* First Perennial Library Edition. New York: Perennial Library, 1987.

Reprint of the 1962 edition.

B188 _____. *O'Neill.* New York: Applause Theater Book Publishers, 1999.

Reprint of the 1962 edition.

B189 Gelb, Barbara. *So Short a Time: A Biography of John Reed and Louise Bryant.* New York: Norton, 1973.

The relevant chapters are 5, 6, 7, 8 (pp. 76-125) and 11 (pp. 184-91), covering the period of Reed's and Bryant's connection with O'Neill. There is no documentation except for a short final acknowledgment page which refers to material Arthur and Barbara Gelb had covered in their *O'Neill*.

B190 Gillett, Peter J. "O'Neill and the Racial Myths." In *Eugene O'Neill: A Collection of Criticism.* Ed. Ernest G. Griffin. New York: McGraw, 1976. 45-58.

Sees the "Negro" plays — *Thirst, Dreamy, Jones, Chillun,* and *Iceman* — as showing progressive development in O'Neill's rendition of blacks. At first the black is primitive with only the superficial covering of civilization (*Thirst*), but by *Iceman,* we see, in Joe Mott, a black who is on equal terms with the other inhabitants of Harry Hope's. Most attention is paid to *Chillun,* which is seen as a play about racial relations in America: the play suggests that happiness is only gained when the black man surrenders to the white myths.

B191 Gilmore, Thomas B. *Equivocal Spirits: Alcoholism and Drinking in Twentieth-Century Literature.* Chapel Hill: U of North Carolina P, 1987.

Applies the principles of Alcoholics Anonymous to literary criticism and, for our purposes, to O'Neill (in the chapter called "*The Iceman Cometh* and the Anatomy of Alcoholism"). Argues that *Iceman* is a parody of AA principles, that, in fact, only Larry and Hickey are alcoholics — the other characters are simply drunks.

Bloom, Steven F. Rev. *Eugene O'Neill Newsletter* 11.3 (1987): 22-24.

B192 Girdhari, V. T. "Eugene O'Neill's Emperor Jones: Dual Character of Minority in America." In *T. S. Eliot & Eugene O'Neill: The Dream and the Nightmare.* Eds. V. R. N. Prasad, et al. New Delhi: Ajanta, 1991. 158-62.

Sees *Jones* as a play which symbolizes "O'Neill's attack on contemporary society that has made the individual what he is." "We end up pitying and not condemning Jones. He is destroyed by the conflict of two cultures," as well as by the "conflicts of impulse in his nature."

B193 Goldstein, Malcolm. *The Political Stage: American Drama and Theater of the Great Depression.* New York: Oxford UP, 1974.

Scattered references to *Chillun, Anna, Days, Desire, Jones, Ape, Brown, Iceman, Journey, Misbegotten, Electra,* and *Interlude.* The preface admits that "the two giants of the period, Eugene O'Neill and Thornton Wilder, receive only brief mention in relation to many of their inferiors whose dramatic themes fall within the range of the book."

B194 Golub, Spencer. "O'Neill and the Poetics of Modernist Strangeness." In *Eugene O'Neill's Century: Centennial Views on America's Foremost Tragic Dramatist.* Ed. Richard F. Moorton, Jr. Westport, CT: Greenwood, 1991. 17-39.

Views *Journey* as O'Neill's attempt to reinvent the family by "defamiliarization," or "making [it] strange." And we are expected to see the play through the eyes of Shklovsky, Bergson, Husserl, Lacan, Bakhtin, and others.

B195 Goodwin, Donald W. *Alcohol and the Writer.* Kansas City: Andrews and McMeel, 1988.

American writers in the first half of the twentieth century were particularly susceptible to alcoholism. No surprise, then, that O'Neill gets his own chapter (pp. 123-37), wherein Goodwin looks at O'Neill's ethnicity, early life, temperament, heredity, even his profession, to find the reasons for his addiction. All may have contributed to the problem.

Bloom, Steven F. Rev. *Eugene O'Neill Review* 13.2 (1989): 97-105.

B196 Goyal, Bhagwat S. *The Strategy of Survival: Human Significance of O'Neill's Plays.* Ghazibad [India]: Vimal, Prakashon, 1975.

A "revised version" of the author's 1970 doctoral dissertation (Agra U, India), which sensitively and intelligently studies the relationship between O'Neill's themes and techniques. The revisions — the only parts of the book that fall within the scope of this annotation — involve a slight increase in the number of items in the bibliography and two quotations in Chapter 8, neither of which alters, as the author admits, his original thesis. Covers the whole range of O'Neill's plays.

B197 Grabes, Herbert. "The Legacy of Eugene O'Neill." In *New Essays on American Drama.* Eds. Gilbert Debusscher and Henry I. Schvey. Costerus New Series, 76. Amsterdam: Rodopi, 1989. 29-40.

Assesses O'Neill's influence on subsequent writers in terms of theme and presentation and finds that influence wide spread.

B198 Grabher, Gudrun M. "Sinful Silence? Ethical Implications of Concealment in Eugene O'Neill's *Strange Interlude.*" In *Semantics of Silence in Linguistics and Literature.* Eds. Gudrun M. Grabher and Ulrike Jessner. Anglistische Forschungen, 244. Heidelberg: Universitätsverlag C. Winter, 1996. 353-63.

Considers silence in literature as theme and strategy and concludes that "in O'Neill's play [*Interlude*] silence is, indeed, of ontological significance. It creates a void that is vicious in that it deprives the characters of the possibility to attribute meaning to their being."

B199 Grace, Sherrill E. *Regression and Apocalypse: Studies In North American Literary Expressionism.* Toronto: U of Toronto P, 1989.

Contains a chunky chapter (pp. 82-116) on O'Neill, "Eugene O'Neill: The American Georg Kaiser," which fathoms the possible links between the American playwright and his German contemporary. Looks at common influences, opportunities O'Neill had for exposure to the German Expressionist's work, and at O'Neill's Expressionistic plays. The broader study attempts to demonstrate the variety of expressionistic writing in Canada and the United States and includes dramatic and non-dramatic writers. Pictures of O'Neill's plays in production and ample notes are included.

B200 Granger, Bruce. "Eugene O'Neill: Man of the Theatre." In *America — Austriaca: Beiträge zur Amerikakunde.* Vol. 3. Ed. Klaus Lanzinger. Vienna: Wilhelm Braumuller, 1974. 24-32.

Concentrates on the stage craft and theatrical techniques of O'Neill's plays.

B201 Grawe, Paul H. *Comedy in Space, Time, and the Imagination.* Chicago: Nelson-Hall, 1983. 221-35.

A general discussion of *Iceman*, which is categorized as a sombre comedy, a "social comedy," where no character is central. Discusses the groups that the characters belong to and the love/hate relationships between them. Sees Hickey as a threat to the denizens' survival rather than a saviour and comments on the parallels between Hickey and Christ. Hickey's ministry, though, has the opposite effect of Christ's.

B202 Greenfield, Thomas Allen. *Work and the Work Ethic in American Drama 1920-1970.* Columbia: U of Missouri P, 1982.

Scattered references to O'Neill. Though he wrote on the periphery of the issues of work and the work ethic, O'Neill avoided addressing them in *Caribbees, Zone,* and *Ape,* while *Journey* and *Interlude* (despite Jane Bonin's *Major Themes*) "although concerned in part with materialism, do not take on the problem of work in any meaningful manner." The "dramatic tension between home values and work values is exploited much more fully" in *Mansions.*

B203 Griffen, William D. *The Book of Irish Americans.* New York: Random House, 1990.

In a section about the O'Neills of the 15th and 16th centuries, headed "O'Neill of Tyrone" (pp. 207-300), the author is cheered by the thought that Eugene O'Neill, despite himself, was Irish.

B204 Griffin, Ernest G., ed. *Eugene O'Neill: A Collection of Criticism.* New York: McGraw, 1976.

The editor contributes a 20-page introduction on O'Neill's life and career. Reprints 13 essays, and parts of books, only two of which — Gillett's and Asselineau's — fall within the scope of this work.

Robert J. Andreach's "O'Neill's Women in *The Iceman Cometh*"

Roger Asselineau's "*Desire Under the Elms*: A Phase of O'Neill's Philosophy" (See B12)

Eric Bentley's "Eugene O'Neill's Pietà"

Travis Bogard's "*The Iceman Cometh*"

Frederic I. Carpenter's "Eugene O'Neill, the Orient, and American Transcendentalism"

Edwin A. Engel's "Ideas in the Plays of Eugene O'Neill"

Peter J. Gillett's "O'Neill and the Racial Myths" (See B190)

Ernest G. Griffin's "Eugene O'Neill: An Introduction to His life and Career"

Elder Olson's "Modern Drama and Tragedy: A View of *Mourning Becomes Electra*"

John H. Raleigh's "*Mourning Becomes Electra* and *A Touch of the Poet*"

Timo Tiusanen's "Through the Fog into the Monologue: *Long Day's Journey into Night*"

Egil Törnqvist's "Parallel Characters and Situations in *Long Day's Journey into Night*"

Otis W. Winchester's "Eugene O'Neill's *Strange Interlude* as a Transcript of America in the 1920's"

B205 Hadomi, Leah. *The Homecoming Theme in Modern Drama.* Lewiston, NY: Edwin Mellen, 1992.

Chapters on Ibsen's *Ghosts,* Miller's *Death of a Salesman,* Albee's *Who's Afraid of Virginia Woolf?,* Pinter's *The Homecoming,* Shepard's *Buried Child,* and (pp. 5-48) *Journey.* Hadomi analyzes the play as a work, in part, about the return of the prodigal child Edmund. Father and son are reconciled and sibling rivalry exposed in an archetypal drama.

B206 Hahn, Emily. *Mabel: A Biography of Mabel Dodge Luhan.* Boston: Houghton, 1977.

A fairly hasty survey of Luhan's life. Chapters 5, 6, and 7 deal with her connection with John Reed and the artistic and radical-political scene of New York in the second decade of the 20th century. Though the author acknowledges materials in the Beinecke Rare Book Collection at Yale as sources, her bibliographical notes refer only to published and generally accessible books. One reference to O'Neill.

B207 Halfmann, Ulrich, ed. *Eugene O'Neill: Comments on the Drama and the Theater: A Source Book.* Studies & Texts in English 7. Tübingen: Gunter Narr, 1987.

Halfmann has brought together and edited 83 contemporary reviews of O'Neill's plays (mostly reprinted from early magazines and newspapers) and interviews, 50-some letters or excerpts of letters from the playwright, some inscriptions, manuscript notes and other material for this volume. His appendix contains lists of dramatic and non-dramatic writings, a chronological list of letters by O'Neill included in the volume, a list of published set designs, a chronological list of books on O'Neill, an index of names and titles, and an analytic subject index. The rationale for the collection (153 items) was whatever "contributed to our understanding of O'Neill's work, *Weltanschauung,* or theory of art." A rich collection.

Chothia, Jean. Rev.-essay. *Journal of American Studies* 23 (1989): 311-14. (See A120)

Shafer, Yvonne. Rev. *Theatre Research International* 17.2 (1992): 166.

Wilkins, Frederick C. Rev. *Eugene O'Neill Newsletter* 12.2 (1988): 68-71.

B208 _____. "'With Clenched Fist...': Observations on a Recurrent Motif in the Drama of Eugene O'Neill." In *Eugene O'Neill and the Emergence of American Drama.* Ed. Marc Maufort. Costerus New Series, 75. Amsterdam: Rodopi. 1989. 107-21.

Discusses what might have gone unnoticed by even the most avid readers of O'Neill's work — the recurring image of the clenched fist, a symbol of rebellion, despair, desire.

B209 Hall, Ann C. *"A Kind of Alaska": Women in the Plays of O'Neill, Pinter and Shepard.* Carbondale: Southern Illinois UP, 1993. 17-53.

A book based on a 1988 doctoral dissertation (see C46) devotes a chapter to the female characters in *Journey, Iceman,* and *Misbegotten,* finding that "unlike the women in *The Iceman Cometh* who haunt their men from their imprisonment behind the glass and unlike Evelyn and Mary Tyrone who have internalized the female mirror and are shattered by it, Josie consciously chooses the Madonna role. Consequently, Josie is the most fully present character in the O'Neill canon."

Mandl, Bette. Rev. *Eugene O'Neill Review* 17.1-2 (1993): 205-06.

B210 _____. "'Gawd, you'd think I was a piece of furniture': O'Neill's *Anna Christie.*" In *Staging the Rage: The Web of Misogyny in Modern Drama.* Eds. Katherine Burkman and Judith Roof. Madison, NJ: Fairleigh Dickinson UP, 1998.

With periodic reference to Luce Irigaray, Hall weighs O'Neill's hits and misses in his creation of the female character Anna Christopherson. That he used a woman's viewpoint is a plus; that he presumed to do so a minus. The argument? "That O'Neill uses such moments [the heterosexual happy ending of the play] not to endorse the patriarchal expectations regarding femininity, but instead ... to highlight how they misrepresent women in an inherently misogynistic fashion." By the end of the play Anna has disturbed stereotypical expectations and the patriarchal universe, so we're not to conclude she has capitulated when she turns to Mat. She is on "another voyage" in her "quest for her identity."

B211 Hammerman, Harley J. *Eugene O'Neill: A Centennial Celebration.* St. Louis, MO: Washington U Libraries, 1988.

The title page bears the following: "An Exhibit Drawn from the Private Collection of Harley J. Hammerman, MD." The exhibit was mounted at the Olin Library of Washington University, and consisted of a selection from Dr. Hammerman's collection of O'Neilliana, including first editions, limited editions, photographs, letters, manuscripts, and playbills.

B212 Hayashi, Tetsumaro, ed. *Eugene O'Neill: Research Opportunities and Dissertation Abstracts.* Jefferson, NC: McFarland, 1983.

Includes Robert L. Tener's "Eugene O'Neill: Research Opportunities," (q.v.) and (pp. 22-144) a list with, where available, the abstracts of the dissertations on O'Neill completed between 1928 and 1980 (139 of them) arranged chronologically. Hayashi's sources are *Dissertation Abstracts International.*

B213 Heilman, Robert Bechtold. *The Iceman, the Arsonist, and the Troubled Agent: Tragedy and Melodrama on the Modern Stage.* Seattle: U of Washington P, 1973. 72-114.

The characters of the book's title refer to types: the iceman is the victim who opts out, the arsonist is the aggressive vengeful destroyer, and the troubled agent is the vigorous man who is disturbed by what he does. Chapter Four deals with O'Neill. It is divided into sections on 15 plays: *Iceman, Interlude, Electra, Touch, Journey, Misbegotten, Mansions, Horizon, Chillun, Jones, Desire, Brown, Lazarus, Days,* and *Dynamo. Iceman* is not a tragedy because of the men's weakness in not being able to live with self-knowledge. The other plays in varying ways and to varying degrees reflect the same view of man — *Electra* and *Journey,* with *Iceman,* being O'Neill's most characteristic. Believes O'Neill's characters do not achieve tragic status, not because they try and fail, but because they undertake too little.

B214 Heller, Adele, and Lois Rudnick, eds. *1915, The Cultural Moment: The New Politics, the New Woman, the New Psychology, the New Art & the New Theatre in America.* New Brunswick, NJ: Rutgers UP, 1991.

Inspired by a four-day conference in Provincetown, Massachusetts, in June of 1987, to commemorate the founding of the Provincetown Players, this very handsome and well-illustrated volume covers the five topics listed in its subtitle in five parts contributed to by 16 specialists — Part V (pp. 217-59) focuses inward on Provincetown specifically, with frequent reminders of the O'Neill connection. A sixth part includes texts of the first four plays produced by the original players in 1915 (and performed at the 1987 conference) and Barbara Gelb's "Eugene O'Neill in Provincetown" (pp. 309-15, excerpted from her talk given at the 1987 conference) in which she gives a reprise of the relevant parts of the Gelbs' *O'Neill.*

Wilkins, Frederick C. Rev. *Eugene O'Neill Review* 16.1 (1992): 126-29.

B215 Henderson, Mary C. *Theater in America.* New York: Abrams, 1986.

With over 200 years of theatrical history to address, this work must be limited in its focus on O'Neill. Nonetheless, Henderson says inarguably that for most "O'Neill's name is synonymous with American theater." Since the work is divided into job categories/theatrical functions, references to the playwright are scattered. However, the author does include a five-page assessment of his canon, the focus being, predictably, on *Journey.*

Shafer, Yvonne. Rev. *Eugene O'Neill Newsletter* 11.3 (1987): 26-27.

B216 _____. *Theater in America.* 1986. New York: Abrams, 1996.

A revision of the 1986 edition.

B217 Herr, Linda. "Theater and the Critics." In *Eugene O'Neill's Century: Centennial Views of America's Foremost Tragic Dramatist.* Ed. Richard F. Moorton, Jr. Westport, CT: Greenwood, 1991. 207-11.

Explores the traditionally problematic and hostile relationship between theater artists and critics.

B218 Higgs, Robert J. *Laurel and Thorn: The Athlete in American Literature.* Lexington: Kentucky UP, 1981. 55-62.

Considers Gordon Shaw of *Interlude* as an athlete-hero, using Lord Raglan's characteristics to define the traditional hero. "O'Neill looks at the hero archetypically and appears to conclude that the hero has his real being in woman for whom he strives in all his undertakings, that the antipathy on the part of the mind man toward the hero is to some extent sour grapes, but that the hero with all his systems of honor is rather inflexible, hence quite superficial and, possibly … a bore." Also touches on *Abortion.*

B219 Hilleary, Roger. *Tao House: Eugene O'Neill's Ideal Home.* Monterey, CA: Hilleary and Petko, 1988.

Unavailable.

B220 Hinden, Michael. *Long Day's Journey into Night: Native Eloquence.* Masterwork Studies Series. Boston: Twayne, 1990.

Following the format for the series, Hinden's work gives a chronology of the author's life and works, discusses *Journey*'s importance, composition and critical reception, and addresses key critical questions raised by the work. A selected bibliography is also provided.

Wilkins, Frederick C. Rev. *Eugene O'Neill Review* 14.1-2 (1990): 114-17.

B221 Hirsch, Foster. *Eugene O'Neill: Life, Work, and Criticism.* The Authoritative Studies in World Literature Series. Fredericton, NB [Canada]: York, 1986.

Neither an article nor a book-length study, Hirsch's contribution may properly be termed a pamphlet, an introduction to the playwright and his work. Included are a biography, a list of O'Neill's plays, an overview of his canon, an assessment of his achievement, and a modest annotated bibliography.

Wilkins, Frederick C. Rev. *Eugene O'Neill Newsletter* 12.2 (1988): 68-71.

B222 Hoffmann, Gerhard. "Eugene O'Neill: America's Nietzschean Playwright." In *Nietzsche in American Literature and Thought.* Ed. Manfred Pütz. Columbia, SC: Camden House, 1995. 197-221.

Looks at the Nietzschean notions — eternal recurrence, self-overcoming, perspectivism, and affirmation of life — that influenced the playwright, and the philosophic notions with which O'Neill took issue or which he modified, in discussions of *Lazarus* and *Brown,* though Nietzsche's influence is not restricted to these two plays, as the essay points out. O'Neill's treatment of two recurring interests — "the function of pipe dreams and the role of pity, and their integration into the struggle between life and death after God is pronounced dead" — shows his indebtedness to Nietzsche and the playwright's uniqueness.

Levin, Eric. Rev. *Eugene O'Neill Review* 20.1-2 (1996): 155-58.

B223 Hori, Mariko. "Author, Actor, Audience: The Metatheatrical Elements in the Late Plays of Eugene O'Neill." In *Eugene O'Neill in China: An International Centenary Celebration.* Westport, CT: Greenwood, 1992. 121-28.

Proclaims the purpose is to apply one of Richard Hornsby's six categories of metatheater, role playing within the role, to O'Neill's late plays and look at its impact on the audience.

B224 Houchin, John H., ed. *The Critical Response to Eugene O'Neill.* Critical Responses in Arts and Letters Series, no. 5. Westport, CT: Greenwood, 1993.

Each number in the series presents "a documentary history of the critical reception" of its subject's major works. In Houchin's collection are 75 newspaper or magazine reviews

from Heywood Broun's 1917 *New York Tribune* review of *Cardiff* to John Simon's 1988 *New York Magazine* review of *Journey*— in all touching base for 35 plays. In addition there are reprints of 17 critical essays or parts of books. The items falling within our scope (all reprints) are:

Judith Barlow's "O'Neill's Many Mothers" (See B23)

Clive Barnes' reviews of the 1973 *Iceman* and of the 1981 *Journey* (See E249 and E305)

Linda Ben-Zvi's "Freedom and Fixity" (See A33)

Steven Bloom 's review of a 1986 *Journey* (See E325)

Robert Brustein's review of 1985 *Iceman* (See E256).

Harold Clurman's reviews of 1977 *Anna* (See E87) and of 1973 *Brown* (See E191).

Stephen L. Fluckiger's "The Idea of Puritanism…" (See A219)

Michael Hinden's "*The Birth of Tragedy* and *The Great God Brown*" (See A305)

T. E. Kalem's review of 1977-78 *Touch* (See E523)

Jack Kroll's review of 1976 *Journey* (See E287)

Bette Mandl's "Absence as Presence…" (See A396)

S. Georgia Nugent's "Masking Becomes Electra" (See A478)

Laurin Porter's "*A Touch of the Poet*" (excerpted from her *Banished Prince* (See B331)

John Raleigh 's "Communal, Familial, and Personal Memories" (See A524)

James A. Robinson's "Metatheatrics of *A Moon for the Misbegotten*" (See B361)

John Simon's review of 1984 *Misbegotten* (See E416)

John Simon's review of 1988 *Wilderness* and *Journey* (See E55).

Thomas F. Van Laan's "Singing in the Wilderness…" (See A668)

Douglas Watt's review of 1975 *Chillun* (See E84)

Frederick C. Wilkins' review of 1984-85 *Interlude* (See E511)

In the introduction we are provided with an overview of O'Neill's critical development. There is a proper-noun index.

Frank, Glenda. Rev. *Eugene O'Neill Review* 17.1- 2 (1993): 211-14.

B225 Houseman, John. *On Stage: Selected Theater Reviews from the "New York*

Times," 1920-70. Eds. Bernard Beckerman and Howard Siegman. New York: Arno, 1973.

Includes: Alexander Woollcott's reviews of *Horizon*, 4 Feb. 1920, pp. 7-8; *Jones*, 7 Nov. 1920, pp. 13-14; *Anna*, 3 Nov. 1921, pp. 23-24; *Ape*, 21 Feb. 1922, pp. 26-27. Stark Young's review of *Desire*, 12 Nov. 1924, pp. 48-49. Brooks Atkinson's reviews of *Brown*, 25 Jan. 1926, pp. 63-64; *Interlude*, 31 Jan. 1928, pp. 85-87; *Electra*, 27 Oct. 1931, pp. 127-29; *Wilderness*, 3 Oct. 1933, pp. 142-43; *Iceman*, 9 May 1956, pp. 377-78; *Journey*, 8 Nov. 1956, pp. 378-79. Howard Taubman's review of *Interlude*, 13 Mar. 1963, pp. 449-51.

B226 Hsia, An Min. "Cycle of Return: O'Neill and the Tao." In *Eugene O'Neill's Critics: Voices from Abroad*. Eds. Horst Frenz and Susan Tuck. Carbondale: Southern Illinois UP, 1984. 169-73.

A reprint; see A326.

B227 Humphrey, Robert E. *Children of Fantasy: The First Rebels of Greenwich Village*. New York: John Wiley, 1978.

Psychobiographies of Max Eastman, Floyd Dell, Hutchins Hapgood, John Reed, and George Cram Cook, all O'Neill contacts.

B228 Ikeuchi, Yasuko. "Two Popular O'Neill Plays Staged in Japan: *Ah, Wilderness!* and *Desire Under the Elms*." In *Eugene O'Neill in China: An International Centenary Celebration*. Eds. Haiping Liu and Lowell Swortzell. Westport, CT: Greenwood, 1992. 255-64.

Gives an overview of O'Neill's popularity in Japan, which, not surprisingly, waxed and waned with the political climate.

B229 Jackson, Esther M. "O'Neill the Humanist." In *Eugene O'Neill: A World View*. Ed. Virginia Floyd. New York: Ungar, 1979. 252-56.

Sees O'Neill's plays of the 1920s and 30s as reflecting the New Humanism of Irving Babbitt, Paul Elmer More, and Jacques Maritain.

B230 Jařab, Josef. "The Lasting Challenge of Eugene O'Neill: A Czechoslovak View." In *Eugene O'Neill: A World View*. Ed. Virginia Floyd. New York: Ungar, 1979. 84-100.

Covers O'Neill's Czechoslovakian career, his production history, and the shifting of attitudes about his work. Gives a partial list of productions from 1925-75.

B231 Jensen, George H. "Eugene O'Neill." In *Twentieth-Century American*

Dramatists. Ed. John MacNichols. *The Dictionary of Literary Biography* 7. Detroit: Gale Research Company, 1981. 39-65.

An overview of O'Neill's life, summaries of the plays, useful lists of first productions and publications. The bibliography ("References") is solid though slightly eccentric.

B232 Jilthe, M. F. "The Trauma of Belonging on [*sic*] *The Hairy Ape*." In *T. S. Eliot & Eugene O'Neill: The Dream and the Nightmare*. Eds. V. R. N. Prasad, et al. New Delhi: Ajanta, 1991. 163-70.

In Yank we see "the picture of one who in the world of wealth — which is not his — tries to seek his identity desperately, and finds it only in death."

B233 Jones, Betty Jean. "Directing the Plays of Eugene O'Neill — Style, Substance, and Synthesis." In *Eugene O'Neill in China: An International Centenary Celebration*. Eds. Haiping Liu and Lowell Swortzell. Westport, CT: Greenwood, 1992. 223-29.

Offers advice on what to consider when reading an O'Neill play for production. Style (internal coherence), substance (meaning), and synthesis (unity) are the director's foci.

B234 Josephson, Lennart. *A Role: O'Neill's Cornelius Melody*. Stockholm Studies in the History of Literature, 19. Trans. Alan Blair. Atlantic Highlands, NJ: Humanities, 1978.

Despite awkwardnesses in the prose style and frequent statement of the obvious, the book gives a careful analysis of the whole play. As the title indicates the focus is on Melody — sources in real life, literary motivation, change at the end of the play. [Originally published in Swedish; see D147]

B235 Kauffmann Stanley. *Persons in the Drama: Theater Criticism and Comment*. New York: Harper, 1976.

A collection of Kauffmann's reviews originally published in *The New Republic, World, Performance, Horizon,* and *The American Scholar*. Includes *Journey*, pp. 133-34 (12 June '71), *Wilderness*, pp. 136-39 (11 Oct. '75), and *Misbegotten*, pp. 134-36 (26 Jan. '74). For scattered comments on productions see his index.

B236 Kellner, Bruce. *The Last Dandy, Ralph Barton: American Artist, 1891-1931*. Columbia: U of Missouri P, 1991.

The other side of the story, Barton being the man Carlotta left for O'Neill.

Mellow, James R. Rev. *New York Times Book Review* 8 Dec. 1991: 13.

B237 Kemp, Harry. *Poet of the Dunes.* Provincetown, MA: Cape Cod Pilgrim Memorial Association, 1988.

Kemp's poetry, mostly about the Cape. The first volume of what is planned as a series of reprints of Cape Cod classics. For those interested in O'Neill's friends and in the ambience of his Provincetown.

Brooks, Marshall. Rev.-note. *Eugene O'Neill Newsletter* 12.2 (1988): 71.

B238 Kennedy, Andrew R. *Dramatic Dialogue: The Duologue of Personal Encounter.* Cambridge: Cambridge UP, 1983. 180-93.

Discusses the different shapes and conventions of dialogue in drama from Aeschylus to the present. Studies in detail the dialogue of personal encounter between protagonists to conclude that in *Journey* and *Hughie* the dialogue reflects the need for self-disclosure, and in general the later O'Neill reflects "special gifts for personal idiom in 'the vernacular' and for embodying personal encounter in dialogue."

B239 Khan, A. G. "The Changing Roles of Electra and Clytemnestra." In *T. S. Eliot & Eugene O'Neill: The Dream and the Nightmare.* Eds. V. R. N. Prasad, et al. New Delhi: Ajanta, 1991. 121-28.

Considers the Electra impulse in O'Neill's play and concludes that Lavinia is "a characteristically O'Neillian statement on the theme of waste that preoccupied the creative imaginations" of O'Neill's contemporaries.

B240 Khan, Hameed. "Transgression and Transcendence: Family in *Desire Under the Elms.*" In *T. S. Eliot & Eugene O'Neill: The Dream and the Nightmare.* Eds. V. R. N. Prasad, et al. New Delhi: Ajanta, 1991. 151-57.

"It is, thus, in this mundane domestic context [the macro-microcosm of the family] that O'Neill develops his major concerns such as death, fate, greed, lust, love, loss of faith," etc.

B241 Khare, R. R. *Eugene O'Neill and His Visionary Quest.* New Delhi: Mittal, 1992.

Sees O'Neill's "tragic vision as a quest for happiness." Happiness is the "escape" from the terrible "compulsions of this physical life" into "an ideal state ... through death." The death-wish in O'Neill's plays is an expression of the urge toward death. The "tragic career"

of his characters is "a sustained quest for happiness." Though many of O'Neill's plays are touched on, *Iceman* and *Journey* receive most attention. An appendix of nearly 40 pages treats of O'Neill and Shakespeare as "Kindred Souls in Quest of Happiness."

B242 Kimbel, Ellen. "Eugene O'Neill as Social Historian: Manners and Morals in *Ah, Wilderness!*" In *Critical Essays on Eugene O'Neill.* Ed. James J. Martine. Boston: G. K. Hall, 1984. 137-45.

A look at O'Neill's comedy in terms of how the play reflects traditional values (home, family, respectability, success) at the early part of the century. Argues the play testifies as to how much we have lost.

B243 King, W. Davies, ed. *"A Wind Is Rising": The Correspondence of Eugene O'Neill and Agnes Boulton.* Rutherford, NJ: Fairleigh Dickinson UP, announced for 1999.

See Primary Works section, G56.

B244 Kobernik, Mark. *Semiotics of the Drama and of the Style of Eugene O'Neill.* Foundations of Semiotics Ser. 19. Ed. Achim Eschbach. Amsterdam: John Benjamins, 1989.

States the purpose forthwith: "To develop and apply a new method of analyzing texts in order better to understand them and their author. This approach takes into consideration many signifying systems of signs as such, and this is semiotic." If only the rest of the work were that lucid. Explaining the theoretical basis for the study, Kobernik then turns his attention to six O'Neill plays: *Anna, Desire, Interlude, Electra, Journey,* and *Touch,* with additional analysis of *Anna, Desire,* and *Journey* to follow. Providing graphs, charts, and other graphics in his impenetrable analysis, Kobernick attempts an interpretation of the matrices in Chapter Nine, his final chapter. See C65.

B245 Konick,   Marcus. "Eugene O'Neill and Puritanism." In *Eugene O'Neill in China: An International Centenary Celebration.* Eds. Haiping Liu and Lowell Swortzell. Westport, CT: Greenwood, 1992. 13-20.

Rates O'Neill's attitude toward religions: Catholicism, "which comes off best," and Protestantism, which "comes in for little but criticism," and Puritanism, in particular, which "is portrayed as critical, loveless, joyless, and eternally frigid."

B246 Koreneva, Maya. "Eugene O'Neill and the Traditions of American Drama." In

20th Century American Literature: A Soviet View. Trans. Ronald Vroon. Moscow: Progress, 1976. 143-59.

O'Neill consciously aimed at inspiring American drama. Though the book's subtitle is suggestive, the essay is not Marxist in slant. O'Neill is treated mostly as technician whose contribution to drama was his experimentation. Arthur Miller, Paul Green, and Lillian Hellman are introduced for ambience; later dramatists (Albee for example) to suggest O'Neill's influence.

B247 _____. "One Hundred Percent American Tragedy." In *Eugene O'Neill: A World View.* Ed. Virginia Floyd. New York: Ungar, 1979. 145-71.

Treats of the reception of O'Neill's plays in Russia. Tairov of the Kamerny Theatre found O'Neill's personal vision and dramatic sense matching his own. Maintains that O'Neill's social vision was instrumental in the Russian appreciation of his work, but so was his handling of tragedy — his experiments culminating in the 100-percent American tragedy *Journey.*

B248 _____. "Eugene O'Neill and the Ways of American Drama." In *Russian Eyes on American Literature.* Eds. Sergei Chakovsky and Thomas Inge. Jackson: UP of Mississippi, 1992. 103-25.

A contextual assessment of the playwright's work, wherein Koreneva looks at O'Neill's connection to his contemporaries and at his uniqueness.

B249 _____. "Leo Tolstoy's *The Power of Darkness* and Eugene O'Neill's *Desire Under the Elms.*" In *Eugene O'Neill in China: An International Centenary Celebration.* Eds. Haiping Liu and Lowell Swortzell. Westport, CT: Greenwood, 1992. 89-96.

Discusses Abbie's killing of her child in *Desire* in light of a similar scene in Tolstoy's work, in particular how the errant characters achieve redemption.

B250 Krafchick, Marcelline. "All God's Chillum Play Games." In *Eugene O'Neill in China: An International Centenary Celebration.* Westport, CT: Greenwood, 1992. 231-38.

Addresses the spousal games Jim and Ella Harris resort to in *Chillun.*

B251 Kurokawa, Yoshiteru. "Directing *Mourning Becomes Electra* in Japan." In *Eugene O'Neill in China: An International Centenary Celebration.* Eds. Haiping Liu and

Lowell Swortzell. Westport, CT: Greenwood, 1992. 265-68.

Explains why *Electra* was selected and what changes were made to ready it for the Japanese stage.

B252 Lahr, John. "Eugene O'Neill: Selling the Sizzle." In *Light Fantastic: Adventures in Theatre.* New York: Dell Publishing, 1996. 199-206.

Originally written for the *New Yorker,* the essay combines an enthusiastic response to the 1992-93 *Anna* and an interview with Natasha Richardson. There is an insightful comparison of this production with O'Neill's original intentions.

B253 Lal, D. K. *Myth and Mythical Concept in O'Neill's Plays.* New Delhi: Atlantic, 1992.

A reworking of Lal's 1985 doctoral dissertation (see C66), this book addresses Greek myth, religious myth, the Oedipus Complex and archetypes, new myths, and symbolic imagery in O'Neill's canon. Predictably the plays that are focal are: *Electra, Desire, Brown, Lazarus, Dynamo,* and *Journey.* Included is a dated bibliography, the most recent entries being from the early 1970s. See C66.

B254 Larabee, Ann E. "'Meeting the Outside Face to Face': Susan Glaspell, Djuna Barnes, and O'Neill's *The Emperor Jones.*" In *Modern American Drama: The Female Canon.* Ed. June Schlueter. Rutherford, NJ: Fairleigh Dickinson UP, 1990. 77-85.

Looks at O'Neill's play in light of the work of Provincetown playwrights Djuna Barnes and Susan Glaspell. As in *Jones,* works by these female playwrights focused on exile and "revised marginality into a position of aliveness, creativity, and linguistic freedom, constrained not only by society but by dramatic representation itself." Larabee looks to Glaspell's *The Verge* and Barnes's *Nightwood* to prove her point.

B255 Lawson, Lewis A. "Yank Smith's Fall: A Sartrean Reading of *The Hairy Ape.*" In *Sense and Transcendence: Essays in Honour of Herman Servotte.* Ed. Ortwin de Graef, et al. Louvain, Belgium: Leuven UP, 1995. 163-73.

In asserting that the play is about being and man's response to it, Lawson traces Yank's struggle with consciousness and reflectivity in an Existentialist vocabulary.

B256 Lazarus, A. L., ed. *A George Jean Nathan Reader.* Cranbury, NJ: Associated U

Presses, 1990/Rutherford, NJ: Fairleigh Dickinson UP, 1990.

O'Neill figures prominently in this reader, which features a photograph of the playwright, letters from O'Neill to the critic, and a profile of O'Neill by Nathan. Though the information on O'Neill is not new, the book provides a one-stop look at the relationship between playwright and critic. Most impressive — the book includes essays in criticism, profiles on theatrical persons, letters, a photo gallery, and an index — is the almost 140 pages of glossary.

Connolly, Thomas F. Rev. *Eugene O'Neill Review* 15.2 (1991): 119-21.

B257 Leech, Clifford. "O'Neill in England — from *Anne Christie* to *Long Day's Journey into Night*: 1923-58." In *Eugene O'Neill: A World View*. Ed. Virginia Floyd. New York: Ungar, 1979. 68-72.

An appreciation of O'Neill's English career as Leech saw the playwright's work being performed from the 1920s on. Leech died before completing the essay.

B258 Lewis, Ward B. *Eugene O'Neill: The German Reception of America's First Dramatist.* German Studies in America, 50. Berne: Lang, 1984.

Shows how German productions of O'Neill's plays interpreted them in such a way as to "illuminate the cultural attitudes and national sensibilities both of the audience and the playwright himself." Claims to concentrate on performance and reception of plays, but covers scholarship as well — scrupulously. Treatments are chronologically arranged in order of their appearance in Germany: *Anna, Jones, Ape, Desire, Chillun, Brown, Interlude, Electra, Wilderness, Iceman, Misbegotten, Journey,* and *Touch.*

O'Neill is seen early on as old-fashioned and derivative, though *Desire* and *Chillun* were modestly successful and *Interlude* very much so. After World War II *Electra* was triumphant. From 1953 until the mid-1960s, O'Neill's reputation was at a peak, especially in regard to his four last plays. He still receives more attention in Germany than any other English language playwright with the exception of Shakespeare.

B259 _____. "Politics and a Proletarian Tragedy: A Comparative Analysis of the Reception of Eugene O'Neill's *The Hairy Ape* in Germany and in the United States." In *Eugene*

O'Neill in China: An International Centenary Celebration. Eds. Haiping Liu and Lowell Swortzell. Westport, CT: Greenwood, 1992. 59-69.

Discusses the 1986 Berlin production (Theatre at Lenin Square) of *Ape*, which generated widely divergent critical comment based on what critics perceived as the political nature of O'Neill's work and compares it to the reception of the original 1922 New York production when the political overtones were largely ignored.

B260 Li, Gang. "O'Neill's Understanding of Chinese Thought in *Marco Millions*." In *Eugene O'Neill in China: An International Centenary Celebration.* Eds. Haiping Liu and Lowell Swortzell. Westport, CT: Greenwood, 1992. 37-47.

Taking Robinson's *Eugene O'Neill and Oriental Thought* as his starting point, Li expands slightly on Taoist and Confucian influence in *Marco.*

B261 Lichtenberg, Joseph D. "The Late Works and Styles of Eugene O'Neill, Henry James, and Ludwig van Beethoven." In *Psychoanalysis: The Vital Issues.* Eds. John E. Gedo and George H. Pollock. Vol. 1. New York: International Universities P, 1984. 297-319. 2 vols.

A psychoanalyst views the parallel careers of O'Neill, James and Beethoven. None showed "great promise as a significantly creative person," each followed in his father's footsteps, each suffered a trauma in middle life which interrupted the progress of his art, each, then, reevaluated his art and, in expressing his inner traumas rather than a political or social agenda, achieved far more than he had previously.

B262 Lind, Ilse Dusoir. "Faulkner's Use of Poetic Drama." In *Faulkner, Modernism, and Film: Faulkner and Yoknapatawpha, 1978.* Eds. Evans Harrington and Ann J. Abadie. Jackson: UP of Mississippi, 1979. 66-81.

From the 1978 annual Faulkner conference. Makes a detailed comparison between *Chillun* and *A Light in August*, indicating some influences on Faulkner.

B263 Liu, Haiping, and Lowell Swortzell, eds. *Eugene O'Neill in China: An International Centenary Celebration.* Contributions in Drama and Theatre Studies, 44. Westport, CT: Greenwood, 1992.

The proceedings of the O'Neill Centennial Celebration, Nanjing, PRC, 1988: 30 presentations, a panel discussion, keynote address and prefatory material about the conference. The presentations are listed below.

Judith Barlow's "Building Characters: Eugene O'Neill's Composition Process" (See B25)

Jean Chothia's "Register and Idiolect in *The Iceman Cometh* and *Long Day's Journey into Night* " (See B96)

William R. Elwood's "Eugene O'Neill's *Dynamo* and the Expressionist Canon" (See B147)

Virginia Floyd's "Eugene O'Neill's *Tao Te Ching*: The Spiritual Evolution of a Mystic" (See B167)

Mariko Hori's "Author, Actor, Audience: The Metatheatrical Elements in the Late Plays of Eugene O'Neill" (See B223)

Yasuko Ikeuchi's "Two Popular O'Neill Plays Staged in Japan: *Ah, Wilderness!* and *Desire Under the Elms* " (See B228)

Betty Jean Jones's "Directing the Plays of Eugene O'Neill — Style, Substance, and Synthesis" (See B233)

Albert E. Kalson and Lisa M. Schwerdt's "Eternal Recurrence and the Shaping of Eugene O'Neill's Dramatic Structure" (A reprint; see A348)

Marcus Konick's "Eugene O'Neill and Puritanism" (See B245)

Maya Koreneva's "Leo Tolstoy's *The Power of Darkness* and Eugene O'Neill's *Desire Under the Elms*: A Road to Redemption" (See B249)

Marcelline Krafchick's "All God's Chillun Play Games" (See B250)

Yoshiteru Kurokawa's "Directing *Mourning Becomes Electra* in Japan" (See B251)

Ward B. Lewis' "Politics and a Proletarian Tragedy: A Comparative Analysis of the Reception of Eugene O'Neill's *The Hairy Ape* in Germany and the United States" (See B259)

Gang Li's "O'Neill's Understanding of Chinese Thought in *Marco Millions* " (See B260)

Felicia Hardison Londre's "Dramatic Tension Between Expressionistic Design and Naturalistic Acting in *The Emperor Jones* " (See B264)

Wenpei Long's "How Does O'Neill Fare in China?" (See B265)

Marc Maufort's "Mirrors of Consciousness: Narrative Patterns in O'Neill's *The Iceman Cometh* " (See B283)

James S. Moy's "Eugene O'Neill's *Marco Millions*: Desiring Marginality and the Dematerialization of the Orient" (See B306)

Thomas D. Pawley's "The Black World of Eugene O'Neill" (See B323)

Zhiji Ren's "The Uses of Pessimism: Some Random Thoughts about Eugene O'Neill's *Misbegotten* and Ibsen's *Peer Gynt* (See B356)

James A. Robinson's "*Iceman* and *Journey*, *Yin* and *Yang*: Taoist Rhythm and O'Neill's Late Tragedies" (See B363)

Robert K. Sarlós' "Eugene O'Neill and the Provincetown Players: Watershed in American Theatre" (See B372)

Lowell Swortzell's "*The Emperor Jones* as a Source of Theatrical Experimentation, 1920s-1980s" (See B419) and his "Introduction from the United States" (A reprint; see A649)

Jianqui Sun's "O'Neill in a Chinese Classroom: *Before Breakfast*— Good Starting Point" (See B417)

Egil Törnqvist's "Ingmar Bergman and *Long Day's Journey into Night* (See B430)

Paul Voelker's "Eugene O'Neill, World Playwright: The Beginnings" (See B441)

Daniel J. Watermeier's "*The Iceman Cometh* Twice: A Comparison of the 1946 and 1956 New York Productions" (See B450)

Jean Anne Waterstradt's "Three O'Neill Women: An Emergent Pattern" (See B453)

Bower, Martha. Rev. *Eugene O'Neill Review* 17.1-2 (1993): 208-11.

B264 Londre, Felicia Hardison. "Dramatic Tension Between Expressionistic Design and Naturalistic Acting in *The Emperor Jones*." In *Eugene O'Neill in China: An International Centenary Celebration*. Eds. Haiping Liu and Lowell Swortzell. Westport, CT: Greenwood, 1992. 183-97.

Provides a look at some of the more famous productions of *Jones* (as well as the Missouri Repertory Theatre's 1988 production) and argues that the play's naturalistic acting and expressionistic design are both a challenge and a strength of the play.

B265 Long, Wenpei. "How Does O'Neill Fare in China?" In *Eugene O'Neill in China: An International Centenary Celebration*. Eds. Haiping Liu and Lowell Swortzell. Westport, CT: Greenwood, 1992. 249-54.

Explains what O'Neill plays were popular in China, and when. "Well" is his answer to the titular question.

B266 Mandl, Bette. "Theatricality and Otherness in *All God's Chillun Got Wings*." In *Feminist Rereadings of Modern American Drama*. Ed. June Schlueter. Rutherford, NJ: Fairleigh Dickinson UP, 1989. 48-56.

Argues that both the power and the limitations of *Chillun* derive from its use of polarities, that the play's form dictates how the "psychological and social elements converge in the play."

B267 Manheim, Michael. *Eugene O'Neill's New Language of Kinship*. Syracuse: Syracuse UP, 1982.

Shows that characters in O'Neill's early works are variations on the playwright's family. Does not read biography into the plays but extrapolates it from them. Also discusses the language of kinship — the alternating between affection and hostility which is so typical of family relations. Observes that in the playwright's middle period (the 1920s) the characters withdrew from each other, but in the late plays, when O'Neill had come to terms with his family, the language of kinship resurfaces.

B268 _____. "The Transcendence of Melodrama in O'Neill's *The Iceman Cometh*." In *Critical Essays on Eugene O'Neill*. Ed. James J. Martine. Boston: G. K. Hall, 1984. 145-58.

Discusses characters' pasts and concludes that the stories we hear of the former lives of these characters are melodramatic in that they all "hint of intrigue, and they all assume a fixed ethical framework and a struggle between protagonists and antagonists." Hickey is like Parritt in that he "is living a single melodrama." Hickey sees himself as a protagonist, but in the course of the play confronts his contradictory selves and achieves self-recognition, which the other characters do not. Slade unlike others, recognizes that there is no absolute past but only conflicting interpretations of it: he lives in the "unmelodramatizable" present.

B269 _____. "The Transcendence of Melodrama in *Long Day's Journey into Night*." In *Perspectives on Eugene O'Neill: New Essays*. Ed. Shyamal Bagchee. Victoria, BC: U of Victoria P, 1988. 33-42.

Argues that O'Neill's masterpiece is "a true tragedy precisely because it does not reduce existence to 'good' and 'evil' alternatives." However familiar we become with the characters in this play, they "remain inscrutable to us."

B270 _____. "Eugene O'Neill and the Founders of Modern Drama." In *Eugene O'Neill and the Emergence of American Drama*. Ed. Marc Maufort. Costerus New Series, 75. Amsterdam: Rodopi, 1989. 47-57.

Beginning with the premises that serious American drama emerged from serious European drama of the 19th and early 20th centuries and that American drama was a reaction to melodrama, Manheim looks to Ibsen's *The Wild Duck*, Strindberg's *Miss Julie*, Chekhov's *The Three Sisters*, and O'Neill's *Journey* to show that in their unpredictability these plays are "distinctly post-melodramatic."

B271 _____, ed. *The Companion to Eugene O'Neill*. Cambridge Companions to Literature series. Cambridge: Cambridge UP, 1998.

Besides front and back matter (chronology, list of works, select bibliography), there are 16 "specially commissioned" studies of O'Neill's life, intellectual and theatrical milieus, his canon, its production history, as well as essays on "special topics" (including one that aims to undermine the notion that O'Neill is a great world dramatist). The work "attempts to be comprehensive." The sixteen studies are listed below.

Judith E. Barlow's "O'Neill's Female Characters" (See B26)

Normand Berlin's "The Late Plays" (See B39)

Stephen A. Black's " 'Celebrant of Loss': Eugene O'Neill 1888-1953" (See B49)

Jean Chothia's "Trying to Write the Family Play: Autobiography and the Dramatic Imagination" (See B97)

Kurt Eisen's "O'Neill on Screen" (See B144)

Donald Gallup's "A Tale of Possessors Self-Dispossessed" (See B182)

Michael Manheim's "The Stature of *Long Day's Journey Into Night*" and "O'Neill Criticism" (See B273 and B272)

Brenda Murphy's "O'Neill's America: The Strange Interlude between the Wars" (See B308)

Margaret Loftus Ranald's "From Trial to Triumph: The Early Plays" (See B352)

James A. Robinson's "The Middle Plays" (See B364)

Edward L. Shaughnessy's "O'Neill's African and Irish-Americans: Stereotypes or 'Faithful Realism'" (See B386)

Egil Törnqvist's "O'Neill's Philosophical and Literary Paragons" (See B432)

Ronald Wainscott's "Notable American Stage Productions" (See B449)

Daniel J. Watermeier's "O'Neill and the Theatre of his Time" (See B451)

Matthew H. Wikander's "O'Neill and the Cult of Sincerity" (See B458)

Maufort, Marc. Rev. *Modern Drama* 41.4 (1998): 657-58.

B272 _____. "O'Neill Criticism." In *The Companion to Eugene O'Neill*. Ed. Michael Manheim. Cambridge Companions to Literature series. Cambridge: Cambridge UP, 1998. 236-43.

A Cook's tour through O'Neill studies. Although critical works (books first, then essays) are of most importance, there is more on offer: bibliographies, biographies, collections of merit. Thumbnail descriptions of works of special importance; for others, groupings by subject or by critical slant. For scholar and aficionado alike.

B273 _____. "The stature of *Long Day's Journey into Night*." In *The Companion to Eugene O'Neill*. Ed. Michael Manheim. Cambridge Companions to Literature series. Cambridge: Cambridge UP, 1998. 206-16.

The one play given its own chapter in the book, it is shown as possessing a kind of rhythmic fluctuation of contradictions, which are designed to reflect the range of forces operating on the characters to make *Journey* "the epitome of tragedy in our time."

B274 Manocchio, Tony, and William Petitt. "The Tyrone Family." In *Families Under Stress: A Psychological Interpretation*. London: Routledge, 1975. 102-28.

Studies families as treated by Shakespeare, Rattigan, Arthur Miller, Albee, and O'Neill, each as a case study. Says the Tyrones form a closed family the interaction of whose members is realistically and accurately representative of real neople and then suggests alternative behaviors that might have resolved their problems.

B275 Manvell, Roger. *Theatre and Film: A Comparative Study of the Two Forms of Dramatic Art, and the Problems of Adaptation of Stage Plays into Film*. Rutherford: Fairleigh Dickinson UP, 1979. 106-19, 253-58.

In one section Manvell studies films made from plays by Shaw, Chekhov, O'Neill, Winter, Strindberg, Pinter, Albee, and Weiss. Considers Sidney Lumet's 1962 film adaptation of *Journey*, summarizing the play and discussing the innovations and alterations in the film. Concludes that *Journey* "seems the case of a play most efficiently rendered, rather than transmitted into film, thus losing some of its overwhelming quality in the process, though by no means all." Considers the cast "extraordinary," but finds the Irish family that O'Neill describes eluding the actors. Elsewhere he reviews the Frankenheimer film of *Iceman*: the casting is "superb" (exception: Lee Marvin, who gives a "somewhat heavy performance"). Applauds Robert Ryan's acting as "sensitive." Thinks the play's weakness lies in the characterization of Hickey which "appears too schematic, too much of a dramatic device imposed on the other, more profound characters."

B276 Martine, James J., ed. *Critical Essays on Eugene O'Neill*. Critical Essays on American Literature series. Boston: G. K. Hall, 1984.

All essays, except Egri's, were previously unpublished. See the list below. Martine's introduction is a solid bibliographical bonus.

Steven F. Bloom's "Empty Bottles, Empty Dreams: O'Neill's Use of Drinking and Alcoholism in *Long Day's Journey into Night*" (See B54)

Jackson R. Bryer's "'Peace is an Exhausted Reaction to Normal': O'Neill's Letters to Dudley Nichols" (See B82)

Steven E. Colburn's "*The Long Voyage Home*: Illusion and the Tragic Pattern of Fate in O'Neill's *S. S. Glencairn* Cycle" (See B102)

Frank R. Cunningham's "Romantic Elements in Early O'Neill" (See B115)

Péter Egri's "'Belonging Lost': Alienation and Dramatic Form in Eugene O'Neill's *The Hairy Ape*" (A reprint; see A180)

B. S. Field, Jr.'s "Concrete Images of the Vague in the Plays of Eugene O'Neill" (See B155)

Ellen Kimbel's "Eugene O'Neill as Social Historian: Manners and Morals in *Ah, Wilderness!*" (See B242)

Michael Manheim's "The Transcendence of Melodrama in O'Neill's *The Iceman Cometh*" (See B268)

Laurin Roland Porter's "*Hughie*: Pipe Dream for Two" (See B330)

Carl E. Rollyson, Jr.'s "Eugene O'Neill: The Drama of Self-Transcendence" (See B365)

June Schlueter and Arthur Lewis' "Cabot's Conflict: The Stones and the Cows in O'Neill's *Desire Under the Elms"* (See B375)

Lisa M. Schwerdt's "Blueprint for the Future: *The Emperor Jones"* (See B378)

Joseph S. Tedesco's "Dion Brown and His Problems" (See B421)

Susan Tuck's "The O'Neill-Faulkner Connection" (See B435)

B277 Maufort, Marc. "Communication as Translation of the Self: Jamesian Inner Monologue in O'Neill's *Strange Interlude*." In *Communiquer et Traduire: Hommages à Jean Dierick*. Eds. Gilbert Debusscher and Jean-Pierre van Noppen. Brussels: Editions de l'Université de Bruxelles, 1985. 319-28.

Finds in *Interlude* unacknowledged echoes of Henry James in the use of "the realistic inner monologue as a medium to communicate the human flow of consciousness" and refers to *The Portrait of a Lady* to exemplify the correspondences. O'Neill's monologue "differs from its Jamesian equivalent as it is separated from the dialogue by means of insets." Like James, though, "O'Neill wishes to suggest, through oppositions and alternating rhythms, the human flow of consciousness." Also, like James's monologue, O'Neill's unifies the work by "establishing the importance of a central consciousness." But though "James is primarily concerned with psychological issues, O'Neill makes efforts to rise from the personal to the general and to formulate a compelling statement on the metaphysical predicament of mankind."

B278 _____. "Eugene O'Neill and the Shadow of Edmond Dantès: The Pursuit of Dramatic Unity in *Where the Cross Is Made* (1918) and *Gold* (1920)." In *American Literature in Belgium*. Ed. Gilbert Debusscher. Costerus, 66. Amsterdam: Rodopi, 1988. 89-97.

The point of the article is succinctly stated at the beginning. Says Maufort, "I propose to demonstrate that while the playwright's quest [to avoid melodramatic trappings] ends in a melodramatic fiasco in *Gold*, his endeavors are rewarded in *Where the Cross Is Made*." While both plays resemble *The Count of Monte Cristo*, *Cross* "achieves a greater originality."

B279 _____. "American Flowers of Evil: *Long Day's Journey into Night* and Baudelaire." In *New Essays on American Drama*. Eds. Gilbert Debusscher and Henry I. Schvey. Costerus New Series, 76. Amsterdam: Rodopi, 1989. 13-28.

Sees "a confluence of vision between the two authors, manifesting itself in parallels in mood and tensions." "O'Neill's explicit or implicit allusions to the French poet serve to reinforce the general mood of sadness and disintegration pervading *Long Day's Journey into Night*."

B280 _____, ed. *Eugene O'Neill and the Emergence of American Drama*. Costerus New Series, 75. Amsterdam: Rodopi, 1989.

The presentations at the May 1988 international conference on Eugene O'Neill, held at Han-sur-Lesse, Belgium are listed below.

Judith Barlow's "Mother, Wife, Friend, and Collaborator: Carlotta Monterey and *Long Day's Journey into Night* " (See B24)

C. W. E. Bigsby's "O'Neill's Endgame" (See B44)

Jackson R. Bryer's "Eugene O'Neill's Letters to Donald Pace: A Newly Discovered Correspondence" (See B83 and G38)

Jean Chothia's "Theatre Language: Word and Image in *The Hairy Ape* " (See B95)

Mel Cobb's "O'Neill, or Sunny Days and Starry Nights: An Original Play" (See B100)

Ulrich Halfmann's "'With Clenched Fist…': Observations on a Recurrent Motif in the Drama of Eugene O'Neill" (See B208)

Michael Manheim's "Eugene O'Neill and the Founders of Modern Drama" (See B270)

Marc Maufort's "*Typee* Revisited: O'Neill's *Mourning Becomes* Electra" (See B281)

Marie-Claire Pasquier's "You Are One of Us, You Are a Russian" (See B321)

John Henry Raleigh's "Strindberg and O'Neill as Historical Dramatists" (See B348)

James A. Robinson's "Buried Children: Fathers and Sons in O'Neill and Shepard" (See B362)

Susan Harris Smith's "Actors Constructing the Audience: *Hughie's* Post-Modern Aura" (See B406)

Egil Törnqvist's "From *A Wife for a Life* to *A Moon for the Misbegotten*: On O'Neill's Play Titles" (See B428)

Paul Voelker's "Success and Frustration at Harvard: Eugene O'Neill's Relationship with George Pierce Baker (1914-1915)" (See B440)

Frederick C. Wilkins' "'Arriving with a Bang': O'Neill's Literary Debut" (See B460)

Mandl, Bette. Rev. *Eugene O'Neill Review* 15.1 (1991): 107-09.

B281 _____. "*Typee* Revisited: O'Neill's *Mourning Becomes Electra* and Melville." In *Eugene O'Neill and the Emergence of American Drama*. Ed. Marc Maufort. Costerus New Series, 75. Amsterdam: Rodopi, 1989. 85-96.

Shows numerous "points of confluence" between Melville's *Typee* and O'Neill's *Electra*. This material is reworked and published in Maufort's *Songs on American Experience: The Vision of O'Neill and Melville* (Lang, 1990). See the next entry.

B282 _____. *Songs of American Experience: The Vision of O'Neill and Melville*. American University Studies Series, 24. New York: Peter Lang, 1990.

Assessing O'Neill's work in light of Melville's, Maufort looks for "traces of confluence" rather than "verified elements of influence." His chapters consider the authors' autobiographical journeys, sea work, concern with tensions between land and sea, focus on Yankees and Puritans, tragedy, realism, and Americanness. Though 31 O'Neill plays are touched on, most attention is given to *Ape*, *Cardiff*, *Electra*, *Iceman*, and *Journey*. An impressive bibliography. See C78.

Cunningham, Frank R. Rev. *Modern Drama* 36 (1993): 169-70.

Martine, James J. Rev. *Eugene O'Neill Review* 15.1 (1991): 109-12.

B283 _____. "Mirrors of Consciousness: Narrative Patterns in O'Neill's *The Iceman Cometh*." In *Eugene O'Neill in China: An International Centenary Celebration*. Eds. Haiping Liu and Lowell Swortzel. Westport, CT: Greenwood, 1992. 165-73.

Studies *Iceman*'s "novelistic interior monologues," focusing on the structural patterns they generate throughout the play and concluding that "intricate use of the monologic genre" creates a challenge for producers—how to translate these patterns into effective drama.

B284 _____. "Like a Saint's Vision of Beatitude: Vision and Narration in O'Neill." In *The Force of Vision*. Eds. Earl Miner and

Torv Haga. Vol. 3 of the Proceedings of the XIIIth Congress of the International Comparative Literature Association. Tokyo: ICLA, 1995. 179-86.

Maufort's purpose: "I would argue that the unmasking process to which Edmund alludes in this rendition of his mystical communion with the sea duplicates the methods O'Neill used to reveal the secret souls of his protagonists in *Long Day's Journey into Night*." O'Neill reveals his characters' psyches "through a skillful use of the narrative interior monologue technique."

B285 McArthur, Benjamin. *Actors and American Culture, 1880-1920*. Philadelphia: Temple UP, 1984.

Stresses the "show biz" world of Richard Mansfield, Edward H. Sothern, Edwin Booth, Julia Marlowe, Ethel Barrymore, Joseph Jefferson and James O'Neill. Carefully documents the careers, reputations, labors, and standing in the community of actors of O'Neill's youth.

B286 McDonough, Edwin J. *Quintero Directs O'Neill*. Chicago: a cappella, 1991.

"Reconstructs the 13 O'Neill plays which Quintero directed, based on published criticism and reviews, memoirs, and personal interviews of producers, actors, designers, and stage managers." The book follows a chronological sequence and provides information about the scripts and premieres before each play's discussion. See C80.

Wilkins, Frederick C. Rev. *Eugene O'Neill Review* 15.2 (1991): 121-23.

B287 Meyers, Jeffrey. *Edmund Wilson: A Biography*. Boston: Houghton Mifflin, 1995. Indexed.

O'Neill doesn't figure largely in this biography, but he was an acquaintance, and Mary Blair, who starred in *Diff'rent*, *Ape*, *Desire* and *Chillun*, receives her own chapter (pp. 84-105) as one of Wilson's wives.

B288 Miller, Alice. *Banished Knowledge*. Trans. Leila Vennewitz. New York: Doubleday, 1990.

Includes a discussion of *Journey* in Miller's analysis of child abuse and its generational effects.

B289 Miller, Jordan Y. *Eugene O'Neill and the American Critic*. 2nd ed. Hamden, CT: Archon, 1973.

A revision of Miller's 1962 *Eugene O'Neill and the American Critic: A Summary and Bibliographical Checklist.* Rather more than a checklist since the second bibliography is annotated. This edition omits the long essay "Eugene O'Neill and the American Critic" in order to allow room for the bibliographical increases of the period since his first edition. Covers O'Neill scholarship and criticism through 1972. The bibliography of secondary materials is nearly 40 percent larger than that of the first edition. The index (most valuable) is 30 percent larger.

B290 _____. "Expressionism: The Waste Land Enacted." In *The Twenties: Fiction, Poetry, Drama.* Ed. Warren French. Deland, FL: Everett/Edwards, 1975. 439-54.

Surveys the appearance of expressionism. There are chapters devoted to *Jones,* "the first genuinely expressionistic play in this country," and *Ape.* Other plays which some might think expressionistic, Miller sees as "stylized" because by his definition, expressionism is concerned with the contemporary, gives a sense of immediacy, and avoids realistic themes.

B291 _____. "The Other O'Neill." In *The Twenties: Fiction, Poetry, Drama.* Ed. Warren French. Deland FL: Everett/ Edwards, 1975. 455-73.

The recurring motif in this collection of essays is the waste-land, which for O'Neill meant the "sickly pale underside of life." Miller treats the 1920s as O'Neill's apprenticeship years, years of experimentation which eventually led to *Journey* and *Iceman.* The strongest sense in O'Neill's work at this time was a sense of dismay at the world around him.

B292 _____, and Winifred Frazer. *American Drama Between the Wars: A Critical History.* New York: G. K. Hall, 1991.

O'Neill gets part of Chapter Two (pp. 37-45) and the whole of Chapter Three (pp. 46-97) in this theater history, in which his contributions to the larger drama are noted. As the title of the book suggests, only his early and middle period plays are considered. A chronology of events, notes and an extensive bibliography add to the usefulness of this informative, general history.

B293 Miller, Ronald R. "O'Neill's *Servitude,* Shaw's *Candida,* and the Comic Vision." In *Text and Presentation* [U of Florida Department of Classics 1987 Comparative Drama Conference Papers]. Ed. Karelisa Hartigan. Vol. 8. New York: University P of America, 1988. 147-56.

Argues that if O'Neill had Ibsen in mind when he conceived of *Servitude,* he turned to Shaw's *Candida* as a model for "both the work's dramatic progression and its comic resolution." In both plays the male authority figures come to realize their own pretensions and to acknowledge their spouses' contributions to the relationship.

B294 _____. "From Scenario to Script: O'Neill's Use of History in *A Touch of the Poet* and *More Stately Mansions.*" In *Text and Presentation.* Ed. Karelisa Hartigan. Lanham, MD: UP of America, 1990. 65-71.

Looks at O'Neill's vision of history and concludes that in these two plays O'Neill used "human consciousness as the crucible of history." "In the final versions of *A Touch of the Poet* and *More Stately Mansions* Eugene O'Neill wrote history plays in which the principal actors are concerned less with the making of history than with the apprehension and reconstitution of history within the montage of consciousness."

B295 _____. "Eugene O'Neill's First Transcultural Epic: 'Universal History' in *The Fountain.*" In *Staging Difference: Cultural Pluralism in American Theatre and Drama.* Ed. Marc Maufort. American University Studies Series, 25. New York: Lang, 1995. 99-109.

Looks at *The Fountain* in light of H. G. Wells's *Outline of History,* with its division of mankind into "heliolithic" agrarian people and the "Aryan" nomads inhabiting grasslands and deserts. *The Fountain* shows the intercultural conflict of these groups.

B296 Miller, Terry. *Greenwich Village and How It Got That Way.* New York: Crown, 1990.

A coffee table book in which O'Neill is mentioned primarily because of his association with the Provincetown Players.

B297 Miller, William. *Dorothy Day: A Biography.* San Francisco: Harper, 1982. 103-19.

Does not document his book: much comes from interviews with Dorothy Day and access to her personal journals and many family letters. Reacts to the Agnes Boulton and Malcolm Cowley views of Dorothy Day and suggests that Josie Hogan was in part based on her.

B298 Misra, K. S. *Modern Tragedies and Aristotle's Theory.* New Delhi: Vikas, 1981. 185-206.

Half the book discusses Aristotle's theory of tragedy. Half applies the theory to modern practice, concentrating mainly on Synge, Galsworthy, R. C. Sherriff, Masefield, O'Neill, and T. S. Eliot. Chapter 10 concerns *Ape*, which is seen as reflecting Aristotelian principles in every way except in Yank's lack of "spiritual and mental stature" (compensated for by his "mental tension and resolute opposition" to fate), and in the absence of that "effect of exaltation which great tragedy produces" (this lacking because "O'Neill's conclusion . . is pessimistic"). In his analysis of the play, Misra explicitly uses a Jungian approach.

B299 Moorton, Richard F., Jr., ed. *Eugene O'Neill's Century: Centennial Views on America's Foremost Tragic Dramatist.* Contributions in Drama and Theatre Studies, 36. Westport, CT: Greenwood, 1991.

A collection of 13 lectures given at Connecticut College, New London, in 1988, under the general title of "Collaborations III" (the others involved in the collaboration were the Eugene O'Neill Theatre Center and the city of New London — O'Neill's boyhood home). The collection is noteworthy because of the diversity of the specialists contributing: two professors of English, three of theater arts, two of psychology, a Germanist, two classicists, and so on.

Roger Brown's "Causality in O'Neill's Late Masterpieces" (See B76)

Burton L. Cooper's "Some Problems in Adapting O'Neill for Film" (See B112)

Spencer Golub's "O'Neill and the Poetics of Strangeness" (See B194)

Linda Herr's "Theater and the Critics" (See B217)

Richard F. Moorton Jr.'s "The Author as Oedipus in *Mourning Becomes Electra* and *Long Day's Journey into Night*" (A reprint; see A451)

Richard F. Moorton Jr.'s "Eugene O'Neill's American *Eumenides* " (A reprint; see A452)

Georgia S. Nugent's "Masking Becomes Electra: O'Neill, Freud, and the Feminine" (A reprint; see A478)

Kristin Pfefferkorn's "Searching for Home in O'Neill's America" (See B325)

Jeffrey Elliott Sands's "O'Neill's Stage Directions and the Actor" (See B370)

Richard B. Sewall's "Eugene O'Neill and the Sense of the Tragic" (See B382)

Lowell Swortzell's "'Get My Goat': O'Neill's Attitude toward Children and Adolescents in His Life and Art" (See B418)

Rita Terras' "A Spokesperson for America: O'Neill in Translation" (See B423)

Jane Torrey's "O'Neill's Psychology of Oppression in Men and Women" (See B433)

B300 Mordden Ethan. *The American Theater.* New York: Oxford UP, 1981.

Surveys the whole of American theater history in 340 pages. Scattered comments on O'Neill and O'Neill productions.

B301 Morse, David. "American Theatre: The Age of O'Neill." In *American Literature Since 1900.* Ed. Marcus Cunliffe. The History of Literature in the English Language 9. London: Barrie and Jenkins. 1975. 73-103.

Surveys the drama of the 1920s and 30s beginning and ending with O'Neill, who dominates the era. Paragraphs on the major plays of the period. Notes that important drama was in the interstices of commercial American theater — and had little immediate impact.

B302 _____. "American Theatre: The Age of O'Neill." In *American Literature Since 1900.* Ed. Marcus Cunliffe. 1975. Rev. ed. New York: Peter Bedrick, 1987. 53-78.

Cunliffe's book has been revised/updated. Chapter 3, Morse's essay, assesses Eugene O'Neill's contributions to American theater as well as those of his contemporaries. Though O'Neill's role in the founding of an American theater is often overstated, he did invest the drama with a psychological credibility theretofore lacking.

B303 Morse, Donald E. "The 'Life Lie' in Three Plays by O'Neill, Williams and Miller." In *Cross-Cultural Studies: American, Canadian and European Literatures, 1945-1985.* Ed. Mirko Jurak. Ljubljana [Yugoslavia]: The English Department, Filozofska fakulteta, Edvard Kardelj University of Ljubljana, 1988. 273-77.

In an article so brief one gets only a glimpse of *Iceman*, Morse argues that Hickey's illusions had no place in the cultural life of America in the 1940's, although American playwrights were fascinated by illusions. His assertion seems contradictory, even though he gives Hickey's friends more credit than he does their counterparts in *A Streetcar Named Desire* and *Death of a Salesman*. The spelling can be jarring to the meticulous.

B304 Mottram, Eric. "Eugene O'Neill." In *American Drama*. Ed. Clive Bloom. New York: St. Martin's, 1995. 21-45.

Chapter Two offers a "comprehensive introduction" to O'Neill. Geared to students who require "detailed but clear information," the essay gives an overview of O'Neill's canon and places his work in its context.

B305 Mounier, Catherine. "Notes on the 1967 French Production of *The Iceman Cometh*." In *Eugene O'Neill's Critics: Voices from Abroad*. Eds. Horst Frenz and Susan Tuck. Carbondale: Southern Illinois UP, 1984. 163-68.

Draws parallels between O'Neill's play and Ibsen's *The Wild Duck* and O'Neill's play and Beckett's *Waiting for Godot*. Then discusses the production directed by Gabriel Garran. Notes that the production was intellectual and comments on how Garran made his actors familiarize themselves with the Bowery. Garran wanted simple sets, a heavy atmosphere, and clothing as close to O'Neill's description as possible.

See D177.

B306 Moy, James S. "Eugene O'Neill's *Marco Millions*: Desiring Marginality and the Dematerialization of the Orient." In *Eugene O'Neill in China: An International Centenary Celebration*. Eds. Haiping Liu and Lowell Swortzell. Westport, CT: Greenwood, 1992. 29-36.

Finds fault with O'Neill's creation of a "Utopian Orient" in *Marco* and says that as a result of O'Neill's myopia, the "play lacks emotional intensity"—despite Kukachin's death and Kublai's grief.

B307 Murphy, Brenda. *American Realism and American Drama, 1880-1940*. Cambridge: Cambridge UP, 1987.

In a book which tries to answer two questions—whether there exists a literary definition of dramatic realism upon which criticism of realistic plays can be based and whether the theoretical ideas of these earlier realists influenced the writers of realistic plays who dominated the American theater between the two world wars—Murphy devotes a chapter, "The Cutting Edge" (pp. 112-31) to O'Neill's realism. *Iceman* and *Journey* get further mention in the last chapter, "The Final Integration." Concludes that "O'Neill's later plays are supremely important documents in the development of dramatic realism not be-

cause they mark his 'return to realism' but because they become his final achievement of inventing a realistic structure in which to represent his dynamic realism of character while maintaining the illusion of reality in all elements of that representation."

Connolly, Thomas F. Rev. *Eugene O'Neill Newsletter* 12.2 (1988): 65-67.

B308 _____. "O'Neill's America: The Strange Interlude between the Wars." In *The Companion to Eugene O'Neill*. Ed. Michael Manheim. Cambridge Companions to Literature series. Cambridge: Cambridge UP, 1998. 135-47.

Touch, Mansions, Electra, Diff'rent, Marco, Dynamo, and especially *Interlude* are used to illustrate the argument that O'Neill has often been miscast in being viewed mainly as a writer of the universal, to be compared with only those on the world stage. He is here first an American—in background, in life, in themes, in his interests, in the theatrical traditions in which, and against which, he writes.

B309 Murray, Christopher. "O'Neill and 'The Ultimate Wound': An Essay on Tragedy." In *Eugene O'Neill in Ireland: The Critical Reception*. Ed. Edward L. Shaughnessy. Contributions in Drama and Theatre Studies Series, 25. Westport, CT: Greenwood, 1988. 183-93.

Focuses on O'Neill's tragic vision and concludes that "the shape he provided for his narratives was tragic in the sense that mankind is therein invariably disclosed as doomed to fail or to lose the promise of happiness. It is a tragic sense that is both classical and Celtic."

B310 Murray, Edward. "Eugene O'Neill." *The McGraw-Hill Encyclopedia of World Drama*. Vol. 4. New York: McGraw-Hill, 1984. 22-40.

The story of O'Neill's life and career, an introduction to his works, summaries of 24 of the plays with dates of composition and publication and locations of first productions, plus a bibliography that goes up to 1978.

B311 Musser Charles. "Troubled Relations: Robeson, Eugene O'Neill, and Oscar Micheaux." In *Paul Robeson: Artist and Citizen*. Ed. Jeffrey C. Stewart. New Brunswick, NJ: Rutgers UP and the Paul Robeson Cultural Center, 1998. 81-104.

Robeson's connections with O'Neill during the *Jones* and *Chillun* period. Charles Gilpin has a brief appearance (and Marcus

Garvey a briefer one in the notes). Micheaux's film *Body and Soul* is treated as asking the viewer "to make specific comparisons" with *Jones* and *Chillun*.

B312 *The New York Times Directory of the Theater.* New York: Arno, 1973.

Lists all plays reviewed in the *Times* through 1970. Especially good index.

B313 Olson, Sara. *The Eugene O'Neill National Site, California.* Harpers Ferry, WV: National Park Service, US Department of the Interior, 1983.

Government pamphlet.

B314 Olsson, Tom. "O'Neill and the Royal Dramatic." In *Eugene O'Neill: A World View.* Ed. Virginia Floyd. New York: Ungar, 1979. 34-60.

Surveys the history of O'Neill in Sweden from the 1920s through the 1970s, especially at the Royal Dramatic Theater in Stockholm.

B315 Ooi, Vicki C. H. "Transcending Culture: A Cantonese Translation and Production of O'Neill's *Long Day's Journey into Night*." In *The Languages of Theatre: Problems in the Translation and Transposition of Drama.* Ed. Ortrun Zuber. Oxford: Pergamon, 1980. 51-68.

Speaks of the difficulties of translating *Journey* into Chinese because the impossibility of separating people from their culture (feeling, language, thought) militates against the simple translation of words: western families' nuances are too foreign to the Chinese. Concludes (ambiguously) that if it were possible to surmount these obstacles, O'Neill's play would appeal on the grounds of its universality.

B316 Orlandello, John. *O'Neill on Film.* London: Associated UP, 1982.

Examines in nine chapters the film versions of nine O'Neill plays: *Anna, Interlude, Jones, Wilderness* (and the version called *Summer Holiday*), *Voyage, Electra, Desire, Journey,* and *Iceman.* An introduction briefly surveys O'Neill's connection with films. The conclusion generalizes about the reasons for Hollywood's failure in converting O'Neill to the screen — partly irreconcilable differences between stage and screen, partly different perceptions of what the plays meant. Maintains that *Voyage, Iceman,* and *Journey* are effective as films because of sympathetic directing and advances in cinematography. Contains a "Fil-

mography." Does not discuss *Ape* or *Recklessness* (*The Constant Woman*) because the film of the first was not, then, available and the second is not well preserved.

B317 Orr, John. *Tragic Drama and Modern Society: Studies in the Social and Literary Theory of Drama from 1870 to the Present.* Totowa, NJ: Barnes and Noble, 1981.

Part IV, chapters 9, 10, and 11, "American Tragedy and the American Dream," covers O'Neill, Arthur Miller, and Tennessee Williams. Chapter 9 (pp. 165-82), "Eugene O'Neill I: The Living Tragedy," deals with *Ape, Jones, Anna,* and *Chillun* wherein the striking formal elements confirm that these plays, despite their potential universality, are primarily social statements. Chapter 10 (pp. 183-205), "Eugene O'Neill II: The Life Remembered," sees *Iceman* and *Journey* as tragedies which find their force in contemporary American conditions — capitalism and the family and the failure of American dreams.

B318 Otero, Rosalie. *Guide to American Drama Explication.* New York: G. K. Hall, 1995. 234-89.

The 55 pages on O'Neill in this unannotated bibliography are arranged alphabetically by play title listing only items connected with individual plays.

B319 *The Oxford Illustrated History of Theatre.* Ed. John Russell Brown. Oxford: Oxford UP, 1997.

For annotation see B75.

B320 Papke, Mary E. *Susan Glaspell: A Research and Production Sourcebook.* Modern Dramatists Research and Production Sourcebooks, No. 4. Westport CT: Greenwood, 1993.

A work that cannot escape an overlap with O'Neill studies. The range of the bibliographies is from 1896 — Susan Glaspell's earliest known newspaper articles and college magazine essays — to 1992. The index includes over 100 O'Neill references.

B321 Pasquier, Marie-Claire. "You Are One of Us, You Are a Russian." In *Eugene O'Neill and the Emergence of American Drama.* Ed. Marc Maufort. Costerus New Series, 75. Amsterdam: Rodopi, 1989. 77-83.

Considers the ways in which the Russian soul and O'Neill's are simpatico by looking at the playwright's reception in Russia.

B322 Patki, Y. K. "*Macbeth* and *The Emperor Jones*: A Comparative Study." In *T. S.*

Eliot & Eugene O'Neill: The Dream and the Nightmare. Eds. V. R. N. Prasad, et al. New Delhi: Ajanta, 1991. 141-50.

Points to several (sometimes forced) points of comparison between the two plays: visions (apparitions), guilt, dress, imagery, etc.

B323 Pawley, Thomas D. "The Black World of Eugene O'Neill." In *Eugene O'Neill in China: An International Centenary Celebration.* Eds. Haiping Liu and Lowell Swortzell. Westport, CT: Greenwood, 1992. 137-48.

Takes a look at the O'Neill plays which focus on blacks — those set in the Caribbean, not the Lower East Side of New York.

B324 Perry, Thomas Amherst. *A Bibliography of America Literature Translated into Romanian with Selected Romanian Commentary.* New York: Philosophical Library, 1983.

Pages 124-25, 171, and 265 list 18 plays by O'Neill published in Romanian between 1939 and 1968, and include a secondary bibliography of 19 articles and one book in Romanian on O'Neill and his plays.

B325 Pfefferkorn, Kristin. "Searching for Home in O'Neill's America." In *Eugene O'Neill's Century : Centennial Views on America's Foremost Tragic Dramatist.* Ed. Richard F. Moorton, Jr. Westport, CT: Greenwood, 1991. 119-43.

Considers the various cultural implication of the word *home* and applies these to *Journey.*

B326 Pfister, Joel. *Staging Depth: Eugene O'Neill and the Politics of Psychological Discourse.* Chapel Hill: U of North Carolina P, 1995.

In the foreword, Alan Trachtenberg describes Pfister's approach: "He practices a skeptical criticism here, one that refuses to take the author at his word and looks instead under and beyond the author's words and the mentality they project in search of cultural sources and historical causes. Pfister re-places O'Neill within the history of a precise segment of the middle class desire, aspiration and self-doubt, joins O'Neill not only to a social history of shifting fortunes in the early twentieth century but also to an intellectual history of shifting values and outlooks during the period (the 1910s and 1920s especially) when corporate capitalism consolidated its domain and control within U.S. culture." While the book includes a perhaps superfluous chronology of

O'Neill's life, it also has never-before published pictures of the playwright, a 20-plus page bibliography, and 60-some pages of notes.

Combs, Robert. Rev. *Eugene O'Neill Review* 20.1-2 (1996): 147-48.

B327 Pilkington, John, ed. *Stark Young: A Life in the Arts — Letters, 1900-1962.* Baton Rouge: Louisiana State UP, 1975.

Scattered references to O'Neill.

B328 Pitavy, François. "Writing in Eugene O'Neill's *Strange Interlude,* Writing out *Strange Interlude.*" In *Transatlantic Encounters: Studies in European-American Relations Presented to Winfried Herget.* Eds. Udo J. Hebel and Karl Ortseifen. Trier [Germany]: Wissenschaftlicher, 1995. 269-78.

Looks at various definitions of *interlude* ("an entertainment of a light or farcical character introduced between acts of an old mystery or morality play," "an intervening or interruptive space of time," "an interval") and applies the definitions to the play. Concludes that the play, which borders on the novelistic, "may be seen as precisely the book Marsden the novelist has not written and will not write. O'Neill could be the Other of Marsden: the novelist who carries out what Marsden ... just dreamed and failed to achieve." "Inconclusive though it may be, *Strange Interlude* can be seen as emblematic of a provisional, incomplete, unsatisfactory, yet necessary attempt in that endless quest for *ex-pression.*"

B329 Popovich, Helen Hauser, and James Roland Keller. "Desire and Strife: The Violent Families of Eugene O'Neill." In *The Aching Hearth: Family Violence in Life and Literature.* Eds. Sara Munson Deats and Tallent Lagretta Lenker. New York: Insight, 1991. 189-98.

A stroll through O'Neill's canon to find examples of psychological and physical domestic abuse. The authors conclude that the playwright's work shows keen understanding of the problem and its causes.

B330 Porter, Laurin Roland. "*Hughie*: Pipe Dream for Two." In *Critical Essays on Eugene O'Neill.* Ed. James J. Martine. Boston: G. K. Hall, 1984. 178-87.

Ties *Hughie* to its predecessor *Iceman* and shows that both plays provide "cultural insights" and reveal O'Neill's personal experiences. Notes that Erie Smith, like Hickey, is at least partially based on Jamie O'Neill, that in both plays family life is negatively depicted, and that both plays "search for transcendence, a strategy for breaking the stranglehold of time."

B331 _____. *The Banished Prince: Time, Memory, and Ritual in the Late Plays of Eugene O'Neill*. Theater and Dramatic Studies Series, 54. Ann Arbor: UMI, 1988.

Looks at *Touch, Mansions, The Calms of Capricorn, Iceman, Hughie, Misbegotten* and *Journey* and considers time, memory, and ritual therein. Concludes that for O'Neill's characters "the hope that the past can be recovered in the future, and the fear that it cannot, keeps them forever beggars standing outside the door, afraid to enter and unable to leave."

Wilkins, Frederick C. Rev. *Eugene O'Neill Review* 13.2 (1989): 113-16.

B332 _____. "Self-Deception as Theme in O'Neill's Late Plays." In *Readings on Eugene O'Neill*. Ed. Thomas Siebold. The Greenhaven Press Literary Companion Series. San Diego: Greenhaven, 1998. 67-72.

Abridged from Chapter One of *The Banished Prince: Time, Memory, and Ritual in the Late Plays of Eugene O'Neill*. See above, B331.

B333 Prachand, Leena. "Politics of Gender in *All God's Chillun got Wings* and *Desire Under the Elms*." In *Literature and Politics in Twentieth Century America*. Eds. J. L. Plakkoottam and Prashant K. Sinha. Hyderabad [India]: American Studies Research Center, 1993. 79-85.

Looks at *Desire's* and *Chillun's* female characters to conclude that, at least in these plays, O'Neill fails to go beyond gender stereotypes.

B334 Pradhan, Narindar S. *Modern American Drama: A Study in Myth and Tradition*. New Delhi: Arnold-Heinemann, 1978.

Originally a dissertation (U of Utah, 1972). Deals with the Edenic or Adamic myth as it relates to the work of 20th-century American dramatists — especially of Mac-Leish, Arthur Miller, Odets, O'Neill, Wilder, Tennessee Williams. The chapter headings are: "The Garden," "Innocence," "The Fall," "The Fortunate Fall," and "Quest for Paradise." *Wilderness* and *Dynamo* are touched on in "Innocence." Seventeen other O'Neill plays are dealt with in the last chapter (especially pp. 122-29), where the quest, for O'Neill, has become "almost a cult, a force in human affairs that seems to dominate all other aspects of life." It is a "dream or craving for the ideal," and is "the strength and weakness" of O'Neill's characters. In the early plays it is the dream of escape. Of *Ape, Brown* and *Marco* we are asked what would have happened if the dreams of the early plays had been realized? Answer: tragic defeat. References to *Cardiff, Caribbees, Horizon, Voyage, Ape, Zone, Brown, Ile, Marco, Interlude, Lazarus, Iceman, Journey, Touch, Wilderness, Dynamo, Desire,* and *Electra*.

B335 Prasad, Hari Mohan. *The Dramatic Art of Eugene O'Neill*. New Delhi: Associated, 1987.

Originally submitted as a thesis in 1977, this book is a survey and justification of O'Neill's art. Prasad takes up O'Neill's dramatic heritage, use of symbols, masks, and dialogue. He attempts to show that O'Neill's art is traceable to the "coalescence of vision and technique" and concludes that "the form or art pattern of his theatre is not an accidental phenomenon but the result of a constant pursuit to create a new and relevant mode of contemporary dramatic idiom." Very dated sources.

B336 Prasad, Sheela. *Tradition and Experiment in the Plays of Eugene O'Neill*. New Delhi: Capital, 1991.

Explores "the true nature of O'Neill's genius in the light of his persistent endeavours to evolve the proper theatrical language for his ever-growing and ever-changing theatrical needs." Maintains that, while much attention has been paid to O'Neill's experimentation, less has focused on "his reworking of the traditions of dramatic writing," her interest. The discussion spans the canon. Formerly a dissertation based on a very dated bibliography.

B337 Prasad, V. R. N., et al., eds. *T. S. Eliot & Eugene O'Neill: The Dream and the Nightmare*. New Delhi: Ajanta, 1991.

Capitalizing on the centennials of Eliot's and O'Neill's births, this volume contains 20 essays, 11 of them O'Neillian. Despite the four editors listed, the book's editing is slipshod. The individual essays draw on very dated bibliographies. For annotations, see under the authors' names in this section.

Madhvi Apte's "Three O'Neill Translations in Marathi" (See B11)

Satish Deshpande's "The Sense of Guilt in *The Emperor Jones* " (See B123)

V. T. Girdhari's "Eugene O'Neill's Emperor Jones: Dual Character of Minority in America" (See B192)

M. F. Jilthe's "The Trauma of Belonging on [sic] *The Hairy Ape*" (See B232)

A. G. Khan's "The Changing Roles of Electra and Clytemnestra" (See B239)

Hameed Khan's "Transgression and Transcendence: Family in *Desire Under the Elms* " (See B240)

Y. K. Patki's "*Macbeth* and *The Emperor Jones*: A Comparative Study" (See B322)

V. R. N. Prasad's "Passion and Possession in O'Neill's *Desire Under the* Elms" (See B338)

D. V. K. Raghavacharyulu's "O'Neill's *More Stately Mansions*: The Cycle of American History" (See B344)

K. G. Ranveer's "Eugene O'Neill's Treatment of Black Experience" (See B354)

Prashant K. Sinha's "Versions of Orestes Figure in *Mourning Become Electra, The Family Reunion* and *The Flies*" (See B402)

B338 Prasad, V. R. N. "Passion and Possession in O'Neill's *Desire Under the Elms.*" In *T. S. Eliot & Eugene O'Neill: The Dream and the Nightmare.* Eds. V. R. N. Prasad, et al. New Delhi: Ajanta, 1991. 115-20.

The desire to possess is a "primitive instinct" in this play. "Possessiveness and greed are such compulsive habits that they rudely violate all known codes of morality and social conduct."

B339 Press, Marcia. "Black Man–White Woman: The 'Lynch Pattern' as Morality Play." In *Text and Presentation* [Univ. of Florida Comparative Drama Conference Papers]. Ed. Karelisa Hartigan. Lanham: University P of America, 1988. 57-68.

Argues that though the punishment for violating society's taboo against the black man-white woman relationship — lynching — is passé, the taboo is still with us, "embedded in our literature." Discusses *Chillun* as a play in which both the black man and the white woman must be symbolically punished for daring to enter into a relationship.

B340 Putzel, Steven D. "Whiskey, Blarney and Land: Eugene O'Neill's Conceptions and Misconceptions of the Irish." In *Literary Interrelations: Ireland, England and the World*. Eds. Wolfgang Zach and Heinz Kosok. Tübingen: Gunter Narr, 1987. Vol. 3 of *Studies in English and Comparative Literature*. Gen.

eds. Michael Kenneally and Wolfgang Zach. 125-31.

Addresses the stereotypes of the Irish in O'Neill's work — where the playwright hits and where he misses the mark. Part of the proceedings of the 1984 conference of the International Association for the Study of Anglo-Irish Literature.

B341 Quintero, José. *If You Don't Dance They Beat You.* Boston: Little, Brown, 1974.

Quintero's autobiography. In Chapter 14 Quintero recalls his first bout with *Iceman*, preparing it for the Circle in the Square. Chapter 16 recalls a meeting with Shane O'Neill. The chapter also covers *Misbegotten* and, briefly, *Desire*. Chapters 18-21 deal with the *Journey* and *Hughie* productions. Throughout are recollections of meetings with Carlotta O'Neill. No index.

B342 _____. *Lines in the Palm of God's Hand: Eugene O'Neill and I.* Fullerton, CA: South Coast P, 1989.

Seventeen-page "collection" "prepared in honor of the centennial celebration of the birth of Eugene O'Neill." A limited edition of 250 copies.

B343 Raghavacharyulu, D. V. K. "Waiting for Hughie." In *Studies in American Literature: Essays in Honour of William Mulder*. Eds. Jagdish Chander and Narindar S. Pradhan. Delhi: Oxford UP, 1976. 43-51.

Notes that the plotting of the action in *Hughie* is like that of *Iceman* and *Journey*—confessional. Finds the play also like Beckett's *Waiting for Godot* in its revelation of "human disjuncture and absurdity": O'Neill's play however has "tidings of the miraculous" in that Charlie and Erie do succeed in establishing human contact in the face of the void as Charlie is transformed into Hughie.

B344 _____. "O'Neill's *More Stately Mansions*: The Cycle of American History." In *T. S. Eliot & Eugene O'Neill: The Dream and the Nightmare.* Eds. V. R. N. Prasad, et al. New Delhi: Ajanta, 1991. 76-99.

Looks at O'Neill's dissatisfaction with American materialism as evidenced in *Mansions*. "The central theme of the play is an extension of the idea developed in *A Touch of the Poet*, namely the loss of one's ideal self in the corruptive process of attaining worldly success and the gradual entropy of the aspiring nature of the sensitive individual in the possessive tendency of all power."

B345 Raleigh, John Henry. "Eugene O'Neill." In *Sixteen Modern American Authors.* Ed. Jackson R. Bryer. [Vol. 1]. Rev. ed. New York: Norton, 1973. 417-43. Vol. 2. Durham, NC: Duke UP, 1990. 480-518.

Volume 1, but never so called, is a revision of *Fifteen American Authors* (1969). Volume 2, "A Survey of American Criticism Since 1972" in this case means an updating of Volume 1. The books are designed to follow the pattern, used originally in *Eight American Authors,* of a narrative account of the bibliographical status of the writers under consideration, the account being divided into 5 sections: bibliography, editions, letters, biography, criticism. 16MAA introduces a sixth, supplementary, section. In Volume 1 these supplements contain the material that makes the work an updating of 15MAA, bringing us to about 1972. Volume 2 covers from 1973 to 1985, the supplements adding coverage to 1988. Raleigh's chapter, though focusing on 1973-85, also salvages a number of pre-1973 items missed in earlier bibliographies. His supplement (pp. 515-18) comments on 15 books, most from the years 1985-88.

B346 _____. "The Irish Atavism of *A Moon for the Misbegotten.*" In *Eugene O'Neill: A World View.* Ed. Virginia Floyd. New York: Ungar, 1979. 229-36.

Phil Hogan's personality, family relationships, and situation are modeled on the archetypal Irish peasant.

B347 _____. "The Last Confession: O'Neill and the Catholic Confessional." In *Eugene O'Neill: A World View.* Ed. Virginia Floyd. New York: Ungar, 1979. 212-28.

Explores the influence on his late plays of O'Neill's early Catholic training — the need to confess and seek forgiveness.

B348 _____. "Strindberg and O'Neill as Historical Dramatists." In *Eugene O'Neill and the Emergence of American Drama.* Ed. Marc Maufort. Costerus New Series, 75. Amsterdam: Rodopi, 1989. 59-75.

Compares and contrasts O'Neill's and Strindberg's interest in history to find that while they had much in common, they had even more essential differences. Ultimately he finds that "what Strindberg and O'Neill were both striving for as historical dramatists was to show, in the words of the familiar saying: history is but the lengthened shadow of a man."

B349 Ranald, Margaret Loftus. *The Eugene O'Neill Companion.* Westport, CT: Greenwood, 1984.

Aimed at "both a general and scholarly audience," this book includes analyses of O'Neill's plays and characters, biographies of those closely associated with the playwright, and casts of original productions, as well as appendices listing a chronology of plays, and film, musical, operatic, and balletic adaptations. Encyclopedic in nature, the book is an important reference tool.

B350 _____. "Eugene O'Neill." In *International Dictionary of Theater-2.* Ed. Mark Hawkins-Dady. Detroit: Gale, 1994. 720-25.

A biographical sketch of, a list of works by (collections and stage works), bibliographies on, selected criticism about and a thumbnail assessment of the canon of O'Neill. Sketches O'Neill's achievement in terms of his intellectual and technical range. Short passages on race relations, mythology, the use of masks, experimentation with dramatic form, family relationships.

B351 _____. "Eugene Gladstone O'Neill (1888-1953)." In *American Playwrights, 1880-1945: A Research and Production Sourcebook.* Ed. William W. Demastes. Westport, CT: Greenwood P, 1995. 323-47.

Forty playwrights are treated in this work, each averaging 13 pages of attention. O'Neill rates 24. The article gives a "biographical overview," covers the "premières and significant revivals" and receptions of 17 major plays (*SS Glencairn* is treated as one) in 300-word essays for each, assesses O'Neill's career in about 800 words, describes the archival sources, and concludes with almost eight pages of bibliography. Most helpful to the student, but even publishing O'Neillians will find the bibliography useful.

B352 _____. "From Trial to Triumph: The Early Plays." In *The Companion to Eugene O'Neill.* Ed. Michael Manheim. Cambridge Companions to Literature series. Cambridge: Cambridge UP, 1998. 51-68.

A study of the evolution of O'Neill's plays: growing out of vaudeville skits, reflecting in their obsession with violence and suicide the melodrama of popular theater, but moving towards a notion of "total theatre" where "character, theme, and mood become interdependent." Touches on O'Neill's growing concern with his plays' addressing mature issues and experimenting with ways to engage his audiences. O'Neill's early career — from the beginnings through *Desire*.

B353 _____. "An Overview of O'Neill's Plays." In *Readings on Eugene O'Neill*. Ed. Thomas Siebold. The Greenhaven Press Literary Companion Series. San Diego: Greenhaven, 1998. 44-50.

Reprint of her essay "Eugene O'Neill" in *International Dictionary of Theater-2*, ed. Mark Hawkins-Dady, Gale, 1994. See B350.

B354 Ranveer, K. G. "Eugene O'Neill's Treatment of Black Experience." In *T. S. Eliot & Eugene O'Neill: The Dream and the Nightmare*. Eds. V. R. N. Prasad, et al. New Delhi: Ajanta, 1991. 171-75.

Commends O'Neill for being one of the few [white] American playwrights "who considers the Black American worthy to be treated as a subject of art." Nonetheless, O'Neill has "provided no positive image of the blacks through his art."

B355 Reiter, Seymour. *World Theater: The Structure and Meaning of Drama*. New York: Horizon, 1973.

Two pages in this book are relevant to O'Neill. The discussion of *Ape* notes that the play "is close to the traditional concept of tragedy." Yank is superior to those about him, has a tragic flaw, and undergoes a recognition before he suffers a catastrophe.

B356 Ren, Zhiji. "The Uses of Pessimism: Some Random Thoughts about Eugene O'Neill." In *Eugene O'Neill in China: An International Centenary Celebration*. Eds. Haiping Liu and Lowell Swortzell. Westport, CT: Greenwood, 1992. 43-47.

Addresses the playwright's regression from hope to despair and looks at *Hughie* and *Journey* as plays which manifest O'Neill's themes of "dreams as opposed to reality and noncommunication as opposed to understanding."

B357 Rich, J. Dennis. "Exile Without Remedy: The Late Plays of Eugene O'Neill." In *Eugene O'Neill: A World View*. Ed. Virginia Floyd. New York: Ungar, 1979. 257-76.

In his last plays O'Neill "ceases his earlier search for transcendence or salvation, and the human effort becomes a search for a means of survival."

B358 Roberts, Nancy L., and Arthur W. Roberts, eds. *"As Ever, Gene": The Letters of Eugene O'Neill to George Jean Nathan*. London: Associated U Presses [Rutherford, NJ: Fairleigh Dickinson UP], 1987.

See Primary Works section, G1.

B359 Roberts, Patrick. "Orestes in Modern Drama: *Mourning Becomes Electra*." In *The Psychology of Tragic Drama*. Ideas and Forms in English Literature 5. London: Routledge, 1975. 170-82.

Primarily a Freudian, approach, so that when the author turns to twentieth-century literature, he must distinguish between unconscious insights explicable by Freud and consciously Freudian insights. Finds *Electra* "the most thoroughgoing and consistent attempt to date to interpret the Orestes myth in the light of Freudian psyche analysis." Points to the interest O'Neill had in the Orestian theme so that no character is judged: each is a victim of his personal compulsions. Although Lavinia is at the center of the play, Orin is the most interesting character. Notes too that the play loses its force as tragedy because of the concern with myth and Freudian interpretation.

B360 Robinson, James A. *Eugene O'Neill and Oriental Thought: A Divided Vision*. Carbondale: Southern Illinois UP, 1982.

Extensive study of how Eastern thought illuminates aspects of O'Neill's art. The western writers O'Neill most admired either paralleled or drew upon Oriental mystical theories: Emerson, Nietzsche, Schopenhauer, and Jung. Theorizes that O'Neill was attracted to Eastern mysticism because he sought a faith to replace his lost Catholicism. Concludes that ultimately O'Neill did not accept Eastern thought but that it still influenced his works.

B361 _____. "The Metatheatrics of *A Moon for the Misbegotten*." In *Perspectives on Eugene O'Neill: New Essays*. Ed. Shyamal Bagchee. Victoria, BC: U of Victoria P, 1988. 61-75.

Defining metatheatrics as a "self-reflexive theatrical style which not only reminds a play's viewers that they are watching a performance, but explicitly explores the conflict between role and self, art and life," Robinson looks at *Misbegotten* for these elements and concludes that the play is a "veiled commentary on his [O'Neill's] chosen medium."

B362 _____. "Buried Children: Fathers and Sons in O'Neill and Shepard." In *Eugene O'Neill and the Emergence of American Drama*. Ed. Marc Maufort. Costerus New Series, 75. Amsterdam: Rodopi, 1989. 151-57.

Suggests that *Buried Child* could be the stepchild of *Desire* since the father-son relationship dramatized therein recalls O'Neill's play.

B363 _____. "*Iceman* and *Journey, Yin and Yang*: Taoist Rhythm and O'Neill's Later Tragedies." In *Eugene O'Neill in China: An International Centenary Celebration*. Eds. Haiping Liu and Lowell Swortzell. Westport, CT: Greenwood, 1992. 21-27.

Looks at *Iceman's* complementary couples and themes of being and nonbeing, life and death and *Journey* to prove that while O'Neill's interest in oriental thought peaked in the 1920s, it lingered. "Driven by the need to resolve conflicts ... O'Neill turned to Taoism."

B364 _____. "The Middle Plays." In *The Companion to Eugene O'Neill*. Ed. Michael Manheim. Cambridge Companions to Literature series. Cambridge: Cambridge UP, 1998. 69-81.

Sees O'Neill as having, in the plays of his middle period (*Brown, Days, Interlude, Lazarus, Marco, Wilderness*) blended the melodrama with naturalism and realism, thereby exposing "the large audiences of mainstream American theatre to the concerns and techniques of European dramatists" and thus setting the stage for "the Ibsenesque moral realism of Miller, the Strindbergian sexual battles of Tennessee Williams, the expressionistic allegories of early Edward Albee, even the absurdist — and mythic — families of later Sam Shepard."

B365 Rollyson, Carl E., Jr. "Eugene O'Neill: The Drama of Self-Transcendence." In *Critical Essays on Eugene O'Neill*. Ed. James J. Martine. Boston: G. K. Hall, 1984. 123-37.

Discusses Lazarus' laughter as a means of transcending self and history and of joining the universal. The Romans in the play represent modern man who is "bound by a linear, historical concept of movement from life to death, whereas archaic man, represented by Lazarus and his followers, sees that life and death are but part of the same life cycle."

B366 Rosenstone, Robert A. *Romantic Revolution: A Biography of John Reed*. New York: Knopf, 1975. 235-77.

Chapters 15 and 16 cover the period during which Reed's and O'Neill's lives crossed, dealing only glancingly with the Bryant-O'Neill affair. Though throughout the book Rosenstone uses much unpublished material, the O'Neill connections depend largely on established publications: Agnes Boulton's *Part of a Long Story*, the Gelbs' *O'Neill*, and Sheaffer's *O'Neill: Son and Playwright* (1968).

B367 Rudnick, Lois Palken. *Mabel Dodge Luhan: New Woman, New Worlds*. Albuquerque: U of New Mexico P, 1984.

Definitive study of the life of Luhan. Chapters 3 and 4 deal with her years in New York City and her association with the bohemian world of art and politics in the second decade of the 20th century. Careful research — especially in the manuscript collections at the Beinecke, Bancroft, Houghton, and Huntingdon libraries. Though there is only one reference to O'Neill — and that is speculative — the study offers much to our understanding of the early O'Neill years.

B368 Ryback, Jeffrey W. *Eugene O'Neill: Dancing with the Devil (1888-1953): A Play for One Person*. Studio City, CA: Players Press, 1990.

See H49.

B369 Sabinson, Harvey. *Darling, You Were Wonderful*. Chicago: Henry Regnery, 1977. 33-40.

Account of a meeting Sabinson had with Carlotta in August 1959: he wanted her permission for his client Lester Osterman to rename his theater, the Coronet, after O'Neill. [This account was reprinted in the advertising supplement to *The New York Times* 7 Sept. 1980: 12, 14, 17.]

B370 Sands, Jeffrey Elliott. "O'Neill's Stage Directions." In *Eugene O'Neill's Century: Centennial Views on America's Foremost Tragic Dramatist*. Ed. Richard F. Moorton, Jr. Westport, CT: Greenwood, 1991. 192-205.

Argues the need to look at O'Neill's stage directions from the actor's viewpoint rather than from the reader's. He takes issue with critics who see the playwright's stage directions as superfluous. See C108.

B371 Sarlós, Robert Karoly. *Jig Cook and the Provincetown Players: Theatre in Ferment*. Amherst: UP of Massachusetts, 1982.

Deals with the beginnings of the Players — from 1915 to 1922. O'Neill and his work then necessarily figure prominently in the book. A well-researched study drawing on interviews and unpublished material as well as published works, the bibliography is helpful as are appendices A, B, and C, which comprise the chronology of productions, a Who's Who of the theater's history, and a description of the playhouse's physical structure.

B372 _____. "Eugene O'Neill and the Provincetown Players: Watershed in American Theatre." In *Eugene O'Neill in China: An International Centenary Celebration.* Eds. Haiping Liu and Lowell Swortzell. Westport, CT: Greenwood, 1992. 177-81.

Sarlós' point is that "Only by analyzing the changes in American theatre and drama that O'Neill and the Provincetown Players advocated in principle, practiced intermittently, and promoted both by direct example and through members who continued working in other theatres does an appropriate assessment of their radical function become possible."

B373 Scanlan, Tom. "Eugene O'Neill and the Drama of Family Dilemma." In *Family, Drama, and American Dreams.* Westport, CT: Greenwood, 1978.

Describes O'Neill as dealing "predominantly with domestic drama": he is the playwright who "traces the warring impulses of security and freedom in the American family."

B374 Schevill, James. *Break Out: In Search of New Theatrical Environments.* Chicago: Swallow, 1973. 190-97.

In recalling a visit to Tao House after O'Neill's death, the author decides the Chinese influence on O'Neill was a strong element in his last plays. Chinese philosophy helped him to control his dreadful illness and gave him the capacity to reconcile the "polarities of existence" exhibited by his characters in *Journey, Iceman,* and *Hughie.*

B375 Schlueter, June, and Arthur Lewis. "Cabot's Conflict: The Stones and the Cows in O'Neill's *Desire Under the Elms." Critical Essays on Eugene O'Neill.* Ed. James J. Martine. Boston: G. K. Hall, 1984. 111-14.

The cows and the stones with which Ephraim Cabot is identified represent two ways of living — the easy life (cows) and the hard life (stones). Both attract him and are a source of moral conflict. At the end Cabot is tempted to turn his cows loose, but he opts for the harder life — to continue on the farm.

B376 _____, **ed.** *Feminist Rereadings of Modern American Drama.* Rutherford, NJ: Fairleigh Dickinson UP, 1989.

Feminist critics address five male "canonical" playwrights. One of the playwrights is O'Neill. The three O'Neillians are listed below.

Suzanne Burr's "O'Neill's Ghostly Women" (See B87)

Anne Flèche's "'A Monster of Perfection': O'Neill's Stella" (See B160)

Bette Mandl's "Theatricality and Otherness in *All God's Chillun Got Wings"* (See B266)

Connolly, Thomas F. Rev. *Eugene O'Neill Review* 14.1-2 (1990): 117-20.

B377 Schroeder, Patricia R. *The Presence of the Past in Modern American Drama.* Rutherford, NJ: Fairleigh Dickinson UP, 1989. 29-52.

Among playwrights discussed in this book on the presence of the past in drama are Thornton Wilder, Arthur Miller, Tennessee Williams, and O'Neill. The chapter on O'Neill is a romp through various plays which confront the past; the author concludes that O'Neill's "revolt against plot-centered melodrama, his interest in characters who interact and develop, his experiments with antimimetic expository devices, and his ultimate revision of traditional dramatic sequence all enabled him, eventually, to depict a past that includes more than anterior events and affects the present in pervasive and profound ways." Dated bibliography. See C111.

Connolly, Thomas F. Rev. *Eugene O'Neill Review* 13.2 (1989): 105-13.

B378 Schwerdt, Lisa M. "Blueprint for the Future: *The Emperor Jones."* In *Critical Essays on Eugene O'Neill.* Ed. James J. Martine. Boston: G. K. Hall, 1984. 72-77.

Studies the levels on which man interacts — the personal, the social, and the impersonal — in *Jones* and traces these levels in later O'Neill plays.

B379 Scovell, Jane. *Oona: A Biography of Oona O'Neill Chaplin.* New York: Warner Books, 1998.

An account of the life of O'Neill's only daughter. Nothing new to O'Neillians — the first six chapters depend almost exclusively on standard O'Neill biographical studies (Sheaffer, the Gelbs, Bowen, Agnes Boulton, and so forth) — but a good read.

B380 Sellars, Peter. "The Importance of Being Unproducible." In *Strindberg, O'Neill and the Modern Theatre.* Eds. Claes Englund and Gunnel Bergström. Jönköping [Sweden]: Tryckeri AB Småland, 1990. 63-70.

The two great playwrights were "damaged people" who showed that "damaged" is what real people are: that "normality" is what is abnormal.

B381 Sewall, Richard. *The Vision of Tragedy.* New Haven: Yale UP, 1980. 161-74.

Journey is seen as exploring an area of contemporary life rich with "tragic potential" and reaching out toward "cosmic concerns." The "Tyrones Become Every Family."

B382 _____. "Eugene O'Neill and the Sense of the Tragic." In *Eugene O'Neill's Century: Centennial Views on America's Foremost Tragic Dramatist.* Ed. Richard F. Moorton, Jr. Westport, CT: Greenwood, 1991. 3-16.

A discussion of tragedy and the tragic in *Journey.* The sources behind "the tragic set of his mind"—Conrad, Greek tragedy, Shakespeare, "the morose poets whom Edmund and Jamie quote so frequently"—are addressed. Finds that in this play, following years of experimentation, O'Neill "comes back to where he started: the simple, direct dramatization of a life situation he knew all too well—his own."

B383 Shafer, Yvonne. *American Women Playwrights, 1900-1950.* New York: Peter Lang, 1995.

Scattered comments on or references to O'Neill, *Cardiff, Desire, Jones, Ape, Journey,* and *Interlude.* See the index where O'Neill receives more lines than any other except George S. Kaufman (who is helped by Connelly and Hart).

B384 Shaughnessy, Edward L. *Eugene O'Neill in Ireland: The Critical Reception.* Contributions in Drama and Theatre Studies Series, 25. Westport, CT: Greenwood, 1988.

Part One puts O'Neill's canon in context by discussing the cultural and familial, dramatic and thematic connections to Ireland and providing the production history of the playwright's work. Part Two gives us six Irish essays (five are reprints) on O'Neill, spanning the period 1926-88. An appendix notes productions in the Republic of Ireland and in Northern Ireland, 1922-1987. The one previously unpublished essay, and falling within this work's scope, is Christopher Murray's "O'Neill and 'The Ultimate Wound': An Essay on Tragedy" (See B309)

The reprints are:

"Danger in Dublin," Editorial condemning O'Neill and others, *The Catholic Bulletin,* Apr. 1926

St. John Ervine's "*Mourning Becomes Electra.*" *London Observer* 13, 20, 27 Mar. 1932

("There is … a poet in Mr. O'Neill, though his note is becoming fainter and fainter")

"Audience Cheered Actresses." Rev. (*Electra*) *Irish Independent* 26 Oct. 1938

"O'Neill Play a Triumph." Rev. (*Wilderness*) *Irish Press* 13 Dec. 1962

Denis Donoghue's "The Force Behind." Excerpted from *The Ordinary Universe: Soundings in Modern Literature.* Macmillan, 1968 151-60.

Wilkins, Frederick C. Rev. *Eugene O'Neill Review* 13.1 (1989): 87-90.

B385 _____. *Down the Nights and Down the Days: Eugene O'Neill's Catholic Sensibility.* Notre Dame: U of Notre Dame P, 1996.

Two concerns are at the core of his book—O'Neill's Catholic sensibility "which informed the playwright's moral vision and … the theme of sin and redemption, as it appears in the canon." His approach is as much biographical as critical. In Part One, "The Reluctant Apostate," Shaughnessy looks at the playwright's religious background and the milieu into which he was born. In Part Two, "Catholic Sensibility and Thematic Development," Shaughnessy applies Catholic teaching to works from O'Neill's early, middle, and late periods.

Breslow, Maurice. Rev. *Modern Drama* 41 (1998): 484-86.

Flynn, Joyce. Rev. *Eugene O'Neill Review* 21.1-2 (1997): 173-74.

B386 _____. "O'Neill's African and Irish-Americans: Stereotypes or 'Faithful Realism'?" In *The Companion to Eugene O'Neill.* Ed. Michael Manheim. Cambridge Companions to Literature series. Cambridge: Cambridge UP, 1998. 148-63.

Shaughnessy's answer? "In affairs of the theatre O'Neill's integrity was unassailable. His black and Irish-Americans must be seen as a 'faithful realism.'" Evidence is found in *Dreamy, Jones, Chillun, Iceman, Ape, Anna, Touch, Journey, Misbegotten,* and the *Glencairn* plays.

B387 Sheaffer, Louis. *O'Neill: Son and Artist.* Boston: Little, Brown, 1973.

The second volume in Sheaffer's definitive biography. Meticulously researched and documented. Based on letters, documents and interviews. Focuses on O'Neill's psyche and his relationship with his family.

B388 _____. *O'Neill: Son and Artist.* 1973. New York: AMS, 1988.

A reissue of the second volume of Sheaffer's definitive biography of O'Neill.

B389 _____. *O'Neill: Son And Artist.* 1973. New York: Paragon House, 1990.

A paperback edition of the second volume of Sheaffer's definitive biography.

B390 _____. *O'Neill: Son and Playwright.* 1968. New York: Paragon House, 1988.

The paperback reissue of the first volume of Sheaffer's definitive biography.

B391 _____. *O'Neill: Son and Playwright.* 1968. New York: AMS, 1988.

A reissue of the first volume of Sheaffer's definitive biography of O'Neill.

B392 Shipley, Joseph T. *The Art of Eugene O'Neill.* 1928. Philadelphia: Folcroft, 1977.

A reprint.

B393 _____. *The Crown Guide to the World's Great Plays: From Ancient Greece to Modern Times.* New York: Crown, 1984.

A revised and updated edition of *Guide to Great Plays,* 1956. Brief notes, thumb-nail summaries, excerpts from critics' responses, histories of first productions of *Horizon, Jones, Anna, Desire, Interlude, Electra, Wilderness, Iceman, Journey, Misbegotten, Touch,* and *Mansions.* Includes personal responses to individual plays. In a section entitled "O'Neill's Posthumous Plays" (that is, "A Tale of Possessors Self-Dispossessed"), he describes his own contribution to the Swedish productions of O'Neill.

B394 Shurr, William E. "American Drama and the Bible: The Case of Eugene O'Neill's *Lazarus Laughed.*" *The Bible and American Arts and Letters.* Vol. 3 of *The Bible in American Culture.* Ed. Giles Gunn. Philadelphia: Fortress, 1983. 83–103.

The theme of the book and of the series is carried through modern American drama with special attention given to *Lazarus.* Treats of the story as found in John and Luke; then discusses O'Neill's handling. Finds that O'Neill celebrates generic rather than individual immortality. What gives life to the play is its blending of traditional interpretations with modern influences — Nietzsche and Whitman. (Sees echoes of Whitman in Lazarus' language and sense of "cosmic consciousness.")

B395 Siebold, Thomas, ed. *Readings on Eugene O'Neill.* The Greenhaven Press Literary Companion Series. San Diego: Greenhaven, 1998.

Reprints, excerpts, or abridgements of some seminal essays or passages from books (with titles changed to "enhance the editorial purpose") on O'Neill. There is a a biographical essay on the playwright, a chronology, a brief bibliography, and an index. "Designed for young adults," a note tells us that some items "may have been edited for content, length, and/or reading level." Of the 20 selections included seven fall within the scope of this bibliography — those by Abbott, Berlin, Bloom, Floyd, Porter, Ranald, and Torrey.

Anthony S. Abbott's "Themes in O'Neill's Plays" (See B3)

Roger Asselineau's "The Quest for God in *Desire Under the Elms* " (A reprint; see B12 and B13)

Normand Berlin's "O'Neill's Accomplishments" (See B36)

Steven F. Bloom's "Alcohol and Addiction in *Long Day's Journey into Night* " (See B54)

Robert Brustein's "Family Connections in *Long Day's Journey into Night* "

Oscar Cargill, N. Bryllion Fagin, and William J. Fisher's "A Critical Assessment"

Winifred Dusenbury's "Loneliness in *Mourning Becomes Electra* "

Edwin A. Engel's "O'Neill's Harmonious Vision in *Ah, Wilderness!* "

Jerome Ellison's "O'Neill's Treatment of Religion"

Doris V. Falk's "Character Conflicts in *A Moon for the Misbegotten* "

Virginia Floyd's "Expressionism in *The Emperor Jones* " (See B165)

Horst Frenz's "The Tragic Vision in *The Iceman Cometh* "

John Gassner's "A Modern Playwright"

Jay L. Halio's "The Illusion of Home in O'Neill's Plays"

Laurin Porter's "Self-Deception as a Theme in O'Neill's Late Plays" (See B331)

John Henry Raleigh's "Race Relations in *All God's Chillun Got Wings* "

Margaret Loftus Ranald's "An Overview of O'Neill's Plays" (See B350)

Rolf Scheibler's "Spiritual Love in *A Moon for the Misbegotten* "

Egil Törnqvist's "O'Neill's Relationship to the Theater"

Jane Torrey's "The Role of Women in O'Neill's Plays" (See B434)

B396 Sienicka, Marta. "O'Neill in Poland." In *Eugene O'Neill: A World View.* Ed.

Virginia Floyd. New York: Ungar, 1979. 101-14.

A history of O'Neill productions in Poland. Maintains that though O'Neill is not an influence on Polish theater, he is still a presence and an influence on Polish sensibility.

B397 Simon, Bennett. *Tragic Drama and the Family: Psychoanalytic Studies From Aeschylus to Beckett.* New Haven: Yale UP, 1988. 177-211

Simon's thesis is "that great tragic drama is fueled by the problematic of the birth and death of the family. The begetting of children within a family is the only sure way open to mortals to gain immortality. At the same time, the passions, rivalries, conflicts, and consequent ambivalence of relationships within the family engender a destructiveness that threatens extinction as much as does the 'natural' fact of death." Not surprising, then, that among the chapters on Aeschylus' *Oresteia*, Euripides' *Medea*, Shakespeare's *Lear* and *Macbeth*, and Beckett's *Endgame*, is one on *Journey* in which Simon discusses the efforts of characters to build bridges in an attempt to undo the damage they have inflicted on one another. Father and sons turn to their shared appreciation of drama and poetry in their struggle to find common ground. Simon notes that poetry as therapy is only transitorily remedic.

Mandl, Bette. Rev. *Eugene O'Neill Review* 13.1 (1989): 90-92.

B398 Simon, John. *Uneasy Stages: A Chronicle of the New York Theatre, 1963-1973.* New York: Random, 1975.

Review-essays covering the seasons' productions (beginning with Spring 1963). The essays, which originally appeared in slightly different form in *Commonweal*, *The Hudson Review*, and *New York* magazine between 1963 and 1975, include reflections on the Actors Studio *Interlude* (Summer 1963), *Misbegotten* (Summer-Autumn 1968), *Journey* (Spring 1971), and *Brown* (Winter 1972-73). The comments about the plays and the productions are brief (two to four paragraphs) but insightful.

B399 Singh, Avadhesh K. *The Plays of Eugene O'Neill.* New Delhi: Creative, 1991.

Takes a chronological stroll through O'Neill's canon in search of myths and symbols — ancient, classical, Christian, contemporary American. "They are raw material for a body of his writings whose schematization

was explicitly and distinctly his own, and can be discerned in all the phases of his creative endeavour."

B400 Singh, Tejpal. *Eugene O'Neill: Quest for Reality in His Plays.* New Delhi: National Book, 1987.

In a work that seems oblivious to more recent scholarship (good gracious, Sheaffer is missing from the bibliography!), Singh assails the canon to discuss O'Neill's search for a non-material reality. He concludes that the playwright "dramatized the cosmic reality in the form of the dialectical relationship between land and sea" in the sea plays; "sought to discover the psychic dimension of human reality by dialectically depicting the anguish of suffering man in a capitalist society" in his expressionistic plays; "dramatized the distortions and perversions in human personality wrought by the rigidities and dogmatic beliefs of Puritanism" in his New England plays; portrayed the spiritual vacuity of the greedy in his Cycle plays; and returned to the self as his subject in his autobiographical play.

B401 Sinha, C. P. *Eugene O'Neill's Tragic Vision.* Atlantic Highlands, NJ: Humanities, 1981.

The introduction tries to "evolve a modern aesthetic of tragedy in order to study O'Neill's tragic vision from a new perspective." Chapters 2 and 3 discuss O'Neill as an artist who suffered and who then gave shape to suffering. The fourth chapter says that the O'Neill tragic hero suffers, not because of his pride, but because he fails to realize his ideal. Chapter 5 argues that O'Neill responds to the "dynamics of change. He moves from negation to affirmation, from rejection of God to acceptance."

B402 Sinha, Prashant K. "Versions of the Orestes Figure in *Mourning Becomes Electra, The Family Reunion* and *The Flies*." In *T. S. Eliot & Eugene O'Neill: The Dream and the Nightmare.* Eds. V. R. N. Prasad, et al. New Delhi: Ajanta, 1991. 100-14.

Finds similarities in these plays. All are influenced by Freudian psychology, all have external agents of remorse and guilt, and "in variant forms these plays analyze the attempt of the character to either disguise his identity or to transform it or to comprehend the remarkable change it has undergone."

B403 Smith, Madeline, and Richard Eaton, eds. *Eugene O'Neill: An Annotated*

Bibliography, 1973-1985. Garland Reference Library of the Humanities, 860. New York: Garland, 1988.

An annotated bibliography covering the period 1973 (when Jordan Miller's work *Eugene O'Neill and the American Critic* ends) through 1985. Included are Books and Parts of Books in English, Dissertations, Periodical Publications in English, Foreign Language Publications, English Language Productions and Reviews, Foreign Language Productions and Reviews, Miscellany, Editions of Primary Works, and Translations. An author/play-title index is provided.

Wilkins, Frederick C. Rev. *Eugene O'Neill Newsletter* 12.2 (1988): 68-71.

B404 _____, eds. *Eugene O'Neill in Court: Documents in the Case of Georges Lewys v. Eugene O'Neill, et al.* American University Studies, series 24. American Literature, 41. New York: Lang, 1993.

See Primary Works section, G12.

B405 Smith, Susan Valeria Harris. *Masks in Modern Drama.* Berkeley: U of California P, 1984.

A wide ranging study of the use of masks in, mostly, twentieth-century theater, touching on some 200 plays, both European and American. Sees masks as stage devices or as textual metaphors. Since the organization of the study is thematic, remarks on O'Neill are scattered (here the index is very useful), but cover, briefly, *Ape, Chillun, Jones, Mariner, Fountain* and *Days,* and, to a greater extent, *Lazarus* and *Brown.* Demonstrates that O'Neill "clearly knew the European experiments in masked subjective projection" and observes that *Brown* is "the most thorough, labored exploration" of modern stage masking. See C115.

B406 _____. "Actors Constructing an Audience: *Hughie's* Post Modern Aura." In *Eugene O'Neill and the Emergence of American Drama.* Ed. Marc Maufort. Costerus New Series, 75. Amsterdam: Rodopi, 1989. 169-80.

Looks at *Hughie* as a play which "straddles that interesting and ambiguous moment at which the subtle shift from modern [certitude of despair, self-absorption, and the simultaneous expression of self-confidence which is coextensive with self-loathing] to post-modern [the self-assertion of the private mind in what Newman calls 'an ideology of discomfiture, in which irony functions as the intellectual's only sentiment'] occurs."

B407 _____. *American Drama: The Bastard Art.* Cambridge Studies in American Theatre and Drama. Cambridge: Cambridge UP, 1997.

A book for all those interested in the history of the teaching of America drama and in the continuing tensions between drama and theater, between literature (text) and performance. O'Neill is not a feature player in this study (if anyone deserves that billing, it is George Pierce Baker, not as O'Neill's teacher but as legitimizer of the theater in higher education), but he does have a part: first as token playwright in American literature courses and anthologies, then as "the first serious American playwright," eventually as "the savior of American drama." And although no one section of the book is given to him, still O'Neill has (after "American Drama") the longest single entry in a very sizeable index, with mentions averaging one in every five pages. A good antidote to those books that depend much on subjectivity.

B408 Sochatoff, A. Fred. "Two Modern Treatments of the Phaedra Legend." In *In Honor of Austin Wright.* Eds. Joseph Baim, et al. Pittsburgh: Carnegie-Mellon UP, 1972. 80-86.

Both O'Neill's *Desire* and T. C. Murray's *Autumn Five* (1924) make use of the Phaedre story but must modify it because of the importance in the original of Hippolytus' devotion to Artemis (purity, charity), ignoring Aphrodite (sensuality). To modernize, O'Neill uses a keyword, *desire,* and variations on it throughout the play: desire for the land, for security, for revenge, sexual release, perpetuation of the family, understanding. But, though a tragedy, *Desire* still offers a note of exaltation at the end.

B409 Spånberg, Sven-Johan. "The Pre-Raphaelite Woman in O'Neill's *Long Day's Journey into Night.*" In *Stockholm Studies in English.* Vol. 2. Eds. Ishrat Lindblad and Magnus Ljung. Stockholm: Almqvist and Wiksell, 1986. 773-84.

O'Neill's many literary references in *Journey* are used to substantiate Spånberg's claim that the pre-Raphaelite woman, honored in verse and prose (Rossetti, Swinburne), was also O'Neill's ideal woman. Mary Tyrone, his greatest female character, represents his obsession with the literary figure. She is beautiful and alluring because she is helpless, vulnerable, and dependent, both on drugs and on the men in her life. This article is of interest for its focus on a literary icon which O'Neill modernizes by adding psychological elements to her makeup.

B410 _____. "The Pre-Raphaelite Woman in O'Neill's *Long Day's Journey into Night*." In *Proceedings from the Third Nordic Conference of English Studies, 25-27 Sept. 1986.* Vol. 2. Eds. Ishrat Lindblad and Magnus Ljung. Stockholm: Almqvist and Wiksell, 1987. 773-84.

See B409.

B411 _____. "Male Speech, Female Silence: The Question of Power in Browning's 'Andrea del Sarto,' Morris's 'The Hill of Venus,' and O'Neill's *Long Day's Journey into Night*." In *From Runes to Romance: A Festschrift for Gunnar Persson on His Sixtieth Birthday, November 9, 1997.* Acta Universitatis Umensis/Umeå Studies in the Humanities, 140. Uppsala: Swedish Science P, 1997. 199-208.

"How O'Neill, in his rewriting of the play from his early notes through a 6000 word scenario and two typescripts to the final printed version ... shaped Act IV so that the use of absence, silence and rupture of communication to present Mary's relationship with her husband and sons becomes much more consistent": this takes up three paragraphs — slightly over a page of the total essay.

B412 Stanley, William T. *Broadway in the West End: An Index of Reviews of American Theatre in London 1950-1975.* Westport, CT: Greenwood, 1978.

Primarily a research tool, it is rich with information about productions and offers occasionally short but valuable insights into the popularity of English productions.

B413 Stein, Rita, and Friedhelm Rickert. "Eugene O'Neill." *Modern American Dramatists: A Library of Criticism.* Vol. 1. New York: Ungar, 1984. 52-78.

An "overview of the critical reception of the dramatist from the beginning of his career up to the present time through excerpts from reviews, articles, and books." Some 30 excerpts are arranged chronologically, starting with one from Edmund Wilson (1922) and continuing through selections from Chabrowe, Chothia, and Floyd.

B414 Stewart, Jeffrey C., ed. *Paul Robeson: Artist and Citizen.* New Brunswick, NJ: Rutgers UP and the Paul Robeson Cultural Center, 1998.

A collection of essays by different contributors covering the life, career, and significance of Robeson. Besides a dozen scattered references to O'Neill, *Jones*, and *Chillun*, there is the chapter noted below.

Charles Musser's "Troubled Relations: Robeson, Eugene O'Neill, and Oscar Micheaux" (See B311)

B415 Stroupe, John H., ed. *Critical Approaches to O'Neill.* AMS Studies in Modern Literature, 17. New York: AMS, 1988.

A collection of essays published on the centennial of O'Neill's birth. All are reprints. The Roy and Stroupe essays were published too early to fall within the scope of this work.

Thomas P. Adler's "'Daddy Spoke to Me!': Gods Lost and Found in *Long Day's Journey into Night* and *Through a Glass Darkly*" (See A9)

John Chioles's "Aeschylus and O'Neill: A Phenomenological View" (See A117)

Michael Hinden's "When Playwrights Talk to God: Peter Shaffer and the Legacy of O'Neill" (See A314)

Michael Manheim's "O'Neill's Transcendence of Melodrama in *A Touch of the Poet* and *A Moon for the Misbegotten*" (See A401)

Joseph J. Moleski and John H. Stroupe's "Jean Anouilh and Eugene O'Neill: Repetition as Negativity" (See A447)

Joseph J. Moleski's "Eugene O'Neill and the Cruelty of Theater" (See A446)

James A. Robinson's "Taoism and O'Neill's *Marco Millions*" (See A546)

Albert Rothenberg and Eugene D. Shapiro's "A Defense of Psychoanalysis in Literature: *Long Day's Journey into Night* and *A View from the Bridge*" (See A557)

Emil Roy's "The Archetypal Unity of Eugene O'Neill's Drama"

Louis Sheaffer's "Correcting Some Errors in Annals of O'Neill" (See A605, A606, and A607)

John H. Stroupe's "O'Neill and the Creative Process: A Road to Xanadu"

Stephen M. Watt's "O'Neill and Otto Rank: Doubles, 'Death Instincts,' and the Trauma of Birth" (See A695)

Mandl, Bette. Rev. *Eugene O'Neill Review* 13.1 (1989): 92-95.

B416 Styan, J. L. *Modern Drama in Theory and Practice.* 3 vols. Cambridge: Cambridge UP, 1981.

Vol. 1. Realism and Naturalism: The chapter called "Realism in America: Early Variations" (pp. 122-36) makes some comments about *Iceman* and *Journey*. *Iceman* was patterned on Gorky's *Lower Depths*, but it is more like Chekhov's works in its negligible and inconclusive plot. *Journey* and *Misbegotten* show that O'Neill had settled into an "intense, obsessed" realism. Vol. 3. Expressionism and Epic Theater: The chapter entitled "Expressionism in America: O'Neill" (pp. 97-111) attempts to put O'Neill's expressionistic works in the context of experimental theater of the 1920s. Has Robert Edmond Jones as the agent for O'Neill's experiments: he kept the playwright abreast of what was happening abroad. In *Jones* Brutus achieves self-knowledge considers *Chillun* as a "psychological study of a mixed marriage." *Ape, Brown, Lazarus,* and *Electra* are also touched on.

B417 Sun, Jianqui. "O'Neill in a Chinese Classroom: *Before Breakfast*—A Good Starting Point." In *Eugene O'Neill in China: An International Centenary Celebration*. Eds. Haiping Liu and Lowell Swortzell. Westport, CT: Greenwood, 1992. 269-74.

Sun explains her pedagogical approach to O'Neill, which begins with *Breakfast*.

B418 Swortzell, Lowell. "'Get My Goat': O'Neill's Attitude toward Children and Adolescents in His Life and Art." In *Eugene O'Neill's Century: Centennial Views on America's Foremost Tragic Dramatist*. Ed. Richard F. Moorton, Jr. Westport, CT: Greenwood, 1991. 145-63.

Looks at O'Neill's youth, his relationships with his children, and his plays in which children appear and concludes that the playwright's fictional children are generally "meddlesome nuisances who got his goat."

B419 _____. "*The Emperor Jones* as a Source of Theatrical Experimentation, 1920s-1980s." In *Eugene O'Neill in China: An International Centenary Celebration*. Eds. Haiping Liu and Lowell Swortzell. Westport, CT: Greenwood, 1992. 199-209.

Surveys the many different kinds of innovative treatments *Jones* has put up with: it has been an opera and a musical and a film, and been adapted to the marionette theater and choreographed for modern dance, and turned into an audio recording. All of which goes to "prove that collaborators are ever ready to reassess and reexpress O'Neill's still challenging theatrical myth."

B420 Szondi, Peter. *Theory of the Modern Drama: A Critical Edition*. Theory and History of Literature 29. Ed. and trans. Michael Hays. Minneapolis: U of Minnesota P, 1987. 81-83.

Translation of Szondi's *Theorie des modernen Dramas* (Frankfurt am Main: Suhrkamp, 1974). One short but dense section is entitled "*Monologue intérieur* O'Neill." On the difference between the *Interlude* monologues and the *à part* (the "aside"): O'Neill is not just a psychological dramatist; he is also "a descendant of Zola"—a naturalist—"who now only registers, machinelike, the outer and inner speech provided by individuals in the unfree space of genetic and psychological laws."

B421 Tedesco, Joseph S. "Dion Brown and His Problems." In *Critical Essays on Eugene O'Neill*. Ed. James J. Martine. Boston: G. K. Hall, 1984. 114-23.

Uses a Jungian approach to analyze *Brown* which sets the teeth of the usual Nietzschean critics on edge.

B422 Tener, Robert L. "Eugene O'Neill: Research Opportunities." In *Eugene O'Neill: Research Opportunities and Dissertation Abstracts*. Ed. Tetsumaro Hayashi. Jefferson, NC: McFarland, 1983. 3-21.

Discusses the 139 dissertations on O'Neill, completed between 1928 and 1980, sketching out the lines of research and schools of thought that he is able to infer from them. The last three-plus pages point to possible future lines of research: the matter of O'Neill's artistry, studies in characterization, textual studies, the relationship between O'Neill and his contemporaries, his influence on others, his work in other media. See B212.

B423 Terras, Rita. "A Spokesman for America: O'Neill in Translation." In *Eugene O'Neill's Century: Centennial Views of America's Foremost Dramatist*. Ed. Richard F. Moorton, Jr. Westport, CT: Greenwood, 1991. 86-101.

Begins by affirming O'Neill's past and present popularity in Europe and discusses some of the problems encountered by those who seek to translate his work.

B424 Tiusanen, Timo. "O'Neill's Significance: A Scandinavian and a European View." In *Eugene O'Neill: A World View*. Ed. Virginia Floyd. New York: Ungar, 1979. 61-67.

Partly an argument that O'Neill be kept "alive" by being made part of classical theater, partly an observation that O'Neill matured as a dramatist too fast for Americans to keep up with.

B425 ____. "O'Neill and Wuolijoki: A Counter-Sketch to *Electra.*" In *Eugene O'Neill's Critics: Voices from Abroad*. Eds. Horst Frenz and Susan Tuck. Carbondale: Southern Illinois UP, 1984. 174-81. [Though the date 1980 is appended to the essay's title, the editors note that the essay is "published here for the first time."]

Identifies Hella Wuolijoki, female Finnish playwright and contemporary of O'Neill, who, after having viewed *Electra* in 1934, wrote a counter-sketch. Tiusanen discusses her work *Justiina* in terms of its affinities with and departure from O'Neill's play.

B426 Törnqvist, Egil. "Platonic Love in O'Neill's *Welded.*" In *Eugene O'Neill: A World View*. Ed. Virginia Floyd. New York: Ungar, 1979. 73-83.

Argues that the title of *Welded*, which is usually interpreted pejoratively, should really to be taken to suggest love as bonding, not binding. In *Welded*, love is the expression of a platonic concept as found in *The Symposium*.

B427 ____. "Strindberg and O'Neill." In *Structures of Influence: A Comparative Approach to August Strindberg*. Ed. Marilyn Johns Blackwell. Studies in the Germanic Languages and Literatures, 98. Chapel Hill: U of North Carolina P, 1981. 277-91.

Surveys the evidence for Strindberg's influence on O'Neill as found in the standard publications, theses, and dissertations. O'Neill's familiarity with Strindberg was considerable even though he probably never saw any of Strindberg's plays performed. Discusses O'Neill's plays — both early and late — in terms of the Strindbergian influence. Notes that O'Neill said he saw his own situation in terms of Strindberg's depiction of family relationships and that O'Neill admired Strindberg's "power to deal with modern psychological problems in a dramatically convincing and arresting way."

B428 ____. "From *A Wife for a Life* to *A Moon for the Misbegotten:* On O'Neill's Play Titles." In *Eugene O'Neill and the Emergence of American Drama*. Ed. Marc Maufort. Costerus New Series, 75. Amsterdam: Rodopi, 1989. 97-105.

The ever-insightful Törnqvist ponders the significance of some O'Neill titles and concludes that the playwright was "one of the most imaginative creators of play titles."

B429 ____. "Strindberg and O'Neill and Their Impact on the Dramatists of Today." In *Strindberg, O'Neill and the Modern Theatre*. Eds. Claes Englund and Gunnel Bergström. Jönköping [Sweden]: Tryckeri AB Småland, 1990. 14-24.

Makes his argument by showing how a contemporary Swedish playwright, Lars Norén, reflects the influence of both Strindberg and O'Neill in structure, subject, theme, and genre, and, lastly, how the two giants have become themselves "myths" of the theater.

B430 ____. "Ingmar Bergman and *Long Day's Journey into Night.*" In *Eugene O'Neill in China: An International Centenary Celebration*. Westport, CT: Greenwood, 1992. 241-48.

Reviews Ingmar Bergman's then recent 1988 production of *Journey* explaining the reasons behind its success.

B431 ____. "Playwright on Playwright: Per Olov Enquist's Strindberg and Lars Norén's O'Neill." In *Documentarism in Scandinavian Literature*. Eds. Poul Houe and Sven-Hakon Rossel. Internationale Forschungen zur Allgemeinen und Vergleichenden Literaturwissenschaft, 18. Amsterdam: Rodopi, 1997. 155-64.

Treats of two plays about the lives of playwrights — Enquist's 1975 play about Strindberg and Norén's *And Grant Us the Shadows* (*Och ge oss skuggorna*) about O'Neill, which opened at the Royal Dramatic Theater in Stockholm in 1991. The importance to Norén of O'Neill's plays (*Journey* is "an incredible play") is seen in his own family plays, but especially in *And Grant Us The Shadows*, set in 1949, at a fictional reprise of O'Neill's sixty-first birthday. The play works out the relationships between O'Neill, Carlotta, Eugene, Jr., and Shane, in ways parallel with the relationships between the characters of *Journey*, and of course between the real O'Neills.

B432 ____. "O'Neill's Philosophical and Literary Paragons." In *The Companion to Eugene O'Neill*. Ed. Michael Manheim. Cambridge Companions to Literature series. Cambridge: Cambridge UP, 1998. 18-32.

Surveys the thinkers who contributed to the intellectual and artistic environment that helped to form O'Neill's thought — especially Nietzsche, Ibsen, Strindberg.

B433 Torrey, Jane. "O'Neill's Psychology of Oppression in Men and Women." In *Eugene O'Neill's Century: Centennial Views of America's Foremost Dramatist.* Ed. Richard F. Moorton, Jr. Westport, CT: Greenwood, 1991. 165-70.

In O'Neill's plays Torrey finds fodder for raising the issues of race, class, and gender oppression in her psychology classes.

B434 _____. "The Role of Women in O'Neill's Plays." In *Readings on Eugene O'Neill.* Ed. Thomas Siebold. Literary Companion Series. San Diego: Greenhaven, 1998. 60-66.

A reprint of her essay in *Eugene O'Neill's Century: Centennial Views on America's Foremost Tragic Dramatist,* ed. Richard F. Moorton, Jr., 1991. See above.

B435 Tuck, Susan. "The O'Neill-Faulkner Connection." In *Critical Essays on Eugene O'Neill.* Ed. James J. Martine. Boston: G. K. Hall, 1984. 196-206.

Speculates on where Faulkner may first have encountered O'Neill's work, with which he was clearly familiar. Then she traces the parallels between Faulkner's "The Sailor" and O'Neill's *Glencairn;* "The Longshoreman" and *Jones* and *Chillun;* "The Kid Learns" and *Cardiff; The Sound and the Fury* and *Interlude; As I Lay Dying* and *Jones; Sanctuary* and *Jones* and *Ape;* and *Light in August* and *Chillun.*

B436 Tynan, Kathleen. *The Life of Kenneth Tynan.* London: Weidenfeld, 1987.

One paragraph (but well worth the reading) on *Journey* and the Olivier production of that play.

B437 Vaillant, George E. *The Wisdom of the Ego.* Cambridge: Harvard UP, 1993.

A clinician's look at the playwright's psyche (pp. 266-83). Vaillant examines O'Neill's ego — his defense mechanisms, his creativity, which attempts to bring order out of chaos, and his adult development, when a capacity for intimacy renders possible a satisfying career, which, in turn, makes regeneration possible. "How the vagrant Gene's acting out of 1908-1912 became the Nobel laureate Eugene O'Neill's sublimated masterpiece *Long Day's Journey into Night* of 1940 is an odyssey of psychological recovery."

B438 Vena, Gary. *O'Neill's* The Iceman Cometh: *Reconstructing the Premiere.* Theater

and Dramatic Studies Series, 47. Ann Arbor: UMI, 1988.

Revisits the 1946 premiere of *Iceman,* directed by Eddie Dowling. His reconstruction looks at the cast, textual changes, rehearsals, the production itself and reviews. This is a version of Vena's 1984 New York University dissertation; see C125.

Chothia, Jean. Rev.-essay. *Journal of American Studies* 23 (1989): 311-14. (See A120)

Wilkins, Frederick C. Rev. *Eugene O'Neill Newsletter* 12.2 (1988): 63.

B439 _____. *O'Neill's* The Iceman Cometh: *Reconstructing The Premiere.* 1988. Lewiston, NY: Edwin Mellen, 1992.

A reprint; see above, B438.

B440 Voelker, Paul. "Success and Frustration at Harvard: Eugene O'Neill's Relationship with George Pierce Baker (1914-1915)." In *Eugene O'Neill and the Emergence of American Drama.* Ed. Marc Maufort. Costerus New Series, 75. Amsterdam: Rodopi, 1989. 15-29.

Takes another look at the relationship between mentor and protégé during O'Neill's brief stay at Harvard and concludes that if O'Neill got nothing more than "the method of work" and "encouragement to continue," his year at Harvard was not wasted.

B441 _____. "Eugene O'Neill, World Playwright: The Beginnings." In *Eugene O'Neill in China : An International Centenary Celebration.* Eds. Haiping Liu and Lowell Swortzell. Westport, CT: Greenwood, 1992. 99-109.

The Movie Man and *Sniper* are discussed as plays which reflect O'Neill's "political and pessimistic" vision elaborated on in *Iceman* years later.

B442 Vogel, Dan. *The Three Masks of American Tragedy.* Baton Rouge: Louisiana State UP, 1974. 41-54.

Discusses what is unique and what is cohesive about American tragedy. Short examinations of *Desire* and *Electra* as American tragedies. Sees the masks of American tragic heroes as the masks of Oedipus Tyrannos (O'Neill's heroes), or Christ or Satan.

B443 Voglino, Barbara. *"Perverse Mind": Eugene O'Neill's Struggle with Closure.* Rutherford, NJ: Fairleigh Dickinson UP, 1999.

Originally a doctoral dissertation. See C127 for an annotation.

B444 Vorlicky, Robert. *Act Like a Man: Challenging Masculinities in American Drama.* Ann Arbor: U of Michigan P, 1995. 90-102.

This book is about "the power that is exercised by, contested by, and occasionally shared by American men." Not surprising is Vorlicky's choice of O'Neill's *Hughie* as a play to be discussed. Pages 90-102 constitute the bulk of the discussion, though there are scattered references to O'Neill and to this play throughout. He concludes that herein "O'Neill masterfully captures this absence of intimacy that the male-cast canon continually uncovers in male communication." But *Hughie* differs from most male-character plays in showing men's desire for self-revelation as well as their frustration over the failure of intimacy.

Vena, Gary. Rev. *Eugene O'Neill Review* 20.1-2 (1996): 148-52.

B445 Vorse, Mary Heaton. *Time and the Town.* Ed. Adele Heller. New Brunswick: Rutgers UP, 1991.

New edition of a classic history of Provincetown. Vorse, a resident of the town for 30-plus years, records the changes she saw. Included in her book is anecdotal material of interest to the O'Neillian, including descriptions of the real life inspiration for Capt. and Mrs. Keeney.

Wilkins, Frederick C. Rev. *Eugene O'Neill Review* 16.1 (1992): 129-30.

B446 [Vorse, Mary Heaton]. *Autobiography of an Elderly Woman: Anonymous.* 1911. Wainscott, NY: Pushcart, 1995.

A reprint originally published in 1911; its author is identified only in the "Afterword," by Dorothy Grumbach. Mary Heaton Vorse's story includes her life in Provincetown during the early years of the twentieth century.

B447 Wainscott, Ronald H. *Staging O'Neill: The Experimental Years, 1920-34.* New Haven: Yale UP, 1988.

"This book examines the accomplishments, failures, problems, and solutions of the professional directors in league with designers who produced the first performances of O'Neill's plays from 1920 to 1934." Twenty-two plays are covered in the book, which draws its material from photographs, letters, telegrams, promptbooks, clippings, publicity materials, drawings, etc. See C129.

Shafer, Yvonne. Rev. *Theatre History Studies* 9 (1989): 170-73.

Wilkins, Frederick C. Rev. *Eugene O'Neill Review* 13.1 (1989): 95-97.

B448 _____. *The Emergence of the Modern American Theater 1914-1929.* New Haven: Yale UP, 1997.

Tensions between the American theater and the national government in the period leading up to the Great Depression: actors' strike, red scare, censorship. Of course O'Neill figures in. Forty or so references, scattered throughout between pages three and 177, to him and/or *Anna, Ape, Brown, Chillun, Desire, Diff'rent, Horizon, Jones, Marco, Mariner, Welded.* Sixty-nine pages of useful back matter.

Coakley, James. Rev. *Comparative Drama* 33.2 (1999): 306-08.

Vanden Heuvel, Michael. Rev. *Modern Drama* 40.4 (1997): 556-58.

B449 _____. "Notable American Stage Productions." In *The Companion to Eugene O'Neill.* Ed. Michael Manheim. Cambridge Companions to Literature series. Cambridge: Cambridge UP, 1998. 96-115.

Surveys important American productions of some two dozen O'Neill plays, focusing on scenic design and acting-directing to find that "the plays ... have had a most uneven production history," but kudos for directing to Robert Edmond Jones, Philip Moeller, and José Quintero.

B450 Watermeier, Daniel J. "*The Iceman Cometh* Twice: A Comparison of the 1946 and 1956 Productions." In *Eugene O'Neill in China: An International Centenary Celebration.* Westport, CT: Greenwood, 1992. 211-22.

Considers the reasons behind the indifferent reception of the 1946 *Iceman* and the critical acclaim garnered by the 1956 production.

B451 _____. "O'Neill and the Theatre of his Time." In *The Companion to Eugene O'Neill.* Ed. Michael Manheim. Cambridge Companions to Literature series. Cambridge: Cambridge UP, 1998. 33-50.

The theater between the Civil War and the years immediately after the World War I — the years of James and Eugene O'Neill. The goal was profit, the means entertainment, the standard what the public was satisfied with. The nearest approach to something more advanced was scenic realism which, however, only masked the immaturity of content. Then with experimental theater and early O'Neill came the first glimmerings of a growing up.

B452 Waters, Joy Bluck. *Eugene O'Neill and Family: The Bermuda Interlude.* Toronto: U of Toronto P, 1992.

Conjures up life in Bermuda in the O'Neill era. Rich in atmosphere and detail (some of it as it relates to O'Neill is first read about here). Waters as the present owner of the O'Neill home, Spithead, is especially qualified to talk of its history, and the O'Neill connection with Bermuda — a connection that continued as far as Agnes, Shane and Oona were concerned long after the playwright had moved on.

B453 Waterstradt, Jean Anne. "Three O'Neill Women: An Emergent Pattern." In *Eugene O'Neill in China: A Centenary Celebration.* Eds. Haiping Liu and Lowell Swortzell. Westport, CT: Greenwood, 1992. 111-19.

Looks at the characters of Nina Leeds, Lavinia Mannon and Josie Hogan to show how O'Neill's concept of woman changed as his art developed.

B454 Watson, Steven. *Strange Bedfellows: The First American Avant-Garde.* New York: Abbeville P, 1991.

Extremely well-illustrated story of Greenwich Village as early American Artistic Center. The first section covers the roots of "Bohemia" in Chicago, Harvard, Paris, London, New York, and Florence. Thereafter (pp. 122-357) the focus is on "The Village." Business matter at the end of the volume includes a "cast of characters" and a "modern chronology: 1900-20," and a 12-page index, small print, three columns per page. Though O'Neill is by no means central, the work is useful for ambience. Also a good read.

B455 Weathers, Winston. "Eugene O'Neill and the Tragic Word." In *The Broken Word: The Communication Pathos in Modern Literature.* New York: Gordon & Breach, 1981. 93-108.

This is a version of his article "Communications and Tragedy in Eugene O'Neill" in *ETC: A Review of General Semantics* (July 1962): 148-60. The introductory chapters of the book observe that the last century may be characterized by the growing awareness of the breakdown in communication owing to the loss of faith in old and certain ties and a consequent loss of semantic understanding. In Chapter 6, pp. 93-108, it is argued that O'Neill's plays are chiefly concerned with problems of communication.

B456 Wells, Arvin R. "Beyond the Horizon." In *Insight I: Analyses of American Literature.* 2nd ed. Eds. John V. Hagopian and Martin Dolch. Frankfurt am Main: Hirschgraben-Verlag, 1975. 186-93.

A study guide for use in German schools, which examines 50 works of 31 American writers. O'Neill is represented by *Horizon.* Summaries of O'Neill's career; slight analysis by a writer who has a low opinion of O'Neill's work; then questions and answers about the plays.

B457 White, George Cooke. *Journal of George Cooke White: A Chronicle of the Production of Eugene O'Neill's* Anna Christie *in the People's Republic of China, September-October, 1984.* [Beijing?: s.n.], 1984.

Anna becomes *An Di* in this Chinese version. See A706 and F2.

B458 Wikander, Matthew H. "O'Neill and the Cult of Sincerity." In *The Companion to Eugene O'Neill.* Ed. Michael Manheim. Cambridge Companions to Literature series. Cambridge: Cambridge UP, 1998. 217-35.

In this essay, chosen by the editor to give another side to the picture, Wikander becomes the devil's advocate: O'Neill is not the paramount American dramatist he is cracked up to be. His characters are stereotypical, his ideas watery, his writing style inept. His lack of trust in and respect for actors results in overdirecting, in too much exposition and interpreting (he writes novels, not plays). And so on. No stone is left unturned.

B459 Wilkins, Frederick C. "The Pressure of Puritanism in O'Neill's New England Plays." In *Eugene O'Neill: A World View.* Ed. Virginia Floyd. New York: Ungar, 1979. 237-44.

Finds the conflict in O'Neill's New England plays between his Irish Catholicism and the Puritan culture — the former allowing for redemption and the latter offering no consolation.

B460 _____. "'Arriving with a Bang': O'Neill's Literary Debut." In *Eugene O'Neill and the Emergence of American Drama.* Ed. Marc Maufort. Costerus New Series, 75. Amsterdam: Rodopi, 1989.

Looks at the early O'Neill — *The Web, Warnings, Fog,* and *Recklessness* — and spots among the minuses some plusses — "some breathtaking moments of both power and poetic intensity far surpassing anything in American drama before 1914."

B461 Williams, Raymond. *Drama from Ibsen to Brecht.* 2nd rev. ed. of *Drama from Ibsen to Eliot.* Harmondsworth: Penguin, 1973. 250-52 and 335-39.

Fleeting references to *Journey* and *Electra.* Part I discusses the three major dramatists of the period: Ibsen, Strindberg, and Chekhov. Part II deals with the Irish dramatists: from Synge, Yeats, and Joyce to O'Casey. O'Neill's work is treated in the third section, under experimental drama.

B462 Wilmeth, Don B. *The American Stage to World War I: A Guide to Information Sources.* Detroit: Gale, 1978.

Items 253, 771, 1131, 1132, and 1133 concern James O'Neill, Sr.

B463 Wilson, Garff B. *Three Hundred Years of American Drama and Theatre.* Englewood Cliffs, NJ: Prentice-Hall, 1973.

Touches lightly on O'Neill's contribution to American theater history in this Cook's tour.

B464 Wilson, Robert N. "Eugene O'Neill: The Web of Family." *The Writer as Social Seer.* Chapel Hill: U of North Carolina P, 1979. 72-88.

Eight essays by a sociologist whose thesis, that literature can help one to understand society, is illustrated in part by a discussion of *Journey* (Chapter 17). Notes the "isolation and inwardness of the family unit" in the play and the characters' confusion about their roles and values.

B465 Wolter, Jürgen C. "Eugene O'Neill: The Plays in Context." In *Twentieth-Century Theatre and Drama in English*: *Festschrift for Heinz Kosok on the Occasion of his 65th Birthday.* Ed. Jurgen Kamm. Trier [Germany]: Wissenschaftlicher, 1999. 647-61.

Takes issue with the notion that O'Neill was reclusive: O'Neill was "firmly anchored to the world he lived in." Describes O'Neill's responsiveness to politics, to "modernism" (concerns with the "fragmentation of human experience and the concomitant epistomological skepticism"), to the contemporary theater, and to the need to use his own experience in his writing. Surveys the whole canon.

B466 Worthen, W. B. *Modern Drama and the Rhetoric of Theatre.* Berkeley: U of California P, 1992.

The O'Neill portion — it is not a separate chapter, though the table of contents suggests differently — plays out the thinking of the whole book: that a play, or production, involves an artifice (in the word's best sense) recognized and shared almost complicity by the physical stage, the text, the actors, and the audience. *Brown*, *Ape*, *Interlude*, *Journey*, and *Iceman* are attended to in six pages (63-69), where we learn that the non-realism of O'Neill's earlier years produced "bizarre and unwieldy plays," not ones that were "manifestly part of the same dramatic project as *Iceman* and *Journey*," which were, in brief, "the exfoliation of an unconscious and intensely private, and interior self in the public action of the theatre."

B467 Yarrison, Betsy Greenleaf. "The Future in the Instant." *To Hold a Mirror to Nature: Dramatic Images and Reflections.* Ed. Karelisa V. Hartigan. Vol. 1. Washington, DC: UP of America, 1982. 137-60. [Papers from the U of Florida Dept. of Classics Comparative Drama Conference].

The thesis that "dramatic tempo animates, measures out, and gives meaning to the movement of dramatic action through time" and "mediates between empirical reality and the virtual reality of the stage world" is illustrated by special reference to *Jones* and *Uncle Vanya* because their "maximal use of the potential theatricality of the spoken word" makes "easy to document and to measure" "the phenomenal existence of tempo."

B468 Yu, Beongcheon. *The Great Circle: American Writers and the Orient.* Detroit: Wayne State UP, 1983. 141-58.

Devotes a chapter to O'Neill's interest in the East. First surveys the work done in this area; then discusses how the plays of the early and middle periods reflect O'Neill's interest in the Eastern vision. Asserts that O'Neill's mysticism did not cease with *Electra* but that thereafter it "turned inward, nurturing his mystical vision itself."

B469 Zucker, Wolfgang M. "The Return of Demons." In *Continuities and Discontinuities: Essays in Psychohistory.* Ed. Shirley Sugerman. Madison, NJ: Drew UP, 1977. 44-57.

Says in the paragraph devoted to *Jones* that the myth of demonism asserts itself when Brutus falls at the feet of the god he no longer believes in — the nomos, the reality he has accepted for most of his life.

C. Dissertations (English)

C1 Adam, Julie. "Versions of Heroism in Modern American Drama: Selected Plays by Miller, Williams, Anderson and O'Neill." U of Toronto, 1988.

Revisits the old debate on the death of tragedy by looking at new definitions of heroism and tragedy and concludes that for Miller, Williams, Anderson and O'Neill "redefinitions of heroism offer an affirmative view of humanity and are meant to counteract a pervasive spirit of degeneration and an overwhelming existential malaise."

C2 Ali, Mohamed El Shirbini Amed. "Eugene O'Neill and His Critics." U of New Mexico, 1998.

Addresses the playwright's vicissitudinous critical reception from the 1930s to the 1990s — in particular "critics' evaluation of O'Neill's early plays, Greek-myth plays, language, development of women characters, and naturalism and his late autobiographical plays."

C3 Anderson, Elizabeth L. "Pathetic Elements in O'Neill's Characters." Florida State U, 1972.

Applies Aristotle's definition of tragedy to O'Neill's *Desire, Electra, Iceman, Journey.* Concludes that the actions of the characters are not noble and that the characters are, therefore, pathetic.

C4 Arai, Anuar Mohd Nor. "The Journeying Souls: The Verbal and Visual Quest in Metaphysical Theater and Film." U of Southern California, 1983.

Terms the modern theater of Strindberg, O'Neill, Ionesco, and Beckett, and the films of Bergman "pilgrimage dramas," wherein is evidenced a concern with "the abyss of fate," "the authors' own doubles," and the "dance of nostalgia." The authors in their works confront despair and "fears of life and death"

through a metaphorical journey into self — a journey that may result in an exorcism of demons and in illumination. The journey, then, is a form of confession and therapy.

C5 Babcock, Francis Granger. "Rewriting the Masculine: The National Subject in Modern American Drama." Louisiana State U, 1993.

Relies on the theories of Jacques Lacan and the Frankfurt school to place the drama of O'Neill, Tennessee Williams, and Arthur Miller in a "broader historical context." Babcock's focus is American maleness as delineated in the drama and as it altered with periods of economic crisis and technological innovation.

C6 Bai, Niu. "The Power of Myth: A Study of Chinese Elements in the Plays of O'Neill, Albee, Hwang, and Chin." Boston U, 1995.

Marco and Albee's "The Sandbox" are studied as plays by Westerners which address Chinese cultural myths in order to critique Western culture. Frank Chin and Henry Hwang, Chinese playwrights, in their work decry the use of Chinese cultural myths (Charlie Chan and the like), stereotypes which privilege the Caucasian.

C7 Barlow, Judith Ellen. "Three Late Works of Eugene O'Neill: The Plays and the Process of Composition." U of Pennsylvania, 1975.

How O'Neill wrote during the period 1939-43, by an examination of the different versions of drafts of *Iceman, Journey,* and *Misbegotten.* The study reveals that characters are more sympathetic in the final versions. In *Iceman* and *Misbegotten,* characters become less biographical in final versions, but in *Journey,* they become more so. Also, in final versions, there is an increased emphasis on the major character, a lessened emphasis on secondary characters.

C8 Bergeron, Jill Stapleton. "Codependency Issues in Selected Contemporary American Plays." Louisiana State U, 1992.

Points to childhood abuse — verbal, sexual, physical — as the principal cause of codependency. Looking at plays by Tennessee Williams, Arthur Miller, Edward Albee, Marsha Norman, and at O'Neill's *Journey*, Bergeron argues that familiarity with the nature of codependency can illuminate the plays.

C9 Bernard, Kathy Lynn. "The Research Library of Eugene O'Neill." U of Massachusetts, 1977.

This study concludes that O'Neill was a careful reader and researcher, with a strong interest in history, philosophy, religion, shipbuilding, sailing, and literature. Two unfinished plays are analyzed to show the influence of his reading upon his creativity — "Shih Huang Ti" and "Don Juan-Philip II." Then finished works are looked at to show how ideas came to fruition — *Fountain, Marco, Lazarus, Touch, Mansions, Touch* and *Electra* are used to show how widely he used his personal library, which is catalogued herein. Additional illustrations are drawn from *Iceman, Misbegotten*, and *Journey*.

C10 Bishoff, Robert R., Jr. "Changing Perspectives: An American Tragedy from Literature to Film." U of Massachusetts, 1974.

Argues that film can complement a writer's work. Compares dramatic literature and film — how meaning is communicated in each medium — and analyzes written and film versions of *Journey* and *Anna*.

C11 Bloom, Steven Frederic. "Empty Bottles, Empty Dreams: O'Neill's Alcoholic Drama." Brandeis U, 1982.

Examines the "realistic details with which the dramatist depicted the effects of habitual heavy drinking" and considers "the significance of alcoholism as a central feature of O'Neill's mature dramaturgy." Finds that O'Neill's portrayal of alcoholism and alcoholics in *Iceman, Touch, Misbegotten, Journey* is consistent with "clinical observation" made subsequent to the time of the plays' composition. Holds, however, that O'Neill goes farther than verisimilitude by integrating the idea of alcoholism "into his vision" and by capturing the "despairing paradox of the human condition" in the contrast between "the romantic myth" about drinking and its reality.

C12 Bower, Martha E. Gilman. "The Making of Eugene O'Neill's Cycle Plays: An Analysis of O'Neill's Writing Process and Gender Role Reversal." U of New Hampshire, 1986.

Looks at *Touch, Mansions, The Calms of Capricorn*, and "Hair of the Dog" in light of the playwright's notes to discover that female characters in these plays have attributes usually ascribed to men. Also studies O'Neill's creative process as he moved from notes to final play. Includes transcriptions and summaries of many of those notes.

C13 Brennan, Joseph J. "The Comic in the Plays of Eugene O'Neill: The Use of Characterization, Situation, and Language in Relation to Henri Bergson's Theory of Comedy." New York U, 1974.

Uses Bergson's definition of comedy to show that *Wilderness* is not the only play in O'Neill's canon to be thought comic. Analyzes plays with comic elements in early, middle, and late periods.

C14 Brown, Susan Rand. "'Mothers' and 'Sons': The Development of Autobiographical Themes in the Plays of Eugene O'Neill." U of Connecticut, 1975.

Traces O'Neill's development to its apex — the late plays which record his relationship with his mother without falsification. Considers the sea plays, *Horizon, Straw, Welded, Diff'rent, Fountain, Marco, Lazarus, Dynamo, Days, Mansions, Iceman,* and *Journey*.

C15 Burr, Suzanne. "Ghosts in Modern Drama: Ibsen, Strindberg, O'Neill and their Legacy." U of Michigan, 1987.

Ghosts appear in the aforementioned's works in order to convey a character's "hauntedness and self-alienation." In arguing her thesis, Burr shows the influence of Strindberg and Ibsen on O'Neill.

C16 Butler, F. Jay. "Eugene O'Neill's Use of Symbolism in Eight Major Experimental Plays." Loyola U, 1973.

Studies the use of symbolism in *Ape, Chillun, Desire, Interlude, Brown, Electra, Iceman,* and *Journey*, and finds symbolism is used to extend the boundary, scope, and meaning of O'Neill's plays beyond the limits of mere realism. Symbols function to universalize the playwright's themes. O'Neill used symbolism experimentally in three areas: setting, character, and plot.

C17 Byrd, Robert E., Jr. "Unseen Characters in Selected Plays of Eugene O'Neill, Tennessee Williams, and Edward Albee." New York U, 1998.

In addition to traditional use of the ancient dramatic device of the unseen character — to move the plot and to provide reference for emotional or humorous speeches — American playwrights have used the technique to add "a second order of reality, a super-realm that surrounds and touches the world of on-stage action." In O'Neill's plays super-realm is the past.

C18 Cai, Yongchun. "O'Neill: A Study of Taoist Ideas in O'Neill's Plays and his Influence upon Modern Chinese Drama." U of Alberta, 1997.

Oriental Taoist principles, such as the incompatibility of dualism between man's materialism and spiritualism, the beginning and return of all divergent existence and the ideal of detachment and transcendence over life and death, are explored in two of the middle-period plays, *Marco* and *Lazarus*. Cai also looks at the influence of the American playwright on Chinese playwrights Hung Shen and Cao Yu.

C19 Castro, Donald Frank. "A Phenomenological Approach to the Concept of Genre." Washington State U, 1978.

Consists of four related essays — related in terms of their subject, genre, and their common perspective, phenomenology. The fourth essay, "Autobiographical Drama: A Phenomenological Deception" discusses *Journey, The Glass Menagerie,* and *After the Fall* as comprising a new or previously unrecognized genre — autobiographical drama.

C20 Chirico, Miriam Madeleine. "Speaking with the Dead: O'Neill, Eliot, Sartre and Mythic Revisionary Drama." Emory U, 1998.

Looking at modern dramas which retell the Orestes myth, Chirico analyzes *Electra,* Sartre's *Les Mouches*, and Eliot's *The Family Reunion* as examples of revisionary writing. The work of Northrop Frye, Claude Levi-Strauss, Harold Bloom and others are referenced.

C21 Cline, Gretchen Sarah. "The Psychodrama of the 'Dysfunctional' Family: Desire, Subjectivity, and Regression in Twentieth-Century American Drama." Ohio State U, 1991.

Plays by O'Neill (*Journey*), Arthur Miller, Tennessee Williams, and Marsha Norman are considered as Cline evaluates the family relationships using psychoanalytic, feminist and existential approaches. Her purpose, in part, is to show the relevance of psychoanalysis, feminism, and philosophy to literary studies.

C22 Collins, Marla Del. "Communicating the Creative Process: A Non-Aristotelian Perspective on Eugene O'Neill and the Women in his Life." New York U, 1998.

Demonstrates how a non-Aristotelian perspective influenced not only her aesthetic choices while creating the personae of Eugene O'Neill and the women in his life (within the text of her play, *The Lovers and Others of Eugene O'Neill*), but also served as a trifocal lens through which to analyze O'Neill, the man, and the women. Uses three approaches to her subject — "general semantics, postmodern feminist philosophy, and the unifying principle of transformation."

C23 Collins, Theresa M. "A Life of Otto H. Kahn, 1867-1934." New York U, 1998.

O'Neill factors into this biography of Kahn in that he and other writers — Hart Crane and Ezra Pound — helped define the philanthropist as a "Kublai" Kahn (*Marco*). Since Kahn was prominent in both the world of finance and art, Collins raises the question of how we fashion public images.

C24 Como, Robert Michael. "The Evolution of O'Neill's Tragic Vision." U of Toledo, 1982.

Nietzsche's influence on O'Neill went beyond the thematic (the concern of most previous critics). Finds the formal implications in Nietzsche's tension between the Apollonian and Dionysian forces in life manifest in O'Neill's writing from the early sea plays through *Iceman*. To "suggest primitive man's intimate relationship to the ebb and flow of life," "O'Neill set many of his early dramas away from civilization" — in the jungle or on the sea. Settings for *Ape* and *Iceman* suggest the estrangement of modern man from the reality of his existence.

C25 Conklin, Robert Brian. "The Performance of Folly in Plays by O'Neill, Williams, and Shepard." Ohio State U, 1992.

Examines *Jones, Marco,* and *Iceman*, as well as several plays by Williams and Shepard, to discover that "the fool in these plays assumes a more authoritative part," bringing into question "the problem of performative power." "By focusing on the on-stage performance situations, in which the fool is a verbal performer," Conklin examines "how the American theatre reproduces specific cultural values through the representations of the American family on stage."

C26 Corrigan, Ralph L., Jr. "The Function of the Green World in Selected Plays by Eugene O'Neill." Fordham U, 1973.

Explores O'Neill's themes of disharmony with and alienation from the natural world. O'Neill's answer lies in man's attempt to find the peace and harmony of the primitive state. Man either dreams of a substitute for nature or journeys to a "sacred grove" to rediscover harmony. Follows with a chronological discussion of O'Neill's changing attitude about the possibility of finding a simple, satisfying life.

C27 Cutler, Janet Klotman. "Eugene O'Neill on the Screen: Love, Hate, and the Movies." U of Illinois, 1977.

Treatments of *Anna, Jones, Journey, Iceman,* and *Voyage* as movie adaptations and art. Concludes that the films, like O'Neill's plays, are uneven.

C28 Dakoske, Mary B. "Archetypal Images of the Family in Selected Modern Plays." U of Notre Dame, 1980.

Draws on both British and American drama to study familiar archetypes in modern drama. Discusses O'Neill's *Journey,* among others, in terms of Jungian archetypes.

C29 Dennery, Thomas. "Social Reform and the American Theater, 1880-1920." Michigan State U, 1974.

Surveys the extent of social concern in the American theater by a look at the plays of the period 1880-1920, the reviews in the *New York Times, New York Dramatic Mirror,* and *Theatre,* other reviews in popular and literary magazines and the works of such figures as Walter Pritchard Eaton, Brander Matthews, William Winter, James Huneker, George Jean Nathan and others. Finds considerable interest in social issues from 1880-1900, a decline of interest thereafter, for half a decade, then regrowth of interest, owing to the influence of the Muckrakers, the Progressive Party (organized in 1904) and efforts to establish a socialist theater in New York. The eventual heirs of these concerns were the Washington Square and Provincetown Players, who rejected social reform, advocating more fundamental changes in American society.

C30 Diamond, George Saul. "The Ironic Use of Melodramatic Conventions of *The Count of Monte Cristo* in the plays of Eugene O'Neill." Lehigh U, 1977.

Discusses the characteristics of melodrama in general and of *The Count* in particular. Looks at early O'Neill—*Cardiff, Zone, Rope,* and *Cross*—for early melodrama influence.

C31 Eisen, Kurt Richard. "Melodrama and Novelization in the Plays of Eugene O'Neill." Boston U, 1990.

Argues, based on theorists of the novel and those of melodrama, that O'Neill "subverts the simple unified self of melodrama, dismantling the moral and psychological opposites on which melodrama depends." Plays considered include *Brown, Journey,* and *Iceman.*

C32 Elliott, Thomas S. "Eugene O'Neill: Art as Religious Quest." U of Oklahoma, 1994.

Argues that O'Neill's canon derived from a lifelong religious quest and that an understanding of his biography is a sine qua non to understanding that canon. His focus is, surprisingly, *Brown.*

C33 Erickson, Steven Craig. "The Drama of Dispossession in Selected Plays of Six Major American Playwrights." U of Texas-Dallas, 1991.

"Through the analysis of selected plays by Eugene O'Neill, Arthur Miller, Tennessee Williams, Edward Albee, David Mamet, and Sam Shepard, this dissertation examines the condition of dispossession as it manifests itself within three thematic areas: the self, the home, and the environment." *Horizon* and *Journey* are the O'Neill plays under discussion.

C34 Fechter, Steven Jerome. "The Impossible Love: A Study of the Incest Theme in the Plays of Ibsen, O'Neill, and Shepard." CUNY, 1993.

Investigates this theme in *Desire* and *Misbegotten* and in works by Ibsen and Shepard. In O'Neill's plays characters search for union with the mother-figure in nature, in other women and in death.

C35 Fisher, Kerk. "The Front Porch in Modern American Drama: The Promise of Mobility in O'Neill, Williams, and Inge." U of Georgia, 1989.

Studies 26 plays written between 1906 and 1985, including *Electra,* in which the focus of the action is the front porch.

C36 Flèche, Anne. "Countering Realism in U.S. Drama: O'Neill and Williams." Rutgers U, 1989.

The O'Neill part of the dissertation deals with *Journey* and *Iceman.* Considers O'Neill's "desire to represent non-being" through a look at character, dialogue, and time. For a fuller annotation see her book.

C37 Fleckenstein, Joan Pazereskis. "Eugene O'Neill's Theatre of Dionysus: The Nietzschean Influence upon Selected Plays." U of Wisconsin, 1973.

Analyzes *Jones, Ape, Fountain, Marco, Brown,* and *Lazarus* in terms of Nietzschean influence — death of God, eternal recurrence, the will to power, the transvaluation of values, and the Superman.

C38 Fleming, William P., Jr. "Tragedy in American Drama: The Tragic Views of Eugene O'Neill, Tennessee Williams, Arthur Miller, and Edward Albee." U of Toledo, 1972.

Develops a modern concept of tragedy, specifically as it relates to American drama. O'Neill's final plays present the Force which makes life tragic, mysterious and different for every man.

C39 Frank, Glenda. "Family Masks: Father-Child Relationships in the Plays of Eugene O'Neill." CUNY, 1992.

Analyzing eight plays from O'Neill's early effort *Bread and Butter* to his masterpieces *Journey, Iceman,* and *Touch,* Frank argues that "O'Neill deliberately adopted the family as a laboratory" wherein he explored philosophical and dramatic ideas. Concludes that "in *Iceman* alone does O'Neill probe the myths surrounding the father-child relationship as psychically wounded sons try to resolve conflicts through surrogate fathers." The family dramas are seen as phased dramatic experiments, sometimes in paired plays like Ibsen's early work. Considers sources and influences as well as staging.

C40 Frank, Robin Jaffee. "Charles Demuth Poster Portraits: 1923-1929." Yale U, 1995.

This art history dissertation discusses the "series of eleven emblematic portraits, which he [Demuth] called 'posters' to honor friends prominent in the avant-garde circles of New York." One portrait was of O'Neill, and so

the relationship between the playwright and painter is addressed.

C41 Friedman, Lois M., O.S.F. "The 'Dark Night of the Soul' in Selected Dramas by Three Modern Catholic Authors." Purdue U, 1977.

Describes the criteria for evaluating the depth and authenticity of the mystical experience. O'Neill's technique for conveying the dark night is to use the divided self. Concludes that O'Neill fails to portray deep and authentic spiritual experiences.

C42 Gray, Cecilia Dolores. "Achievement as a Family Theme in Drama." Oregon State U, 1978.

A dissertation in Sociology which analyzes *Journey* and *Death of a Salesman* to test propositions regarding family achievement — what sustains it.

C43 Gunnon, Bonnie Jo. "A Narrative Psychotherapeutic Approach to the Human Relationship Dilemma: Attachment/Separation-Fusion/Isolation with Implications for the Meaning of Intimacy as Revealed through the Character of Mary Tyrone in Eugene O'Neill's *Long Day's Journey into Night.*" U of Wisconsin-Madison, 1993.

Psychoanalyzes the core of the character Mary Tyrone on intrapsychic, interpersonal, and existential levels.

C44 Hagan, John. "Film/Literature Interface and the Status of the Scenario: A Consideration of Film Texts by J. M. Barrie, Eugene O'Neill, H. G. Wells, and Vladimir Nabokov." New York U (Cinema Studies, Tisch School of the Arts), 1996.

"Delineates the types of functions which the scenario form has served in cinema and literary practice." Film scenarios written by Wells, Nabokov, Barrie, and O'Neill are considered to determine the scenario's relationship to both literary and film modes of discourse.

C45 Hagy, Boyd Frederick. "A Study of the Changing Patterns of Melodramas That Contributed to American Playwriting From 1920-50." Catholic U, 1978.

Fourteen 20th-century plays — among them *Horizon* (1920) and *Desire* (1924) — are discussed to prove Hagy's thesis that 19th-century melodrama made valuable contributions to 20th-century American drama.

C46 Hall, Ann Christine. "'A Kind of Alaska': The Representation of Women in the

Plays of Eugene O'Neill, Harold Pinter, and Sam Shepard." Ohio State U, 1988.

Relies on the work of Jacques Lacan, Jacques Derrida, Luce Iragaray, and other feminist post-structuralist critics to offer an explanation for O'Neill's female characterization in *Iceman, Journey,* and *Misbegotten.*

C47 Hambright, Jeanne K. "The Journey Out: Contributions of German Dramatic Expressionism in the Social Protest Plays of Eugene O'Neill." Tufts U, 1971.

Studies Wedekind and O'Neill — the first as a contributor to Expressionism, the second as a borrower from. Both were influenced by Nietzsche, Marx, and Freud, and found in Expressionism a means of conveying their political and psychological ideas. *Jones, Ape, Chillun, Desire, Marco, Brown, Lazarus, Interlude, Dynamo, Electra,* and *Days* are considered.

C48 Hanson, Eugene Kenneth. "Earth Mother/Mother of God: The Theme of Forgiveness in the Plays of Eugene O'Neill." Claremont U, 1978.

O'Neill's plays deal with a quest for forgiveness from a woman, usually a mother, who represents O'Neill's rejected Catholicism. O'Neill's protagonists want a restoration of the relationship they once knew with the Virgin. However the Mother-figure, like O'Neill's own mother, fails, and the hero turns to other women, often prostitutes. They too fail, and the hero joins the misbegotten. The only hope of salvation is through art.

C49 Hart, Doris. "An Historical Analysis of Three New York Productions of *Long Day's Journey into Night.*" New York U, 1982.

Compares the major New York productions of *Journey*: the 1956 Broadway premiere, the 1971 off-Broadway production, and the 1976 Bicentennial production. Comparison is in terms of interpretations on the part of directors, actors, and designers. Separate chapters for each production. Sources were interviews with actors and actresses — Jason Robards, Zoe Caldwell, Paddy Croft — and stage managers, and technical designers, talks presented by directors, including José Quintero, and materials from the Theatre Collection at Lincoln Center, including scrapbooks, reviews, and a videotape of the 1971 production. The final chapter concludes, among others things, that *Journey* is a masterpiece which for each generation is likely to yield new significance.

C50 Hechler, Marilyn E. "Past and Present in American Drama: The Case of Eugene O'Neill and Sam Shepard." SUNY-Stony Brook, 1989.

Analyzes *Journey, Electra* and *Brown* and plays by Shepard to show that "the dualistic combination of realism and romance that is characteristic of American fiction is characteristic of American drama as well."

C51 Hemmeter, Gail Carnicelli. "Eugene O'Neill and the Languages of Modernism." Case Western Reserve U, 1984.

Studies language in O'Neill's work, language which has often been ignored or denigrated as stilted, repetitious. O'Neill was experimenting with language as he was with form — creating a new language out of the remnants of melodrama, naturalism, and expressionism.

C52 Herrmann-Miller, Eileen Jean. "Eugene O'Neill: The Misprized Modernist." U of California-Davis, 1998.

"Claims O'Neill's position among Modernist writers, by examining his connections to the Greek theater, as well as his variegated language."

Looks to other writers — Eliot, Pound, Yeats — to argue the case for O'Neill's Modernism, especially in *Desire, Electra, Iceman,* and *Journey.*

C53 Herzog, Callie Jeanne. "Nora's Sisters: Female Characters in the Plays of Ibsen, Strindberg, Shaw, and O'Neill." U of Illinois-Urbana, 1982.

Sees Ibsen's Nora as the source for the women of Strindberg, Shaw, and O'Neill. Women characters are described as types. Each playwright blends several types to produce major characters. But though the creative methods are similar, their aims are different: where Ibsen, Strindberg, and Shaw write to challenge conventional attitudes about women, O'Neill creates to reaffirm the conventional attitudes.

C54 Hinden, Michael C. "Tragedy: the Communal Vision: A Critique and Extension of Nietzsche's Theory of Tragedy with Attention Devoted to the Early Plays of Eugene O'Neill." Brown U, 1971.

Concentrates on Nietzsche's ideas expounded in *The Birth of Tragedy.* His fourth and last chapter deals with the plays of O'Neill's "Nietzschean Period" — *Jones, Ape, Chillun, Desire,* and *Brown.*

C55 Hodin, Mark Mitchell. "Legitimate Theater and the Making of Modern Drama in America." U of Wisconsin-Madison, 1995.

Asserts that "the historical formation of a middlebrow stance ... was a key episode in the social emergence of modern drama in America." O'Neill figures in Hodin's conclusion: that the "audience fascination with Belasco's public image helped shape the popular-critical reception of Eugene O'Neill in the 1920s."

C56 Hsia, An Min. "The Tao and Eugene O'Neill." Indiana U, 1980.

Asserts that O'Neill's mysticism is essentially Taoist. Lists the basic tenets of Taoism and discusses *Marco, Lazarus, Interlude, Fountain, Brown* as illustrating these tenets.

C57 Hunt, Doris Ann. "Dialects of the Black Characters in the Plays of Eugene O'Neill." U of Florida, 1977.

The introduction raises the question of whether O'Neill's handling of dialects was accurate. Examines O'Neill's use of dialect and concludes that O'Neill did use black dialect well — especially in Brutus Jones's speech.

C58 Hurley, Daniel F. "The Failed Comedies of Eugene O'Neill." Louisiana State U, 1973.

Studies O'Neill's canon for the playwright's changing attitude toward his characters. Playwright's view was comedic but changed to pathetic. Humor in the later plays drains, and we're left with a residue of agony.

C59 Jensen, George Henry. "The Eugene O'Neill-Theatre Guild Correspondence." U of South Carolina, 1977.

Edits the correspondence between the Theatre Guild and O'Neill from 1927-51. The letters reveal O'Neill's attitude toward his contemporaries, and toward the theater, his relationships with his producers, and his instructions for Guild productions of *Mansions, Interlude, Dynamo, Electra, Days, Iceman, Wilderness.*

C60 Jiji, Vera M. "Audience Response in the Theater: A Study of Dramatic Theory Tested Against Reviewers' Responses to the Plays of Eugene O'Neill." New York U, 1972.

Studies the first night responses to O'Neill's plays produced between 1920 and 1967 to determine if the responses were intrinsic (based on what was in the play) or extrinsic (focused in the mind of the viewer).

Concludes that the societal importance of a play has a great effect upon its reception.

C61 Johnstone, Rosemarie. "The Alcoholism of the Text." U of Minnesota, 1995.

Works by Ernest Hemingway, Anne Sexton, Jack Spicer, and O'Neill are surveyed for the authors' articulation of alcoholism. Uses *Journey* and works by other writers to move literary discussion of alcoholism out of the realm of biography and into epistemological and social realms.

C62 Jordan, John Wingate. "An Examination of the Plays of Eugene O'Neill in Light of C. G. Jung's *Collected Works* and Recorded Conversations." U of Houston, 1980.

Compares Jung's writing with the most experimental O'Neill dramas written between 1916 and 1931. In certain instances O'Neill's stage directions and dialogue coincide verbatim with Jung's words. Finds Jungian influence in *Thirst, Fog, Warnings, Horizon, Anna, Jones, Ape, Desire, Marco, Dynamo, Fountain, Lazarus, Interlude, Electra.*

C63 Karadaghi, Mohamad R. "The Theme of Alienation in Eugene O'Neill's Plays." U of California, 1971.

Argues that alienation is the most consistent of O'Neill's themes. O'Neill sought a cure for this modern illness in liquor, pipe dreams, insanity, and regression into childhood. Analyzes *Cardiff, Horizon, Anna, Jones, Ape, Chillun, Desire, Brown, Interlude, Dynamo, Electra, Iceman, Touch, Journey, Misbegotten.* Finds in first 11 plays man's alienation from God is in the foreground of the play. In the last four it recedes to the background.

C64 Kemper, Susan C. "The Novels, Plays, and Poetry of George Cram Cook, Founder of the Provincetown Players." Bowling Green State U, 1982.

Studies the philosophical ideas and literary techniques expressed in works of George Cram Cook — two novels, two full-length plays, and a book of poetry (excludes collaborations and deals only with published work).

C65 Kobernick, Mark. "Semiotics of the Drama and the Style of Eugene O'Neill." U of Michigan, 1983.

Discusses the "non-verbal signifying systems" in O'Neill's plays — *Anna, Desire, Interlude, Electra, Journey, Touch.* Six semiotic dimensions have been found inherently valuable and adaptable to a controlled form for this kind of study: theatrical semiotic systems, motifs, dramatis personae configuration, personal awareness level, communicative functions, and Aristotelian divisions. The study "theoretically grounds, then illustrates, the collection of the data and their interpretation at three structural levels: the segment, the whole play, and the selected corpus."

C66 Lal, D. K. "Myth and Mythical Concept in O'Neill's Plays." Kumaun U, 1985.

A dissertation later (in 1992) to be revised and published. For annotation see Books and Parts of Books.

C67 Landis, Robyn Gay. "The Family Business: Problems of Identity and Authority in Literature, Theory and the Academy." U of Pennsylvania, 1990.

Discusses the family as "both a fictional topic and a theoretical conceit," considering it as a "model of patriarchal identity and authority" (enter O'Neill), and finally looks at alternative domestic models offered by women authors.

C68 Levin, Eric Mathew. "Postmodern Considerations of Nietzschean Perspectivism in Selected Works of Eugene O'Neill." U of Oregon, 1996.

O'Neill's *Fountain, Marco,* and *Days* are examined "in light of Nietzschean perspectivism. Each play is contextualized within O'Neill's body of work, summarized and examined in terms of traditional literary and production criticism." Finally, a perspectivist approach is considered.

C69 Lichtman, Myla Ruth. "Mythic Plot and Character Development in Euripides' *Hippolytus* and Eugene O'Neill's *Desire Under the Elms:* A Jungian Analysis." U of Southern California, 1979.

Analyzes the two plays using Jung's psycho-philosophical concepts of "myth" and "symbol." Each play is studied in terms of the playwright, the historical time of the play's conception, and the psychological climate of the time. Both plays, in reflecting the psychological climates of their times, reflect man's quest for savage power.

C70 Lieberman, Joseph Alphonsus. "The Emergence of Lesbians and Gay Men as Characters in Plays Produced on the American Stage from 1922 to 1954." CUNY, 1981.

"A 1927 Penal Code prohibition on the statute books of New York State had prohibited [the presentation of] dramatic depictions of lesbian[s] and gay men as characters in Broadway plays." The law remained on the books until 1967. This dissertation treats of some 32 plays produced between 1922 and 1952 in which such characters appeared: among them *The Children's Hour, A Streetcar Named Desire, Tea and Sympathy, Camino Real,* and O'Neill's *Interlude* (pp. 198-203). The information Lieberman offers about Charles Marsden, O'Neill's attitude towards the character, the originals on whom Marsden was based derive from Sheaffer's *Son and Artist* with bolstering from O'Neill's text. Observes that the reviewers of both the 1928 and 1963 New York productions "reacted to Marsden almost as unsympathetically as do the other characters in *Strange Interlude* and that none of the reviewers identified Marsden as gay."

C71 Lischer, Tracy Kenyon. "The Passive Voice in American Literature: Vehicle for Tragedy in Brown, Hawthorne, O'Neill, Wharton, and Frost." Saint Louis U, 1977.

Looks to O'Neill's *Electra* and other works by other American writers to show that Americans devalue the female capability. The result in literature is a divided self, a person who can't assimilate the intuitive female principle and the reflective masculine nature: when the nourishing female principle is needed, the protagonist remains passive or weds action to passion only in death.

C72 Long, Deborah Marie. "The Existential Quest: Family and Form in Selected American Plays." U of Oregon, 1986.

Argues that O'Neill's *Journey,* Arthur Miller's *Death of a Salesman,* and Tennessee Williams' *Cat on a Hot Tin Roof* "exhibit strikingly similar characteristics in regard to each playwright's manipulation of dramatic form" and that the plays present "an identical vision of reality." To support her thesis, Long applies tenets of Existentialism to the plays.

C73 Longhofer, Julie Eakins. "Journeyman's Stage: Rehistoricizing O'Neill, His Audience, and the American Family in the 1920s." U of Illinois at Urbana-Champaign, 1996.

Employs New Historicism "to examine how the American theatre reproduces specific cultural values through the representations of the American family on stage. *The First Man* (1922), *Desire Under the Elms* (1924), and *Strange Interlude* (1928) enact and debate revisionary family structures. Through conflicts over obstacles to reproduction, who will control reproduction, and what form the next generation will take, these plays challenge the status quo of the 'traditional' American family in the 1920s."

C74 Lowel, Marleen Julia. "Herman Melville and Eugene O'Neill in Search of a Nocturnal Paradise: The Myth of Dionysus Rediscovered." George Washington U, 1988.

Considers the similarities between the playwright and novelist and finds the link in their attachment to the Dionysus myth. Melville's *Moby Dick, Mardi,* and *Redburn* are compared to O'Neill's *Journey, Lazarus,* and *Misbegotten.*

C75 Mahmoud, Mahamed A. "A Stylistic, Sociolinguistic, and Discourse Analysis of Linguistic Naturalism in Selected Plays of Arthur Miller and Eugene O'Neill." U of Delaware, 1985.

Suggests that language used by Miller and O'Neill, which has been largely ignored by scholars, bears a strong likeness to the language used by the uneducated classes they depict. Their characters' language is orally-based, so it is often fragmented, repetitive, and formulaic.

C76 Mandel, Josef Lorenz. "Gerhart Hauptmann and Eugene O'Neill: A Parallel Study of their Dramatic Techniques in Selected Naturalistic Plays." U of North Carolina at Chapel Hill, 1977.

Discusses the parallels in three plays of O'Neill and three of Hauptmann and contrasts their techniques. Where O'Neill sees psychological forces as precipitating catastrophe, Hauptmann sees sociological forces. But both write Naturalistic drama and both give us characters subject to a life of suffering and despair.

C77 Mar, Margaret Yang. "Eugene O'Neill and George Jean Nathan: Playwright and Critic." New York U, 1992.

"This research is aimed at examining the possible link between the criticism of Nathan and the development of serious American drama as represented in the major plays of O'Neill." Looks at works from the early, experimental, and mature periods.

C78 Maufort, Marc. "Visions of the American Experience: The O'Neill-Melville Connection, I & II." Free U of Brussels, 1987.

Ambitious 606-page, two-volume dissertation which studies the similarities (confluences) between Melville and O'Neill, including autobiographical tendencies in their writing, their criticism of Puritanism, their innovative concepts of tragedy, and their attitude toward the sea.

C79 McCown, Cynthia Pasquinelli. "Stage Business: The Portrayal of the Businessman and Business Culture by Representative American Playwrights, 1900-1929." Indiana U, 1992.

"By examining the selected works of Broadway playwrights whose popularity was evidence of their ability to parlay art into commercial success, this study presents an audit of the businessman's prestige as perceived by eminent playwrights of the day." Looks at the plays of Clyde Fitch, Charles Klein, George M. Cohan, Edward Sheldon, R. C. Megrue and Walter Hackett, Elmer Rice, O'Neill, Phillip Barry, Sidney Howard, George S. Kaufman and Marc Connelly, Sophie Treadwell, and S. N. Behrman.

C80 McDonough, Edwin Joseph. "Quintero Directs O'Neill: An Examination of Eleven Plays of Eugene O'Neill Staged by José Quintero in New York City, 1956-1981." New York U, 1986.

Later to be updated and published as *Quintero Directs O'Neill* (1991; Books and Parts of Books), McDonough's dissertation, fortified by interviews with Jason Robards, Colleen Dewhurst and Quintero, analyzes the success of the Quintero-directed O'Neill plays over a quarter of a century.

C81 McNicholas, Mary V., O.P. "The Quintessence of Ibsenism: Its Impact on the Drama of Eugene Gladstone O'Neill." Indiana U, 1971.

Finds the influence of Strindberg on O'Neill to be much exaggerated and says that Ibsen's themes and techniques discussed in George Bernard Shaw's *Quintessence*, as well as Shaw's own ideas, reverberate throughout O'Neill's work from early plays to late.

C82 Meade, Robert F. "Jung's Incest Fantasy and the Deleterious Dreams in the Late Plays of Eugene O'Neill." Fordham U, 1994.

Studies the debilitating effects of clinging to pipe dreams in O'Neill's later plays. Referring to Carl Jung's *Psychology of the*

Unconscious, Meade shows how avoidance behaviors are the offspring of the "universal desire to return to the mother womb."

C83 Mihelich, Christine, I.H.M. "The Rite of Confession in Five Plays by Eugene O'Neill." U of Pittsburgh, 1977.

Discusses *Electra, Interlude, Iceman, Journey, Misbegotten* as confessional plays, wherein the characters confess their guilt to persons they have injured or to sympathetic proxies. The study assumes that O'Neill's recollection of the ritual prompted him to use the technique.

C84 Miller, Lance Berry. "Gone West: Landscapes of the Imaginary in Modern American Drama." Stanford U, 1996.

"Theorizes a 'westering desire' in the mythoi of history and the psyche, in which a Lacanian psychoanalytic model of desire as the impossible return to the (M)other is in both collision and collusion with continued variations on the Puritan typological model as God the Father's dispensation of history. René Girard's theory of 'sacred violence' is used to analyze the relationship of fraternal rivalry to the mythic conflicts of westering desire." O'Neill's *Desire* and *Horizon* are among the works referenced.

C85 Miller, Robert Royce. "Tragedy in Modern American Drama: The Psychological, Social, and Absurdist Conditions in Historical Perspective." Middle Tennessee State U, 1975.

The object is to examine the major 20th-century dramatists as reflecting those same concerns that attract contemporary poets, novelists, and short story writers. Deals with *Jones* as reflecting the 20th-century concern with self-identification.

C86 Miller, Ronald Rush. "Eugene O'Neill's Vision of American History: A Study of the Cycle Plays." U of Wisconsin-Madison, 1987.

Argues that *Touch, Mansions* and *The Calms of Capricorn* are works that reflect the "playwright's creation of modern dramatic forms for the treatment of history."

C87 Nash, William Alan. "The Homecoming Motif in Selected Works of Eugene O'Neill." U of Utah, 1975.

Premise: man has since earliest times sought to overcome his alienation from nature and has attempted through the archetypal pattern of withdrawal and return to integrate himself in nature. Discusses the treatment of

this idea in *Horizon, Jones, Ape, Lazarus, Electra, Journey,* and *Misbegotten.*

C88 Newlin, Keith. "Melodramatic Naturalism: London, Garland, Dreiser, and the Campaign to Reform the American Theater." Indiana U, 1991.

Finds the roots of naturalistic drama in melodrama and shows the relevance of Jack London, Hamlin Garland, and Theodore Dreiser to the development of American drama. Their work helped prepare audiences for the appreciation of O'Neill's innovations.

C89 Onunwa, Paschal U. "Eugene O'Neill: The Evolution of Racial Justice and Brotherhood in Five Plays." Fordham U, 1988.

Thirst, Dreamy, Jones, Chillun and *Iceman* are considered for their racial statements. Concludes that O'Neill is the first American playwright to focus on racism.

C90 Orlandello, John Richard. "Stage to Screen: Film Adaptations of the Plays of Eugene O'Neill." U of Michigan, 1976.

The problems of adapting O'Neill's plays to film, and the advantages and disadvantages of the star system.

C91 Pahnichaputt, M. L. Ananchanok. "The Image of Home in Five American Literary Works." U of Denver, 1977.

Unlike the English literary tradition which celebrates the warmth of home, American literature pictures the home negatively — as a place of confinement, a threat to freedom, where familial conflicts result in alienation. Eventually the houses are burnt, sold, divided up into apartments, or abandoned. Works discussed include *The House of Seven Gables, Giants of the Earth, Absalom, Absalom!, Journey,* and *Death of a Salesman.*

C92 Pampel, Brigitte C. "The Relationship of the Sexes in the Works of Strindberg, Wedekind, and O'Neill." Northwestern U, 1972.

Studies the attitudes of Strindberg, Wedekind, and O'Neill toward male-female relationships, focusing on marriage, prostitution, and sexual repression. These writers differed from previous writers because they underscored man's sexual nature. O'Neill emphasized the psychological motivation and dwelled on natural desires and the frustration resulting from an inability to fulfill desires. Although O'Neill reflected Strindberg's pessimism, his characters seek relationships of love and understanding.

C93 Papa, Lee. "Staging Communities in Early Twentieth-Century American Labor Drama (Eugene O'Neill, John Howard Lawson, Maxwell Anderson, Upton Sinclair, Clifford Odets)." U of Tennessee, 1995.

"Using labor historiography as basis, this study demonstrates how labor drama reveals a deep desire for the worker to engage with and form communities with other workers. The plays of the movement attempt to extend that community from the stage to the audience in the theatre." It is the labor movement that provided a bridge between the Little Theatre Movement and the drama of the 40s and 50s. Odets' *Waiting for Lefty* and O'Neill's *Ape* are "canonical texts of the movement."

C94 Peregrim, John J. "A Dialogue of the Self: On the Nature of Theatrical Monologue and Self-Articulation." U of California-Berkeley, 1993.

"An examination of theatrical monologue from performance and communication perspectives, demonstrating that monologue and dialogue are not antonyms, but share a set of structural features common to all communicative utterances." *Hughie* (as well as plays by Beckett, Brecht, and Gray) is considered.

C95 Phillips, Julien Lind. "The Mask: Theory and Practical Use in the Plays of Eugene O'Neill." U of Minnesota, 1977.

Touches on *Jones, Fountain,* and *Marco,* but concentrates on *Ape, Mariner, Chillun, Brown, Lazarus, Electra, Days.* The focus is on how masks indicate symbolic values. O'Neill's masks were successful in providing a separate dramatic element, in reinforcing plot and theme, and in forcing the actor to expand his art, but the masks are limited as tools for conveying meaning.

C96 Pickering, Christine P. "The Works of Eugene O'Neill: A Greek Idea of the Theatre Derived from the Philosophy of Friedrich Nietzsche." East Texas State U, 1971.

O'Neill's conception of drama was based on a Greek concept of theater which he derived from Nietzsche. Analyzes 45 O'Neill plays for Nietzschean influence.

C97 Pike, Frank. "Confession as an Implicit Structuring Device in the Plays of Eugene O'Neill." U of Minnesota, 1980.

Studies confession as a structuring device in *Cardiff, Jones, Brown, Dynamo, Wilderness, Days, Touch, Hughie, Journey, Iceman, Misbegotten.*

C98 Poulard, Regina Fehrens. "O'Neill and Nietzsche: The Making of a Playwright and Thinker." Loyola U, 1974.

Explains the influence of Nietzschean philosophy as expressed in *The Birth of Tragedy* and *Thus Spake Zarathustra* on O'Neill. O'Neill's acceptance of Nietzschean ideas changed during the course of his career; in O'Neill's last period, the playwright fused Nietzschean thinking with the ideas of Thomas à Kempis' *Imitation of Christ.*

C99 Press, Marcia. "That Black Man-White Woman Thing: Images of an American Taboo." Indiana U, 1989.

O'Neill is one of several authors (Faulkner, Wright, Baldwin, Walker, and Styron are others) referenced in this work which focuses on the almost "obsessive concern with the idea or image of intimate contact between a black man and a white woman." Concludes that "through the rhetoric of gender hierarchies embedded in the black man-white woman taboo, writers, white and black, negotiate the racial terms of American 'manhood.'"

C100 Ratliff, Gerald Lee. "An Examination of the Parabolic Nature of 'Suffering' in Selected Plays of Eugene O'Neill 1913-23." Bowling Green State U, 1975.

Considers O'Neill's work during this ten-year period and concludes that his use of biblical allusion is less important than his use of biblical analogue, that he is a Christian playwright-prophet (a point implicit in his treatment of suffering as man's saving grace), and that his unique contribution to the world of literature is his ability to focus on suffering as leading to a gospel of salvation.

C101 Reid, John Louden. "On O'Neill's Own Terms: A Study of the Playwright's Last Dramas." U of California at Berkeley, 1973.

Touch, Mansions, Iceman, Journey, Hughie, Misbegotten use the mythologizing technique developed in O'Neill's earlier plays. Each reflects a central mythic event: *Touch* (Narcissus), *Mansions* (a Kafkaesque fairy tale), *Iceman* (the Harrowing of Hell), *Journey* (the artist's soul conjured from incantatory natural rhythms), *Hughie* (classical elegy and Irish wake), *Misbegotten* (black Irish joke). Four of the plays—*Iceman, Misbegotten, Touch, Journey*—reproduce the four main movements of Greek tragedy and the four steps in the Catholic Sacrament of Penance. These four plays collectively imply a workable contemporary religious stance.

C102 Reifield, Beatrice Ann. "A Theory of Tragicomedy in Modern Drama." Pennsylvania State U, 1976.

Explores the theory of tragicomedy in modern drama, distinguishing between the tragicomic moment and the tragicomic play. Plays by Chekhov, Pirandello, Beckett, and O'Neill are analyzed to show recurring patterns of plot structure, character depiction, and tone.

C103 Rich, J. Dennis. "Eugene O'Neill: Visions of the Absurd." U of Wisconsin, 1976.

Analyzes O'Neill's plays from the perspective of the absurd. The playwright's ideas were influenced by Kierkegaard, Nietzsche, Sartre, Camus, as well as by the American literary and philosophical traditions of Emerson, Hawthorne, Poe, Melville, Thoreau, and Whitman. *Thirst, Cardiff, Jones, Brown* are examined for absurdist influence. In the final stage of O'Neill's career, the struggle to discern the transcendental principle appears to cease and living is affirmed.

C104 Robinson, James Arthur. "O'Neill's Expressionistic Grotesque: A Study of Nine Experimental Plays by Eugene O'Neill." Duke U, 1975.

Discusses *Jones, Ape, Chillun, Desire, Brown, Lazarus, Interlude, Dynamo,* and *Days* in light of the grotesque. Also, surveys O'Neill biography for his early acquaintance with the grotesque and compares O'Neill's use of it to Ionesco's, Genet's, Beckett's, and others.

C105 Roland, Lauren Kay. "Biography and Culture in the Later Plays of Eugene O'Neill." U of Detroit, 1976.

Asserts that the two enterprises of O'Neill's late years — the cycle of 11 plays and the autobiographical works — were not separate endeavors but successive stages in O'Neill's effort to achieve salvation. The search for transcendence in these plays is ultimately a religious quest reflecting the spiritual longings of O'Neill.

C106 Ross, Gwendolyn DeCamp. "Comic Elements in the Late Plays of Eugene O'Neill." U of Tulsa, 1975.

Shows how O'Neill employs comic elements in his late plays to intensify a tragic condition or to point out man's tragic condition in a real rather than an ideal way. Although American by birth, O'Neill was imbued with the Irish comic tradition. Focuses on the use of language to create comedy, the use of character as vehicle for comedy, and the use of situation to create comic effect. Plays considered are *Iceman, Touch, Mansions, Journey, Wilderness,* and *Misbegotten.*

C107 Ryba, Mary Miceli. "Melodrama as a Figure of Mysticism in Eugene O'Neill's Plays." Wayne State U, 1977.

The sources of O'Neill's mysticism were the Roman Catholic Church, Nietzsche, and Oriental traditions, all of which agree on the pattern, if not the goal, of mysticism. The pattern of O'Neill's mysticism conforms more to the pattern of melodrama than to tragedy.

C108 Sands, Jeffrey Elliott. "Eugene O'Neill's Stage Directions." U of Illinois at Urbana-Champaign, 1989.

"An attempt to discover the means by which O'Neill uses his stage directions to guide the actor in his presentation of a role." Sands discusses O'Neill's relations with actors and directors, explains how the actor's perspective is distinct from the literary, and includes "an analysis of how the stage directions reveal O'Neill's method of guiding the actor in the preparation and presentation of the role."

C109 Schiavi, Michael R. "Staging Effeminacy in America." New York U, 1998.

Looks at *Interlude* and *Journey* and plays by Tennessee Williams, Larry Kramer, David Drake, and others to explore "ways in which theatrical configurations of effeminacy inform both its social and dramatic representation in twentieth-century America."

C110 Schmitt, Patrick E. "*The Fountain, Marco Millions,* and *Lazarus Laughed*: O'Neill's 'Exotics' as History Plays." U of Wisconsin-Madison, 1985.

Though the above plays are, "removed temporally, spatially, and culturally from O'Neill's other works," they "convey O'Neill's vision of American history and shape the form of his other history plays."

C111 Schroeder, Patricia Richards. "The Presence of the Past in Modern American Drama." U of Virginia, 1983.

Examines the experiments of four modern American playwrights in their attempts with "dramatic structures ... to portray a past that influences and partly constitutes present stage reality." O'Neill is seen as trying out methods of exposition to define the relationship between past and present. His early plays use "antimimetic expository techniques — to explore the nature of a character's past"; in the later plays the "past becomes an obsession of the characters and the exposition itself ... the central dramatic action."

C112 Shea, Laura. "Child's Play: The Family of Violence in Drama of O'Neill, Albee, and Shepard." Boston U, 1984.

Examines six plays by three playwrights as representing a peculiarly modern feature in American drama — violence in the family. Sees violence as signifying a cultural system's attempt to "reassert its own integrity and difference, and thus its identity." *Journey* is O'Neill's contribution to the study.

C113 Shim, Jung Soon. "Self vs. Tradition: Images of Women in Modern American and Korean Drama." U of Hawaii, 1984.

Three Korean and three American playwrights (including O'Neill) of the 1920s through 1970s represent two societies' "perceptions of and attitudes towards women, their changing roles, morality and values... ." Concludes that "most of the female characters ... experienced an identity crisis because of the conflict between their own self-aspirations and traditional role expectations"; that male playwrights reflect "culturally stereotypical ideas about women"; and that American playwrights show women as having a "relatively stronger sense of individuality."

C114 Smith, Madeline Catherine. "Eugene O'Neill and Sacramental Ritual." West Virginia U, 1982.

O'Neill used rituals of the Roman Catholic Church to structure his plays: Ritual of Baptism (in *Anna, Fountain, Dynamo*); Communion (in *Lazarus, Iceman, Journey*); Confession (in *Cardiff, Jones, Electra, Misbegotten, Iceman)*; and Marriage (in *Welded, Days, Chillun, Servitude*).

C115 Smith, Susan Valeria Harris. "Masks in the Modern Drama." Northwestern U, 1979.

Since Jarry's *Ubu Roi* (1896) about 225 Western plays by playwrights such as Brecht, Cocteau, Genet, Ionesco, O'Neill, Pirandello, and Yeats have used masks. Categorizes the uses of the masks: to satirize; to suggest ritual and myth and invest the theater with a communal spirit; to suggest man's inner life; to suggest the public or false face. Appendix lists some 200 modern plays using masks.

C116 Sohn, Dong-Ho. "Dilemma of Representation in Modern Theater: The Case of Chekhov, O'Neill, Ionesco, and Beckett." U of Minnesota, 1994.

Jones is discussed in an examination of the twentieth-century transition from realistic to postrealistic representation in drama. This is a process of internalizing the subject and spatializing the form, signaling the crisis of representation in modern theater. The discussion ascribes the dilemma of theater to the loss of the Christian myth.

C117 Song, Nina. "Death in the Tragedies of William Shakespeare and Eugene O'Neill." SUNY-Albany, 1988.

O'Neill's *Interlude, Electra, Iceman*, and *Journey* and four tragedies by Shakespeare are the focus of this dissertation, which studies the death wish, the theme of love as death, and the theme of death-in-life.

C118 Sproxton, Birk Ernest. "Subversive Sexuality in Four Eugene O'Neill Plays of His Middle Period." U of Manitoba, 1982.

Sees the period 1926-32 as needing special attention because O'Neill was then involved in a "sex research study" and in "analyzing conflicts in his family background" as well as writing plays. Of the plays of the period, *Lazarus, Interlude,* and *Dynamo* are for various reasons artistic failures, but these together with his one success — *Electra* — bring O'Neill to the forefront "as a major figure in the sexual revolution in American literature and an incisive critic of his culture."

C119 Stelly, Thomas Stuart. "Major American Playwrights and Exotic Materials: Eugene O'Neill, Clifford Odets, William Saroyan, Ed Bullins, and Sam Shepard." U of Southwestern Louisiana, 1987.

Assesses the reasons why playwrights might select exotic locations and characters from subcultures for their plays instead of middle-class locations and characters.

C120 Sturm, Clarence. "Scholarly Criticism of Eugene O'Neill in Periodicals, 1960-1975, with a Bibliographical Overview of the American and German Studies." Oklahoma State U, 1977.

A research tool which contains four main divisions: 1) An introductory essay reviewing the state of O'Neill studies as reflected in scholarly articles in English from 1960-75; 2) Abstracts of articles mentioned in the introduction; 3) A bibliography of scholarship about O'Neill in German since 1920; 4) Biographical data containing important dates in O'Neill's life.

C121 Swanson, Margaret Millen. "Irony in Selected Neo-Hellenic Plays." U of Minnesota, 1979.

Studies works by O'Neill (*Electra*), Eliot, Sartre, Gide, Cocteau, and Ionesco, all derived from Greek drama. In Greek drama, the tension is between God and man, but in contemporary drama the tension is between conflicting aspects of man. Contemporary writers see no definite solutions, offer only tentative ones. Also, finds that in contemporary theater, judge and victim, who are distinct in Greek drama, may merge into a single character or protagonist.

C122 Swanson, Mary Stewart. "The Themes of Time and Mortality in the Dramas of Eugene O'Neill." U of Minnesota, 1977.

Attempts to find some development of attitude about mortality and immortality in O'Neill's work. Sees in the early plays (*Thirst, Sniper, Cardiff*), an obsession with dying, but in the later plays (*Touch, Mansions, Iceman, Journey, Misbegotten, Hughie*) O'Neill's acceptance of death.

C123 Sweet, Harvey. "Eugene O'Neill and Robert Edmond Jones: Text into Scene." U of Wisconsin, 1974.

Studies the contribution of Jones to the form of American theater. Tries to devise a vocabulary for discussion and a context for evaluation. Three collaborations with O'Neill are considered. Chapter I surveys O'Neill's career in New York theatre; Chapter II studies Jones's development in professional theater throughout America. Chapters III-V consider designs for *Desire, Electra* and *Iceman*.

C124 Tuck, Susan. "Eugene O'Neill and William Faulkner." Indiana U, 1984.

Asserts Faulkner's enthusiasm for O'Neill and studies the latter's influence on the novelist. Points out the similarities in the two writers' work, the impact of the *Glencairn* plays, *Ape*, and *Jones* on Faulkner's New Orleans tales, "analyzes expressionistic elements borrowed from O'Neill in *As I Lay Dying*," discusses black characterization in *Chillun* and *Light in August*, and compares *Electra* with *Absalom, Absalom!* and *The Sound and the Fury* with *Journey*.

C125 Vena, Gary A. "Eugene O'Neill's *The Iceman Cometh*: A Reconstruction of the 1946 Theatre Guild Production." New York U, 1984.

Reconstructs the first performance of the Theatre Guild's *Iceman*, at the Martin Beck Theater, 9 Oct. 1946, using interviews with some of the principals, promptbooks, photographs, newspaper accounts, rehearsal texts, and ground plans as sources. An appendix "offers a line-by-line account of the modifications of O'Neill's original text in relation to the script which emerges in performance" and "synopsizes more than forty-five reviews of the premiere performance."

C126 Voelker, Paul Duane. "The Early Plays of Eugene O'Neill: 1913-1915." U of Wisconsin, 1975.

Analyzes the early plays and concludes that from the beginning O'Neill saw his work as a combination of the literary and the theatrical. George Pierce Baker's influence was not negative, may even have been salutary. Demonstrates that O'Neill developed increasing competence in the use of setting, lighting, sound effects, blocking, and in plot structure, pacing, and rhythm in early plays.

C127 Voglino, Barbara. "The Evolution of Closure in the Plays of Eugene O'Neill." Fordham U, 1998.

Concludes that "O'Neill's facility with closure evolved most significantly with regard to completing the structures of his plays more appropriately, rendering reversals of character more credible through better preparation, employing ambiguity more purposefully, and abandoning theatricality for fidelity to life." Looks at nine plays to arrive at her conclusion: *Horizon, Anna, Desire, Dynamo, Days, Electra, Iceman, Journey, Misbegotten* (with separate chapters for all but *Dynamo* and *Days*).

C128 Voigt, Maureen Frances. "Rank, Ibsen, and O'Neill: Birth Trauma and Creative Will in Selected Plays." Ohio State U, 1992.

Applies Otto Rank's theories of birth trauma and creative will to *Journey, Iceman*, and *Desire* and works by Ibsen. Anxiety over separation at birth is resolved by creative people, who "live within their own egos." Ibsen and O'Neill projected the universal trauma of birth separation onto their characters.

C129 Wainscott, Ronald H. "A Critical History of the Professional Stage Direction of the Plays of Eugene O'Neill, 1920-1934." Indiana U, 1984.

"Traces the development of stage direction" in O'Neill's plays from 1920-34: 22 productions, beginning with *Horizon* and concluding with *Days*. The study "describes and evaluates what was most difficult for the directors, as well as what was most unusual, innovative, and historically significant." There was a maturation in directing in that period, which corresponded with the development of serious drama.

C130 Walker, Herbert Kenneth, III. "Symbolism in the Later Plays of Eugene O'Neill." Ball State U, 1978.

Accounts for the disparity between the early and later plays by examining the simplicity of action and the unity of symbol and action in *Touch, Iceman, Journey*. Agrees with Eric Bentley that O'Neill's early plays are ineffective because of the pretentiousness of his ideas, symbols, and themes. *Iceman* and *Touch* are successful because characterization is developed, plots are simple, and theme arises from action and character. In *Journey* O'Neill perfected the use of symbol.

C131 Walker, John Wittington. "Mechanization and Caricature in the Aesthetics of Expressionism." U of Oregon, 1998.

Examines the "sudden intensification of violent spectacle in the modern art of Europe and the United States as a revolt against social conditions of advanced technological modernization." Examples drawn from works by Elmer Rice, Sophie Treadwell, Bertolt Brecht, Dashiell Hammett, and O'Neill's *Ape*.

C132 Walker, Julia Ann. "Character, Commodity Fetishism, and the Origins of Expressionism on the American Stage." Duke U, 1995.

Challenges "the assumption that American theatrical Expressionism was a minor offshoot of the German movement, arguing that what came to be called 'Expressionism' in the United States derived in large part from nineteenth-century American acting traditions and their legacy on the twentieth-century popular stage." *Ape* and *Jones* are among the plays discussed, works by Elmer Rice, John Howard Lawson, and Sophie Treadwell being others.

C133 Wang, Qingxiang. "Who Troubled the Waters: A Study of the Motif of Intrusion in Five Modern Dramatists: John Millington Synge, Eugene O'Neill, Edward Albee, Tennessee Williams, and Harold Pinter." Indiana U of Pennsylvania, 1991.

Works by these playwrights furnish Wang with fodder for his study of "pattern, function, extent, and meaning of the intrusion," which ultimately reveal the playwrights' literary values. The motif of intrusion is favored by these dramatists "because it provides them with the opportunity to present crises, conflicts, and frustrations of individuals in modern society." Unlike earlier playwrights who offered resolutions, these refuse to provide answers to the frustrations and insecurities of the time.

C134 Watkinson, Sharon Anne Onevelo. "An Analysis of Characters in Selected Plays of Eugene O'Neill According to Erik H. Erikson's Identity Theory." New York U, 1980.

Touch, Mansions, Iceman, Hughie, Journey, Misbegotten are treated in terms of Erikson's theory of identity. When he wrote *Journey*, O'Neill dispersed identity disorders among all four characters.

C135 White, Leslie. "Eugene O'Neill and the Federal Theatre Project." New York U, 1986.

Contends that the Federal Theatre Project's productions of O'Neill plays from 1936-39 helped to establish the playwright's reputation. Included in the appendices are the Theatre Project's production histories.

C136 Williams, Julia Willa Bacon. "Eugene O'Neill: The Philos-Aphilos of a Mother's Eternal Son." U of Michigan, 1978.

The effects on O'Neill of learning of his mother's addiction were several — alcoholism, guilt, a death-wish, Jekyll and Hyde personality, obsession with cathartic writing, and exorbitant demands on wives. Traces the intensity of his angst as it reverberates throughout his canon, and the philos-aphilos relationship in his plays

C137 Witt, Jonathan Ronald. "Fearless Audiences: How Modern American Literature Flatters Us." U of Kansas, 1996.

O'Neill figures only briefly in this dissertation addressing the treatment of "lowly, unheroic" protagonists in literature. Witt discusses the problems such characters create for their creators (works by Arthur Miller, Tennessee Williams and O'Neill are looked at) and the effect they have on the audience. Also addressed are theories of comedy and an explanation of "how comedy offers a solution that risks flattering audiences in other ways, as when excessive comic deflation turns into smug satire." Finally, Mark Twain's *The Adventures of Huckleberry Finn* and Flannery O'-Connor's short stories are discussed in terms of the effect the novel's and short stories' comedy elicit.

C138 Wolkowitz, Alfred David. "The Myth of the Atridae in Classic and Modern Drama." New York U, 1973.

Studies the development of the Atridae myth from its Homeric sources to its use in 20th-century adaptations. Deals with the works of eight 20th-century playwrights who treated of the myth — including O'Neill's *Electra*.

C139 Zhang, Yuan-Xia. "Eugene O'Neill's Orientalism and the Search for Life: An Americanized Taoistic Response." Marquette U, 1995.

More Taoism in O'Neill. "This study joins with the earlier Eugene O'Neill scholarship that establishes the validity and significance of Orientalism in O'Neill's plays." Works of the playwright's early, middle, and late periods are considered.

D. Scholarship and Criticism (Foreign Language)

Articles (D1 — D98)

D1 Abiteboul, Maurice. "Civilisation et régression dans *L'Empereur Jones* d'Eugene O'Neill et *Vacances d'été* de Francis Ebejer: le progrès est-il un mythe?" *Commonwealth Essays and Studies* [Dijon] 10.1 (1987): 49-56.

D2 Alagna, Giulia. "L' Aside in *Strange Interlude.*" *Blue Guitar* 2 (1976): 219-31.

D3 Andrenacci Maldini, Silvana. "*L'Imperatore Jones* di Eugene O'Neill, ovvero il tallone di Achille." *Silarus: Rassegna Bimestrale di Cultura* [Salerno] 40.201 (1999): 34-46.

D4 Bakošová-Hlavenková, Z. "Film a divadlo." *Bratislava* 21 (1979): 24.

Concerns the Prague production of *Voyage.*

D5 Bauzyte, Galina. "Eschilas ir Judzino o'Nylo dramaturgija." *Literatura*: Lietuvos TSR Aukstuju Mokyklu Mokslo Darbai [Vilnius, Lithuanian S.S.R., U.S.S.R.] 20.3 (1978): 36-39.

D6 Bérubé, Renald. "Eugene O'Neill." *Liberté* [Montreal, Quebec] 99 (1975): 42-65.

D7 *Bol'shaia Sovetskaia Entsiklopediia.* 3d ed., vol. 18, s.v. "O'Neill, Eugene." Moscow: Sovetskaia Entsiklopediia Publishing House, 1974.

For an annotation see A122.

D8 Brantsaeter, Per L. "Eugene O'Neill-Hans skuespil og hans virkelighet." *Samtiden: Tidsskrift for Politikk, Litteratur og Samfunnssporsmal* 83 (1974): 166-72.

D9 Bremer, J. M. "De weerklank van Electra's schreeuw." *Lampas: Tijdschrift voor nederlandse-classici* 26.1 (1993): 49-72.

D10 Bruna, O. "Theater, das von sich reden macht." *Theater der Zeit* [Berlin] 8 (1979): 34-38.

D11 Buzduganov N. "Interesni proiavi na mladite." *Teatur* [Sofia] 3 (1977): 34-35.

Concerns a production of *Desire* at the Dramaticheskom teatre, Sofia.

D12 Cagliero, Roberto. "O'Neill e la problematicita del canone." *Quaderni di Lingue e Letterature* [Verona, Italy] 17 (1992): 27-33.

D13 Camilucci, Marcello. "Il dramma dell' Interiorita: *Strano interludio.*" *Studium* [Italy] 69 (1973): 201-09.

D14 Conradie, P. J. "*Mourning Becomes Electra* en O'Neill se Griekse droom." *Standpunte* [Capetown] 127 (1977): 17-36.

D15 Cosentino, Giacomo. "Ephraim Cabot e la visione tragica di E. O'Neill." *Ragioni critiche* 29-32 (1987): 21-28.

D16 Ćośic, Ileana. "Judžin O'Nil: Velikan svoje epohe." *Scena* [Yugoslavia] 16.1-2 (1980): 147-67.

D17 Deng, Shihuan. ["On O'Neill's *Mourning Becomes Electra* (Tragic Trilogy)"]. *Foreign Literature Studies* [China] 36.2 (1987): 85-90.

D18 Di Giuseppe, Rita. "*Anna Christie* e la dialettica della menzogna vitale." *Quaderni di Lingue e Letterature* [Verona, Italy] 17 (1992): 63-83.

D19 Dinu, Mihai. "Continuité et changement dans la stratégie des personnages dramatiques." *Cahiers de Linguistique Théorique et Appliquée* 10 (1973): 5-26.

Solomon Marcus' idea for investigating dramatic works with methods developed from distributional linguistics is applied to 14 plays, including *Journey.*

D20 Donahue, Francis. "Eugene O'Neill e la tragédia moderna." *Revista de teatro* 465 (1988): 20-21.

D21 _____. "Llamada a escena." *Atenea: Revista de ciencia, arte y literatura de la universidad de Concepción* [Chile] 457 (1988): 119-30.

D22 Dubost, Thierry. "Renaissance dans *Strange Interlude*." *Americana* 12 (1995): 69-81.

D23 Dumitrescu, C. "*Fire de Poet* de Eugene O'Neill." *Teatru* [Bucharest] 11 (1978): 31-32.

Concerns a Romanian production of *Touch*.

D24 Egri, Péter. "Csehov és O'Neill (Eugene O'Neill: Utazás az éjszakába)." *Filolâogiai Kèozlèony* 24 (1978): 231-35.

D25 _____. "Az amerikai álom természetrajza és társadalomtörténete: Eugene O'Neill drámaciklusáról." *Filolâogiai Kèozlèony* 31 (1985): 57-78.

D26 Filip, Traian. "Relatii editoriale cu România." *Manuscriptum: Revista Trimestriala Editata de Muzeul Literaturii Romane* [Romania] 11.1 (1980): 166-68.

D27 Fridshteïn, Iu. "Lorens Oliv'e v p'ese O'Nila." *Teatr* [Russia] 10 (1973): 127-28.

Observations about the National Theatre (London) production of *Journey*.

D28 Gelb, Barbara. "Dzheïson Robards, Iudzhin O'Nil." *Amerika* [Russia] 19 Jan. 1975: 33-37.

Translation of her article on Jason Robards. See A255.

D29 Gierow, Karl Ragnar. "*Lång dags färd var fel pjäs*." *Svenska Dagbladet* [Stockholm] 1 Apr. 1973: n. pag.

D30 Gorshkova, V. "Krakh illiuziï." *Teatr. zhizn'* [Russia] (1977): 14-15.

D31 Ichinose, Kazuo. "Performance text tôshite no *Hughie*: Togaki wo tôshite." *Eigo-Seinen* 134 (1988): 412-13.

D32 Ishizuka, Koji. "Sakusha 'Fazai' no Jiden Geki: Yoru eno Nagai Tabiji Saikô." *Eigo-Seinen* 134 (1988): 414-16.

About autobiographical features in *Journey*.

D33 Ito, Akira. "On Edmund Tyrone in *Long Day's Journey into Night*." *Gengo Bunkabu Kiyaô.* [Japan] 17 (1989): 195-217.

D34 Jones, Sumie. "Nire no Kokage no Ykubo." *Eibungaku* 21 (Mar. 1992): 66-80.

D35 Jordt, Heinrich. "Sucht und Charakter." *Jahrbuch der Wittheit zu Bremen* 18 (1974): 169-88.

D36 Katsu, Kenichiro. "*The Great God Brown*: A False Mask." *Chu Shikoko/Studies in American Literature* [Hiroshima] 27 (June 1991): 37-48.

Pages 37-47 are in Chinese; p. 48 contains a summary in English which argues that *Brown* is more satisfying to the reader than to the viewer.

D37 Kerjan, Liliane. "*Strange Interlude* ou les vertiges de la fièvre tierce." *Etudes anglaises* 48.4 (1994): 427-35.

D38 Kisselintcheva, X. "Les problèmes dans la dramaturgie d'Eugene O'Neill et Sean O'Casey." *Literaturna Misul* 30.4 (1986): 96-104.

D39 Koike, Misako. "O'Neill Kenkyu — Genjo to Kadai." *Eigo-Seinen* [Tokyo] 119 (1973): 548-50.

D40 Koljević, Nikola. "Postanak i Razvoj Americke Drama," and "Tri Velikana Americke Drame." *Pozorište* 25 (1983): 415-55.

D41 Koreneva, M. "Zhizn' i tvorchestvo Iudzhina O'Nila v otsenke kritikov i biografov, 1970-e gody: Obzor." *Sovrem. Khudozh. Iit. za rubezhom* [Russia] 2 (1977): 107-13.

D42 Kostov, K. "Namereniia i vŭzmozhnosti." *Teatur* [Sofia] 4 (1977): 18-20.

Concerns a production of *Desire* in Bulgaria.

D43 Kreutzer, Eberhard. "Eugene O'Neills *Bound East for Cardiff*: Genese, Struktur und Kontext eines paradigmatischen Einakters." *Anglistik und Englischunterricht* 28 (1986): 33-47.

D44 Krykunova, Natalia. "Khto stoït' naïbluzhche do zirok?: Trahichne v amerykans'kiï drami." *Slovo i Chas* [Ukrainian] 6 (1990): 69-73.

D45 Kusuhara, Tamoko. "Nihon ni okeru O'Neill-geki no Juyô." *Eigo-Seinen* 134 (1988): 420-22.

D46 Lagerroth, Ulla-Britta. "Ny nordisk forskning om drama och teater." *Samlaren* 100 (1979): 200-15.

D47 Liao, Kedui. ["On *The Hairy Ape*"]. *Foreign Literature Studies* [China] 33.3 (1986): 25-31.

D48 _____. ["On O'Neill's *Marco Millions*"]. *Foreign Literature Studies* [China] 38.4 (1987): 40-45, 102.

D49 Lindman-Strafford, Kerstin. "Modern som martyr." *Finsk-Tidskrift* [Turku, Finland] 7 (1989): 414-23.

D50 Liu, Haiping. ["On the Later Creations of Eugene O'Neill"]. *Foreign Literature Studies* [China] 31.1 (1986): 73-79.

D51 Maillard, Michel. "Les Electres modernes." *Magazines Littéraires* [Paris] 360 (1997): 43-46.

D52 Marconi, Emo. "Il testo teatrale e la sua rappresentazione." *Testo: Studi di teoria e storia della letteratura e della critica* 12 (1986): 17-42.

D53 Maufort, Marc. "Visions du nouveau monde: Eugene O'Neill et Herman Melville." *Revue belge de philologie et d'histoire/Belgisch Tijdschrift voor Filologie en Geschiedenis* [Wezembeek, Belgium] 65.4 (1986): 1003-04.

D54 _____. "Eugene O'Neill: Dramaturge américain." *L'Artichaut* 5.1 (1987): 3, 9-14, and 5.2 (1987): 10-16.

D55 _____. "A la recherche d'un réalisme irréel: Symbolisme des couleurs dans l'oeuvre d'Eugene O'Neill." *Figures du noir au blanc* 6-7 (1990-91): 197-212.

D56 Medvedeva, N. P. "O zhanrovom svoeohrazii p'esy Iu. O'Nila *Strannaia interliudiia*" [The Originality of Genre of O'Neill's Play *Interlude*]. *Sbornik nauchnykh Trudov Sverdlovskogo pedagogicheskogo instituta* [Russia] 319 (1979): 88-94.

D57 Meged, Matti. "Shlosha Mishorim: Machaze Ehad (al Ish ha-kerah Ba le-O'Neill)." *Bama* 64-65 (1975): 25-42.

D58 Monova, D. "Tŭrseniiata na kolektivo." *Teatŭr* [Sofia] 7 (1978): 33-35. Concerns a production of *Desire* in Vratsa, Bulgaria.

D59 Morvan, Françoise. "A Propos d'une expérience de traduction: *Désir sous les ormes* d'Eugene O'Neill." *TTR /Traduction, terminologie, redaction: Etudes sur le texte et ses transformations* [Montreal] 7.2 (1994): 63-92.

D60 Müller, Kurt. "Aspekte des Modernen in den frühen See-Einaktern Eugene O'Neills." *Amerika-studien* 34.4 (1989): 391-402.

D61 Mutô, Shûji. "O'Neill to Bokushin." *Eigo-Seinen* 134 (1988): 417-19.

D62 Mylov, V. "Esli by ne O'Nil ... ." *Tiumen. pravda* [Russia] 17 July 1976: n. pag. Concerns the Omsk production of *Desire*.

D63 Nastić Radmila. "Sva božja deca ... Judžina O'Nila." *Pozoriéste* 29 (1987): 99-103.

D64 Ohkawa, Tetsuo. ["Gothicism in Some Plays of Eugene O'Neill"]. *Chu Shikoku Studies in American Literature* [Hiroshima, Japan] 26 (1990): 76-83.

D65 Ouyang, Ji. ["The American Playwright Eugene O'Neill and the Philosophy of Laozi"]. *Foreign Literature Studies* [China] 33.3 (1986): 103-08.

D66 _____. ["O'Neill, an American Playwright Who Bemoans the Fate of Mankind"]. *Foreign Literature Studies* 42.4 (1988): 3-11.

D67 Pacheco, Gilda. "*Hairy Ape* de Eugene O'Neill: Un enfoque diferente." *Káñina* 12.1 (1988): 103-07.

D68 _____. "Un enfoque feminista sobre *Viaje de un Largo Dia Hacia la Noche.*" *Filología y Lingüística* 14.1 (1988): 75-80.

D69 Paduano, Guido. "Manierismo e struttura psicologica nell'esperienza greca di Eugene O'Neill." *Annali della Scuola Normale Superiore di Pisa. Classe di lettere e filosofia* 3.2 (1973): 761-816.

D70 Pinaev, Sergei Mikhailovich. "*Tragicheskaia simbolika Iudzhina O'Nila.*" *Filologicheskie-Nauki* [Moscow] 6 (1989): 30-38.

D71 Pitavy-Souques, Danièle. "L'Intruse: Stratégie du désir dans *Desire Under the Elms* et *A Streetcar Named Desire.*" *Coup de Théâtre* [Publication du Centre de Recherches sur les Arts Dramatiques Anglo-Saxons Contemporains] 3 (1983): 17-27.

D72 Plett, Heinrich F., and Renate Plett. "New York: Variationen über das Thema Metropolis im amerikanischen Drama der Zwanziger Jahre." *Zeitschrift für Literaturwissenschaft und Linguistik* 12 (1982): 103-33.

D73 Quiroga, Osvaldo. "Eugene O'Neill, un mensaje humanista que perdura." Suplemento literatura. *La Nacion* [Buenos Aires] 20 Nov. 1988, sec. 4a: 6+.

D74 Reiss, Walter. "Die Weltliterarische Leistrunge Maksim Gor'kijs bei der Schaffung einer Dramenpopöe: M. Gorkijs ... i drugie-Zyklus im Vergleich zu M. Krlezas Glembajevi und O'Neills *Mourning Becomes Electra.*" *Wissenschaftliche Zeitschrift der Humboldt-Universität zu Berlin: Gesellschafts-und-Sprachwissenschaftliche Reiche* 28 (1979): 347-51.

D75 Scheller, Bernhard. "O'Neill und die Rezeption Spätbürgerlich-kritischer Dramatik." *Zeitschrift für Anglistik und Amerikanistik* 23 (1975): 314-21.

D76 _____. "Lass doch Sara lachen." *Theater der Zeit* [Berlin] 5 (1978): 29-30. Concerns a production of *Touch* in Rostock, Germany.

D77 Seidel, Margot. "Goethes Faust und O'Neill." *Archiv für das Studium der Neueren Sprachen und Literaturen* 219 (1982): 365-72.

D78 _____. "Der Einfluss asiatischer Religionen auf Eugene O'Neill." *Zeitschrift für Anglistik und Amerikanistik* 34.1 (1986): 47-59.

D79 Shelmaru, T. "Dolgii den' yxodit v noch' Iu. O'Nila: (Teatr im. Sturdzy-Bulandry)." *Rumyn. Lit.* [Russia] 3 (1976): 129-31. Concerns the San Francisco touring company's production in Russia of *Desire*.

D80 Sichert, Margit. "Die Moderne, das Unbewusste und der Traum: O'Neills *The Emperor Jones*." *Amerikastudien* [Munich] 34.4 (1989): 403-12.

D81 Sirakov, Martin. "Teâtrât na bunta i tragičnija sviat na Judzin O'Nijl" [The theatre of rebellion and tragic world of Eugene O'Neill]. *Godisnik na VITIZ 'Kr Sarafov'* 13 (1973): 217-36.

D82 Sittler, Loring. "*The Emperor Jones*— ein Individuationspross im Sinne C. G. Jungs?" *Amerikstudien* 23.1 (1978): 118-30.

D83 Spasova, E. "Na Kamerna Stsena." *Teatŭr* [Sofia] 4 (1979): 26-28. Concerns a production of *Misbegotten* in the city of Gabrovo, Bulgaria.

D84 Stanciu, Virgil. "O'Neill si renasterea tragediei." *Steaua* [Bucharest] 37.12 (1986): 44.

D85 Stefanov, O. "Dva spektaklia." *Teatŭr* [Sofia] 2 (1977): 30-32. Concerns a production of *Desire* in Bulgaria.

D86 Thébaud, M. "Délivrez-nous d'O'Neill." *Le Figaro* 23 Nov. 1982: 29.

D87 Törnqvist, Egil. "De Bewerking von de realiteit: Het Historie Drama." *Scenaríum* 4 (1980): 9-20. Includes examples from Ibsen, Strindberg, Brecht, and O'Neill.

D88 Treĭmanis, G. "Poesiia sotsial'nogo i psikhologicheskogo obobshcheniia." *Golos Rigi* [Riga] 25 Aug. 1975: n. pag.

D89 Uchino, Tadashi. "O'Neill no melodramatism." *Eigo-Seinen* 134 (1988): 409-11.

D90 Ueno, Seiichiro. ["The Romance Characteristic in O'Neill's Plays."] *Studies in English and Literature* [Japan] 23 (1973): 17-37.

D91 Vianu, Lidia. "O'Neill." *Secolul XX* [Romania] 168-69 (1975): 140-51.

D92 Voĭtkevich, N. "Dolgoe puteshestvie v noch." *Teatr* [Russia] (1973): 66-69.

D93 Vysots'ka, Natalia. "Dotork do fatumu." Vsesvit: Zhurnal Inozemnoi *Literatury* [Kiev] 11 (Nov. 1988): 139-42. [Ukrainian]

D94 Wawrzyniak, E. K. "Rozgrzebywanie prezeszłości." *Teatr* [Warsaw] 22 (1977): 1-7. Concerns a Polish production of *Journey*.

D95 Weckermann, Hans Jürgen. "Das Haus Pyncheon und das Haus Mannon: der amerikanische Einfluss in O'Neills *Mourning Becomes Electra*." *Literatur in Wissenschaft und Unterricht* 21 (1988): 202-15.

D96 Xia, Yinying. ["Exploration of O'Neill's Philosophy of Life"]. *Foreign Literature Studies* 37.3 (1987): 76-81.

D97 Zapf, Hubert. "Drama und Postmoderne: Zur Aktualität Eugene O'Neills." *Forum Moderne Theater* 3 (1988): 142-54.

D98 Zmudzka, E. "Przyjazie na pewno." *Teatr* [Warsaw] 24 (1976): 8-9.

Books and Parts of Books (D99—D225)

D99 Abe, Hiroshe. "Eugene O'Neill." In *America Bungaku no Ji Kotenkai 20-seiki no America Bungaku II*. Ed. Toshihiko Ogata. Kyoto: Yamaguchi, 1982. 205-39.

D100 Ahrends, Günter. *Traumwelt und Wirklichkeit im Spätwerk Eugene O'Neills*. Heidelberg: Winter, 1978.

D101 Bach, Gerhard. *Susan Glaspell und die Provincetown Players: die Anfänge des Modernen amerikanischen Dramas und Theaters*. Frankfurt am Main: Lang, 1979.

D102 _____. "O'Neills Provincetown connection: Zur Aufhellung einer zum Mythos stilisierten Beziehung." In *Eugene O'Neill 1988: Deutsche Beiträge zum 100. Geburtstag des amerikanischen Dramatikers*. Ed. Ulrich Halfmann. Tübingen: Narr, 1990. 34-47.

D103 Bécsy, Tamás. *Utazás az éjszakába. A drámamodellek és a mai dráma*. Budapest: Akadémiai, 1974. 294-300.

D104 Borchers, Hans. "'Those Profound Hidden Conflicts of the Mind': Zur Rezeption psychoanalytischer Konzepte in O'Neills Dramen *Strange Interlude* und *Mourning Becomes Electra*." In *Eugene O'Neill 1988: Deutsche Beiträge zum 100. Geburtstag des amerikanischen Dramatikers*. Ed. Ulrich Halfmann. Tübingen: Narr, 1990. 87-108.

D105 Brumm, Ursula. "Eugene O'Neills Familiendrama *Long Day's Journey into Night*. Bericht über Kolloquien der Kommission für literatur-wissenschaftliche Motif und Themenforschung 1991-94." In *Familienbildung als Schicksal: Wandlungen eines Motivbereichs in der neueren Literatur*. Abhandlungen der Akademie der Wissen-schaften in Göttingen: Philologisch-Historische Klasse; Folge 3, no. 219. Ed. Theodor Wolpers. Göttingen: Vandenhoeck & Ruprecht, 1996. 275-85.

D106 Brüning, Eberhard. *Eugene O'Neill und die Mündigkeit des amerikanischen Theaters*. Sitzungsberichte der sächsischen Akademie der Wissenschaften zu Leipzig. Philologisch-historische Klasse, B. 130, H. 2. Berlin: Akademie-Verlag, 1990.

Lewis, Ward B. Rev. *Eugene O'Neill Review* 20.1-2 (1996) 158-61.

D107 Castro, Ginette. "Les Femmes dans le théâtre d'O'Neill: essai d'interprétation féministe." In *Annales*. Center for Research on English-speaking America of the U of Bordeaux: Talence, 1977. 131-58.

D108 Comarnescu, Petru. "Introducere la *Straniul interludiu* (1939)." In *Scrieri despre Teatru*. Ed. Mircea Filip. Iași [Romania]: Junimea, 1977. 97-148.

Reprint of an essay first published in 1939.

D109 _____. *O'Neill si renasterea tragediei*. Cluj-Napoca: Editura Dacia, 1986.

D110 Cortina, José Ramón. *Ensayos sobre el teatro moderno*. Madrid: Editorial Gredos, 1973.

D111 Dalgard, Olav. *Teatret i det 20. hundredåret*. Oslo: Det Norske Samlaget, 1976.

An expanded version of an earlier work. Includes a brief introduction to O'Neill.

D112 Digeser, Andreas. "Dialogstrukturen in Eugene O'Neills *Long Day's Journey into Night*." In *Eugene O'Neill 1988: Deutsche Beiträge zum 100. Geburtstag des amerikanischen Dramatikers*. Ed. Ulrich Halfmann. Tübingen: Narr, 1990. 119-38.

D113 Dneprova, I. "Problema nravstvennogo dualizma chělovecheskoi prirody v pŏzdnei dramaturgii Iudzhina O'Nila i ee sootnoshenie *s khudozhestvennym metodom pistelia*." In *Nekotoyre filologicheskie aspekty amerikannstiki*. Moscow: n.p., 1978. 289-309.

D114 Döblin, Alfred. "Eugene O'Neill." In *Ein Kerl Muss eine Meinung haben. Berichte und Kritiken 1921-1924*. Olten, Freiburg im Breisgau: Walter Verlag, 1976. 214-16.

D115 Drimba, Ovidiu. "Eugene O'Neill." In *Teatru de la origine si Pînă azi* [The Theater from its Origin to the present]. Bucharest: Albatros, 1973. 345-48.

D116 Dubost, Thierry. "Masques et miroirs dans *A Touch of the Poet* de Eugene O'Neill." In *Masques et miroirs dans le monde anglo-saxon*. Ed. Josette Leray. Caen: Presse Universitaire de Caen, 1996. 151-62.

D117 Egri, Péter. *A Költeszet valósága* [The Reality of Poetry]. Budapest: Publishing House of the Hungarian Academy of Sciences, 1975.

D118 _____. *Elidegenedés és drámaforma: az amerikai álom társadalomtörténete és lélekrajza O'Neill drámaciklusában*. Modern Filológiai füzetek 45. Budapest: Akadémiai Kiadó, 1988.

D119 Fateeva, S. P. "Pozdnee tvorchestvo Iudzhina O'Nila." In *Issledovaniia po romanskoĭ i germanskoi filologii*. Kiev: n.p., 1975. 47-51.

Concerns the later works of O'Neill.

D120 Fejlková, Katerina. *Eugene O'Neill, Mesíc pro smolare: [Prilezitostny tisk k premiere 20. 12. 1994 ve Stavovskem divadle]*. Prague: Národní Divadlo, Princo, 1994.

D121 Filipowicz-Findlay, Halina. *Eugene O'Neill*. Warsaw: Wiedza Powszechna, 1975.

D122 Frenz, Horst, and Mary Gaither. "Amerikanische Dramatiker auf den Bühnen und vor der Theaterkritik der Bundesrepublik." In *Nordamerikanische Literatur im deutschen Sprachraum seit 1945. Beiträge zu ihrer Rezeption*. Eds. Horst Frenz and Hans-Joachim Lang. Munich: Winkler, 1973. 79-102.

D123 _____, **and John Hess.** "Die nordamerikanische Literatur in der Deutschen Demokratischen Republik." In *Nordamerikanische Literatur im deutschen Sprachraum seit 1945. Beiträge zu ihrer Rezeption*. Eds. Horst Frenz and Hans-Joachim Lang. Munich: Winkler, 1973. 171-99.

D124 Fridshteĭn, Iuriĭ Germanovich, and Vladimir Andreevich Skorodenkoed, eds. and comps. *Iudzhin O'Nil: bibliograficheskii ukazatel'.* Pisateli zarubezhnykh stran. Moscow: Kniga, 1982.

An introduction covers O'Neill's career. Primary and secondary bibliographies, including translations. International in scope. Immensely useful for non-English language material.

D125 Fried, Herwig. "Power/play: Nietzsche und O'Neill." In *Eugene O'Neill 1988: Deutsche Beiträge zum 100. Geburtstag des amerikanischen Dramatikers.* Ed. Ulrich Halfmann. Tübingen: Narr, 1990. 203-20.

D126 Furukawa, Hiroyuki. "Chihei no Kanata." In *Eibungku to no Deai.* Ed. Naomi Matsuura. Kyoto: Showado, 1983. 185-205.

D127 Genieva, E. Iu. "O'Neill, Eugene." In *Bol'shaia Sovetskaia Entsiklopediia.* Ed.-in-Chief A. M. Prokhorov. 3rd ed. Vol. 18. Moscow: Sovetskaia Entsiklopediia Publishing House, 1974-76. 31 vols. 455-56. [Translated as *The Great Soviet Encyclopedia* New York: Macmillan/ London: Collier Macmillan.]

Horizon is seen as a study in psychology, *Ape* (trans. 1922) is about the dehumanization of the individual in a capitalist society, *Chillun* (trans. 1924) one of the first plays to focus on American racism, *Desire* (trans. 1927) a variation on the "classic tragedy of property." There are references to *Electra* and *Journey* in the entries for "U.S. Literature," Vol. 24, p. 688, and "U.S. Theatre," Vol. 24, p. 697.

D128 Gilli, Stefano. "Il lungo viaggio di Edipo." In *La letturatura in scena: il teatro del Novecento.* Ed. Giorgio Barberi Squarotti. Turin: Tirrenia, 1985.

D129 Grabes, Herbert. "Das amerikanische Drama nach O'Neill." In *Die Amerikanische Literatur der Gegenwart: Aspekte und Tendenzen.* Ed. Hans Bungert. Stuttgart: Reclam, 1977. 28-48.

Surveys from the 40s to the 60s, from Broadway to off-off. O'Neill, Miller and Williams are dealt with under the rubric of "The psychological drama and its extension in the 1950s."

D130 _____. "Das Vermächtnis Eugene O'Neills." In *Eugene O'Neill 1988: Deutsche Beiträge zum 100. Geburtstag des amerikanischen Dramatikers.* Ed. Ulrich Halfmann. Tübingen: Narr, 1990. 236-50.

D131 Griga, Stefano Bajma. "Ibsen e il giovane O'Neill." In *Alla origine della drammaturgia moderna: Ibsen, Strindberg, Pirandello: atti de convegno internazionale, Torino … 1985.* Genoa: Costa and Nolan, 1987. 178-85.

D132 _____. *La crisi dell'American Dream: Per una rilettura del teatro borghese di Eugene O'Neill.* Turin: Tirrenia Stampatori, 1987.

D133 Grimm, R. "O'Neills Aufhebung der europäischen Moderne. Naturalismus und Nietzscheanismus in *A* [sic] *Long Day's Journey into Night.*" In *Drama und Theater im 20. Jahrhundert.* Eds. H. D. Irmscher and W. Keller. Göttingen: Vanderhoeck & Ruprecht, 1983. 252-58.

D134 Haas, Rudolf. "Eugene O'Neill: *The Iceman.*" In *Das Amerikanische Drama.* Ed. Paul Goetsch. Düsseldorf: Bagel, 1974. 86-105.

D135 _____. "Das moderne Drama in Amerika als amerikanisches Drama." In *Die Amerikanische Literatur der Gegenwart: Aspekte und Tendenzen.* Ed. Hans Bungert. Stuttgart: Reclam, 1977. 112-21.

D136 _____. "Zugange zum englischen und amerikanischen Drama." In *Theorie und Praxis der Interpretation: Modellanalysen englischer und amerikanischer Texte.* Grundlagen der Anglistik und Amerikanistik 5. Berlin: Schmidt, 1977. 190-226.

D137 Halfmann, Ulrich. "Eugene O'Neill: *Beyond the Horizon.*" In *Das Amerikanische Drama.* Ed. Paul Goetsch. Düsseldorf: Bagel, 1974. 27-49.

D138 _____. "Formen und Tendenzen des sozialcritischen amerikanischen Drama der zwanziger und dreissiger Jahre." In *Das amerikanische Drama.* Ed. Ger-"hard Hoffmann. Bern: Francke, 1984. 144-81.

D139 _____. "Eugene O'Neill: eine Bibliographie." In *Eugene O'Neill 1988: Deutsche Beiträge zum 100. Geburtstag des amerikanischen Dramatikers.* Ed. Ulrich Halfmann. Tübingen: Narr, 1990. 251-62.

Highly selective bibliography of primary and secondary material. Good reminder that O'Neill scholarship is not restricted to what is in English.

D140 _____. "'With Clenched Fist…' Beobachtungen zu einem rekurrierenden Motiv in Dramen Eugene O'Neills." In

Eugene O'Neill 1988: Deutsche Beiträge zum 100. Geburtstag des amerikanischen Dramatikers. Ed. Ulrich Halfmann. Tübingen: Narr, 1990. 188-202.

D141 _____, ed. *Eugene O'Neill 1988: Deutsche Beiträge zum 100. Geburtstag des amerikanischen Dramatikers.* Mannheimer Beiträge zur Sprach-und Literaturwissenschaft, 20. Tübingen: Gunter Narr, 1990.

Lewis, Ward B. Rev. *Eugene O'Neill Review* 14.1-2 (1990): 110-13.

D142 Hebel, Udo J. "'Superior in Unity and Economy'?: Produktivitat, Komplexitat und Konventionalitat einer gattungssuber-schreitenden Wirkungsstruktur amerikanischer Einakter seit Eugene O'Neill und Susan Glaspell." In *Kurzformen des Dramas: Gattungspoetische, epochenspezifische und funktionale Horizonte.* Eds. Winfried Herget and Brigitte Schultze. Mainzer Forschungen zu Drama und Theater, 16. Tübingen: Francke, 1996.

D143 Hoffmann, Gerhard. "Eugene O'Neill: *Mourning Becomes Electra.*" In *Das Amerikanische Drama.* Ed. Paul Goetsch. Düsseldorf: Bagel, 1974. 50-87.

D144 _____. "Auffassungsweisen und Gestaltungskategorien der wirklichkeit im Drama: zum tragischen, komischen, satirischen, und Grotesken bei O'Neill." In *Amerikanisches Drama und Theater im 20. Jahrhundert.* Eds. Alfred Weber and Siegfried Nevweiler. Göttingen: Vandenhoeck and Ruprecht, 1975. 60-123.

D145 _____. "Eugene O'Neill: Realismus, Expressionismus, Mystizismus." In *Das Amerikanische Drama.* Ed. Gerhard Hoffmann. Bern: Francke, 1984. 76-120.

D146 Ichinose, Kazuo. "Sengo no Eugene O'Neill." In *Sengo Amerika Engeki no Tenkai.* Eds. Kuniaki Svenaga and Koji Ishizuka. Tokyo: Bun'eido, 1983. 155-80.

D147 Josephson, Lennart Hjalmar. [_____]. Acta Universitatis Stockholmiensis, 19. Stockholm: Almqvist & Wiksell International, 1977.

The English title is *A Role: O'Neill's Cornelius Melody.* (For an annotation, see B234.)

D148 Juhl, Peter. "Eugene O'Neills *The Hairy Ape*: Bemerkungen zu Sinn und Struktur des Dramas." In *Theater und Drama in Amerika: Aspekte und Interpretationen.* Eds. Edgar Lohner and Rudolf Haas. Berlin: Schmidt, 1978. 235-53.

D149 Kaes, Anton. "Charakterisierung bei O'Neill und Kaiser." In *Expressionismus in Amerika: Rezeption und Innovation.* Tübingen: Niemeyer, 1975. 102-07.

D150 _____. "Expressionismus und der frühe O'Neill." In *Expressionismus in Amerika: Rezeption und Innovation.* Tübingen: Niemeyer, 1975. 74-87.

D151 Kappel, L. "Der Fluch im Haus des Atreus: Von Aischylos zu Eugene O'Neill." In *Antike Mythen in der europäischen Tradition.* Ed. Heinz Hofmann. Tübingen: Attempto, 1999.

D152 Kindermann, Wolf. "'Most Stubborn and Irreconcilable Social Rebel': O'Neill und die Arbeiterbewegung." In *Eugene O'Neill 1988: Deustche Beiträge zum 100. Geburtstag des amerikanischen Dramatikers.* Ed. Ulrich Halfmann. Tübingen: Narr, 1990. 177-87.

D153 Kohler, Klaus. *Der Antiheld bei Eugene O'Neill und seine Vorformen im europäischen Drama seit Henrik Ibsen.* Dresden: Progressmedia, 1998.

D154 Kónya, Judit. "Utazás az éjszakába." In *Kalandozás a dramaturgia világában.* Ed. Géza Hegedüs and Judit Kónya. Budapest: Gondolat, 1973. 240-52.

Concerns *Journey.*

D155 Koreneva, M. M. *Tvorchestvo Iudzhina O'Nila i puti amerikanskoĭ Dramy.* Moscow: Nauka, 1990.

D156 Künstler, Gustav. "Vom Wesenskern des dramatischen Kunstwerks als Vision der Menschheitskatastrophe — Beispiele von: O'Neill, Christopher Fry, Cocteau, Brecht, Lorca, Eliot, Georg Kaiser." In *Interpretationen: De Aussage dramatischer und lyrischer Werke.* Vienna: Schroll, 1976. 88-113.

Essays by the late Gustav Kunstler, several, including the above previously unpublished: *Iceman, Mourning.*

D157 Lange, Wigand. *Theater in Deutschland nach 1945: zur Theaterpolitik der amerikanischen Besatzungsbehorden.* Frankfurt am Main: Lang, 1980.

Scattered references to O'Neill, especially pages 363-68, 446-56, and 459-61.

D158 Legault, Anne. *O'Neill: Théâtre.* Outremont, Québec: VLB, 1990.

D159 Lev, Sverdlin. *Stat'i. Vospominaniia.* Eds. N. A. Velekhova and A. G. Obraztsova. Moscow: Iskusstvo, 1979. 117-19, 160.

D160 Lévy, Ghyslain. *Eugene O'Neill: Ou l'inconvenence de vivre.* Paris: Anthropos: Diffusion Economica, 1994.

D161 Liao, K'o-tui. *Ao-ni-erh hsi chü yen chiu lun wen chi.* Beijing: Chung-kuo hsi chü ch'u pan she: Hsin hua shu tien Pei-ching fa hsing so fa hsing, 1988.

D162 Libman, V. A. *Amerikanskaia literatura v russkikh perevodakhi kritike.* Moscow: Nauka, 1977. 186-88.

D163 Link, Franz H. *Dramaturgie der Zeit.* Freiburg: Rombach, 1977.

D164 *Literatura S.SH.A. XX veka: Opyt tipologicheskogo ssledovaniia.* Moscow: Nauka, 1978. 22-27.

D165 Liu, Haip'ing. *Chung Mei wen hua tsai hsi chü chung chiao liu: Ao-ni-erh yü Chung-kuo.* Nanking: Nan-ching ta hsüeh ch'u pan she: Fa hsing Chiang-su sheng hsin hua shu tien, 1988.

D166 _____. *Yujin-Ao-ni'er Lun Xiju* [Eugene O'Neill Commenting on Theater]. Beijing: People's Literature and Art P, 1999.

D167 Liubimova, E. "Iudzhin O'Nil i Dzhordzh Krem Kuk — opyt tvorcheskogo sodruzhestva: (Iz istorii teatra 'Provinstaun')." In *Problemy Zarubezhnogo teatra i teatrovedeniia.* Moscow: n.p., 1977. 62-77.

D168 Lohner, Edgar, and Rudolf Haas, eds. *Theater und Drama in Amerika: Aspekte und Interpretationen.* Berlin: Schmidt, 1978. 9-41.

D169 Lung, Wen-p'ei. *Yu-chin Ao-ni-erh p'ing lun chi.* Shanghai: Shang-hai wai yü chiao yü ch'u pan she: Hsin hua shu tien Shang-hai fa hsing so fa hsing, 1988.

D170 Malikov, V. "Trilogiia O'Nila." In *O'Nil Iu. Traur — uchast' Elektry.* Moscow: n.p., 1975. 214-29.

About Alekseev's translation of *Electra.*

D171 Markov, P.A. *O Teatre.* 4 vols. Moscow: Iskusstvo 1974-1977. 1: 490-91; 2: 98-100, 132, 295-96; 3: 191-92, 212, 334-35, 357-59.

D172 Mednikova, E. *Three American Plays.* Moscow: n.p., 1973.

Includes a preface to and commentary on a translation of *Journey.*

D173 Melchinger, Siegfried. "Die Yankee-Elektra: O'Neill und Aischylos — vergleichende Bemerkungen." In *Theater und Drama in Amerika: Aspekte und Interpretationen.* Eds. Edgar Lohner and Rudolf Haas. Berlin: Schmidt, 1978. 254-62.

D174 Mennemeier, Franz Norbert. "Eugene O'Neill." In *Das moderne Drama des Auslandes: Interpretationen.* Düsseldorf: Bagel, 1976. 43-65.

D175 Milfull, John. "Die Stummen Gewalten: über die Sprachlosigkeit der Sprachbegabten: 'stumme Stücke' von Beckett, Handke und Müller." In *Handke: Ansätze — Analysen — Anmerkungen.* Ed. Manfred Jürgensen. Bern: Francke, 1979. 165-71.

D176 Morel Montes, Consuela. *El teatro desde una perspectiva psicológica: Lo psicoanalítico y el texto dramático.* Santiago [Chile]: Escuela de Teatro de la Pontificia Universidad Católica de Chile, 1991.

D177 Mounier, Catherine. "Le Marchand de glâce est passé d'Eugene O'Neill et la Mise-en-scène de Gabriel Garran au Théâtre de la Commune d'Aubervilliers." In *Les Voies de la Création théâtrale.* Eds. Denis Bablet and Jean Jacquot. Paris: CNRS, 1975. 65-105.

Excerpted and translated into English in Frenz and Tuck's *Eugene O'Neill: Voices from Abroad.*

D178 Müller, Kurt. "Die Behandlung der Rassen — und Klassen problematik in den expressionistischen Stücken O'Neills." In *Konventionen und Tendenzen der Gesellschaftskritik in expressionistischen amerikanischen Drama der zwanziger Jahre.* Neue Studien zur Anglistik und Amerikanistik, 9. Frankfurt: Lang, 1977. 97-127.

D179 _____. "Vorurteils und Stereotypenkritik in *The Emperor Jones* und *The Hairy Ape:* Aspekte der Wirkungsstruktur in den expressionistische Dramen Eugene O'Neills." In *Eugene O'Neill 1988: Deutsche Beiträge zum 100 Geburtstag des amerikanischen Dramatikers.* Ed. Ulrich Halfmann. Tübingen: Narr, 1990. 48-65.

D180 _____. *Inszenierte Wirklichkeiten: die Erfahrung der Moderne im Leben und Werke Eugene O'Neills.* Darmstadt: Wissenschlaftliche Buchgesellschaft, 1993.

D181 Müller, Wolfgang. "Der Bewusstseinsstrom im Roman und auf der Bühne: James Joyces *Ulysses* und Eugene O'Neills *Strange Interlude.*" In *Amerikanisierung des Dramas und Dramatisierung Amerikas: Studien zu Ehren von Hans Helmcke.* Eds. Manfred Siebald and Horst Immel. Frankfurt am Main: Lang, 1985. 115-29.

D182 Nascimento, Abdias do. "Teatro negro del Brasil: una experiencia socio-racial."

In *Popular Theater for Social Change In Latin America: Essays in Spanish and English*. Ed. Gerardo Luzuriaga. Los Angeles: UCLA Latin American Center, 1978. 251-69.

Reprint of an article published in *Conjunto: [Revista de] teatro Latinoamericano* [Havana] 9 (1971): 14-28.

D183 Nazirzadah Kirmani, Farhad. *Guzarah?garayi "Iksprisyumism" dar adapiyat-i namayishi: hamrah ba tarjumah-i namayishnamah-?i numunah, Maymun-i pashmalu* "The Hairy Ape, 1922," *nivishtah-'i Ujin Unil; Eugene O'Neill, 1988-1953.* Tehran: Surush, 1989.

On expressionism in drama.

D184 Nugel, Bernfried. "Dichtungskritik in O'Neills *A Touch of the Poet.*" In *Eugene O'Neill 1988: Deutsche Beiträge zum 100. Geburtstag des amerikanischen Dramatikers.* Ed. Ulrich Halfmann. Tübingen: Narr, 1990. 139-57.

D185 _____. "Von Elektra zu Lavinia: Eugene O'Neills Konzeption der Titelfigur in *Mourning Becomes Electra.*" In *Frauen und Frauendarstellung in der englischen und amerikanischen Literatur.* Ed. Theresa Fischer-Seidel. Tübingen: Narr, 1991. 295-318.

D186 Obraztsova, A. G. *Sovremennaia angliiskaia stsena.* Moscow: Nauka, 1977. 167-69.

D187 Olsson, Tom J. A. *O'Neill och Dramaten* [with a summary in English]. Stockholm: Akademilitteratur, 1977.

Recounts the Royal Dramatic Theater's staging of O'Neill's plays from 1923 on, but devotes most space to the *Journey, Touch, Hughie,* and *Mansions* productions. Includes correspondence between Carlotta O'Neill and Karl Ragnar Gierow. Sources, among others, are the RDT's archives.

D188 Oswald, Josef. "*The Discordant, Broken, Faithless Rhythm of Our Time:" Eine Analyse der späten Dramen Eugene O'Neills.* Neue studien zur Anglistik und Amerikanistik 21. Frankfurt am Main: Lang, 1980.

D189 Pašteka, Julius. "Aspekty moderného tragična: metamorfózy tragédie v západnej dramatike." In *Estetické paralely umenia: štúdie o divadle, dramatike a filme.* Bratislava: Veda, 1976. 201-45.

References to *Anna, Jones, Dynamo, Lazarus, Electra,* and *Brown.* See especially pp. 201-03, 205-07. Indexed.

D190 _____. "Podoby a problémy moderného herectva: Tvár a maska v divadle i vo filme." In *Estetické paralely umenia: štúdie o divadle, dramatike a filme.* Bratislava: Veda, 1976. 51-74.

Throughout, but see especially pages 66-71. Indexed.

D191 Pellettieri, Osvaldo, and George William Woodyard. *De Eugene O'Neill al 'Happening': Teatro norteamericano y teatro argentino: 1930-1990.* Cuadernos del GETEA 6. Buenos Aires: Galerna, 1995.

D192 Pinaev, S. M. [Sergei Mikhailovich]. "*Na dne* M. Gor'kogo *i Rznoschik l'da griadet* Iu O'Nila: k voprosu o problematike i ideinom svoeobrazii p'es." In *Vopr. gor'kovedeniia: (P'esa Nadne).* Gorki [Russia]: n.p., 1977. 59-71.

D193 _____. "O nekotorykh osobennostiakh dramaturgicheskoĭ tekniki Iudzhina O'Nila: (Semantika sveta i osveshcheniia)." In *Iazyk i stil'.* Volgargrad [Russia]: n.p., 1977. 100-09.

D194 _____. "Kvoprosu o nekotorykh osobennostiakh khudozhestvennoĭ struktury dram Iu. O'Nila i T. Uil'iamsa." In *Voprosy romanticheskogo metoda i stilia.* Kalinin [Russia]: n.p., 1978. 145-52.

On O'Neill and Tennessee Williams.

D195 _____. "O dramaturgicheskoĭ tekhnike Iu. O'Nila i T. Uil'iamsa." In *Literaturnye sviazi i problema vzaimoponimaniia.* Gorki [Russia]: n.p., 1978. 30-48.

D196 _____. *Iudzhin Gladston O'Nil: k 100-letiiu so dniarozhdeniia. Novoe v zhizni, nauke, tekhnike.* Seriia Literatura 5. Moscow: Izd-vo "Znznie," 1988.

D197 Reif-Hülser, Monika. "Überlegungen zur Funktion der Pipe Dreams in O'Neills Dramen." In *Eugene O'Neill 1988: Deutsche Beiträge zum 100. Geburtstag des amerikanischen Dramatikers.* Ed. Ulrich Halfmann. Tübingen: Narr, 1990. 158-76.

D198 Romm, Anna S. *Amerikanskaya dramaturgiya pervoi poloviny xx veka.* Leningrad: Iskusstvo, 1978.

D199 Rühle Günther. *Theater in unserer Zeit.* Frankfurt am Main: Suhrkamp, 1976.

D200 Santraud, Jeanne-Marie. *Stephen Crane, Eugene O'Neill, John Hawkes.* Paris: Presses de l'Université de Paris-Sorbonne, 1995.

D201 Sarrazac, Jean P. "Le roman dramatique familial d'Eugene O'Neill." In *Théâtres intimes: Essais.* Arles: Actes Sud, 1989. 47-63.

D202 Schäfer, Jürgen. *Geschichte des Amerikanischen Dramas.* Stuttgart: Kohlhammer, 1982.

D203 Schmitt-von Mühlenfels, Astrid. "O'Neills *Mourning Becomes Electra*: vom Drama zur Literaturoper." In *Eugene O'Neill 1988: Deutsche Beiträge zum 100. Geburtstag des amerikanischen Dramatikers.* Ed. Ulrich Halfmann. Tübingen: Narr, 1990. 109-18.

D204 Seidel, Margot. *Bibel und Christentum im dramatischen Werk Eugene O'Neills.* Studien zur englischen und amerikanischen Literatur 3. Frankfurt am Main: Lang, 1983.

D205 _____. *Aberglaube Bei O'Neill.* Frankfurt am Main: Lang, 1984.

D206 Sichert, Margit. "O'Neills *The Great God Brown* und die unausweichliche Ambiguität des Psychodramas." In *Eugene O'Neill 1988: Deutsche Beiträge zum 100. Geburtstag des amerikanischen Dramatikers.* Ed. Ulrich Halfmann. Tübingen: Narr, 1990. 66-86.

D207 Sin, Sug-won. *Yujin Onil.* Chakkaron ch'ongso 14. Seoul: Munhak kwa Chisongsa, 1988.

D208 Smirnov, B. A. *Teatr S.SH.A. XX veka: ucheb. posobie.* Leningrad: gos. in – t teatra, musyki i Kinematografii, 1976. 43-58. On O'Neill and the development of realism in the American theater.

D209 So, Yong-duk. *Eugene O'Neill ui kuk e nat'anan sooe yangsang kwa chaa tamgu.* Seoul T'ukpyolsi: Hansin Munhwasa, 1992.

D210 Stuby, Anna Maria. "Tragödie und Privateigentum zu *Desire Under the Elms* von Eugene O'Neill." In *Gulliver: deutsch-englische Jahrbücher* 3. Berlin: Argument, 1978. 78-96.

D211 Suyama, Shizuo. "Eugene O'Neill *Iceman Kitaru*: Moo Hitori no Sisyphe to Kankyaku no Shisei." In *Bungaku to Amerika: Ohashi Kenzaburo Kyoju Kinen Kanreki Ronbunshu.* Vol. 3. Tokyo: Nanundo, 1980. 297-312.

D212 Thies, Henning. *Namen im Kontext von Dramen: Studien zur Funktion von Personennamen im englischen, amerikanischen und deutschen Drama.* Frankfurt: Lang, 1978.

D213 Tiusanen, Timo. *Linjoja: tutkielmia kirjallisuudesta ja teaterista.* Helsinki: Otava, 1977.

D214 Tokushu. "Yujin Oniru." In *Gendai Engeki 10.* Tokyo: Eichoshashinsha, 1989.

D215 Tsimbal, I.S. "Tragediia otchuzhdeniia." In *Nauka o teatre.* Leningrad: n.p., 1975. 260-76. About a production of *Desire*.

D216 _____. "Ot O'Nila – k sovremennoĭ amerikanskoĭ drame: Preemstvennost' problematiki." In *Sotsial'naia tema v sovremennom zarubezhnom teatre i kino.* Leningrad: n.p., 1976. 103-20.

D217 _____. "Rannie 'Morskie' miniatiury Iudzhina O'Nila Parokhod Glenkern: Iz nabliudenniĭ nad stilem pisatelia." In *Analiz stilia zarubeshnoĭ; khudozhestvennoi i nauchnoĭ literatury.* Leningrad: n.p., 1978. I: 97-105.

D218 _____. "Negritianskaia tema v dramaturgii O'Nila: (*Imperator Dzbons*)." In *Problemy realizma v zarubezhnom teatral'nom iskusstve.* Leningrad: n.p., 1979. 11-21.

D219 Vodă-Căpusan, Maria. "Mască si destin la Eugene O'Neill." In *Teatru şi Mit.* Cluj: Dacia, 1976. 96-111.

D220 Wauschkuhn, Doris. *Literarischer Dialekt und seine Funktion zur Begrundung einer dramatischen Tradition im Werk von John Millington Synge und Eugene O'Neill.* Studien zu Texten und Ideen der europäischen Moderne, ser. 13. Trier: Wissenschaftlicher, 1993. Originally a doctoral dissertation; see D238.

D221 Weigel, Robert G. "Theatralik und Melodramatik: Komparative Bemerkungen zu Franz Grillparzers *Des Meeres* und der *Liebe Wellen* und Eugene O'Neills *Anna Christie*." In *Für all, was Menschen je erfahren, ein Bild, ein Wort und auch ein Ziel: Beiträge zu Grillparzers Werk.* Ed. Joseph P. Strelka. New Yorker Beiträge zur österreichischen Literaturgeschichte, 2. Bern: Peter Lang, 1995.

D222 Wolter, Jürgen. "'Throw Everything Overboard': O'Neills früheste Stücke." In *Eugene O'Neill 1988: Deutsche Beiträge zum 100. Geburtstag des amerikanischen Dramatikers.* Ed. Ulrich Halfmann. Tübingen: Narr, 1990. 13-33.

D223 Yamana, Hsoji. *Jidin to Chinkon: Yujin Oniru kenkyu.* Tokyo: Seibido, 1987.

D224 Yi, Hae-rang. *Pam uro ui kin yororul t'eksut'urohan Yi Hae-rang yonch'ul kyojong.* Seoul: Hyondae Kyouk Ch'ulp'anbu, 1986.

D225 Zapf, Hubert. "Drama und Dekonstruktion: Eugene O'Neill als Kulturkritker." In *Eugene O'Neill 1988: Deutsche*

Beiträge zum 100. Geburtstag des amerikanischen Dramatikers. Ed. Ulrich Halfmann. Tübingen: Narr, 1990. 221-35.

Dissertations

D226 Dubost, Thierry. "L'Homme et le monde dans le théâtre de Eugene O'Neill." Université de Paris–Sorbonne, 1993.

D227 Ilmberger, Hans. "Das Meer im Werk Eugene O'Neills." Universität Hamburg, 1984.

D228 Kneževič, Debora Julii. "Eugene O'Neill na pražskem jevišti" [Eugene O'Neill in the Prague Theater]. Unpublished Thesis. Charles U [Prague], 1978.

D229 Medvedeva, N. P. "Tvorcheskie iskaniia Iu. O'Nila 20-kh godov i stanovlenie amerikanskoĭ natsional'noĭ dramy." Gorki State U [Russia], 1974.

D230 Müller, Henning. "Theater im Zeichen des kalten Krieges. Üntersuchungen zur Theater und Kulturpoliti in den Westsektoren Berlins 1945-1953." U of Berlin [West], 1976.

D231 Pardo Gutiérrez, Nieves. "La Tragedía en el teatro norteamericano actual: O'Neill, Miller y Albee." U of Madrid, 1975.

D232 Pinaev, S. M. "Khydozhestvennaia Struktura dram Iu. O'Nila: K probleme Konflikta i ego dramaturgicheskogo voploshcheniia." Avroref. Diss. na soisk. uchën. step. kand. filol. nauk. Moscow, 1979.

D233 Shamina, V. B. "Mif i amerikanskaia drama: Iu. O'Nila. Traur — uchast' Elektry, T. Uil'iams. Orfeĭ spuskaetaia v ad." Avtoref. Diss. na soisk. uchën. step. kand. filol. nauk. Leningrad, 1979.

D234 Soulier, Anne Marie. "Le Héros et son double dans les pièces masquées d'Eugene O'Neill: *The Great God Brown* et *Mourning Becomes Electra*." U of Strasbourg, 1984.

D235 Szabó, Klará. "O'Neill tragediafogasa a kortarsi elmeletek tukreben." Jozsef Attila Tudomanyegyetem, H., 1979.

O'Neill's tragic theory in the light of other contemporary ideas.

D236 Szigeti, Gabriela. "L'Expressionnisme européen et un de ses reflets outre-atlantique: l'oeuvre d'Eugene O'Neill." Université de Paris-Sorbonne, 1985.

D237 Tsimbal, I. S. "Teatr Iudzhina O'Nila." Avtoref. Diss. na Soisk ychën. step. kand. iskusstvovedeniia. Leningrad, 1977.

D238 Wauschkuhn, Doris. "Literarischer Dialekt und seine Funktion zur Begrundung einer dramatischen Tradition im Werk von John Millington Synge und Eugene O'Neill." Justus-Liebig-Universität Giessen, 1992.

E. Productions (English)

E1 *Abortion* with *Cardiff* and *The Movie Man* Playwright's Theater Festival of O'Neill; Provincetown Playhouse; New York City; 3-8 Aug. 1999.

E2 *Ah, Wilderness!* Long Wharf Theater; New Haven, CT; Opened 20 Dec. 1974; Then Circle in the Square; New York City; Opened 18 Sept. 1975 for 77 performances; Dir.—Arvin Brown; Settings—Steven Rubin; Costumes—Bill Walker; Lights—James Gallagher/Ronald Wallace; Artistic Dir.—Theodore Mann; Tommy Miller—Kevin Ellicott/Glenn Zachar; Mildred—Christine Whitmore; Arthur—Paul Rudd; Essie—Geraldine Fitzgerald; Nat—William Swetland; Richard—Richard Backus; Lily—Teresa Wright; Sid Davis—John Braden; David McComber—Emery Battis/John Drischell; Nora—Linda Hunt; Wint Selby—Sean G. Griffin; Belle—Susanne Lederer; Bartender—Stephen Mendillo; Salesman—Don Gantry; Muriel McComber—Susan Sharkey/Swoozie Kurtz.

Barnes, Clive. "Theater: A Magical *Ah, Wilderness!*" *New York Times* 23 Dec. 1974: 32.

Enthusiastic about this production in all areas. *Wilderness* is "a delicate, even sweet, but troubled fantasy."

_____. The Theater/"O'Neill's Only Comedy." *New York Times* 19 Sept. 1975, sec. 2: 5.

The play is a "nostalgic threnody," the production enchanting." Direction tries to "underplay the American aspects of the play." Solid acting. A little bit of *Life with Father*.

Beaufort, John. Theatre Reviews. *Christian Science Monitor* 26 Sept. 1975; *NYTCR* 1975: 212-13.

The production is a "glowing" revival of a "warm, sun-dappled play."

Clurman, Harold. Theatre. *Nation* 4 Oct. 1975: 317-18.

Finds the production skillfully directed by Arvin Brown. Especially liked Geraldine Fitzgerald as Mrs. Miller and Teresa Wright as Aunt Lily. Faulted its being too contemporary and Richard Backus for playing his character for laughs.

Davis, Curt. Rev. *Encore* 3 Nov. 1975: 35-36.

Gill, Brendan. "Paradise Enow." *New Yorker* 29 Sept. 1975: 100.

The production was "exceptionally attractive." Director Brown cut little and Richard Backus played his role with "exemplary tact."

Gottfried, Martin. Theater/"*Ah, Wilderness!*—A Magic Spell." *New York Post* 19 Sept. 1975; *NYTCR* 1975: 211.

Comments on the light and dark sides of O'Neill and says of this production that it is "shamelessly sentimental and entirely charming." O'Neill is like Norman Rockwell.

Hughes, Catharine. "*Ah, Wilderness!* (Oh, O'Neill?)." *America* 1 Nov. 1975: 283-84.

The play is a pleasant celebration of a charming past, but the characters are one-dimensional. Also finds it verbose and essentially dull, but a positive print of the negative we see later in *Journey*.

Kauffmann, Stanley. "Stanley Kauffmann on Theatre." *New Republic* 11 Oct. 1975: 22-23.

"O'Neill's ode to middle-class respectability ... whose emptiness he so fiercely exposed elsewhere." The casting is generally bad with the exception of William Swetland.

Kerr, Walter. "A Long Day's 'Wilderness.'" *New York Times* 28 Sept. 1975, sec. 2: 5.

Original (1933) production charmed by its novelty and by its star, George M. Cohan. Now the play must be seen against the knowledge of *Journey*, and, therefore, our response to it is to what isn't in the play. The work itself is bland, but the production is generally solid except that it lacks "variation or progression" and Uncle Sid is badly cast.

Kissel, Howard. The Theatre. *Women's Wear Daily* 19 Sept. 1975; *NYTCR* 1975: 210.

"One of the most solid, durable and satisfying of O'Neill's works and one of the treasures of the American theater." Like other O'Neill works this one is dominated by the image of woman as whore or mother. The production is "splendid" and the cast "superb."

Mallet, Gina. "Sweet Dreams." *Time* 6 Jan. 1975: 93.

Thinks the play should have been cut, but commends Brown's staging, calling the production a "meticulous revival."

Novick, Julius. Rev. *Village Voice* 29 Sept. 1975: 105.

O'Connor, John J. Rev. *New York Times* 13 Oct. 1976: 86.

The easy tendency of the play to become cloying and sentimental is avoided by this production's realistic treatment of the characters — who can be "taken seriously." The only directional error was in using the "soft focus" cliché.

Pacheco, Patrick. Rev. *After Dark* Nov. 1975: 30+.

The production was "relaxed," the ensemble "brilliant," and the play "enchanting theater."

Rich, Alan. "Long Day's Joy Ride." *New York* 6 Oct. 1975: 68-69.

The play has "miscalculations, some of them crucial, but the spirit of Eugene O'Neill's only comedy does fitfully show through." O'Neill's writing is gracious, unlike so much of his "waterlogged prose," but, without Brown's cuts, would be too long. Direction is generally sympathetic to O'Neill except in the dinner scene which is played for laughs. Finds the actors good to excellent, though Richard is badly cast.

Watt, Douglas. "This Wilderness Paradise Enow." *Daily News* 19 Sept. 1975; *NYTCR* 1975: 210.

Finds this comedy "our richest comedy" and approves of the production.

Wilson, Edwin. The Theater. "The Past as it Perhaps Never Was." *Wall Street Journal* 19 Sept. 1975; *NYTCR* 1975: 213.

Thinks that after writing this play, O'Neill used more humor and returned to realism.

E3 *Ah, Wilderness!* Summer 1975 on tour; Barbara Bel Geddes; Richard Kiley; Donna Pescow.

E4 *Ah, Wilderness!* Waynesburg College; Waynesburg, PA; 21 Oct. 1975; Dir.— Rev. Gilbert V. Hartke.

E5 *Ah, Wilderness!* Lyric Players Theatre; Belfast, Northern Ireland; 26 Sept. 1976; Dir.— Edward Golden.

E6 *Ah, Wilderness!* alternating with *Journey* Milwaukee Repertory Theater Co.; Milwaukee, WI; 18 Nov. 1977-18 Jan. 1978; Dir.— Irene Lewis; Design — R.A. Graham; Richard Miller/Edmund Tyrone — Anthony Heald; Essie/Mary — Regina Davis; Nat/James — Robert Burr; Uncle Sid/Jamie — Ronald Frazer.

Kalson, Albert E. "Review of *Ah, Wilderness!* and *Long Day's Journey into Night.*" *Educational Theatre Journal* 30 Oct. 1978: 422-24.

Notes that the productions were performed in tandem with the same actors and setting. This doubling allows the audience to see into the dark corners of *Wilderness* and adds depth to *Journey*.

Noth, Dominique Paul. Rev. *New York Theatre Review* Jan. 1978: 34.

E7 *Ah, Wilderness!* Playmakers Repertory Co.; University of North Carolina at Chapel Hill; Closed 2 Apr. 1978; Dir.— Tom Haas.

E8 *Ah, Wilderness!* Heights Players; Brooklyn Heights, NY; 8-23 Sept. 1978; Dir.— Roy Clary.

E9 *Ah, Wilderness!* American Conservatory Theatre; San Francisco, CA; Opened 31 Oct. 1978; Toured Hawaii 12-25 June 1979;; Played Tokyo 30 June-9 July 1979; Dir.— Allen Fletcher.

E10 *Ah, Wilderness!* Arena Stage Washington, DC; 1 Dec. 1978-7 Jan. 1979; Dir.— Edward Cornell.

E11 *Ah, Wilderness!* Whole Theatre Company; Montclair, NJ; 4 May-3 June 1979; Dir.— Ron van Lieu.

E12 *Ah, Wilderness!* The Young Company of Ontario; George Ignatieff Theatre; Toronto, ONT; 11-21 July 1979; Dir.— Graham Harley.

E13 *Ah, Wilderness!* Boston University Stage Troupe; Hayden Hall, Boston University; Boston, MA; 26 Oct.-3 Nov. 1979.

E14 *Ah, Wilderness!* Apple Corps; New York City; 8 Nov.-Dec. 1979; Dir.— Will Maitland Weiss.

E15 *Ah, Wilderness!* Dunster House; Harvard University; Cambridge, MA; 6-15 Mar. 1980.

E16 *Ah, Wilderness!* Wisdom Bridge Theatre; Chicago, IL; 19 Mar.-20 Apr. 1980; Dir.—R. Falls.

E17 *Ah, Wilderness!* American Theatre Company; Tulsa, OK; 21 Mar.-5 Apr. 1980; Dir.—James E. Runyan.

E18 *Ah, Wilderness!* American Conservatory Theatre; San Francisco, CA; 8 Apr.-30 May 1980; Dir.—A. Fletcher.

E19 *Ah, Wilderness!* Assumption College; Worcester, MA; 20-22 Apr. 1980; Dir.—Donald H. Letendre.

E20 *Ah, Wilderness!* Ringling Museums Court Playhouse; Asolo State Theater; Sarasota, FL; Closed 1 May 1980; Dir.—John Reich.

E21 *Ah, Wilderness!* Barter Theater; Abingdon, VA; 18 June-29 Aug. 1980; Dir.—Jeff Meredith.

E22 *Ah, Wilderness!* Polka Dot Playhouse; Bridgeport, CT; 4-26 July 1980.

E23 *Ah, Wilderness!* Penn State University Resident Theater; Pavilion Theater; University Park, PA; 17 July-3 Aug. 1980.

E24 *Ah, Wilderness!* Hangar Theater; Cass Park; Ithaca, NY; 5-16 Aug. 1980.

E25 *Ah, Wilderness!* Seattle Repertory Theatre; Seattle, WA; 31 Dec. 1980-25 Jan. 1981; Dir.—Daniel Sullivan.

E26 *Ah, Wilderness!* Boars Head Theater; Lansing Center for the Arts; Lansing, MI; 12 Feb.-1 Mar. 1981.

E27 *Ah, Wilderness!* Studio Arena Theatre; Buffalo, NY; 13 Feb.-14 Mar. 1981; Dir.—Geoffrey Sherman.

E28 *Ah, Wilderness!* Indiana Repertory Theatre; Indianapolis, IN; 24 Apr.-16 May 1981; Dir.—David Rotenberg.

E29 *Ah, Wilderness!* Lakewood Theater Company; Skowhegan, ME; Summer 1981.

E30 *Ah, Wilderness!* South Coast Repertory; Costa Mesa, CA; Closed 18 Oct. 1981; Dir.—Martin Benson.

Hanson, Eugene K. Rev. *Eugene O'Neill Newsletter* 6.1 (1982): 45-48.

The production is a "rousing success" and the casting "generally" good. Bemoans the lack of other O'Neill comedies since this one is so good.

E31 *Ah, Wilderness!* Marymount Theater; Manhattan, NY; 11-14 Nov. 1981; Dir.—Michael Jameson.

E32 *Ah, Wilderness!* Department of Undergraduate Drama; New York University; New York City; 31 Mar.-3 Apr. 1982; Dir.—Penelope Hirsch.

E33 *Ah, Wilderness!* Trinity Theatre Ltd.; Trinity Lutheran Church; New York City; 7-31 Oct. 1982; Dir.—Dale Kaufman.

E34 *Ah, Wilderness!* GeVa Theatre; Rochester, NY; 26 Mar.-17 Apr. 1983.

E35 *Ah, Wilderness!* Roundabout Theater Co.; Haft Theater; New York City; 14 June-24 July 1983; Dir.—John Stix; Setting—Kenneth Foy; Costuming—Gene K. Lakin; Lighting—Ron Wallace; Music—Philip Campanella; Nat Miller—Philip Bosco; Essie—Dody Goodman; Arthur—John Dukakis; Richard—Scott Burkholder; Mildred—Kelly Wolf; Tommy—Mark Scott Newman; Lily—Laurinda Barrett David; Sid Davis—Robert Nichols; McComber—Joseph Leon; Muriel—Liane Langland; Wint Selby & Bartender—Robert Curtis-Brown; Belle—Jean Hackett; Nora—Bernadette Quigley; Salesman—Scott Gordon Miller.

Bennetts, Leslie. Rev. *New York Times* 8 July 1983, sec. C: 3.

As Essie, Dody Goodman, despite the importance of Richard and even Nat, draws the audience's "warmest response."

Rich, Frank. Rev. *New York Times* 29 June 1983, sec. C: 21.

Our way of seeing *Wilderness* has changed since the appearance of *Journey*: now we look for the shadows to peak—and sometimes they do. Though the play is "flimsily constructed ... O'Neill was masterly at tucking the sorrows in slyly."

Simon, John. Rev. *New York* 18 July 1983: 62-63.

The direction by John Stix was mediocre, the acting essentially the same, but then again so is the play. The play's humor is forced.

E36 *Ah, Wilderness!* Angus Bowmer Theatre Festival; Ashland, OR; 11 Sept.-30 Oct. 1983; Dir.—Jerry Turner.

E37 *Ah, Wilderness!* The Players; Castleton State College; Fine Arts Center; Castleton, VT; 30 Nov.-3 Dec. 1983.

E38 *Ah, Wilderness!* McCarter Theatre Company; Fine Arts Center; Princeton, NJ; 18 Jan.-5 Feb. 1984; Dir.—Margaret Booker.

E39 *Ah, Wilderness!* Alumnae Theatre; Toronto, ONT; 22 Mar.-7 Apr. 1984.

E40 *Ah, Wilderness!* Community Theater Company; East Hampton, NY; Opened 4 May 1984.

E41 *Ah, Wilderness!* Body Politic Theatre; Chicago, IL; 13 Sept.-21 Oct. 1984; Dir.—James O'Reilly.

E42 *Ah, Wilderness!* **in repertory with** *Journey* San Diego Repertory Theatre; San Diego, CA; 4 Oct.-18 Nov. 1984; Dir.—Douglas Jacobs; Design—Dan Dryden; Sid Davis—Ric Barr; Lily Miller—Barbara Murray; Essie Jo Ann Reeves; Mildred—Amy Herzberg; Richard—Thom Murray; Tommy—Jonathan Grantham; Nat—William Anton; Arthur—Wayne Tibbetts; Wint Selby—Wayne Tibbetts.

E43 *Ah, Wilderness!* Kennedy Theatre; University of Hawaii; Honolulu, HI; 18 Apr.-3 May 1985; Dir.—Glenn Cannon; Richard Miller—Daniel Kelin; Essie—Meg Roach; Nat—Dean Turner; Lily—Sylvia Hormann-Alper; Sid Davis—Wayne Kischer.

E44 *Ah, Wilderness!* Hartford Stage Company.; Hartford, CT; 28 May-30 June 1985; Dir.—Mary B. Robinson.

E45 *Ah, Wilderness!* East Coast Theater Co.; Kennebunk, Lower Village, ME; 19 June-2 Aug. 1986; Dir.—Janet O'Donnell.

E46 *Ah, Wilderness!* The Alliance Theatre School of Atlanta; The Fifth Annual Theatre Festival; Madison-Morgan Cultural Center; Madison, GA; 8-10 Aug. 1986; Dir.—David Devries; Stage Design—Bill Harrison; Lighting and Sound—David Brewer; Costuming—Yvonne K. Lee; Nat Miller—Allen O'Reilly; Essie—Anne Dudenhofer; Lily—Wendy Bennett; Mildred—Laura Tietjen; Sid Davis—Neil Williams.

Lewis, Ward B. Rev. *Eugene O'Neill Newsletter* 10.2 (1986): 41-42.

The actors—university trained and selected for an actor intern program—were mostly too young for the roles in which they were cast, while the audience saw the play with the "eyes of today."

E47 *Ah, Wilderness!* Purdue University Theatre's entry; American College Theatre Festival; 6-9 Nov. 1986; Dir.—Jim O'Connor; Scene Designer—I. Van Phillips; Richard Miller—Randy McPherson; Mildred—Anne Sermon; Tommy—Keith Cavanaugh; Essie—Patricia O'Connell; Nat—

Steven Gilborn; Lily—Mary Lowry; Sid Davis—Dale E. Miller; Belle—Erica Tobolski; Muriel McComber—Rhonda Reeves.

Fisher, James. Rev. *Eugene O'Neill Newsletter* 10.3 (1986): 38-39.

A "crippled" production because of the director's search for "relevance" (the play's values are dated) and the "hollow performances of the four mature characters" (the Equity actors were far outshone by the student members of the cast).

E48 *Ah, Wilderness!* Winchester (MA) Unitarian Players; 1-9 May 1987; Dir.—Karen Barton; Richard Miller—Eric Mortenson; Lily—Ellen Knight; Arthur—Peter Maust; Sid Davis—Dirck Stryker.

Connolly, Thomas F. Rev. *Eugene O'Neill Newsletter* 11.3 (1987): 32.

This production "compensated for technical limitations by means of a solid ensemble performance." Commends in particular the performances of Mortenson and Stryker.

E49 *Ah, Wilderness!* American Heartland Theater; Kansas City, MO; 24 June-2 Aug. 1987.

E50 *Ah, Wilderness!* The People's Light and Theatre Company; Malvern, PA; 8-26 July 1987; Dir.—Abigail Adams.

E51 *Ah, Wilderness!* Virginia Stage Company; Norfolk, VA; 13-31 Oct. 1987.

E52 *Ah, Wilderness!* Berkeley Repertory Theatre; Berkeley, CA; Closed 3 Dec. 1987.

E53 *Ah, Wilderness!* Merrimack Repertory Theater; Lowell, MA; 19 Feb.-13 Mar. 1988.

E54 *Ah, Wilderness!* The Studio Theatre; Washington, DC; 16 Mar.-17 Apr. 1988; Dir.—Robert Moss; Costumes—Ric Thomas Rice; Set—Daniel Conway; Muriel—Mary Lechter; Richard—Michael Wells.

E55 *Ah, Wilderness!* **and** *Journey*
[for differences in directing and casting and separate reviews see *Journey*—E331]

Yale Repertory Theatre; New Haven, CT; 22 Mar.-21 May 1988. Dir.—Arvin Brown; Costumes—Jane Greenwood; Nat Miller—Jason Robards; Essie—Colleen Dewhurst; Richard—Raphael Sbarge; Lily—Elizabeth Wilson; Sid Davis—George Hearn; David McComber—William Cain; Belle—Annie Golden; Nora—Jane Macfie.

Nightingale, Benedict. Rev. *New York Times* 12 June 1988, sec. 2: 1.

Compares productions and interpretations of *Journey* or *Wilderness*; mostly received opinion about O'Neill.

Simon, John. Rev. *New York* 11 July 1988: 48-49.

"Disappointing." By comparison with earlier productions, Arvin Brown is "less nimble, the cast is less felicitous."

Wilkins, Frederick C. Rev. *Eugene O'Neill Newsletter* 12.1 (1988): 68-70.

Reviews both plays and judges *Wilderness* the winner. Superb acting, including "the most believable and three-dimensional Richard."

E56 *Ah, Wilderness!* and *Journey* (in repertory) Yale Repertory Theatre Production that closed in New Haven on 21 May reopened on 8 June 1988 at the Neil Simon Theatre, 250 W. 52nd Street, New York City.

E57 *Ah, Wilderness!* Dickinson College; Carlisle, PA; Apr. 1988; Dir.— Sheila Hickey Garvey.

E58 *Ah, Wilderness!* Portsmouth Academy of Performing Arts; Portsmouth, NH; 19-22 May 1988.

E59 *Ah, Wilderness!* Berkeley Repertory Theater; Berkeley, CA; 9 Sept.-3 Dec. 1988; Dir.— Ron Lagomarsino.

E60 *Ah, Wilderness!* Department of Theatre Arts; California State University; Long Beach, CA; 7-15 Oct. 1988; Dir.— G.L. Shoup.

E61 *Ah, Wilderness!* Dallas Theater Center at Arts District Theatre; Dallas, TX; 11 Oct.-6 Nov. 1988; Dir.— Ken Bryant; Set Design — Eugene Lee; Artistic Dir.— Adrian Hall; Nat Miller — Nesbitt Blaisdell; Essie — Anne Gerety; Lily — Beverly May; Richard — Michael Cobb; Mildred — Tate Anderson; Arthur — Stephen Kalstrup; Tommy — Nicholas Stone; Muriel McComber — Alison Stone; Sid Davis — Randy Moore.

Porter, Laurin. Rev. *Eugene O'Neill Review* 13.1 (1989): 72-74.

Though the production "was a worthy candle on O'Neill's one hundredth birthday cake" and the innovative set commendable, she finds Richard's climactic monologue "weary, flat, stale and unprofitable, and his posturing monotonous."

E62 *Ah, Wilderness!* Hill Top Players; Kelly Theater/Hall of Fine Arts; 29 Oct.-6 Nov. 1988; West Liberty State College; West Liberty, WV.

E63 *Ah, Wilderness!* Ohio University Players; Monomoy Theatre; Chatham, MA; 4-8 July 1989.

E64 *Ah, Wilderness!* Lakewood Theatre; Madison, ME; 6-15 July 1989.

E65 *Ah, Wilderness!* Gettysburg Theater Festival; Gettysburg, PA; 20-29 July 1989.

E66 *Ah, Wilderness!* Porthouse Theater Company; Blossom Music Center; Cuyahoga Falls, OH; 21 July-13 Aug. 1989.

E67 *Ah, Wilderness!* Wheelock Family Theatre; Boston, MA; 9-25 Feb. 1990; Dir.— Susan Kosoff; Set/Lighting — Stephen Childs; Nat Miller — Peter Battis; Essie — Jane Staab; Arthur — Tony Butler; Richard — Jared Waye; Mildred — Rachel Martin; Lily — Jenny Sterlin; Tommy — Fred Melo; Sid Davis — Kevin Belanger; Muriel McComber — Jeri Hammond; Belle — Monique McIntyre.

Bloom, Steven F. Rev. *Eugene O'Neill Review* 14.1-2 (1990): 89-94.

While the production kept pace with the goal of the company — to present plays suitable for family viewing — it ignored the darker implications of the play and gave the audience (Bloom quoting the *Boston Globe*) a "Miller Lite" version.

E68 *Ah, Wilderness!* Blackfriars Theater; Providence College; Providence, RI; 30 Mar.-8 Apr. 1990.

E69 *Ah, Wilderness!* Summer Resident Theater, AEA; University of Arizona; Tucson, AZ; 5 June-7 July 1990. [Subsequently at Galvin Playhouse, Arizona State University, Tempe, 11 and 13 July]

E70 *Ah, Wilderness!* Pioneer Playhouse; Danville, KY; 3-14 July 1990.

E71 *Ah, Wilderness!* Huron Playhouse; Bowling Green State University; Huron, OH; 24-28 July 1990.

E72 *Ah, Wilderness!* Stratford Festival/Avon Theatre; Stratford, ONT; 28 July-10 Nov. 1990; Dir.— Vivian Matalon; Costumes — John Pennoyer; Set — John Ferguson; Nat Miller — Roland Hewgill; Essie — Susan Wright; Richard — Andrew Dolha; Lily — Barbara Bryne; Sid Davis — Douglas Rain.

Connolly, Thomas F. Rev. *Eugene O'Neill Review* 15.2 (1992): 114-18.

A rave review for a rousing production. Rain was "brilliant," the production "great theatre," the ensemble "marvelous," etc.

E73 *Ah, Wilderness!* Boars Head: Michigan Public Theater; Lansing, MI; 7 Apr.-1 May 1994.

E74 *Ah, Wilderness!* TheatreWorks at Mountain View Center for the Performing Arts; Palo Alto, CA; 20 July-21 Aug. 1994; Dir.—Robert Kelley.

E75 *Ah, Wilderness!* Weathervane Theatre; Whitefield, NH; 10 Aug.-3 Sept. 1994.

E76 *Ah, Wilderness!* Oasis Theater Co. at The Playground; 230 E. Ninth Street; New York City; 13 July-13 Aug. 1995.

E77 *Ah, Wilderness!* Studio Arena Theater; Buffalo, NY; 12 Sept.-14 Oct. 1995; Dir.—Gavin Cameron-Webb.

E78 *Ah, Wilderness!* Wabash College; Crawfordsville, IN; 4-7 Oct. 1995; Dir.—Michael Abbott; Nat Miller—James Fisher.

E79 *Ah, Wilderness!* Powerhouse Theatre (Milwaukee Rep); 19 Oct.-26 Nov. 1995; Dir.—Gavin Cameron-Webb.

E80 *Ah, Wilderness!* Theatrical Outfit; Atlanta, GA; 1-26 May 1996; Dirs.—Tom Key, Janice Akers, and Kate Warner; Artistic Dir.—Tom Key; Sets/Costuming—Leslie Taylor; Nat Miller—Tom Key; Essie—Judith Robinson; Richard—Derek Manson; Arthur—Simon Key; Lily—Megan McFarland; Sid Davis—Christopher Ekholm; Belle/Irish Maid—Elizabeth D. Wells; Wint/Salesman—Bart Hansard.

Lewis, Ward B. Rev. *Eugene O'Neill Review* 19.1-2 (1995): 158-60.

The success of this professional not-for-profit company's production of *Wilderness* was owing to the excellent interpretation of the role of Richard, engaging staging, and period costuming.

E81 *Ah, Wilderness!* National Asian American Theatre Co.; Mint Theatre; 311 W. 43rd St.; New York City; 18 July-3 Aug. 1997; Dir.—Stephen Stout; Nat Miller—Mel Glonson; Essie—Wai Ching Ho; Richard—Andrew Pang; Sid Davis—Ron Nakahara; Muriel McComber—Mayumi Rinas; Nora/Belle—Jennifer Kato; Bartender—Evan Lai.

MacLean, Robert Simpson. Rev. *Eugene O'Neill Review* 22.1-2 (1998): 200-01.

"The production proved that the group's aim of illustrating 'the abiding qualities of human nature' is being reached."

E82 *Ah, Wilderness!* Vivian Beaumont Theatre, Lincoln Center; New York City; 27

Mar. 1998; Dir.—Daniel Sullivan; Settings—Thomas Lynch; Lighting—Peter Kaczorowski; Richard Miller—Sam Trammell; Essie—Debra Monk; Nat—Craig T. Nelson; Muriel—Tracy Middendorf.

MacLean, Robert Simpson. Rev. *Eugene O'Neill Review* 22.1-2 (1998): 201-02.

"Although the play is the least like other O'Neill plays, its popularity is well-deserved as this fine production ... well attested."

Shafer, Yvonne. Rev. *Eugene O'Neill Review* 21.1-2 (1997): 186-90.

Crediting the director with establishing this production's "holiday mood," the review focuses on the innovative sets and the interaction among the characters to explain the ensemble's success.

E83 *Ah, Wilderness!* Huntington Theatre Company; Boston, MA; 15 May-14 June 1998; Dir.—Kyle Donnelly; Richard Miller—James Waterston; Nat—Jordon Charney; Muriel McComber—Careena Miller.

Cummings, Scott. Rev. *Eugene O'Neill Review* 21.1-2 (1997): 198-200.

Finds little to recommend this sentimental production or, indeed, the play. The staging is "flat," the "design ill-conceived," and the characters "innocuous boobies." Concludes that were it not for O'Neill's stature in American drama, this play would have been relegated to the "scrapheap."

E84 *All God's Chillun Got Wings* Circle in the Square; New York City; Opened 20 Mar. 1975 for 53 performances; Dir.—George C. Scott; Setting—Ming Cho Lee; Costuming—Patricia Zipprodt; Lighting—Thomas Skelton/Ronald Wallace; Artistic Dir.—Theodore Mann; Children—Ginny Binder, Beatrice Dunmore, Helen; Jennings, Kathy Rich, Derrell Edwards; Mickey, as a child—Jimmy Balo; Joe, as a child—Robert Lee Grant; Jim, as a child—Carl Thomas; Shorty, as a child—Tommy Gilchrist; Ella, as a child—Susan Jayne; Shorty—Ken Jennings; Joe—Tim Pelt; Mickey—Tom Sminkey; Jim Harris—Robert Christian; Ella Downey—Trish Van Devere; Vino—Chuck Patterson; Mrs. Harris—Minnie Gentry; Hattie Harris—Vickie Thomas; Street People—Alice Nagel, Ted Snowden, Arthur French,; Verona Barnes, Robert Earl Jones, Garcie Carroll; Harmonica player—Craig

Wasson; Singers — Chuck Patterson, Craig Wasson.

Barnes, Clive. "*All God's Chillun* at Circle in the Square." *New York Times* 21 Mar. 1975: 30; *NYTCR* 1975: 290-91.

The play is dated in its handling of racial themes. O'Neill's lines are like "dead rocks." The production's emphasis on the elements of melodrama, of violence was "heavy-handed." Trish Van Devere was not "at home" as Ella; Robert Christian as Jim performed exquisitely. The settings were "flawless."

Beaufort, John. "*All God's Chillun.*" *Christian Science Monitor* 3 Apr. 1975; *NYTCR* 1975: 292.

The play with its "stumbling compassion and inevitably dated attitudes" should be read rather than staged. Direction was "heavy-handed."

Carmody, Deidre. "Seeing *God's Chillun* for What It Is." *New York Times* 17 Feb. 1975: 28.

Contrasts the contemporary view of the play as concerned with fundamental human emotions (an encoded treatment of the playwright's parents' relationship) with the 1924 popular view of the play as advocating interracial marriage. These comments anticipate the production (to be previewed 28 Feb.).

Clurman, Harold. "Theatre." *Nation* 12 Apr. 1975: 442-43.

Although *Chillun* is not one of O'Neill's best plays, it is not without merit. Compares James and Mary Tyrone's relationship to Ella and Jim Harris' and Con and Nora Melody's to Jim and Ella's. In the present production Robert Christian as Jim gives "one of the most memorable performances of the season." Also thought Trish Van Devere as Ella good, but found Scott's direction difficult to judge.

Gill, Brendan. "The Theatre." *New Yorker* 31 Mar. 1975: 47-48.

The roles are "thankless" and the actors have not given "exceptional life" to them. Jim and Ella are caricatures of O'Neill's father and mother.

Gottfried, Martin. Theater/"Oh, Mr. Scott!" *New York Post* 1 Mar. 1975; *NYTCR* 1975: 291.

The handling of racial themes is dated, the production badly cast, badly directed, badly staged.

Kalem, T. E. "Haunted House." *Time* 31 Mar. 1975: 61.

Suspects that *Chillun* has been revived for its topicality and that we are expected to respond to a play which does not elicit a deep response: O'Neill's prose is "dead-battery"; neither Robert Christian nor Trish Van Devere projects the torment that the roles expect.

Kerr, Walter. "O'Neill's Uneasy Study in Black and White." *New York Times* 30 Mar. 1975, sec. 2: I.

Finds *Chillun* "ambivalent about its theme" and "a skeletal piece." Scott makes a "bold attempt" at directing the play — creating a "quasi-poetic dream-state." This is successful in the first half but not in the second. The evening is "evocative" nonetheless.

Probst, Leonard. NBC Radio. 20 Mar. 1975; *NYTCR* 1975: 293.

A "chilling, powerful drama, strongly directed and acted, and fully absorbing."

Sanders, Kevin. WABC-TV 7. 20 Mar. 1975; *NYTCR* 1975: 293.

O'Neill's "worst" play, dated and "unactable." Imaginative direction.

Sharp, Christopher. The Theatre/"*All God's Chillun Got Wings.*" *Women's Wear Daily* 24 Mar. 1975; *NYTCR* 1975: 292.

Stresses less "the racial issues than the emotions that reduce the races to a common denominator." The director "turned what could have been a brilliant evening into only a decent one." The emphasis is on pathos, not something out of Aeschylus. Trish Van Devere is "excellent"; Robert Christian "over-directed."

Simon, John. Rev. *New York* 7 Apr. 1975: 78, 80

The revival of the play is a "major disaster" and the play itself a "clinker." The problems are not the topic (miscegenation) but "the psychological inconsistencies and improbabilities," "rickety stagecraft" and "leaden language." Scott's direction is no help.

Watt, Douglas. "O'Neill Rarity in Weak Revival." *Daily News* 21 Mar. 1975; *NYTCR* 1975: 290.

The play is "unsuccessful." The performance lacks "tension and rhythm." The play is "as crude in outline and clumsy in speech" as is O'Neill's worst. The setting was good but the acting was not.

Wilson, Edwin. The Theatre/"*All God's Chillun Got Wings.*" *Wall Street Journal* 29 Mar. 1975: *NYTCR* 1975: 292.

A play marked by "faulty construction and theatrical extravagance." In this production melodrama was given too much opportunity to control things.

E85 *All God's Chillun Got Wings* Horace Mann Theater; Columbia University; New York City; 21-23 Oct. 1982; Dir.— Virlana Tkacz.

E86 *Anna Christie* Soho Repertory (off off Broadway); New York City; 30 Jan. 1976.

E87 *Anna Christie* Imperial Theatre; New York City; Opened 14 Apr. 1977 for 124 performances; Dir.— José Quintero; Decor and Lighting — Ben Edwards; Costuming — Jane Greenwood; Johnny-the-Priest — Richard Hamilton; Longshoremen — Edwin McDonough/Vic Polizos; Larry — Ken Harrison; Postman — Jack Davidson; Chris Christopherson — Robert Donley; Anna — Liv Ullmann; Marthy Owen — Mary McCarty; Sailors — Vic Polizos/Ken Harrison; Johnson — Jack Davidson; Mat Burke — John Lithgow.

Barnes, Clive. "Theater/Liv Ullmann's *Anna Christie*." *New York Times* 15 Apr. 1977, sec. 3: 3; *NYTCR* 1977: 278.

"A clumsy play" that can be made to work since O'Neill provided "scarecrows" that can be clothed by inventive actors. Ullmann was "born for *Anna Christie*."

Beaufort, John. Theater Reviews/"A Powerful O'Neill on Broadway." *Christian Science Monitor* 20 Apr. 1977; *NYTCR* 1977: 279.

Superlatives.

Clurman, Harold. Theatre. *Nation* 30 Apr. 1977: 538-39.

The plot is banal as are most of the characters. Although Liv Ullmann looks the part, she is quintessentially not Anna. Support actors Robert Donley and John Lithgow are good and Quintero's direction intelligent, but the production as a whole "does not speak to the inner voice."

Gill, Brendan. "Mal de Mer." *New Yorker* 25 Apr. 1977: 92.

The play is "coarsely conceived, coarsely constructed, coarsely composed." This production makes one feel "battered not purged." Faults Ullmann for "failing to command the stage," Donley for his near indecipherable accent, and John Lithgow for being "at a loss" in the impossible role of Mat.

Gottfried, Martin. Theater/ "What's a Nice Girl Like Liv Doing in a Play Like This?" *New York Post* 15 Apr. 1977; *NYTCR* 1977: 281.

The play is bad; the direction is "corny;" the design is inept; and the supporting cast doesn't support. The only excuse for the play is Liv Ullmann, and for her there is only praise.

Kalem, T. E. "Liv in Limbo." *Time* 25 Apr. 1977: 84; *NYTCR* 1977: 282.

The play is "a cheap, cosmetic come-on of a drama." Rates the production a failed effort — largely because almost everthing is wrong with the play. Approves of Liv Ullmann's performance.

Kauffmann, Stanley. "Stanley Kauffmann on Theatre." *New Republic* 7 May 1977: 22-23.

"*Anna* is an example of early 20th-century American naiveté about realism." But it has elements that anticipate O'Neill's maturity. Of this production the direction was unimpressive as was the acting, with the exception of Robert Donley.

Kerr, Walter. "There's More to *Anna Christie* Than This Production Knows." *New York Times* 24 Apr. 1977, sec. 2: 5.

Liv Ullmann is talented, but miscast. She doesn't look like any of the things she tells us she is — defeated, tired, cynical. Robert Donley's performance is "all one color and all one key." John Lithgow as Mat Burke is a "real howler."

Kissel, Howard. The Theater/"*Anna Christie*." *Women's Wear Daily* 15 Apr. 1977; *NYTCR* 1977: 279-80.

Insists that O'Neill's plays have to be seen not read. The 1922 *Anna* has much that is "quaint and dated," but "the metaphor of the sea gives the play a poetry" that lifts it above its stilted dialogue and "soap operatic plot." Superlatives for the production.

Kroll, Jack. "Liv's Anna." *Newsweek* 25 Apr. 1977: 89.

Unenthusiastic about Donley's Chris but thought Lithgow and Ullmann were excellent. *Anna* is a "heavy, hooting scow of a play."

Mayer, David. Rev. *Plays and Players* 27.3 (1979): 30-31.

This production proves that while on paper O'Neill has many faults — tin ear, leaden philosophizing, clumsy asides and soliloquizing — still on the stage his plays have "a crude vitality and disturbing turbulence."

Probst, Leonard. NBC Radio. 14 Apr. 1977: *NYTCR* 1977: 282.

The play is "rambling, awkward, early O'Neill," but it is made "memorable" by Liv Ullmann.

Rich, Alan. Rev. *New York* 12 May 1977: 68-69.

Anna stands at a turning point in O'Neill's work between the "dark, terse personal melodramas," and the sea plays, on the one hand, and the experimental plays of the 1920s, on the other. Finds the plot and language deficient, but the current production better than the play.

Rogoff, Gordon. "The Mere Human Props of Eugene O'Neill." *Saturday Review* 28 May 1977: 38-39.

Approves of the casting—especially Liv Ullmann—but maintains the play itself is clumsy, the action forced and the characters stereotypes. Thinks the play came at a good point in O'Neill's career. With the country looking for a serious playwright, how could someone "grumbling about fate and hammering away at destiny miss?"

Watt, Douglas. "To See Liv Is to Luv Her." *Daily News* 15 Apr. 1977; *NYTCR* 1977: 278-79.

As in all O'Neill "there is an awesome power at work beneath the surface of this somewhat old-fashioned melodramatic triangle." The production is "something to see, and its star ... [Liv Ullmann] someone to take home."

Wilson, Edwin. The Theater/"*Anna Christie.*" *Wall Street Journal* 19 Apr. 1977; *NYTCR* 1977: 282.

The play is old-fashioned and awkward, but it has some of the strength O'Neill is capable of and some of his themes which we find in later plays. Liv is "well-directed" and "ably supported." She is a "joy to behold."

E88 *Anna Christie* Royal Shakespeare Company at The Other Place; Stratford-upon-Avon; Opened 18 Sept. 1979; also May-Sept. 1980; Dir.—Jonathan Lynn; Design—Saul Radomsky; Lighting—Leo Leibovici; Johnny-the-Priest—Ian East; Larry—Ian McNeice; Chris Christopherson—Fulton MacKay; Anna—Susan Tracy; Marthy Owen—Lila Kaye; Mat Burke—Gareth Thomas.

E89 *Anna Christie* New England Repertory Theatre; Worcester, MA; 23 Oct.-15 Nov. 1981; Dir.—John Knowles.

E90 *Anna Christie* St. Nicholas Theater Company; Chicago, IL; 18 Nov.-20 Dec. 1981; Dir.—Cynthia Sherman.

E91 *Anna Christie* American Folk Theater; Richard Allen Center for Culture and Art; New York City; 5-24 Apr. 1983; Dir.—Bob Sickinger.

E92 *Anna Christie* Your Theatre; New Bedford, MA; 19-29 Sept. 1984; Dir.—Cynthia J. Messier; Anna Christopherson—Linda Sue McCallester; Chris—Edward J. Maguire; Mat Burke—Gregory F. Leonard.

E93 *Anna Christie* Seventh Sign Theatre Company; Good Shepherd-Faith Presbyterian Church; New York City; Closed 18 May 1985; Dir.—Anthony Osnato.

E94 *Anna Christie* Ohio University Players; The Monomoy Theatre; Chatham, MA; 4-8 Aug. 1987; Dir.—Cigdem Onat; Set Design—Ron Gottschalk; Lighting—Timothy D. Latners; Anna Christopherson—Jane Gabbert-Wilson; Chris—Matt DeCaro; Mat Burke—Jeffrey Baumgarten.

Connolly, Thomas. Rev. *Eugene O'Neill Newsletter* 11.3 (1987): 33.

Calling this production "splendidly mounted," Connolly, nonetheless, wonders whether the "quasi-feminist" interpretation isn't undone by the "happy ending." Particularly noteworthy in this production were the "fine technical touches."

E95 *Anna Christie* Arena Players Repertory Theatre; East Farmingdale; Apr. 1988.

E96 *Anna Christie* Dramateurs; Lafayette, CA; 30 Sept.-5 Nov. 1988.

E97 *Anna Christie* Horse Cave Theatre; Horse Cave, KY; 8 Oct.-18 Nov. 1988; Dir.—Laura Fine.

E98 *Anna Christie* American Stanislavski Theatre; Trinity Presbyterian Church; New York City; 6-23 Apr. 1989; Dir.—Sonia Moore.

E99 *Anna Christie* The Bathhouse Theatre; Seattle, WA; 24 Oct.-10 Dec. 1989; Dir.—Marjorie Nelson.

E100 *Anna Christie* Long Wharf Theatre; New Haven, CT; 13 Mar.-29 Apr. 1990; Dir.—Gordon Edelstein.

E101 *Anna Christie* Young Vic Theatre; London, UK; June 1990; Dir.—David Thacker; Anna Christopherson—Natasha Richardson; Chris—John Woodvine.

E102 *Anna Christie* George Street Playhouse; New Brunswick, NJ; 26 Oct.-17 Nov. 1991.

E103 *Anna Christie* Roundabout Theatre Company; New York City; 23 Dec.

1992-28 Feb. 1993; Dir.— David Leveaux; Setting — John Lee Beatty; Lighting — Marc B. Weiss; Anna Christopherson — Natasha Richardson; Chris — Rip Torn; Mat Burke — Liam Neeson; Marthy Owen — Anne Meara.

Corless, Richard. Rev. *Time* 25 Jan. 1993: 66.

The play "finally finds its sea legs." Natasha Richardson "makes Anna a fighter, battered on the wheel of men's lust but still defiantly erect."

Frank, Glenda. Rev. *Chelsea Clinton News* 28 Jan.-3 Feb. 1993: 7.

Lahr, John. "Selling the Sizzle." *New Yorker* 1 Feb. 1993: 99-102.

See B252.

Lyons, Donald. "Saints and Sinners." *New Criterion* 11 Mar. 1993: 56-60.

"This exciting new production of *Anna Christie* at the Roundabout seizes on what is living in the play — the drive of the central pair, Anna and her brutish Irish stoker, Mat, toward redemption — and downplays what is dated — the sodden maunderings of Anna's father, Chris Christopherson, about sea and fog." The play itself is a "valuable" O'Neill play, but not a great one.

O'Neill, Michael C. Rev. *Eugene O'Neill Review* 16. 2 (1992): 114-19.

Gives an approving if restrained nod to the production, finding the director's "stubborn" fidelity to the text a wise decision in light of the principals, Richardson and Neeson, but less judicious as applied to Rip Torn, whose "questionable Swedish accent" and "embarrassed mumble" make for a less than convincing Chris.

Vena, Gary. Rev. *Eugene O'Neill Review* 16.2 (1992): 108-14.

Faults the director for "lack of vision," the actors for giving generally "lack lustre" performances, and the "theatre's auditorium-like sterility" for creating a, well, less than moving theatrical experience.

E104 *Anna Christie* San Jose Repertory Theatre; San Jose, CA; 9 Mar.-6 Apr. 1997.

E105 *Anna Christie* StageWest; Springfield, MA; 16 Apr.-4 May 1997; Dir.— Greg Leaming.

E106 *Anna Christie* Arena Stage; Washington, DC; 9 May-15 June 1997; Dir.— Liviu Ciulei.

E107 *Anna Christie* Focus Theatre; Dublin; 4-12 May 1998; Dir.— Leon Halligan; Setting — Robert Lane; Lighting — Marcus Costello; Anna Christopherson — Aoibhinn Gilroy; Chris — Sean Treacy; Mat Burke — Ger Carey; Marthy Owen — Margaret Toomey.

E108 *Before Breakfast* Chichester Festival; England; July 1978; Dir.— Sylvia Miles.

E109 *Before Breakfast* see *Three Lost Plays of Eugene O'Neill (Breakfast, Wife, Cross)*

Nameless Theater; 125 W. 22nd St.; New York City; Closed 19 Nov. 1978; Dir.— Michael Alexander.

E110 *Before Breakfast* American Theatre Arts Conservatory; Los Angeles, CA; Fall 1981; Dir.— Barry Bartle.

Hanson, Eugene K. Rev. *Eugene O'Neill Newsletter* 6.1(1982): 45-48.

The production failed for two reasons: "the development of the character of Mrs. Rowland was all wrong," and the director chose to make Alfred an on-stage presence for the duration of the play.

E111 *Before Breakfast* No Smoking Playhouse; New York City; Closed 15 Dec. 1985; Dir.— Francisco Rivela.

E112 *Before Breakfast* with *Dreamy* and *Cross*

The Winter Company; Tower Theatre; Massachusetts College of Art; Boston, MA; 13-26 Feb. 1986; Dir.— Kenneth MacDonald; Mrs. Rowland — Paula Jowanna; Dreamy — Michael Jones; Mammy Saunders — Georgette Leslie; Irene — Zakiya Alake; Capt. Bartlett — Chuck Brining; Sue — Jen MacDonald; Nat — Richard Callahan; Dr. Higgins — Peter Whitten.

Connolly, Thomas F. Rev. *Eugene O'Neill Newsletter* 10.1 (1986): 34-36.

When the production stuck to the text (*Cross* and *Dreamy*), it was successful. When it didn't (*Breakfast*), it was not. Since the hand of Alfred never appeared in the latter, the audience was left to wonder whether he exists. Nonetheless, these three short plays "revealed that O'Neill's short early plays are theatrically viable and can move contemporary audiences if the playwright's instructions are faithfully heeded."

E113 *Before Breakfast* and *Hughie*

South Street Theater; 424 W. 42nd Street; New York City; Opened 17 May 1988.

E114 *Before Breakfast* Common Basis Theatre Company; New York City; Fall 1994;

Dir.— Amy Coleman; Mrs. Rowland —
Donna Jason.

McLean, Robert S. Rev. *Eugene O'Neill
Review* 17.1-2 (1994): 167-69.

Double billed with Pinter's *The Lover*,
O'Neill's play was "expertly acted and directed."

E115 *Before Breakfast* C. Walsh Theatre; Boston, MA; 13 May 1995; Dir.— Tom
McDermott; Mrs. Rowland — Mary Wadkins.

E116 *Before Breakfast* with *Hughie,
Recklessness* and *Web*

Playtime Series 59; Theater-Studio; 750
Eighth Avenue at 46th Street; New York City;
16-21 Sept. 1995; Dir.— A.M. Raychel.

E117 *Before Breakfast* Bas Bleu Theatre Company; Fort Collins, CO; 12 Oct.-4
Nov. 1995; Dir.— Warren Sherrill; Set Design — Cristal Martinez and Ric Lantz; Mrs.
Rowland — Lisa Rucker.

Jones, Laura. Rev. *Eugene O'Neill Review*
19.1-2 (1995): 156-58.

The decision to pair this play with Susan
Glaspell's *Trifles* elicited from the audience a
sympathy for Mrs. Rowland at odds with
O'Neill's intent. Nonetheless, Glaspell would
probably be pleased and, "perhaps hers is simply the better play."

E118 *Beyond the Horizon* McCarter
Theater Company; Fine Arts Center; Princeton,
NJ; 10 Oct. 1974; Producing Dir.— Michael
Kahn; Setting — Robert U. Taylor; Lighting —
David F. Segal; Robert Mayo — Richard Backus;
Andrew — Edward J. Moore; James — Hugh
Reilly; Kate Mayo — Laurinda Barrett; Ruth
Atkins — Marta Tucci; Capt. Dick Scott — Paul
Larson; Mrs. Atkins — Camila Ashland; Mary —
Sharon Chazin; Ben — Michael Houlihan; Dr.
Fawcett — Daniel Saltzer.

Barnes, Clive. "*Beyond the Horizon.*"
New York Times 12 Oct. 1974: 18.

O'Neill "stammers out miracles" and this
is one of them. The play is simple on the surface but contains themes which recurred in
O'Neill for the next 30 years.

E 119 *Beyond the Horizon* 78th Street
Theater Lab; New York City; Closed 18 Nov.
1979; Dir.— Christian Renaud.

E120 *Beyond the Horizon* Theatre Exchange; New York City; 26 Mar.-2 Apr. 1981;
Dir.— Charles Clubb.

E121 *Beyond the Horizon* ATA Theatre; New York City; Closed 25 Apr. 1981;
Dir.— James Jennings.

E122 *Beyond the Horizon* Queens
College Little Theatre; Flushing, NY; 18-20
Mar. 1982.

E123 *Beyond the Horizon* Source Theatre Company; Washington, DC; 8 Nov.-7
Dec. 1985.

E124 *Beyond the Horizon* Connemara
Players; ATA Theatre; 314 W. 54th St.; New
York City; 29 Jan.-2 Feb. 1986.

E125 *Beyond the Horizon* Nucleo
Eclettico Theater; Boston, MA; Closed 2 Aug.
1986; Dir.— Joe DeGuglielmo.

E126 *Beyond the Horizon* Palmer Auditorium; Connecticut College; New London,
CT; 19-21 Nov. 1987; Dir.— Rick Scott.

E127 *Beyond the Horizon* Independence Theater Co.; Fort Lee Historic Park;
Fort Lee, NJ; 9 July-14 Aug. 1988.

Klein, Alvin. Rev. *New York Times* 7
Aug. 1988, sec. 12: 21.

E128 *Beyond the Horizon* The Berk-
shire Public Theatre; Pittsfield, MA; 29 Sept.-
5 Nov. 1988; Dir.— Frank Bessell; Set — Bud
Clark; Mrs. Atkins — Irene McDonnell; Mary
Mayo — Leah Lotto; Ruth — Eliza Bond;
Robert — Noel Hanger; Andrew — Barney
Moran; Elder Mayos — Amy Judd and
Glen Barrett; Captain Scott — Bruce T. Mac-
Donald.

Wilkins, Frederick C. Rev. *Eugene
O'Neill Newsletter* 12.3 (1988): 48-50.

Congratulates the effort and commends
the result. Not often is this O'Neill play produced, but this skillfully directed effort shows
that "the play has more than enough vitality
and substance to deserve regular production."

E129 *Beyond the Horizon* Hilberry
Theatre; Wayne State University; Detroit,
MI; Fall-Winter 1995; Dir.— James Thomas;
Robert Mayo — Karl Kippola; Ruth — Peggy
Johns; Andrew — David Haig/Dwight Tolar;
James — David Orley.

Field, Brad. Rev. *Eugene O'Neill Review*
20.1-2 (1996): 163-66.

Though Thomas studied with Quintero,
his direction of this college production gets
only a tepid endorsement. Nonetheless, David
Orley, as James Mayo, is "striking."

E130 *Beyond the Horizon* Chain
Lightning Theatre; New York City; Winter
1997/1998; Dir.— David Travis.

Shafer, Yvonne. Rev. *Eugene O'Neill Review* 22.1-2 (1998): 205-08.

"This production was very pleasing in so many ways." Casting was "solid," with "a good ensemble feeling."

E131 *Beyond the Horizon* Horizon Productions; Producers Club; 358 W. 44th St.; New York City; 22 Nov.-6 Dec. 1998; Dir.— Rafael DeMussa; Andrew Mayo — Britt Lafield; Robert — Rafael DeMussa; James — Jaime Sanchez; Kate — Fidelma Murphy; Ruth Atkins — Sandra Trullinger; Sarah — Janet Hoskins; Capt. Dick Scott — Gabriel Walsh; Ben/Dr. Fawcett — Bill Vartus.

MacLean, Robert Simpson. Rev. *Eugene O'Neill Review* 22.1-2 (1998): 209-10.

"A sincere performance." "A cast from a variety of backgrounds," resulting in an ensemble of Irish, Hispanic and other accents.

E132 *Bound East for Cardiff* see *The Sea Plays of Eugene O'Neill (Caribbees, Zone, Cardiff* and *Voyage)* Long Wharf Theater; New Haven, CT; Opened 28 Mar. 1978.

E133 *Bound East for Cardiff* see *The Long Voyage Home (Caribbees, Cardiff, Zone and Voyage)* National Theatre Company; Cottesloe Theatre; London; 20 Feb. 1979-17 Mar. 1979; revived Jan. 1980.

E134 *Bound East for Cardiff* Tufts Arena Theater; Medford, MA; Spring 1981; Dir.— Sean Skilling.

E135 *Bound East for Cardiff* see *Six Plays of the Sea (Cardiff, Voyage, Zone, Ile, Rope, Cross)* Apple Corps Theatre Company; New York City; Closed 2 May 1982; Dir.— Skip Corris.

E136 *Bound East for Cardiff* see *Sea Plays at Monte Cristo (Cardiff, Voyage, Zone, Ile, Cross, Rope)* "Monte Cristo"; 305 Pequot Avenue; New London, CT; 26 Sept.-14 Nov. 1985.

E137 *Bound East for Cardiff* see *Four Plays of the Sea (S.S. Glencairn)* Just So Productions; San Francisco, CA; 27 Apr.-17 June 1988.

E138 *Bound East for Cardiff* see *The Sea Plays (Cardiff, Caribbees, Voyage, and Zone)* The Willow Cabin Theater Company; Intar II Theater; New York City; 3-20 Nov. 1988.

E139 *Bound East for Cardiff* Provincetown Art Association; Provincetown Playhouse Theater Co.; Summer 1996; Dir.— Eisenhauer.

E140 *Bound East for Cardiff* with *Abortion* and *The Movie Man* Playwright's Theater Festival of O'Neill; Provincetown Playhouse; New York City; 3-8 Aug. 1999.

E141 *Bread and Butter* Playwright's Theatre Festival of Eugene O'Neill; The Provincetown Playhouse; New York; 28 Aug.-11 Sept. 1998.

Frank, Glenda. Rev. *Back Stage* 11 Sept. 1998: 56.

E142 *Chris Christophersen* The Goodman Theatre; Chicago, IL; 1982 Season.

E143 *Desire Under the Elms* ACSTA The Village Church (off off Broadway); New York City; 9 Mar. 1974 till the 2nd week in April; Dir.— Sonia Moore; Ephraim Cabot Philip G. Bennett; Eben — Bill Baker; Abbie — Cathy Brady.

Thompson, Howard. "Ibsen and O'Neill." *New York Times* 12 Apr. 1974: 18.

Applauds the ACSTA ensemble "whose artful, unified sensibility continues to give one of the steadiest theater glows in town."

E144 *Desire Under the Elms* Queensboro Community College; Opened 14 Mar. 1974 for seven performances.

E145 *Desire Under the Elms* Academy Festival Theatre; Lake Forest, IL; June 1974; Dir.— Vinnette Carroll; Cicely Tyson.

Zimmerman, Paul D. Rev. *Newsweek* 24 June 1974: 76-77.

Calls the production with its mostly black cast an "interesting experiment," one, however, which was not entirely successful.

E146 *Desire Under the Elms* Jean Cocteau Repertory (off off Broadway); 11 Oct. 1975.

E147 *Desire Under the Elms* ACSTA The Village Church (off off Broadway); New York City; 9 Jan. 1976.

E148 *Desire Under the Elms* San Francisco American Conservatory Theater; Academy Theater; Playing in Moscow [Soviet Union]; Opened 27 May 1976; Artistic Dir.— William Ball.

Powers, Dennis. "The Russians said Hello to Dolly Levi." *New York Times* 5 Sept. 1976, sec. 2: 5 and 24.

Comments on the reception given the ACT in Russia. Notes that its two productions — one was *Desire*— were excerpted for Soviet TV.

Report on ACT in Russia. *New York Times* 8 June 1976: 28.

ACT's production of *Desire (Lyubov pod Viasami)* in Russia is getting full-house reception. Russian translation comes through earphones at each seat. During the three-week tour, the company will also perform in Riga and Leningrad.

E149 *Desire Under the Elms* Asolo Theatre; Ringling Art Museum; Sarasota, FL; 1977 Season; Dir.— Richard Fallon.

Frazer, Winifred. Rev. *Eugene O'Neill Newsletter* 1.3 (1978): 17-18.

Discusses O'Neill's two-level set and the way in which the set of this production differs, then recommends future experimenting with ways to produce O'Neill.

E150 *Desire Under the Elms* Gainesville Little Theatre; Gainesville, FL; 5-15 Apr. 1978; Dir.— Craig Hartley.

Frazer, Winifred. Rev. *Eugene O'Neill Newsletter* 2.2 (1978): 16.

Maybe the director had read Frazer's review of the Asolo production. In any case his set as she describes it seems quite sophisticated.

E151 *Desire Under the Elms* Royall Tyler Theatre; University of Vermont; Burlington, VT; 18-21 Oct. 1978.

E152 *Desire Under the Elms* Playwrights Horizons; Queens; New York City; 13 Oct.-4 Nov. 1979; Dir.— Irene Lewis.

E153 *Desire Under the Elms* Dartmouth Players; Warner Bentley Theater; Hopkins Center; Hanover, NH; 26 Feb.-1 Mar. 1980; Dir.— Robert Berlinger.

Wilkins, Frederick. Rev. *Eugene O'Neill Newsletter* 4.1 (1980): 25-26.

The set was "effective," " lighting directions ... superbly executed," characterization quite mature (the actors were college students). "The production was a blend of spurts — of highs and lows with no fully sustained emotional arcs."

E154 *Desire Under the Elms* Guthrie Theater; Minneapolis, MN; 23 Aug.-22 Nov. 1980; Dir.— George Keathley.

Voelker, Paul D."Lust Under Some Elms: *Desire* at the Guthrie." *Eugene O'Neill Newsletter* 4.3 (1980): 9-12.

Notes the compromises necessitated because the Guthrie has a different kind of stage set up from the one O'Neill wrote for and the director a leaning toward ultra-realism that played down O'Neill's symbolism. And other matters that left Voelker dissatisfied.

E155 *Desire Under the Elms* American Stanislavsky Theater; [off off Broadway]; New York City; 1982.

E156 *Desire Under the Elms* Tacoma Actors Guild; Tacoma, WA; 4-27 Feb. 1982; Dir.— William Becvar.

E157 *Desire Under the Elms* V. A. Smith Chapel Theatre; 656 Sixth Ave.; New York City; Opened 12 Feb. 1982; Dir.— Sonia Moore.

E158 *Desire Under the Elms* with songs by Micki Grant; [off off Broadway]; Urban Arts Theatre; 30 Apr.-23 May 1982; Dir.— Vinnette Carroll.

E159 *Desire Under the Elms* Pennsylvania Stage Company; Allentown, PA; 16 Feb.-13 Mar. 1983; Dir.— Gregory S. Hurst.

E160 *Desire Under the Elms* Indianapolis Repertory Theatre; Indianapolis, IN; 15 Mar.-10 Apr. 1983; Dir.— Tom Haas; Design — Ming Cho Lee.

Tuck, Susan. Rev. *Eugene O'Neill Newsletter* 7.1 (1983): 15-19.

Uninspired performances, but an impressive set with mechanically controlled wall panels so that they could be shifted quickly.

E161 *Desire Under the Elms* Bay Players; Duxbury, MA; 11-19 Nov. 1983; Dir.— Maggie McGovern.

E162 *Desire Under the Elms* Roundabout Theatre Company (Stage One); New York City; 20 Mar.-3 June 1984; Dir.— Terry Schreiber; Scenic Designer — Michael Sharp; Ephraim Cabot — Lee Richardson; Eben — Lenny Von Dohlen; Simeon — Tom Spiller; Peter — Patrick Meyers; Abbie — Kathy Whitton Baker.

E163 *Desire Under the Elms* East-West Fusion Theatre Center; for Far East-West Studies; Sharon, CT; Opened mid-June 1984; Dir.— Balwant Gargi.

E164 *Desire Under the Elms* Rand Theater; University of Massachusetts; Amherst, MA; 11-20 Oct. 1984; Dir.— Edward Golden; Abbie — Danielle DiVecchio; Eben — John Campbell Finnegan; Ephraim — Harry Mahnken.

Wilkins, Frederick C. Rev. *Eugene O'Neill Newsletter* 8.3 (1984): 31-33.

On the performance as a whole: "Faithful, briskly paced ... the liveliest I have seen."

E165 *Desire Under the Elms* Hartford Stage Company; Hartford, CT; 19 Apr.-19 May 1985; Dir.— Mary K. Robinson.

E166 *Desire Under the Elms* Horse Cave Theatre; Horse Cave, KY; 5 July-25 Aug. 1985; Dir.— Warren Hammack.

E167 *Desire Under the Elms* Florida Repertory Theatre; West Palm Beach, FL; 2 Jan.-2 Feb. 1986; Dir.— Keith Baker.

E168 *Desire Under the Elms* Open Door Theater; Jamaica Plain, MA; 7 Aug.-6 Sept. 1986; Dir.— David Mold.

E169 *Desire Under the Elms* Schaubühne Company of West Berlin; National Theatre; London; 6 May-20 June 1987; Dir.— Patrick Mason; Designer — Joe Vanek; Ephraim Cabot — Tom Hickey; Eben — Colin Firth; Abbie — Carmen Du Sautoy.

Kalson, Albert E. Rev. *Eugene O'Neill Newsletter* 11.2 (1987): 36-40.

Acknowledging the chemistry between Firth and Du Sautoy, this blunt review says the actors deserve a "less confusing setting" than the production, Schaubühne's offering along with *Ape*, furnishes. Ultimately, predicts that this interpretation "will have no afterlife."

E170 *Desire Under the Elms* Palmer Auditorium; Connecticut College; New London, CT; 3-5 Mar. 1988; Dir.— Linda Herr.

E171 *Desire Under the Elms* Denver Center Theater Co.; Denver, CO, and Japan; 4-21 Oct. 1989 (Followed by a tour of cities of Japan in November); Dir.— Donovan Marley; Set Design — Richard Hay; Ephraim Cabot — Jim Baker; Eben — Scott Quintard; Simeon — William Breener; Peter — Mick Regan; Abbie Putnam — Jacqueline Antaramian.

Fink, Joel G. Rev. *Eugene O'Neill Review* 13.2 (1989): 85-89.

While crediting the "consistently professional caliber of the acting," Fink faulted the removal of "all the elements that might identify the locale as New England, or even as specifically American." As O'Neill created her, Abbie was not, after all, Armenian, as she is in this production. Why? asks the reviewer.

Osada, Mitsunobu. Rev. *Eugene O'Neill Review* 13.2 (1989): 82-84.

Speaks to the reception of the Denver Center Theatre Company's production of *Desire* in Japan. The Japanese appreciate that the spirit of Eben's mother is pervasive, but they have a harder time with the infanticide.

E172 *Desire Under the Elms* Kestrel, Inc.; Clearwater, FL; 31 May-23 June 1990; Dir.— Nan Colton.

E173 *Desire Under the Elms* Merrimack Repertory Theater; Lowell, MA; 2-25 Nov. 1990.

E174 *Desire Under the Elms* Tovstonogov Great Academic Drama Theater; St. Petersburg, Russia; Sept. 1995.

E175 *Desire Under the Elms* Peccadillo Theater Co.; Kraine Theatre; New York City; 10 July-3 Aug. 1997; Dir.— Dan Wackerman; Abbie Putnam — Devora Millman; Eben Cabot — Carl Jay Cofield; Ephraim — George Bartenieff.

MacLean, Robert Simpson. Rev. *Eugene O'Neill Review* 22.1-2 (1998): 210-13.

As the three Cabot sons were played by black men, the play acquires "a unique subtext in O'Neill's story of familial deceit and exploitation."

E176 *The Dreamy Kid* Di Pinto Di Blu (Off Off Broadway); New York City; 1975-76 Season.

E177 *The Dreamy Kid* see *Before Breakfast* and *Where the Cross Is Made* The Winter Company; Tower Theatre; Massachusetts College of Art; Boston, MA; 13-26 Feb. 1986.

E178 *Dynamo* The Impossible Ragtime Theater (Off Off Broadway); New York City; 29 Oct. 1976; Dir.— George Ferencz; Setting — Bill Stabile; Lighting — John Gisondi; Hutchins Light — Frank Hamilton; Amelia Light — Helen Breed; Reuben Light — Ray Wise; Mae Fife — Rosemary Foley; Ramsey — David Tress; Ada — Shelley Wyant.

Gussow, Mel. Rev. *New York Times* 2 Nov. 1976, sec. C: 22.

The play is "overwrought, the dialogue thunderstruck," yet the work "survives as a play of ideas." This production "makes *Dynamo* throb with renewed energy."

E179 *The Emperor Jones* Perry Street Theater; New York City; Opened by 22 Sept. 1977; Dir.— Donald J. Schulte/Vasek Simek; Ritual Dance Choreography — Randy Thomas; Afro-Cuban Score — Eric Diamond; Brutus Jones — Rodney Hudson; Smithers — Philip Karnell.

Baker, Rob. Rev. *After Dark* Nov. 1977: 94.

The acting was "exemplary."

Gussow, Mel. Off Off Broadway. *New York Times* 23 Sept. 1977, sec. C: 5.

Endorses the production and play. Political events and personalities [Idi Amin] make the play even more meaningful. Commends the acting. Is Jones mocking "whitey" when he uses "blackspeak"?

Hill, Holly. Rev. *New York Theatre Review* Nov. 1977: 94.

_____. Rev. *New York Theatre Review* Dec. 1977: 40.

Wilkins, Frederick C. Rev. *Eugene O'Neill Newsletter* 1.3(1978): 18-19.

Summarizes reviews of this production.

E180 *The Emperor Jones* Seven Ages; New York City, and on tour; 1977.

E181 *The Emperor Jones* Masque and Gown of Bowdoin College; Brunswick, ME; Feb. 1979; Dir.— Peter Honchaurk.

E182 *The Emperor Jones* American Theatre Experiment; Fordham University Theatre; New York City; 10-22 Sept. 1979; Brutus Jones — Stephen D. Agins.

E183 *The Emperor Jones* Fusion Project; 28th St. Theater; 4-16 Oct. 1982.

E184 *The Emperor Jones* American Music Theater Festival; Philadelphia, PA; 23 June-5 July 1984; Dir.— Donald McKayle; Music by Coleridge Taylor Perkinson.

E185 *The Emperor Jones* SUNY-Purchase; Purchase, NY; 18-22 and 25-29 July 1984; Dir. and choreographer — Donald McRayle; Brutus Jones — James Earl Jones.

E186 *The Emperor Jones* The Wooster Group; Performing Garage; New York City; 24 Sept.-17 Oct. 1992; Dir.— Elizabeth LeCompte; William Dafoe and Peyton Smith.

E187 *The Emperor Jones* The Wooster Group; Performing Garage; New York City; 15 Sept.-1 Oct. 1995; Dir.— Elizabeth LeCompte.

E188 *The Emperor Jones* The Wooster Group; Performing Garage; New York City; Mar. 1998; Dir.— Elizabeth LeCompte.

Brustein, Robert. Rev. *New Republic* 27 Apr. 1998: 28-30.

Frank, Glenda. Rev. *Back Stage* 13 Mar. 1998: n. pag.

MacLean, Robert Simpson. Rev. *Eugene O'Neill Review* 22.1-2 (1998): 213-16.

Dancing, electronic props "in great abundance" (television screens, actors with mikes, amplified voices), white women in "crude blackface," Jones presented as "an oreo cookie." Enough said.

E189 *The First Man* Stage Left, Inc.; New Vic Theatre; 2nd Ave. and 14th St.; New York City; 10-28 Oct. 1984; Dir.— Ray Hubener.

Vena, Gary. Rev. *Eugene O'Neill Newsletter* 8.3 (1984): 28-29.

A "fledgling company" and its "youngish actors" attempt a fledgling play by a youngish playwright with predictable results.

E190 *Four Plays of the Sea (S.S. Glencairn — Caribbees, Cardiff, Voyage, Zone)* Just So Productions; San Francisco, CA; 27 Apr.-17 June 1988; Dir.— Michael Cawelti with Marc Bruno.

Mason, Jeffrey D. Rev. *Eugene O'Neill Newsletter* 12.2 (1988): 79-80.

Caribbees, *Cardiff*, *Voyage*, and *Zone*, staged aboard the schooner C.A. Thayer, are "daring and faithful" to the playwright's vision, "a sterling example of San Francisco theatre and a sincere tribute to O'Neill." Of the four one-acts in production, *Caribbees* proved to be the weakest.

E191 *The Great God Brown* Phoenix Repertory Company; 149 W. 45th St.; The Lyceum Theater; New York City; Opened 10 Dec. 1972 for 19 performances; Dir. Harold Prince; Scenery — Boris Aronson; Costuming & Masks — Carolyn Parker; Lighting — Tharon Musser; William Brown — John Glover; Mrs. Brown — Bonnie Gallup; Mr. Brown — Paul Hecht; Dion Anthony — John McMartin; Mrs. Anthony — Charlotte Moore; Mr. Anthony — James Greene; Margaret — Katherine Helmond; Cybel — Marilyn Sokol; Older Son — Robert Phelps; Younger Son — Thomas A. Stewart; Older Draftsman — Bill Moor; Younger Oraftsman — Clyde Burton; Committee — David Dukes/Peter Friedman/Ellen Tovatt; Policeman — Curt Karabalis.

Clurman, Harold. Theatre. *Nation* 1 Jan. 1973: 28-29.

"Though a rather confusing play," it has a certain staying power. It's about "personal torment" that, however, "acquires an extension in social meaning." The fault with this production is that "Brown's centrality in the play has not been realized." The characters lack dimension or depth so that the theme and conflict have been trivialized. Still, O'Neill's voice is not entirely lost.

E192 *The Great God Brown* Germinal Theatre; Denver, CO; Fall 1977; Dir.— E. Baierlein.

MacKay, Brenda. Rev. *New York Theatre Review* Dec. 1977: 32.

E193 *The Great God Brown* Laurie Theatre; Brandeis University; Waltham, MA; 11-15 Apr. 1984; Dir.—David Wheeler; Billy Brown—Christopher Scheithe; Margaret—Gayle Keller; Billy's Mask—Bump Heeter; Dion's Mask—Norm Silver.

E194 *The Great God Brown* Department of Theatre; SUNY-Albany; Albany, NY; 20-23 Nov. 1985; Dir.—Jarka Burian.

E195 *The Great God Brown* **(staged reading)** Yale School of Drama; Monte Cristo Cottage; New London, CT; 14 Apr. 1988; Dir.—David DeRose.

E196 *The Great God Brown* California State University; Hayward, CA; 17-26 Nov. 1988.

E197 *The Great God Brown* Wesleyan University; Middletown, CT; 14-16 Nov. 1991; Dir.—Howard Fishman.

E198 *The Great God Brown* Abe Burrows Theatre; Tisch School for the Arts; New York University; New York City; 10-19 Dec. 1991; Dir.—Marcus Stern.

E199 *The Great God Brown* Chain Lightning Theatre Company at One Dream Theatre; New York City; 17 Feb.-16 Mar. 1997.

Frank, Glenda. Rev. *Back Stage* 7 Mar. 1997: 38.

E200 *The Hairy Ape* with *Ile* and *Voyage* Morgan's Bar; 134 Reade Street; New York City; Jan. 1976. With J.R. Horne, John Michaiski, Judith Gero, Robert Boardman, Ryan Kelley, Peter Jolly, Dan Emerich, Melissa Sutherland, Mary Shortkroff, Michael Zuckerman

Gussow, Mel. Rev. *New York Times* 14 Jan. 1976: 17:4.

Voyage is played with the bar at Morgan's used as the central prop. The plays are introduced by sea chanties.

E201 *The Hairy Ape* Impossible Ragtime Theater; (off off Broadway); New York City; 10 Jan. 1976; Artistic Dirs.—Ted Story and George Ferencz; Dir.—George Ferencz; Environment—Ron Daley and George Ferencz; Lighting—John Gisondi; Parasite—Pattie Baker; Jail Guard—Louis Braunstein; Paddy—Richard Carballo; Political Prisoner—Spencer Cohen; Mildred's Aunt—Cynthia Crane; Secretary I.W.W.—Greg Fabian; Parasite—Margaret Flanagan; Second Engineer—Jonathan Foster; Lang—Jonathan Frakes; Cop—Drew Keil; Mildred Douglas—

Annette Kurek; Parasite—Karen L. Pontius; Parasite—Kristen Richards; Yank—Ray Wise; Fourth Engineer—Stephen Zuckerman.

Rich, Alan. Rev. *New York* 15 Mar. 1976: 75.

The play is a bad one: what's its point—"rich is bad and poor is good? An ignorant brute is a happy brute?" Nonetheless, Ragtime Theater and George Ferencz produced O'Neill "agreeably" and "intelligently."

E202 *The Hairy Ape* Hanover College Theatre; of Indiana at Tao House; Danville, CA; July 1976; Staged by Tom G. Evans; Yank—Jim Baird.

Wilkins, Frederick C. Rev. *Eugene O'Neill Newsletter* 1.3 (1978): 19-20.

Tao House's first play: "an auspicious debut." "The play was simply mounted in a rebar iron cage which could quickly change its contours as needed to become" the different settings: "at the end of each scene, the actors dropped their roles, changed the shape of the cage, and then, at a signal, recommenced the play."

E203 *The Hairy Ape* Hopkins Center; Dartmouth College; Hanover, NH; 8-29 Aug. 1979; Dir.—Michael Rutenberg.

Wilkins, Frederick C. Rev. *Eugene O'Neill Newsletter* 3.3 (1980): 9-10.

Paddy's "lengthy Scene-One aria" is "uttered to harmonica accompaniment with all action temporarily frozen around him"; Yank's ejection from the IWW headquarters (scene 7) is done in slow motion; other bits—all combine to make a "memorable production."

E204 *The Hairy Ape* Studio Theatre Production; Washington Square; New York University; New York City; 16-26 June 1982; Dirs.—Rob Mulholland and Harold Easton.

Wilkins, Frederick C. Rev. *Eugene O'Neill Newsletter* 6.2 (1982): 47-49.

As usual, Professor Wilkins finds something good to say about the production ("thought-provoking"), but when the problems are in the staging and in the language ("Take the language—please!"), it's a strain to be positive.

E205 *The Hairy Ape* 725 Broadway Theatre; New York City; 27 Oct.-5 Nov. 1983.

E206 *The Hairy Ape* Strider Theater, Runnels Union; Colby College; Waterville, ME; 7-9 Feb. 1985; Dir.—Susan Perry.

E207 *The Hairy Ape* Wilma Theatre; Philadelphia, PA; 12 Mar.-21 Apr. 1985; Dir.—Blanka Zizka.

E208 *The Hairy Ape* Nelke Theatre; Brigham Young University; Provo, Utah; 19-21 Mar. 1987; Dir.—Nathan Criman.

E209 *The Hairy Ape* American Blues Theatre; Bailiwick Theatre; Chicago, IL; July 1987; Dir.—William Payne.

E210 *The Hairy Ape* Pittsburgh Public Theater; Pittsburgh, PA; Fall 1987; Dir.—George Ferencz.

E211 *The Hairy Ape* Berkeley Repertory Theatre; Berkeley, CA; 5-29 Nov. 1987; Dir.—George Ferencz; Score—Max Roach; Yank—Sam Tsoutsouvas.

E212 *The Hairy Ape* Theater-Studio; 750 8th Ave.; New York City; 23 Jan.-1 Feb. 1988; Dir.—A. M. Raychel.

E213 *The Hairy Ape* William Redfield Theater; New York City; 7-22 Oct. 1988; Dir.—Anthony DiPietro.

E214 *The Hairy Ape* Mainstage, Alumni Hall; Western Maryland College; Westminster, MD; 3 Mar. 1989; Dir.—Ronald Miller; Costumes—Steven Miller; Set Design—Ira Domser.

Stevens, Ray. Rev. *Eugene O'Neill Review* 13.1 (1989): 70-72

Miller's direction was "eclectic in style, combining traditional elements of Greek choric drama, expressionistic devices common in the early '20s, and stylistic elements suggestive of William Butler Yeats' experiments with ritual drama" ... and relied upon contrasts, some suggested by the playwright, others directorial innovation. Ultimately the interpretation proved effective.

E215 *The Hairy Ape* Theatre 22; New York City; 1-18 Aug. 1991; Dir.—S. Armus.

E216 *The Hairy Ape* La Jolla Playhouse; San Diego, CA; 13 July-22 Aug. 1993; Dir.—Matthew Wilder; Design—Robert Brill; Lights—David S. Thayer; Yank—Mario Arrambide; Paddy—Jan Triska; Long—Mark Harelik; Mildred Douglas—Micha Espinosa.

Hanson, Eugene Kenneth. Rev. *Eugene O'Neill Review* 17.1-2 (1993): 169-73.

Gives high marks to this production due largely to the direction. Among Wilder's innovations was the substitution of a naked man as the hairy ape in the last scene, an innovation that rescues the play from a comedic finish.

E217 *The Hairy Ape* Globe Theatre; San Diego, CA; Summer 1993.

E218 *The Hairy Ape* Odyssey Theatre Ensemble; Los Angeles, CA; Oct.-19 Dec. 1993; Dir.—Michael Arabian.

E219 *The Hairy Ape* The Wooster Group; Performing Garage; SoHo; New York City; 29 Nov.-17 Dec. 1995; Dir.—Elizabeth LeCompte; Design—Jim Clayburgh; Yank—Willem Dafoe; Mildred—Kate Valk; Her Aunt—Peyton Smith; again in 1996 then again at Selwyn Theatre New York City; 21 Mar.-25 May 1997.

Brustein, Robert. Rev. *New Republic* 12 May 1997: 19-21.

MacLean, Robert S. Rev. *Eugene O'Neill Review* 21.1-2 (1997): 175.

At the Group's Performing Garage in Soho in 1995 and 1996, this production deserved high praise. In its current and more impersonal location (Selwyn Theatre), it loses much.

E220 *Hughie* Lolly's Theater Club; (off off Broadway); New York City; 9 Aug. 1973.

E221 *Hughie* American Theatre Company; (off off Broadway); New York City; 9 Nov. 1973.

E222 *Hughie* Chicago-at-the-First; Chicago Center; Chicago, IL; Opened in Apr. 1974; Then John Golden Theatre; New York City; Opened 11 Feb. 1975; Presented by Jay Julien and Sidney Eden; Dir.—Martin Fried; Setting—James E. Maronek; Lighting—Bengt Nygren; Night Clerk—Peter Maloney; Erie Smith—Ben Gazzara.

Anon. Rev. *New York* 3 Mar. 1975: 64-65.

Thinks of *Hughie* as an unfinished work, and if Robards couldn't do much with it, what can Ben Gazzara expect to do.

Barnes, Clive. Stage: "O'Neill's *Hughie*." *New York Times* 9 Apr. 1974: 35.

Reviewing one of the Chicago performances, Barnes finds the play among O'Neill's "finest achievements." Gazzara "is absolutely right for Erie Smith."

_____. "O'Neill's *Hughie* and David Milton's *Duet*." *New York Times* 12 Feb. 1975: 48; *NYTCR* 1975: 355.

"Brief but perfect ... celebrating in lean, even brisk language, the spirit of man's hopeful failure." Enthusiastic over the production in all respects (seems not to sense that the night clerk is anything but a pair of ears).

Beaufort, John. Theater/"Gazzara Duo." *Christian Science Monitor* 21 Feb. 1975; *NYTCR* 1975: 355.

Discusses the themes of loneliness and lost illusions. Gazzara "exposes the hollowness behind the braggadocio." The night clerk is his audience.

Clurman, Harold. Theatre. *Nation* 15 Mar. 1975: 314-15.

Hughie is "one of O'Neill's most admirable small-scale accomplishments." Finds Ben Gazzara "successful in playing ... [Erie] for laughs."

Gill, Brendan. The Theatre. *New Yorker* 24 Feb. 1975: 95.

Notes that without the background film and sound track we miss the important "bitter humor" that the hotel clerk's own fantasies are just "as vivid as Smith's and even more pitiful."

Gottfried, Martin. Theater/"Gazzara Revives O'Neill." *New York Post* 12 Feb. 1975; *NYTCR* 1975: 354.

The play is "second-rate," rambles, but ends touchingly. Erie is a "slight variation on Hickey."

Hughes, Catharine. "Revival of (some of) the Fittest." *America* 22 Mar. 1975: 219-20.

The play is "distinctly second drawer," Hughie a "one-dimensional" character.

Kerr, Walter. "Looking into O'Neill's Mirror in *Hughie*." *New York Times* 23 Feb. 1975, sec. 2: 1.

Hughie is really a mirror—"a pair of credulous eyes." Erie creates a new Hughie out of the Nightclerk.

Morrow, Lance. "The Uses of Illusion." *Time* 22 Apr. 1974; *NYTCR* 1974: 356.

Gazzara plays Erie "superbly."

Probst, Leonard. NBC-Radio. 11 Feb. 1975; *NYTCR* 1975: 357.

Gazzara lacks "the depth to penetrate Hughie," is "leaden and monotonous."

Sanders, Kevin. WABC-TV. 11 Feb. 1975; *NYTCR* 1975: 357.

"A very good example of very bad O'Neill." Erie is "another one of O'Neill's relentlessly boring drunks, who tells his "desolately dull story." The play is a "long, rambling harangue," "has no context to give it resonance, no layers to give it depth." "Gazzara tries his best" but....

Thompson, Howard. "O'Neill's *Hughie* is Star Gazzara." *New York Times* 18 Aug. 1974: 40.

An announcement (erroneous) that *Hughie* is scheduled to open at the Booth Theater, New York City, 15 Oct., starring Ben Gazzara, in his first stage appearance in the city since 1963, when he played in the Actors Studio revival of *Interlude*. Gazzara, interviewed by phone, finds Erie Smith, despite his losing streak, "a prince of a man, brave in the face of defeat, and the play, unlike a lot of O'Neill, does end on a note of hope."

Watt, Douglas. "Gazzara Shines in Slim Twin Bill." *Daily News* 12 Feb. 1975; *NYTCR* 1975: 354.

Sometimes funny but "hardly seems worth the effort." The night clerk is a "sounding board" for Erie, who is "a character in search of a play."

E223 *Hughie* No Smoking Playhouse; 354 45th St.; New York City; Dec. 1978; Dir.—Frank Girardeau.

E224 *Hughie* Old Creamery Theatre Company; Garrison, IA; 7-8 Dec. 1979.

E225 *Hughie* Hudson Guild Theatre; (off off Broadway); 441 W. 26th St.; New York City; 14 Jan.-5 Feb. 1980; Dir.—David Kerry Heefner.

E226 *Hughie* National Theatre; Cottesloe; London; 22 Jan.-Apr. 1980; Dir.—Bill Bryden; Design—Hayden Griffen; Lighting—Andy Phillips; Erie Smith—Stacy Keach; Night Clerk—Howard Goorney.

Gow, Gordon. Rev. *Plays and Players* 275 (1980): 22-23.

Speaks well of the play and of the production. Keach is "gripping" as Erie Smith. Observes that Charles Hughes goes "off into imaginative flights of his own," but doesn't say how the audience could know.

Taylor, John Russell. "London." *Drama: The Quarterly Theatre Review* 136 (1980): 37-48.

Finds Stacy Keach a "formidable actor" who needs "something more substantial ... to stretch his powers." The play is "not very complex" but "quite clever."

E227 *Hughie* Studio Theatre Production; Washington Square; New York University; New York City; 27-30 Jan. 1980; Dir.—Rob Mulholland.

E228 *Hughie* Black Swan Theatre; Oregon Shakespearean Festival; Ashland, OR; July-Sept. 1980.

E229 *Hughie* Great Lakes Shakespeare Festival; Lakewood Civic Auditorium; Cleveland, OH; 7, 9-10, 15, 20 Aug. and 4, 7 Sept. 1980.

E230 *Hughie* Hyde Park Festival Theater; Hyde Park, NY; 17-21 June 1981; Later White Barn Theater; Westport, CT; 16-18 Oct. 1981; Erie Smith — Jason Robards; Night Clerk — Jack Dodson.

E231 *Hughie* **double-billed with** *The Stranger* South Street Theater; 424 W. 42nd St.; (off off Broadway); New York City; 4 Nov.-6 Dec. 1981; Dir.— Gino Giglio; Setting — Bob Phillips; Lighting — Malcolm Sturchio; Sound — Amy Steindler; Erie Smith — Michael Fischetti; Night Clerk — Frank Geraci.

Gussow, Mel. Rev. *New York Times* 1 Jan. 1982: 15.

Finds Michael Fischetti's Erie Smith particularly effective. Nightclerk Frank Geraci is good as well. Giglio's direction is "resourceful."

E232 *Hughie* **double-billed with** *Caribbees* Studio Theatre Productions; Washington Square; New York University; New York City; 26-30 Jan. 1982; Dirs.— Rob Mulholland and Harold Easton.

E233 *Hughie* American Repertory Theatre; Cambridge, MA; 7 Apr.-6 May 1983; Dir.— Bill Foeller; Erie Smith — John Bottoms; Night Clerk — Richard Spore.

Connolly, Thomas F. Rev. *Eugene O'Neill Newsletter* 7.1 (1983): 20-21.

"Neither the director nor the actors succeeded completely in making the transition from separateness to communion wholly believable."

E234 *Hughie* One Act Theatre Company; San Francisco, CA; 23 Mar.-5 May 1984; Dir.— Tom McDermott.

E235 *Hughie* Provincetown Playhouse; Provincetown, MA; 20-21 Sept. 1984; Dir.— John MacDonald; Erie Smith — Stephen Joyce; Night Clerk — Robert Zukerman.

E236 *Hughie* East West Players (Second Stage); Los Angeles, CA; 11-21 June 1987.

E237 *Hughie* '92 Theater; Wesleyan University; Middletown, CT; 17-19 Mar. 1988 and; Meetinghouse; Chester, CT; 24-26 Mar. 1988; Dir.— Peter Loffredo.

E238 *Hughie* Long Island Stage Company; Hempstead, NY; 19 Apr.-8 May 1988.

E239 *Hughie* **with** *Breakfast* South Street Theater; 424 W. 42nd Street; New York City; Opened 17 May 1988.

E240 *Hughie* Germinal Stage; Denver, CO; 12 May-12 June 1988; Dir.— Ed Baierlein.

E241 *Hughie* Eugene O'Neill Theatre Festival (CA); Nanjing, PRC; June 1988.

E242 *Hughie* The Belfry Theatre; Victoria, BC; 1-17 Dec. 1988; Dir.— Alex Diakun; Set Design — Ted Roberts; Lighting — Marsha Sipthorpe; Costuming — Christine Thomson; Clerk — Tom McBeath; Erie Smith — Stuart Margolin.

Black, Stephen A. Rev. *Eugene O'Neill Review* 13.1 (1989): 74-76.

This play, coupled in production as it was with Gogol's *The Gamblers* and the resulting bill called *Snake Eyes*, "went very well." Margolin in particular supplied the production with an excellent Erie.

E243 *Hughie* Lunchtime Performances; Peacock Theatre; Dublin; 18-21 July 1989; Dir.— Ms. Friel; Erie Smith — O.Z. Whitehead; Night Clerk — Gerard McSorley.

E244 *Hughie* Apple Corps Theater; New York City; 7-30 Apr. 1989; Dir.— Susan Flakes.

E245 *Hughie* Trinity Repertory Theatre; Providence, RI; 12-22 Aug. 1993; Erie Smith — Jason Robards; Night Clerk — Jack Dodson.

E246 *Hughie* **with** *Breakfast, Recklessness,* **and** *Web* Playtime Series 59; Theater-Studio; 750 Eighth Avenue at 46th Street; New York City; 16-21 Sept. 1995; Dir.— A.M. Raychel.

E247 *Hughie* Long Wharf Theatre [Revived Los Angeles, 1999 q.v]; New Haven, CT; 2-21 July 1996; Dir.— Al Pacino; Costuming — Candice Donnelly; Erie Smith — Al Pacino; Night Clerk — Paul Benedict.

Canby, Vincent. Rev. *New York Times* 23 Aug. 1996, sec. C: 1, 20.

"Plays like a footnote" to *Iceman*. "The word 'pipe dream' is never used, but pipe dreams are the subject." Of Pacino's performance, "Bravo!"

Garvey, Sheila Hickey. Rev. *Eugene O'Neill Review* 20.1-2 (1996): 173-78.

Examines the set, costumes, and casting of this production and looks to earlier successes (with Robards, with Gazzarra) to conclude this one measures up. "One has to conclude if actors of the caliber of Jason Robards, Ben Gazzara and Al Pacino have found *Hughie* an acting challenge, then this brief and compact piece has many fascinating worlds in it worthy of continued exploration."

McLean, Robert Simpson. Rev. *Eugene O'Neill Review* 20.1-2 (1996): 178-80.

Heaps high praise on this production, calling it "wonderful," and on Pacino in particular for his insight into the play and character of Erie. But most noteworthy is the "harmonious integration of theatrical crafts."

Nemsers, Cindy. "Critical Decisions: Theaters vs. Reviewers." *Theater Week* 7 Oct. 1996: 34-37.

Steyn, Mark. "Beckett and the Broadway Playwright." *New Criterion* 15 Oct. 1996: 41-45.

While Circle in the Square was declaring bankruptcy and cancelling its 1996-97 season, the summer filler was playing to packed houses. The reason is Al Pacino's production of *Hughie*, which provided the audience with "a full, absorbing, immensely satisfying evening." Pacino's performance comes as a refreshing change after his less-than-impressive appearance in recent movies. As Erie Smith, the actor "pulls off a rare feat ... he shrinks the room." As director of the production Pacino blunders, though, in opting to put Charlie's lines through the reverb chamber on the sound system.

E248 *Hughie* Mark Taper Forum [Revival of 1996 New York production]; Los Angeles, CA; 23 June-25 July 1999; Dir.—Al Pacino; Erie Smith—Al Pacino; Night Clerk—Paul Benedict.

E249 *The Iceman Cometh* Circle in the Square/Joseph E. Levine Theatre; Preview 9 Dec. 1973; Opened 13 Dec. 1973 for 85 performances; Dir.—Theodore Mann; Set—Clarke Ducham; Lighting—Jules Fisher; Rocky Pioggi—Joseph Ragora; Larry Slade—Michael Higgins; Hugo Kalmar—David Margulies; Willie Oban—Walter McGinn; Harry Hope—Stefan Gierasch; Joe Mott—Arthur French; Don Parritt—Stephen McHattie; Cecil Lewis—Jack Gwillim; Piet Wetjoen—George Ebeling; James Cameron—Tom Aldredge; Pat McGloin—Rex Everhart; Ed Mosher—Patrick Hines; Margie—Marcia Savella; Pearl—Jennie O'Hara; Cora—Lois Smith; Chuck Morello—Pierrino Mascarino; Theodore Hickman (Hickey)—James Earl Jones; Moran—Gene Fanning; Lieb—Ronald Siebert.

Anon. Rev. *New York* 31 Dec.-7 Jan. 1974: 84.

Finds the set and costumes "fine," the lighting "good." The blocking "works." But the cast is indifferent in ability, inadequate in interpretation, and undistinguished—except for James Earl Jones, who as Hickey, is "impossible."

Barnes, Clive. Rev. *New York Times* 14 Dec. 1973: 54.

Mann's direction is "careful, reverent but lacks something in immediacy." James Earl Jones as Hickey "was all right but all wrong": seemed as if he were "selling insurance rather than dreams."

Clurman, Harold. Theatre. *Nation* 5 Jan. 1974: 29-30

It is the ambiguity of *Iceman* that holds the viewer's attention.

Gill, Brendan. "Stars in Your Eyes." *New Yorker* 24 Dec. 1973: 56.

The production risks odious comparison with the 1956 "Circle" production and the American Film Theatre version.

Gottfried, Martin. The Theatre/"*The Iceman Cometh.*" *Women's Wear Daily* 14 Dec. 1973; *NYTCR* 1973: 149-50.

The play is technically a "mess," and too long for its needs, the production badly directed and Jones inadequate as Hickey.

Holder, Geoffrey. Rev. NBC-TV. 13 Dec. 1973; *NYTCR* 1973: 151.

The play is "great ... where everyone suffers ... and you suffer with them." Jones is "brilliant and inspired." Higgins is "haunting and penetrating."

Kalem, T. E. "Agon of the Sad Cafe." *Time* 24 Dec. 1973: 57.

The actors, with the exception of Jones, are like puppets. Jones's performance is "disconcertingly and divisively strong."

Kerr, Walter. "The *Iceman* Is Absent Too Much." *New York Times* 23 Dec. 1973, sec. 2: 3.

Enthusiastic about Jones's Hickey, but finds that there are vast portions of the play which must simply be "endured," especially the segments without Jones. The play should however be seen.

Kroll, Jack. Theater. *Newsweek* 31 Dec. 1973; *NYTCR* 1973: 150.

A play one either loves or doesn't. Kroll loves it, but finds Jones ineffective as Hickey.

Simon, John. "Theatre Chronicle." *Hudson Review* 27 (1974): 82-90.

Director Mann either chose poor actors or miscast good ones. Jones as Hickey is implausible.

Watt, Douglas. "O'Neill's *Iceman*: A Spellbinder." *Daily News* 14 Dec. 1973; *NYTCR* 1973: 148.

"Enthralling play," "absorbing revival," a "spellbinder."

Watts, Richard. Theater/"O'Neill's Defense of Illusions." *New York Post* 14 Dec. 1973; *NYTCR* 1973: 148.

Ranks this play as "only slightly beneath those other masterpieces," *Journey* and *Mourning*. Jones is not up to his standard.

Wilson, Edwin. The Theater/"Harry Hope's Hopeless Bar." *Wall Street Journal* 21 Dec. 1973; *NYTCR* 1973: 149.

Mostly kudos for Jones.

E250 ***The Iceman Cometh*** Aldwych Theatre; Royal Shakespeare Company; London; Opened 18 June 1976; Dir.— Howard Davies; Design— Chris Dyer; Lighting— David Hersey; Harry Hope— Norman Rodway; Ed Mosher— Harry Towb; Pat McGloin— Raymond Marlowe; Rocky— Bob Hoskins; Chuck— David Daker; Piet Wetjoen— Hal Galili; Cecil Lewis— Richard Simpson; Jimmy Tomorrow— John Warner; Joe Mott— Cy Grant; Larry Slade— Patrick Stewart; Hugo Kalmar— Patrick Godfrey; Willie Oban— Gary Bond; Don Parritt— Kenneth Cranham; Pearl— Patti Love; Margie— Paola Dionisotti; Cora— Lynda Marchal; Hickey— Alan Tilvern; Moran— Larry Hoodekoff; Lieb— Karl Held.

Gussow, Mel. "Stage View." *New York Times* 18 July 1976, sec. 5:1.

London reviews were enthusiastic but anyone who has seen Robards' Hickey will be dissatisfied. Alan Tilvern "falls far short of encompassing" Hickey's character. The others in the cast are not effective.

Lambert, J. W. Rev. *Drama: The Quarterly Theatre Review* 122 (1976): 51-53.

Well done but not well enough to dispel irritation with O'Neill's repetitiveness. Tilvern as Hickey, "the most desperate of hollow men," "looked strangely like a rough-diamonded Nixon."

Mairowitz, David Zane. "*The Iceman Cometh*." *Plays and Players* 23 (1976): 17.

The play is a "masterpiece despite great structural flaws and a second-rate 'philosophy.'" But the production is timid, doing nothing to overcome the flaws, and so the play "lumbers and wallows."

Wardle, Irving. Rev. *Times* 21 June 1976: 13d.

Sees *Iceman* as O'Neill's transition play standing between two phases of O'Neill's dramatic career, the early, secretly autobiographical plays, like *Dynamo, Brown*, and the later, after O'Neill "came out into the open" with *Journey*. Notes that the theme, "that mankind in general are kept going by their dreams" is Ibsen's, in *The Wild Duck*, but O'Neill blurs the theme's universality by placing it in the "context of alcoholic futility." The production is "altogether a rich extension" to the Royal Shakespeare Company repertory.

E251 ***The Iceman Cometh*** Loretto-Hilton Repertory Theatre; St. Louis, MO; 13 Oct.-11 Nov. 1978; Dir.— Davey Marlin-Jones.

E252 ***The Iceman Cometh*** National Theater; Cottesloe; London; Opened Mar. 1980; Dir.— Bill Bryden; Design— Hayden Griffin; Music— John Tams; Hickey— Jack Shepherd/Robert Stephens; Rocky Pioggi— John Satthouse; Larry Slade— Niall Toibin; Hugo Kalmar— Tony Haygarth; Willie Oban— James Grant; Harry Hope— JG Devlin; Joe Mott— Oscar James; Don Parritt— Kevin McNally; Cecil Lewis— Frederick Treves; Piet Wetjoen— Jeffrey G. Chiswick; James Cameron— Gawn Grainger; McGloin— Brian Glover; Margie— Edna Dore; Pearl— Ann Lynn; Ed Mosher— Derek Newark; Cora— Morag Hood; Morello— Brian Protheroe; Moran— John Tams; Lieb— Elliott Cooper & Anthony Falkingham.

Hayman, Ronald. Rev. *Plays and Players* 27.6 (1980): 23.

Generally unenthusiastic. The production was awkwardly conceived and Hickey badly cast. The handling of the large number of people on stage was inept.

Taylor, H. Hobson, Jr. Rev. *Drama: The Quarterly Theatre Review* 135 (1980): 35-36.

The production refreshes, strengthens, and fills one with the "high tragic significance of life." Admittedly O'Neill's phrases are "lame," "pretentious," and "repetitive," but the play ranks with *Othello* and the *Agamemnon*. Hickey's scene is like the Last Supper with Hickey "a destructive Christ rendering through an equivocal gospel sordid misery into a yet more miserable sordidness."

E253 ***The Iceman Cometh*** New Theater; (Hasty Pudding Playhouse); Holyoke St.; Cambridge, MA; 10-27 Apr. 1980; Dir.— Larry McCarthy.

E254 *The Iceman Cometh* Trinity Square Repertory Company; Providence, RI; 30 Jan.-29 Feb. 1981; Dir.—Philip Minor.

Wilkins, Frederick C. Rev. *Eugene O'Neill Newsletter* 5.1(1981): 15-17.

Observes: "Not that the production uncovered new truths about, or highlighted new revelations in, O'Neill's play," but still is strongly positive about the production.

E255 *The Iceman Cometh* Sea View Playwrights' Theatre; Staten Island, NY; 29 Sept.-2 Oct. 1983.

E256 *The Iceman Cometh* American National Theater; Eisenhower Theater; Kennedy Center; Washington, DC; 31 July-14 Sept. 1985; Then Lunt-Fontanne Theatre; Broadway; New York City; 21-29 Sept. 1985; Dir.—José Quintero; Scenery—Ben Edwards; Costuming—Jane Greenwood; Prods.—Lewis Allen, James Nederlander,; Stephen Orchard, Ben Edwards; Hickey—Jason Robards; Larry Slade—Donald Moffat; Harry Hope—Barnard Hughes; Rocky Pioggi—John Pankow; Joe Mott—Roger Robinson; Chuck Morello—Harris Laskawy; Margie—Natalie Nogulich; Don Parritt—Paul McCrane; Gen. Wetjoen—Frederick Neumann; Cora—Caroline Aaron; Willie Oban—John Christopher Jones; Hugo Kalmar—Leonard Cimini; Pat McGloin—Pat McNamara; Ed Mosher—Allen Swift; Cecil Lewis—Bill Moor; Pearl—Kristine Nielsen; Jimmy Tomorrow—James Greene.

Brown, Joe. "*The Iceman Cometh* Again." *Washington Post* Weekend 16 Aug. 1985: 7.

The cast is "excellent." Robards' 30-minute monologue is a "tour de force." Ben Edwards' set suggests a "patina of neglect." The play, itself, is as "monumental (and slow-going) as a glacier."

Brustein, Robert. "On Theatre: Souls on Ice." *New Republic* 28 Oct. 1985: 41-43.

"The play resonates." "Fine cast." Wishes "that Quintero had been a little bolder in his approach." "The productions is a re-tread of the one staged in 1956, as if nothing had happened to the theatre in 30 years."

Henry, William A., III. "Recreating a Stage Legend." *Time* 14 Oct. 1985: 75.

The Quintero-Robards revival of *Iceman*, 28 years after the 1956 Quintero-Robards *Iceman*, is a "triumph," thanks to a "superb cast."

Wilkins, Frederick C. "Family Reunion at the Bottom of the Sea." *Eugene O'Neill Newsletter* 9.3 (1985): 23-28.

Ensemble is "superb"; Robards reprised his role of Hickey "brilliantly." Of Quintero and Robards: "I doubt that we shall see their like again."

E257 *The Iceman Cometh* [Washington-New York production]; Doolittle Theatre; Los Angeles, CA; 12 Feb.-9 Mar. 1986; Dir.—José Quintero; Hickey—Jason Robards.

E258 *The Iceman Cometh* Oregon Shakespearean Festival; Ashland, OR; 29 July-19 Oct. 1988 (in repertory); Dir.—Jerry Turner; Costuming—Jeannie Davidson; Lighting—James Sale; Set—John Dexter; Music—Todd Barton; Hickey—Paul Vincent O'Connor (replacing Denis Arndt); Larry Slade—Richard Elmore; Ed Mosher—Philip Davidson; Don Parritt—Larry Paulsen; Jimmy Tomorrow—Douglas Markkanen; Joe Mott—J.P. Phillips.

Black, Stephen A. Rev. *Eugene O'Neill Newsletter* 12.3 (1988): 51-52.

"The Ashland Festival *Iceman* came close enough to being excellent for its flaws to aggravate more than they might in a mediocre performance." Among those flaws were a falling off in momentum in medias res and a badly miscast Parritt.

E259 *The Iceman Cometh* Goodman Theatre; Chicago, IL; 4 Sept.-3 Nov. 1990; Dir.—Robert Falls; Hickey—Brian Dennehy; Harry Hope—Jerome Kilty; Larry Slade—James Cromwell.

E260 *The Iceman Cometh* Germinal Stage; Denver, CO; Feb. 1992; Dir.—Ed Baierlein; Hickey—Richard Lyons; Larry Slade—Ed Baierlein; Harry Hope—Stephen R. Kramer; Hugo Kalmar—John Seifert; Piet Wetjoen—Douglas White; Joe Mott—Erik Brodnax; Rocky Pioggi—Joseph Abramo; Chuck Morello—Michael Vernard-Winn; Cecil Lewis—James Mills; Jimmy Tomorrow—John Fortin; Willie Oban—Eric Field.

Zeiger, E. James. Rev. *Eugene O'Neill Review* 16.1 (1992): 111-15.

Calling the production "accurate and effective," a "qualified success," Zeiger pointed to its unevenness. While some interpretations of character were highly credible, even brilliant, others missed the mark. The inaudibility of characters' lines and the small stage were also problematic.

E261 *The Iceman Cometh* Abbey Theatre; Dublin; Oct.-7 Nov. 1992; Hickey—Brian Dennehy; Larry Slade—Donald Moffat.

E262 *The Iceman Cometh* Long Wharf Theatre; New Haven, CT; 17 May-26 June 1994; Dir.—Arvin Brown; Hickey—Al Pacino.

E263 *The Iceman Cometh* Almeida Theatre; London; [Revived in New York City in 1999, see E264]; 2 Apr.-23 May 1998; Dir.—Howard Davies; Hickey—Kevin Spacey; Larry Slade—Tim Pigott-Smith.

Berlin, Normand. Rev. *Eugene O'Neill Review* 21.1-2 (1997): 190-98.

Places this production in context and finds that it does not disappoint. "Howard Davies had the most skilled of actors, who allowed him to regulate the mixture of comedy and tragedy, controlling the tempo; in short, orchestrating the whole as Quintero so effectively did in 1956. Things came together beautifully: director, stage designer, English actors, Hollywood star, space, sound."

Lynch, Vivian Valvano. Rev. *Irish Literary Supplement: A Review of Irish Books* 18.2 (1999): 4.

Spacey, as set against Robards, "might just provide the theatre world with another definitive O'Neill interpreter."

Morley, Sheridan. Rev. *International Herald Tribune* 18 Sept. 1998.

"Spacey sees the Iceman as a weird mix of Billy Graham and Willy Loman."

Nightingale, Benedict. Rev. *New York Times* 10 May 1998, sec. 2: 2, 9.

Spacey's Hickey is understated. The ending with its "joyous relief" after Hickey's leaving is "the most original moment in a consistently striking performance."

E264 *The Iceman Cometh* Brooks Atkinson Theater [Revival of London production, see E263]; New York City; Spring 1999.

E265 *Ile* The Quaigh; Quaigh Theater; 808 Lexington Ave. (at 62d St.); Jan. 1976; Dir.—Mary Tierney. With William Hickey, Peter Hadreas, Brian Dennehy, James De Marse, Evelyn Seubert, Jere Allen, Ralf Nemec

E266 *Ile* played with *Voyage* and *Ape* Morgan's Bar; 134 Reade St.; New York City; Jan. 1976.

E267 *Ile* played with *Voyage* Source at the ASTA; 507 8th St. SE; Washington, DC; Aug. 1978; Dir.—Camille David.

E268 *Ile* see *Six Plays of the Sea (Cardiff, Voyage, Zone, Ile, Rope, Cross)*

Apple Corps Theatre Company; New York City; Closed 2 May 1982; Dir.—Skip Corris.

E269 *Ile* see *Sea Plays at Monte Cristo (Cardiff, Voyage, Zone, Ile, Cross, Rope)* "Monte Cristo"; 305 Pequot Ave.; New London, CT; 26 Sept.-14 Nov. 1985.

E270 *Ile* and *In the Zone* Leamy Hall Auditorium; Mohegan Community College; New London, CT; 25-27 Feb. 1988.

E271 *Ile* see *The Sea Plays (Zone, Voyage,* and *Ile)* Rand Theater; University of Massachusetts at Amherst; 20-29 Oct. 1988; Dir.—Edward Golden.

E272 *Ile* and *The Long Voyage Home* Provincetown Repertory Theatre; 1-18 Aug. 1996; Dir.—José Quintero; Olson—Ken Hoyt; Capt. Keeney—Richard Mover; Mrs. Keeney—Alison Crowley; Steward/Fat Joe—William J. Devany; Slocum/Driscoll—Jerry O'Donnell.

Peterson, William M. Rev. *Eugene O'Neill Review* 20.1-2 (1996): 70-72.

"Quintero's direction of this excellent cast endowed the two texts with startling power." Changes that Quintero implemented were lauded as softening the plays' melodrama.

E273 *In the Zone* see *The Sea Plays of Eugene O'Neill* Long Wharf Theater; New Haven, CT; Opened 28 Mar. 1978.

E274 *In the Zone* see *The Long Voyage Home (Caribbees, Cardiff, Zone,* and *Voyage)* National Theatre Company; Cottsloe Theatre; London; 20 Feb. 1979, et al.

E275 *In the Zone* played with *Voyage* Spectrum; 277 Park Ave. South; Spring 1979; Dir.—Norman Morrow.

E276 *In the Zone* Ensemble Company; New Haven, CT; 23-26 July 1980.

E277 *In the Zone* see *Six Plays of the Sea (Cardiff, Voyage, Zone, Ile, Rope, Cross)* Apple Corps Theatre; New York City; Closed 2 May 1982; Dir.—Skip Corris.

E278 *In the Zone* see *Sea Plays at Monte Cristo (Cardiff, Voyage, Zone, Ile, Cross, Rope)* "Monte Cristo"; 305 Pequot Ave.; New London, CT; 26 Sept.-14 Nov. 1985.

E279 *In the Zone* and *Ile* Leamy Hall Auditorium; Mohegan Community College; New London, CT; 25-27 Feb. 1988.

E280 *In the Zone* see *Four Plays of the Sea (S. S. Glencairn)* Just So Productions; San Francisco, CA; 27 Apr.-17 June 1988.

E281 *In the Zone* see *The Sea Plays (Zone, Voyage,* and *Ile)* Rand Theater; University of Massachusetts at Amherst; 20-29 Oct. 1988; Dir.— Edward Golden.

E282 *In the Zone* see *The Sea Plays (Cardiff, Caribbees, Zone,* and *Voyage)* The Willow Cabin Theater Company; Intar II Theater; New York City; 3-20 Nov. 1988.

E283 *Long Day's Journey into Night* National Theatre Company; London; 21 Dec. 1971-8 Jan. 1973 (122 performances in rep.); James Tyrone — Laurence Olivier; Mary — Constance Cummings; Jamie — Dennis Quilley; Edmund — Ronald Pickup.

Clarke, Gerald. Viewpoints. *Time* 12 Mar. 1973: 67-68.

Touches on the background of "America's greatest play." Olivier and Cummings both handle well the contrarities of the characters they play. Quilley and Pickup are adequate.

Gautier, J. J. Rev. *Le Figaro* 14 Sept. 1973: 21.

E284 *Long Day's Journey into Night* (off off Broadway); Actors Studio; New York City; 10 Dec. 1973 for nine performances.

E285 *Long Day's Journey into Night* (off off Broadway); Hudson Guild Theater; New York City; Dec. 1974.

E286 *Long Day's Journey into Night* Thorndike Theatre; London; Winter 1974; Frank Grimes, Trevor Bannister as the brothers Tyrone.

E287 *Long Day's Journey into Night* Kennedy Center; Washington, DC; Then Brooklyn Academy of Music; New York City; 28 Jan.-8 Feb. 1976; Dir.— Jason Robards; Setting — Ben Edwards; Costuming — Jane Greenwood; Lighting — Ken Billington; James Tyrone — Jason Robards; Mary — Zoe Caldwell; Jamie — Kevin Conway; Edmund — Michael Moriarty; Cathleen — Lindsay Crouse.

Barnes, Clive. "Long Day's Journey into Greatness." *New York Times* 29 Jan. 1976: 26; *NYTCR* 1976: 343.

Robards as Tyrone is "unable to reach the pain of the play." The play dawdles under his direction but can survive even bad handling.

Feingold, Michael. "Robards Returns to O'Neill's *Journey*." *New York Times* 25 Jan. 1976, sec. 2: 5.

Journey is the "greatest American play," partly because it is "the least pleasant." Mixed response to the Robards-directed production.

Zoe Caldwell is the best, Robards is competent as Tyrone, but sons Kevin Conway (Jamie) and Michael Moriarty are lacking.

Gottfried, Martin. "An Endless Night in Brooklyn." *New York Post* 29 Jan. 1976; *NYTCR* 1976: 346.

The play overrated, the plotting blurry. Characterization was "heavy except for Zoe Caldwell's Mary."

Gussow, Mel. Rev. *New York Times* 22 Dec. 1975: 44.

Writes on Jason Robards as actor in and director of *Journey*. Robards previously saw the Jamie-Tyrone-Mary trinity as the core of the play. Now he finds Edmund focal.

Kissel, Howard. The Theatre/"*Long Day's Journey into Night*." *Women's Wear Daily* 29 Jan. 1976, *NYTCR* 1976: 345.

American tragedy hinges on the lack of resolution, on the back of any "new wisdom and therefore of the need to accept pain." *Journey* "begins with false hopes and ends with bitter wisdom." This production is "soundly paced and sensitively acted." "Solid, honest, and deeply responsive to the extraordinary riches of the play."

Kroll, Jack. "The Haunted Tyrones." *Newsweek* 9 Feb. 1976: 52-53.

The production, which was originally staged for the Kennedy Center, is "absolute reality." The play entitles O'Neill to "sit in the shade with Sophocles."

Oliver, Edith. "Journey into Brooklyn." *New Yorker* 9 Feb. 1976: 78.

Doesn't find *Journey* a masterpiece, but compliments this production, which Mary dominates.

Probst, Leonard. NBC-Radio. 29 Jan. 1976.

The play is great, although this is not the finest production. Nonetheless, it is a "memorable" one. "Slow to start." Direction is "soft and bland."

Sterrit, David. "Dramatic Star Also Makes Directing Debut." *Christian Science Monitor* 5 Feb. 1976; *NYTCR* 1976: 344.

A "gloomy" play, "difficult to bring off." This production is slack in pace, but Mary looms large.

Tucker, Carl. "O'Neill Explores the Wilderness of Despair." *Village Voice* 9 Feb. 1976: 99.

Journey is boring, obvious, uneventful, goes nowhere, and has a creed of hopelessness, but though an unlikely masterpiece, it is still one.

Watt, Douglas. "A Divided Homefront." *Daily News* 29 Jan. 1976; *NYTCR* 1976: 344.

The play towers, the cast is "stellar" but doesn't quite gel. Zoe Caldwell's Mary is thoughtfully portrayed to emphasize the "spitefulness underlying her sad addiction."

Wertheim, Albert. Rev. *Educational Theatre Journal* 23 (1976): 122-24.

The production turns the play into a character study of Mary and considers her effect on others. Script cuts eliminate the Catholicism and the references to the Virgin Mary and the convent days. The characters' main concern is in curing her. Such "slanting … need not … necessarily do the original disservice."

E288 *Long Day's Journey into Night* Creative Arts Center; West Virginia University; Morgantown, WV; Apr. 1976; Dir.— John Whitmore.

E289 *Long Day's Journey into Night* Ahmanson Theater; Los Angeles, CA; Feb. 1977; Dir.— Robert Fryer; James Tyrone— Charlton Heston; Mary— Debora Kerr; Tyrone sons— Andrew Prine, George Burke.

Flatley, Guy. "At the Movies." *New York Times* 11 Feb. 1977, sec. 3: 9.

Notes that the role of Tyrone is "histrionically taxing, minimally lucrative."

Murray, William. "A Long Day's Journey to the Bar." *New West* 14 Mar. 1977: 19-20.

Calls the cutting of *Journey* "artistic rape." O'Neill was not a slick writer and required time to develop the ideas. Charlton Heston had "gall" to attempt the role of James Tyrone, played by such eminent actors as Olivier and March. Andrew Pine and Robert Burke but "dimly impersonate" the Tyrone boys.

E290 *Long Day's Journey into Night* Shubert Theatre; Boston, MA; 3-5 May 1977; Dir.— Michael Kahn; Tyrone— José Ferrer; Mary— Kate Reid.

E291 *Long Day's Journey into Night* Provincetown Playhouse on the Wharf; Goswold St.; Provincetown, MA; Summer 1977.

E292*Long Day's Journey into Night* **alternating with** *Wilderness* Milwaukee Repertory Theatre Company; Milwaukee, WI; 4 Nov. 1977-22 Jan. 1978; Dir.— Irene Lewis; Design— R.A. Graham; Richard

Miller/Edmund Tyrone— Anthony Heald; Essie/Mary— Regina Davis; Nat/James— Robert Burr; Uncle Sid/Jamie— Ronald Frazer.

E293 *Long Day's Journey into Night* Academy Theatre; Atlanta, GA; 23 Mar.-21 Apr. 1978; on tour 7 Sept.-1 Oct. 1978; Dir.— F. Wittow.

E294 *Long Day's Journey into Night* George St. Playhouse; New Brunswick, NJ; 24 Nov.-16 Dec. 1978.

E295 *Long Day's Journey into Night* American Stanislavski Theatre; Greenwich Mews Theatre; 141 W. 13th St.; New York City; 1 Dec. 1978-21 May 1979; Dir.— Sonia Moore.

E296 *Long Day's Journey into Night* Playmakers Repertory Company; University of North Carolina at Chapel Hill; In rep. 1978-79 Season.

E297 *Long Day's Journey into Night* Cohoes Music Hall; Cohoes, NY; 27 Jan.-8 Feb. 1979; Dir.— L. Ambrosio.

E298 *Long Day's Journey into Night* Haymarket Theatre; Leicester, England; 7-24 Feb. 1979.

E299 *Long Day's Journey into Night* Asolo State Theater; Sarasota, FL; 6 Apr.-12 July 1979; Dir.— Bradford Wallace.

E300 *Long Day's Journey into Night* Queens College Summer Theatre; Flushing, NY; 9-11 Aug. 1979.

E301 *Long Day's Journey into Night* Nassau Repertory; Adelphi Calderone Theater; 22, 23, 29 Feb. and 1, 7, 8, 14, 15Mar. 1980; Dir.— Clinton J. Atkinson; Setting— Kenneth Hollamon; Mary Tyrone— Catherine Byers; James— Patrick Beatey; Jamie— Brian Evers; Edmund— Mark Arnott; Cathleen— Nancy Elizabeth Kammer.

Klein, Alvin. "Theater in Review." *New York Times* 2 Mar. 1980, sec. 21: 4-5.

The staging is "fragmented"; the production lacks a "sense of momentum." There is "no tragic fiber." A disservice to O'Neill.

E302 *Long Day's Journey into Night* Avon Theatre, Stratford Festival; Stratford, ONT; In rep. 4 Oct.-8 Nov. 1980; Dir.— Robin Phillips; Setting— Susan Benson; Lighting— Michael J. Whitefield; James Tyrone— William Hutt; Mary— Jessica Tandy; Edmund— Brent Carver; Jamie— Graeme Campbell.

Czarnecki, Mark. "The Reign of Dissension." *Macleans* 20 Oct. 1980: 69.

Journey is "more sauna than play," endured because "overexposure to truth is considered good for the soul." Speaks of the "loving twist of the knife," the "hateprompted hug": the clear exposition of all passions. This production is "not great theatre" but good. Hutt's Tyrone is "a masterful portrait," Carver's Edmund is "suitably tender and poetic," but Jessica Tandy overemphasizes Mary's frailty, and Campbell is miscast — his Jamie too robust.

Wilkins, Frederick C. Rev. *Eugene O'Neill Newsletter* 4.3 (1980): 25-27.

"More a reverie and appreciation than a review." Recounts attempts to recapture the power of the Frederic March-Florence Eldridge *Journey,* which turned Wilkins into an "O'Neill acolyte." He comes closest in this production: principals gave "exemplary performances."

E303 *Long Day's Journey into Night*
Virginia Players; Culbreth Theatre; University of Virginia; Charlottesville, VA; 5-13 Dec. 1980; Dir.— Jay E. Raphael.

E304 *Long Day's Journey into Night*
Apple Corps Theatre Company; New York City; 8 Jan.-1 Feb. 1981 Dir.— David O. Glazer.

E305 *Long Day's Journey into Night*
Richard Allen Center for Culture & Art; Common Theater, St. Peter's Church; Then the Public/Anspacher Theatre (Presented by Joseph Papp); New York City; 8 Mar. 1981 (for 87 performances); Dir.— Geraldine Fitzgerald; Set — Paul Scheffler; Lighting — John Matthiessen; James Tyrone — Earle Hyman; Jamie — Al Freeman, Jr.; Mary — Gloria Foster; Edmund — Peter Francis-James; Cathleen — Samantha McKoy.

Barnes, Clive. "*Long Day's Journey into Night.*" *New York Post* 4 Mar. 1981; *NYTCR* 1981: 270-71.

Sees the long day as the "watershed" in the Tyrones' family life.

Brooks, Marshall. Rev. *Eugene O'Neill Newsletter* 5.1 (1981): 10-12.

"Fine cast and intelligent director" helped render this production "exciting."

Gussow, Mel. Theater/"Black Cast Stages O'Neill." *New York Times* 3 Mar. 1981 *NYTCR* 1981: 271-72.

The production presents not a "black" but a "non-ethnic" version of *Journey.* All play

their roles well by stressing relationships rather than atmosphere, and prove that blacks can use the play as well as Irish whites.

Kroll, Jack. "Passionate Journey." *Newsweek* 20 Apr. 1981: 104.

This all-black production works. Sees the play as "both epic and tragic ... an emotional *Iliad* ... that produces the great tragic entity of the modern world — waste, pure human waste."

Sharp, Christopher. The Theatre/"*Long Day's Journey into Night.*" *Women's Wear Daily* 3 Mar. 1981; *NYTCR* 1981: 272.

Motivation is badly established in the first act but good thereafter. Jamie's charm can only show when he is drunk.

Sterrit, David. Theater/"Splendid Black Version of O'Neill Drama." *Christian Science Monitor* 23 Apr. 1981; *NYTCR* 1981: 272-73.

A "drama" for all seasons — that rises above color. "All the performers are splendid" but especially "the consistently touching" Mary.

Watt, Douglas. "*Long Day's Journey into Night.*" *Daily News* 3 Mar. 1981; NYTCR 1981: 271.

The Mary is "exquisite," the Jamie "superb," the Edmund "enormously appealing," the Tyrone "likable but dull." Though the director has not been able "to pull all the strands together," the production (staged in two halves, with cuts) shows "the remarkable."

E306 *Long Day's Journey into Night*
Floorboards Theatre Company Edinburgh; Edinburgh Festival Fringe; Fall 1981; Dir.— Kate Harwood.

Berkowitz, Gerald M. Rev. *Eugene O'Neill Newsletter* 6.3 (1982): 27-28.

While this 50-minute, two-person version of the play was not O'Neill's masterpiece, as an independent work inspired by *Journey,* it "proved an evocative and potentially haunting study." Faults Harwood's direction.

E307 *Long Day's Journey into Night*
S. J. Experimental Theatre; Yale School of Drama; New Haven, CT; 30 Oct.-7 Nov. 1981; Dir.— J. Michael Sparough.

E308 *Long Day's Journey into Night*
Richmond Shepard Theater Studios; Hollywood, CA; Spring 1982.

Hanson, Eugene K. Rev. *Eugene O'Neill Newsletter* 6.3 (1982): 28-29.

"A poor production." Acting, direction, setting — all are wrong.

E309 *Long Day's Journey into Night* Nucleo Eclettico; Boston, MA; Closed 3 Apr. 1982; Dir.— Marco Zarattini.

Brooks, Marshall. Rev. *Eugene O'Neill Newsletter* 6.1 (1982): 42-43.

"Refreshingly honest and intimate" production. Solid acting.

E310 *Long Day's Journey into Night* Denison University Theatre; Granville, OH; 12-20 Nov. 1982; Dir.— William Brasmer.

E311 *Long Day's Journey into Night* Richard Allen Center for Culture & Art; New York City; 18 Nov. 1982; Dir.— Geraldine Fitzgerald.

E312 *Long Day's Journey into Night* North Carolina Shakespeare Festival; High Point, NC; 27 July-31 Aug. 1983; Dir.— Malcolm Morrison; Mary Tyrone — Ann Owens; Edmund — Eric Zwemer; Jamie — Mel Shrawder; James — Max Jacobs.

Lister, Joedy. Rev. *Eugene O'Neill Newsletter* 7.3 (1983): 26-27.

Only Jacobs up to snuff. Mary is "one-dimensional," Edmund "never quite captured the pathos the role calls for," yet "all three actors were strong enough to stand on their own and hold an audience."

E313 *Long Day's Journey into Night* Arts Theatre; London; 5 Apr. 1984; Dir.— Ludovica Villar-Hauser; Mary Tyrone — Darlene Johnson; Jamie — Michael Deacon; James — Trevor Martin; Edmund — Sean Mathias.

E314 *Long Day's Journey into Night* Warehouse Repertory Source Theater; Washington, DC; Closed 15 Apr. 1984; Dir.— Dorothy Neumann.

E315 *Long Day's Journey into Night* Court Theatre; University of Chicago; 12 Apr.-13 May 1984; Dir.— Nicholas Rudall; James Tyrone — Tony Mockus; Jamie — Scott Jaeck; Mary — Peg Small; Edmund — Joseph Guzaldo.

E316 *Long Day's Journey into Night* Intiman Theatre; Seattle, WA; 8 June-7 July 1984; Dir.— Margaret Booker.

E317 *Long Day's Journey into Night* Gateway Playhouse; Wareham, MA; 22 June-14 July 1984; Dir.— George W. Hayden; James Tyrone — Niels Miller; Mary — Dorothy Taylor; Edmund — Richard Giles; Jamie — Roger Kelly.

E318 *Long Day's Journey into Night* Byrdcliffe Theater; Woodstock, NY; 10-15 July 1984.

E319 *Long Day's Journey into Night* in repertory with *Wilderness* San Diego Repertory Theatre; San Diego, CA; 6 Sept.-1 Nov. 1984; Dir.— Sam Woodhouse; Design — Dan Dryden; Mary Tyrone — Jo Ann Reeves; James — Mitchell Edmonds; Jamie — Tavis Ross; Edmund — Thom Murray; Cathleen — Darla Cash.

E320 *Long Day's Journey into Night* Abbey Theatre; Dublin, Ireland; Opened 14 Feb. 1985; Dir.— Patrick Laffan; Design — Alfo O'Reilly; Mary Tyrone — Siobhan McKenna.

E321 *Long Day's Journey into Night* Marian Theatre Pacific Conservatory of the Performing Arts; Santa Maria, CA; Closed 17 Feb. 1985; Dir.— Bernard Kates; Mary Tyrone — Dorothy James; Edmund — Robert Elliot; James — Vincent Dowling.

E322 *Long Day's Journey into Night* Royal Exchange Theatre; Manchester, England; Opened 14 Mar. 1985; Dir.— Braham Murray; Mary Tyrone — Dilys Hamlett; Jamie — Jonathan Hackett; Edmund — Michael Mueller.

E323 *Long Day's Journey into Night* Long Wharf Theatre; New Haven, CT; 1 Mar.-14 Apr. 1985; Dir.— Arvin Brown; Mary Tyrone — Geraldine Fitzgerald.

E324 *Long Day's Journey into Night* New Day Repertory Company; Vassar Institute Theater; New Paltz, NY; 21-24 Aug. 1985.

E325 *Long Day's Journey into Night* Broadhurst Theatre; New York City; 21 Apr.-29 June 1986; Theatre Royal, Haymarket; London; Opened 4 Aug.; Tel Aviv; Opened in Oct.; Dir.— Jonathan Miller; James Tyrone — Jack Lemmon; Mary — Bethel Leslie; Jamie — Kevin Spacey; Edmund — Peter Gallagher; Cathleen — Jodie Lynne McClintock.

Bloom, Steven F. Rev. *Eugene O'Neill Newsletter* 10.2 (1986): 33-39.

Sees little in the production to commend, but finds the fault mainly in the directing. Jonathan Miller's attempt to reduce the play's running time (by about a third) by overlapping of lines and injudicious cutting subverts O'Neill's purposes: he meant for the audience to hear the repetition, to endure the "horrible burden of time weighing on ... [the family's] shoulders and crushing ... [them] to the earth." Indeed any benefit this version offers can come only if it "breeds debate and controversy ... publicity and curiosity" about the original version.

Drucker, Trudy. "The Return of O'Neill's 'Play of Old Sorrow.'" *Eugene O'Neill Newsletter* 10.3 (1986): 21-23.

Saw Lemmon as the "best of all the fine actors" she had seen in the role of James; found fault with several directorial decisions — Mary's wearing instead of carrying the wedding dress in the last act, the pace of delivery of her speech to Cathleen in the third act — but found the overlapping dialogue "true to the spirit of the play."

Honan, William F. Rev. *New York Times* 11 May 1986, sec. 2: 5.

Lemmon, no longer the nice little guy of so many of his roles, plays Tyrone as gruff, growling, snarling, howling.

Kramer, Mimi. Rev. *New Criterion* 5 Sept. 1986: 67-78.

What starts out as a review of Jonathan Miller's *Journey* moves to a diatribe against method acting and finally to a review of *A Practical Handbook for the Actor*, written by a group of young American actors. Of the O'Neill production Kramer says that Lemmon's performance was "nothing less than a miracle, but not because it was great. The miracle lay in the fact that for once the actor wasn't playing himself." Kevin Spacey's and Bethel Leslie's performances were "great," and the overlapping of lines successful, though it must be noted that this assessment comes from one for whom "O'Neill has always been an exercise in tedium."

Wilson, Edwin. Rev. *Wall Street Journal* 30 Apr. 1986: 31.

Finds that Miller's speeding up of the play by means of judicious cutting and overlapping of speeches works remarkably well. Also thinks that the play's "comedic" side has finally been realized.

And see:

Barnes, Clive. Rev. *New York Post* 29 Apr. 1986.

Feingold, Michael. Rev. *Village Voice* 13 May 1986: 97.

Gill, Brendan. Rev. *New Yorker* 12 May 1986: 93-94.

Henry, William A., III. Rev. *Time* 12 May 1986: 97.

Kroll, Jack. Rev. *Newsweek* 5 May 1986: 72-73.

Leech, Michael. Rev. *Plays and Players* Sept. 1986: 11-13.

E326 *Long Day's Journey into Night* Siena Heights College; Adrian, MI; 3-15 Nov. 1986; Dir.— Trudy McSorley; Technical Dir.— Doug Miller; James Tyrone — Doug Marquis; Mary — Elizabeth Klinker; Edmund — Rodney Alexander Terwilliger; Jamie — Grant Neale; Cathleen — Mary Billings.

Manheim, Michael. Rev. *Eugene O'Neill Newsletter* 10.3 (1986): 39.

An uncut production, "the direction was sensitive and intelligent ... the set design ... superb."

E327 *Long Day's Journey into Night* Portland Stage Company; Portland, ME; 7 Feb.-1 Mar. 1987; Dir.— Barbara Rosoff; Set Design & Lights — Arden Fingerhut; Composer — Louis Rosen; Costumes — Susan Tsu; James Tyrone — Ford Rainey; Mary — Helen Stenborg; Edmund — Paul McCrane; Jamie — W. T. Martin; Cathleen — Sarah Bedner.

Wilkins, Frederick C. Rev. *Eugene O'Neill Newsletter* 11.1 (1987): 48-49.

Compliments this production on its faithful, "virtually uncut" version of O'Neill's masterpiece. Noting that Mary was the "bitterest" he had ever seen, Wilkins, nonetheless, found the actors "fully capable" of their roles.

E328 *Long Day's Journey into Night* Octagon Theatre; Alabama Shakespeare Festival; Montgomery, AL; 19 Nov.-13 Dec. 1987; Dir.— Martin L. Platt.

E329 *Long Day's Journey into Night* Berkeley Repertory Theatre; Berkeley, CA; Closed 5 Dec. 1987; Dir.— Jackson Phippin.

E330 *Long Day's Journey into Night* Denver Center Theatre Company; Denver, CO; 4 Jan.-13 Feb. 1988; Dir.— Malcolm Morrison; Jame Tyrone — James Lawless; Mary — Carol Mayo Jenkins; Jamie — Michael Winters; Edmund — Jamie Horton.

Ben-Zvi, Linda. Rev. *Eugene O'Neill Newsletter* 12.1 (1988): 64-66.

"While the Denver Center production never soared, and failed to fully realize the key scenes mentioned, it did not completely sour O'Neill's great play." The director was essentially faithful to the text if not sensitive to its power.

E331 *Long Day's Journey into Night and Ah, Wilderness!* (in repertory) Yale Repertory Theatre; New Haven, CT; 22 Mar.-21 May 1988; Then moved to; The Neil Simon Theatre; 250 W. 52nd St.; New York

City; 6 June 1988 opened; Dir.— José Quintero; Set — Ben Edwards; Lighting — Jennifer Tipton; James Tyrone — Jason Robards; Mary — Colleen Dewhurst; Jamie — Jamey Sheridan; Edmund — Campbell Scott.

Frank, Glenda. Rev. *Westsider* 7-13 July 1988: 12.

Rich, Frank. Rev. *New York Times* 15 June 1988, sec. C: 21.

Colleen Dewhurst's Mary is a "killer," Scott's Edmund a mother's "born victim," Sheridan's Jamie "an innocent straight arrow taken to drink." The staging "illuminates one parent-child axis — Mary and Edmund — more brilliantly than the other." Mary is "almost shockingly unsentimentalized." Quotes Tynan on Mary as "at heart an emotional vampire."

_____. Interview with Quintero. *New York Times* 16 June 1988, sec. C: 21.

Wilkins, Frederick C. Rev. *Eugene O'Neill Newsletter* 12.1 (1988): 68-70.

Unenthusiastic. Attributes his discontent to the "low energy level of the parents." O'Neill's great tragedy did not soar in this interpretation.

E332 *Long Day's Journey into Night*
Indiana Repertory Theater; Indianapolis, IN; 21 Sept.-16 Oct. 1988; Dir.— Tom Haas; Set — Bill Clarke; Costuming — Bobbi Owen; Lighting — Denny Clark; James Tyrone — Michael Lipton; Mary — Bella Jarrett; Jamie — Robert Burns; Edmund — Christian Baskous.

Fisher, A. James. Rev. *Eugene O'Neill Newsletter* 12.3 (1988): 50-51.

Passionless, tedious, inadequate are just some of the adjectives used to describe this production, wherein the key roles of Mary and Edmund are badly cast.

E333 *Long Day's Journey into Night*
Berkeley Repertory Theater; Berkeley, CA; 30 Sept.-5 Dec. 1988; Dir.— Jackson Phippin.

E334 *Long Day's Journey into Night*
New American Theater; Rockford, IL; Closed 9 Oct. 1988; Dir.— J. R. Sullivan.

E335 *Long Day's Journey into Night*
Cincinnati Playhouse; Cincinnati, OH; 27 Oct.-13 Nov. 1988.

E336 *Long Day's Journey into Night*
Syracuse Stage; Syracuse, NY; 18 Nov.-4 Dec. 1988.

E337 *Long Day's Journey into Night*
The Artist's Repertory Theater; Portland, OR;

Spring 1990; Dir.— Allen Nause; Set Design — Dan Handelman; James Tyrone — Ted Roisum; Mary — Vana O'Brien; Jamie — Eric J. Hull; Edmund — Michael R. Welsh; Cathleen — Sarah Fitzpatrick.

Black, Stephen A. Rev. *Eugene O'Neill Review* 14.1-2 (1990): 101-03.

This production gets an enthusiastic thumbs up from Black, who says that O'Brien was the best Mary he had ever seen. "Inobtrusive" direction and "fine sets" contribute to the production's success.

E338 *Long Day's Journey into Night*
Summer Resident Theater, AEA; University of Arizona; Tucson, AZ; 21 June-8 July 1990; [Subsequently at the Galvin Playhouse, Arizona State University, Tempe, 12 and 14-15 July.]

E339 *Long Day's Journey into Night*
Pilgrim Center for the Arts; Seattle, WA; Autumn 1990; James Tyrone — Rick Tutor; Mary — Dee Dee Van Zyl; Jamie — Kevin Lynch; Edmund — Stephen Godwin.

Black, Stephen A. Rev. *Eugene O'Neill Review* 15.1 (1991): 97-99.

Comparing this production to the Seattle Repertory's running the same season, Black prefers this low budget version. Of special interest is the suggestion that Edmund, played as effeminate, is suffering from AIDS, thereby removing the hope tentatively offered by the text. In sum Black found the acting strong (with the exception of Jamie) and the play topical.

E340 *Long Day's Journey into Night*
Seattle Repertory Theatre; Seattle, WA; 5-23 Dec. 1990; Dir.— Michael Engler; James Tyrone — William Biff McGuire; Mary — Marion Ross; Jamie — John Procaccino; Edmund — Patrick Breen; Cathleen — Katie Forgette.

Black, Stephen A. Rev. *Eugene O'Neill Review* 15.1 (1992): 97-99.

Labeling the Seattle Repertory Company, "smugly affluent," Black found little to praise in this production. "And the set was as dissatisfying as the work of the four principals." Ouch!

E341 *Long Day's Journey into Night*
University of Buffalo; Department of Theatre and Dance; Pfeifer Theatre; Buffalo, NY; 17 Jan.-3 Feb. 1991; Dir.— Fortunato Pezziminti; James Tyrone — Saul Elkin; Mary — Barbara Link LaRou; Jamie — Vincent O'Neill;

Edmund — Tom Zindle; Cathleen — Maureen Porter.

Watkinson, Sharon. Rev. *Eugene O'Neill Review* 15.1 (1991): 99-104.

"Despite the shortcomings of the fourth act," and the lack of a setting, this production was solid. Some noteworthy performances.

E342 *Long Day's Journey into Night*
National Theatre at the Lyttleton and the Bristol Old Vic; London; Spring 1991; Dir. — Howard Davies; James Tyrone — Timothy West; Mary — Prunella Scales; Edmund — Stephen Dillane; Jamie — Sean McGinley.

Kingston, Jeremy. Rev. *Times* [London] 23 May 1991: 22.

Finds the true climax, "really the core and revelation," of the play in Act IV with Jamie's warning Edmund against his corrupting counsel.

Peter, John. Rev. *Sunday Times* 24 Feb. 1991, sec. 5: 8.

Moral O'Neill blames all on his father, but artist O'Neill, "more even-handed, redistributes the blame." A "granite" production teaching a "grim lesson: that to learn from your own mistakes means by definition that you learn too late."

E343 *Long Day's Journey into Night*
Royal Dramatic Theatre of Stockholm; Majestic Theatre, Brooklyn Academy of Music; Brooklyn, New York City; 14-16 June 1991; Dir. — Ingmar Bergman.

E344 *Long Day's Journey into Night*
Artists' Cooperative Theatre; Nashville, TN; 22-23 Nov. 1991; Dir. — Rob Daniel; Set — Craig Spain; James Tyrone — Bob O'Connell; Mary — Rona Carter; Jamie — Chris Harrod; Edmund — Johnson West; Cathleen — Betty Reed

Eisen, Kurt. Rev. *Eugene O'Neill Review* 16.1 (1992): 115-17.

Faults the directing and the miscasting of Mary for an "ill-fitting" production.

E345 *Long Day's Journey into Night*
Gem Theatre; Grove Shakespeare Festival; Garden City, CA; 30 Sept.-31 Oct. 1992.

E346 *Long Day's Journey into Night*
The Huntington Theatre Company; Boston, MA; 23 Oct.-22 Nov. 1992; Dir. — Edward Gilbert; James Tyrone — Jack Aronson; Mary — Patricia Conolly; Jamie — Jonathan Walker; Edmund — Robert Sean Leonard.

Connolly, Thomas F. Rev. *Eugene O'Neill Review* 16.2 (1992): 134-41.

Connolly gives this production his imprimatur, finding Patricia Conolly's Mary "a revelation," and, while Jamie did not measure up, the director, Edward Gilbert, is credited with offering "a respectful rather than reverential treatment of the play." The concluding moments of the play were as moving as any he had ever seen.

E347 *Long Day's Journey into Night*
Arena Stage; Washington, DC; 1992-93 Season; Dir. — Joe Dowling.

E348 *Long Day's Journey into Night*
New Theater; Coral Gables, FL; 11 Nov.-11 Dec. 1994.

E349 *Long Day's Journey into Night*
Tom Patterson Theatre; Stratford, ONT; 1994 Season (Festival); 1995 Repertory; Dir. — Diana Leblanc; James Tyrone — William Hutt; Mary — Martha Henry; Jamie — Peter Donaldson; Edmund — Tom McCamus; Cathleen — Martha Burns.

Garebian, Keith. "Following the Arts: Revisionism (Part II): The 1995 Stratford Festival." *Revue Etudes Canadiennes* 31.2 (1996): 166-73.

In a review of several of the Festival's offerings, Garabian says this *Journey* was not on an "even keel." While William Hutt's Tyrone is "certain to become legendary, Miss Henry's touching up of the portrait of Mary from the previous season ended up almost tilting the play into parody." The Edmund and Jamie were balanced and well paired.

McLean, Robert S. Rev. *Eugene O'Neill Review* 17.1-2 (1993): 179-84.

Splendid casting, a "most impressive" production. The audience's rapt attention is a testimony to the production and to the play's power.

E350 *Long Day's Journey into Night*
Arena Stage; Washington, DC; 6 Jan.-12 Feb. 1995; Dir. — Douglas C. Wagner; Design — Ming Cho Lee; Lighting — Scott Zielinski; James Tyrone — Richard Kneeland; Mary — Tana Hicken; Jamie — Casey Biggs; Edmund — Rainn Wilson; Cathleen — Holly Twyford.

Ranald, Margaret Loftus. Rev. *Eugene O'Neill Review* 17.1-2 (1993): 187-92.

"A very solid, distinguished, and memorable" production. "I was totally won over by the pathos" of Mary's regression to childhood "as she curled up in the rocking chair to deliver her final speech."

E351 *Long Day's Journey into Night*
Germinal Stage; Denver, CO; 9 Mar.-9 Apr.
1995; Dir.— Ed Baierlein.

E352 *Long Day's Journey into Night*
Trinity Repertory Company; Providence,
RI; 6 Oct.-19 Nov. 1995; Dir.— Oskar
Eustis.

E353 *Long Day's Journey into Night*
Theatre Royal; Plymouth; Transferred to the
Young Vic; London, UK; Summer 1996;
Dir.— Laurence Boswell; Mary Tyrone —
Penelope Wilton.

E354 *Long Day's Journey into Night*
American Repertory Theatre; Loeb Drama
Center,; Cambridge, MA; 24 May-14 July 1996;
Dir.— Ron Daniels; Set — Michael Yeargan;
Costuming — Catherine Zuber; Lighting —
Frances Aronson; Sound — Christopher Walker;
Stage Manager — Wendy Beaton; James Ty-
rone — Jerome Kilty; Mary — Claire Bloom;
Jamie — Bill Camp; Edmund — Michael
Stuhlbarg; Cathleen — Emma Roberts.

E355 *Long Day's Journey into Night*
(**dramatic reading**) Roundabout Theatre;
New York City; 10 Feb. 1997; Dir.— Stephen
Kennedy. Philip Bosco, Julie Harris, Peter
Gallagher, Tom McCamus.

Verde, Tom. "Long Journey to Oblivion
for [the] O'Neills' Cottage." *New York Times*
10 Feb. 1997, sec. C: 12.

Announces the reading whose purpose is
to raise money for the maintenance of Monte
Cristo Cottage. The reading will also inaugu-
rate a series of 50 O'Neill plays to be produced
by New York University, Yale, the Provincetown Playhouse and the Cottage itself.

E356 *Long Day's Journey into Night*
Jungle Theatre; Minneapolis, MN; 21 Mar.-
31 May 1997; Dir.— Bain Boehlke.

E357 *Long Day's Journey into Night*
Pittsburgh Public Theater; Pittsburgh, PA; 9
Oct.-16 Nov. 1997; Artistic Dir.— Edward
Gilbert; James Tyrone — Tom Atkins; Mary —
Deborah Kipp; Jamie — James Colby; Ed-
mund — James Waterson; Cathleen — Heather
Goldenhersch.

Rawson, Christopher. Rev. *Pittsburgh
Post-Gazette* 12 Oct. 1997, sec. G: 3-4.

Pittsburgh's first *Journey* since 1958, so
the "review" of the production's preview is devoted to introducing the audience to the play
and to its production history.

_____. Rev. *Pittsburgh Post-Gazette* 18
Oct. 1997, sec. D: 8.

"O'Neill's dark passion pulls us into his
Journey."

Scheid, Ed. Rev. *Pittsburgh Post-Gazette*
8 Nov. 1997, sec. B: 6.

E358 *Long Day's Journey into Night*
Merrimack Repertory Theatre; Lowell, MA;
31 Oct.-21 Nov. 1997; Dir.— David G. Kent.

E359 *Long Day's Journey into Night*
Chamber Theatre of Maine; Thomaston, ME;
Oct. 1997; Dir.— Erika Pfander.

E360 *Long Day's Journey into Night*
Dallas Theatre Center; Dallas, TX; 10 Mar.
1998; Dir.— Richard Hamburger; James Tyrone — Michael Kevin; Mary — Barbara Tarbuck; Edmund — Mark H. Dodd; Jamie —
Kurt Ziskie; Cathleen — Tara Gibson.

Shafer, Yvonne. Rev. *Eugene O'Neill Review* 21.1-2 (1997): 182-86.

Gives the production a qualified nod.
Approves of the lighting, setting, and performances by Kevin and Ziskie, but found
Dodd's and Tarbuck's interpretations not altogether satisfying.

E361 *Long Day's Journey into Night*
Gate Theatre; Dublin; 26 Mar.-25 Apr. 1998;
Dir.— Karel Reisz; Setting — Robin Don;
Lighting — Peter Mumford; James Tyrone —
Don Moffat; Mary — Rosaleen Linehan;
Jamie — David Herlihy; Edmund — Andrew
Scott; Cathleen — Sonya Kelly.

E362 *The Long Voyage Home* with *Ile*
and *Ape* Morgan's Bar; 134 Reade St.; New
York City; Jan. 1976; Dir.— Alex Sokoloff;
Musical Dir.— Dan Emerich.

E363 *The Long Voyage Home* see *The
Sea Plays of Eugene O'Neill* Long Wharf
Theatre; New Haven, CT; Opened 28 Mar.
1978.

E364 *The Long Voyage Home* with *Ile*
Source at the ASTA; 507 8th St. SE; Washington, DC; Aug. 1978; Dir.— Bart White-
man.

E365 *The Long Voyage Home
(Caribbees, Cardiff, Zone,* and *Voyage)* Na-
tional Theatre Company; Cottesloe Theatre;
London; 20 Feb.-17 Mar. 1979 (Revived Jan.
1980); Dir.— Bill Bryden; Design — Hayden
Griffen; Lighting — Andy Phillips; Music —
John Tams; Sound — Ric Green; Driscoll —
Niall Toibin; Yank — Dave King; Cocky —
Bill Owen; Smitty — Jack Shepherd;
Olson — Mark McManus; Scotty — Jarnes
Grant; Big Frank, & Fat Joe — Brian Glover;
Davis — Trevor Ray; Paul — John Tams;

Captain and Donkeyman — Howard Goor-
ney; 1st Mate & a Sailor — Peter Armitage;
Jack and Nick — Gawn Grainger; Ivan —
Frederick Warder; Bella — Nadia Cottouse;
Violet — Marsha Miller; Pearl — Shirley Allan;
Freda — Edna Dore; Edna — June Watson.

Elsom, John. "All at Sea." *Listener* 101
(1979): 325.

Finds O'Neill's sea plays inferior to Conrad's and Hughes' sea stories. Notes O'Neill's
clichés — the shanghaied sailor, death at sea.
The production is good, but "unfocused."

Jones, Simon. Rev. *Plays and Players* 26.8
(1979): 24, 29.

O'Neill's romanticism, anarchism, mysticism and acute grasp of social reality are all
displayed, as well as are his tendencies toward
sentimentalism and melodrama. Praises this
production for its fidelity to the original, even
if it is a little ponderous. Yank and Olson are
especially well portrayed.

Taylor, John Russell. "London." *Drama:
The Quarterly Theatre Review* 136 (1980): 41-43.

Review of productions of *Voyage, Hughie,*
and *Iceman* at the Cottesloe. *Voyage* and
Hughie are like dramatic versions of O. Henry
stories — anecdotes with a twist, not great art
but proficiently put together. The small stage
is used efficiently to conjure up a sense of
confinement in the below deck episodes.

E366 *The Long Voyage Home* with
Zone Spectrum; 277 Park Ave. South; Spring
1979; Dir. — Norman Morrow.

E367 *The Long Voyage Home* National
Theatre Company; Cottesloe Theatre; London; Jan. 1980.

Fender, Stephen. "The Fatal Destiny."
Times Literary Supplement 18 Jan. 1980: 62.

Finds the representation of fate "a bit on
the grand side" for such short plays. In
O'Neill's longer plays speeches can produce
an ironic distance between the characters'
public and private selves. In the shorter plays
such speeches become "isolated moments of
rather puzzling beauty."

E368 *The Long Voyage Home* see *Six
Plays of the Sea (Cardiff, Voyage, Zone, Ile,
Rope, Cross)* Apple Corps Theatre Company;
New York City; Closed 2 May 1982; Dir. —
Skip Corris.

E369 *The Long Voyage Home* M.I.T.
Drama Shop; Kresge Little Theater; Cam-
bridge, MA; 4-6 Oct. 1984; Dir. — Robert N.
Scanlan.

Connolly, Thomas F. Rev. *Eugene
O'Neill Newsletter* 8.3 (1984): 35.

"Competent and satisfying performances" elicited from a cast of undergraduates

E370 *The Long Voyage Home* see *Sea
Plays at Monte Cristo* "Monte Cristo"; 305
Pequot Ave.; New London, CT; 26 Sept.-14
Nov. 1985.

E371 *The Long Voyage Home* see
Four Plays of the Sea (S.S. Glencairn) Just
So Productions; San Francisco, CA; 27 Apr.-
17 June 1988.

E372 *The Long Voyage Home* see *The
Sea Plays (Zone, Voyage,* and *Ile)* Rand Theater; University of Massachusetts at Amherst;
20-29 Oct. 1988; Dir. — Edward Golden.

E373 *The Long Voyage Home* see *The
Sea Plays (Cardiff, Caribbees, Zone,* and
Voyage) The Willow Cabin Theater Com-
pany; Intar II Theater; New York City; 3-20
Nov. 1988.

E374 *The Long Voyage Home* with *Ile*
Provincetown Repertory Theatre; 1-18 Aug.
1996; Dir. — José Quintero; Olson — Ken
Hoyt; Capt. Keeney — Richard Mover; Mrs.
Keeney — Alison Crowley; Steward/Fat Joe —
William J. Devany; Slocum/Driscoll — Jerry
O'Donnell.

Peterson, William M. Rev. *Eugene
O'Neill Review* 20.1-2 (1996): 70-72.

"Quintero's direction of this excellent
cast endowed the two texts with startling
power." Changes that Quintero implemented
were lauded as softening the plays' melodrama.

E375 *Marco Millions* Playmakers
Repertory Company; University of North
Carolina at Chapel Hill; 16 Mar.-2 Apr. 1978;
Dir. — Tom Haas.

E376 *Marco Millions* Sharon Playhouse; Sharon, CT; 1-5, 8-12 Aug. 1978.

E377 *Marco Millions* **overlapping
with** *Misbegotten.* See E424 University of
Pittsburgh; Pittsburgh, PA; Spring 1987.

E378 *Marco Millions* Shanghai People's Arts Theatre; PRC; 1988.

E379 *Marco Millions* American Conservatory Theatre; 450 Geary St.; San Francisco, CA; Opened 11 Oct. 1988; Dir. — Joy
Carlin; Costuming — Jovita Chow; Kublai
Khan — Sun Dao Lin.

E380 *A Moon for the Misbegotten* Mer-
maid Theatre; London; 6 Sept.-Nov. 1973;
Dir. — David Leveau; Ian Bannen, Alan Devlin.

E381 *A Moon for the Misbegotten* A Lester Osterman-Richard Horner Production; Morosco; New York City; Opened 29 Dec. 1973; recessed 13 July 1974.; Reopened 3 Sept. 1974 for a total of 314 performances.; Dir.— José Quintero; Setting & Lighting — Ben Edwards; Josie Hogan — Colleen Dewhurst; Mike — Edwin J. McDonough; Phil — Ed Flanders; Jim Tyrone — Jason Robards; T. Stedman Harder — John O'Leary.

Anon. Rev. *Playboy* Apr. 1974: 42, 46.

The production is a "restoration of a classic." The play's place in the O'Neill canon was uncertain until this production. The Dewhurst-Robards pairing is "symbiotic."

Barnes, Clive. Rev. *New York Times* 31 Dec. 1973: 22.

Hails the production as a "landmark," the cast "ideal." Comments on the non-judgmental nature of the play and on the pietà hints: Colleen Dewhurst as the Virgin earth-mother, Robards, as the suffering Tyrone, and Flanders, as the sprightly Phil Hogan, get unqualified raves.

_____. Rev. *London Times* 10 Jan. 1974: 11g.

Speaks only in superlatives — a "landmark production." The play is one of the four that made O'Neill "one of the great playwrights of the modern theatre."

Clurman, Harold. Theatre. *Nation* 19 Jan. 1974: 92-93.

Enthusiastic endorsement of the "best production of the season." Applauds the Robards and Dewhurst performances as well as Flanders', and Quintero's direction.

Gill, Brendan. "Views of Home." *New Yorker* 14 Jan. 1974: 58.

The revival is "superb." Colleen Dewhurst gave the "performance of her life," but Robards was uneasy in his role.

Gottfried, Martin. The Theatre/"*A Moon for the Misbegotten.*" *Women's Wear Daily* 2 Jan. 1974; *NYTCR* 1973: 121.

The staging is listless, the roles have little dimension. Dewhurst gives Josie as much as can be given the thinness of the character. The blocking on the lip of the stage make the production seem like a reading. In this play "O'Neill's writing is at its clumsiest in terms of literacy and boozy philosophizing."

Harris, Leonard. WCBS-TV. 11 Jan. 1974; *NYTCR* 1973: 122.

The play is a "masterpiece." The production "magnificent."

Holder, Geoffrey. NBC-TV. 29 Dec. 1973; *NYTCR* 1973: 121.

Refers to the "great O'Neillian" director and to the acting by "two great American actors" one of whom is "pure brilliance," the other exhibiting "amazing emotional power."

Hughes, Catharine. "The Performance is the Thing." *America* 19 Jan. 1974: 33.

Hails the production, although less enthusiastic about the play itself. Offers to explain why the production is so good, but doesn't — simply appreciates the casting.

Kalem, T. E. "O'Neill Agonistes." *Time* 14 Jan. 1974: 42.

At the Morosco "power, beauty, passion, and truth command the stage." Calls the production an "unmitigated triumph" that Quintero has "beautifully orchestrated." Praises Robards' performance as "a touchstone for all actors to measure themselves by" and says of Dewhurst that "no woman was ever big enough for the part before."

Kauffmann, Stanley. "Stanley Kauffmann on Theatre." *New Republic* 6 Jan. 1974: 22, 34.

Dewhurst was ill-cast, as was Flanders, but Robards was "superb."

Kerr, Walter. "It's a Rich Play, Richly Performed." *New York Times* 13 Jan. 1974, sec. 2: 1.

Is "possibly O'Neill's best." Kudos for Colleen Dewhurst — she's particularly effective with the unfinished lines in the text. Ed Flanders' performance is "stunning." Robards begins "brilliantly." Suggests that the impossibility of a relationship between James Tyrone and Josie Hogan not be disclosed until the fourth act.

Kroll, Jack. "Rev. of *Misbegotten.*" *Newsweek* 14 Jan. 1974: 83.

The review is almost all praise. The "most Irish" of O'Neill's plays with an ambience of Irish Catholicism, puritanism, profanity, love, lust, "sense of self-corruption," "polluted idealism."

Melloan, George. The Theater/"A Dread Secret Unfolds on a Moonlit Porch." *Wall Street Journal* 2 Jan. 1974; *NYTCR* 1973: 119-20.

"A great production, brilliant performances." Quintero works "magic." The play is a rich "fabric of Irish wit and subtle meanings." The O'Neills were knights in Ireland and "the sense of tragedy of kingdoms lost" is deep in their consciousness.

Miller, Jordan Y. Rev. *Kansas Quarterly* 7.4 (1975): 103-05.

Impressed that O'Neill's status has become such that a commercial network would do *Moon* on prime time. Also thinks the performances are of the highest quality, but is still displeased with the play itself. Jamie has no tragic stature and characters are always retracting what they say.

Nathan, Ben. Letter. *New York Times* 20 Oct. 1974, sec. 2: 7.

Finds a "frail, weak-kneed work" in which O'Neill does not make clear "what he had on his mind" until the last act.

Sanders, Kevin. WABC-TV. 29 Dec. 1973; *NYTCR* 1973: 122.

A bleak, dismal story of miserable people set in "Ma and Pa Kettle country."

Simon, John. "Theatre Chronicle." *Hudson Review* 27 (1974): 265-66.

Mixed response. Finds Quintero's directing uninspired, but Dewhurst, Robards, and Flanders marvelous. Censures O'Neill for "uncertain language, with its terrible built-in obsolescence."

Watt, Douglas. "*A Moon for the Misbegotten.*" *Daily News* 31 Dec. 1973; *NYTCR* 1973: 118.

"Stunning revival." The first act "almost pure O'Casey."

Watts, Richard. Theater/*A Moon for the Misbegotten. New York Post* 31 Dec. 1973; *NYTCR* 1973: 118.

"A superb play, superbly done." Notes the humor amidst the tragedy. Josie and James Tyrone, Jr., are "among O'Neill's most brilliant creations." Dewhurst is "right for the role and looks very beautiful;" Robards is "perfect"; Flanders "splendid."

E382 *A Moon for the Misbegotten* Guthrie Theatre; Minneapolis, MN; Opened 8 June 1977, on tour 1978; Dir.—Nick Havinga; Jim Tyrone—Peter Michael Goetz; Josie Hogan—Sharon Ernster; Phil—Richard Russell Ramos.

Eder, Richard. "Review of *A Moon for the Misbegotten.*" *New York Times* 21 July 1977, sec. C: 19.

"In this theatre the stage becomes an actor" that Director Havenga uses to act as a "barometer of Josie's mercurial strength and vulnerability." (She moves forward when she feels strong, back when she feels weak.)

Voelker, Paul D. "A Full Moon in Indianapolis." *Eugene O'Neill Newsletter* 1.3 (1978): 15-17.

Sees the play in the light of *Journey* and O'Neill biography. Too much emphasis on Jim Tyrone: Josie and Hogan are more important to O'Neill's intentions.

E383 *A Moon for the Misbegotten* Oregon Shakespeare Festival Association at Tao House; Danville, CA; 24 & 25 Sept. 1977.

E384 *A Moon for the Misbegotten* Intiman Theatre Company; Seattle, WA; Closed 15 Oct. 1977; Dir.—Margaret Booker.

E385 *A Moon for the Misbegotten* Cohoes Music Hall; Cohoes, NY; 31 Dec. 1977-28 Jan. 1978; Dir.—Tom Greunewald.

E386 *A Moon for the Misbegotten* Foothills Theatre Company; Worcester, MA; 11-29 Jan. 1978.

E387 *A Moon for the Misbegotten* Playmakers Repertory Company; University of North Carolina at Chapel Hill; 16 Mar.-2 Apr. 1978; Dir.—Tom Haas.

E388 *A Moon for the Misbegotten* Berkeley Repertory Theatre; Berkeley, CA; 21 Apr.-28 May 1978; Dir.—M. Leibert.

E389 *A Moon for the Misbegotten* American Stage Festival; Milford, NH; 25-30 July 1978; Dir.—Stanley Wojewodski, Jr.

E390 *A Moon for the Misbegotten* Lyric Stage Company; 54 Charles St.; Boston, MA; 3 Jan.-10 Feb. 1979; Dir.—Sue Bowlin.

E391 *A Moon for the Misbegotten* GeVa Theatre; Rochester, NY; 26 Jan.-18 Feb. 1979.

E392 *A Moon for the Misbegotten* Nassau (NY) Repertory; County Theater (in the Social Services Building); 30, 31 Mar. 1979; Dir.—T.J. Barry; Setting—Ken Hollamon; Lighting—Victor En Yi Tan; Josie Hogan—Caroline Sidney Abady; Phil—Tom Bahring; Jim Tyrone—James Gallagher. With Steve Connor and John Little.

Klein, Alvin. "Theater in Review." *New York Times* 25 Mar. 1979, sec. 21: 11.

Finds the attempt at doing such a difficult play, considering the company's resources, "foolhardy," the performance "ineffectual and woe-begone."

E393 *A Moon for the Misbegotten* Monomoy Theater; Chatham, MA; 1-4 Aug. 1979.

E394 *A Moon for the Misbegotten*
Troupe Theatre; 335 W. 39th St.; 13 Dec.
1979-5 Jan. 1980; Dir.— Geoffrey Sadwith.

E395 *A Moon for the Misbegotten*
Meadow Brook Theatre; Rochester, MI; 3-27
Jan. 1980; Dir.— Charles Nolte.

E396 *A Moon for the Misbegotten* New
England Repertory Theatre; Worcester, MA;
1979-80 Season, closed 9 Mar. 1980; Dir.— Jon
Knowles; Jim Tyrone— James Cooke; Josie
Hogan— Susan McGinley; Phil— Bill McCann.

Brooks, Marshall. Rev. *Eugene O'Neill
Newsletter* 4.1-2 (1980): 26-28.

"Imaginative and full-bodied rendition."
James Cooke was "stunning." Phil Hogan "a
joy." Josie "sublimely earthy, crude and frol-
icking throughout."

E397 *A Moon for the Misbegotten*
Portland Stage Company; Portland, ME;
Closed 18 May 1980; Dir.— Susan Dunlop.

E398 *A Moon for the Misbegotten*
Classic Theater; New York City; Closed 2
Sept. 1980; Dir.— Geoffrey Sadwith.

E399 *A Moon for the Misbegotten*
Bergenstage; Laboratory Theater at Bergen
Community College; Paramus, NJ; 7-30 Nov.
1980; Dir.— Bing D. Bills; Setting— Beeb
Salzer; Lighting— Susan Dandridge; Josie
Hogan— Nora Chester; Phil— Vince O'Brien;
Jim Tyrone— Kelly Fitzpatrick; T. Stedman
Harder— Kevin Gilmartin; Mike Hogan— D.
Peter Moore.

Catinella, Joseph. "Theater." *New York
Times* 23 Nov. 1980, sec. 40: 23.

The production stresses the "twisty
humor and jagged poetry of the play." Approves of the production except for Kelly Fitzpatrick (Jim), who was miscast.

E400 *A Moon for the Misbegotten* Old
Globe Theatre; San Diego, CA; 18 Jan.-22
Feb. 1981.

E401 *A Moon for the Misbegotten*
Main Street Theater; White Plains, NY; 1-15
Mar. 1981; Artistic Dir.— Stephen Rosefield;
Jim Tyrone— Frederic Coffin; Josie Hogan—
Suzanne Collins; Phil— Ian Martin; Mike—
Michael Mantel; T. Stedman Harder—
William Meisle.

Frankel, Haskel. "Theater." *New York
Times* 1 Mar. 1981, sec. 22: lh.

Observes that there are repetition, mo-
notony, and tedium in *Misbegotten* as in *Journey,* but there is also "a dramatic sense,"
adding to the texture of the plays.

E402 *A Moon for the Misbegotten*
Academy Theatre; Atlanta, GA; In repertory
Feb.-May 1981; Tour of the Southeast ended
3 Oct. 1981; Dir.— Frank Wittow.

E403 *A Moon for the Misbegotten*
StageWest; West Springfield, MA; 12 Feb.-7
Mar. 1981; Dir.— Robert Brewer.

E404 *A Moon for the Misbegotten*
Germinal Stage; Denver, CO; 9 July-2 Aug.
1981; Dir.— Ginger Valone.

E405 *A Moon for the Misbegotten*
Woodstock Playhouse; Woodstock, NY; 15-19
and 21-26 July 1981.

E406 *A Moon for the Misbegotten* Mc-
Cadden Theatre Company; American Theatre Arts Conservatory; Los Angeles, CA; Fall
1981; Dir.— Henry Hoffman; Josie Hogan—
Salome Jens; Phil— Stefan Gierasch; Jim Tyrone— Mitchell Ryan.

Hanson, Eugene K. Rev. *Eugene O'Neill
Newsletter* 6.1 (1982): 45-48.

"A heroic and largely satisfying attempt,"
though Ryan "seemed to have difficulty" with
his role and Phil Hogan appeared "distracted
at times."

E407 *A Moon for the Misbegotten* Theatre Project Company; University of Missouri;
St. Louis, MO; 18-21 Feb. 1982; Dir.— F. Syer.

E408 *A Moon for the Misbegotten* Bar-
ton Square Playhouse; Salem, MA; 26 Feb.-3
Apr. 1982; Dir.— David George; Josie
Hogan— Judith Black; Phil— Michael Mc-
Namara; Jim Tyrone— Kerry Brown.

Connolly, Thomas F. Rev. *Eugene
O'Neill Newsletter* 6.1 (1982): 43-45.

"The production did have one serious
flaw: Kerry Brown's performance as Jim Tyrone."

E409 *A Moon for the Misbegotten* 2nd
Story Theatre; Newport, RI; 9 Mar.-25 Apr.
1982.

E410 *A Moon for the Misbegotten*
Playmakers Repertory Company; University
of North Carolina at Chapel Hill; 27 Oct.-14
Nov. 1982; Dir.— Gregory Boyd.

E411 *A Moon for the Misbegotten*
Theatre Calgary; Calgary, Canada; Fall 1982;
Dir.— John Murrell; Phil Hogan— Edward
Atienza; Josie— Janet Wright; Jim Tyrone—
Eric Schneider.

Czarnecki, Mark. "The Endless Quest
for Love." *Macleans* 8 Nov. 1982: 52+

Applauds the director's "judicious" cutting of a half hour of text.

E412 *A Moon for the Misbegotten*
Lyric Stage; Boston, MA; 9 Feb.-13 Mar.
1983; Dir.—Polly Hogan; Phil Hogan—
William Barnard; Josie—Sheila Ferrini; Jim
Tyrone—Ronald Ritchell.

Connolly, Thomas F. Rev. *Eugene
O'Neill Newsletter* 7.1 (1983): 22.

The first half of the performance was
"execrable" ("sloppy blocking, missed lines
and garbled diction"), but Jim Tyrone found
himself midway, returning in the second act to
save the production.

E413 *A Moon for the Misbegotten*
Riverside Studio London; June 1983.

E414 *A Moon for the Misbegotten*
Steppenwolf Theatre; Chicago, IL; 11 May-5
June 1983; Dir.—Jeff Perry; Phil Hogan—
Alan Wilder; Josie—Moira Harris; Jim Ty-
rone—Rick Snyder.

Tuck, Susan. Rev. *Eugene O'Neill
Newsletter* 7.2 (1983): 23-26.

Gives background on the play's performance history. "Steppenwolf's Josie and Phil
worked so well together" that it became clear
"that Jim Tyrone is not the central character."
"He is merely a catalyst for Josie."

E415 *A Moon for the Misbegotten*
Dorset Theater Festival; Dorset Playhouse and
Colony House; Dorset, VT; 21-30 July 1983;
Dir.—John Morrison.

E416 *A Moon for the Misbegotten*
American Repertory Theatre; Cambridge,
MA; 9 Dec. 1983-29 Jan. 1984; Then Cort
Theater; New York City; Opened 1 May 1984;
Dir.—David Leveaux; Josie Hogan—Kate
Nelligan; Phil—Jerome Kilty; Jim Tyrone—
Ian Bannen.

Kroll, Jack. "Courage of Their Convic-
tions." *Newsweek* 23 Jan. 1984: 69.

The play "mixes blarney, melodrama and
… sentimentality in an improbable fusion of
emotional and spiritual power." Kate Nelligan acts "with a savage sophistication … beautiful to behold" and the performance has a
"splendid dynamic variety and lyric intensity."

Simon, John. Rev. *New York* 14 May
1984: n.p.

Does not compare well with the 1973
Robards-Dewhurst production. The set was
more "suited to Sam Shepard than to
O'Neill."

E417 *A Moon for the Misbegotten* Tar-
ragon Theatre; 30 Bridgman Ave.; Toronto;
Opened 8 Oct. 1985; Dir.—Martha Henry;

Josie Hogan—Clare Coulter; Jim Tyrone—
Michael Hogan.

E418 *A Moon for the Misbegotten*
Lyric Players Theatyre; Belfast, Northern Ire-
land; 27 Mar. 1986; Dir.—Richard Digby-
Day.

E419 *A Moon for the Misbegotten* Grove
Theatre Company, Gem Theatre; Garden
Grove, CA; 11 Apr.-10 May 1986; Dir.—
Thomas F. Bradac; Set—Gil Morales; Costum-
ing—Karen J. Weller; Phil Hogan—Daniel
Bryan Cartmell; Josie—Cherie A. Brown;
Mike—Danny Oberbeck; Jim Tyrone—Russ
Terry; T. Stedman Harder—Wayne C. Watkins.

Hanson, Eugene K. Rev. *Eugene O'Neill
Newsletter* 10.2 (1986): 40-41.

Badly cast. Phil should be small and
scrappy—not a gentle hulk. The actor playing James Tyrone was "more distinguished
than dissolute." "Suave … he seemed to belong more to Pigalle than to Broadway." Weak
links show that in O'Neill there is "scant room
for improvising."

E420 *A Moon for the Misbegotten*
Pennsylvania Stage Co.; Allentown, PA; 7
May-8 June 1986; Dir.—Pam Pepper.

E421 *A Moon for the Misbegotten*
Asolo State Theater; Sarasota, FL; Winter
1986; Josie Hogan—Nora Chester; Phil—
Dane Knell; Mike/T. Stedman Harder—Marc
Durso; James Tyrone, Jr.—Terry Layman.

Frazer, Winifred L. Rev. *Eugene O'Neill
Newsletter* 10.2 (1986): 39-40.

Struck by the "close relationship" between Josie and Phil … not exactly incestuous,
but…. "The play is theirs. Jim Tyrone, you
might say, pops in and out." "Superb theater
in the heart of cracker land in north central
Florida."

E422 *A Moon for the Misbegotten* Victor Jory Theatre; Actors Theatre of Louisville
(KY); 6-24 Jan. 1987.

E423 *A Moon for the Misbegotten*
George Street Playhouse; New Brunswick,
NJ; 14 Jan.-8 Feb. 1987

E424 *A Moon for the Misbegotten*
overlapping with *Marco*. See E377. University of Pittsburgh; Pittsburgh, PA; Spring
1987.

E425 *A Moon for the Misbegotten*
Theatrical Outfit; Atlanta, GA; 11 Mar.-12
Apr. 1987; Dir.—David Head; Set—Jeroy
Hannah; Lighting—Liz Lee; Costuming—
Chris Cook; Phil Hogan—Buck Newman;

Josie—Suzi Bass; Mike—Mike McGehee; Jim Tyrone—David Milford; T. Stedman Harder—David de Vries.

Lewis, Ward B. Rev. *Eugene O'Neill Newsletter* 11.3 (1987): 29-30.

Though hailed unanimously by Atlanta theater critics, and rightly so, this production was "a far cry from what O'Neill had conceived or intended." Commending the performance for its acting "tour de force," Lewis faults the elimination of Jim's paternal hatred and isolation for masking the playwright's vision.

E426 *A Moon for the Misbegotten* Theatre Virginia; Richmond, VA; 18 Mar.-11 Apr. 1987.

E427 *A Moon for the Misbegotten* Seattle (WA) Repertory Company; 21 Mar.-18 Apr. 1987.

E428 *A Moon for the Misbegotten* Bermuda Musical and Dramatic Society; Hamilton, Bermuda; Fall 1987; Dir.—Carole Nichols. With Nigel Kermode, Richard Reynell, Beth Hall

E429 *A Moon for the Misbegotten* Sacramento (CA) Theatre Company; 27 Oct.-21 Nov. 1987; Dir.—Kenneth Kelleher; Design—Jerry Reynolds; Lighting—Maurice Vercoutere; Costuming—Michael Chapman; Josie Hogan—Ingrid Gerstmann; Phil—Jack Wellington Cantwell; Jim Tyrone—Randall King; T. Stedman Harder—David DiFrancesco.

Hanson, Eugene K. Rev. *Eugene O'Neill Newsletter* 11.3 (1987): 28-29.

"The production was strong theatre, and did justice to a central part of America's dramatic inheritance," though Gerstmann failed to live up to her promise as Josie and King "failed to turn in a satisfying portrayal of Jim Tyrone."

E430 *A Moon for the Misbegotten* Connemara Players at ATA Sargent Theatre; 314 W. 54th St.; New York City; Closed 26 Mar. 1988; Dir.—Gene Reilly.

E431 *A Moon for the Misbegotten* Magic Theatre; San Francisco, CA; 20 Apr.-5 June 1988; Dir.—John Lion.

E432 *A Moon for the Misbegotten* West Virginia University; Morgantown, WV; Spring 1988; Dir.—Judith Williams.

E433 *A Moon for the Misbegotten* Strand Theatre; Schroon Lake, NY; 8-9 July and 5-7 Aug. 1988.

E434 *A Moon for the Misbegotten* New Jersey Shakespeare Festival; Drew University; Madison, NJ; 15 Oct.-5 Nov. 1988; Dir.—Paul Barry.

E435 *A Moon for the Misbegotten* Nutmeg Theater; University of Connecticut; Storrs, CT; 20-29 Oct. and 8-13 Nov. 1988; Dir.—Edward Golden; Sets—Joan Peters.

E436 *A Moon for the Misbegotten* Portland Repertory Theatre; Portland, OR; 12 Nov.-17 Dec. 1988; Dir.—Tom Ramirez.

E437 *A Moon for the Misbegotten* Theatre-Virginia; Richmond, VA; 9 Feb.-5 Mar. 1989; Dir.—Terry Burgler.

E438 *A Moon for the Misbegotten* Pennsylvania Stage Company; Allentown, PA; 15 Mar.-9 Apr. 1989; Dir.—Donald Hicken.

E439 *A Moon for the Misbegotten* Attic Theare; Detroit, MI; 12 Apr.-7 May 1989; Dir.—Anthony Schmitt.

E440 *A Moon for the Misbegotten* Hartford Stage; Hartford, CT; 27 May-2 July 1989; Dir.—Jackson Phippin; Set Design—Christopher Barreca; Lights—Ken Tabachnick; Mike—Gordon MacDonald; T. Stedman Harder—Terence Caza; Phil Hogan—Robert Symonds; Josie—Maureen Anderman; Jim Tyrone—James Handy.

Wilkins, Frederick C. Rev. *Eugene O'Neill Review* 13.2 (1989): 77-80.

Though the principals were "not all physically consonant with the playwright's descriptions of them...," they "quickly made the roles their own and toppled a purist's initial reservations." Symonds was the star of this "creditable production."

E441 *A Moon for the Misbegotten* Second Studio for Actors; New York City; 21 June-23 July 1989; Dir.—Harv Dean.

E442 *A Moon for the Misbegotten* Abbey Theatre (National Theatre of Ireland); Studio Arena Theatre; Buffalo, NY; 20 Feb.-25 Mar. 1990 and; Spaulding Auditorium; Dartmouth College; Hanover, NH; 27 and 29 Mar. 1990; Dir.—Vincent Dowling; Set Design—Wendy Shea; Josie Hogan—Britta Smith; Phil—David Kelly; Mike—Stuart Dunne; Jim Tyrone—Bosco Hogan; T. Stedman Harder—Dan Monahan.

Manheim, Michael. Rev. *Eugene O'Neill Review* 14.1-2 (1990): 95-100.

"A gem of a set," superior acting, and a production that would be "close to O'Neill's heart" combine to make for a highly successful performance, though the second half lacks the momentum of the first.

E443 *A Moon for the Misbegotten* The Conservatory; Vancouver, BC; 12 Oct.-3 Nov. 1990; Dir.— Nick Tattersall; Artistic Direction— Lee Van Passen; Set Design— J. Lawrence McCarthy; Josie Hogan— Lee Van Passen; Phil— Edward J. Astley; Jim Tyrone— Michael Puttonen; Mike Hogan/T. Stedman Harder— R. Nelson Brown.

Black, Stephen A. Rev. *Eugene O'Neill Review* 14.1-2 (1990): 103-07.

There were small faults with this production (e.g. the lighting), "but the faults were as nothing in the face of the achievement." The relationships among the characters were sensitively depicted and the acting (especially Van Passen's Josie) superior.

E444 *A Moon for the Misbegotten* Theater-by-the-Grove; Waller Hall; Indiana University of Pennsylvania; Indiana, PA; 2-4 and 8-11 Aug. 1990.

E445 *A Moon for the Misbegotten* Williamstown Theatre Festival; Williamstown, MA; Aug. 1990; Dir.— Kevin Dowling; Phil Hogan— Pat Hingle; Josie— Christine Lahti; Jim Tyrone— Jamey Sheridan.

E446 *A Moon for the Misbegotten* Florida Repertory Theatre; West Palm Beach, FL; Spring 1991; Dir.— Richard Edelman.

E447 *A Moon for the Misbegotten* Yale Repertory Theatre; New Haven, CT; 30 Apr.-25 May 1991; Dir.— Lloyd Richards.

E448 *A Moon for the Misbegotten* Merrimack Repertory Theatre; Lowell, MA; 4-26 Oct. 1991.

E449 *A Moon for the Misbegotten* Touchstone Theater; Halsted Theater Center; Chicago, IL; Opened Oct. 1991; at Yale Repertory Theatre; New Haven, CT; 30 Apr.-25 May 1991.

E450 *A Moon for the Misbegotten* Vancouver Playhouse; Vancouver, BC; 8 Oct.-2 Nov. 1991; Dir.— Kathryn Shaw; Josie Hogan— Janet Wright; Phil— Leslie Carlson; Jim Tyrone— Jerry Franken.

Black, Stephen A. Rev. *Eugene O'Neill Review* 16.1 (1992): 118-23.

A "fundamentally incoherent" production. "Problems in the individual characterizations made for specific problems in the interactions between Josie and Jim."

E451 *A Moon for the Misbegotten* Philadelphia Drama Guild; Annenberg Center; Zellerback Theater; 14 Apr.-17 May 1992; Dir.— Mary B. Robinson.

E452 *A Moon for the Misbegotten* Pittsburgh Public Theater; Pittsburgh, PA; 23 Apr.-31 May 1992; Dir.— Lee Sankowich.

E453 *A Moon for the Misbegotten* South Jersey Regional Theater; Somers Point, NJ; 23 Apr.-10 May 1992.

E454 *A Moon for the Misbegotten* Heritage Repertory Theater; University of Virginia; Charlottesville, VA; 17 June-8 Aug. 1992 [in repertory].

E455 *A Moon for the Misbegotten* Pearl Theatre Company; New York City; 9 Sept.-24 Oct. 1992; Dir.— Allan Carlsen; Josie Hogan— Joanne Camp; Phil— Frank Lowe; James Tyrone, Jr.— Paul O'Brien; T. Stedman Harder— Arnie Burton.

_____. Rev. *Eugene O'Neill Review* 16.2 (1992): 146-48.

"A few scenes have not aged well"; nonetheless, "the moonlit tryst remains spellbinding." Advises a Josie more befitting the text (ample) and more chemistry between Josie and Jim in the confessional scene.

Frank, Glenda. Rev. *Westsider* 1-7 Oct. 1992: 17+

E456 *A Moon for the Misbegotten* Grand Theatre; London, ONT; 19 Feb.-13 Mar. 1993; Dir.— Martha Henry; Setting— Ange Zhang; Josie Hogan— Mary Walsh; Phil— Roland Hewgill; Mike— Andy Jones; Jim Tyrone— Colm Fiore; T. Stedman Harder— Hardee T. Lineham.

Lane, Harry. Rev. *Eugene O'Neill Review* 16.2 (1992): 141-46.

A tepid endorsement: "In spite of its limitations, the Grand Theatre's production served O'Neill's play well, with perceptive design choices, and some excellent direction and acting."

E457 *A Moon for the Misbegotten* Center Stage; Baltimore, MD; Spring 1993; Dir.— Lisa Peterson; Josie Hogan— Cherry Jones.

Rose, Lloyd. Rev. *Washington Post* 8 Jan. 1993, sec. C: 2.

The director "deconstructs" the play to produce a sort of "Brechtian O'Neill, an oxymoron if ever there was one ... in short nonsense." The Josie is "wonderful." The play itself mixes "the corny and the emotionally powerful"— but "the corniness *enhances* the emotional power."

E458 *A Moon for the Misbegotten*
Cincinnati Playhouse in the Park; Cincinnati,
OH; 27 Apr.-23 May 1993.

E459 *A Moon for the Misbegotten*
Gloucester Stage Company; Gloucester, MA;
20 July-14 Aug. 1994; Dir.— Grey Johnson.

E460 *A Moon for the Misbegotten* Milwaukee Repertory Theatre; Milwaukee, WI;
20 Jan.-12 Feb. 1995; Dir.— Edward Morgan.

E461 *A Moon for the Misbegotten*
Berkeley Repertory; Berkeley, CA; 31 Mar.-19
May ₤95; Dir.— Michael Bloom.

E462 *A Moon for the Misbegotten* Circle in the Square; New York City; Opened 26
Apr. 1996.

E463 *A Moon for the Misbegotten* Old
Globe Theatre; San Diego, CA; 22 Jan.-2
Mar. 1997.

E464 *A Moon for the Misbegotten*
DubbelJoint Productions; Belfast, Northern
Ireland; Mar.-Apr. 1998; On tour in the Re-
public; Apr. 1998; Dir.— Simon Magill; Set-
ting — Chisato Yoshimi; Lighting — John Rid-
dell; Phil Hogan — John Hewitt; Josie — Billie
Traynor; Mike — Steve Brown; Jim Tyrone —
Sean Campion; T. Stedman Harder — Noel
McGee.

E465 *A Moon for the Misbegotten* Performing Arts Center Stage Theatre; Denver,
CO; 23 Sept.-23 Oct. 1999.

E466 *The Moon of the Caribbees* WPA
Theater (off off Broadway); New York City;
1974-75 Season.

E467 *The Moon of the Caribbees*
American Theater Arts; 133 MacDougal St.;
New York City; 9-26 Nov. 1978.

E468 *The Moon of the Caribbees* see
*The Long Voyage Home (Caribbees, Cardiff,
Zone* and *Voyage)* National Theatre Com-
pany; Cottsloe Theatre; London; 20 Feb.-17
Mar. 1979; Revived Jan. 1980.

E469 *The Moon of the Caribbees* see
*The Sea Plays of Eugene O'Neill ("S.S.
Glencairn")* Long Wharf Theater; New Lon-
don, CT; Opened 28 Mar. 1978.

E470 *The Moon of the Caribbees* Long
Wharf Theatre; New Haven, CT; 9 Mar.-9
Apr. 1979; Dir.— Arvin Brown.

E471 *The Moon of the Caribbees* with
Hughie Washington Square,; New York Uni-
versity; New York City; 27-30 Jan. 1982;
Dir.— Rob Mulholland.

Jiji, Vera. Rev. *Eugene O'Neill Newsletter*
6.1 (1982): 48-49.

In *Caribbees* the student actors were "a
little shaky on their acting legs." "Well inten-
tioned" but amateurish. *Hughie*, conversely,
was "beautifully acted."

E472 *The Moon of the Caribbees* see
Six Plays of the Sea Apple Corps Theatre
Company; New York City; Closed 2 May 1982.

E473 *The Moon of the Caribbees* see
Sea Plays at Monte Cristo "Monte Cristo";
305 Pequot Ave.; New London, CT; 26 Sept.-
14 Nov. 1985.

E474 *The Moon of the Caribbees* see
Four Plays of the Sea ("S.S. Glencairn") Just
So Productions; San Francisco, CA; 27 Apr.-
17 June 1988.

E475 *The Moon of the Caribbees* see
The Sea Plays (Voyage, Zone, Cardiff, and
Caribbees) The Willow Cabin Theater Com-
pany; Intar II Theater; New York City; 3-20
Nov. 1988.

E476 *More Stately Mansions* (British
premiere) Greenwich; London; 19 Sept.-2
Oct. 1974; Dir.— David Giles; Design — Kenneth Mellor; Deborah — Elisabeth Bergner,
replaced by Dorothy Reynolds; Sara — Frances
Cuka; Simon — Gary Bond.

Wardle, Irving. Rev. *Times* 20 Sept.
1974: 8f.

Instead of characters the people of the
play are masks covering the pained opposition
of "assailant-victim, peasant-gentry, mother-
whore." "The play is fired with sexual con-
tempt and the idea that men are corrupted by
female greed." Deborah is a "dry-run" for
Mary Tyrone.

E477 *More Stately Mansions* University of Wisconsin; Madison, WI; 15 Dec.
1980; Dir.— Ronald Miller.

E478 *More Stately Mansions* Irish
Rebel Theatre; Irish Arts Center; New York
City; Through 31 May 1981.

E479 *More Stately Mansions* New
York Theatre Workshop; 79 E. Fourth St.;
New York City; Oct.-Nov. 1997; Dir.— Ivo
van Hove; Artistic Dir.— James C. Nicola;
Designer — Jan Versweyveld; Simon Har-
ford — Tim Hopper; Sara — Jenny Bacon;
Deborah — Joan MacIntosh.

Brantley, Ben. Rev. *New York Times* 8
Oct. 1997, sec. E: 5

A "comic-strip version" of O'Neill's
Mansions.

Drukman, Steven. Rev. *New York Times*
5 Oct. 1997, sec. 2: 5, 18.

Horowitz, Simi. Rev. *Backstage: The Performing Arts Weekly* 3-9 Oct. 1997: 13 and 37.

An interview with Ivo van Hove, in which the director explains that O'Neill "does his thing, I mine" (the sentiment is van Hove's, not the words).

MacLean, Robert S. Rev. *Eugene O'Neill Review* 21.1-2 (1997): 178-82.

Approves the acting, the symbolic and spare set, the direction, and (good heavens!) even the nudity and simulated masturbation.

Shafer, Yvonne. Rev. *Eugene O'Neill Review* 22.1-2 (1998): 218-20.

"Much has been written about the whole question of producing the play at all here and elsewhere." "The contradictory response to the play was clearly evidenced at the end."

Simon, John. Rev. *New York* 20 Oct. 1997: 72.

A "ghastly revival" that has reduced *Mansions* to a "rubble." What O'Neill saw as properly done realistically has by Van Hove's "senseless, vapid pseudo-expressionism" been "trivialized into an olla podrida of cheap theatrics."

E480 *Mourning Becomes Electra* Circle in the Square/Joseph E. Levine Theatre; New York City; Opened 15 Nov. 1972 for 53 performances; Dir.— Theodore Mann; Setting— Marsha L. Eck; Lighting— Jules Fisher; Seth Beckwith— William Hickey; Amos Ames— Hansford Rowe; Louisa— Eileen Burns; Minnie— Jocelyn Brando; Christine— Colleen Dewhurst; Lavinia— Pamela Payton-Wright; Hazel Niles— Lisa Richards; Ezra— Donald Davis; Orin— Stephen McHattie; Peter Niles— Jack Ryland; Adam Brant— Alan Mixon; Josiah Borden— Hansford Rowe; Emma Borden— Jocelyn Brando; Rev. Everett Hills— William Bush; Mrs. Hills— Eileen Burns; Dr. Joseph Blake— Daniel Keyes; Chantyman— John Ridge; Abner Small— William Bush; Joe Silva— Daniel Keyes; Ira Mackel— John Ridge.

E481 *Mourning Becomes Electra* Goodman Theatre; Chicago, IL; 15 Jan. 1976; Dir.— William Woodman; Music Selector— Nick Venden; Lavinia— Laura Esterman; Christina— Rosemary Murphy.

Adler, Thomas P. Rev. *Educational Theatre Journal* 28 (1976): 411-12.

The play is "dime-novel Freud," "a soap opera … with hokum of the worst kind." Contains all "O'Neill's recurrent themes and

motifs" and illustrates "all his strengths and weaknesses." This production emphasizes the melodramatic qualities of the play. The final scene, however, lifts the play almost to the level of the tragic.

E482 *Mourning Becomes Electra* American Conservatory Theatre; San Francisco, CA; 2 Mar.-27 May 1982; Dir.— Alan Fletcher.

E483 *Mourning Becomes Electra* Harvard-Radcliffe Summer Theatre; Loeb Drama Center; Cambridge, MA; 20-31 July 1983; Dir.— Jonathan Magaril.

Wilkins, Frederick C. Rev. *Eugene O'Neill Newsletter* 7.2 (1983): 26-29.

Stripped down version, set in post World War II America, with many roles dropped, but no advantage gained: no "illumination," no hint of Aeschylus, just "tacky minimalism."

E484 *Mourning Becomes Electra* Indiana Repertory Theatre; Indianapolis, IN; 14 Feb.-2 Mar. 1986; Dir.— Tom Haas; Set Design— Christopher H. Barreca; Lighting— Rachel Budin; Costuming— Gail Brassard; Christine Mannon— Janet Sarno; Ezra— Michael Lipton; Orin— Frederick Farrar; Lavinia— Amelia Penland; Brant— Martin LaPlatney; Hazel Niles— Marylou DiFillippo; Peter— Craig Fuller; Seth— Matthew Harrinton.

Fisher, James. Rev. *Eugene O'Neill Newsletter* 10.1 (1986): 33-34.

Though "purists would undoubtedly find the extent of Haas' radical editing a distressing violation of a classic," "inventive staging, strong acting and excellent scenic and costumes designs" enabled the power of O'Neill's work to reveal itself.

E485 *Mourning Becomes Electra* Trinity Repertory Company; Providence, RI; 25 Sep.-25 Oct. 1987; Dir.— Edward Payson Call; Set Design— Robert D. Soule; Lights— John F. Custer; Music— Paul Nelson; Christine Mannon— Barbara Orson; Ezra— Richard Kneeland; Orin— David PB Stevens; Lavinia— Jennifer Van Dyck; Brant— Richard Kavanaugh; Seth— David C. Jones.

Wilkins, Frederick C. Rev. *Eugene O'Neill Newsletter* 11.3 (1987): 34-36.

Despite competent acting, this radically cut production, "was memorable as melodrama but less than the tragedy that O'Neill intended and envisioned." Thinks that only if O'Neill's text is faithfully followed and the proscenium stage utilized might "the true note of tragedy be struck."

E486 *Mourning Becomes Electra* Playmakers Repertory Company; Paul Green Theatre; University of North Carolina at Chapel Hill; 30 Jan.-28 Feb. 1988; Dir.— David Hammond; Executive Producer— Milly S. Barranger; Stage— Desmond Heeley; Scenic Designer— Bill Clarke; Lighting— Robert Wierzel; Seth Beckwith— Paul Tourtillotte; Christine Mannon— Ira Thomas; Orin— David Whalen; Ezra/Chantyman— Maury Cooper; Lavinia— Tandy Cronin; Hazel Niles— Susanna Rinehart; Peter— James Lawson; Adam Brant— Patrick Egan.

Wilkins, Frederick C. Rev. *Eugene O'Neill Newsletter* 12.1 (1988): 66-68.

In appreciation of a successful performance of O'Neill's lengthy trilogy, Wilkins takes off his hat to salute the acting, the direction, and the fidelity to O'Neill's text found in this production.

E487 *Mourning Becomes Electra* Mohegan Community College; New London, CT; 13 Feb. 1988; Dir.— John Basinger.

E488 *Mourning Becomes Electra* College Theater; City College of San Francisco; 50 Phelan Ave.; San Francisco, CA; 16 Sept.-6 Nov. 1988.

E489 *Mourning Becomes Electra* Citizens' Theatre; Glasgow, Scotland; Spring 1991; Dir.— Philip Prowse; Christine Mannon— Glenda Jackson; Lavinia— Georgina Hale; Ezra/Orin— Gerard Murphy.

Stevenson, Randall. Rev. *TLS* 12 Apr. 1991: 16.

Strain as O'Neill might towards infinity, he is undermined "by his drab prosaicness, his inability to find fit words to match [his] characters' passions."

E490 *Mourning Becomes Electra* Arizona Repertory Theatre; University of Arizona; Tucson, AZ; 9 June-11 July 1993; Dir.— Harold Dixon.

E491 *Mourning Becomes Electra* Chain Lightning Theatre; New York City; 24 Sept.-10 Oct. 1993; Dir.— Joseph Millett; Ezra Mannon— Kricker James; Christine— Ginger Grace; Lavinia— Cheryl Horne; Orin— Joel Goldes; Adam Brant— Richard Kinsey; Peter Niles— Burton Fitzpatrick; Hazel— Priscilla Holbrook.

Frank, Glenda. Rev. *Westsider* 7-13 Oct. 1993: 18+.

Ranald, Margaret Loftus. Rev. *Eugene O'Neill Review* 16.2 (1992): 122-27.

Though "the dramaturgy does sometimes creak" yet "overall, this was a memorable occasion, one which left the audience emotionally drained, almost silent, spellbound by the power of an admittedly flawed but extraordinarily visceral experience." Ranald casts an appreciative eye upon the women characters, whose strength "carried the performance."

E492 *Mourning Becomes Electra* Shakespeare Theatre; Washington, DC; 29 Apr.-15 June 1997; Dir.— Michael Kahn.

Kelly McGillis and Ted van Griethuysen

E493 *The Movie Man* see *Three Lost Plays of Eugene O'Neill (Wife, Movie Man and Web)* Lotus Theatre Group; Playhouse 46; 423 W. 46th St. (at St. Clement's Church); New York City; 4-20 Nov. 1982.

E494 *The Movie Man, Shell-Shock, and Thirst* Playtime Series 59; Theater-Studio; 750 Eighth Ave. at 46th St.; New York City; 9-14 Sept. 1995; Dir.— A. M. Raychel.

E495 *The Movie Man,* with *Cardiff* and *Abortion* Playwright's Theater Festival of O'Neill; Provincetown Playhouse; New York City; 3-8 Aug. 1999.

E496 *The Personal Equation* Actors' Studio of New York; Boston, MA; 13 May 1995; Dir.— Stephen Kennedy Murphy.

E497 *Recklessness,* with *Web, Breakfast,* and *Hughie* Playtime Series 59; Theater-Studio; 750 Eighth Avenue at 46th Street; New York City; 16-21 Sept. 1995; Dir.— A. M. Raychel.

E498 *The Rope* see *Six Plays of the Sea (Cardiff, Voyage, Zone, Ile, Rope, Cross)* Apple Corps Theatre Company; New York City; Closed 2 May 1982; Dir.— Skip Corris.

E499 *The Rope* see *Sea Plays at Monte Cristo (Cardiff, Voyage, Zone, Ile, Cross, Rope)* "Monte Cristo"; 305 Pequot Ave.; New London, CT; 26 Sept.-14 Nov. 1985.

E500 *The Rope* Nederlander Television and Film Productions; A&E Network; American Playwrights Theater: The One-Acts.; 7 Dec. 1989; Dir.— Lela Swift; Producer— George Manasse; Set— Tom H. John; Music— Brian Keane; Abraham Bentley— José Ferrer; Annie— Elizabeth Ashley; Luke— Brad Davis; Mary— Donna Vivino; Pat Sweeney— Len Cariou.

Wilkins, Frederick C. Rev. *Eugene O'Neill Review* 13.2 (1989): 94-96.

While appreciative of the effort "especially Ferrer's interpretation of Abraham," Wilkins hopes that A & E and the Nederlanders move on to longer plays in subsequent seasons that are "worthier O'Neill artifacts."

E501 *Sea Plays at Monte Cristo (Caribbees, Cardiff, Voyage, Zone, Ile, Cross,* **and** *Rope)* "Monte Cristo"; 305 Pequot Ave.; New London, CT; 26 Sept.-14 Nov. 1985.

E502 *The Sea Plays of Eugene O'Neill ("S. S. Glencairn": Caribbees, Zone, Cardiff* **and** *Voyage)* Long Wharf Theater; New Haven, CT; Opened by 28 Mar. 1978; Dir.— Edward Payson Call; Artistic Dir.— Arvin Brown; Setting— John Jensen; Lighting— Ronald Wallace; Music— Robert Dennis; CREW OF THE S. S. GLENCAIRN; Driscoll— Robert Lansing; Smitty— David Clennon; Cocky— Emery Battis; Ivan— Peter Iacangelo; Yank— Beeson Carrol; Davis— Frederick Coffin; Max— Owen Hollander; Scotty— Lance Davis; Lamps— Bob Harper; Donkeyman— William Swetland; Olson— William Newman; Paddy— Richard Jamieson; Paul— Dick Sollenberger; First Mate— Edwin J. McDonough; Captain— Victor Argo; THE ISLANDERS; Bella— Carol Jean Lewis; Pearl— C. C. H. Pounder; Susie— Shirley Martelly; Violet— Helen Chivas Hatten; THE LONDONERS; Joe— Owen Hollander; Nick— Lance Davis; Mag— Le Clanche du Rand; Freda— Marlena Lustik; Kate— Nora Chester; Two Stevedores— Bob Harper and Richard Jamieson.

Eder, Richard. Rev. *New York Times* 30 Mar. 1978, sec. C: 15.

The production does not succeed in taking the plays "out of mothballs." The set is good, the actors try hard, but the plays are too difficult to do effectively. The director "has imposed a somnolent rhythm on all four plays." *Caribbees* is the "most clumsily performed" and slightest play, *Zone* not much better.

Wilkins, Frederick C. Rev. *Eugene O'Neill Newsletter* 2.1 (1978): 12-13.

"Lacked the cumulative punch of a full-length play … but did capture the atmosphere which is the play's chief virtue." And "performance by the same actors in the same roles [from play to play] underscored O'Neill's consistency in characterization."

E503 *The Sea Plays (In the Zone, The Long Voyage Home,* **and** *Ile)* Rand Theater; University of Massachusetts at Amherst; 20-29 Oct. 1988; Dir.— Edward Golden; *In the Zone;* Davis— Scott Davison; Smitty— Michael Flood; *The Long Voyage Home;* Olson— Jonathan Jude Duquette; Fat Joe— Dudley Stone; Kate— Amanda Percival; Freda— Jennifer Lavenhar; *Ile;* Captain Keeney— Harry Mahnken; Mrs. Keeney— Christine Adair.

Wilkins, Frederick C. Rev. *Eugene O'Neill Newsletter* 12.3 (1988): 47-48.

Crediting the success of this production, in part, on effective sets and lighting, Wilkins, thinks *Ile* the high point since it included faculty as well as student actors, and concludes that this interpretation of O'Neill's plays "with its skillful blend of sights and sounds and confrontations, disclosed the evocative richness that was O'Neill's from his earliest days as a dramatist."

E504 *The Sea Plays (Cardiff, Caribbees, Voyage,* **and** *Zone)* The Willow Cabin Theater Company; Intar II Theater; New York City; 3-20 Nov. 1988; Dir.— Edward Berkeley; Sets— Paul Cook; Donkeyman— Philip Ashby; Smitty— Mark Piatelli; Paul/Fat Joe— Michael Rispoli; Yank— Craig Zakarian; Nick— Joe Pacheco; Freda— Angela Nevard; Cocky— Doug Broe; Driscoll— Adam Oliensis.

Frank, Glenda. Rev. *Eugene O'Neill Review* 13.1 (1989): 65-68.

This production of *Cardiff, Caribbees, Voyage,* and *Zone* "was a testament to the vitality of O'Neill's early sea plays" in part because "Mr. Berkeley approached the plays not as poetry nor sea adventure, but as dramas about human relationships." In production the reviewer found *Zone* least satisfying, but then so did O'Neill.

E505 *Servitude* Coppertop Theatre; University of Wisconsin Center; Richland, WI; 14-16 Nov. 1981; Dir.— Paul Voelker.

E506 *Servitude* Playwright's Theater Festival of O'Neill; Provincetown Playhouse; New York City; 17-21 Aug. 1999.

E507 *Shell-Shock, The Movie Man,* **and** *Thirst* Playtime Series 59; Theater-Studio; 750 Eighth Ave. at 46th St.; New York City; 9-14 Sept. 1995; Dir.— A. M. Raychel.

E508 *Six Plays of the Sea (Cardiff, Voyage, Zone, Ile, Rope, Cross)* Apple Corps Theatre Company; New York City; Closed 2 May 1982; Dir.— Skip Corris.

E509 *The Sniper* Playwright's Theater Festival of O'Neill; Provincetown Playhouse; New York City; 24-28 Aug. 1999.

E510 *S. S. Glencairn — Four Plays of the Sea (Caribbees, Cardiff, Voyage, Zone)* Willow Cabin Theatre Company; Harold Clurman Theatre; New York City; 8-31 Oct. 1993; Dir.— Edward Berkeley; Design — Miguel Lopez-Castillo; Driscoll — Adam Oliensis; Yank/Fat Joe — Michael Rispoli; Olson — Laurence Gleason; Freda — Angela Nevard; Mag — Charmain Lord; Cocky — Doub Broect.

Carlson, Marvin. Rev. *Eugene O'Neill Review* 16.2 (19): 105-08.

Played together they enrich one another. Settings, acting, and especially the music all earn high marks.

Lyons, Donald. "Young and at Sea." *New Criterion* 12 Nov. 1993: 60-62.

Approves of the Willow Cabin Theatre Company's production of *S.S. Glencairn: Four Plays of the Sea*, the impressive ensemble acting, and the playwright who created the theatrically viable plays. Regrets O'Neill's middle, experimental period (*Interlude, Electra*), but applauds his early works and, of course, his later masterpieces.

E511 *Strange Interlude* Duke of York's Theatre; London; opened 6 Apr. 1984; Then Nederlander Theatre; New York City; 21 Feb.- 5 May 1985; Dir.— Keith Hack; Design — Voytek with Michael Levine; Costuming — Deirdre Clancy; Incidental Music — Benedict Mason; Nina Leeds — Glenda Jackson; Charlie Marsden — Edward Petherbridge; Ned — Brian Cox; Sam Evans — James Hazeldine; Madeline — Caitlin Clarke (in New York only).

Gelb, Barbara. "*Strange Interlude* Returns to Broadway." *New York Times* 14 Feb. 1985, sec. 1: 1, 24.

Kelly, K. Rev. *Boston Globe* 22 Feb. 1985: 21.

Nightingale, Benedict. "Glenda Jackson Grapples with O'Neill's Everywoman." *New York Times* 14 Feb. 1985, sec. 2: 1, 6.

Rich, Frank. Rev. *New York Times* 22 Feb. 1985, sec. C: 3.

Richards, David. "Enduring the Interlude." *Washington Post* 22 Feb. 1985, sec. E: 6.

Simon, John. Rev. *New York* 4 Mar. 1985: 10.

Wilkins, Frederick C. Rev. *Eugene O'Neill Newsletter* 9.1 (1985): 46-49.

"Fresh, even brash approach." Not a "flawless masterpiece." O'Neill's psychology was clearly weak, but not his theatricality. "A performance to cherish."

E512 *Strange Interlude* Channel 13, PTV's "American Playhouse" [A British production based on the London and Broadway stage version of 1984-85 with Jackson and Petherbridge repeating their roles.]; 18, 19, 20 Jan. 1988 (in three segments); Prod.— Philip Barry; Adapted for television — Robert Enders; Nina Leeds — Glenda Jackson; Charles Marsden — Edward Petherbridge; Edmund Darrell — David Dukes; Professor Leeds — José Ferrer; Sam Evans — Ken Howard; Mrs. Amos Evans — Rosemary Harris; The young Gordon — Jadrien Steele; The grown Gordon — Kenneth Branagh.

O'Connor, John J. Rev. *New York Times* 18 Jan. 1988, sec. A: 25+.

Notes that, though the actors' speaking their thoughts may be awkward (no "voice over" as in the 1932 film version), it is ultimately "rewarding." A "period piece" but "theater at its most powerful."

E513 *Strange Interlude* Tampa Players, at the Jaeb Theatre; Tampa Bay Performing Arts Center; Tampa, FL; 10-26 Mar. 1989; Dir.— Bill Lelbach.

E514 *The Straw* The Salamander Repertory Theatre; Walker Street Theater; New York City; 3-26 Nov. 1989; Dir.— Toni Dorfman; Adaptation — Joel Leffert/Toni Dorfman; Bill Carmody — Bud Thorpe; Eileen — Nancy Nichols; Stephen Murray — Joel Leffert; Mrs. Brennan — Cecile Mann.

Frank, Glenda. Rev. *Eugene O'Neill Review* 14.1-2 (1990): 79-85.

After reviewing the play's stage history and O'Neill family associations Frank praises the director's sensitivity to the text and the performance of Joel Leffert as Stephen, but finds that Nancy Nichols "enacted the role of Eileen with one-dimensional, saccharine resignation."

Vena, Gary. Rev. *Eugene O'Neill Review* 13.2 (1989): 89-94.

Cutting the opening scene in the Carmody kitchen was a mistake, and Nancy Nichols "never fully captured the 'wistful sadness' O'Neill ascribes to Eileen." While questioning the choice of plays, Vena applauds the fledgling company's pioneering spirit.

E515 _Thirst_ Experimental Theatre; University of Wisconsin; Madison, WI; 12-15 Apr. 1978; Dir.— Edward Amor; Scenic Designer — Mohammed Paigah; Lit. Advisor — Esther M. Jackson.

Wilkins, Frederick C. Rev. _Eugene O'Neill Newsletter_ 2.2 (1978): 16-17.

Originally produced in 1916, this is the play's first revival. Quoting others Wilkins, who did not see the revival (nor the original), says that the play was considered "cinematic in form and contemporary in theme," "one of the [local] theater events of the year," and successful because of "the setting, designed with uncanny insight by Mohammed Paigah."

E516 _Thirst_ Ashe County Little Theatre; The North Carolina Theatre Conference/Farthing Auditorium; Boone, NC; 8. Nov. 1986; Dir— Robert Franklin; Set — Ricky Brown; Makeup — Phyllis Efford; Technical — Dayne Hodges; A Gentleman — Tom Fowler; A Dancer — Wendy Leland; A Sailor — Rus Cato.

Notice. _The Skyland Post_ (West Jefferson, NC) 12 Nov. 1986:11.

"powerful and unexpected … utterly unlike anything else … an intense and difficult script.…"

Notice. _Jefferson Times_ (Jefferson, NC) 13 Nov. 1986: n.p.

"not recommended for children younger than teenage."

E517 _Thirst, The Movie Man_, and _Shell-Shock_ Playtime Series 59; Theater-Studio; 750 Eighth Ave. at 46th St.; New York City; 9-14 Sept. 1995; Dir.— A. M. Raychel.

E518 _Three Lost Plays of Eugene O'Neill (Breakfast, Wife,_ and _Cross)_ Nameless Theater; 125 W. 22nd Street; New York City; Closed 19 Jan. 1978.

E519 _Three Lost Plays of Eugene O'Neill (Wife, Movie Man,_ and _Web)_ Lotus Theatre Group; Playhouse 46; 423 W. 46th St. (at St. Clement's Church); New York City; 4-20 Nov. 1982; Dir.— Michael Fields.

Wilkins, Frederick C. Rev. _Eugene O'Neill Newsletter_ 6.3 (1982): 24-26.

Happy with the productions, and with _Wife_ ("if one accepts the play as representative of its genre, the melodramatic vaudeville sketch") and _Web_ (occasional "effective mo-

ments"), but thought _Movie Man_ "ham-fisted"; it "should return to a well-deserved oblivion."

E520 _A Touch of the Poet_ Hartford Stage Company; Hartford, CT; Opened 31 Mar. 1974; Dir.— Paul Weidner; Setting — Marjorie Kellogg; Lighting — Peter Hunt; Mickey Maloy — Daniel Snyder; Jamie Cregan — Jack Murdock; Sara Melody — Tana Hicken; Nora Melody — Maureen Quinn; Cornelius Melody — Paul Sparer; Dan Roche — Bernard Frawley; Paddy O'Dowd — Jerry Reid.; Patch Riley — David O. Petersen; Deborah Harford — Barbara Caruso; Nicholas Gadsby — John Leighton.

Barnes, Clive. Rev. _New York Times_ 31 Mar. 1974: 53.

Endorses the production. Notes that the play is typically American — unlike other later O'Neill.

O'Connor, John J. Rev. _New York Times_ Apr. 25, 1974: 79.

Finds the production "cumbersome," and "somewhat laborious," but still "solid and intelligent."

E521 _A Touch of the Poet_ Manhattan Theater Club; (off off Broadway); 1974-75 Season.

E522 _A Touch of the Poet_ York Players; (off off Broadway); New York City; 17 Feb. 1976.

E523 _A Touch of the Poet_ Irish Rebel Theater; (off off Broadway); New York City; Nov. 1976.

E524 _A Touch of the Poet_ Helen Hayes Theatre; New York City; Opened 28 Dec. 1977 for 141 performances.; Dir.— José Quintero; Decor and lighting — Ben Edwards; Costumes — Jane Greenwood; Mickey Maloy — Barry Snider; Jamie Cregan — Milo O'Shea; Sara Melody — Kathryn Walker; Nora Melody — Geraldine Fitzgerald; Cornelius Melody — Jason Robards; Dan Roche — Walter Flanagan; Paddy O'Dowd — Dermot McNamara; Patch Riley — Richard Hamilton; Deborah Harford — Betty Miller; Nicholas Gadsby — George Ede.

"Dear Valentine 'On Stage: Blarney and Bluster.'" _New Leader_ 30 Jan. 1978: 25-26.

Too long, repetitive and indigestible. Impressed with Quintero's direction, but not with Robards' performance.

Barnes, Clive. Theater/"Touching Portrayal of _Poet_ by Robards." _New York Post_ 29 Dec. 1977; _NYTCR_ 1977: 97.

"Too many words ... too many flat words at that." O'Neill "wanders" and "blurs" but has a "vision." Rates production, acting, directing high. The performance gets to the play's "bitter, cynical core."

Beaufort, John. Theater Reviews/"Outside Poet Tops New York Openings." *Christian Science Monitor* 5 Jan. 1978; *NYTCR* 1977: 102.

All superlatives, although "judicious cutting" would be in order.

Clurman, Harold. Theatre. *Nation* 21 Jan. 1978: 60-61.

Doesn't think Quintero fully understands the play: Con Melody's downfall is only meaningful if he isn't a phoney. Robards isn't right for the part.

Eder, Richard. "*A Touch of the Poet* Staged by Quintero on Broadway." *New York Times* 29 Dec. 1977, sec. 3:13; *NYTCR* 1977: 99.

High praise except for Robards' portrayal (or it may have been Quintero's direction) of Con in the first part of the play.

Gill, Brendan. "Overkill." *New Yorker* 9 Jan. 1978: 59.

Though the play was written in O'Neill's prime, it is clumsy.

Gottfried, Martin. "The Cult of the Second-rate." *Saturday Review* 4 Mar. 1978: 41.

Second-rate O'Neill and neither Quintero's directing nor Robards' acting can compensate for its deficiencies.

Kalem, T. E. "Dream Addict." *Time* 9 Jan. 1978: 68.

Touch is "like a tidal wave that seems to purge almost every defect of the play." The Robards/Quintero pairing seems "attuned not only to O'Neill's text but to his troubled soul."

Kauffmann, Stanley. "Stanley Kauffmann on the Theatre." *New Republic* 28 Jan. 1978: 24-25.

Emphasizes that O'Neill was fundamentally concerned with the conflict of cultures: "Irish Catholic versus American Protestant or American godless is at the base of his great dramas." Thinks Quintero and Robards fail to discern this, in so far as they think of Con Melody as *acting* grand: there is no tragedy if he is just acting. Unimpressed with directing and acting — except with Geraldine Fitzgerald.

Kerr, Walter. "Vintage O'Neill — But with the Crucial Ambiguity Missing." *New York Times* 8 Jan. 1978, sec. 2: 5.

Thinks that the meaning of the play has escaped Quintero and Robards: that although men with a touch of the poet may be fools, they are "ambiguously fools." Quintero and Robards fail to suggest that "there is anything to be salvaged from the fantasist's inventive brain." Approves most of Geraldine Fitzgerald and Kathryn Walker.

Kroll, Jack. "Symphony of Despair." *Newsweek* 9 Jan. 1978: 71.

The acting early in the play is "fussy," but improves. The play itself is generally slightly below the great O'Neill works.

Lape, Bob. WABC-TV. 28 Dec. 1977; *NYTCR* 1977: 102.

"Scorching, searing theatre." Robards and Quintero are a "formidable force."

Oliver, Roger W. Rev. *Eugene O'Neill Newsletter* 2.1 (1978): 11-12.

Sharp, Christopher. The Theatre. *Women's Wear Daily* 30 Dec. 1977; *NYTCR* 1977: 98.

"Exotic poetry" but over-written, "a study in blarney." "A bit self-conscious" of its historical setting. Despite a slow start for the play, Robards is "at his best," and the rest of the cast is "outstanding."

Simon, John. Rev. *New York* 16 Jan. 1978: 57-58.

The play is not great but does command our attention. However this production is not worthy. Compliments Kathryn Walker's Sara, says Geraldine Fitzgerald is satisfactory, but objects to Robards as Con and to Quintero's direction.

Watt, Douglas. Theater/"Superb *Touch of the Poet.*" *Daily News* 30 Dec 1977; *NYTCR* 1977: 98.

Lesser play than *Misbegotten* but still "grand enough and fascinating." All superlatives.

Williams, Gary Jay. "Theater in New York: Jason and the Guilt Fleece: *A Touch of the Poet.*" *Theater* 9.2 (1978): 147-48.

Maintains that the ambiguities of the historical setting and the unbiographical characters give richness to the play and spare us the near self-lionizing of *Journey.* Robards is badly cast until his performance at the end when the play becomes interesting.

Wilson, Edwin. The Theater/"Robards Connects Again with O'Neill." *Wall Street Journal* 30 Dec. 1977; *NYTCR* 1977: 100.

Observes the usual O'Neill faults in the play but finds the production sterling.

E525 *A Touch of the Poet* University of Calgary; Canada; 7-11 Feb. 1979; Dir.— Richard Hornby.

E526 *A Touch of the Poet* Ionia Summer Theater; New Rochelle, NY; Summer 1979.

E527 *A Touch of the Poet* Actors Theatre of St. Paul; St. Paul, MN; 7 Feb-1 Mar. 1980; Dir.— George C. White.

E528 *A Touch of the Poet* Lyric Stage; 54 Charles St.; Boston, MA; 20 Feb.-22 Mar. 1980; Dir.— Polly Hogan; Con Melody — Ron Ritchell; Sara — Ann Murphy; Nora — Joan Gale.

Wilkins, Frederick C. Rev. *Eugene O'Neill Newsletter* 4.1-2 (1980): 29-30.

"A rich and satisfying production" whose "highest acting honors" go to the actresses playing Nora and Sara, especially Sara: "Sara grows up in the course of her play, and ... [the actress'] performance traced that development touchingly and persuasively."

E529 *A Touch of the Poet* Centralia College; Centralia, WA; 28 Feb.-8 Mar. 1980; Dir.— Deborah Kellar.

E530 *A Touch of the Poet* Library Theatre; St. Peter's Square; Manchester, England; 1-6 June 1981; Then Neptune Theatre; Liverpool, England; 8-13 June 1981; Dir.— Roland Jaquarello.

E531 *A Touch of the Poet* Intiman Theatre Company; Seattle, WA; 8-26 Sept. 1981; Dir.— Margaret Booker.

Pattin, Deborah Kellar. Rev. *Eugene O'Neill Newsletter* 5.3 (1981): 20-21.

"Impressive," "enthusiastic audiences," "held over by popular demand": the reviewer's comments suggest that the production's success came from the careful exploitation of the play's humor.

E532 *A Touch of the Poet* ANTA Presentation; at Springfield College; Springfield, MA; 8-10, 15-16 Jan. 1982; Dir.— Gini Andrewes.

E533 *A Touch of the Poet* Whole Theatre Company; Montclair, NJ; 12 Oct.-7 Nov. 1982; Dir.— Arnold Mittelman.

E534 *A Touch of the Poet* Roberts Theater; Rhode Island College; Providence, RI; 11-14 Nov. 1982.

E535 *A Touch of the Poet* The American Stage Company; St. Petersburg, FL; 24 Feb.-27 Mar. 1983; Dir.— Kevin Coleman.

E536 *A Touch of the Poet* The Concord Players; Concord, MA; 22 Apr.-7 May 1983; Dir.— Dorothy A. Scheckter.

Brooks, Marshall. Rev. *Eugene O'Neill Newsletter* 7.1 (1983): 19-20.

Con Melody "is a bewildering array of emotions, prejudices, memories, requiring subtle and sudden changes in mood and tone to convey." He "has to be more than an out-of-touch, grandiloquent windbag." In this production, he wasn't.

E537 *A Touch of the Poet* Yale Repertory Theatre; New Haven, CT; 3-21 May 1983; Dir.— Lloyd Richards.

Wilkins, Frederick C. Rev. *Eugene O'Neill Newsletter* 7.1(1983): 22-25.

"I have always found [*Touch*] near perfect on stage, in its telling of a story ... that descends from irresisible comedy to — if not tragedy, at least a pathos that is extremely moving." An "excellent production."

E538 *A Touch of the Poet* Equity Library Theater; New York City; 12-29 Apr. 1984; Dir.— Yvonne Ghareeb; Setting — Dennis Bradford; Con Melody — Gerald J. Quimby; Nora — Helen-Jean Arthur; Sara — Kay Walbye.

E539 *A Touch of the Poet* Berkeley Repertory Theatre; Berkeley, CA; 14 Sept.-2 Oct. 1984; Dir.— Steven Schachter.

E540 *A Touch of the Poet* Department of Theatre; Indiana University; Bloomington, IN; 7-15 Feb. 1986.

E541 *A Touch of the Poet* Detroit (MI) Repertory Theatre; 15 May-22 June 1986.

E542 *A Touch of the Poet* Gateway Players; Wareham, MA; May 1987.

E543 *A Touch of the Poet* Druid Theartre Co.; Galway, Ireland; 15 June 1987; Dir.— Garry Hynes.

E544 *A Touch of the Poet* University of North Carolina at Greensboro; 4-8 Nov. 1987; Dir.— Betty Jean Jones.

E545 *A Touch of the Poet* Civic Arts Repertory Company; Walnut Creek, CA; 22 Jan.-22 Feb. 1988; Dir.— Edward Weingold.

E546 *A Touch of the Poet* The Young Vic and Comedy Theatres; London; 28 Jan. Transferred to the Haymarket; 10 Mar.-May 1988; Dir.— David Thacker; Sara Melody — Rudi Davies; Nora — Vanessa Redgrave; Con — Timothy Dalton; Deborah Harford — Amanda Boxer; Malcolm Tierney, John

McEnery, James Berwick; Shay Gorman, Simon Coady, William Armstrong.

Chothia, Jean. Review-essay. *Recorder* 3.1 (1989): 67-72. (See A119)

Condee, William F. Rev. *Eugene O'Neill Newsletter* 12.2 (1988): 71-76.

Condee's review-essay discusses the "theatrical transplantation" of this play in terms of the director's vision. Thacker shunned preconceived notions of the play, balanced the work's political and psychological issues, and emphasized the Irish-English dichotomy. Redgrave's performance was impressive, but Dalton's and Davies' less so.

Morley, Sheridan. Rev. *International Herald Tribune* 10 Feb. 1988: 7.

"A production that would have glorified the National or the Royal Shakespeare at any time in their history" and "despite its lyrical, rambling verbosity," a play that "reveals an altogether lighter and often sharper O'Neill than the more familiar alcoholic heroics."

Porter, Laurin R. Rev. *Eugene O'Neill Newsletter* 12.1 (1988): 62-64.

"His [Thacker's] *Poet* ... captured with insight and sensitivity the nuances and the subtleties of a complex play. The individual performances were compelling, the ensemble deftly orchestrated from the morning routine at Melody's inn to the Nora-Sara tableau of the final scene." Commends the production for capturing the play's "intensely Irish flavor."

E547 *A Touch of the Poet* Kendall Drama Lab; Southern Connecticut State University; New Haven, CT; 24-27 Feb. 1988; Dir.— Anthony Watts.

E548 *A Touch of the Poet* Academy Theatre; Atlanta, GA; May 1988; Dir.— John Stephens.

E549 *A Touch of the Poet* Theatre Plus at the Jane Mallett Theatre; St. Lawrence Centre; Toronto, ONT; 5 Sept.-1 Oct. 1988; Dir.— Malcolm Black.

E550 *A Touch of the Poet* New Rose Theatre; Portland, OR; 14 Sept.-16 Oct. 1988; Dir.— Twig Webster.

E551 *A Touch of the Poet* Long Wharf Theatre; New Haven, CT; 7 Apr.-17 May 1992; Dir.— Arvin Brown; Design — Michael Yeargan; Lighting — Christopher Akerlind; Mickey Maloy — Eddie Bowz; Jamie Cregan — Jarlath Conroy; Sara Melody — Melissa Leo; Nora — Joyce Ebert; Con — Len Cariou;

Deborah Harford — Alexandra O'Karma; Nicholas Gadsby — Doug Stender.

Garvey, Sheila Hickey. Rev. *Eugene O'Neill Review* 16.2 (1992): 128-32.

"The quality of the performances and direction was so outstanding" that the faults Garvey did find were relatively speaking peccadilloes. Leo's vocal execution was one cause for concern and the inexplicable shifts in temperament in Cariou's interpretation of Con was another.

E552 *A Touch of the Poet* American Repertory Theatre; Cambridge, MA; 7-26 Mar. 1994; Dir.— Joe Dowling; Lights — Frances Aronson; Set Design — Derek McLane; Con — Daniel J. Travanti; Sara — Elizabeth Marvel; Mrs. Harford — Margaret Gibson; Nora — Dearbhla Molloy.

Connolly, Thomas F. Rev. *Eugene O'Neill Review* 17.1-2 (1993): 173-78.

Finds that Travanti's Melody "does not soar," and in fact returned to earth after the first two acts. Also faulted the play's timing, but commended the production's "technical dazzle" and the performance of Dearbhla Molloy as Nora, who "alone of the principals" "etched a brilliant and distinctive performance."

E553 *A Touch of the Poet* Roundabout Theatre Company; New York City; 29 Mar.- 28 May 1995.

E554 *A Touch of the Poet* San Antonio Public Theatre; San Antonio, TX; 1-16 June 1996; Dir.— Barry Pearson; Con Melody — David Connelly; Nora — Sam Carter Gilliam; Sara — Esther Magaloni; Deborah Harford — Maia Adamina; Mickey Maloy — Guy Metzger; Jamie Cregan — Stephen Price.

Fletcher, Anne. Rev. *Eugene O'Neill Review* 20.1-2 (1996): 166-70.

Though the play was offered as a vehicle for current immigrants to find identification in the plight of the immigrant Irish, the interpretation is "sound" and "traditional." Generally commending the cast, Fletcher found them individually strong but failing to interact convincingly. While the costuming was "problematic," the production is "an ambitious undertaking for a fledgling company."

E555 *A Touch of the Poet* Goodman Theatre; Chicago, IL; Closed 8 June 1996; Dir.— Robert Falls; Con Melody — Brian Dennehy; Pamela Payton-Wright and Jenny Bacon.

E556 *A Touch of the Poet* Arena Stage; Washington, DC; 3 Oct.-9 Nov. 1997; Space Theatre; Denver, CO; 10 Dec. 1997-10 Jan. 1998; Dir.— Michael Kahn; Con Melody— Daniel J. Travanti; Sara— Fiona Gallagher; Nora— Tana Hicken; Deborah Harford— Robin Moseley.

Wainscott, Ronald. Rev. *Eugene O'Neill Review* 21.1-2 (1997): 175-78.

"It is unfortunate that such excellent staging and mature performances by the talented women could not be made by a fuller depiction of Cornelius."

E557 *The Web* see *Three Lost Plays of Eugene O'Neill (Wife, Movie Man, and Web)* Lotus Theatre Group; Playhouse 46; 423 W. 46th St. (at St. Clement's Church); New York City; 4-20 Nov. 1982; Dir.— Michael Fields.

E558 *The Web,* with *Breakfast, Hughie,* and *Recklessness* Playtime Series 59; Theater-Studio; 750 Eighth Avenue at 46th Street; New York City; 16-21 Sept. 1995; Dir.— A. M. Raychel.

E559 *Welded* Academy Arts Repertory; 330 E. 56th St.; New York City; Closed 23 Apr. 1978.

E560 *Welded* No Smoking Playhouse; New York City; Closed 10 Nov. 1979; Dir.— Irene Horowitz.

E561 *Welded* Presented by the Summer Session; The Center for Theater Studies; Columbia University; Horace Mann Theater of Teachers College; New York City; 10 June-5 July 1981; Dir.— José Quintero; Setting— Quentin Thomas; Lighting— Michael Valentino; Michael Cape— Philip Anglim; Eleanor— Ellen Tobie; John— Court Miller; Woman— Laura Gardner.

Brooks, Marshall. Rev. *Eugene O'Neill Newsletter* 5.2 (1981): 18-19.

"Really, one must love Eugene O'Neill in order to watch…" etc. Sees Michael Cape as an early dry run at Edmund and Jamie Tyrone.

Gussow, Mel. "In a Sea of Symbolism." *New York Times* 18 June 1981, sec. C: 22.

Pans both the play and the production. Says this play would have buried a lesser playwright. Objects to "sea of symbolism" and the "over wrought language." Adds that Quintero's "heavy-handed" direction is not helpful.

Hinden, Michael. Rev. *Eugene O'Neill Newsletter* 5.2 (1981): 17-18.

"A dispiriting event." Quintero "has taken one of O'Neill's least imaginative plays and mounted it with deadening fidelity." In it O'Neill "fails to dramatize … instead he talks around" whatever.

Simon, John. "Theater." *New York* 29 June 1981: 39.

Although the actors were all professionals, the play came off as a drama school amateur production. Contains "clumsy plotting and elephantine language."

E562 *Welded* 725 Broadway; New York City; Closed 12 Feb. 1984; Dir.— Gregg Brevoort.

E563 *Where the Cross Is Made* see *Three Lost Plays of Eugene O'Neill (Breakfast, Wife* and *Cross)* Nameless Theater; 125 W. 22nd St.; New York City; Closed 19 Jan. 1978.

E564 *Where the Cross Is Made* Harvard Summer Repertory Theatre; Loeb Experimental Theatre; Cambridge, MA; 6-8 July 1978; Dir.— George Hamlin.

Wilkins, Frederick C. Rev. *Eugene O'Neill Newsletter* 2.2 (1978): 17-18.

Has "more than enough thematic material to sustain a one-act play," and this production "brought it to effective life."

E565 *Where the Cross Is Made* see *Six Plays of the Sea (Cardiff, Voyage, Zone, Ile, Rope, Cross)* Apple Corps Theatre Company; New York City; Closed 2 May 1982; Dir.— Skip Corris.

E566 *Where the Cross Is Made* see *Sea Plays at Monte Cristo (Cardiff, Voyage, Zone, Ile, Cross, Rope)* Monte Cristo"; 305 Pequot Ave.; New London, CT; 26 Sept.-14 Nov. 1985.

E567 *Where the Cross Is Made* with *Breakfast* and *Dreamy* The Winter Company; Tower Theatre; Massachusetts College of Art; Boston, MA; 13-26 Feb. 1986.

E568 *Where the Cross Is Made* Colony Theatre; Taylor Hall (Blessed Sacrament Church); 152 W. 71st Street; New York City; Spring 1993 Closed 8 May; Dir.— Mary McGowan.

E569 *A Wife for a Life* see *Three Lost Plays of Eugene O'Neill (Breakfast, Wife, and Cross)* Nameless Theater; 125 W. 22nd St.; New York City; Closed 19 Nov. 1978.

E570 *A Wife for a Life* see *Three Lost Plays of Eugene O'Neill (Wife, Movie Man, and Web)* Lotus Theatre Group; Playhouse 46; 423 W. 46th St. (at St. Clement's Church); New York City; 4-20 Nov. 1982; Dir.— Michael Fields.

F. Productions
(Foreign Language)

F1 *Anna Christie.* Olomouc, Czechoslovakia; Feb. 1979.

F2 *Anna Christie [An Di].* Theater of the Central Academy of Dramatic Arts; Beijing; PRC; 16-21 Oct. 1984; Dir.—George C. White.

F3 *Beyond the Horizon* [Chinese adaptation] Nanjing, PRC; June 1988; Dir.—Xiong Guodong; Robert Mayo—Shi Jinming.

F4 *Desire Under the Elms.* Two productions in Poland between 1972-78.

F5 *Desire Under the Elms [Vágy a szilfák alatt].* József Attila Színház; Budapest; 1974.

F6 *Desire Under the Elms.* Leningrad (?); Date (?); Referred to in a 1975 article..

F7 *Desire Under the Elms [Liubov' pod viasami].* Omskii dramaticheskii teatr; Omsk, USSR; 1975.

Dumma, G. "Strasti pod viasami." *Omskaia pravda* 20 Dec. 1975: n. pag.

Mylov, V. "Esli by ne O'Nil…." *Tiumen. pravda* 17 July 1976: n. pag.

F8 *Desire Under the Elms [Liubov' pod viasami]*— see previous entry. San Francisco Touring Company; Various places in USSR; June-July 1976. Simultaneously in English and (through earphones) Russian.

Damidov, M. "O'Nil i Uaïlder segodnia." *Lit. gaz.* 9 June 1976: n. pag.

Fridshteĭn, Iu. "Amerika smeiushchaiacia i stradalushchala." *Teatr* 2 (1977): 115-18..

Kachalov, N. "Ne tol'ko vesel'e." *Sov. Kultura* 1 June 1976: n. pag.

Liubimova, E. "Osmyslenie proshlogo." *Teatr zhizn'* 18 (1976): 28-29.

Mikhaĭlova, N. "Liubov' i nenavist'." *Ogönek* 25 (1976): 29.

Tsimbal, I. S. "Smeshnoe i tragicheskoe." *Leningr. Pravda* 13 June 1976: n. pag.

F9 *Desire Under the Elms [Lyubov pod viasami].* Len Soviet Palace of Culture; Leningrad, USSR; Date (?); Production referred to in an article dated 5 Sept. 1976.

F10 *Desire Under the Elms.* Dramaticheskom teatre; Sofia, Bulgaria; c. 1977.

F11 *Desire Under the Elms.* Vratsa, Bulgaria; c. 1978.

F12 *Desire Under the Elms [Désir sous les ormes].* Théâtre de l'Athénée-Louis Jouvet; Paris; Opened 9 Jan. 1987; Dir.—Claudia Morin; Translators—Ginette Herry and Claude Lacassagne.

F13 *Desire Under the Elms [Lyubov pod viasami].* Pushkin Theatre; Moscow; Spring 1988; Dir.—Mark Lamos; Performed in Russian.

Interview with Mark Lamos, the American director. *Soviet Life* 8 Aug. 1988: 63-65.

F14 *Desire Under the Elms [Balde Tibbe]* [Punjabi] Chandigarh University; 13 Oct. 1988; Chandigarh, India; Adapted—Balwant Gardi.

F15 *Desire Under the Elms.* Théâtre des Amandiers; Nanterre (Paris), France; 9 Jan.-25 Feb. 1993; Dir.—Matthias Langhoff; Translator—Françoise Morvan.

Dubost, Thierry. Rev. *Eugene O'Neill Review* 16.2 (1992): 150-51.

Despite splendid acting, the production, in placing O'Neill's work somewhere between *Medea* and *Gone with the Wind,* left the audience puzzled and unengaged.

F16 *The Emperor Jones.* Nanjing, PRC; June 1988; Dir.— Feng Changnian.

F17 *The Hairy Ape [Der haarige Affe].* Schaubühne Company of West Berlin; London, England; 9 Nov. 1986; Dir.— Peter Stein; Set Design — Lucio Fanti; Yank-Roland Schäfer.

Massa, Ann. Review-essay. *Modern Drama* 31.1 (1988): 41-51. See A412.

F18 *The Hairy Ape [Den Ludna Gorillan].* Folkteatern; Gavle, Sweden; 15 Nov. 1986; Dir.— Peter Oskarson; Set Design — Peter Holm; Yank — Rolf Lassgård; Paddy — Peter Haber; Long — Ole Ränge; Mildred — Anne-Li Norberg; Aunt — Pia Arnell.

Olsson, Tom J. A. Rev. *Eugene O'Neill Newsletter* 11.1 (1987): 46-48.

The production had a "poetical magic," was "full of vitality," "something to admire."

F19 *The Hairy Ape [Der haarige Affe].* Schaubühne Company of West Berlin; National Theatre; London; Opened 11-16 May 1987; Dir.— Peter Stein; Set Designer — Lucio Fanti; Yank — Roland Schäfer.

Kalson, Albert E. Rev. *Eugene O'Neill Newsletter* 11.2 (1987): 36-40.

"Those who see the Schaubühne *Hairy Ape* will never forget it, but what they will remember will more than likely be its startling stage pictures rather than O'Neill's play." The lesson to be learned from this and from Schaubühne's other offering, *Desire*, is: "Place your trust in the dramatist you are supposedly honoring, not in the ingenuity of a creative concept."

F20 *Hughie.* Kirori Mal College (India); USIS Sponsored; March 1988.

F21 *Hughie [Hughie Nattportiern].* Komediteatern; Stockholm, Sweden; May 1988; Dir./Design — Pi Lind; Erie Smith — Tor Isedal; Night Clerk — Sten Ardenstam.

Wilkins, Frederick C. Rev. *Eugene O'Neill Newsletter* 12.2 (1988): 82-83.

While the actors may not have looked the age of their characters, and while Isedal's mannerisms may have been a bit distracting, the play was a success once more.

F22 *The Iceman Cometh [Le marchand de glâce est passé].* Théâtre de la Commune d'Aubervilliers; Aubervilliers; c. 1975; Mise en scène — Gabriel Garran.

F23 *The Iceman Cometh.* Teatr Dramatyczny; Warsaw; Opened 16 June 1976.

F24 *The Iceman Cometh [Der Eismann kommt].* Deutsches Theater; Berlin, Germany; Opened 27 Mar. 1993; Dir.— Rolf Winkelgrund; Scenery/Costumes — Eberhard Keienburg; Lighting — Hilmar Koppe; Dramaturgs — Maik Hamburger/Annette Reber; Translators — Leopardi/Eckstein; Hickey — Jörg Gudzuhn; Hugo Kalmar — Horst Hiemer; Larry Slade — Dietrich Körner; Harry Hope — Reimar J. Baur.

Earnest, Stephen. Rev. *Eugene O'Neill Review* 16.2 (1992): 132-34.

The success of this production was due to "the level of talent exhibited by the ensemble at the Deutsches Theater."

F25 *The Iceman Cometh.* Frankfurt, Germany; Fall 1993.

F26 *Ile [De l'huile]* and *Where the Cross Is Made [Marque d'une croix].* Comédie de Caen; Caen, France; 1983; Mise en Scène — Claude Yersin.

F27 *Long Day's Journey into Night.* Six productions in Poland between 1972-78.

F28 *Long Day's Journey into Night [Le long voyage vers la nuit].* Théâtre de l'Atelier; Paris; Mar. 1973 Première en hommage à André Barsacq; Mise en Scène — G. Wilson.

F29 *Long Day's Journey into Night* [Russian]

Referred to in a 1973 article.

F30 *Long Day's Journey into Night [Eines langen Tages Reise in die Nacht].* Deutsches Schauspielhaus; Hamburg, Germany; 27 Apr. 1975; Prod./Dir.— Rudolf Noelte; Designer — Ute Meid; Mary Tyrone — Maria Wimmer.

Hensel, Georg. Rev. *Frankfurter Allgemeine Zeitung* 29 Apr. 1975: n. pag.

Michaelis, Rolf. Rev. *Theater heute* 16.6 (1975): 6-8.

Wertheim, Albert. Rev. *Educational Theatre Journal* 28 (1976): 122-24.

The production turns the play into a character study of Mary considering her effect on others. Script cuts eliminate the Catholicism, and the references to the Virgin Mary and the convent days. The characters' main concern is curing Mary Tyrone. Such "slanting need not ... necessarily do the original disservice."

Wiese, Eberhard von. "Orationen für Maria Wimmer und Quadflieg." Rev. *Hamburger Abendblatt* 28 Apr. 1975: n. pag.

F31 *Long Day's Journey into Night [Hosszú ut az éjszakába].* Pesti Színház; Budapest.

F32 *Long Day's Journey into Night.* Wroclaw, Poland; 1977-78.

F33 *Long Day's Journey into Night [Hosszú ut az éjszakába].* Vígszínház; Budapest; 1978.

F34 *Long Day's Journey into Night.* Polish TV; Spring 1978.

F35 *Long Day's Journey into Night [Le long voyage vers la nuit].* Théâtre de l'Atelier; Paris; Mar. 1979.

Gautier, J. J. Rev. *Le Figaro* 21 Mar. 1979: 29.

F36 *Long Day's Journey into Night.* Cinoherni klub; Prague, Czechoslovakia; c. 1979; Dir.—Ladislav Smocek.

F37 *Long Day's Journey into Night [Le long voyage vers la nuit].* Centre Théâtral du Maine; Maine, France; 1983; Mise en Scène—André Cellier.

F38 *Long Day's Journey into Night [Le long voyage vers la nuit].* Théâtre Eclaté d'Annecy; Annecy, France; Jan. 1984; Then Théâtre 13; Paris; 3 Feb. 1984 and into March; Mary Tyrone—Nelly Borgeaud; James—Jean-Marc Bory; Edmund—Jean-Ives Chatelain.

Marcabru, Pierre. Rev. *Le Figaro* 27 Feb. 1984: 33.

Rebeix, Viviane. Rev. Section/Spectacles. *France-Soir* 13 Mar. 1984: 20.

F39 *Long Day's Journey into Night [Lange Dagreis naar de Nacht].* Korrekelder Theatre Company; Bruges, Belgium; 14 Nov. 1986-10 Jan. 1987; Dir.—Julien Schoenaerts; Stage Design and Dutch Translation—Julien Schoenaerts; Costuming—Dominque Wiche; James Tyrone-Julien Schoenaerts; Mary-Reinhilde Decleir; Edmund-Norbert Kaart; Jamie-Carl Ridders.

Maufort, Marc. Rev. *Eugene O'Neill Newsletter* 11.2 (1987): 32-35.

While some reviewers commended the "non-melodramatic" interpretations of the roles of Mary and James, others suggested they "lacked energy." Maufort says of this production (which eliminated the role of Cathleen) that it "was most meritorious in its accurate setting, its skillful translation, its judicious cutting, its 'absurdist' suggestiveness, and its superb presentation of the Edmund-Jamie relationship."

F40 *Long Day's Journey into Night [Lang Dags Fard mot Natt].* Kungliga Dramatiska Teatern; Stockholm, Sweden; Opened 16 Apr. 1988; Dir.—Ingmar Bergman; Sets—Gunilla Palmstierna-Weiss; James Tyrone—Jarl Kulle; Mary Tyrone—Bibi Anderssen; Jamie Tyrone—Thommy Bergren; Edmund Tyrone—Peter Stormare.

Wilkins, Frederick C. Rev. *Eugene O'Neill Newsletter* 12.2 (1988): 83-85.

"Thanks to the innovative genius of Ingmar Bergman, the fresh contributions of his production team, and the splendid ensemble of the performers," the Royal Dramatic Company made a memorable contribution to the O'Neill centennial celebrations. Of note were the director's emphasis on the tendency toward violence of the male characters, the unrealistic set, and the cutting of the play to three hours running time.

F41 *Long Day's Journey into Night* [Chinese] Drama Theatre of the Nanjing Military Sub-area of the People's Liberation Army; Nanjing, PRC; June 1988.

F42 *Long Day's Journey into Night.* Théâtre de la Madeleine; Paris, France; 1992; Dir.—P. Kerbrat.

Dubost, Thierry. Rev. *Eugene O'Neill Review* 16.2 (1992): 148-49.

One critic punned on "Night" to suggest that *Nuit* should have been *Ennui.* Dubost does not dispute him. "The faults were numerous."

F43 *Long Day's Journey into Night.* Moscow Gogol Theatre of Drama; Boston, MA; 12 May 1995; Dir.—Sergey Yashin; Translator—Vitaly Voulf.

F44 *The Long Voyage Home.* Prague, Czechoslovakia; c. 1979.

F45 *Marco Millions [Marco Polo millioi].* Nemzeti Színház; Pécs, Hungary; 1973.

F46 *Marco Millions.* Théâtre Montparnasse; Paris; 1973; Mise en Scène—M. C. Valène.

F47 *Marco Millions.* La Gaité Montparnasse; Paris; 31 July-14 Sept. 1974.

Anon. Rev. *Le Figaro* 31 July 1974: 12.

Gautier, J. J. Rev. *Le Figaro* 14 Sept. 1974: 23.

Olivier, J. J. Rev. *Le Figaro* 14 Sept. 1974: 15.

F48 *Marco Millions [Karori Marco]* [Hindu]

National School of Drama; New Delhi; 16 Oct. 1988; Dir.—Rodney Marriott.

F49 *Marco Millions* National Theatre; Prague, Czechoslovakia; Municipal Theatre; Premiere-11 Feb. 1988; Dir.—Václav Hudeček; Setting—Zbyněk Kolář; Kublai—Miloš Kopecky.

Burian, Jarka M. Rev. *Eugene O'Neill Newsletter* 12.2 (1988): 76-79.

Taking into account that Czech theater insists upon relevance, the reviewer found this production, though faithful to the original text, routine, despite "lavish" costuming and "impressive" sets.

F50 *A Moon for the Misbegotten [Une lune pour les déshérités]*. Théâtre de l'Odéon; Paris; 1973; Mise en Scène—Jacques Rosner.

F51 *A Moon for the Misbegotten [Une lune pour les déshérités]*. Théâtre de l'Odéon; Paris; Feb. 1975; Dir.—Jacques Rosner; Adapted by—Jacqueline Autrusseau; Jim Tyrone—Jacques Destoop; Josie Hogan—Françoise Seigneur; Phil—Michel Aumont.

F52 *A Moon for the Misbegotten [Boldogtalan hold]*. Katona József Színház; Kecskemét, Hungary; 1975.

F53 *A Moon for the Misbegotten [Mone for Livets Stebarn]*. Bergen International Festival of the Arts; Nye Theater; Oslo, Norway; 15 May 1976; Dir.—José Quintero; Josie Hogan—Liv Ullmann; Phil—Espen Skjonberg; Jim Tyrone—Toralv Maurstad.

Waal, Carla. Rev. *Educational Theatre Journal* 28 (1976): 557-58.

The audience's attention was on the relationship between Josie and Hogan. Although the production was energetic and interesting, it was "difficult to follow as a whole."

F54 *A Moon for the Misbegotten [Luna dlia pasynkov sud'by]*. Teatr "Sofiia"; Sofia, Bulgaria; 1977.

Liubimova, E. "Samyĭ iunyĭ v Sofii." *Teatr zhizn* 6 (1977): 21-22.

Shamovich, E., and M. Shvydkoĭ. "Gastroli.—76." *Teatr* 6 (1977): 116-26.

F55 *A Moon for the Misbegotten*. Petr Bezruč Theater; Ostrava, Czechoslovakia; 1978.

F56 *A Moon for the Misbegotten [Luna dlia pasynkov sud'by]*. Gabrovo, Bulgaria; c. 1979.

F57 *A Moon for the Misbegotten [Une lune pour les déshérités]*. Maison des Arts André Malraux; Paris; 10-28 Jan. 1984.

F58 *A Moon for the Misbegotten [Une lune pour les déshérités]*. Théâtre de la Renaissance à Oullins, CAC d'Annecy; Avignon, France; 24-30 June 1987; Dir.—Alain Françon.

F59 *More Stately Mansions [Les châteaux magnifiques]*. Théâtre De l'Ancre; Charleroi, Belgium; Feb. 1990; Dir.—Roumen Tchakarov; Translator—Paul Edmond; Scenic Design—Jean Marie Fievez; Deborah Harford—Janine Patrick; Sara—Anny Czupper; Simon—Christian Crahay.

Maufort, Marc. Rev. *Eugene O'Neill Review* 14.1-2 (1990): 85-89.

While approving this production's set as its "most extraordinary element" and the acting as "superb," Maufort, says the translation, with its numerous cuts, did not do justice to the original. Still, this first production in Belgium must be hailed as one which shows that the play "even though unfinished, can work marvelously on stage."

F60 *More Stately Mansions*. Het Zuidelijk Toneel; Amsterdam; 2-5 June 1994; Dir.—Ivo van Hove.

F61 *Mourning Becomes Electra [Le deuil sied à Electre]*. Paris; Feb. 1974; Adapted by Maurice Cazeneuve.

Walter, Georges. Rev. of Part I. *Le Figaro* 20 Feb. 1974: 29.

_____. Rev. of Part 2. *Le Figaro* 28 Feb. 1974: 29.

F62 *Mourning Becomes Electra [Le deuil sied à Electre]*. Théâtre d'Ivry; Paris; Mar. 1975.

Gautier, J. J. Rev. *Le Figaro* 1 Mar. 1975: 46.

Marcabru, Pierre. Rev. *Le Figaro* 9 Feb. 1975: 21.

F63 *Mourning Becomes Electra [Traur—uchast' Elektra]*. Ivanovskom dramaticheskom teatre; Ivanovo, USSR; 1976.

Tarshish, N. "Imitatsiia tragedii; Pravda zamysla i ispolneniia." *Rabochiĭ krai* [Ivanovo] 29 May and 11 June 1976: n. pag.

F64 *Mourning Becomes Electra [Le deuil sied à Electre]*. Théâtre des Quartiers d'Ivry; Ivry; 1980; Then Le Studio d'Ivry; Paris; 5 Feb.-9 Mar. 1980; Mise en Scène—Stuard Seide; Adapted by—Louis Lanoux.

F65 *Mourning Becomes Electra [Le deuil sied à Electre]*. 8-22 Nov. 1981;

TV FR 3; Dir.— Maurice Cazeneuve; Lavinia — Anna Deleuze.

Rebeix, Viviane.Section/Télévision. Interview with Anne Deleuze. *France-Soir* 21 Nov. 1981: 22.

F66 *Mourning Becomes Electra.* Prague Municipal Theaters; Prague; Opened at the Rokoko Theatre Mar. 1987; Still running in Autumn 1990.

Interview with Mark Lamos, the American director. *New York Times* 22 Jan. 1988: 19.

F67 *Mourning Becomes Electra.* Mahen Theatre; Brno, Czechoslovakia; 20 Apr. 1988; Dir.— Zdeněk Kaloč.

Burian, Jarka M. Rev. *Eugene O'Neill Newsletter* 12.2 (1988): 76-79.

Despite the radical changes (running time just three hours, contemporary and expressionistic setting, minimalization of Puritan and Freudian elements), the production worked, though it is "not the play O'Neill wrote."

F68 *Mourning Becomes Electra [Rouw Siert Electra].* Zuidelijk Toneel Company of Eindhoven; Belgium-Netherlands tour; Apr.-May 1989; Dir.— Ivo van Hove; Trans.— Ger Thijs; Ezra Mannon and Adam Brant — Tom Jansen; Lavinia — Jip Wijngaarden; Christine — Trudy de Jong; Orin — Hans Kesting.

Maufort, Marc. Rev. *Eugene O'Neill Review* 13.2 (1989): 73-77.

Good acting, but production "departed strikingly from O'Neill's intentions," though in some ways interestingly. Nonetheless, the interpretation, stressing as it did expressionistic possibilities, seems unfortunate. "Hardly flawless," but offering some "interesting insights."

F69 *Mourning Becomes Electra.* Prague Municipal Theaters; Prague; Autumn 1990; Dir.— Miroslaw Macháček; Lavinia Mannon — Jana Paulová; Orin — Pavel Rímský. Burian, Jarka M. Rev. *Eugene O'Neill Review* 15.2 (1991): 110-14.

Using a classical Greek rather than Puritan New England ambience and costuming that blended classical, 19th century and modern, the director created "an interesting and effective variant of O'Neill's original text."

F70 *Strange Interlude [Különös közjáték].* Nemzeti Színház; Budapest; 1978.

F71 *Strange Interlude.* Bretania Theatre; Athens; Spring 1985.

F72 *Strange Interlude [L'etrange intermède].* Le Sorano; Théâtre National de Toulouse Midi-Pyrénées; National Theatre of Belgium; Brussels; 12-18 May 1988; Dir.— Jacques Osner; Sets — Max Schoendorff; Charles Marsden — Jean-Claude Dreyfus; Professor Leeds — Jean Bosquet; Nina — Marie-Christine Barrault; Sam Evans — Roger Van Hool; Ned Darrell — Didier Sauvegrain.

Wilkins, Frederick C. Rev. *Eugene O'Neill Newletter* 12.2 (1988): 80-82.

Gives high praise to this cast, and in particular to the convincingly charming Barrault. Despite his rusty French, Wilkins remained "rapt until the bittersweet end."

F73 *Strange Interlude.* National Theatre; Turin, Italy; 1991; Dir.— Luca Ronconi; Design — Margerita Palli; Charles Marsden — Massimo de Francovich; Professor Leeds — Maurizio Gueli; Nina — Galatea Ranzi; Edmund Darrell — Massimo Popolizio; Sam Evans — Riccardo Bini; Mrs. Evans — Paola Bacci.

Carlson, Marvin. Rev. *Eugene O'Neill Review* 16.1 (1992): 105-11.

Massimo de Francovich is the star of the production. Praises Massimo Popolizio and Riccardo Bibi, but finds Galatea Ranzi less satisfying. Commends the "strikingly original and unconventional" settings.

F74 *A Touch of the Poet [Egy igazi úr].* Katona József Színház; Kecskemét, Hungary; 1974.

F75 *A Touch of the Poet.* Hungária Chamber Theatre; Sokonai Theater; Debrecen, Hungary; Spring 1975.

F76 *A Touch of the Poet [Dusha poêta].* Moskovskiĭ dramaticheskiĭ teatr na Maloĭ Bronnoĭ; 1977.

"Dusha poêta." *Teatr. zhizn'* 8 (1977): 2-3.

"Dusha poêta." *Vech. Moskva* 20 Jan. 1977: n. pag.

Garibova, O. "Dusha poêta." *Teatr* 5 (1978): 25-27

Ryzhova, V. "Dusha poêta." *Vech. Moshva* 16 Feb. 1977: n. pag.

Suknanova, T. "Takie raznye sud'by." *Teatr. zhizn'* 2 (1978): 6-7.

F77 *A Touch of the Poet.* Rostock, Germany; c. 1978.

F78 *A Touch of the Poet [Fire de Poet].* Bucharest, Romania; c. 1978.

F79 *A Touch of the Poet.* Hungarian Chamber Theater; Debrecen, Hungary; Spring 1979; Dir.— Antal Rencz.

F80 *A Touch of the Poet [Fast ein Poet].* Renaissance Theatre; Berlin; Nov.-Dec. 1994; Dir.— Gerhard Klingenberg; Design and Costumes — Andreas Rank; Trans.— Michael Walther; Con Melody — Michael Degen; Nora — Elisabeth Orth; Sara — Béatrice Bergner.

Shafer, Yvonne. Rev. *Eugene O'Neill Review* 17.1-2 (1993): 178-79.

Good sets, good ensemble acting and costuming combined to produce "a very satisfying" performance.

F81 *Where the Cross Is Made [Marque d'une croix]* and *Ile [De l'huile].* Comédie de Caen; Caen, France; 1983; Mise en Scène — Claude Yersin.

G. Primary Works
Including Translations

G1 *"As Ever, Gene": The Letters of Eugene O'Neill to George Jean Nathan.* Eds. Nancy L. Roberts and Arthur W. Roberts. London: Associated U Presses [Rutherford, NJ: Fairleigh Dickinson UP], 1987.

Contains the 130 surviving letters from O'Neill to his friend, the critic George Jean Nathan. The letters are carefully annotated.

Included in the book are a general introductory essay, essays covering the four groupings the editors have chosen for the letters, an afterword, and index. The project, the foreword explains, was inspired by Nathan's widow, Julie Haydon Nathan.

Miller, Jordan Y. Rev. *Eugene O'Neill Newsletter* 11.3 (1987): 25-26.

G2 *Beyond the Horizon.* Mineola, NY: Dover Books/Dover Thrift Eds., 1996.

G3 *Beyond the Horizon: A Play in Three Acts.* Bartleby Library, Mar. 1996, republished July 1999. On-line edition [http://www.bartleby.com/132/index.html].

G4 *The Calms of Capricorn: A Play.* Developed from O'Neill's scenario by Donald Gallup. New Haven: Ticknor and Fields, 1982.

Includes a transcription of the scenario. The play was originally to be the first, then the third, play of the Harford family cycle. Gallup corrects spelling, tries to integrate O'Neill's changes of plans, turns indirect speech into direct speech, and fleshes out what O'Neill "merely sketched." The last comprises, perhaps, 15-20 percent of the text.

G5 *Chris Christophersen.* New York: Random House 1982. Foreword by Leslie Eric Comens.

A three-act play, the precursor of *Anna,*

Chris opened in March 1920; its producer hoped to capitalize on the success of *Horizon,* but *Chris* folded the same month. This text is not the stage version, which is not extent, but is from the transcript sent to the copyright office. It is the only surviving *produced* O'Neill play that has never till now been printed.

G6 *The Collected Plays.* London: Jonathan Cape, 1988.

All plays except *Bread and Butter, The Personal Equation, Shell Shock, Chris, Exorcism,* and *Now I Ask You.*

G7 *The Complete Plays.* Ed. Travis Bogard. 3 vols. New York: Library of America, 1988.

Here are the definitive texts of O'Neill's plays, notes on the texts, and a chronology. Volume 1 covers the period 1913 to 1920 and includes 29 plays; Volume 2 covers 1920 to 1931 and includes 13 plays; and Volume 3, covering the period 1932 to 1943, includes eight plays.

Wilkins, Frederick C. Rev. *Eugene O'Neill Review* 12.3 (1988): 45-47.

G8 *"A Comradeship-in-Arms': A Letter from Eugene O'Neill to Arthur Miller."* Introduced by Travis Bogard and Jackson R. Bryer.

Eugene O'Neill Review 17.1-2 (1993): 121-23.

The title of this article is almost as long as the brief letter O'Neill wrote to Miller in response to the latter's invitation to see *Death of a Salesman,* an invitation which, owing to his failing health, O'Neill declined.

G9 *The Emperor Jones.* Mineola, NY: Dover Books/Dover Thrift Eds., 1997.

G10 "Eugene O'Neill: An Early Letter." Ed. Stanford S. Apseloff. *Resources for American Literary Study* 1 (1981): 109-11.

In the Department of Special Collections of the Kent State University Library is a letter from O'Neill to Edward Pierre Loving and his co-editor Frank Shay, giving them permission to use any one of the sea plays or *Dreamy Kid* in their planned anthology. The letter indicates that O'Neill valued *Caribbees* most.

G11 *Eugene O'Neill at Work: Newly Released Ideas for Plays.* Ed. Virginia Floyd. New York: Ungar, 1981.

Gathers 25 of O'Neill's notes and ideas for plays and provides commentary on them. Some of the information on O'Neill was, at the time of publication, new.

Chothia, Jean. Rev.-essay. *Journal of American Studies* 23 (1989): 311-14. For an annotation see A120.

Coppenger, Royston. "The Incomplete Plays of Eugene O'Neill: Floyd's *Eugene O'Neill At Work.*" *Theater* 13.3 (1982): 65-69. For an annotation see A135.

G12 *Eugene O'Neill in Court: Documents in the Case of Georges Lewys v. Eugene O'Neill, et al.* Eds. Madeline Smith and Richard Eaton. American University Studies, series 24. American Literature, 41. New York: Lang, 1993.

Shortly after *Interlude* appeared, O'Neill was sued for plagiarism by aspiring author Georges Lewys who maintained that her novel *The Temple of Pallas Athenae* provided the inspiration for O'Neill's very profitable work. The "Documents in the Case" include O'Neill's own comments and marginalia. The introduction and the textual bridges to the various sections of the book handle background and context.

G13 *Eugene O'Neill, More Stately Mansions: The Unexpurgated Edition.* Ed. Martha Gilman Bower. New York: Oxford UP, 1988.

The uncut version of O'Neill's typescript for *Mansions*. The introduction explains that "included in this unabridged version of *More Stately Mansions* are Act I, Scene i, the beginning of Act 3, Scene ii, and the epilogue. These sections of the play provide not only continuity but also elements essential to the development of character, theme, and plot."

Connolly, Thomas F. Rev. *Eugene O'Neill Review* 13.2 (1989): 105-13.

G14 *Eugene O'Neill: Poems: 1912-1944.* Ed. Donald Gallup. New Haven: Ticknor and Fields, 1980.

Publication of all 72 known poems by O'Neill. Sanborn and Clark's 1931 bibliography had published 30 of them.

G15 *Eugene O'Neill: The Unfinished Plays.* Ed. Virginia Floyd. New York: Continuum, 1988.

The outlines and scenarios for three unfinished O'Neill plays — "The Visit of Malatesta," "The Last Conquest," and "Blind Alley Guy" — which the playwright worked on between 1940 and 1943.

Chothia, Jean. Rev.-essay. *Journal of American Studies* 23 (1989): 311-14. For an annotation see A120.

Wilkins, Frederick C. Rev. *Eugene O'Neill Review* 13.1 (1989): 77-90.

G16 *Eugene O'Neill: Work Diary 1924-1943.* Ed. Donald Gallup. Preliminary ed. 2 vols. New Haven: Yale UP, 1981.

The Work Diaries, based on the "Scribbling Diaries," (all destroyed by O'Neill save for the one for 1925 — here included in the appendix to Vol. 2) are dated notes on when and where plays were produced, inspiration struck, work was done, and whatever seemed worth recording. The first volume covers 1924-1933; the second covers 1934-1943. Also included are various tables in which O'Neill charts the time he spent working and the time he spent abstaining from alcohol and tobacco.

G17 "Eugene O'Neill's Introduction to Hart Crane's *White Buildings*: Why he 'would have done it in a minute but....'" Intro. Marc Simon. *Eugene O'Neill Review* 15.1 (1991): 41-58.

Provides background for the introduction to Crane's volume that O'Neill wrote but reneged on publishing. A glimpse of O'Neill as critic.

G18 "First Love: Eugene O'Neill and 'Boutade.'" Ed. Travis Bogard. *Eugene O'Neill Newsletter* 12.1 (1988): 3-9.

How many young ladies did O'Neill have in mind when he created the character of Muriel McComber? Bogard finds another possible inspiration in Marion Welch ("Boutade") and publishes letters from the youthful O'Neill to the young miss who may have inspired the character in *Wilderness.*

G19 "Founding Father: O'Neill's Correspondence with Arthur Miller and

Tennessee Williams." Intro. Dan Isaac. *Eugene O'Neill Review* 17.1-2 (1993): 124-33.

Isaac, who discovered the O'Neill letter to Arthur Miller in the Harry Ransom Humanities Research Center, describes the circumstances of O'Neill's writing it. Old master and young Turk interact. The O'Neill-Tennessee Williams connection, if there ever was one, is used to flesh out the ambience of the times.

G20 "Four Letters by Eugene O'Neill." Eds. Madeline Smith and Richard Eaton. *Eugene O'Neill Newsletter* 11.3 (1987): 12-18.

Hitherto unpublished letters, to the Romanian critic, translator, and Americanist Petru Comarnescu, discussing the translations into Romanian of *Interlude* and *Electra*.

G21 *Four Plays/Eugene O'Neill*. Franklin Center, PA: Franklin Library, 1978.

A limited edition. Illustrated by Jerry Cosgrove. Contains *Interlude, Electra, Misbegotten, Touch*.

G22 *Four Plays*. Franklin Center, PA: Franklin Library, 1979.

A limited edition. Illustrated by Fred Otnes. Contains *Interlude, Electra, Misbegotten, Touch*.

G23 *Four Plays/Eugene O'Neill*. 1978. Franklin Center, PA: Franklin Library, 1980. See above G21.

G24 *Four Plays by Eugene O'Neill*. New York: Penguin/A Signet Classic, 1998. Contains *Horizon, Jones, Anna, Ape*.

G25 "Greed of the Meek": Scenario for Act One of the First Play of His Eight-Play Cycle, edited and introduced by Donald Gallup. *Eugene O'Neill Review* 16.2 (1992): 5-11.

Having escaped the fires that engulfed much of the playwright's unfinished efforts, the scenario for "Greed of the Meek" is edited, introduced and published herein. Also see Articles section.

G26 *Hughie*. New Haven: Yale UP, 1982.

G27 *The Iceman Cometh*. New York: Limited Editions Club, 1982.

G28 *The Iceman Cometh: A Play*. New York: Vintage Books, 1999.

G29 *The Last Will and Testament of an Extremely Distinguished Dog*. New York: Henry Holt, 1999.

G30 *Long Day's Journey into Night*. 1956. New Haven: Yale UP, 1989.

In this, the sixty-first reprint of the play, departures from the final typescripts of the play (several lines of dialogue and stage directions previously omitted) have been inserted making it the definitive edition.

G31 The Long Voyage Home *and Other Plays*. Mineola, NY: Dover Books, Dover Thrift Eds., 1995.

G32 "A Lost Poem by Eugene O'Neill." Intro. Winifred L. Frazer. *Eugene O'Neill Newsletter* 3.1 (1979): 4-6.

Using internal and external evidence, Frazer concludes that "The American Sovereign," a poem published anonymously in Emma Goldman's *Mother Earth*, was written by O'Neill.

G33 *"Love and Admiration and Respect": The O'Neill-Commins Correspondence*. Ed. Dorothy Commins. Durham, NC: Duke UP, 1986.

Of the 242 letters contained herein, 82 are from O'Neill to Saxe Commins, covering the period 1920 to 1951. Included are letters from Saxe to Carlotta, some letters from Dorothy Commins, Saxe's wife, and segments of Saxe's memoir. The work details the relationship between the playwright and his editor. There is matter concerning O'Neill's divorce from Agnes Boulton, his marriage to Carlotta Monterey, and the deterioration of that marriage into anger and bitterness.

Black, Stephen A. Rev. *Modern Drama* 31.1 (1988): 117-19.

G34 *A Moon for the Misbegotten*. New York: Vintage, 1974.

G35 *More Stately Mansions*. Ed. Martha Bower. New York: Oxford UP, 1988. See G13.

G36 *Nine Plays of Eugene O'Neill*. 1932. New York: Modern Library, 1993.

G37 "The O'Neill-Komroff Connection: Thirteen Letters from Eugene O'Neill." Eds. Madeline Smith and Richard Eaton. *Eugene O'Neill Review* 16.2 (1992): 13-28.

Heretofore unpublished letters from Eugene O'Neill to Manuel Komroff, chronicling the sad dissolution of a once close friendship.

G38 "O'Neill's Letters to Donald Pace: A Newly Discovered Correspondence." Ed. Jackson R. Bryer. In *Eugene O'Neill and the Emergence of American Drama*. Ed. Marc Maufort. Costerus New Series, 75. Amsterdam: Rodopi, 1989. 133-48.

Introduces and edits letters from O'Neill to Donald Pace, who built models of clipper ships to the playwright's specifications. See Books and Parts of Books section.

G39 "O'Neill's Original 'Epilogue' for *A Touch of the Poet.*" Ed. Donald Gallup. *Eugene O'Neill Review* 15.2 (1991): 93-107.

To reveal O'Neill's original conception of *Touch*, Gallup edits and publishes the playwright's epilogue as it was conceived in 1935.

G40 "'Peace Is an Exhausted Reaction to Normal': O'Neill's Letters to Dudley Nichols." Ed. Jackson R. Bryer. In *Critical Essays on Eugene O'Neill.* Ed. James J. Martine. Boston: G. K. Hall, 1984. 33-55.

Nineteen letters and telegrams from O'Neill to Dudley Nichols, sent between 1932 and 1949. They reveal O'Neill's attitude toward film adaptations of his plays, which Nichols worked on: *Voyage* and *Electra*.

G41 *The Plays of Eugene O'Neill.* 3 vols. New York: Random, 1982.

Vol. 1 contains *Cardiff, Voyage, Lazarus, Zone, Ile, Cross, Rope, Dreamy, Fountain, Interlude, Caribbees, Breakfast*. Vol. 2 contains *Electra, Wilderness, Chillun, Marco, Welded, Diff'rent, The First Man, Gold*. Vol. 3 contains *Anna, Horizon, Jones, Ape, Brown, Straw, Dynamo, Days, Iceman*.

G42 *The Plays of Eugene O'Neill.* New York: Random House/Modern Library Giant, 1982.

A reprint of the original *Nine Plays* (Liveright, 1932).

G43 *Return to Life.* Ed. Robert Kastenbaum. The Literature of Death and Dying Series. New York: Arno, 1977.

Includes a reprint of *Lazarus*.

G44 *Selected Letters of Eugene O'Neill.* Eds. Travis Bogard and Jackson R. Bryer. New Haven: Yale UP, 1988.

Bogard and Bryer edit and publish selected letters covering a 50-year period by O'Neill to family members and theatrical persons. The nearly 600 pages of text present letters chronologically and include introductory essays — what O'Neill was about at the time the letters were written. The editors of this volume opt for a judicious approach to annotations — just what is necessary for an understanding of the content of the documents.

Frank, Glenda. Rev. *Westsider* 31 Aug.- 6 Sept. 1989: 11.

Shafer, Yvonne. Rev. *Theatre History Studies* 9 (1989): 170-73.

Wilkins, Frederick C. Rev. *Eugene O'Neill Review* 12.3 (1988): 45-47.

G45 *Selected Letters of Eugene O'Neill.* Eds. Travis Bogard and Jackson R. Bryer. 1988. New Haven: Yale UP, 1994.

A reprint.

G46 *Selected Plays of Eugene O'Neill.* Introduction by José Quintero. Garden City: Doubleday, 1979.

Includes *Anna, Jones, Desire, Interlude, Electra, Touch, Iceman, Misbegotten*.

G47 *Strange Interlude.* Franklin Center, PA: Franklin Library, 1985.

G48 *Ten "Lost" Plays.* New York: Dover, 1995.

A reprint of the 1964 Random House edition. Contains *Thirst, Web, Warnings, Fog, Recklessness, Abortion, Movie Man, Sniper, A Wife for a Life, Servitude*.

G49 "*The Theatre We Worked For*": *The Letters of Eugene O'Neill to Kenneth Macgowan.* Ed. Jackson R. Bryer. New Haven: Yale UP, 1982.

Bryer annotates and publishes in four parts the 157 surviving letters and telegrams that define the relationship between the playwright and theater producer Kenneth Macgowan. The first batch charts the formation of the triumvirate (O'Neill-MacGowan-Robert Edmond Jones). The second reflects the disintegration of the Experimental Theatre. The third reveals O'Neill's personal turmoil as he moved away from Agnes and toward Carlotta. The fourth discloses the decline of the friendship. The four parts are introduced by Travis Bogard.

G50 *Three Plays.* New York: Vintage, 1973.

Contains *Desire, Interlude, Electra*..

G51 *Three Plays of Eugene O'Neill.* New York: Vintage, 1995.

Contains *Anna, Jones, Ape*.

G52 "Tomorrow." *Eugene O'Neill Newsletter* 7.3 (1983): 3-13.

O'Neill's published short story, precursor to *Iceman*.

G53 *A Touch of the Poet.* 1957. New York: Vintage, 1983.

G54 "Two Letters by Eugene O'Neill." Ed. William J. Scheick. *Resources for American Literary Study* 8 (1978): 73-80.

Two letters by O'Neill, now in the Humanities Research Center of the University of Texas at Austin, hitherto unknown. One, to

Lawrence Langner, dated 5 Apr. 1927, talks of the Theatre Guild's upcoming production of *Marco* and anticipates the Guild's possibly staging *Interlude*. The other, to Philip Moeller, dated 19 Aug. 1933, discusses casting for *Wilderness* and notes that it is not a New England play. Commentary by the editor.

G55 *The Unknown O'Neill.* Ed. Travis Bogard. New Haven: Yale UP, 1988.

Publishes heretofore unfamiliar works by the playwright, including *The Personal Equation,* the original version of *Marco Millions,* "The Ole Davil," "The Reckoning," O'Neill's dramatic version of Coleridge's "Rime of the Ancient Mariner," "Tomorrow," "S.O.S." and other O'Neilliana. Bogard edits and introduces the work.

Chothia, Jean. Rev. *Journal of American Studies* 23 (1989): 311-14. For an annotation see A120.

G56 *"A Wind Is Rising": The Correspondence of Eugene O'Neill and Agnes Boulton.* Ed. W. Davies King. Rutherford, NJ: Fairleigh Dickinson UP, announced for 1999.

Most of the correspondence, preserved by Agnes and kept in her house through the 1950s are now at Harvard. Davies' edition includes 295 pieces of correspondence, dating from 1918 through 1928. The letters deal with such topics as the rehearsing of *Horizon,* the death of James O'Neill, the infighting among the Provincetown Players, and the circumstances of the divorce.

TRANSLATIONS

Arabic

G57 *Beyond the Horizon* and *Anna Christie.* Trans. Abdullah Mitwalli. Kuwait: Ministry of Information, 1978.

G58 *Desire Under the Elms [Ragba tahta sagaratad-dardar].* Trans. Abdullah A. Hafez Mitwalli and Mohamed Samir Abdulhamid. Kuwait: Ministry of Information, 1979.

G59 *The Fountain [Al-yanbu].* Trans. Salāh' Izz al-Din. Cairo: Maktabat Masr, 1980.

G60 *Long Day's Journey into Night.* Trans. Amer Al Zohair. Kuwait: Ministry of Information, 1987.

Chinese

G61 *Beyond the Horizon [Ta ti chih ai].* Trans. Chung-i Ku. 1946. Shanghai: Yung hsiang yin shu knan, 1976.

G62 *Beyond the Horizon [T'ien pien wai].* Trans. Huang-wu. Nanjing: Li-chiang ch'u pan she, 1985.

G63 *Desire Under the Elms [Yu hsia chih lien].* Trans. Po-hsin Kuo. Taipei [Taiwan]: Ching sheng wen wu kung ying kung sswu, 1984.

G64 *The Collected O'Neill [Ao-ni-erh chi].* Ed. Travis Bogard. Trans. I-ch'un Wang. Beijing: Sheng huo, tu shu, hsin chih san lien shu tien, 1995. 2 vols.

This appears to be a set of which Vol. 1 has 1295 pages.

G65 *The Emperor Jones [Chung-ssu huang].* Trans. Ching-hui Chung. Hong Kong: Hsiang-kang yen i hsueh yuan hsi chu hsueh yuan, 1989.

G66 *The Iceman Cometh [and Other Plays] [Sung ping ti jen lai le].* Trans. Wen-p'ei Lung. Beijing: Chung-kuo hsi chu ch'u pan she, 1988.

Contains *Iceman, Journey, Touch, Misbegotten,* and one other.

G67 *Long Day's Journey into Night [Ch'ang yeh man man lu t'iao t'iao].* Trans. George Kao. Hong Kong: World Today Press, 1973.

G68 *Long Day's Journey into Night, by Eugene O'Neill [Ou-nai-erh hsi chu hsuian chi. Jih mu t'u yuan].* Trans. Po-hsin Kuo. Taipei [Taiwan]: Ching sheng wen wu kung ying kung ssu, 1973.

G69 *Long Day's Journey into Night.* Taipei [Taiwan]: Hsin Ya, 1976.

G70 *Long Day's Journey into Night [Ch'ang yeh man man lu t'iao t'iao].* Trans. Chih-kao Ch'iao. Hong Kong: Chin jih shih chiehch'u pan she, 1979.

G71 *Long Day's Journey into Night; Desire Under the Elms [Man ch'ang ti lu ch'eng; Yu shu hsia ti lien ch'ing].* Ch'angsha ?; Hu-nan jen min ch'u pan she: Hu-nan sheng hsin hua shu tien fa hsing, 1983.

G72 *Long Day's Journey into Night [Ch'ang yeh man man lu t'iao t'iao].* Trans. George Kao. In *I-fan Pu-ning: 1933 huo chiang....* Taipei [Taiwan]: Yuan ching ch'u pan shih yeh kung ssu, 1987.

One of a series of volumes celebrating the work of Nobel laureates. This volumes includes one play each by Bunin, Pirandello and O'Neill.

G73 *Selections from O'Neill [Ou-nai-erh hsi chu hsuan chi].* Trans. Ying-yu Yen. Taipei [Taiwan]: Ching sheng wen wu kung ying kung ssu, 1980.

Contains *Jones, Anna,* and one other.

Czechoslovakian

G74 *Ah, Wilderness1 [Ach, divoćina].* Trans. Jozef Kot. Bratislava: LITA, 1977.

G75 *Ah, Wilderness1 [Ach, ta léta bláznivá].* Trans. Eva Kondrysová. Prague: Dilia, 1978.

G76 *Desire Under the Elms [Tonha pod jilmy].* Trans. Milan Lukeš. Prague: Dilia, 1976.

G77 *The Great God Brown [Velký boh Brown].* Trans. Jozef Kot. Bratislava: LITA, 1977.

G78 *Moon of the Caribbees [Dlouhá plavba domu].* Trans. Jiri Ornest. Prague: Dilia, 1989.

Dutch

G79 *Long Day's Journey into Night [Lange dagreis naar de nacht].* Trans. Henri Schmabers. Eindhoven: Zuidelijk Toneel Globe, 1987.

G80 *Strange Interlude.* Trans. Gommer Van Rousselt. Antwerp: Dedalus, 1990.

G81 *A Touch of the Poet [Een druppel dichters bloet].* Trans. Walter Van den Broeck. Amsterdam: International Theatre and Film Books, 1994.

Finnish

G82 *Long Day's Journey into Night [Pitkän päivän matka vöhön].* Trans. J. Siltanon. Helsinki: Lovë Kiriat, 1999.

French

G83 *Long Day's Journey into Night [Long voyage du jour à la nuit].* Trans. Françoise Morvan. Paris: L'Arche, 1996.

G84 *Long Day's Journey into Night* and *Hughie [Théâtre complet: Long voyage*

vers la nuit; Hughie]. 1965. Paris: L'Arche, 1989.

German

G85 *Ah, Wilderness1 [O Wildnis1]* Trans. Karl Goldmann. Frankfurt am Main: Hirschgraben, 1973.

G86 *Ah, Wilderness1 [O Wildnis1: eine Komödie der Erinnerung in 3 Akten].* Trans. Inge [——?] and Bettina von Leoprechting. Frankfurt am Main: Fischer-Taschenbuch, 1991.

G87 *All God's Chillun Got Wings [Alle Kinder Gottes haben Flügel: Stück in 2 Akten].* Trans. Leopardi and Eckstein. Frankfurt am Main: Fischer-Taschenbuch, 1991.

G88 *[Anna Christie: Schauspiel in 4 Akten].* Trans. Sibylle Hunzinger. Frankfurt am Main: S. Fischer, 1975.

G89 *Beyond the Horizon [Jenseits vom Horizont: Stück in 3 Akten].* Trans. Leopardi and Eckstein. Frankfurt am Main: Fischer-Taschenbuch, 1991.

G90 *Desire Under the Elms [Gier unter Ulmen: Stück in 3 Teilen].* Trans. Alexander F. Hoffmann and Hannelene Limpach. Frankfurt am Main: Fischer-Taschenbuch, 1990.

G91 *The Emperor Jones [Kaiser Jones].* Trans. Michael Walter. Frankfurt am Main: Fischer-Taschenbuch, 1990.

G92 *The Great God Brown [Der grosse Gott Brown: Stück in 4 Akten mit einem Vor und einem Nachspiel].* Trans. Michael Walter. Frankfurt am Main: Fischer-Taschenbuch, 1992.

G93 *The Hairy Ape [Der Haarige Affe].* Trans. Peter Stein. Frankfurt am Main: Fischer-Taschenbuch, 1992.

G94 *Hughie [Hughie: Stück in ein Akt].* Trans. Ursula Schuh. Frankfurt am Main: S. Fischer, 1973.

G95 *Hughie [Hughie: Stück in ein Akt].* Trans. Leopardi and Eckstein. Frankfurt am Main: Fischer-Taschenbuch, 1992.

G96 *Long Day's Journey into Night [Eines langen Tages Reise in die Nacht: Schauspiel in vier Akten].* Trans. Ursula Schuh and Oscar Fritz Schuh. 1975, 1982, and 1986. Stuttgart: Reclam, 1992.

G97 *Major Plays [Meisterdramen].* Trans. Rita Matthias. Frankfurt am Main: S. Fischer, 1986.

G98 *Marco Millions [Marcos Millionen: Schauspiel].* Frankfurt am Main: S. Fischer, 1977.

G99 *A Moon for the Misbegotten [Ein Mond für die Beladenen: Drama in 4 Akten].* Trans. Marianne Wentzel. Frankfurt am Main: S. Fischer, 1977.

G100 *A Moon for the Misbegotten [Ein Mond für die Beladenen: Schauspiel in 4 Akten].* Trans. Leopardi and Eckstein. Frankfurt am Main: Fischer-Taschenbuch, 1990.

G101 *More Stately Mansions [Alle Reichtumer der Welt: Stück in drei Akten].* Trans. Michael Walter. Frankfurt am Main: Fischer- Taschenbuch, 1995.

G102 *Mourning Becomes Electra [Trauer muss Elektra tragen: eine Trilogie. Die Heimkehr. Die Gejagten. Die Verfluchten].* Trans. Marianne Wentzel. Frankfurt am Main: S. Fischer, 1971-76.

G103 *Mourning Becomes Electra [Trauer muss Elektra tragen].* Marburg: Blindenstudienanst, 1980.

G104 *Mourning Becomes Electra [Trauer muss Elektra tragen: eine Trilogie].* Trans. Michael Walter. Frankfurt am Main: Fischer-Taschenbuch, 1990.

G105 *Mourning Becomes Electra [Trauer muss Elektra tragen: eine Trilogie].* Trans. Michael Walter. Frankfurt am Main: Fischer-Taschenbuch, 1993.

G106 *Strange Interlude [Seltsames Zwischenspiel: Drama in 9 Akten].* Trans. Marianne Wentzel. Frankfurt am Main: S. Fischer, 1977.

G107 *Strange Interlude [Seltsames Intermezzo: Drama in neun Akten].* Trans. Michael Walter. Frankfurt am Main: Fischer-Taschenbuch, 1993.

G108 *A Touch of the Poet [Fast ein Poet: Drama in 4 Akten].* Trans. Ursula Schuh and Oscar Fritz Schuh. 1957. Leipzig: Insel, 1979.

G109 *A Touch of the Poet [Fast ein Poet].* Trans. Michael Walter. Frankfurt am Main: Fischer-Taschenbuch, 1988.

Greek

G110 *All God's Chillun Got Wings [Ola ta Pedia tou Theou ehoun phtera].* Trans. V. Nikolopoulos. Athens: Govostis, 1990.

G111 *Desire Under the Elms [Pothoi kato ap'tis ftelies].* Trans. Dora Volanaki. Athens: Dodoni, 1981.

G112 *The Iceman Cometh [O pagopolis erhetai].* Trans. Marios Ploritis. Athens: Dodoni, 1979.

G113 *Strange Interlude [Paraxeno intermezzo].* Trans. S. Spiliotopoulos. Athens: Govostis, 1989.

Hungarian

G114 *Drámák.* Budapest: Európa Könyvkia, 1974. 2 vols.

Contains *Jones [Jones Császár]* and *Desire [Vágy a szilfák alatt].* Trans. Vajda Miklòs; *Interlude [Különös Közjáték].* Trans. Bányay Geyza; *Electra [Amerika Elektra].* Trans. Ottlik Géza; *Touch [Egy igazi úr].* Trans. Vas István; *Iceman [Eljö a jeges].* Trans. Vajda Miklòs; *Journey [Utazás az éjaza kábá].* Trans. Vas István; *Misbegotten [Boldogtalan hold].* Trans. Vas István. Terminal essay by Almàsi Miklòs.

Icelandic

G115 *Long Day's Journey into Night [Dagleidin lânga inn í nótt].* Trans. Thor Vilhjálmsson. Reykjavík: Bókaútgáfa menningarsjóds og Pjódvinafélagsins, 1983.

Italian

G116 *Long Day's Journey into Night [Lunga giornata verso la notte].* Trans. Bruno Fonzi. Turin: Einaudi, 1977.

G117 *Mourning Becomes Electra [Il lutto si addice ad Elettra].* Trans. Bruno Fonzi. 1962. Turin: G. Einaudi, 1974 and 1977.

G118 *Works: Caribbees, Voyage, etc. [Le Opere: La luna dei Caraibi. I lungo viaggio di ritorno, etc.].* Trans. Bruno Fonzi. Turin: UTET, 1978.

G119 *Chief Works [I Capolavori di Eugene O'Neill: Drammi marini, L'imperatore Jones, Anna Christie, Desiderio sotto gli olmi, Strano interludio, Il lutto si addice ad Elettra, Arriva l'uomo del ghiaccio, Lunga giornata verso la notte].* Trans. Bruno Fonzi. Turin: Einaudi, 1999. 2 vols.

Contains *The Sea Plays, Jones, Anna, Desire, Interlude, Electra, Iceman, Journey.*

Japanese

G120 Desire Under the Elms [Nire no Kokage no Yokubo]. Trans. Inoue Soji. 1974. Tokyo: Iwanami Shoten, 1981.

G121 O'Neill's Works [O'Neill Meisaku-shu]. Trans. Kishi Tetsuo, et al. Tokyo: Hakusuisha, 1975.

Korean

G122 Desire Under the Elms [Nurup namu mit'ui yokmang]. Trans. Kun-sam Lee. Seoul: Kumsong ch'ulp'ansa, 1990.

G123 Desire Under the Elms. [Nurup namu mit'ui yokmang]. Seoul: Ch'longmok, 1994.

G124 Long Day's Journey into Night. Trans. Hae-rang Yi. Seoul: Hyondae Kyoyuk Ch'ulp 'anbu, 1986.

Norwegian

G125 Hughie. Trans. Arne Skouen. Oslo: Norsk rikskringkasting, 1977.

G126 Long Day's Journey into Night [Lang dags ferd mot natt]. Trans. Arthur Klaebo. Oslo: Det Norske teater, 1976.

G127 Long Day's Journey into Night [Lang dags ferd mot natt]. Trans. Svein Selvig. Trondheim: Trondelag Teater, 1980.

G128 Long Day's Journey into Night [Lang dags ferd mot natt]. Trans. Svein Selvig. Bergen: Den Nationale scene, 1985.

G129 Long Day's Journey into Night [Lang dags ferd mot natt]. Trans. Svein Selvig. Oslo: Nationaltheatret, 1999.

G130 A Moon for the Misbegotten [Måne for livets stebarn]. Trans. Kjell Askildsen. Oslo: Nationaltheatret, 1995.

Polish

G131 Teatr. Trans. Kazimierz Piotrowski, et al. Warsaw: Panstwowy Instytut Wydawnicay, 1973.

Contains *Jones, Ape, Chillun, Desire, Brown, Lazarus, Electra, Wilderness, Iceman*.

Portuguese

G132 Long Day's Journey into Night [Longa jornada noite adentro]. Trans. Helena Pessoa. 1980. Sao Paolo [Brazil]: Abril, 1982.

G133 Long Day's Journey into Night [Jornada para a noite: teatro]. (No other information available.)

Romanian

G134 [Four Letters to Petru Comarnescu]. In *Scieri despre Teatru*. Ed. Mircea Filip. Iaşi [Romania]: Editura Junimea, 1977: 149-55.

Dated 20 May 1938, 26 Nov. 1938, 8 Mar. 1939, 12 July 1945, the letters are about translation and publication rights. In one O'Neill discusses critics' views of his work. The letters are in Romanian translations.

Russian

G135 [Long Day's Journey into Night]. *Three American Plays.* Trans. and ed. E. Mednikova. In *Pisateli S. SH. A o Literature.* Moscow: n.p., 1973. 9-127.

Includes "On Tragedy," "Strindberg and Our Theatre," "Theatre and its Means," "Letter to the Kamerny Theater" ["O tragedii," "Strindberg i nash teatr," "Teatr i ego sredstva," "Pis'mo v Kamernyi teatr"]. Trans. Georgii Zlobin. 206-16.

G136 Mourning Becomes Electra [Traur-ucast' Elektry: trilogiia]. Trans. V. Alekseev. Moscow: Iskusstvo, 1975.

G137 Plays [P'esy]. [Selections by O'Neill and Tennessee Wlliams]. Trans. M. Koreneva and Georgii Zlobin. Moscow: Raduga, 1985.

G138 Select Plays [P'esy]. Moscow: Gud'ial, 1999.

Contains *Horizon, Touch, Journey, Anna, Chillun, Desire [Gorizonty tvorchestva, Dusha poeta, Dolgoe puteshestvie v noch', Anna Kristi, Kryl'ia dany vsem detiam chelovecheskim, Liubov' pod viasami].*

Spanish

G139 Before Breakfast [Antes del desayuno]. Trans. Raul Blengio Brito. Montevideo [Uruguay]: La Casa del Estudiant, 1978.

G140 Before Breakfast [Antes del desayuno]. Madrid: Editiones Mk., 1981.

G141 Desire Under the Elms. Days Without End [Deseo bajo los olmos. Dias sin fin]. Trans. León Mirlas. 1984. Barcelona: Ediciones Orbis, 1986.

G142 *Desire Under the Elms. Marco Millions. Welded [Deseo bajo los olmos. Los millones de Marco Polo. Intimamente unidos].* Madrid: Club Internacional del Libro, 1992.

G143 *The Emperor Jones [El Emperador Jones].* Trans. José Carner-Ribalta. Barcelona: Edic. 62, 1984.

G144 *The Great God Brown. Strange Interlude. Mourning Becomes Electra [El gran dios Brown. Extraño interludio. A Electra le siente el luto].* 1934. Trans. León Mirlas. Madrid: Hyspamérica, 1985.

G145 *Long Day's Journey into Night [Largo viaje hacia la noche].* Trans. Ana Antón-Pacheco. 2nd ed. 1986. Madrid: Cátedra, 1992.

G146 *Long Day's Journey into Night [Largo viaje hacia la noche].* Trans. Ana Antón-Pacheco. Barcelona: Altava, 1995.

G147 *Selected Plays [Teatro escogido].* 1958, 1965. Madrid: S.A. de Promoción y Ediciones Club Internacional del libro, 1982. Contains *Horizon, Gold, Diff'rent, Anna, First Man, Welded, Desire, Marco, Brown, Days.*

Swedish

G148 *Anna Christie [Anna Christie].* Trans. Sven Barthel. Helsinki: Yleisradio, 1980.

Thai

G149 *Ah, Wilderness1 [Botlakorn plae ruang wai-wun].* Trans. Suchayadi Tantavanich. Bangkok: Pracpitaya, 1976.

Turkish

G150 *Ile [Yag].* Trans. Avni Givuda. Istanbul: MEB, 1992.

Yugoslavian

G151 *Before Breakfast: A Play in one act [Pred zajtrkom: igra v enem dejanju].* Trans. Janko Moder and Dusan Tomse. N.p.: n.p., 1982.

H. Miscellaneous

H1 *Ah, Wilderness!* Video. Dir. Arvin Brown. With Richard Backus, Geraldine Fitzgerald, William Swetland, Joyce Ebrert, Swoozie Kurtz. Insight Media [www.insight-media.com], 1999. 120 min.

The 1976 Long Wharf Theater production.

H2 *Anna Christie.* With Blanche Sweet. Hollywood Select Video, 1993. 95 min.

Video release of the 1923 silent film.

H3 *Anna Christie.* Recording. Dir. Eric Simonson. With Dwier Brown, Maurice Chasse, Alison Elliot, Stacy Keach, Scott Lowell, Alley Mills. Venice, CA: L.A. Theatre Works, 1999. 1 sound cassette.

H4 *Before Breakfast.* By Thomas Pasatieri. Libretto by Frank Corsaro. With Marilyn Zschau. New York City Opera. New York City. 9 Oct. 1980.

An opera based on O'Neill's play.

H5 *Beyond the Horizon.* Dirs. Michael Kahn and Rick Hauser. With Richard Backus, Maria Tucci, Edward J. Moore, Geraldine Fitzgerald, James Broderick, John Randolph, and John Houseman. PBS. 14 Jan. 1976.

H6 *Beyond the Horizon.* Video. With John Houseman, Geraldine Fitzgerald, and Maria Tucci. Insight Media [www.insight-media.com], 1999. 90 min. A 1975 production.

H7 Campbell, Jack K. *Call for Phillip Morr-r-riss.* [Privately Printed?], 1994.

A play about O'Neill and featuring Carlotta, Agnes, Shane, Oona, James O'Neill and Jamie and a number of O'Neill's characters.

H8 Cheuse, Alan. *The Bohemians: John Reed and his Friends Who Shook the World.* Cambridge: Applewood, 1982.

A novel, told from John Reed's perspective, about his life. Enter O'Neill as a drunkard.

H9 Cobb, Mel. "O'Neill or Sunny Days and Starry Nights: An Original Play." In *Eugene O'Neill and the Emergence of American Drama.* Ed. Marc Maufort. Costerus New Series, 75. Amsterdam: Rodopi, 1989. 181-204.

A one-person play which spans a single day in 1940 in the life of O'Neill as the mature playwright reflects on life and work.

H10 *Desire Under the Elms* [Videocassette]. With Sophia Loren, Anthony Perkins, Burl Ives. Paramount, 1991. 114 min.

A video of the 1957 film.

H11 *Desire Under the Elms.* By Edward Thomas. Libretto by Joe Masteroff. With Michael Best, Carol Todd, William Fleck, Sean Barker, Ken Bridges. Palmer Auditorium, Connecticut College. New London, CT. 10 and 12 Aug. 1978.

An opera based on the play.

H12 *The Emperor Jones* [Audio]. Dir. Theodore Mann. With James Earl Jones. Caedmon, CDL 5341 [1974]. 93 min. Two cassettes. One-track mono.

H13 *The Emperor Jones.* An opera [written 1932]. By Louis Gruenberg. Michigan Opera Theatre. Detroit, MI. Feb. 1979.

H14 *The Emperor Jones* [Radio Play in Ireland]. Radio Telefis Eireann (RTE). Played 1976, 1979, and 1980.

H15 *The Emperor Jones: An Opera.* Vocal Score. English and German. Newton Centre, MA: GunMar Music, 1990.

This, a musical score, was composed originally in 1950.

H16 *The Emperor Jones.* Video. With Paul Robeson and Dudley Digges. Insight Media [www.insight-media.com], 1999. 72 min.

The 1933 film.

H17 *Eugene O'Neill, a Glory of Ghosts* [Recording]. With Jason Robards, Jr.,

Geraldine Fitzgerald, Zoe Caldwell, Blythe Danner. PBS (American Masters Series), 1986. 1 hr., 30 min.

The life of O'Neill traced through his writings, with readings from some of the plays.

H18 *Eugene O'Neill* [Videocassette]. Dir. Malcolm Hossick. Famous Authors Ser., 1993. 30 min.

One of 10 American writers whose lives and works are explored.

H19 *Eugene O'Neill, 1888-1953* [Videocassette]. West Long Branch, NJ: White Star [distr. by Kultur], 1996. 30 min.

The life and career of Eugene O'Neill, photographs of people and places associated with his life.

H20 *Facets of Desire.* Music Score by John Butler. Woodwinds and strings by Alan Hoddinott. Dancers: Kevin McKenzie, Martine van Hamel, Gary Chryst. 25 July 1981.

A dance performance based on *Desire*, at the Pepsico Summerfare '81 Arts Festival, SUNY/Purchase.

H21 **Farrell, Herman Daniel, III.** *Dreams of the Son.* West End Theatre, New York City. Opened 18 July 1984.

A play based on O'Neill's life.

H22 *Fish Story Part I* (based upon *The Emperor Jones*). Dir. Elizabeth LeCompte. With Kate Valk/Willem Dafoe. The Wooster Group, New York. Fall 1992-Winter 1993.

Carlson, Marvin. Rev. *Eugene O'Neill Review* 16.2 (1992): 119-22.

O'Neill, Michael C. Rev. *Eugene O'Neill Review* 16.2 (1992): 114-19.

H23 **Gelb, Barbara.** *My Gene.* With Colleen Dewhurst. The Public Theatre, New York City. 29 Jan.-22 Mar. 1987.

A play about O'Neill and Carlotta's relationship.

Interview with Colleen Dewhurst. *New York Times* 25 Jan. 1987, sec. 2: 3.

Kaplan, Justin. Rev. *New York Times* 30 Jan. 1987, sec. C: 3.

Vena, Gary. Rev. *Eugene O'Neill Newsletter* 11.1 (1987): 19-21.

H24 *The Hairy Ape.* Dir. Yuri Rasovsky. With Danny Goldring. Chicago Radio Theatre production. WNIB, Chicago. 9 Dec. 1974.

A 46-minute adaptation for radio.

H25 *Hughie* [Audiorecording]. Dir. José Quintero. With Jason Robards and Jack Dodson. BARD, 1993.

H26 *The Iceman Cometh.* Dir. John Frankenheimer. With Lee Marvin, Frederic March, Robert Ryan, Jeff Bridges, Bradford Dillman. American Film Theater, 1973.

A film version.

Canby, Vincent. Rev. *New York Times* 30 Oct. 1973: 36

_____. Rev. *New York Times* 11 Nov. 1973: 1, 3.

Cocks, Jay. Rev. *Time* 12 Nov. 1973: 122-23.

Kael, Pauline. Rev. *New Yorker* 5 Nov. 1973: 149-52.

Kauffmann, Stanley. Rev. *New Republic* 7 Nov. 1973: 24, 35-36.

Zimmerman, Paul D. Rev. *Newsweek* 12 Nov. 1973: 119-20.

H27 *The Iceman Cometh* [Audio]. With Lee Marvin. Caedmon, TRS 359, 1973. 228 min. Four discs Stereo.

The original sound track recording of the AFT film of *Iceman*.

H28 *The Iceman Cometh* [Video]. With Jason Robards, Jr., Robert Redford. Insight Media [www.insight-media.com], 1999. Black & white. 240 min.

The 1960 production.

H29 *Ile* [Radio Play in Ireland]. Radio Telefis Eireann (RTE). Played 1974.

H30 *Jimmy Tomorrow.* Adaptation/expansion, by Michael Lynch, of O'Neill's short story "Tomorrow." One Act Theatre Company, San Francisco, CA. 25 May-19 June 1988.

H31 *Journey into Genius* [Audiovideo]. Dir. Calvin Skaggs. With Dylan Baker, Kate Burton, Chris Cooper, and (as Eugene O'Neill) Matthew Modine. WETA-TV [American Playhouse], 1988. Subsequently Sidney, New South Wales: SBS, 1990. 60 min.

Drama tracing O'Neill's early development as an artist.

H32 *Kejsar Jones.* By Sven-David Sandstrom. Librettist/Dir.—Lars G. Thelestam. With Kolbjorn Höiseth. Royal Opera. Stockholm. 29 Sept. 1984.

A chamber dance-opera based on *Jones*.

Olsson, Tom J. A. Rev. *Eugene O'Neill Newsletter* 8.3 (1984): 33-34.

H33 *Last Will and Testament of an Extremely Distinguished Dog.* New York: Henry Holt, 1999.

H34 *Long Day's Journey into Night*
[Radio Play in Ireland]. With Agnew Mc-
Master. Radio Telefis Eireann (RTE). Played
1969, 1977 and 1982.

H35 *Long Day's Journey into Night.*
With Laurence Olivier and Constance Cum-
mings. National Theatre Production. ABC-
TV. 10 Mar. 1973.

O'Connor, John J. Rev. *New York Times*
14 Mar. 1973: 85.

H36 *Long Day's Journey into Night*
[Videocassette]. Dir. Sidney Lumet. With
Katherine Hepburn, Ralph Richardson, Jason
Robards, Jr., Dean Stockwell. Princeton, NJ:
Films for the Humanities: History of the
Drama, Unit 9, 1988. 47 min.

Abridged version of the film.

H37 *Long Day's Journey into Night.*
Dir. Jonathan Miller. With Jack Lemmon,
Bethel Leslie, Peter Gallagher, Kevin Spacey,
Jodie Lynne McClintock. Stamford, CT/Los
Angeles, CA: Vestron Video; Distributed by
Image Entertainment, 1988. Audiovisual: 2
videodiscs (laser optical). 169 min.

The Broadway production, filmed 1987,
and presented on TV (American Playhouse).

H38 *Long Day's Journey into Night*
[Audiovisual]. Dir. David Wellington. With
William Hutt, Martha Henry, Tom McCamus, Peter Donaldson, Martha Burns. Princeton, NJ: Films for the Humanities and Sciences. And Telefilm Canada, 1999. 3
videocassettes. 178 min.

A film of the Ontario's Stratford Festival
production, 1996.

H39 *A Moon for the Misbegotten.* Dir.
José Quintero. With Gordon Rigsby. ABC-
TV. 27 May 1975.

Burke, Tom. Rev. *TV Guide* 24 May
1975: 12-17.

Hendy, Valerie. Preview. *National
Catholic Reporter* 23 May 1975: 12-17.

O'Connor, John J. Rev. *New York Times*
27 May 1975: 59.

H40 *A Moon for the Misbegotten*
[Radio Play in Ireland]. Radio Telefis Eireann
(RTE). Played 1979.

H41 *Mourning Becomes Electra.* Dir.
Nick Havinga. With Joan Hackett and
Roberta Maxwell. PTV — WNET. TV's Great
Performances Series. Adapt. Kenneth Cavan-
der. 6 Dec. 1978-3 Jan. 1979.

O'Connor, John J. Rev. *New York Times*
6 Dec. 1978, sec. C: 26

Romano, John. Preview. *TV Guide* 2
Dec. 1978: 23-24.

H42 *Mourning   Becomes   Electra*
[Radio Play in Ireland]. Radio Telefis Eireann
(RTE). Played 1980.

H43 *Mourning   Becomes   Electra*
[Video]. With Bruce Davison, Joan Hackett,
and Roberta Maxwell. Insight Media
[www.insight-media.com], 1999. 5 episodes,
58 min. each.

A 1979 production.

H44 *New Girl in Town.* Music and
lyrics by Robert Merrill. Book by George Abbott. Equity Library Theater (the Roerich
Museum on Riverside Drive), New York City.
9 Jan. 1975.

A revival of the 1957 musical based on
Anna.

H45 Norén, Lars. *Och ge oss skuggorna*
[*And Grant Us the Shadows*]. Royal Dramatic
Theatre, Stockholm, 1991.

Written 1991? A play about O'Neill,
dealt with in two essays by Törnqvist. See Articles and Books and Parts of Books sections.

H46 *O'Neill* [Videocassette]. Peoria,
IL: The Company. Thomas S. Klise Company, 1985. Also: Insight Media [www.in-
sight-media.com], 1999. 22 min.

Brief introduction to O'Neill and his
greatest plays.

H47 *Reds* [2 Videocassettes]. With
Warren Beatty, Diane Keaton, Jack Nichol-
son, Maureen Stapleton. Paramount, 1998.
195 min.

The video release of the 1981 film about
John Reed. Louise Bryant, Eugene O'Neill
and Emma Goldman are woven into the story.

H48 Roberts, Meade. *Thornhill.* Dir.
John Casavetes. With Ben Gazzara, Patti
Lupone, Carol Kane. Westbeth, NY. Oct.
1983.

A play about O'Neill, developed in a stu-
dio-workshop.

H49 Ryback, Jeffrey W. *Eugene
O'Neill: Dancing with the Devil (1888-1953):
A Play for One Person.* Studio City, CA: Players Press, 1990. [Opened at the American Ensemble Company Theatre, New York City, 26
Feb. 1987, for a run of three weeks, then at the
Vermont Repertory, 20 Mar. 1987, for a run of
three weeks. Ryback played O'Neill in both
productions.]

The ghost of O'Neill comes to the ghost
of the "Hell-Hole" in hopes of meeting the

ghost of Terry Carlin and while waiting tells the story of its/his life and playwriting career.

H50 Scrimgeour, James R. "Photo of Eugene and Carlotta O'Neill: 1929 (poem)." *Eugene O'Neill Review* 15.2 (1991): 108.

Inspired by the handsome couple (the O'Neills were in their love's infancy), Scrimgeour pens an admiring tribute in verse.

H51 *Strange Interlude* [Videocassette]. With Norma Shearer and Clark Gable. MGM/UA Home Video, 1992. 111 min.

A video release of the 1932 film.

H52 *Success* [Videocassette]. PBS [The Irish in America], 1997. 59 min.

Joseph P. Kennedy and Eugene O'Neill exemplify Irish assimilation into American society.

H53 *Take Me Along.* Music and lyrics by Robert Merrill. Book by Joseph Stern and Robert Russell. Revised and adapted by C. T. Perkinson. Dirs. Geraldine Fitzgerald and Mike Malone. Richard Allen Center, Manhattan Community College, New York City. 8 — 25 Mar. 1984.

An all-Black revival of the 1959 musical based on *Wilderness.*

H54 *Take Me Along.* Goodspeed Opera House, East Haddam, CT. 12 Sept. 1984. Then to the Martin Beck Theatre. 15 Apr. 1985, for one performance.

A revival of the 1959 musical based on *Wilderness.*

H55 *A Touch of the Poet.* Dir. Stephen Potter. With Fritz Weaver, Nancy Marchand, Roberta Maxwell, and Carrie Nye. PBS. 24 and 25 Apr. 1974.

H56 *A Touch of the Poet* [Video]. With Nancy Marchand, Fritz Weaver, Roberta Maxwell, Donald Moffat, Carrie Nye, and Robert Phaelen. Insight Media [www.insight-media.com], 1999. 150 min.

Repeat of the 1974 production.

H57 "Two Pen Portraits of Eugene O'Neill, Broadwayite." **Ed.** Frederick C. Wilkins. *Eugene O'Neill Newsletter* 8.2 (1984): 17-19.

Two humorous sketches of O'Neill biography, one by Samuel Marx, the other by Sidney Skolsky. Originally published in 1929 and 1930 respectively.

H58 Wheeler, David. "Here Before ... Eugene O'Neill." *Eugene O'Neill Newsletter* 6.1 (1982): 3-15.

A one-person play spotlighting the character of Eugene O'Neill.

H59 Working in the Theatre [Videocassette]. Dir. Jennifer Johnson-Spence. Panelists: George C. White, Barbara Gelb, Rip Torn, Natasha Richardson. American Theatre Wing & CUNY-TV, 1993. 85 min.

Interviews with members of the Broadway cast of *Anna.*

Index of Authors

Index of Plays

Index of Subjects